HISTORICAL ANALYSIS OF THE CATALAN IDENTITY

Identities. An interdisciplinary approach to the roots of the present
Identités. Une approche interdisciplinaire aux racines du présent
Identidades. Una aproximación interdisciplinar a las raíces del presente

Vol. 6

PETER LANG
Bern · Berlin · Bruxelles · Frankfurt am Main · New York · Oxford · Wien

FLOCEL SABATÉ (ed.)

HISTORICAL ANALYSIS OF THE CATALAN IDENTITY

PETER LANG
Bern · Berlin · Bruxelles · Frankfurt am Main · New York · Oxford · Wien

Bibliographic information published by die Deutsche Nationalbibliothek
Die Deutsche Nationalbibliothek lists this publication in the Deutsche Nationalbibliografie; detailed bibliographic data is available on the Internet at ‹http://dnb.d-nb.de›.

British Library Cataloguing-in-Publication Data: A catalogue record for this book is available from The British Library, Great Britain

Library of Congress Control Number: 2015949621

Institut d'Estudis Catalans

Generalitat de Catalunya
Departament de la Presidència

European Science Foundation
Setting Science Agendas for Europe

Catalan texts were translated into English by Mary Black.

ISBN 978-3-0343-2010-8 pb.
ISSN 2296-3537 pb.

ISBN 978-3-0351-0885-9 eBook
ISSN 2296-3545 eBook

This publication has been peer reviewed.

Contents

Contemporary History

Cross-cutting topics

Preface

Joandomènec Ros
Institut d'Estudis Catalans

At the end of *Notícia de Catalunya*, Jaume Vicens Vives said:

> *El primer resort de la psicologia catalana no és la raó, com en els francesos; la metafísica com en els alemanys; l'empirisme, com en els anglesos; la intel·ligència, com els italians; o la mística, com en els castellans. A Catalunya el mòbil primari és la voluntat d'ésser*[1].

> The first trait of the Catalan psychological makeup is not reason like the French, metaphysics like the Germans, empiricism like the English, intelligence like the Italians or mysticism like the Castilians. In Catalonia, the most important impetus is the drive to be.

Another eminent thinker, Josep Ferrater Mora, in *Les formes de la vida catalana*[2], mentioned the four concepts that he believed defined Catalan culture and society: continuity, *seny* ("wisdom"), measure and irony. When did this drive to be first appear? Were *seny*, measure, irony (we shall leave continuity for later) traits of the earliest Catalans?

This collective volume does not strive to go so far, and it's a lucky thing: the media still report on that grotesque statement made by a Spanish politician claiming that the Spanish nation has three thousand years of history... In the words of this book's coordinator, Flocel Sabaté, the authors of the texts have "tried to untangle the reasons that have kept Catalonia together and somehow prolonged the defining features with which population itself has identified, and which have been the object of outside perception". That is: what we Catalans are like, and what characteristics define us to ourselves and to the world.

Obviously, the first characteristic is being recognised (by ourselves and others) as belonging to a unique nation different to all others. And this

1 Jaume Vicens, *Notícia de Catalunya* (Barcelona: Edicions Destino, 1982, p. 225.
2 Josep Ferrater, *Les formes de la vida catalana i altres assaigs* (Barcelona: Edicions 62, 1980).

happened quite early on, in the Middle Ages (in the late 9th century, based on document sources, or perhaps earlier, although there are no sources to confirm it). While the origin of the words *català* ("Catalan") and *Catalunya* ("Catalonia") are still shrouded in mystery, they were used quite early to distinguish the nationals and the nation. The different authors of this book, which is the outcome of a European research project, survey the advent of these terms over the course of the centuries and the features that were associated with them, and they discuss the unique features that shape the Catalan identity; that is, our hallmarks.

The coordinator of the volume, who was also the lead researcher in the project, recognises that "the political and social model" influences identity, "which […] contributes to consolidating the discourses of collective identity […]. Therefore, the cohesion of a region should be sought not so much in physical or even cultural features but in the evolution and acceptance of the different elements that articulate power and its fit within the land, always superimposed over the social and economic realities".

These social and economic realities are far-ranging, and they are examined by the different authors to a greater or lesser extent. Identification with the land, the language, the religion, the politics, the literature, the history, the law, the flag, industry, Europeanism, associationism, *Nova Cançó*, architecture and art have been the catalysts of our identity at different points in time.

Likewise (as Cristian Palomo, another author, notes), much of Catalan identity comes from the misdeeds of the Spaniards (standing army, civil servants) and the French (invasions, several wars); here I would add the anti-Francoism of the second third of the 20th century. Therefore it is a response to an aggression (physical, against the people and assets, or psychological, against the language, customs and law). This reaction against the outside enemy, which binds a society together, is a well-known phenomenon in human societies, and it poses a disturbing question: should we thank the enemies that our country has had throughout its history for our collective identity? An opposing phenomenon is assimilation, which also occurs and works in the opposite direction: the dilution of the identity of a small or vanquished country within the all-encompassing identity of a larger or victorious one.

This is a clear parallel with a well-known ecological phenomenon, and it is one of the modest handful of non-historical, but instead biological, contributions, that I can make to a fascinating historical treatise of the topic at hand. It refers to the morphological and behavioural differences in the species of living beings of similar ecological niche (that is to say, of function) and morphology in those geographic areas in which their respective distributions overlap: each species tends, through divergent evolution, to differ more from the other that in the situations in which their distribution does not overlap (and, therefore, they do not compete), where behaviour and morphology are more homogeneous. There is a segregation (morphological, ethological, ecological, etc.) to avoid competing for the same resources when the distribution is sympatric[3].

There is yet another factor which merits an ecological interpretation: given that from very early on Catalonia was a country that was frequently transited, as it still is today, what led it to achieve the "Catalanisation" of those who came here from elsewhere either peacefully or through war? What is it about this physical environment, as well as cultural environment (language, character, institutions; that is, the culture) that "grabs" them? Is it the country's *genius loci* that makes it stand out from the other countries on the Iberian Peninsula or Europe and renders it so appealing? (Here we mean *genius loci* not in the classical architectural or artistic sense but precisely as the entire set of features that define the region, the country and Catalan identity).

And finally we have the biological approach. Studies of the DNA of the Y-chromosome of the bearers of around 50 Catalan surnames[4] show, among many other findings, an appearance and later consolidation of the surnames centuries ago, with the family lines that bear these names having a wide variety of backgrounds (Occitanian, German, French, Italian, Arab, Jewish, etc.). Since our earliest days, we have been a melting pot, a country of ethnic diversity. Perhaps now would be the time to add to the historical and geographic names of *Catalunya Vella* ("Old Catalonia") and *Catalunya Nova* ("New Catalonia") *Catalunya Novíssima* ("Extremely New Catalonia") to denote the entire population of the Principality today, a blend of diverse roots and the outcome of this constant integration, yet with the common feelings and objectives of a shared identity.

3 Ramon Margalef, *Ecología* (Barcelona: Omega, 1974).

4 Neus Solé-Morata, Jaume Bertranpetit, David Comas, Francesc Calafell, "Y-chromosome in surname samples: Insights into surname frequency and origin", *European Journal of Human Genetics* (forthcoming); Jaume Bertranpetit, dir., *Un atles genètic i lingüístic dels cognoms catalans* (Barcelona: Institut d'Estudis Catalans, 2014).

Precisely this mixture of different people and cultures in a clearly defined social entity unique from its surroundings is notable, because it seems logical that the features of the original Catalans would have become blurred. The mixture of peoples (and genes) from different places should have homogenised not only the morphological features but also the social and cultural characteristics into a *totum revolutum* in which no particular identity would stand out but instead they would together become more similar to the countries around them, the origin of many of the immigrants. Yet that has not been the case. Instead there has been a kind of adaptation to this *genius loci* mentioned above. It is that "drive to be" that Vicens stressed, and to be different to others and to share with their fellow countrymen aspirations, customs, pursuits and beliefs.

Having reached this point, I cannot fail to mention an imaginary example of cultural isolation in much older human communities than the ones examined in this book, but it may serve to capture how the lack of isolation can dilute those cultural differences. It comes from the original version of *Sapiens. A Brief History of Humankind*:

> For example, there's every reason to believe that a forager band that lived 30,000 years ago on the spot where Madrid now stands would have spoken a different language from one living where Barcelona is now situated. One band might have been belligerent and the other peaceful. Perhaps the Castilian band was communal while the Catalan one was based on nuclear families. The ancient Castilians might have spent long hours carving wooden statues of their guardian spirits, whereas their Catalan contemporaries may have worshiped through dance. The former perhaps believed in reincarnation, while the latter thought this was nonsense. In one society, same-sex sexual relationships might have been accepted, while in the other they were taboo[5].

(The Spanish version of the book[6] – my doing – is faithful to this original, but curiously, in the Catalan version of the same book[7], the places are changed and the customs of their inhabitants are, too: whereas the author makes the comparison between Madrid and Barcelona, the translator makes it between Barcelona and Lleida. Might this be an attempt to make the text more politically correct?).

5 Yuval Noah Harari, *Sapiens. A Brief History of Humankind* (London: Harvill Secker, 2014), p. 57.

6 Yuval Noah Harari, *De animales a dioses*: *Breve historia de la humanidad* (Barcelona: Debate-Penguin Random House, 2014), pp. 60-61.

7 Yuval Noah Harari, *Sàpiens. Una breu història de la humanitat* (Barcelona: Edicions 62, 2014).

But let us return to this book. There may be more aspects we could consider, beyond the historical, linguistic, legal and architectural ones; other cultural traits (myths, literature, music – choral singing, the sardana dance – and art), the economy, the geography, immigration itself, sports, politics…). Some of these issues are addressed in a collective work[8] that shares some of the objectives and authors with this book, and that also concludes that we Catalans have a clearly distinct identity from the peoples around us:

> *s'ha produït en la Catalunya contemporània la fixació d'uns trets identitaris col·lectius que amb una intensitat major o menor han acabat contribuint a la fixació de […] la moderna identitat nacional catalana*[9].

> In contemporary Catalonia, certain collective identity traits have been established which have ended up contributing, more or less intensely, to establishing […] the modern Catalan national identity.

The Institut d'Estudis Catalans (IEC) is also known for being a key piece in the forging of this Catalan identity, especially in the sphere of culture, for over a century. If we survey the IEC's research, activities and publications since it was founded by Enric Prat de la Riba in 1907, we realise that it has shaped the cultural identity of Catalonia and the Catalan-speaking lands through its active research, study, publication and dissemination of scholarship in Catalan in fields like Romanesque art, archaeological excavations, cartography of vegetation, biomedical research, laying the foundation and setting the rules for the Catalan language and geographic studies, to name only a few areas of research.

Aware of the outstanding research that this book has produced, the Presidency of the Institut d'Estudis Catalans did not hesitate to help get it published. It worked with the Department of the Presidency of the Generalitat de Catalunya to produce an English-language version which will ensure that it reaches all points on the globe. The work deserves it, and the historical circumstances that Catalonia is currently experiencing clearly advocate on behalf of this book's second international life.

8 Jordi Casassas, coord., *Les identitats a la Catalunya contemporània* (Cabrera de Mar: Galerada, 2009).

9 Jordi Casassas, "Introducció", *Les identitats a la Catalunya...*, pp. 9-15.

Catalonia among the Longstanding Regions in Europe

Flocel SABATÉ
Universitat de Lleida and Institut d'Estudis Catalans

Why do some territories retain their identity throughout the centuries despite border changes or the lack of state recognition? What are the reasons that bind regions together, and why do they differ from place to place? Is it physical or human geography? In other words, when speaking about regions we are actually speaking about the people who have brought them to life over the centuries and who therefore adapt to different situations of cohesion and survival under motivations that can vary depending on the places or time, through the acceptance of referents and of quite differing values, be they cultural, economic, social, dynastic or others.

When the latest changes in Europe's ideologies and structure in the late 20th century were veering towards models of political articulation that would bring new frameworks between regions and supra-state structures, territorial identifications and referents re-emerged, either spontaneously or induced, yet in all cases they often harked back to longstanding territorial invocations. Historians welcomed the challenge of inquiring into the raison d'être of certain regions' secular identifications precisely as some political scientists were simultaneously revisiting expressions such as neo-medievalism to refer to the return to societies with identifying features that were quite similar to those from prior to 1648, that is, polycentric societies that were characterised by the permeability of borders, the ambiguity of authority, the transnationalism of the elites, a supranational system of values, the transfer of communication and the combination of local identities and globalising authorities[1]. The variety of situations necessitated a comparative analysis which would more deeply explore both the respective studies and the interrelations in order to ascertain what they had in common.

1 Jorg Friedrichs, "The Meaning of New Medievalism", *European Journal of International Relations (Thousand Oaks)*, 7/4 (2001), pp. 475-501; Neil Winn, ed., *Neo-Medievalism and Civil Wars* (London: Frank Cass, 2004).

With this shared goal, in 2007 numerous European historians embarked upon a fruitful joint reflection on these issues. This led to a Europe-wide research project carried out between 2010 and 2013 with the support of the European Science Foundation. The project has been dense and complex while yielding its fruit: eight teams have performed their own research on their respective regions, while a shared reflection was undertaken in order to attain an exchange of relations with which we could define the essential points of the topic at hand. This book is thus the culmination of the efforts of the team of researchers who conducted the specific research on Catalonia as part of this project. We have studiously striven to explore the reasons that have kept Catalonia together and have somehow contributed to the survival of the defining features with which the people have identified themselves, which have also been perceptible outside Catalonia. In this way, inquiring into the cohesion of Catalonia is synonymous with rising to the challenge of revising traditional explanations which might be now obsolete, and to historically analyse Catalan identity using modern scholarly tools and comparing it to its European setting.

1. Research issues

At the turn of the 20th to 21st centuries, a new epistemological approach to the study of history is gaining ground[2] at the same time as a new global vision is being sought[3]. This is clearly the consequence of the worldwide changes taking place at the same time, which are imposing on every society contradictory stimuli swinging between globalization and a reinforcement of the local[4]. All of this dovetails with the striking political changes in the articulation of Europe, especially in terms of the increasing permeability

2 Josep Fontana, *La història després del fi de la història* (Barcelona-Vic: Institut Universitari d'Història Jaume Vicens Vives-Eumo Editorial, 1992).

3 Bruce Mazlish, Ralp Buultjens, *Conceptualizing Global History* (Boulder-San Francisco Oxford: Westview Press, 1993).

4 See, for example: Christiana Stallaert, *Perpetuum Mobile. Entre la balcanización y la aldea global* (Rubí: Editorial Anthropos, 2004).

of the borders among European Union member states and the delegation of competences to supra-state entities. This in itself is shattering the model accepted since the Treaty of Westphalia in 1648[5], which was based on fully independent states behind their respective borders, an approach that had been reinforced since the 19th century[6] by the assumed equivalence of nation and state[7], adapted to a series of specific cases[8], which actually swallowed up supra-national states after World War I[9]. At the same time, the early 20th century ideological alternatives which interpreted the nation-state as an instrument of domination and the encroachment of capitalism in favour of the interests of the bourgeoisie also inevitably referred to packages of collective identity, albeit at times with other referents as well[10].

These identities are based on cultural features that are in the blood of those who participate in them, thus infusing an indelible, non-transferrable mixture of language, nation and people, as Herder posited in the early 19th century[11]. In any event, from a different perspective, a few decades earlier Rousseau advised not only promoting but also basing society on national identities, as he viewed them as remote from the motives of politicians and yet part and parcel of the values that truly keep each society together[12]. Society, therefore, might have a cohesive meaning in itself. Not for nothing: since the 17th century, societies have been expressing a cohesive meaning around the consideration of patriotism, with all the connotations inherent in the belonging and specific feeling of affection entailed in

5 Paul Hirst, Graname Thompson, "Globalization and the Future of the Nation-State", *Economy and Society*, 24/3 (1995), pp. 408-442.
6 Anne-Marie Thiesse, *La création des identités nationales. Europe XVIIIe-XIXe siècle* (Paris: Éditions du Seuil, 2001), pp. 67-158.
7 Gidon Gottlieb, *Nation against State* (New York: Council on Foreign Relations Press, 1993).
8 Timothy Baycroft, Mark Hewitson, eds., *What is a Nation? Europe 1789-1914* (Oxford: Oxford University Press, 2009).
9 Eric Hobsbawm, *Nations et nationalisme depuis 1780. Programme, mythe, réalité* (Paris: Éditions Gallimard, 1990), pp. 243-299.
10 Rosa Luxemburg, *La cuestión nacional* (Barcelona: El Viejo Topo, 1998), p. 90.
11 Adriana Rodríguez, *Identidad lingüística y nación cultural en Johann Gottfried Herder* (Madrid: Ediciones de la Universidad Autónoma de Madrid, 2008), pp. 101-102.
12 Ana M. Cohler, *Rousseau and Nationalism* (New York: Basic Books, 1970), pp. 31-35, 191-195.

identifying with a given human collective and the land it occupies[13]. This nonetheless refers to the notion of collective solidarity that characterises the different organisational aspects of society in the modern centuries[14].

In reality, there is a clear continuity between the Middle Ages and the Modern Age through the concepts of community and social solidarity[15]. Medieval rules are precisely the ones that provide the needed theological, philosophical and legal validity[16], thus complementing the legal formulations that upheld participative figures, which are quite clear in the political system[17]. The often-invoked concern with the common good[18] was found at the core of the respective justifying discourses, which sought a favourable position in the discussion and gestation of the balance of an agreed-upon power as the only possible way of governing[19]. This is the participative formula promoted by the diversity in possession of power, by the roots of the estates, while it is also able to complete the political and social tensions with a painstakingly devised political and legal theory: "ideal government and the mixed constitution", to put it in the consolidated words of James M. Blythe[20].

13 Robert von Friedeburg, "The Problems of Passions and Love of Fatherland in Protestant Thought, Melanchton to Anthusius, 1520s to 1620s", *Studies in Medieval and Renaissance History*, 3/3 (2006), pp. 247-253.

14 Paolo Prodi, Valerio Marchetti, eds., *Problemi di Identità tra Medioevo ed Età Moderna* (Bologna: Clueb, 2001).

15 Keith Stringer, "Social and Political Communities in European History. Some Reflections on Recent Studies", *Nations, Nationalism and Patriotism in the European Past*, Claus Bjorn, Alexander Grant, Keith J. Stringer, eds. (Copenhagen: Academic Press, 1994), pp. 11-12.

16 Pierre Michead-Quantin, *'Universitas'. Expressions du mouvement communautaire dans le Moyen-Age latin* (Paris: Livrairie Philosophique J. Vrin, 1970).

17 Dieter Mertens, *Il pensiero politico medievale* (Bologna: Il Mulino, 1999), pp. 95-132.

18 Matthew S. Kempshall, *The Common Good in Late Medieval Political Thought* (Oxford: Clarendon Press, 1999); Elodie Lecuppre-Desjardin, Anne Laure Van Bruaene, eds., *'De Bono Communi'. The Discourse and Practice of the Common Good in the European City (13th – 16th c.)* (Turnhout: Brepols Publishers, 2010).

19 Flocel Sabaté, "Expressões da representatividade social na Catalunha tardomedieval", *Identidades e Fronteiras no Medioevo Ibérico*, Fátima Regina Fernandes, ed. (Curitiba: Juruá Editora, 2013), pp. 51-61.

20 James M. Blythe, *Ideal Government and the Mixed Constitution in the Middle Age* (Princeton: Princeton University Press, 1992).

Repeatedly since the 13th century, this European context, characterised by group solidarities[21] and representative invocations[22], identified certain collectives as nations, as the bearers of certain shared cultural features[23]. This is the same term that designated specific peoples – *Germanorum natione*[24] – in the classical world and early Middle Ages, the reason why in the 3rd century Tertullian was able to refer to the *natione iudaeorum*, just as in the 12th century Bernard of Clairvaux mentioned Saint Malachy as *natione quidem Hibernus*[25]. Under the parameters of the late Middle Ages, one expected the members of a given nation to show similar behaviours, like a new, higher circle of solidarity[26]. The goal was to capture a unit of behaviour and even feeling, as if it were a single body[27] that had evolved jointly from a specific founding moment in accordance with the coeval justifying narratives[28]. The consolidation of sovereign power over

21 Flocel Sabaté, "Les factions dans la vie urbaine de la Catalogne du XIVème siècle", *Histoire et archéologie des terres catalane au moyen Age*, Philippe Sénac, ed. (Perpignan: Presses Universitaires de Perpignan, 1995), pp. 339-365.

22 Antony Black, *El pensamiento político en Europa, 1250-1450* (Cambridge: Cambridge University Press, 1996), pp. 88-288; Bertie Wilkinson, *The Creation of Medieval Parliaments* (New York-London-Sydney-Toronto: John Wiley and Sons, 1972).

23 Léopold Genicot, *Europa en el siglo XIII* (Barcelona: Editorial Labor, 1973), pp. 127-130.

24 Alfred John Church, William Jackson Brodibb, *The Germania of Tacitus* (London-Cambridge: Macmillan, 1869), p. 62.

25 Tertullianus, "De praescriptionibus adversus haeretico", *Patrologia Latina*, vol. 2, coll. 67 (Database, disc 1); Bernardus Claraevallensis, "Vita S. Malachiae", *Patrologia Latina*, vol. 182, coll. 1079 (Database, disc 5).

26 Flocel Sabaté, "La construcción ideológica del nacimiento unitario de Cataluña", *Castilla y el mundo feudal. Homenaje al professor Julio Valdeón*, 3 vols., María Isabel del Val, Pascual Martínez, eds. (Valladolid: Junta de Castilla and León-Universidad de Valladolid, 2009), vol. 1, pp. 101-102.

27 Flocel Sabaté, "'Amar la nostra nació'", *Sardegna e Catalogna 'officinae' di identità. Riflessioni stoiograpiche e prospetive di ricerca*, Alessandra Cioppi, ed. (Cagliari: Consiglio Nazionale delle Ricerche. Istituto Storico Europeo della Mediterranea, 2013), pp. 15-63.

28 Bernard Guenée, *Occidente durante los siglos XIV y XV. Los Estados* (Barcelona: Editorial Labor, 1973), pp. 65-71.

a specific nation[29] or over a plurality of different ones[30] could not avoid the diversity of power in the conception at the time, leading to the consolidation of the estates[31] and their corollary invocation of representativeness[32]. In the 14th century, the duality between the sovereign and the estates allowed the latter to increasingly be viewed as representative of the "land".

In this way, the political and social model, which entails the need to justify representativeness[33], contributes to consolidating the discourses of collective identity. The institutional approaches that stem therefrom, through the implementation of an articulation over the land, shape it and enable society, territory and institutions to become intertwined. Survival is only guaranteed when the institutional framework matches the social reality already in place, such that the territory becomes a mirror of the social reality and, for that very reason, can host an institutional structure in line with the social, economic and jurisdictional reality[34].

The cohesion of a land, therefore, should be sought not so much in certain physical or even cultural features but in the evolution and acceptance of different elements that articulate power and its fit within the region, always within given social and economic parameters. The bonds between the capitals and their areas of influence create coherent territorial units in a Europe of cities and regions, while the local social and economic elites that set up their interests there also promote discourses that justify their access to political power in order to broaden the scope of their position and that of the territory they formally represent. The culmination

29 Walter Ullmann, *Historia del pensamiento político en la Edad Media* (Barcelona: Editorial Ariel, 1983), pp. 125-216.

30 Gisela Naegle, "Diversité linguistique, identités et mythe de l'Empire à la fin du Moyen Âge", *Revue Française d'Histoire des Idées Politiques*, 36/2 (2012), pp. 264-271.

31 John Watts, *The Making of Polities. Europe 1300-1500* (Cambridge: Cambridge University Press, 2009), pp. 233-238.

32 Henry John Randall, *The Creative Centuries. A Study in Historical Development* (London-New York-Toronto: Longman Green, 1947), p. 248.

33 Susan Reynolds, "Medieval urban history and the history of political thought", *Urban History Yearbook* (Leicester: Leicester University Press, 1982), pp. 15-16.

34 Flocel Sabaté, "Els eixos articuladors del territori medieval català", *L'estructuració territorial de Catalunya. Els eixos cohesionadors de l'espai. V Congrés Internacional d'Història Local de Catalunya (Barcelona, 10 i 11 de desembre de 1999)*, Flocel Sabaté, coord. (Barcelona: L'Avenç, 2000), pp. 44-70.

of this dynamic in institutional formulas consolidates the trajectory. This is a quite coherent dynamic within late medieval ideological parameters, which stand on Roman law, Aristotelian referents and the adaptation of Christianity, thus creating a conceptual context which can fit the different realities. For this reason, even though they wielded similar arguments, the evolutions were so different around Europe, in line with the respective balance of forces that might exist in each place.

In any event, the state consolidations in the Modern Age sought a centrality that collided with the medieval participative models[35]. During the 16th and 17th centuries, the institutional structures with which the whole was governed clearly gained ground in the different European countries, while the different social and territorial referents were integrated, which gave rise to differing degrees of fit with the spatial cohesions inherited from the Middle Ages[36]. In fact, by thus consolidating a superior state framework, the exit of the Middle Ages has been posited as the shift *de la région à la nation* ("from the region to the nation"), meaning the time when all the inferior or intermediate stages lost prominence[37]. However, the levels of solidarity and bonds under the state constructions were retained in many cases and in different scenarios, often coupled with clear socioeconomic capitalities endowed with differing degrees of cultural features and differing levels of social representativeness and political participation.

This constancy gave rise to different formulas of fit and in all cases led to assumptions of collective identity in certain regions which, drew from the appropriate historical tales. This, in turn, led to constant looping between historical explanations and justifying discourses in a different direction, all of them sharing the projection into the past. Clearly, the map of Europe was constantly shifting with contrasting tensions under different interests, with contrasting collective identity discourses which sought justification in a remote historical origin and its evolution. This is a reality

35 Marie Gaille-Nikodimov, ed., *Le Gouvernement mixte. De l'idéal politique au monstre constitutionnel en Europe (XIIIe-XVIIe siècle)* (Saint Étienne: Publications de l'Université de Saint-Étienne Jean Monnet, 2005).

36 Wim Blockmans, André Holenstein, Jon Mathieu, eds., *Empowering Interactions. Political Cultures and the Emergence of the State in Europe 1300-1900* (Fernham-Burlington: Ashgate, 2009).

37 Jean-François Bergier, "De la région à la nation: la construction de l'espace au Moyen Âge", *Les Européens*, Hélène Ahrweiller, Maurice Aymard, dirs. (Paris: Hermann Éditeur des Sciences et des Arts, 2000), pp. 212-213.

that blurs the vision of the past while also spurring the historian's role. The non-negligible challenge of this was captured by Eric Hobsbawm:

> The past is therefore a permanent dimension of the human consciousness, an inevitable component of the institutions, values and other patterns of human society. The problem for historians is to analyse the nature of this "sense of the past" in society and to trace its changes and transformations[38].

2. Our ESF research project

The positing of similar historical roots which, adapted to the respective circumstances, govern the processes of social cohesion and, as a corollary, territorial cohesion, that were shared in medieval Europe led a group of European historians to seek a scientific and institutional framework of collaboration in order to engage in regional research while also enjoying an opportunity to compare their findings. To this end, in 2007, under the coordination of Dick de Boer, medievalists from twelve European universities began to explore the possibilities offered by the European Commission's Seventh Framework Programme to inquire into the Europe' historical roots. Soon, however, we noticed that the ideal framework was the Eurocores Programme, through which the European Science Foundation had been stimulating partnerships among research groups from different countries on common issues since 2005. The specific sub-programme entitled *European Comparisons in Regional Cohesion, Dynamics and Expressions (EuroCORECODE)*, whose first call for participation was being prepared in 2009, took shape as the ideal venue for a comparative study on the formative origins and elements of cohesion of the European regions.

Given this, throughout 2008 and 2009 a group of medievalists from different European research groups held scholarly meetings in Bochum[39] and Wassenaar. The purpose of these meetings was to fine-tune a common research plan in order to seek the elements at the core of the social cohesions that have strengthened numerous regions so much that they have

38 Eric Hobsbawn, *On History* (London: Abacus, 2008), p. 13.

39 My thanks go to Nikolas Jaspert for his interest in our participation in this project.

been able to survive over time and through different historical evolutions, including the articulation of the states under national invocations. To do this, we needed to examine a wide range of factors and compare the most important reasons in each individual case, such as physical space, language and other cultural elements, the importance of dynasty, the dynamics of social cohesion and the discourses legitimising different groups. Therefore, we had to establish a broad, extensive Europe-wide research project that would enable us to more deeply analyse the importance of the different elements in given regions while also comparing them in order to achieve a comprehensive, reliable picture. With these purposes in mind, duly expressed in the research goals, and with a working plan designed Europe-wide, in 2009 we submitted the research project to the European Science Foundation, and it was approved and promoted so that the research could be conducted between 2010 and 2013[40].

Thus it was that in 2010 we embarked upon the studies through a scholarly kick-off meeting held in Copenhagen. Given the obvious complexity stemming from the plurality of factors and the large number of researchers who had to be coordinated in a research project that was actually an entire web of projects in order to gain further insight into each region while also moving towards a view of the whole, it was necessary to devise a specific research project in each of the regions being studied, all under joint academic coordination. These regions included Guelders-Lower Rhine, Bohemia, Livonia, Portugal, Schleswig-Holstein, Silesia, Transylvania and Catalonia[41]. This is a range of regions chosen carefully, within the possibilities afforded by European financing, which enabled us to compare regions where the factors behind cohesion were perceived to be quite varied, and which have evolved under quite diverse historical fates, although the awareness of regional identity has persisted in all of them. Two working levels were proposed, each to be explored over the course of three years: one performed by each team in the respective region they were studying aimed at capturing and outlining the key elements of the process in the

40 *Cuius Regio*. An Analysis of the Cohesive and Disruptive Forces Destining the Attachment of Groups of Persons to an the Cohesion within Regions as a Historical Phenomenon (CURE).

41 Coordinated respectively by Dick de Boer (also the general coordinator), Lenka Bobkova, Anu Mänd, Luis Adâo da Fonseca, Kurt Villads, Roscislaw Zerelik, Cosmin Popa-Gorjanu and the author of these lines.

region, while also taking note of its corresponding evolution; and a second more complex comparative level aimed at attaining a global, Europe-wide perspective that would weigh the different factors that played a role and the reasons why these factors became more or less important depending on the place and the circumstances. For the benefit of scholarly research, we also added a third level by holding scientific meetings with the two other projects that the European Science Foundation was financing within the same sub-programme[42]. This enabled us to attain broader and more extensive comparisons, such as between the founding periods, modern and even contemporary periods and today, as noted in the working meetings held in Glasgow, Alba Iulia and Arnhem between 2012 and 2013.

3. The ESF research project on Catalonia

The dependence of the European Science Foundation's programmes on funds coming from its member states prevented the Spanish research teams from participating in the EuroCORECODE sub-programme[43]. However, Catalonia represents a very specific case in the evolution of European identity. After experiencing a cohesion process in the Middle Ages, during the modern centuries a political and institutional claim for identity was used in a vindicatory sense, which survived under different circumstances in the subsequent centuries. This history initially encourages a contrast with other regions in the Iberian Peninsula which evolved in quite different ways, especially Portugal, which managed to form a state of its own[44]. It also opens up comparisons with other European regions consolidated

42 "Symbols that bind and break communities: Saint's cults as stimuli and expressions of local, regional, national and universalist identities (CULTICSYMBOLS)"; " Un familiarity as signs of European times: scrutinizing historical representations of otherness and contemporary daily practices in border regions (Unfamiliarity)" <www.esf.org/coordinating-research/eurocores.html> (Retrieved 13 August 2013).

43 European Science Foundation. Call for Outline Proposals. European Comparisons in Regional Cohesion, Dynamics and Expressions (EuroCORECODE), <www.esf.org> (retrieved 10 February 2009).

44 Precisely within the same framework, a specific comparative study was performed of Catalonia and Portugal, leading to: Flocel Sabaté, Luis Adao da Fonseca, eds.,

through other factors or through the same factors combined in different ways. For this reason, the presence of Catalonia in a historical research project like this one was deemed important, which is why the ESF kept the Catalan team on the research project even though it initially had to give it the unique status of associate partner in order to avoid the aforementioned institutional conflicts.

The historiographic reasoning that deemed it important to keep Catalonia in a project that strove to analyse the cohesive significance of the European regions determined the importance of Catalonia, as a region within Europe endowed with a particular formative history. Certainly, to begin with, the cohesion of Catalonia does not so much stem from a shared starting point as from a range of neighbouring territories that experienced very similar circumstances in the early Middle Ages, which brought them together while helping them to develop shared cultural traits, beginning with language. This convergent evolution gave shape to the first trait, which leads to an internal assumption as well as an external perception, as was quite clear in the 12th century when the country's social and political cohesion spread at the same time that this territory was perceived from the outside as a unit which received a common name for the first time: Catalonia. In any event, the initial political fragmentation bequeathed a jurisdictional and fiscal weakness to late medieval sovereigns that would result in a mandatory pact between the monarchy and the estates. The latter, in turn, generated a justifying discourse based on their representativeness over a collective that identified with the country, with the land. The balance of power achieved generated specific institutions based on their representativeness of the country's identity. Thus, in the Middle Ages the convergent evolution, external perception, incidence of specific discourses of power and institutional development brought together a region which was grounded upon on its own identity. For this reason, when in the modern centuries the Iberian Peninsula had its own specific experience of the widespread tensions in Europe between the participative forms of government inherited from the Middle Ages and the new absolutist trends, the identity of Catalonia was a highly specific scenario where the institutions, taking refuge in their representativeness of the land, invoked discourses

---

Catalonia and Portugal. The Iberian Peninsula from the Periphery (Bern: Peter Lang Publishers, 2015).

of territorial cohesion. However, the dissolution of Catalonia's own institutions in the 18th century, and even of it as an administrative unit in the 19th century, did not destroy Catalonia's cohesion. Instead, to the contrary, it grew stronger through its identity-based cultural traits.

This long history, from the Middle Ages to the 20th century, first requires historical examination that is attentive to the ideological and cultural evolution in each of the three periods: the Middle Ages, the Modern Age and the contemporary world. For this reason, when I had to devise the ESF research project for Catalonia, I deemed that it had to be based on consolidated research groups that were capable of bringing significant experience to the research in this field. This is how we came to join the forces of three research groups with the utmost scholarly qualifications as consolidated research groups: *Grup de Recerca Consolidat en Estudis Medievals "Espai Poder i Cultura"* ("Consolidated Research Group in Medieval Studies: 'Space, Power and Culture'", 2009 SGR 274), headquartered at the Universitat de Lleida and led by myself; *Manuscrits. Grup de Recerca d'Història Moderna. Identitats, Cultura i Pensament Polític en el Procés de Construcció Nacional Català* ("Manuscripts. Modern History Research Group. Identities, Culture and Political Thinking in the Process of Catalan National Construction", 2009 SGR 808), centred at the Universitat Autònoma de Barcelona under the supervision of Antoni Simon; and the *Grup d'Estudis d'Història de la Cultura i dels Intel·lectuals* ("Study Group on the History of Culture and Intellectuals", 2009 SGR 1130), seated at the Universitat de Barcelona and supervised by Jordi Casassas. Specifically, in the first group the main contributions were from Isabel Grifoll and myself; in the second one they came from Antoni Simon, Ignasi Fernández, Òscar Jané and Cristian Palomo; and in the third one the significant contributions came from Jordi Cassasas, David Cao, Giovanni Cattini and Carles Santacana. Given the importance of such extraordinarily cross-cutting factors such as language, law and art, respectively, we also enlisted the participation of renowned experts in these fields, namely Josep Moran, Tomàs de Montagut and Xavier Barral i Altet, respectively, along with Prim Bertran and Joan Anton Rabella.

The teamwork was encouraged by the European Science Foundation itself, the source of the financing for the trips and activities inherent to this research. Through a competitive application process, the ESF also awarded two additional grants for the translation, publication and dissemination of this research. Likewise, the research project benefited enormously from the sensitivity and collaboration of the Institut d'Estudis Catalans, which validated and promoted the research. Finally, without the backing of the *Departament de la Presidència de la Generalitat de Catalunya*, we would not have had the assistance we needed to disseminate this research internationally.

The outcome of three years of research has been shared at professional gatherings with the members of the other European teams. The Catalan team made major scholarly contributions at the meetings held between 2010 and 2013 in Morbach, Tallinn, Copenhagen, Porto, Groningen, Glasgow, Alba Iulia and Arnhem. At the same time, we sought to share our own studies in order to reach scientific conclusions, which gave rise to two meetings in Lleida in 2011 and 2012, along with a long, intense workday on the 6th of February 2013 at the Institut d'Estudis Catalans headquarters in Barcelona.

This book strives to summarise these studies on the cohesion of Catalonia and, as a corollary, the survival and adaptations of its identity. We honestly believe that compared to preceding stages of research, we have achieved a vision that more closely matches the reality of the historical events, and therefore one that is further from both the temptation to recreate the past and the ageing of the traditional historiographic explanations. It thus contributes to inserting knowledge of this territorial identity into the international concert of historiography, because ultimately what happened in Catalonia fits within the shared dynamics in Europe.

Medieval Roots

The Medieval Roots of Catalan Identity

Flocel SABATÉ
Universitat de Lleida and Institut d'Estudis Catalans

Since the earliest days, history has been used more or less consciously to seek the roots that justify choices and positions in the present time. The looping feedback that this entails can seriously blur our knowledge of the past by situating behind numerous layers of interpretation. Proposals that entail actual deconstructions of the historical language are therefore not mere rhetorical devices but attempts to truly understand the texts in their real context. Plumbing the consciousness of centuries-old collective identifications which have somehow survived until the present stirs up all the perils and yet calls for caution in order to achieve a scientifically rigorous, honest effort. For this reason, it is essential to analyse not only the historical deeds but also the different pathways that have driven how they have been studied in order to look for a hermeneutics that enables us to objectively analyse the events and refashion our analysis of the words used based on full contextualisation in the society in which they were used. Only in this way will we be able to capture the true legacy of the Middle Ages, which is a significant conditioning factor for the ensuing centuries[1]

1. In the quest for the origin of the nation

There is a longstanding tradition of situating the origins of Catalonia in a dynastic move by Wilfred the Hairy in 11th century. In fact, this has been

1 Abbreviations used: ACA, Arxiu de la Corona d'Aragó; ACBE, Arxiu Comarcal del Baix Ebre; ACN, Arxiu Comarcal de la Noguera; ACUR, Arxiu Comarcal de l'Urgell; ADPO, Archives Départementales des Pyrénées-Orientales; AHCB, Arxiu Històric de la Ciutat de Barcelona; AHCG, Arxiu Històric de la Ciutat de Girona; AHCM, Arxiu Històric de la ciutat de Manresa; AML, Arxiu Municipal de Lleida.

repeated since the 12th century based on the *Gesta comitum Barcinonensium*[2], which intentionally[3] insinuated the relationship between the origins of the country and his Barcelona-based dynasty[4]. Throughout the Middle Ages, the story had it that his descendant and successor became *lo primer Comte natural de Barcelona* ("the first natural Count of Barcelona"), as Pere Tomic[5] states in 15th century, in concordance with the 17th century explanations provided by Narcís Feliu de la Peña that Wilfred *mereció con propiedad el título de conde*[6] ("properly deserved the title of count"). He marked a shift, as mentioned in the 19th century *España Sagrada*, from the *gobernadores* ("governors") to *los condes propietarios de Barcelona*[7] ("the counts who owned Barcelona"), the reason why Pròsper de Bofarull believed that the *Genealogía de los condes soberanos de Barcelona* ("Genealogy of the sovereign counts of Barcelona") could only begin with Wilfred the Hairy[8]. In the same vein, the varied popular historical works issued in the first half of the 20th century distinguished two stages: *Els comtes depenents*

2 Stefano M. Cingolani, Robert Álvarez, eds., *Gestes dels comtes de Barcelona i reis d'Aragó – 'Gesta comitum Barchinone et regum Aragonie'* (Santa Coloma de Queralt: Obrador Edèndum, 2012), pp. 62-66.

3 Martin Aurell, "Aux originies de la Catalogne: le mythe fondateur de la Maison de Barcelone dans l'historiographie du XIIe siècle", *Comptes Rendus de Séances de l'Académie des Inscriptions et Belles-Lettres*, 142/1 (1998), pp. 7-18.

4 *En attribuant à Guifred le gouvernment anticipé de toute la Catalogne, le rédacteur des 'Gesta' justifie le regroupement féodal catalan et revindique la vocation du pays à s'étendre aux dépens de l' 'Hispania', glorifiant à l'avance les conquêtes de Ramon Berenguer IV* ("By assigning Guifred the early government throughout Catalonia, the editor of the 'Gesta' justifies the Catalan feudal grouping and the vocation of the country to expand at the expense of the 'Hispania', glorifying the future conquests of Ramon Berenguer IV"). Michel Zimmermann, "Les origines de la Catalogne d'après les 'Gesta comitum Barcinonensium'. Mythe fondateur ou récit étiologique?", *Liber largitorius. Études d'Histoire médiévale offertes à Pierre Toubert par ses élèves*, Dominique Bathélemy, Jean-Marie Martin, eds. (Paris: Droz, 2003), p. 538.

5 Pere Tomic, *Històries e conquistes dels reis d'Aragó e comtes de Barcelona* (Bagà: Centre d'Estudis Baganesos, 1990), p. 100.

6 Narciso Feliu de la Peña, "Fénix de Cataluña, compendio de sus antiguas grandezas", *Hazañas y recuerdos de los Catalanes – Fénix de Cataluña* (Barcelona: Juan Oliveres Impresor, 1846) (facsimile: Extramuros Facsímiles, Seville, 2010), p. 14.

7 Enrique Flórez, Manuel Risco, *España Sagrada*, 56 vols. (Madrid: Real Academia de la Historia, 1959), vol. 29, p. 160.

8 Próspero de Bofarull, *Los condes de Barcelona vindicados*, 2 vols. (Barcelona: Imprenta de J. Oliveres y Monmany, 1836), vol. 1, p. 1.

("the dependent counts") and *Els comtes independents* ("the independent counts"), with Wilfred the Hairy marking the onset this latter stage[9]. Despite this, it is now agreed, as Pi y Arimon said back in the mid-19th century, that Catalonia's definitive independence came in the year 987, after the shift in the Carolingian dynasty with Hugh Capet[10], to whom the count of Barcelona had not paid homage because the Muslim attack on the city just two years earlier had had to be repelled without any assistance from the empire. This was recounted by Font i Segué: *reconquistada la ciutat amb les soles forces catalanes, quedà de fet establerta la independència de la 'Marca'*[11] ("the city [being] reconquered with only the Catalan forces, the de facto independence of the 'March' was established").

The conviction that the count of Barcelona had power over Catalonia as a whole, called the Spanish March[12], enabled the considerations to be extended to all of Catalonia, as reported by Bori Fontestà when he presented *Vifredo el Velloso fundador de la dinastía condal catalana y primero de los condes independientes*[13] ("Wilfred the Hairy founder of the Catalan county dynasty and first of the independent counts"). In fact, as taught in Republican schools, Wilfred the Hairy *és l'heroi nacional de Catalunya*[14] ("is the national hero of Catalonia").

The stabilisation of Wilfred the Hairy's dynasty would lead based on a generic Carolingian concession at the assembly at Quierzy in 877, which enabled it to encompass a broader social reality. This would demonstrate by the tensions felt at the beginning of the 9th century, which were interpreted as a *tendència antifranca* ("anti-Frank tendency") thus *preparant el terrer per a la formació de la Nacionalitat Catalana*[15] ("preparing the ground for the forming of the Catalan Nationality"). Therefore, this begs

9 Damià Ricart, *Història de Catalunya* (Barcelona: Miquel A. Salvatella Editor, 2004).

10 Andrés Avelino Pi, *Barcelona antigua y moderna o descripción e historia de esta ciudad desde su fundación hasta nuestros días*, 2 vols. (Barcelona: Imprenta y Librería Politécnica Tomás Gorchs, 1854), vol. 1, p. 48.

11 Norbert Font, *Història de Catalunya* (Barcelona: Imprenta i Editorial Altés, 1933), p. 47.

12 Flocel Sabaté, "El nacimiento de Cataluña. Mito y realidad", *Fundamentos medievales de los particularismos hispánicos. IX Congreso de Estudios Medievales (2003)* (León: Fundación Sánchez Albornoz, 2005), pp. 265-274.

13 Antonio Bori, *Historia de Cataluña* (Barcelona: Imprenta de Henrich, 1898), p. 41.

14 Ramon Torroja, *Història de Catalunya* (Barcelona: Impremta Elzeviriana-Librería Camí, 1933), p. 31.

15 Norbert Font, *Història de Catalunya*..., p. 44.

the question of whether there was a widespread social reality behind these political approaches. This was studied and accepted by Joseph Calmette, who explains it as a gradual rooting of national identity. Back in 865, Charles the Bald defined the Spanish March as distinct from Septimania. Catalonia would born at that time at the intersection between a given space and a popularly rooted consciousness:

> *Qu'a-t-il fallu pour que, dans le monde carolingien, il se formât une Catalogne? Un élément matériel, c'est-à-dire un cadre territorial; un élément moral, c'est-à-dire une conscience locale. Le cadre territorial a été fourni par le glacis de protection organisé sous Charlemagne par saint Guilhem, duc de Toulouse, sur le rebord méridional des Pyrénées méditerranéennes [...]. Mais l'élément matériel, le territoire n'est pas tout, ce n'est qu'un corps; un élément moral doit s'y ajouter, autant dire une âme.*

> What did it take so that a Catalonia should be formed in the Carolingian world? A material element, that is to say, a territorial framework; a moral element, that is to say, a local consciousness. The territorial framework was provided by the protective shield organized under Charlemagne by Saint William, Duke of Toulouse, on the southern rim of the Mediterranean Pyrenees [...]. But the material element, the territory is not all, it is not a body; a moral element must be added to it, in other words a soul.

Its own identity would lead to a resistance to Carolingian domination, and this same opposition fuelled popular sentiment throughout the 9th century, as Calmette also claimed in 1941, precisely when his country was suffering from an occupation under national discourses: *le sentiment local provoque la compression et la compression exaspère le sentiment local. Ce travail de psychologie collective se poursuit jusqu'au jour tragique qui coûte la vie au dernier des comtes de race franque, Salomon*[16] ("local sentiment causes compression and compression exasperates the local sentiment. This work of collective psychology continued until tragic day that Solomon the last of the counts of the Frankish race, was killed"). Therefore, enfeoffment the Countship of Barcelona to Wilfred the Hairy meant an agreed-upon solution to the situation, a felicitous merger of both stimuli: *la montée du sentiment national dans la marche d'Espagne coïncident avec la poussée féodale qui prend d'autre part son allure accélérée dans la seconde moitié*

16 Joseph Calmette, *L'effondrement d'un Empire et la naissance d'une Europe (IXe-XIe siècles)* (Paris: Aubier-Éditions Montaigne, 1941), pp. 143, 145; Joseph Calmette, *La question des Pyrénées et la Marche d'Espagne au Moyen-Âge* (Paris: J. B. Janin, 1947), pp. 21, 23.

du XIe siècle[17] ("the rise of national sentiment in the March of Spain coincides with the feudal thrust that, on the other hand, takes on an accelerated pace in the second half of the 11th century") The approach had major fallout for decades: Calmette, in Abadal's words published in 1958, *amb justos i ben guanyats títols exercí durant tota la primera meitat del nostre segle una mena de dictadura sobre la primitiva història catalana*[18] ("with fair and well-earned titles, exercised throughout the first half of our century a sort of dictatorship over the primitive Catalan history"). In fact, several decades later, the 1978 monograph by Josep Maria Salrach dedicated to the 8th and 9th centuries was explicitly entitled *El procés de formació nacional de Catalunya*; the title of the first volume was devoted to *domini carolingi* ("Carolingian domination") while the second one was entitled *L'establiment de la dinastia nacional*[19].

However, since the 19th century, numerous authors like Fita and Torras y Baiges posited that, in reality, this territory would not witness full, comprehensive treatment until the 11th century, when the Church's actions came to the fore in the wake of feudalisation, the spread of the constitutions of peace and truce after the 1020s[20] and, most prominently, the "Usatges" or rules handed down by Count Ramon Berenguer I of Barcelona in 1068[21], a veritable *carta constitucional de Catalunya* ("Constitutional charter for Catalonia") in the words of Ferran Valls i Taberner[22]. In Catalonia, feudalism and cohesion would go hand in hand with the Count of Barcelona:

> *Havent pacificat el comtat un cop dominades les revoltes interiors; promulgades per ell, en funció de legislador i asistit dels seus magnats, les normes judicials i feudals dels "Usualia"; posats sota la seva senyoria o en estreta relació d'aliança altres comtes catalans; vencedor de diversos reis sarrains i estimada en molt la seva amistat, particularment pel de Dènia, Ramon Berenguer I havia arribat a l'apogeu*

17 Joseph Calmette, *La question des Pyrénées…*, p. 24.
18 Ramon d'Abadal, *Els Primers Comtes Catalans* (Barcelona: Editorial Vicens-Vives, 1983), p. 3.
19 Josep Maria Salrach, *El procés de formació nacional de Catalunya (segles VIII-IX)*, 2 vols. (Barcelona: Edicions 62, 1978).
20 Josep Torras, *La tradició catalana* (Barcelona: Editorial Selecta, 1966), pp. 139-140.
21 Fidel Fita, "Corte y Usajes de Barcelona en 1064. Textos inéditos", *Boletín de la Real Academia de la Historia*, 16-17 (1890), pp. 389-393.
22 Ferran Valls, "Carta constitucional de Ramon Berenguer I de Barcelona (vers 1060)", *Anuario de Historia del Derecho Español*, 6 (1929), pp. 252-259.

del seu poder i del seu prestigi i estava en el millor moment per donar una consagració legal a l'enaltiment de l'autoritat pública[23].

Having pacified the county after controlling the internal revolts; promoted by him, as a legislator and assisted by his magnates, the legal and feudal norms of the *Usualia*; placed under his lordship or in close alliance with other Catalan counts; defeater of various Sarracen kings and highly esteemed his friendship, especially by the one from Denia, Ramon Berenguer I had reached the peak of his power and his prestige and was at the best moment to give a legal consecration to the praise for the public authority.

With no doubts about the date of the Usatges of Barcelona, mid-20th century historiography kept pinpointing the second half of the 11th century as a milestone, seeing the *conde barcelonés como soberano de un estado que legisla, acuña moneda y se considera heredero de la plenitud soberana que tenía en antiguo rey de Francia*[24] ("the Barcelonan count as the sovereign of a state that legislated, minted money and considered himself heir to the full sovereignty that the old king of France held").

Well into the last third of the 20th century, Pierre Bonnassie accepted this approach, albeit from a materialist hermeneutics[25]. According to the Hegelian scheme, pre-feudal society was shaken by a period of upheaval – *vingt ou trente ans (entre 1030/1040 et 1060)* ("twenty or thirty years [between 1030/1040 and 1060]") – resembling a feudal revolution – *on a l'impression d'assister à un séisme*[26] ("one has the impression of watching an earthquake") –, which would culminate with feudal society as a synthesis of the previous thesis and antithesis. This, in turn, led to the formation of a feudal society over all the countships governed by the Count of Barcelona:

23 Ferran Valls, *Estudis d'història jurídica Catalana* (Málaga: Arxiu de la Biblioteca Ferran Valls i Taberner and others, 1989), p. 60.

24 Federico Udina, "Evolución del poder soberano hasta la unión", *VII Congreso de Historia de la Corona de Aragón (1-6 octubre 1962)*, 3 vols. (Barcelona: Viuda de Fidel Rodríguez Ferrán, 1962), vol. 3, p. 274.

25 Flocel Sabaté, "The Catalonia of the 10th-12th centuries and the historiographic definition of feudalism", *Catalan Historical Review*, 3 (2010), pp. 38-39.

26 Pierre Bonnassie, *Sur la formation du féodalisme catalan et sa première expansion (jusqu'à 1150 environ), dans La formació i expansió del feudalisme català. Actes del col·loqui organitzat pel col·legi Universitari de Girona (8-11 de gener de 1985)*, Jaume Portella, ed. (Girona: Col·legi Universitari de Girona-Universitat Autònoma de Barcelona, 1985-1986), p. 12.

> *C'est la famille comtale de Barcelone qui mène à bien l'œuvre de reconstruction et elle le fait à son seul profit. Désormais, tout et tous, en Catalogne, lui sont directement ou indirectement soumis. Le nouveau régime politico-social ne retient guère du passé que la vieille notion de 'Potestas' qui maintenant s'incarne entièrement dans la personne du prince barcelonais et en fait un être hors du commun. Au-dessous de lui, les pouvoirs s'organisent sur la seule base des liens de dépendance. L'État féodal est né*[27].

> It was the count of Barcelona's family that carried out the reconstruction work, and it did so for its own benefit. Now everyone and everything, Catalonia, was directly or indirectly a subject. The new political and social system did not really retain the old notion from the past of 'Potestas' now fully embodied in the person of the Barcelona Prince and turn him into a political been beyond the common scene. Below him, the powers were organized on the sole basis of links of interdependence. The feudal state was born.

Following this opinion expressed by Pierre Bonnassie, the image of a Catalonia united since the 11th century as imposed by the feudalism of the Count of Barcelona has been repeated almost until today[28]. In reality, the feudal pacts that joined the heads of the countships consolidated not the interference of the Count of Barcelona but his pre-eminence, in a process which instead of putting an end to feudalisation extended it through a society that shared a similar evolution in the different economic, political and cultural facets via a convergent trajectory in around the 12th century[29]. For this

27 Pierre Bonnassie, *La Catalogne du milieu du Xe à la fin du XIe siècle*, 2 vols. (Toulouse: Publications de l'Université de Toulouse – Le Mirail), 1976, vol. 2, p. 732.

28 *Es cierto que a través de estos pactos, realizados entre 1060 y 1070, la totalidad de la Cataluña cristiana se encontraba por primera vez reunida bajo la autoridad de los condes de Barcelona y que éstos no eran vasallos de nadie* ("It is true that through these agreements, made between 1060 and 1070, all Christian Catalonia first came under the authority of the counts of Barcelona and that these were no-one's vassals"). Pere Ortí, "La primera articulación del estado feudal en Cataluña a través de un impuesto: el bovaje (ss. XII-XIII)", *Hispania*, 61/209 (2001), p. 973; *Ramón Berenguer I fue el verdadero creador del principado de Cataluña como un verdadero Estado feudal, como ha señalado P. Bonnassie. Su largo reinado permitió la consolidación de la unidad de todos los territorios catalanes bajo la dirección de Barcelona* ("Ramon Berenguer I was the real creator of the principality of Catalonia as a true feudal state, as pointed out by P. Bonnassie. His long reign allowed the consolidation of the unity of all the Catalan territories under the leadership of Barcelona"). César González, "La multiplicación de los reinos (1035-1072)", *Historia de España de la Edad Media*, Vicente Ángel Álvarez, coord. (Barcelona: Ariel, 2002), p. 204.

29 Flocel Sabaté, *La feudalización de la sociedad catalana* (Granada: Editorial Universidad de Granada, 2007).

reason, during the last few decades of the 20th century, Michel Zimmerman stressed that Catalonia's cohesion did not come until the mid-12th century, precisely when this cultural convergence dovetailed with the rise led by the House of Barcelona, which absorbed other countships, completed the conquest of Islamic territory and secured the royal Crown of Aragon. This set of elements prompted the emergence of a true national sentiment:

> *C'est au milieu du XIIe siècle que se constitue vraiment la principauté catalane; la liturgie politique cristallise un sentiment national; à l'inverse des autres principautés nées au Xe siècle du démembrement du royaume franc, la principauté catalane s'est constituée de bas en haut: la conscience d'une identité y accompagne, y précède sans doute le regroupement territorial*[30].

> It was in the middle of the 12th century that the Catalan principality was really constituted; the political liturgy crystallized a national sentiment; unlike other principalities born in the 10th century from the break-up of the Frankish kingdom, the Catalan principality was formed from the bottom up: an awareness of identity accompanied it and undoubtedly preceded the territorial reunification.

However, the difficulties entailed in consolidating the initiatives of the House of Barcelona in its pretensions to secure taxes and jurisdictions highlighted the foibles of the counts and, more importantly, revealed the plurality of a society in which both the feudal lords and emerging urban elites were coalescing[31]. In this context, Thomas Bisson accepts the existence of a Catalan nation identifiable by its cultural traits since before the 12th century: *La Catalogne appartient à ces pays pour lesquels le concept de nation précédé celui d'Etat. Il n'y pas de doute que la « nation » catalane a existé dès avant le XIIe siècle* ("Catalonia is among those countries where the concept of nation preceded the state. There is no doubt that the Catalan 'nation' existed even before the 12th century"). However, at the same time, this identity would not become politically stable until the shift from the 12th to the 13th centuries: *les élans et progrès de la conscience catalane, loin d'être « achevés » en 1100 ou en 1137, connaissent alors l'ébauche d'une première expression; ils devaient être profondément secoués et accélérés par les*

30 Michel Zimmermann, "Des pays catalans à la Catalogne: genèse d'une représentation", *Histoire et archéologie des terres catalanes au Moyen Âge*, Philippe Sénac, ed. (Perpignan: Presses Universitaires de Perpignan, 1995), p. 80.

31 Flocel Sabaté, "Els primers temps: segle XII (1137-1213)", *Història de la Corona d'Aragó*, 2 vols., Ernest Belenguer, ed. (Barcelona: Edicions 62, 2007), vol. 1, pp. 31-82.

conquêtes et les fondations des premiers comtes-rois (c. 1148-1213)[32] ("the momentum and progress of Catalan awareness, far from being 'completed' in 1100 or 1137, then underwent the beginnings of a first expression; they were deeply shaken and accelerated by the conquests and the foundations of the first counts-kings (c. 1148-1213").

In short, the question of the origin of the nation has led us to note a concatenation of prominent medievalists, each of whom at a given point in time was responsible for a document analysis aimed at detecting the combination of political consolidation and awareness of a common identity shared by the inhabitants of the land. Given these characteristics, the conclusion is always that a nation could indeed be detected. Yet "nation" is a term that does not appear in the documentation analysed; instead, its existence can be deduced by seeing all the aforementioned elements converge, especially popular consciousness, which would be derived from a cultural component that usually precedes a political component. Even though they all concur on this point, the conclusions are diametrically opposed when specifying the point in time when the birth of national identity took place: the late 9th century, the late 10th century, the mid-11th century, the second third of the 12th century, the shift from the 12th to 13th centuries. Such broad disagreement casts doubt on any choice. In reality, bearing in mind that on historiographical matters the questions may condition the answers, we should open up a methodological reflection on whether, during the course of these studies, appropriate questions for an early medieval context were asked.

2. How the country and its inhabitants adopted a common name

In many cases, the affiliations between coronym and demonym, as well as the relationship between them, are quite clear. However, in Catalonia, the question gives rise to discrepancies between philologists and historians, perhaps leading to more questions than answers, with the consequent

32 Thomas N. Bisson, "L'éssor de la Catalogne: identité, pouvoir et idéologie dans une société du XIIe siècle", *Annales. Économies, Sociétés. Civilisations*, 39/3 (1984), p. 455.

uncertainty among the researchers themselves[33]. For this reason, the issue has sometimes been viewed as a dead-end of incessant inquiry, as Joan Vernet stated in 1978: *el nom de Catalunya té uns origens força foscos i no es pot assegurar que cap de les hipòtesis o teories fins ara exposades respongui a la veritat històrica*[34] ("the name Catalonia has rather dark origins and one cannot claim that any assumptions or theories hitherto presented respond to the historical truth"). However, a careful look at the topic leads to conclusions that are not too at odds with the historical approaches.

First of all, from a philological standpoint, we can note coronyms like Cadalen in the south of what is today France, which are considered to come from the same coronymic roots as Catalonia, as the result of Catalan immigration in the 12th century[35]. In other interpretations, however, the name of these Occitan places are taken as the origin of the Catalan name and people: in 1744, when defining the location of *Les Catalans ou Escalens* in the diocese of Montalbà, the following entry was made: *quelques-uns croient que c'est de ce lieu qui étoit autrefois très considérable, que sortirent les premières troupes que firent des conquêtes sur les sarrasins en Espagne, et que c'est de là que la Catalogne a pris son nom*[36] ("some believe that it was from this place that was formerly very large, that the first troops aet out to make conquests from the Saracens in Spain, and it is from there that Catalonia took its name"). The same dictionary then defines the *catalauni* without associating them with the aforementioned coronym, although in the preceding centuries the erroneous location of

33 *Las discusiones y razonamientos acerca del topónimo Cataluña y del étnico catalán, son abundantes e incluso contradictorias, ninguna sin embargo realmente satisfactoria. No es infrecuente tampoco que los estudiosos, aun mostrándose partidarios de una determinada etimología citen o insinúen otras, dando a entender la inseguridad en que se mueven* ("There are abundant and even contradictory discussions and arguments about the place name Catalonia and Catalan ethnicity, however none are really satisfactory. It is not uncommon for scholars, even showing support for a certain etymology, cite or imply other, showing the insecurity in which they move"). Luis Rubio, "Catalán-Cataluña", *Estudios Románicos*, 1 (1978), p. 239.

34 Joan Vernet, "El nom de Catalunya", *Història de Catalunya*, 6 vols. (Barcelona: Salvat Editores, 1978), vol. 2, p. 31.

35 Pierre-Henri Billy, "'Catalán'. Nom de persona", *Congrés Internacional de Toponímia i Onomàstica Catalanes* (Valencia: Publicacions de la Universitat de València, 2001), p. 6.

36 Abbé Expilly, *Dictionnaire géographique, historique et politique des Gaules et de la France*, vol. 2 (Amsterdam: no editor listed, 1764), p. 127.

the Campus Catalaunicus in Languedoc had fostered this association. In reality, the Campus Catalaunicus was located to the west of Champagne, where the coronym bears numerous clearly early medieval references (*Ager Catalaunicus, Campania Cathalaunensis, Campi Catalaunenses, Campania Territorii Catalaunensis, Pagus Catalaunicus*, etc.) in the area near Châlons (Châlons-en-Champagne). Between the 9th and 11th centuries, while the diocese of Châlons covered a large area, the specific district near the city, the grand archdeaconry of Châlons, was known as the *comitatus catalaunensis*[37].

The origin of Catalonia and its name as a transfer from the people and their name initially situated in the Campus Catalaunicus is not a bad fit within the humanistic framework from the late 15th century, which might view it as a contribution similar to the settlement of the Germanic peoples. This is Jeroni Pau's explanation in 1491, which was accepted by Calça in 1588[38] and reproduced by Father Mariana in his reissued *History of Spain*, which facilitated its dissemination for centuries:

> *En la parte de Cataluña se le entregaron* [to Charlemagne] *las ciudades de Gerona y de Barcelona. De donde conviene tomar principios de los condes de Barcelona y de los catalanes, nombrados así de los pueblos Catalaunos puestos en la Gallia Narbonense cerca de la ciudad de Tolosa, que contra los moros hicieron entrada y asiento por aquella parte de España*[39].

> In the part of Catalonia the cities of Girona and Barcelona were handed over [to Charlemagne]. From here the counts of Barcelona and the Catalans started, so named the *Catalaunos* people placed in the Narbonese Gaul near the city of Toulouse, who against the Moors entered and settled that part of Spain.

37 M. J. Desnoyers, "Topographie Ecclésiastique de la France pendant le Moyen Âge et dans les temps modernes jusqu'en 1790. Anciennes subdivisions territoriales des diocèses en Archidiaconés, Archiprêtrés, et Doyannés ruraux. Deuxième partie: Les Belgiques et les Germanies", *Annuaire de la Société de l'Histoire de France*, 23 (1859), pp. 210-211.

38 Calça framed it within the vision of the Catalan people who had liberated themselves from the Muslims and offered themselves to the Carolingians (Jesús Villanueva, "Francisco Calça y el mito de la libertad originaria de Cataluña", *Revista de Historia Jerónimo Zurita*, 69-70 (1994), pp. 75-87).

39 Juan de Mariana, *Historia General de España*, 2 vols. (Barcelona: Imprenta y Librería de Gaspar y Roig Editores, 1852), vol. 1, p. 219.

When Andreu Bosch systematically outlined the seven possible roots of the name Catalonia in 1628, he stressed, as *més rebuda com a més certa* ("the most accepted such as a more truthful"), the link with this place *dels camps Cathalaunos de Aquitania en França lloch y sol a hont és avui lo Limosí* ("from the 'Cathalaunos' fields of Aquitaine in France, where there is today the Limousin region"), thanks to the people who arrived during the campaigns against the Muslim invaders: *succehí quant entraren les differents nacions estranyes a expellir los moros de la Gocia segons los pobladors restaren en ella quiscuna terra, proseguí lo nom, títol y llengua de la mateixa nació restà*[40] ("it happened when the different foreign nations entered to Gotia to expel the Moors, and then the settlers remained on the country and the name, title and Language of the nation remained"). This statement prolongs the humanistic confusion that situated the Campus Catalaunicus near Toulouse, which helped to explain the purported linguistic similarities. In the 19th century, the location of the Campus Catalaunicus was rectified, which helped to debunk this theory due to the distance between Champagne and the places with which it shared linguistic and historical similarities[41]. Nevertheless, in the 20th century Giuliano Bonfante revisited the theory by assessing the move of a tribal branch of *catalauni* to the place that is currently known as Catalonia. The Franks' activity to expel the Muslims was the right occasion to move the population of Châlons towards the Hispanic fringe of Carolingian territory[42]. There is no appropriate documentary support to endorse this view[43], yet it does match the close relationship between Champagne and Catalonia, as both regions were very naturally in touch through Lyon until 877[44].

40 Andreu Bosch, *Sumari, índex o epítome dels admirables i nobilíssims títols d'honor de Catalunya, Rosselló i Cerdanya* (Perpignan: Pere Lacavalleria, Estamper, 1628) (facsimile: Barcelona: Curial, 1974), p. 90.

41 Pascual Madoz, *Articles sobre el Principat de Catalunya, Andorra i zona de parla catalana del regne d'Aragó al 'Diccionario geográfico – estadístico – hiustórico de España y sus posesiones de Ultramar'* (Barcelona: Curial, 1985), p. 430.

42 Giuliano Bonfante, *El nombre de Cataluña* (Buenos Aires: Universidad de Buenos Aires, 1944).

43 This is acknowledged by one of the opinions which recently has expressed its support of this explanation, although based more on popular history than on scholarly research: Lowell Lewis, *Catalonia California Estats Agermanats* (Bloomington: Author House, 2013), pp. 15 and 19.

44 Flocel Sabaté, "Història Medieval", *Història de Catalunya*, Albert Balcells, dir. (Barcelona: L'Esfera dels Llibres, 2004), pp. 108-109.

In reality, the veracity of this explanation should be backed by the concurrent use and continuity of the coronym, which it is not. The supposed uses of the term "Catalonia" in the 9th century have been shown to be false, beginning with the 806 donation to Sant Feliu de Pesillà, located *in comitatu Cathalonia in pago Rossilionensi*[45], which is only referenced in the later copies compiled by Fossà in the 18th century[46]. This was followed by the 844 document which verified the fact that Louis the Pious gave the Count of Barcelona the authority *super totam Catalonia*. Jaime Villanueva called attention to this by noting that *esta es la primera vez que se cree nombrada Cataluña* ("this is the first time that Catalonia is believed to be named"), and then warning that *no salgo fiador de la autenticidad de esta escritura*[47] ("I do not guarantee the authenticity of this writing"). It seems more appropriate for the demonym or ethnic name to precede the coronym, and for this to be reflected when defining certain people. In this sense, we may believe that *en els textos trobem gent que es diu Català abans del segle XI* ("in the texts we find people called Catalan before the 11th century") in the words of Michel Zimmermann[48]. However, these are unusual mentions and somewhat dubious and difficult to verify, beginning with the oldest reference, a delimitation from 917 – *de meridie in vinea Cathalani* – if we accept as valid a document only known through a much later copy from the 18th century[49].

The desire for documents to contain domains and references from the founding epoch is related to the inherent legal underpinnings[50] common

45 Francisco Monsalvatje, *El obispado de Elna*, 4 vols. (Olot: Imprenta y Librería de Ramon Bonet, 1913), p. 82.

46 Paul Aesbicher was aware of the reference when reading Montsalvatge's work, and he limited himself to reproducing it, only adding the note that *me parait bien étrange* ("it seems to me very strange") because of the chronology (Paul Aesbicher, *Estudis de toponimia catalana* [Barcelona: Institut d'Estudis Catalans, 2006], p. 134).

47 Jaime Villanueva, *Viage literario a las iglesias de España*, 22 vols. (Madrid: Real Academia de la Historia, 1850), vol. 13, p. 18.

48 Jordi Barrachina, Jesús Mestre, "Michel Zimmermann: la fascinació per la Catalunya medieval", *L'Avenç*, 125 (1989), p. 65.

49 Lluis G. Constans, *Diplomatari de Banyoles*, 6 vols. (Banyoles: Centre d'Estudis Comarcals de Banyoles, 1985), vol. 1, p. 213.

50 Juan de Churruca, "La relatividad del argumento histórico", *Derecho y argumentación histórica*, Teresa Peralta, dir. (Lleida: Edicions de la Universitat de Lleida, 1999), pp. 20-25.

to the Middle Ages, which mistrusted changes after the early stage[51]. The attempt to justify the Counts of Barcelona's initial dominion over Catalonia as a whole with his leadership in the process of forming the country[52] was the argument sought by late medieval sovereigns who needed to strengthen their ground before the estates[53]. However, the estates, in turn, also found their own likely endorsement in the founding epoch through explanations that strove to determine the subsequent evolution, either because the earliest Aragonese people in Aragon would choose a popular officer called *justicia* before the king[54], or because in Catalonia the origin is pinpointed at the arrival of Otger Cataló, preceding Charlemagne and presiding over nine knights who match the prominent 15th century lineages, with whom he would free the country and grant it a name derived from his own surname. Thus, the importance of noble lineages was underscored, which in any case, as added by another text that aims to appeal to the origins, would then agree with the inhabitants of the country, who came from the people from the villages and cities with whom the barons shared the power of the estates in the late Middle Ages[55]. This explanation, which sprang up in the first half of the 15th century[56] and was quite widespread back then[57], easily links up with the previous explanations of the Campus Catalaunicus

51 Flocel Sabaté, "Els referents històrics de la societat: identitat i memòria", *L'Edat Mitjana. Món real i espai imaginat*, Flocel Sabaté, coord. (Catarroja-Barcelona: Editorial Afers, 2012), pp. 18-19.

52 Flocel Sabaté, "La construcción ideológica del nacimiento unitario de Cataluña", *Castilla y el mundo feudal. Homenaje al profesor Julio Valdeón*, 3 vols., María Isabel del Val, Pascual Martínez, eds. (Valladolid: Junta de Castilla y León-Universidad de Valladolid, 2009), vol. 1, pp. 101-102.

53 Flocel Sabaté, "États et alliances dans la Catalogne du bas Moyen-Âge", *Du contrat d'alliance au contrat politique. Cultures et sociétés politiques dans la péninsule Ibérique à la fin du Moyen Âge*, François Foronda, Ana Isabel Carrasco, eds. (Toulouse: Centre National de la Recherche Scientifique-Université Toulouse–Le Mirail, 2007), pp. 300-301.

54 Agustín Ubieto, *Leyendas para una historia paralela del Aragón medieval* (Saragossa: Institución Fernando el Católico, 1998), p. 337.

55 Berenguer de Puigpardines, *Sumari d'Espanya* (Valencia: Universitat de València, 2000), p. 68.

56 Eulàlia Duran, *Sobre la mitificació dels orígens històrics nacionals catalans* (Barcelona: Institut d'Estudis Catalans, 1991), pp. 14-17.

57 Pere Tomic, *Històries e conquestes dels reis d'Aragó...*, pp. 57-61.

by claiming that Otger came from there, as both Jeroni Pau and Francesc Calça quite vehemently accepted in the 16th century[58].

In the 16th century, too, Zurita reduces Otger Cataló to mere *fábula* ("fable") after he claimed to have examined the documentation[59], an identical opinion to the one which Pierre de la Marca reached the following century after a study of the documentation[60]. This is coherent with Diago being unaware of the purported figure who lent his name to the country[61], and with Bosch, who when mentioning it as the first of the seven etymological possibilities for the name of Catalonia, expressed objections that are coherent with the documentation: *aquesta és la primera opinió, emperò a la veritat de molt temps après de Carles Magne no tingué tal nom* ("this is the first opinion, however the truth is that long after Charlemagne it had no such name"). Bosch also reported on the opinion that the name came from the move of the aforementioned Catalaunics, or other Germanics, the Cats[62], thus supporting the hypothesis formulated by Francesc Comte in 1586[63]. However, these arguments and the dearth of documentation do not deter the criteria and purposes of the majority of historiographers in the modern centuries. This is why the founding role of Otger Cataló became so

58 *Calça supone que los catalaunos, desde su tierra originaria en Aquitania, emigraron a Cataluña en el siglo VIII siguiendo la expedición de Otger y luego las de Carlomagno y Luis el Piadoso. Pocos años después de la reconquista de Barcelona adquirirían el pleno dominio del país, tras reprimir las revueltas goticistas de Aisó (o Ayshun) e 827 e imponerse así a los 'antiguos españoles' (hispani) y a los godos* ("Calça supposes that the catalaunos, from their native land in Aquitaine, emigrated to Catalonia in the 8th century following Otger's expedition and later those by Charlemagne and Louis the Pious. A few years after the reconquest of Barcelona, they would acquire the full domain over the country, after putting down the Gothic revolts of Aisó (or Ayshun) in 827 and imposing themselves over the 'old Spaniards (hispani) and the Goths"). Jesús Villanueva, *Política y discurso histórico en la España del siglo XVIII. Las polémicas sobre los orígenes medievales de Cataluña* (Alicante: Publicaciones de la Universidad de Alicante, 2004), p. 45.

59 Jerónimo Zurita, *Gestas de los Reyes de Aragón*, 2 vols. (Saragossa: Institución Fernando el Católico, 1984), vol. 1, p. 34.

60 Petro de Marca, *Marca Hispanica sive limes hispanicus* (Paris: Franciscum Muguet, 1688) (facsimile, Barcelona: Editorial Base, 1974), coll. 242.

61 Francisco Diago, *Historia de los victoriosísimos antiguos condes de Barcelona* (Barcelona: Casa Sebastián de Cormellas al Call, 1603), pp. 47-48.

62 Andreu Bosch, *Sumari, índex o epítome dels admirables...*, p. 90.

63 Francesc Comte, *Il·lustracions dels Comtats de Rosselló, Cerdanya i Conflent*, ed. Joan Tres (Barcelona: Curial, 1995), pp. 171-172.

prominent, thanks to the enthusiastic reference of Francesc Calça[64], who was followed by authors like Onofre Manescal[65], Jeroni Pujades[66], Diego de Montfar[67], Narcís Feliu de la Peña[68] and, most prominently, Esteve Corbera, who devoted much of his history to Catalonia[69]. The primacy of documentary rigour among the 18th century authors once again led Otger Cataló to be ignored in the works of Masdeu[70] and Florez[71]. During the 19th century not only did Otger Cataló return with Pi i Arimón[72], but he also became quite important thanks to the inflamed romantic positions of Víctor Balaguer[73]. The reference would only be permanently destroyed thanks to the definitive death blow dealt by Antoni Bofarull[74].

In the 15th century, when Pere Miquel Carbonell rejected the name of the country as a derivation of Otger Cataló's actions, he did so by appealing to the need to examine the past upon a well-grounded basis, and he thus refused to reach that far back to find the roots of the name of Catalonia:

64 Calça links it up with the arguments that support the freedoms of Catalonia back in its founding moments (Jesús Villanueva, "Francisco Calça i el mito…", pp. 75-87).

65 Onofre Manescal, *Sermó vulgarment anomenat del Serenissim senyor den Jaume segon, justicier y pacífic rey de Aragó y compte de Barcelona, fill de Pere lo Gran y sa dona Constança sa muller* (Barcelona: Casa Sebastià de Cormellas al Call, 1602), f. 25v.

66 Jerónimo Pujades, *Crónica Universal del Principado de Cataluña*, 8 vols. (Barcelona: Imprenta de José Torner, 1829), vol. 5, p. 16.

67 Diego de Monfar, *Historia de los condes de Urgel*, 2 vols. (Barcelona: Establecimiento Litográfico y Tipográfico de D. José Eusebio Montfort, 1853), vol. 1, pp. 259-264 (into the series, directed by Próspero de Bofarull, *Colección de Documentos Inéditos del Archivo General de la Corona de Aragón*, vol. IX).

68 Narciso Feliu de la Peña, *Anales de Cataluña*, 3 vols. (Barcelona: Imprempta Josep Llopis, 1709), vol. 1, p. 203.

69 Estevan de Corbera, *Cataluña Ilustrada* (Naples: Antonino Gramiñani, 1678), pp. 306-440.

70 Juan Francisco Masdeu, *Historia crítica de España y de la cultura española*, 20 vols. (Madrid: Imprenta de Sancha, 1793), vol. 12, pp. 85-107; Juan Francisco Masdeu, *Historia crítica de España y de la cultura española*, 20 vols. (Madrid: Imprenta de Sancha, 1794), vol. 13, pp. 5-8.

71 Enrique Florez, Manuel Risco, *España Sagrada…*, vol. 29, pp. 149-150.

72 Andrés Avelino Pi, *Barcelona antigua y moderna…*, vol. 2, p. 440.

73 Víctor Balaguer, *Historia de Cataluña y de la Corona de Aragón*, 5 vols. (Barcelona: Librería de Salvador Manero, 1860), vol. 1, pp. 180-191.

74 Antonio de Bofarull, *Historia crítica (civil y eclesiástica) de Cataluña*, 9 vols. (Barcelona: Juan Aleu y Fugarull Editor, 1876), vol. 2, pp. 31-41; Antonio de Bofarull, *Historia crítica (civil y esglesiàstica)...*, vol. 3, pp. 49-66.

> *pot passar com a cosa apòchrifa e de poca fe, majorment que fins al temps de Carolo Calvo emperador no legim aquests noms de catalans, sinó que dita província se nomena, en temps de Carles Mayes e de Loys emperador, de Hespanya gòtthica*[75].
>
> it can be like an apocryphal thing and of little faith, mostly until the time of the Emperor Charles the Bald we do not read these names of Catalans, but this province was called, in the time of Charlemagne and the emperor Louis, the Gothic Spain.

It could easily be deduced that the name of Catalonia is derived from a reference to the Goths: it is the country that was inhabited by this Germanic people, or perhaps by a mixture of Visigoths and Alans, as Jeroni Pau explains in an opinion most likely borrowed from Bishop Margarit[76], which would continue to survive in the background in the 17th century[77]. This proposition was fully accepted in the humanistic climate of the 15th century, when, as consideration of the classical world resumed[78], the overall vision of *Hispania*[79] was accentuated, and with it the core role of the Visigoths, especially as a political and dynastic referent based on the unity and cohesion of the Peninsula[80]. Thus, the name Catalonia is framed within *l'herència goda* that the Catalan humanists revived by participating in *elaboració i difusió d'aquells mites històrics que contribueixen al*

75 *Altres molts grans errors se troben scrites per lo dit mossèn Thomich e altres hòmens il·literats, car han volgut dir e scriure sens fundament algú ne auctors aprovats, històrics o chronistes* ("Other very great errors are found written by the hand of Father Thomich and other illiterate men, because they wanted to say and write without any basis in any approved or historical authors or chroniclers"). Pere Miquel Carbonell, *Cròniques d'Espanya*, 2 vols., Agustí Alcoberro, ed. (Barcelona: Editorial Barcino, 1997), vol. 1, pp. 178 and 181.

76 Eulàlia Miralles, "La posteritat del cardenal Margarit (segles XV-XVII)", *El cardenal Margarit i l'Europa quatrecentista*, Mariàngela Villalonga, Eulàlia Miralles, David Prat, eds. (Rome: L''Erma' di Bretschneider, 2008), pp. 100-101.

77 Andreu Bosch, *Sumari, índex o epítome dels admirables...*, p. 90.

78 Mariàngela Vilallonga, "Humanistas italianos en los manuscritos de Pere Miquel Carbonell", *Humanismo y pervivencia del mundo clásico*, José María Maestre, Luis Charlo, Joaquín Pascual, eds. (Cádiz: Servicio de Publicaciones de la Universidad de Cádiz, 1997), pp. 1217-1226.

79 Mariàngela Vilallonga, "La geografia a Catalunya a l'època del Renaixement", *Estudi General*, 13 (1993), pp. 51-61.

80 Jocelyn N. Hillgarth, "Los godos en la historiografía catalana, antes y en la época de Margarit", *El cardenal Margarit i l'Europa quatrecentista*, Mariàngela Vilallonga, Eulàlia Miralles, David Prat, eds. (Rome: L'Erma' di Bretschneider, 2008), pp. 188-189.

sentit del destí i d'identitat col·lectius i sobretot de continuïtat dinàstica[81] ("preparation and dissemination of those historical myths that contribute to the sense of destiny and group identity and especially to dynastic continuity"). Therefore, it draws from a common *origine regum Hispaniae et Gothorum,* in the words of Joan Margarit[82]. However, as Tate noted, we should avoid the simplistic act of relating the Gothic referent with a desire to unify the Peninsula, because works like those of Bishop Margarit primarily strove to highlight the special relationship between the kings of Catalonia-Aragon and their Gothic predecessors precisely when the latter enjoyed prestige around the Iberian Peninsula, quite different to the image of barbarism that they inspired on the other peninsula, Italy[83].

In any event, this explanation does not contradict the previous ones regarding the birth of the country's name; rather it may complement them by connecting the German origin in the Campus Catalaunicus and the expedition led by Otger, as proposed by Jeroni Pau:

> *Vnde existimatum est a non uulgaribus propter consistentem tum maxime in ea regione Alanam et Gotorum gentem, inceptos appellari Gotalanicos populos, qui nunc Catalani dicuntur; et si quidam ab Augerio quodam, cognomento Catalone, Germanorum duce dictos fuisse scribant, quem ante Caruli Magni tempora non legitimo exercitu ut Sarracenos pelleret Hispaniam intrasse tradunt, militibusque suis Catalanorum nomen indidisse, et paulo mox dum Emporias urbem obsideret occubuisse. Hunc ducem quidam non Germanicae sed Gallicae gentis fuisse ferunt, e Catalaunica regione singulari proelio memorabili. Superiora sane astruere illius temporis scriptores uidentur, qui usque ad Caruli Calui tempora hanc regionem Hispaniam Goticam, et prouinciam Narbonensem Gallogotiam appellant*[84].

At the turn of the 17th century, Pere Gil omits Otger Cataló and instead naturally links up with the Goths and Alans, and then the Franks,

81 Eulàlia Duran, *Sobre la mitificació dels orígens...*, p. 11.

82 Robert B. Tate, *Joan Margarit i Pau, cardenal i bisbe de Girona* (Barcelona: Curial, 1976), pp. 215-222.

83 Robert B. Tate, "Margarit i el tema dels gots", *Actes del Cinquè col·loqui Internacional de Llengua i Literatura Catalanes (Andorra, 1-6 October 1979)*, Jordi Bruguera, Josep Massot, eds. (Barcelona: Publicacions de l'Abadia de Montserrat, 1980), pp. 151, 160-162.

84 Jeroni Pau, "Barcino", *Obres*, ed. Mariàngela Vilallonga (Barcelona: Curial, 1986) <http://www3.udg.edu/ilcc/Eiximenis/html_eiximenis/portal_SH/textos/barcino.pdf>; Jeroni Pau, "Barcino", *Historia de Barcelona fins al segle XV*, Josep Maria Casas, ed. (Barcelona: Fundació Francesc Blasi, 1957), p. 48.

concatenating two successive names: *De Gotholonia que abans se nomenava, dels Gothos y Alanos que juntament lo habitaren: se nomena ara Cathalonia, dels francesos que vingueren de França, dela provincia nomenada Cathalaunia*[85] ("from Gotholonia which previously was named, after the Goths and Alans who jointly inhabited it: it is now called Cathalonia, after the French who came from France, from the province named Cathalaunia").

Even though the addition of criteria such as document comparisons may make the references to Otger Cataló and the Campus Catalaunicus credible, the Gothic reminiscence may be endorsed by the evidence which is at least based on a provable presence, which can then be complemented with linguistic arguments. This explains why the proposed German origin became more prominent in the 19th century, as upheld by Torres Amat:

> *Suponen que los catalanes refugiados en Aquitania en la irrupción sarracénica, trajeron después la lengua al país natural, cuando auxiliados con tropas de Aquitania le reconquistaron, y que de ahí vendría en nombre de 'catalanes', tomado del lugar de 'Cathalens' o de los Campos Catháláunicos. Otros empero le hacen derivar del caudillo de la tropas que vinieron contra los moros, 'Otger Godland; al cual suponen que era gobernador del Lemosín, y vino, dicen, acompañado de los nueve barones a echar a los moros de Cataluña: otros le hacen derivar de las palabras Catos y Alanos, o de Godos y Alanos, pero todo lo dicho carece de sólido fundamento. Lo más probable es que debemos el nombre de Cataluña a los Godos, desde que Ataulfo, firmada la paz con el Emperador Honorio, estableció su Corte en Barcelona, y fundó su reino, llamándolo en su idioma 'Gottland, voz que en la pronunciación Teutónica suena 'Keteland' y en la nuestra 'Cathalan'; en romano vulgar 'Gotholaunia' (que en nuestro acento es 'Cathalonia) y en latí 'Gothia' o 'Gotia'*[86].

> They suppose that the Catalan refugees in Aquitaine after the Saracen invasion brought their own language to the country, when helped by troops from Aquitaine the reconquered it, and that would be where the name of 'Catalans' came from, taking the place of 'Cathalens' or the Campos Catháláunicos. Others however make it derive from the leader of the troops that came against the Moors, 'Otger Godland; who they suppose was the governor of Limousin, and came, they say, accompanied by the nine

85 Josep Iglésies, *Pere Gil, S. J. (1551-1621) i la seva Geografia de Catalunya* (Barcelona: Societat Catalana de Geografia-Institut d'Estudis Catalans, 2002), p. 276.

86 Félix Torras, *Memorias para ayudar a formar un diccionario crítico de los escritores catalanes y dar alguna idea de la antigua y moderna literatura de Cataluña* (Barcelona: Imprenta de J. Verdaguer, 1836), p. 28.

barons to expel the Moors from Catalonia: other make it derive from the words Catos and Alanos, or Godos and Alanos, but everything said lacks a solid foundation. The most probable is that we owe the name of Catalonia to the Goths, since Ataulfo, signing the peace with the Emperor Honorius, set up his court in Barcelona, and founded his kingdom, calling it in his language 'Gottland, a word that in the Teutonic pronunciation sounds like 'Keteland' and in ours 'Cathalan'; in vulgar Roman 'Gotholaunia' (which in our accent is 'Cathalonia) and in Latin 'Gothia' or 'Gotia'.

Therefore, it is understandable that when the arguments about Otger Cataló were fully debunked in the late 19th century, the conviction regarding the Germanic roots survived. This is what Bori Fontestà reported in 1899, referring to the name of Catalonia:

de cuya etimología tanto han discrepado los autores, pues mientras unos quieren hallarla en Otjer Catalón, héroe de existencia puralmente fabulosa, la determina otros, con más acierto, en "Gotholandia", tierra de godos[87].

whose etymology both authors have so disagreed with, because while some want to find it in Otjer Catalón, hero of purely fantasy existence, other determine it, more accurately, in 'Gotholandia' land of Goths.

However, the lack of continuity in the name makes it difficult to sustain such a chronologically remote explanation. The field of philology has sought alternatives around emblematic places that might have determined the coronym. This is nothing new: Lorenzo Valla tried to do so by linking it up with the classical period:

leemos en Plutarco, en la vida de Sertorio, que hubo allí una ciudad ilustre llamada Catalon, y que sus habitantes se llamaban Catalanes. Que más tarde el nombre propagara no es nada extraño, hay numerosos casos semejantes[88].

we read in Plutarch, in the life of Sertorius, that was there an illustrious city called Catalon, and its inhabitants were called Catalans. That the name later spread is not unusual, there are numerous similar cases.

In the 17th century, Andreu Bosc reported on this possible explanation, as he did of Castellón, too[89]. Continuing in the vein of pinpointing a coronym

87 Antonio Bori, *Historia de Cataluña…*, p. 77.

88 Lorenzo Valla, *Historia de Fernando de Aragón*, ed. Santiado López Moreda (Madrid: Akal, 2002), p. 84.

89 Andreu Bosch, *Sumari, índex o epítome dels admirables...*, p. 90.

which lends its name to the territory located beyond it, as in other cases in Europe, in 1942 Paul Aebischer pointed out one of the emblematic gateways to the Barcelona region: Montcada[90]. He also noted the chronological milestone of the birth of the coronym and demonym: *fue en la segunda mitad del siglo XI cuando 'Cathalonia' y 'Catalanus' debieron de empezar a difundirse*[91] ("was in the second half of the 11th century when 'Cathalonia' and 'Catalanus' must have started to spread"). However, while the name may derive from an emblematic entry point, in the 11th century, too, which also witnessed the clashes between the Muslim domains, especially in the western part of the country[92]. it would be understandable for the coronym to derive from the Arabic language, referring to a point from which one could glimpse the country that was the target of aggression. This is the role that Joan Vernet, based on the texts by al-Udri, believed corresponded to an Islamic fortification called Talunyat located on the route between Huesca and Lleida, whose precise whereabouts are impossible to determine today[93]. "Catalonia" would derive from its name. When seeking a meaningful enough point of reference to lend its name to the country that stretches out beyond it, we could also consider on the other border, as Joseph Piel explained, the Occitanian-Provençal etymon *cataluonh*, a way of warning someone to "look into the distance" from a border fortification, although it is difficult to pinpoint where this fortification might have been[94]. At the same time, the linguistic substrate in *cata* has enabled us to view it as a reference to the country and its settlers, who would be seen as belonging to a "land of mountain-dwellers", according to

90 Paul Aebischer, "Autour de l'origine du nom *Catalogne*", *Zeitschrift für Romanische*, 62 (1942), pp. 49-67.

91 Paul Aebischer, *Estudios de Toponimia y Lexicografía románica* (Barcelona: Escuela de Filología, 1948), p. 61.

92 Flocel Sabaté, *L'expansió territorial de Catalunya (segles IX-XII): ¿Conquesta o repoblació?* (Lleida: Edicions de la Universitat de Lleida, 1997), pp. 76-86.

93 Joan Vernet, "¿La más antigua cita de Cataluña?", *Al-Andalus*, 32 (1967), pp. 231-232; Joan Vernet, "El nombre de Cataluña", *Boletín de la Real Academia de las Buenas Letras de Barcelona*, 33 (1969-1970), pp. 133-136; Joan Vernet, "El nom de Catalunya", *Història de Catalunya...*, pp. 31-32.

94 Joseph Piel, "Kleine Besträge zur Katalanischen Toponomastik", *Estudis Romànics*, 13 (1963-1968), pp. 237-244.

the explanation by Ángel Pariente[95]. The same etymon *cata* has served to promote explanations far from any criteria of scientific accuracy in order to link the choronym Catalonia with the sunset[96] or with the Cathars, imagining a displaced Occitan people featured by their beliefs[97].

All of these proposals come from philologists who are seeking a coronym that is logical and coherent with the rules of toponymy, while one that also preferably dovetails in dating the appearance of the name Catalonia and the demonym Catalan in around the 11th century, and in seeking an external reference given the perception that a name would be given to this land from the outside as a way to identify its inhabitants. Along these same lines, Pere Balañà noticed that the first reference to the Catalans appeared in the *Liber Maiorichinus*, which narrated the Pisans' participation in the expedition led by Ramon Berenguer III[98] between 1113 and 1115 to conquer the self-sufficient island of Majorca ruled by Mubashshir[99]. He noted that the invasion invoked the need to put an end to the Muslims' piracy, which must have previously besieged the northeast countships on the Peninsula because they were viewed as the "land of wealth" (*Qat`a al-gunya*) or as the "land of the wealthy" (*Qat`a al-gunya'*), a description which was used by the Majorcans and reproduced by the Pisans, giving rise to the name Catalonia[100]. From that same context of piracy, Miquel Carrasquer recently added the conviction that the name Catalonia may have derived from the same term that is at the root of the word Almogaver (alqattâlûn) after the predatory attacks: "'Català' would then be derived from the word 'qattāl' by adding the Romance adjective-forming suffix

95 Ángel Pariente, "Sobre el origen de 'Catalán' y 'Cataluña'", *Anuario de Filología*, 3 (1977), pp. 373-390.

96 Bienvenido Mascaray, "L'origen lingüístic del topònim 'Catalunya'", *Segre* (25th February 2001), pp. 74-75.

97 José-Fermín Peña, *El misterio de la palabra Cataluña. ¿Cuál es el origen de este enigmático término?* (Madrid: Edición personal, 2011), pp. 43-46.

98 Jaume Vidal, *'Liber Maiorichinus' (Text, traducció, notes i introducció)* (Barcelona: Universitat de Barcelona, PhD Dissertation, 1976).

99 Maria Jesús Rubiera, *La Taifa de Denia* (Alacant: Denia Town Hall-Instituto Juan Gil-Albert of the Diputación Provincial de Alicante, 1988), pp. 113-114.

100 Pere Balañà, "El nom de Catalunya: encara una qüestió pendent", *L'Avenç*, 117 (1989), pp. 39-41; Pere Balañà, "Catalunya, 'la terra de la riquesa'", *Medievalia*, 10 (1992), pp. 44-53.

-an-, whereas the name of the country, Catalunya, is made by adding the Romance suffix -ia to the plural 'qattālūn'"[101].

Joan Coromines had already noticed that everything seemed to begin back in the early 12th century in the *Liber Maiorichinus*. For this reason, he believed that the Italian allies of Ramon Berenguer III needed a term with which they could refer to all their colleagues assembled around the Count of Barcelona, without using any specific demonym[102]. This is why in the composition of the poem praising him, the writers harked back to the literary memory of Lacetania, which would then morph from Lacetani to Catelani and from there to Catalans. The use of this literary term and its spread would actually stem from the need to have a word to name the political and social cohesion that coalesced around the aforementioned armed events[103].

This explanation thus gave both consistency and a new frame to the relationship between Catalonia and Lacetania, which the phonetician Ernst Schopf had posited in scholarly circles in 1919 by briefly noting it as a popular hereditary evolution[104]. In reality, back in 1891, Joaquim Cases Carbó highlighted the phonetic affinity between Lacetanian and Catalan, which would reveal an *afinitat de raça* ("racial affinity") within the research that the author performed to propose a large linguistic and ethnic family within which to set the roots of Catalonia, an exercise that he himself calls *etnogènia catalana* ("Catalan ethnogeny")[105].

101 Miquel Carrasquer, "Etymology of 'Català', 'Catalunya'…", <http://www.academia.edu/3815281/Etymology_of_catala_Catalunya>.

102 Joan Coromines, "Extensió i origen de 'català' i 'Catalunya'", *Estudis*, 2 (1970), pp. 159-170.

103 Joan Coromines, *El que s'ha de saber de la llengua catalana* (Palma de Mallorca: Editorial Moll, 1954), pp. 71-83.

104 Ernst Schopf, *Die konsonantischen Fernwirkungen: Fern-Dissimilation, Fern-Assimilation und Metathesis. Ein Beitrag zur Beurteilung ihres Wesens und ihres Verlaufs und zur kanntnis der Vulgärsprache in den lateinischen Inschriffen der römischen Kaiserzeit* (Göttingen: Vandenhocek & Ruprecht, 1919), p. 196.

105 *La radical llatina 'lacetan' equival a la radical grega λακεταν (laketan) y aquesta forma antiga 'laketan' conté exactament els meteixos elements fònics que la forma moderna 'catalan' no habenthi més diferencia entre amduas que la disposició de las consonants sent la meva conclusió qu'els 'lacetans' o λακετανοι, de qui parlan els antichs com habitant aquesta regió eran no més ni menos els ascendents com a fondo de raça dels catalans qu'are l'habitan : això és lo qu'ens dona l'anàlisi fonètic dels noms d'úns y altres* ("the radical Latin 'lacetan' is equivalent to the

In the late 18th century, Jaume Caresmar confessed his uncertainty regarding the origin of the name of the country and its inhabitants and remarked how this contrasted with Valencia: *no podemos decir de qué lugar toman el nombre los catalanes, como lo podemos decir de donde lo toman valencianos, esto es, por su principal ciudad, Valencia*[106] ("we can not say what place the Catalans take their name from, as we can tell where the Valencians take theirs from, that is, from its main city, Valencia"). Quite meaningfully, this statement is part of a set of deductions on coronyms based on Iberian settlements and comes in the middle of a story about Catalonia that is geographically organised according to these Iberian settlements. Echoing this fascination with the Iberian world, back in the 16th century both Florián de Ocampo and Jerónimo Zurita assumed an origin of the coronym derived *de unos pueblos que antiguamente se llamaron Castellanos, que estaban en la antigua Cataluña, entre los Ausetanos y los Lacetanos*[107] ("of peoples who formerly called themselves Castellanos, who were in the old Catalonia between the Ausetani and the Lacetani"). This is an opinion that spread as the territory's contribution became more accentuated in the historical assessment than contributions from the incoming civilisations, either classical or Germanic. After commenting on the possible Germanic roots of the term, Madoz concludes that: *Nosotros creemos más bien, con Gerónimo Zurita, que este nombre se deriva de los antiguos 'castellanos' o 'catalanos' que nombra Ptolomeo en el centro de Cataluña*[108] ("nevertheless we believe, like Geronimo Zurita, that this

radical Greek λακεταν (laketan) and this old form 'laketan' contains exactly the same phonic elements as the modern 'catalan' form with no greater difference between the two than the distribution of the consonants my conclusion being that the 'lacetans' or λακετανοι, who the ancient ones mentioned as inhabitants of this region were no more or less than the deep ascendants of the race of the Catalans who now inhabit it: that is why we derive from the phonetic analysis of the names of ones and the others"). Joaquim Cases, "Estudis d'etnogenia catalana", *L'Avenç Literari, Artístic, Científic*, 3/1 (1891), pp. 17-18.

106 Jaume Caresmar, *Carta al baron de La Linde* (Igualada: Centre d'Estudis Comarcals d'Igualada, 1979), p. 67; Junta de Comercio de Barcelona, *Discurso sobre la agricultura, comercio e industria del Principado de Cataluña (1780)*, ed. Ernest Lluch (Barcelona: Editorial Alta Fulla, 1997), p. 170.

107 Jerónimo Zurita, *Anales de la Corona de Aragón*, 4 vols. (Valencia: Anubar, 1967), vol. 1, p. 49.

108 Pascual Madoz, *Articles sobre el Principat de Catalunya...*, p. 430.

name is derived more from the ancient 'castellanos' o 'catalanos' named by Ptolemy in the centre of Catalonia").

Based on this purported phonetic affinity, relating the name of Catalonia directly to the castles was suggested back in the 16th century[109], although it received scathing criticism. Quite clearly, Onofre Manescal devoted the philological portrait that always accompanied his proposal to it:

> *és cosa certa que dels molts castells que y a en esta terra, no se a dit Cathalunya y los habitadors dellà Catalans. Primerament perquè de castells no se avian de dir Cathalani ni Cathalans sinó Castellani com se anomena la Província de Castella*[110].
>
> it is true that of many of the castles that there are in this land, they are not called Cathalunya and their inhabitants Catalans. First because the castles should not be called Cathalani nor Cathalans but rather Castellani as it is called the Province of Castile.

Back in the turn of the 19th to 20th centuries, Josep Balari formulated it as centred around not the castles but the lieutenants of the fortresses, the castellans. Showing a fine capacity for historical analysis, he stated that the coronym and demonym were unknown during the early Middle Ages – *los habitantes de la Marca eran apellidados con el nombre gentilicio de 'francos' dentro de España* ("the inhabitants of the March were called by the name of 'Franks' within Spain") – and he reported that:

> *en el feudalismo que se desenvolvió en la Marca se llamaba 'castellanus' al que era meramente guarda o alcaide de un castillo sin tener derecho alguno sobre él, y así como de 'castellanus' proceden en francés 'chastelain' y 'châtelain, así mismo se formó en el bajo-latín de la Marca el nombre 'castlanus', del cual son variantes en catala'l: 'castlà, 'catlà' y `carlà'. El nombre 'castlanus' vino a ser término técnico en la institución feudal para significar el vasallo que tenía el castillo en feudo de otro señor.*
>
> In the feudalism that unfolded in the March he who was merely guard or warden of a castle without any right over him was called 'castellanus', and as 'castellanus' comes from French 'Chastelain' and 'châtelain', likewise the name 'castlanus', was formed

109 Miquel Cortés, *Diccionario Geográfico histórico de la España antigua Tarraconense,* Bética *y Lusitania*, 3 vols. (Madrid: Imprenta Real, 1985), vol. 2, p. 323.

110 Onofre Manescal, *Sermó vulgarment anomenat del Serenissim senyor den Jaume segon, justicier y pacífic rey de Aragó y compte de Barcelona, fill de Pere lo Gran y sa dona Constança sa muller* (Barcelona: Casa Sebastià de Cormellas al Call, 1602), f. 7r.

in the low-Latin of the March of which 'Castlà,' 'Catlà' and 'Carlà' are variants in Catalan. The name 'castlanus' became a technical term in the feudal institution to signify the vassal who had the castle in fief for another man.

Consequently:

cuando el país hubo adquirido fisonomía propia por hallarse constituido bajo el régimen feudal, sus habitantes fueron llamados por otro nombre, catalanes. Este apelativo fue debido a los extranjeros de allende los Pirineos. A ellos hubo de parecer que en esta región pululaban los 'castlanes' o 'catlanes', como atalayas destinados a la defensa de la misma[111].

When the country had acquired its own physiognomy by being constituted under the feudal regime, its inhabitants were called by another name, Catalans. This appellation was due to the foreigners from beyond the Pyrenees. For them they had to think that this region was swarming with 'castlanes' or 'catlanes', as watchtowers for the defence thereof.

This was immediately accepted by historians like Carreras Candi, who warned about *designarse a tots nostres guerrers ab lo generich nom de 'catlans' o 'castelans' d'ahont lo nom de 'Catalunya'*[112] ("designating all our warriors with generic name of 'catlans' o 'castelans' d'ahont the name of 'Catalunya'"). In the field of philology, Luis Rubio supported this opinion by remarking on the parallelism with the rest of the Peninsula: *de esta manera el étnico se vincularía a un proceso análogo y paralelo al del Centro de la Península que se plasmaría en Castilla*[113] ("thus the ethnic would be linked to a similar and parallel process to that of the Centre of the Peninsula that would evolve into Castile"). The castle origin of the name of Catalonia, referring either to the fortifications or more likely to their lieutenants, has been overwhelmingly accepted by historians, who still mentioned it in the second half of the 20th century[114], while the majority

111 José Balari, *Orígenes históricos de Cataluña* (Barcelona: Establecimiento Tipográfico de Hijos de Jaime Jepús, 1899) (facsimile: Valladolid: Editorial Maxtor, 2009), pp. 30-31.

112 Francesc Carreras, "Notes sobre los origens de la enfiteusis en lo territorio de Barcelona', *Revista Jurídica de Catalunya*, 15 (1909), p. 198.

113 Luis Rubio, "Catalán-Cataluña…", p. 267.

114 Pierre Bonnassie, *La Catalogne du milieu du X à la fin du XI siècle*, 2 vols. (Toulouse: Publications de l'Université de Toulouse-Le Mirail, 1976), vol. 2, p. 804; Prim Bertran, "Notes sobre els orígens d'unes poblacions urgellenques: la Fuliola, Boldú

of philologists doubted it and offered objections along the lines already formulated back in the 16th century.

When Andreu Bosc considered this possibility in the 17th century, he related it to the "number of castles"[115]. This was also posited by Enric Guiter, who in 1979 proposed an Arabic root for the Catalans' name which referred to the "inhabitants of castles", thus reflecting the perception of how the Muslims might have seen this land and its inhabitants[116]. The most recent proposal also stresses the number of castles, albeit in a very specific zone in the early Middle Ages, from which it would expand to refer to all of Catalonia[117].

---

i Bellcaire als segles XI i XII", *Ilerda*, 42 (1981), pp. 237-272; Michel Zimmermann "Orígenes y formación de una sociedad feudal (785-1137)", *Història de Cataluña*, Joaquim Nadal, Philippe Wolff, eds. (Vilassar de Mar: Oikos-Tau, 1992), p. 236; Pierre Bonnassie, "Sur la formation du féodalisme catalan et sa première expansion (jusqu'à 1150 environ)", *La formació i expansió del feudalisme català. Actes del col·loqui organitzat pel col·legi Universitari de Girona (8-11 de gener de 1985)*, Jaume Portella, ed. (Girona: Col·legi Universitari de Girona-Universitat Autònoma de Barcelona, 1985-1986), p. 21; Thomas N. Bisson, "L'éssor de la Catalogne: identité, pouvoir et idéologie dans une société du XIIe siècle", *Annales. Économies, Sociétés. Civilisations*, 39/3 (1984), p. 456; Manuel Riu, "El feudalismo en Cataluña", *En torno al feudalismo hispánico* (Ávila: Fundación Sánchez Albornoz, 1989), p. 394.

115 Andreu Bosch, *Sumari, índex o epítome dels admirables...*, p. 90.

116 Enric Guiter, "Catalans – Catalonia", *Revista Catalana*, 44 (1979), pp. 13-14.

117 This would be an area *a caballo entre la 'Gothia' y la 'Marca hispanica', y que ya la 'Historia Wambae' había presentado sembrada de fortalezas: 'Caucoliberi', 'Vulturaria', 'Clausuras' y 'Castrum Libiae'. Su situación junto a la Galia Narbonense, dependiente como ella del antiguo reino de Toledo, la convertían en un ente extraño dentro del reino franco* ("between 'Gothia' and the 'Marca hispanica', and that the 'Historia Wambae' had presented full of fortresses: 'Caucoliberi', 'Vulturaria', 'Clausuras' and 'Castrum Libiae'. Their situation next to the Galia Narbonense, dependent like it on the ancient kingdom of Toledo, would turn it into a strange entity within the Frankish kingdom"). Thus the word Catalonia emerged, with a use that was *de carácter popular, probablemente acuñada en el habla franca meridional ya a fines del siglo X, que pasaría a llamar 'Catalonia/Cathalonia' -es decir el país de los 'catalans'/castellanos- a esta parte concreta del país caracterizada por su encastillamiento* ("popular character, probably coined in southern Frankish tongue spoken until the late 10th century, which would call 'Catalonia/Cathalonia' -that is the land of the 'Catalans'/Castilians to this particular part of the country characterized by its castle building"). Rafael Barroso, Jesús Carrobles, Jorge Morín, "Toponimia altomedieval castrense, Acerca del origen de algunos corónimos de España", *e-Spania*, 15 (2013), p. 21. However, we should note that even though this research was published in a prestigious online scholarly journal, it suffers from

However, in reality, the weight and impact exerted by the castles lies not so much in their obviously high number[118] but in their role in articulating the land and the society in the northeast Iberian Peninsula during the 11th and 12th centuries. The occupation of the borderland, which was viewed first as a no-man's land in the 10th century and then as a zone to be conquered in the 11th[119], led to the establishment of a dense, inextricable web of bounded castles[120], with no solution of continuity[121] throughout the

a surprising lack of knowledge of the bibliography and a serious dearth of suitable contextualisation of the period studied, which unquestionably undermines the value of its proposed contributions.

118 Andres Giménez Soler, as always, is clear and vehement when stating that a large number of castles cannot justify the name of Catalonia: *Tengo por etimología cierta y científica la de Zurita y por falsa y popular la de Balari: los reconquistadores de Aragón, de Navarra, de Castilla y León habitaban como los de Oriente y todos construían fortalezas, incluso los no españoles o peninsulares; llenos están de ruinas de edificaciones de esta clase Francia e Italia, las costa de todo el Mediterráneo, las orillas del Danubio y del Rin; los bereberes tienen sus calas y sus 'tirremts': ¿era posible que una costumbre universal caracterizase un pueblo, hasta el punto de darle nombre? Ese nombre, además, suena cuando la reconquista está ya terminada; cuando en el territorio catalán no se siente la necesidad de levantar castillos, y es caso curioso el de prevalecer un nombre cuando cesa la causa y que no tuviese eficacia ni para desterrar uno de los antiguos cuando el motivo vivía en todo auge* ("I have for certain and scientific etymology that of Zurita and false and popular that of Balari: the reconquerers of Aragon, Navarre, Castile and León lived like those from the East and all built forts, even the non-Spanish or peninsular; full of ruins of buildings of this sort are France and Italy, the entire Mediterranean coast, the banks of ther Danube and the Rhine; Berbers have their coves and 'tirremts': was it possible that a universal custom characterised a people, to the point of naming them? That name, moreover, sounds when the reconquest was finished; when in Catalonia no need was felt to erect castles, and it is curious case of a name prevailing when its cause ceases and that did not have the power to banish one of the old ones when the motive was experiencing its heyday"). Andrés Giménez, "La frontera catalano-aragonesa", *II Congreso de Historia de la Corona de Aragón dedicado al siglo XII. Huesca, 26 to 29 April 1920*, 2 vols. (Huesca: Imprenta viuda de Justo Martínez, 1922), vol. 1, p. 472.

119 Flocel Sabaté, *L'expansió territorial de Catalunya...*, pp. 68-76.

120 Flocel Sabaté, "Ocupació i poblament de la Catalunya Nova", *Atles d'Història de Catalunya*, Víctor Hurtado, Jesús Mestre, eds. (Barcelona: Edicions 62, 1995), p. 80.

121 Flocel Sabaté, "El marc històric", *Catalunya Romànica*, 28 vols. (Barcelona: Fundació Enciclopèdia Catalana, 1992), vol. 19, pp. 308-322; Flocel Sabaté, "L'organització territorial i jurisdiccional", *Catalunya Romànica*, 28 vols. (Barcelona: Fundació Enciclopèdia Catalana, 1997), vol. 24, pp. 306-324; Flocel Sabaté, "Territori i

entire land[122]. The feudal area established after the 11th century in all of Catalonia, both Old and New, spread a complete, systematic web of castle districts in extraordinary detail[123], with the corresponding assignment of the entire territory and all its inhabitants[124]. The bounded castle became the basic jurisdictional cell[125] and was built in preferential reference to the location of places[126]. Most prominently, a pyramid of castellans developed in each of the bounded castles[127]. The castellanies articulated the fit between the castle lieutenant and the lord, which resulted in military duties that shaped the entire basic defensive and armed structure of the country for centuries[128], along with rights to taxation that spread and disseminated a dense web of castellan income, for centuries as well, which was spread and affected by all the fragmentation, durability and transference inherent in feudalism[129]. The process that turned Catalonia into a web of bounded castles and castellanies based on deeds and incomes is part of a dynamic that was shared concurrently among all the countships, as they all, in their different facets, coalesced between the 11th and 12th centuries[130].

---

jurisdicció", *Catalunya Romànica*, 28 vols. (Barcelona: Fundació Enciclopèdia Catalana, Barcelona, 1997), vol. 24, pp. 48-65.

122 Flocel Sabaté, "Las tierras nuevas en los condados del nordeste peninsular (siglos X-XII)", *Studia Historica. Historia Medieval*, 23 (2005), pp. 146-153.

123 Flocel Sabaté, "La castralització de l'espai en l'estructuració d'un territori conquerit (Urgell, Pla d'Urgell, Garrigues i Segrià)", *Urtx*, 11 (1997), pp. 8-40.

124 Flocel Sabaté, *El territori de la Catalunya medieval. Percepció de l'espai i divisió territorial al llarg de la Catalunya medieval* (Barcelona: Fundació Salvador Vives Casajuana, 1997), pp. 87-94.

125 It would remain so for centuries: Josep Maria Pons, *Recull d'estudis d'Història jurídica catalana* (Barcelona: Fundació Noguera, 1989), pp. 341-352.

126 Flocel Sabaté, "Limites et ville dans la Catalogne médiévale", *Connaître et delimiter l'espace local au Moyen Âge*, Nacima Baron-Yelles, Stéphane Boissellier, François Clement, Flocel Sabaté, eds. (Lille: Presses Universitaires du Septentrion, forthcoming).

127 Flocel Sabaté, *Fiscalitat i feudalisme (Tàrrega, 1329: recompte i reestructuració)* (Barcelona: Rafael Dalmau Editor, 1991), pp. 16-35.

128 Flocel Sabaté, "La tenencia de castillos en la Cataluña medieval", *Alcaidías y fortalezas en la España medieval*, José Vicente Cabezuelo, ed. (Alcoy: Editorial Marfil, 2006), pp. 76-136.

129 Flocel Sabaté, "Les castlanies i la comissió reial de 1328", *Estudios sobre renta, fiscalidad y finanzas en la Cataluña bajomedieval*, Manuel Sánchez ed. (Barcelona: Consejo Superior de Investigaciones Científicas, 1993), pp. 177-241.

130 Flocel Sabaté, *El territori de la Catalunya medieval* (Barcelona: Fundació Salvador Vives Casajuana, 1997), pp. 273-281.

This is the context in the sights of those who referred to the Count of Barcelona in the *Liber Maiorichinus* in the early 12th century. It is not an improvisation, rather they compiled the demonyms that they were beginning to find at the time as referents for a group with a precise geographic location; thus, the demonym preceded the coronym[131]. The document reveals an increase in references in the first third of the 12th century, and *a partir de 1136, y durante toda la segunda mitad del siglo XII, la forma 'Catalani' (como aposición o apellido), Català', Catalán, Catalanus, etc., ya menudea*[132] ("from 1136, and during the second half of the twelfth century, the form 'Catalani' [as an apposition or surname], 'Català', 'Catalán', 'Catalanus', etc., were becoming frequent"), the reason why we can posit the earliest oral uses in around the 11th century[133].

Seen thus as a descriptor from the outside perspective, the spread of the demonym and the coronym as a referent used from the outside[134] would be facilitated by the projections outward in the 12th century, most prominently in Occitania, but also further inland on the Peninsula through the lineages that would place themselves at the service of the monarchs from León and Castile[135], along with the expansion of troubadour culture[136]. As Billy said, in the Provençal regions, this would be the nickname of those who came from the south[137]. In fact, in this zone there are signatories like *Arnal Catalan, Geral de Cataliung* in the early 12th century, thus showing continuity with the middle (*Guillem Català*) and end

131 Federico Udina, "La última hipótesis sobre el nombre de Cataluña", *Études de Civilisation Médiévales (IX-XI siècles). Mélanges offeretes à Edmon Réné Laborde* (Poitiers: Université de Poitiers, no date), p. 689.

132 Federico Udina, "Cataluña y su corónimo, así como el étnico 'catalán' aparecen en el siglo XI", *Estudios de Edad Media de la Corona de Aragón*, 6 (1956), p. 15.

133 Josep Maria Salrach, *Història dels Països Catalans. 1. Dels orígens a 1714* (Barcelona: Edhasa, 1982), p. 9.

134 Luis Rubio, "Catalán-Cataluña...", p. 256.

135 Ernesto Fernández-Xesta, *Un magnate catalán en la corte de Alfonso VII. 'Comes Poncius de Cabreira, Princeps Çemore* (Madrid: Prensa y Ediciones Iberoamericanas, 1991).

136 Ramon Menéndez, *Poesía juglaresca y juglares. Aspectos de la historia literaria y cultural de España* (Madrid: Espasa-Calpe, 1969).

137 Pierre-Henri Billy, "'Catalán'. Nom de persona", *Congrés Internacional de Toponímia i Onomàstica Catalanes* (Valencia: Publicacions de la Universitat de València, 2001), pp. 5-7.

of that same century (*B. Catalani, Raimundus Catalan, Catalanus*)[138]. We should note that, at the same time, the andronym also accompanied the repopulations of Tortosa and Lleida in the third quarter of the century, as *Bernardus Catalani* was documented in the latter city in 1174, and a neighbourhood was described as *in carrera publica ante domum de Catalanis* in 1176[139], while in Tortosa there were negotiations in 1163 for the *terre Guillelmi Catalani Barchinonensi*[140]. In fact, in Barcelona itself in 1160, and nearby in places like Valls in 1150, we can document names like *Guillelmi Catalani*[141] and *Petri Catalani*[142], respectively.

In the second half of the century there are prominent figures with this surname, such as *frater Pere Catala*, the Hospitaller who served as the commander of Alguaire between 1185 and 1187[143]. However, a territory-based patronymic must have been used by families with no higher indicators of honours; this would explain its use in popular echelons of society, which are not as thoroughly documented. As late as 1259, this surname was used, for example, by *Bernardus Catalani*, who was one of the *homines de Uliano qui erant homines proprii et solidi domini episcopi* in Ullà[144].

The female name "Catalana" also spread rather early. In Tortosa in 1152, Ramon de Pujalt gave houses to *Raimundo de Copons et fratri tuo Guilelmo de Copons et uxori tue que appellatur Catalana*[145]. Likewise,

138 Maria Teresa Ferrer, Manuel Riu, dirs., *Tractats i negociacions diplomàtiques de Catalunya i de la Corona catalanoaragonesa a l'edat mitjana* (Barcelona: Institut d'Estudis Catalans, 2009), vol. 1/1, pp. 280, 306, 377, 406.

139 Agustí Altisent, *Diplomatari de Santa Maria de Poblet. Volum I Anys 960-1177* (Barcelona: Abadia de Poblet-Departament de Cultura de Generalitat de Catalunya, 1993), pp. 363, 413.

140 Antoni Virgili, *Diplomatari de la catedral de Tortosa (1062-1193)* (Barcelona: Fundació Noguera, 1997), p. 183.

141 Jesús Alturo, *L'arxiu antic de Santa Anna de Barcelona del 942 al 1200 (Aproximació històrico-lingüística)*, 3 vols. (Barcelona: Fundació Noguera, 1985), vol. 2, p. 361.

142 Pere Puig, Vicenç Ruiz, Joan Soler, *Diplomatari de Sant Pere i Santa Maria d'Ègara Terrassa, 958-1207* (Barcelona: Fundació Noguera, 2001), p. 385.

143 Jesús Alturo, *Diplomatari d'Alguaire i del seu monestir santjoanista, de 1076 a 1244* (Barcelona: Fundació Noguera, 1999), pp. 145, 149-150.

144 Josep Maria Marques, Jaume de Puig, Albert Serrat, *El 'Cartoral de Rúbriques Vermelles' de Pere de Rrocabertí, bisbe de Girona (1318-1324)* (Barcelona: Fundació Noguera, 2009), pp. 252-253.

145 Agustí Altisent, *Diplomatari de Santa Maria de Poblet...*, p. 131.

this was the name of the daughter of Bernat de Montesquiu, who had taken issue with the bishop of Barcelona over possession of the castle of Montmell until the agreement reached in 1181[146]. It was also applied to the daughter of Pere and Ermesenda, in Santa Eulàlia Provençana, documented in 1179, who received her dowry in 1188. Likewise, in the following decade Ermessenda de Torrenova also had a daughter with the same name[147]. By the beginning of the 13th century, the name was quite widespread: *ego Catalana, per me et per meos* closed a sale in Sarral in 1203[148], and soon thereafter it spread to a broad geographic region which extends to the areas of Lleida[149], Tortosa[150] and Girona[151].

Back in the 19th century, authors like Bori Fontestà claimed that the mid-12th century was *cuando aparece en las crónicas el nombre de Cataluña*[152] ("when the name of Catalonia appears in the chronicles"). And, in fact, the literary testimony of this use is quite extensive, primarily thanks to the troubadours[153]. At that time, the same sovereign governed two territories simultaneously, and the dynasty's inability to impose a common system reveals that the true locus of gravity was in each of the respective societies[154]. That is when the coronym Aragon extended from the Pyrenees to encompass the different areas conquered since the late 11th century, which had initially been juxtaposed even when mentioned. Now, also another single coronym, Catalonia, encompassed the eastern regions. The king struggled to preside over both lands and strove to define his pre-eminence over each of them, as stated by Peter the Catholic in

146 Maria Pardo, *Mensa episcopal de Barcelona (878-1299)* (Barcelona: Fundació Noguera, 1994), p. 66.

147 Jesús Alturo, *L'arxiu antic de Santa Anna de Barcelona...*, pp. 39, 87-88, 209-210.

148 Josep Maria Sans, *Col·lecció diplomàtica de la Casa del Temple de Barberà (945-1212)* (Barcelona: Departament de Justícia de la Generalitat de Catalunya, 1997), p. 308.

149 Jesús Alturo, *Diplomatari d'Alguaire i del seu monestir santjoanista...*, p. 283.

150 Antoni Virgili, *Diplomatari de la catedral de Tortosa (1193-1212). Episcopat de Gombau de Santa Oliva* (Barcelona: Fundació Noguera, 2004), p. 374.

151 Esteve Pruenca, *Diplomatari de Santa Maria d'Àger* (Barcelona: Fundació Noguera, 1995), p. 140; Josep M. Marques, *Col.lecció diplomàtica de Sant Daniel de Girona (924-1300)* (Barcelona: Fundació Noguera, 1997), p. 242.

152 Antonio Bori, *Historia de Cataluña...*, p. 77.

153 Luis Rubio, "Catalán-Cataluña...", pp. 256-263.

154 Flocel Sabaté, "Els primers temps: segle XII (1137-1213)...", pp. 62-65.

1198 over the whole Catalonia: *per tota Cathaloniam, videlicet a Salsis usque ad Ilerdam*[155].

The duality between Aragon and Catalonia was constantly respected in the monarch's practice, as shown by Alfonso the Chaste in his 1194 will, which mentioned *terrarum Aragonis et Cathalonie*, or when he let *fillium meum regem Petrum cum regno Aragonis et Cathalonie*[156]. This territorial duality meant that the executors who had to enforce this will explicitly had to choose: some *de regno Aragonie* and others *de Cathalonia*[157]. It was actually a perennial referent. In 1169, Alfonso the Chaste had enjoyed power over *catalanorum et aragonensium*, and in 1176 he confirmed his father's donations *tam in regno Aragonis quam in Chatalonia*[158]. His subjects, as stated in 1179, were *hominibus vestris Aragonis vel Catalonie aut Provincie*[159]. For this reason, the following is recounted about the tensions between King Alfonso the Chaste and the Viscount Ponç de Cabrera in 1189: *acquindamento facto secundo die, hoc est die lunis, iusse sunt omnes cavalcate tocius Aragonis et Catalonie ut venirent ad depopulandam et dissipandam ubique totam terran Poncii de Capraria*[160].

Quite naturally, when the Viscount of Béarn, Guillem Ramon de Montcada, was preparing his will in 1215, he specified where he wanted to be buried, considering the three regions over which he held dominion: *dimito corpus meum ad sepeliendum monasterio de Sanctis Crucibus, si in regno Aragone vel in Cataulania obiero, et si in Guaschonia, Sancte Marie de Oloro*[161]. In fact, the entrenchment of the coronym led to the assumption and perception of common practices among those living there. Thus, it was possible to speak about the customs of the nobles of Catalonia, as well as the

155 Gener Gonzalvo, *Les Constitucions de Pau i Treva de Catalunya (segles XI-XIII)* (Barcelona: Departament de Justícia de la Generalitat de Catalunya, 1994), p. 109.

156 Antoni Udina, *Els testaments dels comtes de Barcelona i dels reis de la Corona d'Aragó. De Guifré Borrell a Joan II* (Barcelona: Fundació Noguera, 2001), pp. 114-115.

157 Jesús Alturo, *L'arxiu antic de Santa Anna de Barcelona...*, pp. 193.

158 Luis Rubio, "Catalán-Cataluña...", pp. 259, 255.

159 Maria Teresa Ferrer, Manuel Riu, dirs., *Tractats i negociacions diplomàtiques de Catalunya...*, p. 391.

160 Ramon Chesé, *Col·leccio diplomàtica de Sant Pere d'Àger fins 1128* (Barcelona: Fundació Noguera, 2011), p. 938.

161 Joan Papell, *Diplomatari del Monestir de Santa María de Santes Creus (975-1225)*, 2 vols. (Barcelona: Fundació Noguera, 2005), vol. 2, p. 761.

customs of the bishoprics of Catalonia. This can be seen in the 1178 royal endowment to the cathedral of Tortosa, when the sovereign agreed that

> *in omnibus eclesiis sui episcopatus Dertusensis episcopus habeat potestatem introducendi, disponendi et ordinandi quoscumque clericos voluerit et nullos nisi quos voluerit secundum antiquam et laudabilem consuetudinem episcopatuum Cathalonie*[162].

Apparently, the nobles may have entered the 13th century claiming to the monarch that they mutually agreed on *consuetudinem Catalonie*[163].

This perception is compatible with the jurisdictional exceptions that were being allowed. On the one hand, the troubadour Bertran de Born reflected a duality between Catalans and Aragonese: *e desse que serem vengut,/mesclar s'a.l torneis pel chambo/e.lh catala e.lh d'Arago/tombaran soven e menut*[164] ("and when we will arrive/the tournament's struggle over the fields will start/and Catalans and Aragone will fell down often and quickly"). Yet at the same time he remarked upon the uniqueness of Urgell: *Aragones fan gran dol/catala e cilh d'Urgel/quar non an qui los chapdel*[165] ("the Aragonese are in big grief/the Catalan and this one from Urgell/have not who helped"). When settling her differences with the Hospitallers in 1199, the Countess Elvira of Urgell quite clearly referred to *omnes querimonias quas uchusque habui de Ospitali et de omnibus hominibus suis in Aragone vel in Urgello et adhuc etiam in Katalonia, per me et per me comitem Ermengaudum et per omnes nostros homines*[166]. In fact, the monarch may himself have referred to his domain as *in tota Cathalonia* while also specifying which countships had jurisdictional exceptions, such as *comitatu Rossilionis, comitatu Ceritanie et Confluenti o comitatu Palariense*[167].

The consolidation of the House of Barcelona contributed to territorial cohesion, which was simultaneously undergoing the same synergies of

162 Antoni Virgili, *Diplomatari de la catedral de Tortosa...*, p. 376.

163 Maria del Carmen Álvarez, *La Baronia de la Conca d'Odena* (Barcelona: Fundació Noguera, 1990), p. 176.

164 Martin de Riquer, *Los trovadores. Historia literaria y textos*, 3 vols. (Barcelona: Editorial Planeta, 1983), vol. 2, p. 691.

165 Jordi Ventura, *Alfons el Cast, el primer comte-rei* (Barcelona: Editorial Aedos, 1961), p. 191.

166 Jesús Alturo, *Diplomatari d'Alguaire i del seu monestir santjoanista...*, p. 205.

167 Antoni Udina, *Els testaments dels comtes de Barcelona...*, pp. 114-115.

approximation thanks to the extraordinary dynamism of both the nobles and barons and the ascendant men of the villages and cities, each of whom was gaining ground over a territory as it was being organised. Thus, the country's name culminated a period of coalescence which lent a specific cohesion which was perceived both internally and externally. As Michel Zimmermann warned, it is important to *réfléchir sur cet 'anonymat' de la Catalogne jusqu'au XIIe siècle*[168] ("think about this 'anonymity' of Catalonia up to the 12th century").

3. Keys to interpreting the 9th to 12th centuries: Convergent evolution, cohesion and perception

Taking advantage of the defeat of the Visigoth kingdom after the Islamic invasion, Pepin's dynasty emerging power resumed its southward expansion in the 9th century. Its army crossed the borders that had been the focal point of tensions with the Visigoths[169] and declared itself their heir[170], consolidating a conquest framed as the Christian liberation against the Muslim invaders[171], followed by full cultural and political assimilation[172]. The occupation of Barcelona in the early 9th century enabled boundaries to be established which opened up to the unruly lands beyond the Llobregat

168 Michel Zimmermann, "Aux origines de la Catalogne. Géographie politique et affirmation nationale", *Le Moyen Age*, 89/1 (1983), p. 6.

169 Claudio Sánchez, "Observaciones a unas páginas sobre el inicio de la Reconquista", *Cuadernos de Historia de España*, 47-48 (1968), pp. 346; Luis García, "Algunas observaciones sobre los pueblos pirenaicos en la Baja Antigüedad", *Segon Col·loqui Internacional d'Arqueologia de Puigcerdà (Puigcerdà, 1976)* (Puigcerdà: Institut d'Estudis Ceretans, 1978), pp. 320-322.

170 Michel Zimmermann, "Les gots et l'influence gothique dans l'empire carolingien", *Les Cahiers de Sant-Michel de Cuxa*, 23 (1992), pp. 31-46.

171 Michel Zimmermann, "Conscience gothique et affirmation nationale dans la genèse de la Catalogne (IXe-XIe siècles)", *L'Europe héritière de l'Espagne wisigothique* (Madrid: Casa de Velázquez, 1992), pp. 51-67.

172 Flocel Sabaté, "El nacimiento de Cataluña. Mito y realidad", *Fundamentos medievales de los particularismos hispánicos. IX Congreso de Estudios Medievales (2003)* (Ávila: Fundación Sánchez Albornoz, 2005), pp. 224-227.

and Cardener Rivers[173]. The framework of interaction in all respects stretched between the Llobregat and the Rhone Rivers on one side, facilitating the relationship with Lyon, and from there to near Burgundy; while on the other side it involved quite an intense relationship with the area around Toulouse, which was part of the political milieu of Aquitania[174]. The territory was organised into countships whose leaders also accumulated other titles and fully participated in the play of tensions inside the empire[175]. What characterised these southern lands was not so much singularisation but full integration within the Carolingian empire as a whole, although they were not a specific territorial entity: there was no solution of continuity to the north, as shown in Rasès, for example, which in the 9th century was governed sometimes by the leader of Roussillon, other times by the leader from Carcassonne, and coveted, at least in part, by the counts of Conflent and Cerdagne[176]. Neither was very distinguishable when seen from beyond their southern border; everything was *Ifranja* from the Muslim vantage point[177]. The dynastic tensions within the empire actually concealed a fragmentation of power which signalled the seigniorial roots being laid and regional fragmentation, which in turn led to the empire's inability to attain overall articulation. For this reason, the division of the empire in 840, with the lands located to the northeast of the Iberian

173 Michel Zimmermann, "Le concept de Marca Hispanica et l'importance de la frontière dans la formation de la Catalogne", *La Marche Supérieure d'Al-Andalus et l'Occident Chrétien*, Philippe Sénac ed. (Madrid: Casa de Velázquez-Universidad de Zaragoza, 1991), pp. 29-48.

174 Ramon d'Abadal, *Dels visigots als catalans* (Barcelona: Edicions 62, 1986), pp. 155-157.

175 Josep Maria Salrach, *El procés de formació nacional de Catalunya...*, vol. 1, pp. 27-120.

176 André Bonnery, "El Capcir i el Donasà. El marc històric", *Catalunya Romànica*, 28 vols. (Barcelona: Fundació Enciclopèdia Catalana, 1996), vol. 25, pp. 213-214.

177 *Es per tant incorrecte dir que 'Ifranj' és equivalent a 'catalans', encara que els inclogui, perquè abraça també tots els habitants dels territoris carolingis, sense precisions, si més no fins al segle X* ("It is therefore incorrect to say that 'Ifranj' is equivalent to 'Catalan', although it includes them, because it also embraces all the inhabitants of the Carolingian territories, without greater details, at least until the 10th century"). Míkel de Epalza, "Descabdellament polític i militar dels musulmans a terres catalanes [segles VIII-XI]", *Symposium Internacional sobre els orígens de Catalunya (Segles VIII-XI)*, 2 vols. (Barcelona: Real Academia de Buenas Letras de Barcelona, 1991), p. 54.

Peninsula in the *Francia Occidentalis*, did not put a halt to the tensions and collapse of royal authority. In 878, King Louis II granted Count Wilfred of Cerdagne and Urgell the countships of Barcelona, Osona and Girona. This was the last royal designation to the counts in the region, owing to the monarch's own debility[178].

Thus began an introspective period, with counts who were physically settled in countships which were now – in the shift from the 9th to the 10th centuries – quite stable and accepted into the territorial organisation around the capital[179]. Every count based his power on God – *gratia Dei comes* –, was succeeded by his descendants, presided over the demarcation as his own – *comitato nostro* – and managed the *fiscus comitalis* with full authority, which enabled him to instigate policies of cessions and privatisations. Carolingian power was the higher referent: the counts' visits to the royal court took place until 953[180], and the royal deeds to protect goods and rights were most likely repeated until 986[181]. The end of the Carolingian dynasty in 987[182] contributed to sanctioning a dynamic that Hugh I, Count of Empúries, summarised perfectly in 1019: *potestatem quam reges ibi pridem habuerint, iste Hugo comes ibi habebat*[183]. This was perceived externally, with the Count of Barcelona treated as the sovereign by Córdoba's rulers in the 10th century[184].

178 This is not so different to the region directly to the north: *Dans les années qui suivirent la mort de Charles le Chauve* (877), *les apparences d'autorité royale dans le Midi se dissipèrent rapidement* ("In the years that followed the death of Charles the Bald (877), the appearances of royal authority in the south quickly dissipated"). Philippe Wolff, "Le Midi franc et seigneurial", *Histoire du Languedoc*, Philippe Wolff, ed. (Toulouse: Éditions Privat, 2000), p. 131.

179 Flocel Sabaté, "Els eixos articuladors del territori medieval català", *L'estructuració territorial de Catalunya. Els eixos cohesionadors de l'espai. V Congrés Internacional d'Història Local de Catalunya (Barcelona, 10 i 11de desembre de 1999)*, Flocel Sabaté, coord. (Barcelona: L'Avenç, 2001), p. 51.

180 Ramon d'Abadal, *Els primers comtes catalans...*, pp. 297-298.

181 José Rius, *Cartulario de 'Sant Cugat' del Vallés*, 4 vols. (Barcelona: Consejo Superior de Investigaciones Científicas, 1945), vol. 1, pp. 145-148.

182 Dominique Barthélemy, *Nouvelle Histoire des Capétiens, 987-1214* (Paris: Éditions du Seuil, 2012), pp. 13-67.

183 Petro de Marca, *Marca Hispanica sive limes hispanicus*, Paris, 1688 (facsimile: Barcelona: Editorial Base, 1998), coll. 1014.

184 Juan Vernet, "El 'statu quo' internacional de Barcelona en el siglo X", *Festgabe für Hans-Rudolf Singer zum 65 Gerburstag am 6 April 1990 überreicht vos*

Throughout the 10th century, the counts' houses strove to strengthen their respective lineages and assets, settle the framework of interaction with the neighbouring entities – with no dearth of boundary disputes among countships[185] – and establish internal balances, given the overwhelming seigneurialisation of the society (the counts were faced with strengthened *vicecomes et seniores*)[186], which led to serious tensions mid-century[187]. The rise of the lineages of the viscounts and vicars and of the Church hierarchy projected over the borderland, which they occupied and transformed into a chain of bounded castles that attracted peasants bound to them by exactions. The inherent rise in agriculture[188] and the systematic organisation of the castles[189] infused a new physiognomy onto the ancient disorderly land and turned it into the foundation of the emergence of renewed lineages[190].

seinen Freunden und Kollegen, Martin Forstner, ed. (Frankfurt-am-Main: Peter Lang Publishers, 1991), pp. 515-516.

185 Albert Benet, *El procés d'independència de Catalunya (897-989)* (Sallent: Institut d'Arqueologia-Història i Ciències Naturals, 1988), pp. 20-40; Joan Blasi, *Els obligats comtes de Cerdanya (798-1117)* (Sant Vicenç de Castellet: El Farell Edicions, 1999), p. 152.

186 José María Font, *Cartas de población y franquicia de Cataluña*, 2 vols. (Madrid-Barcelona: Consejo Superior de Investigaciones Científicas, 1983), vol. 1, p. 18.

187 Josep Maria Salrach, "El comte Guifré de Besalú i la revolta de 957. Contribució a l'estudi de la noblesa catalana al segle X", *II Assemblea d'Estudis sobre el comtat de Besalú. Actes* (Olot: Amigos de Besalú y su Condado, 1973), pp. 3-36; Ramon d'Abadal, *Els comtats de Pallars i Ribagorça. Segona part* (Barcelona: Institut d'Estudis Catalans, 1985), p. 385 ; Cebrià Baraut, "Els documents del segle IX i X, conservats a l'Arxiu Capitular de la Seu d'Urgell", *Urgellia*, 2 (1979), p. 98.

188 Josep Maria Salrach, "Défrichement et croissance agricole dans la Septimanie et le Nord-est de la Péninsule Ibérique", *La croissance agricole du Haut Moyen Age. Chronologie, modalités, géographie. Dixièmes journées internationales d'histoire, 9-10 septembre 1988* (Auch: Centre culturel de l'Abbaye de Flaran, 1990), pp. 132-151.

189 Flocel Sabaté, "Occuper la frontière du nord-est péninsulaire (Xe-XIIe siècles)", *Entre Islam et Chrétienté. La territorialisation des frontières, XIe-XVIe*, Stéphane Boissellier, Isabel Cristina Ferreira Fernandes, eds. (Rennes: Presses Universitaires de Rennes, forthcoming).

190 Flocel Sabaté, "Estructura socio-econòmica de l'Anoia (segles X-XIII)", *Acta historica et archaeologica Mediaevalia*, 13 (1992), pp. 176-203; Antoni Virgili, "El Penedès: un espai conquerit; un espai de conqueridors", *De la Marca Hispànica a les terres de marca: el Penedès. XVII Jornades d'estudis penedesencs*, Roger Benito, ed. (Vilafranca del Penedès: Institut d'Estudis Penedesencs, 2008), pp. 9-24.

Precisely the 11th century expansion, not into empty territory but alongside Islamic society, transformed the new lands into a rather attractive place where the acquired rights and revenues rooted the people perennially, including the jurisdictional monopoly stemming from the new feudal ways.[191] The agreements regulating[192] the castellans' rank emerged in each castle tenancy[193], while they also articulated the power inside each countship[194] and the pacts with which the concurrent tensions among countships were smoothed over[195]. It is the institutional framework which reflects the pre-eminence of the Count of Barcelona, albeit without allowing him to meddle whatsoever in the other countships.

This proximity is nonetheless a reflection of a gradual convergent dynamic among countships which were facing similar circumstances. First of all, they participated in the Carolingian domain based on the shared and enhanced cultural inheritance from the *Gotia*[196], drawing significantly from Visigoth law[197] as a useful code until the 12th century[198]. Some believe that life in the countships reflected *més a un model de tradició hispano-gòtica que no pas carolingi*[199] ("a model of Hispano-Gothic tradition more than Carolingian"). At the same time, both the art and the language, though straying further from the myth of the single founding

191 Flocel Sabaté, "Frontera peninsular e identidad (siglos IX-XII)", *Las Cinco Villas aragonesas en la Europa de los siglos XII y XIII. De la frontera natural a las fronteras políticas y socioeconómicas (foralidad y municipalidad)*, Esteban Sarasa, ed. (Saragossa: Institución Fernando el Católico, 2007), pp. 85-91.

192 Adam J. Kosto, *Making Agreements in Medieval Catalonia. Power, Order, and the Written Word, 1000-1200* (Cambridge: Cambridge University Press, 2001), pp. 9-218.

193 Flocel Sabaté, "La tenencia de castillos en la Cataluña medieval...", pp. 76-80.

194 Flocel Sabaté, *La feudalización de la sociedad catalana...*, pp. 67-69.

195 Flocel Sabaté, "El nacimiento de Cataluña...", p. 236.

196 Michel Zimmermann, "Les gots et l'influence gothique...", p. 37.

197 Michel Zimmermann, "L'usage du droit wisigothique en Catalogne du IX au XII siècle: Approche d'une signification culturelle", *Mélanges de la Casa de Velázquez*, 9 (1973), pp. 233-281.

198 Aquilino Iglesia, "Ley y costumbre en la Cataluña altomedieval", *El Dret Comú i Catalunya. Actes del V Simposi Internacional (Barcelona, 26-27 May 1995)* (Barcelona: Fundació Noguera, 1996), p. 220.

199 Frederic Udina, "El llegat i la consciència romano-gòtica. El nom d'Hispania", *Symposium internacional sobre els orígens de catalunya (Segles VIII-XI)*, 2 vols. (Barcelona: Memorias de la Reial Academia de Buenas Letras de Barcelona, 1991-1992), vol. 2, p. 195.

root because the art stemmed from a variety of local contributions[200] and the language from evolutions from Latin which retained indelible regional features[201] or had traits that remained in the linguistic substrates[202], showed concordant social evolutions which would lead to a similar Romanesque[203] and a common pre-Catalan language, although one that was unique compared to the linguistic cohesion around Occitanian achieved directly to the north[204]. One could certainly detect a gradual *sédimentation d'un espace culturel*[205] ("sedimentation of a cultural space"). This joint cultural and linguistic evolution denotes frequent contact, which is coherent with surging economic evolution backed by agricultural expansion, as evidenced by the spread of mills and the manufacture of metal tools, benefitting from the strategic location for trade between Andalusia and northern Europe. Coherently, similar strategies were pursued towards the outside, both with the Muslim neighbours and in the quest for new poles of support, such as contact with Rome[206]. The agreements among the different counts' houses are clearly reflected in the fact that 39.39% of dynastic marriages were reached among them[207].

200 Xavier Barral, *Contra l'art roman? Essai sur un passé réinventé* (Paris: Librairie Arthème Fayard, 2006), pp. 102-104.

201 Antoni Maria Badia, "L'Alt Urgell i el català occidental naixent", *Actes del Cinquè Col·loqui Internacional de Llengua i Literatura Catalanes (Andorra, 1-6 d'octubre de 1979)*, Jordi Bruguera, Josep Massot, eds. (Barcelona: Publicacions de l'Abadia de Montserrat, 1980), pp. 349-377.

202 Xavier Terrado, "Llengua, identitat i territori. La Ribagorça comtal", *L'Edat Mitjana. Món real i espai imaginat*, Flocel Sabaté, coord. (Catarroja-Barcelona: Editorial Afers, 2012), pp. 71-78.

203 Eduard Carbonell, "Algunes reflexions sobre l'arquitectura a Catalunya a l'entorn de l'any mil", *Simposi Internacional d'Arquitectura a Catalunya. Segles IX, X i primera meitat de l'XI* (Girona: Universitat de Girona, 1994), pp. 121-129.

204 Josep Moran, "La llengua catalana en els seus orígens i en relació amb altres llengües de l'Europa carolíngia", *Catalunya a l'època carolíngia. Art i cultura abans del romànic (segles IX i X)* (Barcelona: Museu Nacional d'Art de Catalunya, 1999), pp. 129-130.

205 Michel Zimmermann, *Écrire et lire en Catalogne (IXe-XIIe siècle)*, 2 vols. (Madrid: Casa de Velázquez, 2003), vol. 2, pp. 619-832.

206 Ramon d'Abadal, *Com Catalunya s'obrí al món mil anys enrere* (Barcelona: Rafael Damau Editor, 1988), pp. 53-59.

207 Flocel Sabaté, "La noció d'Espanya en la Catalunya medieval", *Acta historica et archaeologica Mediaevalia*, 19 (1998), pp. 375-390.

The pre-eminence of the Count of Barcelona is primarily based on optimal location – ruling over three entities with three prosperous church centres: Barcelona, Girona and Vic – along with the right degree of border openness and boundless maritime potential. For this reason, the gradual social cohesion strengthened the organisational importance of the Count and city of Barcelona. His leadership in the campaign against Mallorca in 1113 and the Pisans' perception of seeing the *catalanicus heros* or *catalanensis dux* in it is quite indicative of this[208]. Throughout the course of that century, the Count of Barcelona added other counts' houses (Besalú, Cerdagne-Berga, Roussillon, Pallars Jussà) to his domain, led the conquests against the Islamic domains of Tortosa and Lleida, stressed his influence over the North side of the Pyrenees, reached the royal Crown of Aragon and undertook an arrangement to rationalise and manage the inherent rights and revenues[209]. Over the course of the preceding centuries, a border expansion which originated in a variety of countships which had fostered jurisdictional breakdown and cessions in taxation and jurisdictions inherent to feudal development, imposed a fragmented, plural reality which the Count of Barcelona had to respect, even as he strove to consolidate his pre-eminence over it. This pre-eminence would seek its foundations in the two realities that took root in the country concurrently: feudalism and the urban dynamic. The values that permeated the former – "solidarities, faith, honor and shame"[210] – were complemented by those of the latter, from which elites emerged that claimed representativeness over coalesced urban collectives and who, springing from a variety of provenances, became businessmen-investors who moved quickly towards the integration of profit and economic gain[211]. In this climate, the Church enhanced its role in society from the context of reform, which led to a renewed legal articulation[212] and the introduction of Canons Regular and

208 Jaume Vidal, *'Liber Maiorichinus'*..., p. 52.

209 Thomas N. Bisson, *Fiscal Accounts of Catalonia under the Early Count-Kings (1151-1213)*, 2 vols. (Berkeley-Los Angeles-London: University of California Press, 1984).

210 Thomas N. Bisson, *Tormented Voices. Power, Crisis and Humanity in Rural Catalonia, 1140-1200* (London: Harvard University Press-Cambridge Mass, 1998), pp. 120-138.

211 Flocel Sabaté, *Història de Lleida. Alta edat mitjana* (Lleida: Pagès Editors, 2003), pp. 335-366.

212 Santiago Bueno, "El concepte i la regulació canònica del patrimoni eclesiàstic a Catalunya entre els segles XII i XIV", *El dret comú i Catalunya. Actes del X Simposi*

new orders[213] while also emblematically reviving the metropolitan cathedral of Tarragona, thus breaking its ties with Narbonne, which remained in Elne[214]. Generally speaking, if the 12th century has already been defined as a crossroads where *the Origins of European Government*[215] can be pinpointed, cohesion was achieved in Catalonia thanks to the confluence of social and economic dynamics diverse enough to leave weak fronts that remained open to dispute, beginning with the management of power.

In short, the downfall of the Carolingian empire in the 9th century led to the de facto independence of a series of countships which shared similar circumstances and engaged in an evolution within a similar scenario. In the 10th and 11th centuries, this facilitated approximations in the spheres of culture, economics, society and politics, which in turn generated an environment and axiology shared by a people who coexisted in the same physical and social space. The cohesion thus achieved was significant enough to be perceived from the outside. The advent of Catalonia in the 12th century culminated the previous journey and sanctioned it through the internal and external perception of the dynamic of social and spatial uniqueness[216]. The inherent tensions and contradictions continued to evolve based on the framework of economic vitality, social dynamics and

Internacional (Barcelona, 2-3 de juny de 2000). La superació d'un sistemàtica: el Dret patrimonial, Aquilino Iglesia, ed. (Barcelona: Associació Catalana d'Història del Dret 'Jaume de Montjuïc', 2001), pp. 140-150.

213 Flocel Sabaté, "Església, religió i poder a l'edat mitjana", *Església, societat i poder a les terres de parla catalana* (Valls: Cossetània Edicions, 2006), pp. 26-31.

214 Lawrence McCrank, "La restauración eclesiástica y reconquista en la Catalunya del siglo XI: Ramon Berenguer I y la sede de Tarragona", *Analecta Sacra Tarraconensia*, 49-50 (1976-1977), pp. 2-3; Antoni Pladevall, *La metròpoli de Tarragona. Nou-cents anys de la seva restauració medieval* (Barcelona: Facultat de Teologia de Barcelona, 1991), pp. 30-32.

215 Thomas N. Bisson, *The Crisis of the Twelfth century. Power, Lordship and the Origins of European Government* (Princeton-Oxford: Princeton University Press, 2009).

216 I have borrowed the parameters from the geography of perception: Yi-Fu Tuan, *Topophilia. A Study of Environmental Perception. Attitudes and Values* (Englewood Cliffs: Prentice-Hall, 1974); Paul Y. Villeneuve, "Géographie de la perception et méthode dialectique", *Cahiers de géographie de Québec*, 29/77 (1985), pp. 241-260; Yi Fu Tuan, "Environment, behaviour and thought", *The Behavioural Environment. Essays in Reflection, Applications and Re-evaluation*, Frederick W. Boal, David N. Livingstone, eds. (London-New York: Routledge, 1989), pp. 77-81.

the quest for balances of power, as captured in the 12th century, which in turn led to new cohesive formulas that would blossom in the forthcoming centuries.

4. The Catalan nation

After the presence of *catalani* in the Pisan *Liber Maiorichinus* from 1114 and the country's later coronym, Bernard Guenée made the comparison that the names *'Polonia' y 'Catalonia' nacieron para designar Estados ya existentes. Por el contrario, 'Francia' fue muy anterior al reino que acabó por calificar*[217] ("'Poland' and 'Catalonia' were born to designate existing states. On the contrary, 'France' was much earlier than the kingdom which labelled after"). Apart from the fact that this claim requires some nuancing, it implies that behind each coronym lies a combination of a centralised political power and a consciously unique collective. This refers to the perception and acceptance of a collective identity which we can call a 'nation' in that it defines a set of individuals born in the same place; that is, 'nation' refers to shared generation by birth[218]. In this sense, Léopold Génicot posited that in 13th century Europe *la nación era, pues, un sentimiento naciente*[219] ("the nation was therefore a growing feeling").

The elements that shape a nation stem from the shared day-to-day lives of the group itself and thus have common features. We cannot fail to mention Francesc Eiximenis: when praising the Catalan nation in the 14th century he referred to the fact that it observed better customs than neighbouring nations in aspects such as food, drink and table manners, adding that *la nació catalana era eximpli de totes les altres gents cristianes*

217 Bernrad Guenée, *Occidente durante los siglos XIV y XV. Los Estados* (Barcelona: Editorial Labor, 1973), p. 58.

218 Natalia Vega, *Estudio sintáctico-semántico de los verbos de nacimiento en el latín 'gigno', 'nascor' y 'orior'* (Bogotá: Universidad Nacional de Colombia, Bachelor's thesis, 2007), p. 14.

219 Léopold Genicot, *Europa en el siglo XIII* (Barcelona: Labor, 1976), p. 130.

en menjar honest e en temprat beure[220] ("the Catalan nation was example to all other Christian people in honest food and drink in moderation"). Nation and demonym were used synonymously, with the inherent axiological and cultural aspects, including language, the reason why *nació e llengua* ("nation and language") are often equated with each other[221].

In 1369, King Peter the Ceremonious expressed his indignation that the Sardinian uprising was led by the judge of Arborea, Mariano IV, whose education had been paid for by King Alfonso the Benign, who had brought him to Catalonia and left him in the hands of *dos cavalers catalans e donà-los per maestres qui els nodrissen a les nostres maneres e lo mostressin servir lo senyor rei nostre pare e nós e amar la nostra nació*[222] ("two Catalan knights and gave them as teachers to feed him with our manners and showed him how to serve our lord the king our father and to love our nation"). Therefore, all of these distinctive features make up our ways of being and doing *nostres maneres* ("our manners") and given that these features define us as a nation, the nation becomes a collective, abstract entity which can be loved. Or it can be hated by our rivals, just as we hate our enemies' nation: the 1409 campaign in Sardinia was conducted to *aniquilar i abatre la detestable i fàtua rebel·lió de la nació sarda*[223] ("annihilate and beat down the detestable and foolish rebellion of the Sard nation"). Clearly, the nations competed with each other. The purpose, as Ferdinand I said in 1413, was for the policy to ensure that *nostra nació ne serà amada, temuda e honrada*[224] ("our nation shall be loved, feared and honoured"). In the concert of nations, if King Alfonso the Magnanimous pursued a Mediterranean foreign policy that hindered Catalan trade, it would lead, as warned by representatives of the city of Barcelona in 1422, *los navilis e mercaderia diminueixen e los guanys e*

220 Francesc Eiximenis, *Terç del Crestià*, ch. 372 (Francesc Eixmenis, *Lo Crestià. Selecció*, ed. Albert Hauf (Barcelona: Edicions 62, 1983), pp. 147-148).

221 AML, llibre d'actes, 398, f. 19v; AHCB, fons municipal, B-VI, book 1, f. 103r.

222 Ricard Albert, Joan Gassiot, *Parlaments a les corts catalanes* (Barcelona: Editorial Barcino, 1928), pp. 37-38; Pere Miquel Carbonell, *Cròniques d'Espanya...*, vol. 2, p. 138; Francisco Gimeno, "Escribir, leer, reinar. La experiencia gráfico-textual de Pedro IV el Ceremonioso (1336-1387)", *Scritura e civiltà*, 22 (1998), p. 215.

223 ACA, Cancillería, reg. 2220, f. 75r.

224 ADPO, 1B-209, sheet 9, unnumbered folio.

profits se'n porten altres nacions[225] ("the ships and merchandise diminish and the profits are taken by other nations"). Precisely, in 1471 Bishop Margarit explained the civil war that was drawing to a close as a result of the jealousy and vengeance of other nations, which had previously been harmed by the expansion of the Catalan nation, such that

> *moltes d'elles dittes nacions nos fossen infestissimes e exosses e en la nostra preclara natio han volgut exercir les venjances de les injúries e dans que de la dita nostra preclara natió per lo passat havien rebuda*[226].

> many of these nations fought against our prestigious nation and then they have wished to revenge the injuries and damages received in the past from our prestigious nation.

This approach is coherent with the speech that the same prelate had delivered before the courts in 1454, painting Catalonia's successes as a string of heroic deeds by the Catalan nation:

> *Aquesta és aquella benaventurada, gloriosa e fidelíssima nació de Catalunya, qui per lo passat era temuda per les terres e mars; aquella qui ab sa feel e valent espasa ha dilatat l'imperi e senyoria de la casa d'Aragó; aquella conquistadora de les illes Balears e regnes de Mallorques e de València, llançats los enamics de la fe cristiana, aquella Catalunya qui ha conquistades aquelles grans illes de Itàlia, Sicília e Sardenya, les quals los romans en llurs primeres batalles ab los cartaginesos tan trigaren conquistar e en les quals arbitraven estar gran e la major part de llur estat; aquella qui aquelles vetustíssima e famosíssima Atenes, d'on és exida tota elegància, eloqüència e doctrina dels grecs, e aquella Neopàtria, havia convertides en sa llengua catalana; aquella Catalunya qui diversos reis veïns de França e Espanya, e altres, ha tots fugats e perseguits e mesos a total extermini; aquella Catalunya qui sots lo rei en Pere, llavors regnant, s'és defesa contra tots los prínceps del món, cristians e moros, los quals tots li foren enamics. Per los quals e altres singulars mèrits, que comptar seria superfluïtat, aquell bon rei en Martí, en la cort de Barcelona coronà la dita nació e li apropià per les sues singulars fidelitats aquell dit del psalmista: 'Gloriosa dicta sunt de te, Catalonia'.*

> This is that blessed, glorious and very loyal nation of Catalonia, who in the past was feared on land and on the seas; that with which its loyal and valiant sword has

225 Damien Coulon, *Barcelone et le grand commerce d'Orient au Moyen Âge. Un siècle de relations avec l'Égypte et la Syrie-Palestine (ca. 1330–ca. 1430)* (Madrid-Barcelona: Casa de Velázquez-Institut Europeu de la Mediterrània, 2004), p. 61.

226 Francesc Carreras, *Pere Joan Ferrer, militar y senyor del Maresme* (Barcelona: Imprempta La Renaixensa, 1892), p. 104.

spread the empire and lordship of the house of Aragon; that conqueror of the Balearic Islands and kingdoms of Majorcas and of Valencia, expelled the enemies of the Christian faith, that Catalonia that has conquered those great islands of Italy, Sicily and Sardinia, which the Romans in their first battles against the Carthaginians took so long to conquer and then liked to be and to center the major part of their states; that which that ancient and so famous Athens, where all elegance, eloquence and doctrine of the Greeks were born; and also Neopàtria, that had converted to its Catalan language; that Catalonia which various neighbouring kings of France and Spain, and others, has expelled and pursued and put in total extermination; that Catalonia that under king Peter, then reigning, vanquished the attacks suffered from against all the princes of the world, Christians and Moors, who were all its enemies. For these and other singular merits, that it would be superfluous to list, the good king Martin corresponded the singular fidelity of the nation crowning it, in the parliament of Barcelona, with the words spelled by the psalmist: 'Gloriosa dicta sunt de te, Catalonia'.

These efforts led to an adhesion felt by all the members of the nation, who may even be requested to shed their blood, that is, to endanger their lives to prove their loyalty to the sovereign and to exalt the nation:

Ni es deu algú meravellar si aquesta dita fael nació, ultra totes altres, crida la conservació de sos privilegis, així com aquella qui els ha guanyat ab sa fidelíssima aspersió de sang e en aquesta sua inmaculada fidelitat[227].

Nor should anyone wonder if this faithful nation, among all other nations, calls for the conservation of its privileges, as well as those who have won throughout the most faithful ab healthy sprinkling of blood and sweat into this immaculate loyalty.

In any event, the nation has collective behaviours and feelings which call for and should receive the support of its members. In fact, the successes of one of its members should be shared by everyone, in coherence with the collective solidarity existing in all spheres. This was set forth by King Peter in 1357, right after the Catalan Dominican Nicolau Rossell was elevated to the rank of cardinal,

de la qual cosa és estada feta gran gràcia e fort assenyalada a nós e a tota nostra nació, car jassia que y hagués cardenal d'Espanya, tota vegada era castellà, e de nostra nació jamés no n'i havia haüt tro ara, e com nos convenga que·l dit cardenal vaia en cort de Roma, de guisa que sia honor nostra e de la nostra nació.

227 Ricard Albert, Joan Gassiot, *Parlaments a les corts catalanes...*, pp. 209, 212.

> this generated many graces and was very recognized to us and to the whole nation, because although some cardinal from Spain existed, he was always a Castilian and never any cardinal existed from our nation until now, and it is convenient for us that the new cardinal goes to the Roman court, because this will be a big honour for us and for our nation.

In reality, a practical outcome of this was expected, because precisely at the time of the war with Castile, Catalonia needed a voice of its own in Rome: *per les grans messions que havem fetes e.ns convé fer per rahó de la guerra*[228] ("for the great missions that we have done and that we need to do because of the war").

In the anonymous *consueta del misteri de la gloriosa Santa Ágata* ("the custom book of the mystery of the glorious Saint Agatha"), Quincià addresses the saint and asks her: *digau, donzella, prestament/qui sou vós i de quina gent; jo vull saber la nació/i vostra condició*[229] ("tell me maiden, quickly/who are you and from which people; I want to know the nation/and your condition"). Therefore, everyone has a familiar level and belongs to a nation. With this naturalness, it is coherent that when finding themselves in distant and often strange lands, groups would band together based on the affinity of the nation to which they belonged. This is what happened with the groups of teachers and students in the universities (*Studium Generale*), which were articulated into nations from the earliest times[230]. For this reason, the Saint Clement College created by Cardinal Gil Álvarez de Albornoz in Bologna in 1363 to house students from the Spanish kingdoms, hosted a specific *natio catalanorum*[231]. More spectacularly, the expansion in trade after the 13th century was accompanied by the establishment of consulates *dels catalans* ("of the Catalans") or *de la nació catalana* ("of the Catalan Nation"), designated by the city of

228 Antoni Rubió, *Documents per l'història de la Cultura Catalana Mig-eval*, 2 vols. (Barcelona: Institut d'Estudis Catalans, 1908), vol. 1 (facsímil: Barcelona: Institut d'Estudis Catalans, 2000), p. 181.

229 "Consueta del Misteri de la Gloriosa Santa Ágata", *Teatre medieval i del Renaixement*, ed. Josep Massot (Barcelona: Edicions 62-La Caixa, 1993), p. 97.

230 Maria de Pilar Rábade, *Las universidades en la Edad Media* (Madrid: Arco libros, 1996), p. 28.

231 Pascual Tamburri, "España en la Universidad de Bolonia: vida académica y comunidad nacional (siglos XIII-XIV)", *Espacio, Tiempo y Forma. Serie III. Historia Medieval*, 10 (1997), pp. 295-299.

Barcelona, according royal concessions in 1266 and 1268[232]. The *consules Cathalorum* in Ragusa, attended not only to Catalans. It explicitly had authority over:

> *omnes et singulos Cathalanos et alios subditos et naturales dicti domini Regis de dictis suis regonis et terris et insulis ad dicta civitatem Raguxii et eius territorium et districtum navigantes seu aplicantes aut appelantes aut in eis mercantes, negotiantes seu residentes*[233].

Similarly, the consulate of the *nació de catalans* ("nation of catalans") in Málaga was charged with matters related to *mercaderes catalanes e mallorquines e valencianos* ("Catalan and Majorcan and Valencian merchants") the latter numerically predominant[234], just as the aforementioned nation of Catalans in Bologna hosted students from all over the Crown of Aragon[235]. Assimilation was, in fact, quite widespread: the defenders of Benedict XIII in Avignon in 1408 were viewed as *catalanos*[236]; the pontificate of the Valencian Callixtus III was described as a *regnano chatalani*[237]; and popularly, *Catalani' erano detti allora quanti proveniano dal regno iberico (Aragona, Catalogna, Valenza, Baleari)*[238]. This globalisation had to do with the prestige and pre-eminence initially accorded the Catalans

232 Maria Teresa Ferrer, "El Consolat de Mar i els Consolats d'Ultramar, instruments i manifestació de l'expansió del comerç català", *L'expansió catalana a la Mediterrània a la baixa edat mitjana*, Maria Teresa Ferrer, Damien Coulon, eds. (Barcelona: Consejo Superior de Investigaciones Científicas, 1999), pp. 67-71.

233 Nenad Fejic, *Шпанци у дубровнику у средњем веку* (Belgrade: Просвета, p. 207).

234 José María Ruiz, "El consulado catalán de Málaga en época de los Reyes Católicos", *En la España Medieval*, 10 (1987), pp. 423-433.

235 Pascual Tamburri, "España en la Universidad de Bolonia...", pp. 295-299.

236 Francisco de Moxó, "La coyuntura económica catalana-aragonesa y el repliegue de Benedicto XIII de Porto Venere a Port Vendres (1403-1408)", *Jornades sobre el Cisme d'Occident a Catalunya, les Illes i el País Valencià (Barcelona – Peníscola, 19-21 April 1979). VI Centenari del Cisma d'Occident"*, 2 vols. (Barcelona: Institut d'Estudis Catalans), vol. 1, 1986, p. 119.

237 Eugenio Dupré-Theseider, "La política italiana di Alfonso il Magnanimo", *IV Congreso de Historia de la Corona de Aragón*, 2 vols. (Palma de Mallorca: Diputación Provincial de Mallorca, 1955), vol. 1, p. 234.

238 Vincenzo d'Alessandro, "Spazio geografico e morfologie sociali nella Sicilia del basso Medioevo", *Commercio, finanza, funzione pubblica. Stranieri in Sicilia e in Sardegna nei secoli XIII-XV*, Marco Tangheroni ed. (Naples: Gisem Liguori Editore, 1989), p. 7.

in line with their larger volume and its leadership shown in Sardinia and Sicily, which equated anything that was part of the culture as *cosa catalana*[239] ("Catalan thing"). At the same time, the use of speech itself helped to assimilate those who spoke the same language[240] as Catalans and to distinguish them from the Aragonese, who may have been part of the Crown of Aragon and attended by the same consulates but expressed themselves in a different language[241].

Attention to similarities is a common part of all national representations: the nation of the Castilians on Mallorca[242] tended to any *mercader castellà o portogalès o altre generació d'Espanya*[243] ("Castilian or Portuguese merchant or other procreated from Spain"). In fact, in all *Studia Generalia* the teachers and students were gathered into nations that already existed, such as in Paris, with a division into four nations: French, Picardy, Norman and English or German[244]. At the Council of Constance in 1416, the Spanish nation included the Portuguese, Castilians and members of the Crown of Aragon, including Sardinians and Sicilians. Castile's protest over this situation was only voiced when major internal discrepancies arose regarding the stances adopted on the Church schism[245]. This disfigured any traces of identity. By offering their natural services, the consulates themselves identified the term 'nation' with their own group. The consulate of the Catalan nation, in Bruges since 1320, moved to Antwerp

239 Amadeo Serra, "'È cosa catalana'. La Gran Sala de Castelnuovo en el contexto mediterráneo", *XVI Congresso Internazionale di Storia della Corona d'Aragona. Celebrazioni Alfonsine*, 2 vols., Guido D'Agustino, Giulia Buffardi eds. (Naples: Paparo Edizioni-Comune di Napoli, 2000), vol. 1, pp. 1787-1799.

240 Coral Cuadrada, "Oci i diversió a les societats preindustrials: l'exemple català a la baixa edat mitjana", *XI Jornades d'Estudis Històrics Locals. Espai i temps d'oci a la història (Palma, 1992)* (Palma de Mallorca: Govern Balear, 1993), p. 323.

241 Nenad Fejic, *Шпанци у дубровнику у средњем...*, pp. 114-276.

242 Pau Cateura, "El consulado medieval de Castilla en el reino de Mallorca", *Actas del II Congreso de Historia de Andalucia (Córdoba, 1991)* (Córdoba: Consejería de Cultura y Medio Ambiente de la Junta de Andalucía-Obra Social and Cultural Cajasur, 1994), pp. 289-296.

243 István Szászdi, "Sobre el consulado castellano de Mallorca en la Baja Edad Media", *Anales de la Universidad de Alicante. Historia Medieval*, 10 (1994-1995), p. 218.

244 Jean-Philippe Genet, *La mutation de l'éducation et de la culture médiévales*, 2 vols. (Paris: Seli Arslan, 1999), vol. 1, pp. 216-217.

245 Alan Ryder, *Alfonso el Magnánimo, rey de Aragón, Nápoles y Sicilia (1396-1458)* (Valencia: Edicions Alfons el Magnànim-Generalitat Valenciana, 1992), pp. 80-81.

in 1527[246]. When on the latter date *lo consol y mercadés de nostra nasió* ("the consul and merchants of our nation") had to consider how to act against those who *avia fet contra la nassió den voller rompre los privilegis de la dita nassió* ("had done against the nation of wanting to break the privileges of this nation"), and asked that the guilty party *fos banit de la dita nassió* ("be banned from this nation"), we tend to interpret this latter term as meaning from their own group. This occurred again when it was determined that *en l'església del Carme de la present villa d'Anvés faga de dir cada dilluns una misa cantada de rèquiem per les ànimes difuntes dels nostres antipasats q.aquesta nasió an fundada e per totes les altres venides*[247] ("in the church of the Carmel in this town of Antwerp it must say every Monday a sung requiem mass for the defunct souls of our ancestors that have founded this nation and for all the others that have come").

The malleability of the term never fails to refer to identity as something felt and shared. Thus, the term 'nation' remained fully valid as a way to designate cohesive groups regardless of their corresponding political power. This is what we can observe in the Parliament ("Courts") of 1454: when stating that the cause of the irresolution of the evils they were suffering was the lengthy absence of the king, who had been in Italy since 1432[248], Bishop Margarit stated that *jau la dita nació catalana, quasi vídua, e plora la sua desolació ensemps ab Jeremie profeta, e espera algú qui l'aconsol* ("this Catalan nation lies, almost widowed, and weeps its desolation together with the prophet Jeremiah, and awaits someone to console it") and immediately appeared to address to the king to say him: *e creu, senyor, aquesta quasi vídua nació de Catalunya que per la sua innada fidelitat meresca de vostra majestat e de tot altre senyor ésser ben tractada*[249] ("and believe, my lord, this almost widowed nation of Catalonia for its innate loyalty deserves to be well treated by your majesty and all other lords"). The comparison of a nation to a body, and even as having feelings, captures a unity in itself without the need for a king, beyond asking this

246 Pablo Desportes, "El consulado catalán de Brujas (1330-1480)", *Aragón en la Edad Media*, 14-15 (1999), pp. 375-381.

247 Antonio Paz, *Serie de los más importantes documentos del Archivo y Biblioteca del Excmo. Señor Duque de Medinaceli, 2ª Serie bibliográfica* (Madrid: Imprenta de Blass, 1922), pp. 483, 481.

248 Alan Ryder, *Alfonso el Magnánimo, rey de Aragón…*, pp. 230-231.

249 Ricard Albert, Joan Gassiot, *Parlaments a les corts catalanes...*, pp. 211-212.

king to participate in the common goal of favouring the nation, especially when different nations tend to coexist under the same sovereign[250]. This is also the case of the Cismarine Crown of Aragon, which Pere Miquel Carbonell saw as made up of *lo rey e nostra nació aragonesa, valenciana e catalana*[251] ("the king and our Aragonese, Valencian and Catalan nation").

In short, 'nation' expresses a cohesive set of traits, especially cultural and axiological ones, which make the group unique in its awareness of itself and its perception from the outside. It leads to an identity which is believed to be eternal and motivates the conscious adhesion of its members, in line with the dynamic in other parts of Europe at the same time: *viene intrapreso il tentativo di saturare eticamente ed emozionalmente l'idea di nazione, cioè di collegare con la nazione vincole de fedeltà morali o giuridici*[252] ("an attempt is undertaken to saturate ethically and emotionally the idea of nation, that is to connect links of moral or legal loyalty to the nation"). In this sense, it can be considered an internally binding term which distinguishes between nation and political power but merges both to achieve similar goals, just as was happening at the same time in Germany, for example[253]. Understandably, in clashes with the sovereign, the members of the nation seek other binding referents and they thus present themselves on behalf of not the nation but the name of the soil where it lies: the land[254].

250 Gisela Naegle, "Diversité linguistique, identités et mythe de l'empire à la fin du moyen âge", *Revue Française d'Histoire des Idées Politiques*, 36/2 (2012), pp. 264-267.

251 Pere Miquel Carbonell, *Cròniques d'Espanya...*, vol. 2, p. 170.

252 Dieter Mertens, *Il pensiero politico medievale* (Bologna: Il Mulino, 1999), p. 129.

253 Caspar Hirschi, *The Origins of Nationalism. An Alternative History from Ancient Rome to Early Modern Germany* (Cambridge: Cambridge University Press, 2012), pp. 167-169.

254 Flocel Sabaté, "L'idéel politique et la nation catalane: la terre, le roi et le mythe des origines", *La légitimité implicite*, Jean-Philippe Genet, ed. (París: Publications de la Sorbonne, forthcoming).

5. Political articulation of the nation: The Catalan land

'Land' ("*terra*") designates physically homogenous places, and for this reason in both the 13th and 14th centuries it was usually used to refer to traditional entities (*in terrae Rossilinis, Vallespirii, Ceritanie et Confluentum*[255]) or recently created ones (*procurador general de la terra del Marquesat*[256]) ("Attorney General of the land of Marquesat") or to identify the domains of a baron (*en la terra del noble en Pere de Ffonoyllet*[257]) ("in the land of the noble Peter of Fonolleda") or to describe anything that happened in *la seva terra*[258] ("his land"). Consequently, one could also speak about *la terra del rei*[259] ("the king's land"). However, if the king wanted to consolidate power over the entire country backed by his Romanist jurists who theorised the *general jurisdicció que ha en son regne*[260] ("the general jurisdiction that the king has in his kingdom"), he had to impose the fact that his land was all the whole Catalonia, as James II clearly proclaimed in 1298: *omnibus hominibus totius Regni sunt terri domini regis*[261]. This identification is extremely widespread in all countries, because just as the enemies of the sovereign *minabant ingredi in terram domini regis*[262], one could refer to the *terra regis Francie*[263], the *tierra del Rey de Castiella*[264] ("land of the King of Castile") or what happened *in terra Regis Granate*[265].

If there is an invasion, the enemies *dampniffiquen la terra*[266] ("damaged the land") and proceed *en gran dampnatge de la terra*[267] ("with great damage to the land"). Correspondingly, it must be defended with

255 ADPO, 1B-10, parchment 1271.
256 ACA, Cancillería, reg. 2219, f. 62v.
257 AHCG, I.1.2.1, file 1, book 2, f. 98v.
258 ACA, Cancillería, reg. 363, f. 30v.
259 AHCM, fons del veguer, book 3, not numbered.
260 Pere Albert, "Commemoracions", *Usatges de Catalunya i Commemoracions de Pere Albert* (Barcelona: Els nostres clàssics, 1933), p. 185.
261 ACA, Monacals-Hisenda, reg. 892, f. 41r.
262 ADPO, 1B-172, f. 3r.
263 AHCM, fons del veguer, book 3, not numbered.
264 ACA, Cancillería, reg. 14, f. 93r
265 ACA, Cancillería, reg. 236, f. 70r.
266 ACBE, Comú I, 26.
267 AHCG, I.1.2.1, file 7, book 1, f. 51v.

les hosts de la terra[268] ("the hosts of the land") to protect everything that the space itself might contain, such as the *moltons de la terra*[269] ("sheep of the lands"), *bones carns primals e de la terra*[270] ("good primal meats of the land") or the *lana de la terra*[271] ("wool of the lands"). The land, therefore, encompasses both its products and people and can therefore be understood as an entity in itself, a whole. For example, a slave with the appropriate permit to circulate may *anar per la terra*[272] ("move around the land"). Given the very definition of 'land', we can clearly see a duality with regard to the king. This occurred naturally in the city of Lleida in 1390, when it strove to fend off a possible invasion from the troops from the north of the Pyrenees[273] *per bon profit e utilitat del senyor rey e de la terra*[274] ("for the good advantage and usefulness of [our] lord the King and the land"). In reality, the interests of the two may not dovetail: in 1396 the government of Valencia wrote to the king complaining that in the tax requirements it was unclear *quan la terra n·és calumniada e quant ne ve a profit de vos, senyor*[275] ("when the land is damaged and when it makes a profit for you, lord"). Consequently, the ascendant municipal governments may have clashed with the king because of his tax requirements, invoking the good of the land as a reason for their opposition, that is *per la gran pobresa que és en la terra* ("the great poverty that there is in the land"), as the town council of Tàrrega claimed in 1361[276]. In 1336, concerned that jurisdictional fragmentation would rupture the jurisdictional homogeneity needed by the exercise of the justice and consequently damage the city's interests over its surroundings, the government of Girona warned the king

268 AHCG, I.1.2.1, file 2, book 1, f. 6v.
269 AML, llibres d'actes, book 460, f. 7r
270 AML, llibres d'actes, book 398, f. 44r
271 ADPO, 1B-367, f. 34v.
272 AHCB, fons municipal, B-I, book 18, f. 14r.
273 Flocel Sabaté, "Companyies estranyes d'armes qui eren entrades en lo Principat", *Catalunya, seconde moitié du XIVè siècle* (forthcoming).
274 AML, llibres d'actes, book 403, loose sheet between 6v and 7r.
275 Josep Maria Roca, "Memorial de greuges que'ls missatgers de la ciutat de València presentaren al rey Johan I d'Aragó", *Boletín de la Real Academia de Buenas Letras de Barcelona*, 11 (1924), p. 76.
276 ACUR, fons municipal de Tàrrega, llibres del consell, book 3, f. 6r.

that if he consented to this situation for any longer *tota aquesta terra seria perjudicada*[277] ("all this land would be harmed").

Those who spoke on behalf of the land could institutionalise its voice, which was equated with the land itself. This is clearly implicit in different large noble jurisdictions. The local estates' coordination to respond collectively to the demands of the corresponding lord, or perhaps to submit grievances to him, as paradigmatically occurred in the countship of Urgell[278], was institutionalised in some entities. This gave voice to the estates under a clear municipalist profile and thus stabilising their interlocution with their corresponding lord under the invocation of the land, either the *Consell de la Terra a les Muntanyes de Prades*[279] ("Council of the Land in the Mountains of Prades") or the *Vista general de la terra* ("General View of the Land") in the so-called Lands of the Marquisate, in Camarasa[280].

Therefore, it should come as no surprise that those who negotiated with the monarch not only invoked their concern with the land but also assumed representation of and identification with it. These were nobles and barons who had consolidated their jurisdictional rights, which had been well-shielded since 1283[281], and municipal governments which represented villages and cities whose elites had socially and economically intertwined surrounding regions whose size was directly proportional to the might of the city[282]. The weak jurisdictional and tax bases upon which the Barcelona dynasty trying to govern all of Catalonia in the 12th century was grounded led to a 13th century which witnessed both the economic rise of cities and tensions over power, expressed in five major withdrawal of homage to James I and to Peter the Great[283]. The monarchs' efforts

277 AHCG, I, 1.2.1, file 1, book 2, f. 51v.

278 Flocel Sabaté, *El territori del comtat d'Urgell* (forthcoming).

279 Torrell de Reus, Ignasi Planes, *Llibre de Prades* (Prades: Ajuntament de la Vila Comtal de Prades, 1982), p. 78.

280 Dolors Domingo, *Una frontera interior. Montgai i Butsènit a l'edat mitjana* (Lleida: Edicions de la Universitat de Lleida, 2014), pp. 126-154.

281 José Luis Martín, *Economía y sociedad en los reinos hispánicos de la baja edad media*, 2 vols. (Barcelona: El Albir, 1983), vol. 1, pp. 242-253.

282 Flocel Sabaté, "Ejes vertebradores de la oligarquía urbana en Cataluña", *Revista d'Història Medieval*, 9 (1998), pp. 127-151.

283 Flocel Sabaté, "Poder i territori durant el regnat de Jaume I. Catalunya i Aragó", *Jaume I. Commemoració del VIII centerani de naixement de Jaume I*, Maria Teresa Ferrer, ed. (Barcelona: Institut d'Estudis Catalans, 2011), pp. 62-80.

to institutionally strengthen their power, especially in the two decades before and the two decades after the shift from the 13th to 14th centuries, were flung aside in view of the challenges that the monarchy had to face throughout the 14th century[284]. The monarch failed in his attempts to lay the groundwork of a stable taxation system[285], and the need for cash led first to a transfer of assets through leaving the patrimony as warranty for loans ("*carta de gràcia*"), which lowered the presence of the royal jurisdiction to percentages that were virtually inoperable: in 1392 only 13.43% of the land and 22.17% of the population fell within the royal orbit, while the remainder was a jurisdictional mosaic which escaped the hands of the king[286]. And yet at the same time, this led the sovereign to depend on extraordinary subsidies that had to be granted by the estates[287], which led to serious indebtedness by the taxpaying municipal entities. This circumstance is assumed to be behind the negotiations that led to the king's acceptance of numerous demands and guarantees[288].

This increasingly fraught situation with a weak monarch depending on the estates characterised the reality in Catalonia within the context of late medieval power: it was based on agreements or pacts reached among those who wielded power, which was institutionalised all over Europe under the image of sovereigns meeting with the estates in parliament[289]. The representativeness claimed by the participants, heralded as the major

284 Flocel Sabaté, "L'augment de l'exigència fiscal en els municipis catalans al segle XIV: elements de pressió i de resposta", *Col·loqui Corona, municipis i fiscalitat a la baixa edat mitjana*, Manuel Sánchez, Antoni Furió, eds. (Lleida: Institut d'Estudis Ilerdencs, no date), pp. 423-426.

285 Manuel Sánchez, *El naixement de la fiscalitat d'Estat a Catalunya (segles XII-XIV)* (Vic-Girona: Eumo Editorial-Universitat de Girona, 1995), pp. 49-118.

286 Flocel Sabaté, "Discurs i estratègies del poder reial a Catalunya al segle XIV", *Anuario de Estudios Medievales*, 25 (1995), pp. 632-633.

287 Manuel Sánchez, "1289/92 y 1342/44: dos fechas cruciales en la evolución de la fiscalidad real y urbana en Cataluña", *XVI Jornades d'Estudis Històrics Locals. El Regne de Mallorca a l'època de la dinastía privativa*, Pau Cateura, ed. (Palma de Mallorca: Institut d'Estudis Balearics, 1998), pp. 67-84.

288 Manuel Sánchez, Pere Ortí, eds., *Corts, parlaments i fiscalitat a Catalunya: els capítols del donatiu (1288-1384)* (Barcelona: Departament de Justicia de la Generalitat de Catalunya, 1997).

289 Bertie Wilkinson, *The Creation of Medieval Parliaments* (New York-London-Sydney-Toronto: John Wiley and Sons, 1972).

contribution of the medieval political system[290], meant that the estates spoke not only on their own behalf but also on behalf of the entire land. Hence the duality: *la terra davant del monarca*[291] ("the land in front of the monarch"). Each of the elements in this binomial would seek discourses grounding them within the ideas that were circulating around Europe as a whole to sustain the primacy of the prince[292] or to support the fact that the base of society and all political legitimacy rests on the social collective[293], the root of the demand for participation in the management of governance[294]. Yet in any case, the pacts were achieved based on the respective forces with which the agreement was reached, that is, based on the weakness of the monarchy and the ascendancy of the estates.

Among them, the nobles and barons regarded the rise of the cities with mistrust. In the courts of Perpignan of 1350-1351, on behalf of the knights of the vicary ("the royal administrative unit") of Barcelona and El Vallès, Berenguer Santvicenç warned the king that *per semblants empreniments e ontes sien vengudes totes les comunes que vuy són en lo món*[295] ("all the communes current existed in the world became throughout similar threats and embarrassments"). He was referring to the dire consequences of the villages' and cities' use of force against outside jurisdictions, a practice, however, which would become more accentuated in the late 14th century and even more so in

290 "The idea of representation in the political sense was not prominent, though it existed in the Ancient World, but as a fundamental political principle it is a gift of a Middle Ages to ourselves" (Henry John Randall, *The Creative Centuries. A Study in Historical Development* (London-New York-Toronto: Longman Green and Co., 1947), p. 248.

291 Oriol Oleart, "La terra davant del monarca. Una contribució per a una tipología de l'assemblea estamental catalana", *Anuario de Estudios Medievales*, 25/2 (1995), pp. 593-615).

292 Jacques Krynen, "Droit romain et état monarchique. A propos du cas français", *Représentation, pouvoir et royauté à la fin du moyen âge*, Joël Blanchard, ed. (Paris: Picard, 1995), pp. 13-23.

293 Igor Mineo, "Cose in comune e bene comune. L'ideologia della comunità in Italia nel tardo medioevo", *The Languages of Political Society. Western Europe, 14th-17th Centuries*, Andrea Gamberini, Jean-Philippe Genet, Andrea Zorzi, eds. (Rome: Viella, 2011), pp. 39-67.

294 Diego Quaglioni, "La souveraineté partagé au Moyen Âge", *Le gouvernement mixte. De l'idéal politique au monstre constitutionnel en Europe (XIIIe-XVIIe siècle)*, Marie Gaille-Nikodimov ed. (Saint-Étienne: Publications de l'Université de Saint- Étienne, 2005), pp. 15-24.

295 *Cortes de Cataluña* (Madrid: Real Academia de la Historia, 1896), vol. 1/2, p. 444.

the ensuing century, thus highlighting the armed forces that the municipal governments were capable of mobilising in order to impose their jurisdictional homogenisation without so much as a glance to outside jurisdictions[296]. In turn, nobles and barons could force the sovereign to recognise their full right and capacity to not only collect revenues and enjoy jurisdictions but also to fully exercise the *regiment de gent*[297] ("gouverment over people") within their domains. However, beyond this recognition, they did not generate any overall discourse about the country alternative to the monarch's discourse, as if they were capable of promoting the men of the villages and cities[298].

Certainly, the doctrine generated after the 13th century explaining, as Marsilius of Padua did, that the source of power *est le peuple, qui par délegation le transmet à l'empereur*[299] ("is the people, who by delegation transmit it to the emperor") and that therefore, following now with Baldus de Ubaldis, the *populus liber* can indeed not even recognise any higher domain than the city itself, if it wishes to[300]. These ideas found a very suitable receptacle in the concurrent spiritualist currents, especially from the same Franciscans who were integrating the market economy into urban Christian ethics[301]. The strong influence of the spiritualist Franciscan currents in Catalonia[302], drawing from *l'élaboration d'une ecclésiologie*

296 Flocel Sabaté, *El sometent a la Catalunya medieval* (Barcelona: Rafael Dalmau Editor, 2007), pp. 69-132.

297 José Ángel Sesma, "La nobleza bajomedieval y la formación del estado moderno en la Corona de Aragón", *La nobleza peninsular en la Edad Media* (Ávila: Fundación Sánchez Albornoz, 1999), p. 373.

298 Flocel Sabaté, "États et alliances dans la Catalogne du bas Moyen-Âge", *Du contrat d'alliance au contrat politique. Cultures et sociétés politiques dans la péninsule Ibérique à la fin du Moyen Âge* (Toulouse: Université Toulouse-Le Mirail, 2007), pp. 308-355.

299 Jeannine Quillet, *La Philosophie Politique du Songe du Vergier (1378). Sources Doctrinales* (Paris: Librarie Philosophique J. Vrin, 1977), p. 52.

300 Joseph Canning, *The Political Thought of Baldus de Ubaldis* (Cambridge: Cambridge University Press, 1987), pp. 96-97.

301 Giacomo Todeschini, "Ordini mendicanti e linguaggio ético-politico", *Etica e política: le teorie dei frati mendicanti nel due e trecento* (Spoleto: Centro Italiano di Studi sull'alto medievo, 1999), pp. 3-27.

302 Martin Aurell, "Eschatologie, spiritualité et politique dans la confédération catalano-aragonaise (1282-1412)", *Actes du 27e colloque de Fanjeaux* (Fanjeaux: Centre d'études supérieures de civilisation médiévale-Université de Poitiers, 1992), pp. 191-235.

contractuelle coherent with *la politique théologienne du contrat*[303] ("the development of a contractual ecclesiology coherent with the theologian policy of the contract") established the ideal framework to easily fit with the coeval context of rising urban society[304]. At the same time, it was internalising a specific adaptation of the notion of common good[305] which grafted the different levels of political theory[306] and practice[307] and was mirrored in the idealised German and especially Italian communal models[308]. Indeed, the author with the greatest influence both at the court[309] and in bourgeois society[310], Francesc Eiximenis, explained that the community itself is the basis of power, as it chooses its governor and reaches the corresponding pacts according to its own interests:

> *Nota que com cascuna comunitat per son bon estament e per son millor viure elegís viure sots senyoria, que cascun pot presumir que cascuna comunitat féu ab sa pròpia senyoria patis e convencions profitosos e honorables per si matexa principalment, e aprés per aquell o per aquells a qui donà la potestat de son regiment. Assò appar per tal car la comunitat no alagí senyoria per amor del regidor, mas elegí regidor per amor de si matexa*[311].

303 Alain Boureau, "Pierre de Jean Olivi et l'émergence d'un théorie contractuelle de la royauté au XIIIe siècle", *Représentation, pouvoir et royauté à la fin du moyen âge*, Joël Blanchard, ed. (Paris: Picard éditeur, 1995), pp. 174-175.

304 Flocel Sabaté, "Municipio y monarquía en la Cataluña bajomedieval", *Anales de la Universidad de Alicante. Historia medieval*, 13 (2000-2002), pp. 261-281.

305 Flocel Sabaté, "Expressoês da representatividade social na Catalunya...", pp. 55-58.

306 Matthew S. Kempshall, *The Common Good in Late Medieval Political Thought* (Oxford: Clarendon Press, 1999).

307 Elodie Lecuppre-Desjardin, Anne-Laure Van Bruaene, eds., *De Bono Communi. The Discourse and Practice of the Common Good in the European City (13th-16th c.)* (Turnhout: Brepols Publishers, 2010).

308 Flocel Sabaté, "La civiltà comunale del medioevo nella storiografia spagnola", *La civiltà comunale italiana nella storiografia internazionale*, Andrea Zorzi, ed. (Florence: Firenze University Press, 2009), pp. 120-121.

309 Paolo Evangelisti, "Credere nel mercato, credere nella *res publica*. La comunità catalano-aragonese nelle proposte e nell'azione politica di un esponente del francescanesimo mediterraneo: Francesc Eiximenis", *Anuario de Estudios Medievales*, 33/1 (2003), p. 74.

310 Josep Hernando, "Obres de Francesc Eiximenis en biblioteques privades de la Barcelona del segle XV", *Arxiu de Textos Catalans Antics*, 26 (2007), pp. 390-392.

311 Francesc Eiximenis, *Dotzè llibre del Crestià*, ch. 156 (Francesc Eixmenis, *Dotzè Llibre del Crestià I.1*, ed. Xavier Renedo [Girona: Universitat de Girona-Diputació de Girona, 2005], p. 338).

> Note that as each community for its good state and to live better chooses to live under lordship, and that each one can claim that each community agreed with its respective lordship different agreements and accords, which were profitable and honourable first for itself and secondary for that o those whose the power of government was ceded. This happened because the community did not choose the lordship by love to the ruler, but it chose the ruler by love to itself.

Therefore, coherent with the rise of the villages and cities and with the ability to generate a suitable justifying discourse, the land tended to be run by the municipalities, and their concern with the government of the country came to affect the very core of the monarchic system: succession. When John I died suddenly in 1396, the possible doubts regarding whether he should be succeeded by his daughter Johanna, who was married to the powerful Count of Foix and Viscount of Béarn and Castellbò, or by his brother Martin, the co-regent of Sicily, were quelled because the local authorities of the city of Barcelona took pains to sway the estates towards Prince Martin[312]. They immediately went to the wife of Prince Martin so he could assume the lieutenancy and be advised *en la conservació e bon estament de la terra*[313] ("in the conservation and good estate of the land"), while setting up a council to adopt *provisions que'ls parega esser profitoses en defensió e conservació de la terra* ("provisions what seem to be profitable in the defence and conservation of the land"). In their conviction that they represented and were of the land, just before proceeding to read the deceased king's will numerous municipal representatives, nobles and ecclesiasts stated that if it ran counter to rights of the chosen successor, *no consentian ans hi dissentien expressament*[314] ("they did not consent, but they disagreed expressly").

When King Martin then died in 1410 without a direct, legitimate successor, the estates once again took over the choice of his successor. Because of the institutional distance between the regions of the crown and interference from the respective social issues, this triggered a crisis that would not come to a head until two years later through what was called the

312 Flocel Sabaté, "Regnat de Martí I. El goven del territori i els bàndols", *Martí I l'Humà, el darrer rei de la dinastia de Barcelona (1396-1410). L'interregne i el Compromís de Casp*, Maria Teresa Ferrer, ed. (Barcelona: Institut d'Estudis Catalans, 2015), pp. 71-83.

313 AHCB, fons municipal, B-I, book 27, f. 29r.

314 *Cortes de Cataluña* (Madrid: Real Academia de la Historia, 1901), vol. 4, pp. 257, 262.

Compromise of Caspe[315]. Apart from the candidate that ended up prevailing[316], it became clear that, as Pere Tomic described, *fou lo XI Rey de Aragó e Comte de Barçelona elegit per la terra*[317] ("the 11th King of Aragon and Count of Barcelona was elected by the land").

Later on, during the reign of the second-born son of the king chosen at Caspe, John II, there were tensions *entre lo senyor rey e la terra* ("between the king and the land"), which they tried to remedy by establishing a *concòrdia del senyor rey ab la terra*[318] ("concord of the king with the land"). The following year, this agreement, signed in Vilafranca del Penedès in 1461[319], would be violated by the monarch, the reason why the representatives of the land removed him from power, in view of the contumacy of the king and to show that the sovereignty was in their hands. When the king rejected this move, it led to a civil war which inflamed the existing social tensions[320]. In the midst of the conflict, the candidate chosen by the estates to be king, *lo senyor Rey en Pere Quart*[321] ("the lord King, Peter [the] Fourth"), died after designating his successor in his will, his sister's son, Prince John of Portugal[322]. This decision was rectified by the representatives of the estates, who *elegiren en rey d'Aragó e comte de*

315 Flocel Sabaté, "Per què hi va haver un Compromís de Casp?", *Els valencians en el Compromís de Casp i en el Cisma d'Occident*, Ricard Bellvesser, ed. (Valencia: Institució Alfons el Magnànim- Diputació Provincial de València, 2013), pp. 45-119.

316 Flocel Sabaté, "El Compromís de Casp", *Història de la Corona d'Aragó*, 2 vols. Ernest Berenguer, ed. (Barcelona: Edicions 62, 2007), vol. 1, pp. 287-304.

317 Pere Tomic, *Històries e conquestes dels reis d'Aragó...*, p. 261.

318 Josep Maria Sans, dir., *Dietaris de la Generalitat de Catalunya*, 10 vols. (Barcelona: Departament de la Presidència de la Generalitat de Catalunya, 1994), vol. 1, p. 163.

319 François Foronda, "Emoción, contrato y constitución. Aproximación a los intentos (pre)constitucionalistas en la Europa de los años 1460 (Sentencia de Medina del Campo, Concordia de Vilafranca del Penedès y Tratado de Saint-Maur-des-Fossés)", *Por política, terror social*, Flocel Sabaté, ed. (Lleida: Pagès Editors, 2013), pp. 211-219.

320 Flocel Sabaté, "El poder soberano en la Cataluña bajomedieval: definición y ruptura", *Coups d'État à la fin du Moyen Âge? Aux fondements du pouvoir politique en Europe occidentale*, François Foronda, Jean Philippe Genet, José Manuel Nieto eds. (Madrid: Casa de Velázquez, 2005), pp. 509-515.

321 Jesús Ernest Martínez-Ferrando, *Pere de Portugal "rei dels catalans" vist a través dels registres de la seva cancelleria* (Barcelona: Institut d'Estudis Catalans, 1936), p. 123.

322 Andreu Balaguer, *Don Pedro, el Condestable de Portugal, considerado como escritor, erudito y anticuario (1429-1466). Estudio histórico-bibliográfico* (Girona: Imprenta de Vicente Dorca, 1881), p. 53.

Barchinona lo il·lustríssimo senyor en Renat, rey de Sicília e comte de Prohença[323] ("chose the king of Aragon and count of Barcelona the very illustrious lord Renate, king of Sicily and count of Provence"), thus showing that the sovereignty lay not in the monarch but in the land.

Even though oligarchic interests held in just a few hands lay behind the invocation of the land[324], the justification in the representation of a land identified by itself versus the monarch contributed to the country's cohesion and personality. Clearly, the land, with its voice expressed by those who claimed to represent it, was capable of affecting the Crown's core institutions. Therefore, we should more closely examine the mutual influence and feedback that this approach had on the institutions, both those of the king and those of the land.

6. The institutions of the king and of the *General*

In 1301, James II established a network of royal districts that for the first time covered all of Catalonia: the *vegueries* ("vicaries"), ruler by a vicar[325]. This was part of the discourse of securing the power of the king as the sovereign over the entire land. Initially it was accepted with few misgivings by the other powers, because, in accordance with the courts of 1283, the royal vicars could never enter the areas within the barons' jurisdiction, even if they fell within their demarcation[326]. The establishment of the *vegueries* was not based on an exercise of the king's chancellery but on royal adaptation to the socioeconomic reality: the vicars were housed in the prominent royal villages and cities, and the *vegueries* matched those villages and cities' radii of projection. This synchrony situated the king's officers within the orbit of and

323 Josep Maria Sans, dir., *Dietaris de la Generalitat de Catalunya...*, vol. 1, p. 188.
324 Joan Lluis Palos, *Catalunya a l'imperi dels Àustria. La pràctica de govern (segles XVI i XVII)* (Lleida: Pagès Editors, 1994), pp. 300-304.
325 Flocel Sabaté, "La divisió territorial de Catalunya: les vegueries", *Història. Política, societat i Cultura dels Països Catalans*, 13 vols., Borja de Riquer, ed. (Barcelona: Enciclopèdia Catalana, 1996), vol. 3, pp. 304-305.
326 Flocel Sabaté, "El veguer a Catalunya. Anàlisi del funcionament de la jurisdicció reial al segle XIV", *Butlletí de la Societat Catalana d'Estudis Històrics*, 6 (1995), pp. 147-159.

practically subjugated the rising municipal powers, yet it also guaranteed the feasibility, stability and survival of the system in that it reflected a reality of the human relations between the villages and their spheres of influence. For this reason, the web of *vegueries* started to be used in the country's joint dealings and in the location of the places, and they emerged from the Middle Ages accepted by everyone as the demarcation system in Catalonia, including by the barons who held jurisdictional capacity[327].

The unified treatment of Catalonia had characterised the inorganic high royal delegations under the reign of James I[328]. This figure close to the monarch, whom he represented over the whole Catalonia became stable as the royal lieutenant under Peter the Great (1276-1285), and remained in place under Alfonso the Liberal (1285-1291), alternating between lieutenancy, vice-regency and attorney general, the latter the name used during the early years of James II's reign. In 1301, an attorney general over the Crown as a whole was chosen in the person of the successor, along with a specific vice-regent for Catalonia. This is the combination that remained in place until 1344, with the exception of the period 1303-1304, when there was an attempt to divide Catalonia into four supra-*vegueries*. After attempting a division into three governates between 1344 and 1347, on the latter date an attorney general for Catalonia was adopted until 1358, when the attorney general was appointed for the entire Crown and a vice-regency for Catalonia. This formula stabilised in 1363 under governmental appointment, with the governor general of the Crown of Aragon in the figure of the successor, and the vice-regencies of the government in every territory, where they became known popularly as governors. In the ensuing decades, the ordinary court of governance and the political influence of the governor consolidated the institution, while the governor general increasingly became a matter of protocol[329]. The government of Catalonia thus became an institution that was wholly equated with the political management of the entire country: in 1410, the governor general could be done away with, but not the governor[330].

327 Flocel Sabaté, "Els eixos articuladors del territori medieval..., pp. 55-70.

328 Jesús Lalinde, *La gobernación general en la Corona de Aragón* (Saragossa: Institución Fernando el Católico, 1963), pp. 3-40.

329 Flocel Sabaté, "La governació al Principat de Catalunya i als comtats de Rosselló i Cerdanya", *Anales de la Universidad de Alicante. Historia Medieval*, 12 (1999), pp. 21-62.

330 *Cortes de Cataluña* (Madrid: Real Academia de la Historia, 1905), vol. 9, pp. 67-77.

Under James I, too, the figure of a bailiff who coordinated the actions of his counterparts around Catalonia also took shape[331], as institutionalised in 1283 through the figure of the general bailiff of Catalonia[332]. His permanent action in the region, with both ordinary actions and extraordinary interventions, highlighted how the institution was equated with the specific territory of Catalonia[333].

As part of Peter the Great's same organising impetus, in 1283 the Master Rational was established as the auditor of the Crown of Aragon[334]. However, in the late 14th century, the unity of the office was fragmented with the consolidation of regional document deposits[335], and by 1410 the Master Rational was clearly delegating to territorial lieutenants, such as the one in Valencia. This marks the beginning of the territorial fragmentation of this post[336]. In fact, this regionalisation began to spread everywhere, even to the royal counsel, which came to be structured by each of the territories making up the Crown in the 1430s[337]. This dynamic only served to stress the Crown's inability to achieve cohesiveness while also highlighting the dynamic of each of the societies, enhancing their respective territorial cohesion.

Historiography situates the point of departure of the Parliaments or Courts which summoned the representatives of the estates upon the king's convocation precisely in the rudimentary assembly of 1214[338]. Due to their representative function, the courts consolidated the image of Catalonia as a community and institutionalised its influence at the highest levels of political power through its division into branches, which usually first sought agreement

331 Flocel Sabaté, "Poder i territori durant el regnat de Jaume I...", p. 106.

332 Tomàs de Montagut, "El baile general de Cataluña (notas para su estudio)", *Hacienda Pública Española*, 87 (1984), pp. 73-84.

333 Flocel Sabaté, "Les castlanies i la comissió reial de 1328...", pp. 177-241.

334 Tomàs de Montagut, *El mestre racional a la Corona d'Aragó (1283-1419)*, 2 vols. (Barcelona: Fundació Noguera, 1987), vol. 2, pp. 69-425.

335 Rafael Conde, *Reyes y archivos en la Corona de Aragón. Siete siglos de reglamentación y praxis archivística (siglos XII-XIX)* (Saragossa: Institución Fernando el Católico, 2008), pp. 62-64.

336 Carlos López, *Patrimonio regio y orígenes del maestre racional del reino de Valencia* (Valencia: Generalitat Valenciana, 1998), pp. 31-34.

337 Flocel Sabaté, "Corona de Aragón", *La época medieval: administración y gobierno* (Tres Cantos: Istmo, 2003), p. 351.

338 Thomas N. Bisson, *L'impuls de Catalunya. L'època dels primers comtes-reis (1140-1225)* (Vic: Eumo Editorial, 1997), pp. 154-157.

amongst themselves and then later negotiated with the king[339]. Precisely, the courts of 1283 permanently limited the supreme legislative capacity, which the monarch could not use without the agreement of the estates:

> *Si nos vel successores nostri constitucionem aliquam generalem seu statutum facere voluerimus in Catalonia, illam vel illud faciamus de approbacione et consensu prelatorum, baronum, militum et civium Catalonie vel ipsis vocatis maioris et sanioris partís eorumdem*[340].

Until the culmination achieved at the courts of Barcelona in 1599, the parliamentary meetings completed the legal articulation that would restrict the monarch's absolute pretensions, as any legislative intention obligatorily had to be complemented by the representative and legislative personality of the estates gathered in parliament[341]. In this way, the courts channelled the specific fit between the monarch and the country, and Ramon d'Abadal thus defined them as *la qüestió bàsica de l'Estat medieval català*[342] ("the basic question of the medieval Catalan State").

Given the monarch's weakness and his dependence on subsidies, the 14th century witnessed the coalescence of courts called by the sovereign to discuss the economic petition at hand[343]. The conviction that they represented not the respective estates but the land, or the country, was thus channelled through the courts. As explicitly revealed in the courts of Barcelona in 1368, the estates' attitudes towards the king make it clear that *Catalunya, com a comunitat política, està representada, no tan sols pel monarca, sinó també pel conjunt dels tres estaments de la Cort*[344]

339 Josep Maria Gay, "La creació del dret a Corts i el control institucional de la seva observança", *Les corts a Catalunya. Actes del congrés d'història institucional (28, 29 i 30 d'abril de 1988)* (Barcelona: Departament de Cultura de la Generalitat de Catalunya, 1991), pp. 90-91.

340 *Cortes de Cataluña* (Madrid: Real Academia de la Historia, 1896), vol. 1/2, p. 145.

341 Tomàs de Montagut, "Pactisme o absolutisme a Catalunya: les grans institucions de governs (s. XV-XVI)", *Anuario de Estudios Medievales*, 19 (1989), pp. 669-679.

342 Ramon d'Abadal, *Pere el Cerimoniós i els inicis de la decadència política de Catalunya* (Barcelona: Edicions 62, 1987), p. 123.

343 Manuel Sánchez, *Pagar al rey en la Corona de Aragón durante el siglo XIV* (Barcelona: Consejo Superior de Investigaciones Científicas, 2003), pp. 215-338.

344 Tomàs de Montagut, *Les institucions fiscalitzadores de la Generalitat de Catalunya (Des dels seus orígens fins a la reforma de 1413)* (Barcelona: Sindicatura de Comptes de Catalunya, 1996), p. 103.

("Catalonia as a political community, is represented not only by the monarch, but also by all three estates of the Court").

In the negotiations, the estates recalled their concern for the country, revisiting the usual invocations in municipal governments when they justified their actions. In 1329, the juries of Girona stated in their decisions: *Se sien esforçats e se forsen de procurar so qui és profités a tot lo general de la terra*[345] ("they have strained and continue to strain for seeking what is better off for the whole general of the land"). With this global orientation, the term "general" referred to the courts[346]: in the courts of Cervera in 1359, King Peter the Ceremonious acknowledged that he would give satisfaction *pro gravaminibus per generale Cathalonia nunc in curiam quam celebramus in Cervaria*[347]. At these same courts, the estates made their aid conditional upon retaining their oversight of their entire course through a deputation of the courts, that is, a *Diputació del General*[348] ("General Deputation"). In a dramatic circumstance for the crown as it had to collect aid in order to deal with the Castilian invasion[349], in 1363 the king transferred control of the economic aid to the deputations which were established in each of the three territories after 1365[350]. The initially temporary nature of this arrangement soon became permanent through the concatenation of aid, the establishment of public debt and the participation in politics based on economic capacity[351]. Thus, a different taxation system

345 AHCG, I.1.1.1, file 1, book 1, f. 1r.

346 Jaume Sobrequès, "L'estat català a la baixa edat mitjana: les Corts, la Generalitat i el Consell de Cent", *Cuadernos de Historia Económica de Cataluña*, 18 (1978), p. 45.

347 Federico Udina, *Privilegios reales concedidos a la ciudad de Barcelona* (Barcelona: Archivo General de la Corona de Aragón, 1971), p. 117.

348 Maria Teresa Ferrer, *Els orígens de la Generalitat de Catalunya (1359-1413)* (Barcelona: Departament de Vicepresidència de la Generalitat de Catalunya, 2009), pp. 7-23.

349 Mario Lafuente, *Dos Coronas en guerra. Aragón y Castilla (1356-1366)* (Saragossa: Grupo de Investigación Consolidado CEMA, 2012), pp. 96-149.

350 Montserrat Fibla, "Les corts de Tortosa i de Barcelona 1365- Recapte del donatiu", *Cuadernos de Historia Económica de Cataluña*, 19 (1978), pp. 97-127.

351 Federico Udina, "Préstamo de cinco galeras por la Generalidad al infante Martín", *Martínez Ferrando Archivero. Miscelánea de estudios dedicados a su memoria* (Madrid: Asociación Nacional de Bibliotecas, Archivos y Arqueólogos, 1968), pp. 487-489.

to that of the king emerged[352], meant the establishment of a state fiscal system that was in the hands not of the sovereign but of the estates[353]. The monarch could neither proceed jurisdictionally nor impose exactions in much of Catalonia, and the General Deputation was the only institution that covered the entire country on tax matters[354] and even held other jurisdictional competences that it could hold, as attempted with the persecution of fugitive slaves[355]. Having to separate the taxation of all three territories led to the establishment of internal customs, with a clear demarcation of the boundaries between Aragon, Valencia and Catalonia[356]. The establishment of a stable seat in Barcelona in the early 15th century[357] and the institutional reform of 1413[358] only served to sanction and institutionally consolidate the General Deputation as a singular body among the large European monarchies, justified through the permanent representation of the courts[359].

With this stability, the General Deputation became at least a permanent indicator of the legal personality *de la terra* ("of the land") and thus beyond the effective control of the institution of the oligarchy through an

352 Enric Guinot, "El patrimoni reial al País Valencià a inicis del segle XV", *Anuario de Estudios Medievales*, 22 (1992), pp. 487-489.

353 José Ángel Sesma, "Fiscalidad y poder. La fiscalidad centralizada como instrumento de poder en la Corona de Aragón (siglo XIV)", *Espacio, Tiempo y Forma*, 4 (1989), pp. 461-463.

354 José Luis Martín, "Nacionalización de la sal y aranceles extraordinarios en Cataluña (1365-1367)", *Anuario de Estudios Medievales*, 3 (1966), pp. 515-524.

355 Flocel Sabaté, "Gli schiavi davanti alla giustizia nella Catalogna bassomedievale", *Schiviatù e servaggio nell'economia europea, secc. XI-XVIII*, Simonetta Cavaciocchi, ed. (Florence: Firenze University Press, 2014), pp. 401-402.

356 José Ángel Sesma, "La fijación de fronteras económicas entre los estados de la Corona de Aragón", *Aragón en la Edad Media*, 5 (1983), pp. 141-163.

357 Albert Estrada, *Una casa per al General de Catalunya* (Barcelona: Generalitat de Catalunya, 2000), pp. 35-54.

358 Isabel Sánchez de Movellán, *La Diputació del General de Catalunya (1413-1479)* (Barcelona: Generalitat de Catalunya-Institut d'Estudis Catalans, 2004), pp. 99-460.

359 *Catalunya constituïa (com els altres estats de la Corona, i també Navarra) un exemple perfecte – potser el més elaborat, junt amb alguns principas alemanys, esp. Württemberg- de 'Ständestaat' ('estat estamental')* ("Catalonia constituted [like other states of the Crown, and also Navarre] a perfect example – perhaps the most elaborate, together with some German principalities, esp Württemberg- of a 'Ständestaat' ['corporative state']"). Víctor Ferro, *El Dret Públic Català. Les Institucions de Catalunya fins al Decret de Nova Planta* (Barcelona: Eumo Editorial, 1987), p. 244.

access system that combined co-optation with insaculation, as regulated in 1455[360]. Precisely, striving to extend its room for manoeuvre, the courts meeting in Lleida in 1461 established an explicit *Consell representant el Principat de Catalunya* ("Representative Council of the Principality of Catalonia") which would not survive the Civil War, but whose very name was justified by its full representation of the country[361] – it took decisions and framed itself as *los diputats del General e Consell llur representants lo Principat de Catalunya*[362] ("the members of the General and Council and their representatives the Principality of Catalonia"), even though socially the power remained in the interests of the few, oligarchic hands[363].

If political and administrative institutions are always a mirror of a society's organisational capacity, late medieval Catalonia found its organisations of governance to be both the route that channelled its territorial specificity within the Crown of Aragon as a whole and the tool with which to endow the capacity invoked by those who framed themselves as the representatives of the land with content.

Coherently, this bond with Catalonia would soon become a requirement for those who had to hold public posts. The courts of 1292 determined that *vicarius, baiulus et curia et quilibet alius officialis qui ius habeat reddere de uno ad alium in Cathalonia et in Regno Maiorice et dictis insulis et assessor eorum in sint Cathaloni.* It was also stablished that the hight representatives of the king (the general procurators) had *consiliarios et judicis Cathalanos in factis Cathalonie*, precisely *pro eo quia Catalano scient melius consuetudines et observantias Cathalonie.* And the courts of 1333 referred to this to clarify a general sense of those whose jurisdictions were affected: *pro eo quia Catalano scient melius consuetudines et observantias Cathalonie*[364]. The measure certainly concurred with the practice followed in all domains, both royal and baronial. In 1418, when the seigniory of Balaguer was reorganised under the new lords who replaced the

360 Flocel Sabaté, "Corona de Aragón…", pp. 386-387.

361 Josep Maria Sans, dir., *Dietaris de la Generalitat de Catalunya...*, vol. 1, p. 161.

362 *Memorias de Don Enrique IV de Castila. Tomo II, Colección diplomática de la crónica de Don Enrique IV* (Madrid: Real Academia de la Historia, 1835, p. 259.

363 Carme Batlle, *La crisis social y económica de Barcelona a mediados del siglo XV*, 2 vols. (Barcelona: Consejo Superior de Investigaciones Científicas, 1973), vol. 1, p. 353.

364 *Cortes de Cataluña* (Madrid: Real Academia de la Historia, 1896), vol. 1/1, pp. 155-156 and 309.

deposed counts of Urgell, the city demanded *que·ls veguer, sotszveguer, batlle, assessor e qualsevol altres oficials ordinaris qui regiran la jurisdicció del dit senyor en la dita ciutat sien e haien a ésser originaris e nadius del Principat de Cathalunya*[365] ("that the vicar, under-vicar, bailiff, legal assessor and any other ordinary officials who run the jurisdiction of said lord in this city be and have to be from and natives of the Principality of Catalonia"). This dynamic, which was well entrenched in the 14th century, matched what was happening in nearby lands such as Béarn[366], but in other states of the Crown, too, the internal, separate cohesion of each of their constituent territories was coming to the fore[367]. Tellingly, the legal framework sprang from the land: before taking possession of the seigniory of Balaguer, in 1419 Prince John agreed that he would apply justice *segons dret comú e o de la terra o de la dita ciutat*[368] ("according to common law and of the land or this city").

7. The geographic shell: Spain

In the early Middle Ages, the countships of the northeast of the Iberian Peninsula, in line with the other Christian domains in the north of the Peninsula[369], equated Spain with Al-Andalus, even though the Church

365 ACN, Fons Balaguer, *Pergamins Diversos*, n. 71.

366 Dominique Bidot-Germa, "Le discours national des officiers publics et des représentants aux États dans la principauté de Béarn au XVe siècle (1391-1517)", *Les variantes du discours régionaliste en Béarn*, Jean-Pierre Barraqué, Christian Thibon, eds. (Orthez: Ed. Gascogne, 2005), p. 60.

367 José A. Armillas, Enrique Solano, "Proyección del poder real sobre Aragón en la construcción del absolutismo (1495-1645)", *La Corona de Aragón y el Mediterráneo. Siglos XV-XVI*, Esteban Sarasa, Eliseo Serrano, eds. (Saragossa: Institución Fernando el Católico, 1997), pp. 333-339.

368 Dolors Domingo, *Pergamins de Privilegis de la ciutat de Balaguer* (Lleida: Edicions de la Universitat de Lleida-Institut d'Estudis ilerdencs, 1997), p. 190.

369 Pablo Álvarez, "El concepto de España según los cronicones de la Alta Edad Media", *Príncipe de Viana*, 3/6 (1942), pp. 150-154; Antonio Linage, "Las raíces medievales de la diferenciación española", *Actas del Cuarto Congreso Internacional de Hispanistas (Salamanca, 1971)*, 2 vols. (Salamanca: Asociación Internacional de

maintained the traditional uniform treatment which identified the entire Peninsula as *Hispania*. The Church's influence, and the change in the balances and geographic profile on the Peninsula in the 12th century helped to ease the spread of the classical view[370]. The assumption of the peninsular perspective combined perfectly with political plurality: in 1240, the Grand Commander of the Hospitallers on the entire Peninsula presented himself as *fratri Reonbaldo maiori comendatori qinque regnorum d'Ispannyam ordinis Hospitalis Santi Iohannis Iherusalem*[371]. Sharing parameters, in the 13th century James I would speak about *los cinc regnes d'Espanya* ("the five kingdoms of Spain") in his chronicle and presented himself as *rei d'Espanya* ("king of Spain") whose actions would lead him to be *honrada tota Espanya*[372] ("honoured all over Spain"). This is simply a spatial referent, not a political design[373]. Apparently, in the ensuing century, Francesc Eiximenis would stress three ports *en Spanya, Mallorques, Sibília e València*[374] ("in Spain, Majorca, Seville and Valencia"). This was quite a common observation: when there were fears of a Marinid invasion in 1338, in Catalonia there was talk of *propter passagium Regis Marrochiorum ad partes Ispanie*[375].

In 1394, the vicar of Barcelona took action against *I hom castellà apellat 'lo patit espanyol' delat que aportava les gents a jugar*[376] ("one

---

Hispanistas-Consejo General de Castilla y León-Universidad de Salamanca, 1982), vol. 2, p. 133.

370 Flocel Sabaté, "La noció d'Espanya en la Catalunya medieval", *El comtat d'Urgell a la Península Ibèrica*, Flocel Sabaté, ed. (Lleida: Pagès Editors, 2002), pp. 121-122.

371 María Luisa Ledesma, "Colección Diplomática de Grisén (Siglos XII y XIII)", *Estudios de Edad Media de la Corona de Aragón*, 10 (1975), p. 64.

372 *Llibre dels feits del rei En Jaume I*, ch. 478, 105, 535 (*Llibre dels feits del rei En Jaume I*, ed. Ferran Soldevila [Barcelona: Institut d'Estudis Catalans, 2007], pp. 469, 198, 507, respectively).

373 A diplomatic space in which different kingdoms, even the conquered and colonized kingdoms of al-Andalus, have a right to enjoy the negotiation of their differences, a position evinced also by the absence of the notion of crusade in the Chronicle (Alexander Ibarz, "The idea of Spain in the Chronicle of Jaume I (c. 1270): Interregnal rivalry, culture and geo-politics in the Crown of Aragon", *La Corónica*, 37/2 [2009], p. 100).

374 Francesc Eiximenis, *Dotzè llibre del Crestià*, ch. XXV (Francesc Eiximenis, *Dotzè llibre del Crestià*, ed. Xavier Renedo..., p. 75).

375 AHCG, I.1.2.1, file 3, book 2, f. 24r.

376 ACA, Reial Patrimoni, Mestre Racional, 1549, f. 26v.

Castilian man named "the small Spanish", accused because led the people to play"), while two years earlier, in 1392, the judges of Tortosa proceeded *en la acusació proposada contra Domingo lo castellà*[377] ("in the accusation proposed against Domingo the Castilian"). In reality, in Catalonia those who came from the kingdom of Castile were called Castilians (*castellans*) – *I castellar qui posava en son hostal*[378] ("One Castilian who were in their hostal") – because of their political affiliation and the language they spoke. In 1363, in the town of Tàrrega, which was under the seigniory of the Count of Trastámara and was housing Castilian troops leftover from their interventions in the French uprising, those men were described as *castellans*[379] ("Castilians"). All of the King of Castile's subjects tended to be known as *castellans* ("Castilians"), regardless of their provenance: in 1384 the royal almoner stated that he had provided economic sustenance *a sor Gueralda ab sa companyona, de la Terça Regla, castellanes de Còrdova, qui anaven en Roma*[380] ("to sister Gueralda with her companion, of the Third Order, Castilians from Cordoba, who were on their way to Rome"), and in 1394 the vicar of Barcelona took action against *P. de Carmona, castellà qui està als Tayers, delat que havia muller en Sibilia e havia presa altra muller en Barcelona*[381] ("P. of Carmona, Castilian who is in the 'Tayers', accused that he had a wife in Seville and another wife in Barcelona"). In order to use the same language, the name Castilian could be applied to subjects of other kingdoms, as perhaps was the case with *Johan de Navarra, castellà* who was in Barcelona in 1394[382], although the Aragonese were always known according their region: *I hom aragonès delat de una mort* ("on Aragonese man accused for a death") was said in Perpignan in 1386[383].

The intensification of political relations between Catalonia and other territories on the Peninsula in the 15th century[384] had a clear corollary in

377 ACBE, Paeria i Vegueria II, 61, f. 77v.

378 ACA, Reial Patrimoni, Mestre Racional, 1549, f. 15vr.

379 ACUR, Tàrrega collection, council book 3, f. 41r.

380 Agustí Altisent, *L'almoina reial a la cort de Pere el Cermoniós. Estudi i edició dels manuscrits de l'almoiner fra Guillem Deudé, monjo de Montserrat (1378-1385)* (Poblet: Abadia de Poblet, 1969), p. 208.

381 ACA, Reial Patrimoni, Mestre Racional, 1549, f. 28v.

382 ACA, Reial Patrimoni, Mestre Racional, 1549, f. 20r.

383 ACA, Reial Patrimoni, Mestre Racional, 1526, f. 39v.

384 Jaume Vicens, *Juan II de Aragón (1398-1479): monarquía y revolución en la España del siglo XV* (Pamplona: Urgoiti Editores, 2003), pp. 29-188.

the cultural perspective. Adopting humanistic parameters, it pinpointed the geographic and historical referent as the Peninsula as a whole, as mentioned by Catalan writers like Jeroni Pau[385]. In fact, the geographic framework of the Peninsula remained in the popular mind-set: with its governance plan, the 'Busca' group in Barcelona proclaimed that it was striving to reinforce the position in the city of Barcelona of *aquella qui és en Spanya cap de llibertat*[386] ("that who in Spain is the liberty's capital"). In turn, the perception from the outside concurred with the overall vision: *Summa summarum, is Hyspanien gar eyn buesser lant*, as Arnold von Harff summarised[387]. Travellers made comparisons reflecting this perception: when he was in Burgos, Popielovo spoke about a market that sent products *a toda España* ("all over Spain"), and when he visited Barcelona he noted that *si se pueden encontrar hermosas mujeres en todas partes de España, por cierto las hay más aquí que en cualquier otro lugar*[388] ("if you can find beautiful women in all parts of Spain, by the way there are more here than anywhere else"), just as Jerónimo Münzer said that Valencia is the *principal población de España*[389] ("the main city of Spain"). In this context, the Catalans was seen as a singular group within Spain as a whole, according the Alfonso the Magnanimous' entrance in Naples in 1443 described by Antonio Beccadelli the Panormita: *Post hos veniebant Hispani, hi quos Latini Celtiberos vulgo Cathalano vocitamos*[390].

At the same time, Catalonia had the common like of the Gothic origins, sharing the basic traits attributed to them with the entire Iberian Peninsula, beginning with religion: *en lo temps dels Gots tornaren a la fe chrestiana en la dita terra de Hispanya o en la mes part*[391] ("in the time of the Goths the

385 Mariàngela Vilallonga, "La geografia a Catalunya...", pp. 54-55.

386 Carme Batlle, "La ideología de la 'Busca'. La crisis municipal de Barcelona en el siglo XV", *Estudios de Historia Moderna*, 5 (1955), pp. 194-195.

387 Antonio Antelo, "Caballeros centroeuropeos en España y Portugal durante el siglo XV", *Espacio, tiempo y forma*, 4 (1989), p. 57.

388 Miguel Ángel Ladero, "Nicolás de Popielovo, viajero por tierras hispánicas (1484-1485)", *Iacobus*, 9-10 (2000), pp. 102, 109.

389 Jerónimo Münzer, *Viaje por España y Portugal* (Madrid: Ediciones Polifemo, 1991), p. 21.

390 Antonio Panormitae, "De dictis et factis Alphonsis Regis", *De Regibus Siciliae et Apuliae in queis et nominatim de Alfonso, rege Aragonum*, Felinus Sandeus, ed. (Hanaus: Typis Wechelianis apud Heredes Ioannis Aubrii, 1640), p. 99.

391 Pere Tomic, *Històries e conquestes dels reis d'Aragó...*, pp. 49-50.

Christian faith returned to this land of Hispania or to the greatest part"). In this orientation, one can see the *reivindicació d'una primera manifestació patriòtica i nacional* in 15th century Catalonia[392], yet at the same time there was a simultaneous appeal to the continuity of the common roots to the benefit of the Castilian crown, as explicitly stated by Sánchez de Arévalo in his *Historia Hispanica*: *quodmodo in regno quod hodie appellatur Castellae et Legionis residet titulus et nominatio regum Hispanie*, and therefore, *solum autem regem Castellae vocant Hispaniae regum*[393]. In reality, though it appeared to be merely a dynastic unification without any institutional consequences[394], the unification of the Peninsula under the same throne in 1479 had huge cultural repercussions by confirming and strengthening Castile's importance and axiology[395], which were assumed to be the expression of its teleological pre-eminence over the Peninsula as a whole[396].

After 1479, the dynastic unification gave the sovereigns a list of titles which were simplified in practice as *rey e reyna de España*[397] ("king and queen of Spain"). This was the outside perception as well: the government

392 Eulàlia Duran, *Sobre la mitificación dels orígens...*, p. 11.

393 Robert B. Tate, *Ensayos sobre la historiografía peninsular del siglo XV* (Madrid: Gredos, 1970), pp. 95-96.

394 Antoni Simón, *La Monarquía de los Reyes Católicos. Hacia un Estado hispánico plural* (Madrid: Temas de Hoy, 1996), pp. 12-14.

395 *Tota una literatura s'estava convertint en vehicle de supremacia cultural – la supremacia del castellà –, corroborada pel zel per la realització d'una unitat panibèrica i per l'impuls de l'orgull nacionalista. Promogut per l'onada de messianisme que va caracteritzar la cultura espanyola del segle XV, el mateix esperit d'autosuficiència cultural que va mantenir autors com Juan del Encina aïllats de l'influx italianitzant, va consolidar l'oficialitat del castellà en perjudici del català i de les altres llengües que havien prosperat en el territori peninsular* ("a whole literature was becoming a vehicle of cultural supremacy -the supremacy of Castilian, corrobarated by the zeal for building a pan-Iberian unit and promoting nationalistic pride. Promoted by the wave of messianism that characterized Spanish culture in the fifteenth century, the spirit of cultural self-sufficiency maintained authors like Juan del Encina isolated from the Italianate influx, consolidated official role of Castilian to the detriment of Catalan and the other languages that had thrived in land of the peninsula"). Peter Cczzella, "Pere Torroella i Francesc Moner: aspectes del bilinguïsme literari (catalano-castellà) a la segona meitat del segle XV", *Llengua & Literatura*, 2 (1987), p. 106.

396 Luis Fernández Gallardo, "Lengua e identidad nacional en el pensamiento político de Alfonso de Cartagena", *e-Spania*, 12/2 (2012), <http://e-spania.revues.org/21012>.

397 Antonio de la Torre, "El concepto de España durante el reinado de los Reyes Católicos", *Revista de la Biblioteca, Archivo y Museo*, 23/68 (1954), pp. 13-14.

of Genoa addressed the king of Granada in 1482 to report *de le novità le quali al presente occurreno tra la vostra maiestà e il serenissimi re de Spagna*[398] ("from the news that right now are happening between your majesty and the most serene King of Spain").

In the meantime, King Ferdinand II of Aragon and V of Castile accepted geographic plurality and institutional diversity according to the medieval notion of space and power. This, therefore, concatenated the reference to Spain and the plurality of constituent kingdoms and nations over which he presided, surely imbued with teleological missions reminiscent of the messianic traditions that converged in him[399]. For this reason, in 1484 he commented that he had his *las manos agora en esta sancta empresa de Granada, por echar d'esta Espanya estos infieles moros* ("the hands foretell in this holy endeavour of Granada, to remove these infidel Moors from Spain") at the same time that he spoke about *el reyno de Sicilia, tan apartado d'estos nuestros reynos de Espanya* ("the kingdom of Sicily, so far from these our kingdoms of Spain") and that he was addressing *universis et singulis consulibus mercatoribus tam cathalanorum et castellanorum quam etiam quarumvis aliarum nacionum horum nostrorum Hispanie regnorum ac aliorum subtitorum nostrorum*[400].

The fact that the different nations shared the same Spanish monarch fostered mutual tensions over each party's rights, as can clearly be seen abroad in cities where nation each had its own consulate. This is why in 1488 King Ferdinand equalised the rights of the two consulates in Bruges, *a ffin que todos los vasallos nuestros tengan y gozen de unos mismos privilegios*[401] ("so that all our vassals have and enjoy the same privileges"). In fact, he was also trying to instil common action in the consular representations, as they were now linked not only to trade interests but also

398 Roser Salicrú, "La embajada de 1479 de Pietro Fieschi a Granada: nuevas sombras sobre la presencia genovesa en el sultanato nazarí en vísperas de la conquista castellana", *Atti dell'Accademia Lugure di Scienze e Lettere*, 54 (1997), p. 361.

399 José Ángel Sesma, *Fernado de Aragón, Hispaniarum rex* (Saragossa: Gobierno de Aragón, 1992), pp. 209-210.

400 Antonio de la Torre, *Documentos sobre relaciones internacionales de los Reyes Católicos*, 6 vols. (Barcelona: Consejo Superior de Investigaciones Científicas, 1950), vol. 2, pp. 154, 163,145, respectively.

401 Pablo Desportes, "El consulado catalán de Brujas...", p. 390.

to the Crown's diplomatic needs, just as in Rome at the same time[402]. And at home, some voices watched as major possibilities opened up within the new framework, such as the municipal counsellor of Valencia: when celebrating the enthronement of the new King Ferdinand in 1479, he explained that *per no ésser Spanya juncta ab la dita casa sereníssima de Aragó, érem molt vexats*[403] ("for Spain not being together with this most Serene house of Aragon, we were were much harassed").

In the same period, the 1472 defeat of the Catalan civil war by those who had posed as the representatives of the land, to the extreme of deposing the monarch[404], and the acceptance of a king who since 1479 added the Crown of Aragon to the Crown of Castile he already held[405], did not substantially alter either the institutional framework[406] or its justifying discourse. After the war, the legal thinking had to resolve the fit between royal, territorial and community authority and power[407]. Yet at the same time, it would not move towards approaches involving pactism or contractualism favourable to the monarch, as had proposed by Belluga in Valencia[408]. Instead, the representative discourse would remain in place, invoking the identity and capacity of the land itself in accordance with its secular roots. Above and beyond the arguments, the ordinary operation of the representative institutions left no room for doubt: *la conservació del Principat de Catalunya consisteix en lo General de Catalunya* ("conservation of

402 José Manuel Nieto, "La nación española de Roma y la embajada del comendador santiaguista Gonzalo de Beteta (1484)", *Anuario de Estudios Medievales*, 28 (1998), pp. 109-117.

403 Miguel Gual, "Valencia ante la muerte de Juan II de Aragón", *Saitabi*, 33-34 (1949), p. 272.

404 Alan Ryder, *The Wreck of Catalonia. Civil War in the Fifteenth century* (Oxford: Oxford University Press, 2007), pp. 210-225.

405 Jaume Vicens Vives, *Historia crítica de la vida i reinado de Fernando de Aragón* (Saragossa: Institución Fernando el Católico, 2007), pp. 471-523.

406 Flocel Sabaté, "Capitulació de Pedralbes", *Enciclopèdia de Barcelona*, 4 vols. (Barcelona: Enciclopèdia Catalana, 2006), vol. 3, p. 319.

407 Manuel J. Peláez, *Catalunya després de la guerra civil del segle XV* (Barcelona: Curial, 1981), pp. 199-205.

408 Carlos López, "Teoría y práxis del contrato político en el reino de Valencia. Del interregno a la conquista de Nápoles", *Du contrat d'alliance au contrat politique. Cultures et sociétés politiques dans la péninsule Ibérique à la fin du Moyen Âge*, François Foronda, Ana Isabel Carrasco, eds. (Toulouse: Centre National de la Recherche Scientifique-Université Toulouse-Le Mirail, 2007), pp. 402-403.

the Principality of Catalonia consists of the General of Catalonia"), as was claimed in Cervera back in the 16th century[409]. In fact, the oligarchic social fabric had changed little, and access to power and the institutions remained under apparently identical parameters[410].

In this way, the justifying discourse, which appealed to the secular roots of identity cohesion and to the specific ordinary institutions, would survive in Catalonia as it entered a new context. Precisely the shift from the 15th to the 16th centuries witnessed how the sovereign became the receptacle of cultural and ideological baggage that contained the conviction of a specific peninsular and monarchic cohesion[411]. Headway was needed in the quest for new balances within a new scenario in which the king, now invoking a Spanish monarchy, neither was in Catalonia nor would need its subsidies to finance his undertakings.

8. Conclusion: A medieval legacy

The controversy in modern Europe between the purposes of mixed governments versus the rise in absolutism[412] found a very specific scenario in

409 Joan Lluis Palos, *Catalunya a l'imperi dels Àustria. La pràctica de govern (segles XVI i XVII)* (Lleida: Pagès Editors, 1994), pp. 328-329.

410 Carme Batlle, "La oligarquía de Barcelona a fines del siglo XV: el partido de Deztorrent", *Acta historica et archaeologica Mediaevalia*, 7-8 (1986-1987), pp. 321-335.

411 *Todos los aspectos ideológicos mencionados [...] – el gobierno centralizado, la lengua como instrumento del imperio, la historiografía de los funcionarios, la apelación a la herencia visigoda, etc. – confluyen y se refuerzan mutuamente en el último decenio del siglo XV y el primero del XVI* ("All the ideological aspects mentioned [...] – the centralised government, language as an instrument of empire, the historiography of officials, the appeal to the Visigoth inheritance, etc. come together and reinforce each other in the last decade of the 15th century and the first of the 16th"). Alan Deyermond, "La ideología del Estado moderno en la literatura española del siglo XV", *Realidades e imágenes del poder. España a fines de la Edad Media*, Adeline Rucquoi, eds. (Valladolid: Ámbito, 1988), p. 192.

412 Marie Gaille-Nikodimov, *Le gouvernement mixte. De l'idéal politique au monstre constitutionnel en Europe (XIIIe-XVIIe siècle)* (Saint-Étienne: Publications de l'Université de Saint-Étienne, 2005).

Catalonia: not only would the controversity circulate through institutions that had survived from the Middle Ages, but after the 16th century the legal underpinnings rested upon the invocation of a legitimising medieval order – with its milestones in the supposed Carolingian concessions to the inhabitants of Barcelona in 844, the constitutions of 1283 and the Compromise of Caspe of 1412. In the 17th century, the controversy over the model of state led to not only armed but also dialectical confrontation, with discussions that largely centred on the medieval roots of the country and the consequences and obligations derived therefrom.

The true roots of this legacy are veiled in the circumstances in which the late medieval discourse of power was forged, which had enabled the position of an oligarchy to be justified by invoking the representativeness of an identity-based collective. The fit between the ideology of power in late medieval political thinking and the particular situation of the relationship between the sovereign and the estates in Catalonia facilitated the emergence of an extraordinarily coherent institutional framework and justifying discourse. The first step was a long pathway throughout the centuries which brought society closer and made it more cohesive, leading to an internal awareness and an external perception. The second step was a particular stabilisation defined in terms of the institutional balance of power and the justifying arguments around collective representativeness. Both milestones were to define the subsequent developments in a different way, shaping a legacy that would experience quite different circumstances to the ones in which it was born.

Modern History

The Centuries Ushering in Modernity: Identity, State and Nation

Antoni Simon
Universitat Autònoma de Barcelona and Institut d'Estudis Catalans

The centuries of the Modern Age are a crucial period in the construction of the modern Spanish state and the way Catalonia's historical formation articulated it. It is a historical period characterised by three major touchstone "moments": 1) the dynastic union of the branches of the House of Trastámara reigning in the Crown of Aragon and the Crown of Castile, which territorially compacted the medieval kingdoms on the Iberian Peninsula in the late 15th century; 2) the revolutionary crisis of 1640, which led to the failure of an early Spanish "national" project defined in peninsula-wide terms; and 3) the War of the Spanish Succession and the transition from the aggregative, institutionally plural Habsburg monarchy to another which consolidated a much more unified central area – Spain; this monarchy bore the absolutist, centralising hallmark of the Bourbon dynasty but also encompassed the dominant forms of governance in the political culture of the Castilian court.

As is common knowledge, in the late 15th century, the Catholic Kings turned Castile into the political locus of a new monarchy. However, there was no political or institutional integration, nor was there any process of merging the incipient national identities that had developed in the different peninsular kingdoms during the Middle Ages, which were now dynastically united. The institutional and governing structures common to each historical formation were left in place with few substantial changes until the Bourbon triumph in the War of the Spanish Succession. The lack of legal, institutional, monetary and linguistic-cultural unity hindered a compact territory recognised as such from being distinguished either individually or collectively. The diversity and fragmentation of the legal rights and privileges entailed in any given territory also shaped mental boundaries that were difficult to overcome. However, Castile's centrality left Catalonia and all the territories on the periphery of the monarchy in general under a twofold subjugation: to the Crown and to a central government established in Madrid since 1561, which was basically controlled by Castilian political staff.

In the waning decades of the 16th century, the process of the legitimisation and constitutionalisation of the Spanish monarchy entered a crucial phase. Numerous deeds and historical developments became shared elements of reflection among the intelligentsia at the Castilian court, including the Spanish Habsburgs' disassociation from the imperial title, the upheaval of the rebellion in the Netherlands and fears of its disruptive chain effects, the incorporation of Portugal, the crisis of the Castilian human and material bases, and the enormous costs entailed in maintaining a monarchy that spanned the entire planet.

Within the range of theoretical options proposed to "conserve" the state and retain its power, the idea of Spain – formulated in peninsula-wide terms – as a political community began to gain momentum. Spain would be a medium-sized, territorially compact state endowed with common cultural and historical ties. These characteristics were fully in line with the ideals posited by the doctrine of the reason of state in Europe on the issue of conserving the monarchies. At the same time, this idea of Spain was the heir to the historical-mythical formulations of the medieval and Renaissance Castilian chroniclers, who aspired to reconstruct the Gothic unity lost by the Muslim invasion in the 8th century.

From that moment on, proposals for institutional, fiscal and legislative unification started to emerge, all with a heavy Castilian bias, which ultimately more closely resembled a proposal for annexation and assimilation than for integration. The coalescence and budding awareness of these ideas among the circles at the monarchy's Castilian court was deep and important. Thus, during the ministry of the Count-Duke of Olivares, there was an attempt to try a set of military-fiscal and institutional reforms in political practice which combined a political model with absolutist tendencies with the constitution of a state centre that was equated with Spain.

As this political and identity-based concept of Spain was beginning to take shape in the centre of the peninsula, Catalonia was experiencing major transformations in the realms of demographics-economics and institutions-ideology. In the second half of the 16th century, there was a famous reform of the human and material bases of the Principality and a rising articulation of the land around its capital, Barcelona. In parallel, during those same decades the distance between the Crown and the ruling classes in the Principality became increasingly clear. Conversely, the *Diputació del General* ("General Deputation") and the *Consell de Cent* ("Council of One Hundred") were institutions that were becoming increasingly representative of the Catalan community and less beholden to royal power. The strengthening of these institutions – administratively, symbolically, etc. – as well as the rise of the Generalitat's taxation-financial system, enabled a web of interests and complicities to be woven that spread to broad swaths of Catalan society.

Within this historical setting, there was a clear strengthening of Catalan national identity with medieval roots. This conscious notion of a Catalan nation was reflected in the historical and legal arguments that accompanied battles between the Crown and the Catalan institutions over jurisdiction or sovereignty. In parallel, a political culture would take root among the ruling groups – and among broad sectors of the middle classes – in which the defence of the laws and institutions of the "land" would become the prime political value. The economic, cultural, linguistic and historical thinking of the day would nurture and reflect the idea that Catalonia was the Catalans' political homeland.

After the second third of the 17th century, when the fight for hegemony over Europe among the Spanish Habsburgs and the French Bourbons entered its decisive phase, the military factor dashed the delicate balances upon which the Spanish monarchy's constitutional model had been grounded. The arguments regarding the "need" for and "conservation" of the state spurred the absolutist, uniformising tendencies of the governing circles in the Castilian court, who saw intermediate powers which interfered with royal authority as hurdles that had to be eliminated or levelled.

In the Catalonia of 1640, the military and fiscal pressure from the government of Madrid collided with a political culture which viewed the Catalans' institutions and "freedoms" as fundamental political and identity values. This led to the 1640 Revolution and the Catalan Revolt against the Spanish monarchy and its alliance with Bourbon France.

Although the identity factor (with the Catalonia-Castile-Spain contrast as the fundamental referent) permeated the political and intellectual debate, it was not what triggered the Catalan Revolt of 1640-1652. However, once the hostilities had begun, the national factor gained extraordinary force and momentum, sowing the seeds of strong Catalan-Castilian and Catalan-French counter-identities among broad swaths of Catalonia's society.

In fact, a kind of concatenation or chain reaction had been unleashed which we can find until the end of the War of the Spanish Succession. The political conceptualisation of Spain and the absolutist tendencies of its central government encouraged uniformising policies which were met with energetic resistance in the Catalan political community, whose own institutional, symbolic-identity and cultural referents had already matured during that same period. What was fostered by Spain's military presence on Catalan soil to achieve the objectives and ideals of a far-away dynasty and a Castilianised political centre was precisely a "national" shock that made any project aimed at identity unification even more unfeasible.

At the start of the 18th century, the Catalan constitutional dispute once again came to the fore in the wider arena of European international politics. However, as so often claimed, the Catalans' choice in 1705 had not a Spanish "horizon" but a Catalan "sovereignist" one, in the sense that its main political objective was to recover the self-governance of its land lost in 1652.

The outcome of the War of the Spanish Succession was to instate a political model in Catalonia with an absolutist framework, in contrast to the pactist nature in its historical tradition. This absolutist model also aspired to politically and legally construct a Spanish union or nation cut of Castilian cloth, where alternative powers and loyalties had no place. However, despite the Catalans' defeat in the War of the Spanish Succession and the harshness of the subsequent repression, we can nonetheless detect unequivocal symptoms of the persistence of Catalan national identity in the 18th and early 19th centuries. This persistence would prove that the national identities of certain historical groups can survive even when they are not protected by their own institutional and legal structures. Historical memory, cultural-symbolic factors and emotional factors as well had a deep, hardy substrate, at least in Catalonia.

"Catalans" and "Spaniards": Two Chosen Peoples for a Single Promised Land[1]

Antoni SIMON
Universitat Autònoma de Barcelona and Institut d'Estudis Catalans

1. Background

As is common knowledge, throughout the century spanning the mid-16th and mid-17th centuries, the relationships between the Catalan historical formation and the centre of power at the Castilian court which determined the fate of the Spanish Habsburg monarchy entered into a phase of tensions which ultimately led to the rupture of 1640.

The outbreak of political and institutional clashes, and ultimately military confrontations, which characterised this period was accompanied by divergences in the realm of ideas, symbols and cultural and identity referents. More specifically, it has been noted how in this period an Iberia-wide project quite well defined as Spain as a political community was being supported by the circles at the Castilian court[2] as Castilian identity became the metaphor for Spanish national identity[3]. That is, especially after the

1 Abbreviations used: BC, Biblioteca de Catalunya; BNE, Biblioteca Nacional de España.

2 Primarily: Antoni Simon, *Construccions polítiques i identitats nacionals. Catalunya i els orígens de l'estat modern espanyol* (Barcelona: Publicacions de l'Abadia de Montserrat, 2005), pp. 53-133; Mateo Ballester, *La identidad española en la Edad Moderna (1556-1665). Discursos, símbolos y mitos* (Madrid: Tecnos, 2010).

3 See: Irving A. A. Thompson, "Castilla, España y la monarquía: la comunidad política de la *patria natural* a la *patria nacional*", *España, Europa y el mundo atlántico*, Richard L. Kagan, Geoffrey Parker, eds. (Madrid: Marcial Pons, 2001), pp. 177-216, especially, p. 197 (first edition Cambridge University Press, 1995); on the changes in the political vocabulary of the period which led to the emergence of this concept of Spanish fatherland, see: Irving A. A. Thompson, "La Monarquía de España: la invención de un concepto", *Entre Clio y Casandra. Poder y sociedad en la monarquía hispánica durante la Edad Moderna*, Javier Guillamón, Domingo Centenero, Julio David Muñoz, eds. (Murcia: Universidad de Murcia, 2005), pp. 31-56.

end of the 16th century, the intelligentsia at the Castilian court developed a Spanish "national" project that sought to construct a state base in the former Iberia that was institutionally compact and, in the longer term, compact in terms of identity as well. However, this Spanish "national" project was built upon a diverse reality in terms of both institutions and identity. Specifically in Catalonia, the political, institutional and ideological clashes with the Castilian court stemming from the contrast between two divergent models of state (one constitutionalist and the other with absolutist tendencies) were accompanied by the strengthening of two equally distinct national identities – the Castilian identity extended metaphorically to encompass the Spanish identity, and the Catalan identity – which the war from 1640-1652 would do nothing other than revive and pit against each other.

Regarding this process of divergence and confrontation, in this study we shall focus on an ideological element which – according to the parameters of the system of cultural values at that time – endowed both of these national identities with moral force and political rationality: the sacralisation of these identities based on the idea that both the Catalans and the Spaniards were God's "chosen" people.

It is common knowledge that ideas about an ethnic choice or a divine covenant were fairly common in the processes of constructing European national identities in both the Catholic and Protestant worlds[4]. However, I believe that a joint analysis of the cases of Catalonia and Spain poses some features of particular interest:

1. First of all, unlike, say, in the Netherlands, where freedom from the shackles of Spanish political domination was also a religious liberation, in Catalonia and Spain the clash of the two models of state and their inherent national identities arose in societies that shared the same religion: Catholicism.

4 Primarily: David Novak, *The Election of Israel: The Idea of Chosen People* (Cambridge: Cambridge University Press, 1995); William Hutchinson, Hartmut Lehmann, eds., *Many are Chosen: Divine Election and Western Nationalism* (Minneapolis: Fortress Press, 1994); Steven Grosby, "The Chosen People of Ancient Israel and the Accident: Why Does Nationality Exist and Survive?", *Biblical Ideas of Nationality. Ancient and Modern* (Winona Lake: Eisenbrauns, 2002), pp. 91-119; Anthony D. Smith, *Chosen Peoples* (Oxford: Oxford University Press, 2003).

2. Secondly, one could consider whether in societies that experienced the Counter-Reformation, as Catalan and Spanish societies did, the controlled dissemination of the Bible made the idea that the nation itself was the successor of the Israelite people less intense than in Protestant societies. Likewise, on this point, one could also consider whether or not the anti-Judaism that permeated the Catalan and Spanish societies stanched these comparisons between the national identities on the Iberian Peninsula and the Jewish people.

2. "The Spaniards": God's chosen people in the age of the "Law of Grace". Their superiority over the Jewish people

Within the leafy tree of Spanish political thinking on the reason of state in this period, the identification of the "Spaniards" as God's chosen people was closely tied to the theorisations which posited a political ideal or horizon grounded upon a universal monarchy where secular power and spiritual power converged[5].

The Calabrian Tomasso Campanella was one of the first to state clearly and directly that the Spaniards were the people chosen by Divine Providence to carry out the ideals of a universal theocratic monarchy. At the turn of the 17th century, this restless Dominican friar claimed in the preface to *La monarquia Hispánica* that the:

5 This idea of a universal monarchy, which is not exclusive to Hispanic thought, can be interpreted as a theocratic version of the doctrines of reason of state and proof that these doctrines were still imbued with categories from medieval political culture. See: Richard Tuck, *Philosophy and Government 1572-1561* (Cambridge: Cambridge University Press, 1993), chapter 3; Pablo Fernández, *Fragmentos de monarquía* (Madrid: Alianza, 1992), p. 168 and thereafter. Still, by the first half of the 17th century, the idea of a universal monarchy had ceased to be a referent or common point of European political thinking. See: John M. Headley, "The Demise of Universal Monarchy as a Meaningful Political Idea", *Imperium, Empire, Reich Ein Konzept politischer Herrchaft in deutsch-britischen Vergleich*, Franz Bosbach, ed. (Munich: Saur, 1999), pp. 41-58.

> *Monarquía universal, venida de Oriente a Occidente de mano de los asirios, persas, medos, griegos y romanos (estos últimos divididos en tres cabezas del águila imperial), llegó por último a los españoles, a quienes tras larga servidumbre y guerra el Hado les concedió todo*[6].
>
> The universal monarchy, coming from East to West by the Assyrians, Persians, Medes, Greeks and Romans (the latter divided into the three heads of the imperial eagle), finally reached the Spaniards, whom fate has granted everything after a long servitude and war.

And, in fact, the process of legitimisation and conceptualisation of the Spanish monarchy which took place in the late 16th and early 17th centuries was characterised by a strong religious tone. In his *Tomo Primero de la Conveniencia de las dos Monarquías Católicas* of 1612, Juan de la Puente claimed that the monarchy of Spain was the universal church of the present time the way Israel had been in the past, and that the medieval centuries of reconquest from the Muslims were the founding period of the Spanish "ecclesiastical monarchy":

> *Vivieron los antiguos Españoles, descendientes de Tubal, retirados en las montañas de España [...] Estos invencibles Montañeses, hijos del primer poblador, en la ocasión y año señalado [714 d.c.] intentaron restaurar la tierra que el Cielo les tenia prometida*[7].
>
> The old Spaniards, descendants of Tubal, lived in the mountains of Spain [...] These invincible Mountaineers, children of the first settler, on the occasion and important year [714 AD] attempted to restore the land which Heaven had promised them.

6 Cited by: Tomas Campanella, *La Monarquía Hispánica* (Madrid: Centro de Estudios Constitucionales, 1982), p. 7 (translation, prologue and notes by Primitivo Mariño). Campanella's *Monarquía Hispanica*, written in around 1598-1600, was a highly influential work, even before the printing press had been invented. It was published for the first time in a German version by de C. Besold in 1620, reissued in 1623 and 1630, and later was released in several Latin version. Regarding the dates of Campanella's works (Stilo, Calabria 1568- Paris 1639), see: Luigi Firpo, *Bibliografia degli scritti di ommaso Campanella* (Turin: Bona, 1940); Regarding his thinking, see primarily: John M. Headley, *Tommaso Campanella and the transformation of the World* (Princeton: Princeton University Press, 1997).

7 Juan de la Puente, *Tomo Primero de la Conveniencia de las dos Monarquías católicas, la de la Iglesia Romana y la del Imperio español, y defensa de la Precedencia de los Reyes católicos de España a todos los Reyes del Mundo* (Madrid, 1612), book 3, ch. 26, p. 368. See: Eva Botella, *Monarquía de España: discurso teológico 1590-1685* (Madrid: Ediciones de la Universidad Autónoma de Madrid, PhD Dissertation, 2006).

One year later, the Benedictine friar Juan de Salazar unquestionably drew inspiration from Campanella to write in the prologue to his *Política española* (1619) that *comenzando la Monarquía universal en el Oriente, de las manos de asirios, medos, persas griegos y romanos, vino a parar en las de los españoles* ("The universal Monarchy having begun in the East at the hands of the Assyrians, Medes, Persians, Greeks and Romans, came to rest in the land of Spaniards"). However, Salazar added from his own opinion that *la voluntad divina se la concedió con mayores ventajas que a los predecesores*[8] ("Divine will was granted [to the Spaniards] with greater advantages than to their predecessors").

The intention guiding Salazar was to make a total apologia for the Spanish state as a historical reality, arguing that from the start of the reconquest of the Muslims, it had become larger and stronger thanks to its religious underpinning. As a way of proving that the "Spaniards" were God's chosen people, Juan de Salazar pointed out the multiple comparisons which could be drawn between the history of the Spaniards and the people of Israel, as well as the existing analogies between the Spanish kings and chiefs and those of the Jewish people. In the fourth chapter or "proposition", Juan de Salazar related:

> *Los sucessos, casi símiles en todos los tiempos, y el modo singular que Dios ha tenido en la elección y gobierno del pueblo español, declaran ser su pueblo escogido en la ley de gracia, como lo fue el electo, en tiempo de la escrita.*
>
> The events, almost identify in all times, and the unique way God had chosen and governed the Spanish people chosen in the Law of Grace, like de elect, in the time of the writing.

In that chapter, he equated Don Pelayo with Moses, Bernardo de Carpio with Gideon, Rodrigo de Vivar with Samson, Charles V with David, Philip

8 Juan de Salazar, *Política española* (Logroño: Diego Mares, 1619), p. 19. I have cited from the edition by the Centro de Estudios Políticos y Constitucionales with a prologue by Miguel Herrero García (Juan de Salazar, *Política española* (Madrid: Centro de Estudios Políticos y Constitucionales, 1997), which, in turn, is a reprint of the one issued in 1945. The citation is on p. 19. Regarding Salazar's oeuvre, see: Alberto Montoro, *Fray Juan de Salazar, moralista político 1619* (Madrid: Escelicer, 1972); Pablo Fernández, *Materia de España. Cultura política e identidad en la España moderna* (Madrid: Marcial Pons, 2007), pp. 96-102; Mateo Ballester, *La identidad española...*, pp. 281-287.

II with Solomon, the Kings Garcia V of Navarra, Ramiro I of Aragon and Ferdinand I of Castile, all of them the sons of Sancho III the Great of Navarra, with the Maccabee brothers Simon, Judah and Jonathan[9]. However, at the end of his comparison, Salazar proclaimed the superiority of the Spaniards over the Hebrews, because unlike the latter, ever since the 8th century Muslim invasion the settlers of the former Iberia had never strayed from the pathway set by God:

> *En lo que es faltar a sus obligaciones, no se le parece; ni se le asimila en adorar el becerro en el desierto; ni en reverenciar el ídolo Moloch; ni en humillarse, como hicieron las diez tribus de Israel ante Bel; ni ha adorado jamás a otro Dios que al verdadero, vivo y eterno, porque desde que escarmentando en cabeza de Witiza, volvió sobre sí la nación y la semilla española, después de la general pérdida de España y miserable esclavitud y servidumbre de los moros, en cuyas manos la entregó el Señor para remedio suyo, no ha admitido España herejía ni ha negado la propiedad de Dios*[10].

> Regarding not fulfilling their obligations, they do not resemble each other; nor do they resemble each other in worshipping the golden calf in the desert; nor in revering the pagan god Moloch; nor put to shame, like the ten tribes of Israel before Bel; nor in never worshipping any other God but the true one, living and eternal, because, after to be chastised in the Witiza's head, the Spanish nation return over itself and seed, after the general loss of Spain and miserable bondage and servitude under the Moors, into whose hands was leaved by the Lord for its remedy, Spain has not permitted any heresy nor denied the property of God.

Ten years later, another Benedictine monk, Father Benito de Peñalosa y Mondragón, devoted chapters seven, eight and nine of his *Libro de las cinco excelencias del español que despueblan España para su mayor potencia i dilatación* (1629) to explaining how the Spaniards spread the Catholic faith around the world, which was *oficio y prerrogativa que tenia el pueblo de Dios escogido*[11] ("the role and prerogative that God's chosen people possessed"). Peñalosa said that Yahweh had first entrusted this sacred mission to the Jewish people, but that now it was being performed

9 Juan de Salazar, *Política española…*, pp. 73-89.

10 Juan de Salazar, *Política española…*, p. 88.

11 Benito de Peñalosa, *Libro de las cinco Excelencias del Español que despueblan a España para su mayor potencia y dilatación* (Pamplona: Carlos de Labayén, 1629), f. 22 and following. Regarding Peñalosa's work, see: Mateo Ballester, *La identidad española...*, pp. 287-291.

by the Spaniards imitating the apostles, even if this meant the depopulation of Spain: *De quan glorioso es el despueblo de España, por causa que sus naturales vayan a ganar almas para poblar al cielo* ("the inhabitants of Spain are so glorious that they are going seeking souls for populating the Heaven implying the depopulation of the Spain"), An in this divine mission, the Spaniards had an advantage over the Jewish people because in addition to preaching the word of God around Europe, Asia and Africa as the sons of Israel had done, they were also spreading the word of God around the Americas. Likewise, the superiority of the Spaniards over the Israelites could clearly be seen in the sacrifices of the "infinite" Spanish martyrs who died every day, while *muy pocas vezes fueron mártires los Hebreos por defender la ley de Dio* ("Very rarely were the Hebrews martyred for defending God's law") Finally, in this comparison, which was always favourable to the Spaniards, Peñalosa also argued that while the Jewish people preached the Written Law, the Spaniards were spreading the Law of Grace, which was *más general, más clara, más perpétua, más viva y graciosa, que no la suya particular, enigmática y obscura*[12] ("more general, clearer, more perpetual, than their own, enigmatic and obscure").

Neither Juan de Salazar nor Benito Peñalosa bothered to hide a smouldering anti-Judaism in their works which led them to censure certain ethical features of the Jewish people and praise their expulsion ordered by the Catholic Kings in 1492[13]. Likewise, as Mateo Ballesteros has noted, the core goal common to both works was to highlight that while the divine choice of the Jewish people had been contingent and temporary, the choice of the Spaniards was permanent and everlasting[14].

12 Benito de Peñalosa, *Libro de las cinco Excelencias…*, f. 33, 23, 23v.

13 Regarding the anti-Judaism that permeated the period and its connotations in politics and ideology, see: Juan Ignacio Pulido, *Injurias a Cristo. Religión, política y antijudaísmo en el siglo XVII* (Alcalá de Henares: Universidad de Alcalá, 2002); also: Juan Hernández, *Sangre limpia, sangre española. El debate de los estatutos de limpieza (siglos XV-XVII)* (Madrid: Cátedra, 2011).

14 Mateo Ballester, *La identidad española…*, p. 290.

3. The Habsburgs: The dynasty chosen by God to put an end to heresy

Apart from the explicit formulations which directly equated the Spaniards with God's chosen people, the political thinking in the Spanish Counter-Reformation used other biblical referents which sought the same providentialist objective yet at least partly avoided the ethically awkward comparison with the Jewish people.

As is common knowledge, one of the fundamental features of Spanish political thinking in the age of the reason of state was the exaltation – to mythification – of the Crown-Church or king-religion binomial[15]. In fact, in Spanish political treatises we can find numerous analogies comparing David, Solomon and other kings from the dynasty of Israel to the Habsburg monarchs even earlier and more frequently than comparisons of the *Spaniards* with the Jewish people[16]. These analogies had appeared in authors in the mid-16th century such as the Erasmist Felipe de la Torre, whose *Institución de un Rey Cristiano* compared Charles V with King David and Philip II with Solomon:

> *La magestad del Emperador como un segundo David, ha en sus días emprendido grandes guerras, dado grandes batallas y mantenido grandes exércitos a título de servir a Dios y reprimir los Philisteos y enemigos de la Yglesia. Ha puesto allende d'esto muy grande diligencia por cobrar el Arca del Testamento y edificar a Dios su Templo. Y finalmente en sus dias ha resignado en V.M. el imperio y mando de todos sus reynos como también David en Salomón. Resta pues agora que V.M. como otro*

15 See: Julián Viejo, "Ausencia de política. Ordenación interna y proyecto europeo en la Monarquía católica de mediados del siglo XVII", *Monarquía, imperio y pueblos en la España Moderna*, Pablo Fernández, ed. (Alicante: Caja de Ahorros del Mediterráneo-Universitat d'Alacant, 1997), pp. 615-630; by the same author: Julián Viejo, "Razón de estado católica y monarquía hispànica", *Revista de Estudios Politicos*, 104 (1999), pp. 233-244; and for an overview of the intertwine between religion and politics in Spanish political thinking, Xavier Gil, "Spain and Portugal", *European Political Thought 1450-1700*, Howell Lloyd, Glenn Burgess, Simon Hodson, eds. (New Haven-London: Yale University Press, 2007), pp. 416-457, see, especially, pp. 439-457.

16 Regarding the analogy between Philip II and Solomon, see: José Rafael de la Cuadra, "King Philip of Spain as Solomon the Second. The Origins of Solomonism of the Escorial in Netherlands", *The Seventh Window*, Wim de Groot, ed. (Hilversum: Verloven Publishers, 2005), pp. 169-180.

segundo Salomón edifique a Dios con mucha paz el templo que a Nuestro Señor no plugo que el emperador su padre lo edicase, como tampoco a David se lo permitió[17].

The majesty of the Emperor as a second David, has in his days undertaken great wars, given great battles and maintained great armies to serve God and repress the Philistines and enemies of the Church. Beyond of this, he promotes with big diligence to collect the Ark of the Testament and erect the Temple to God. And finally in his days has resigned in Your Majesty the empire and ruled over all his reigns like David did in Salomon. It just rest to wait for that His Majesty, such as a second Salomon, build peaceful peace the temple for God that Our Lord did not wish that the his father the emperor built, such as neither permited to David.

Biblical comparisons sometimes also appeared in historical and genealogical works which starting in the mid-16th century sought to glorify the Habsburgs. This includes written works by Italian, German and Spanish authors like Jerónimo Bossi, Gerardo de Roo, Wolfgang Kiliano, Diego Tafurí de Lequile, Nicolás Vernulaei and Father Pablo de Granada[18].

17 Felipe de la Torre, *Institución de un Rey Cristiano colegida principalmente de la Santa Escritura y de sagrados Doctores* (Antwerp: Casa de Martín Nuncio, 1556), f. 94v-95. The core of Felipe de la Torre's discourse revolves around the figure of the prince who, as a Christian ruler, must maintain justice and religion in his kingdom while using the Sacred Scriptures as the primary guide for his governance. Regarding Felipe de la Torre and his works, see: José Antonio Maravall, "La oposición político-religiosa a mediados del siglo XVI. El erasmismo tardío de Felipe de la Torre", *Homenaje a Xavier Zubiri*, 2 vols. (Madrid: Editorial Moneda y Crédito, 1970), vol. 2, pp. 295-320, reproduced in: José Antonio Maravall, *La oposición política bajo los Austrias* (Barcelona: Ariel, 1972), pp. 53-92, which notes that *Institución de un rey Christiano*, Felipe de la Torre *adelanta, como empresa doctrinal las que más tarde llevarán a cabo Márquez y Bossuet* (p. 66) ("it advanced, such as doctrinal task, the activities later done by Márquez and Bossuet"); by the same author: José Antonio Maravall, *Antiguos y modernos. La idea de progreso en el desarrollo inicial de una sociedad* (Madrid: Sociedad de Estudios y Publicaciones, 1966), p. 521 and following; Ronald W. Truman, *Spanish Treatises of Government, Society and Religion in the Time of Philip II* (Leiden: Brill, 1999), pp. 69-89.

18 Jerónimo Bossi, *La genealogía della gloriosissima Casa d'Austria* (Venice: G. B. et M. Sessa Fratelli, 1560); Gerardo de Roo, *Annales Rerum Belli Domique ab Austriacis Habspurgicae gentis Principibus, a Rudolpho primo usque ad Carolum V, gestarum* (Oeniponto: Agricola, 1592); Wolfgang Kiliano, *Serenissimorum Austriae Ducum, Archiducum, Regum, Imperatorum Genealogía…* (Augsburg: Kilian, 1623); Diego Tafurí de Lequile, *Pissima atque Augustissima Domus Austriaca...* (Innsbruck: Excudebat Michael Wagnerus, 1640); Nicolás Vernulaei, *Virtutum Augustissimae gentis Austriacae, Libri Tres* (Leuven: Typis Iacobi Zegeri, 1640); Pablo de Granada,

In the process of the legitimisation of the monarchy of Spain underway in the late 16th century, the idea of a universalist monarchy in which the Spanish people would be God's "chosen" people often came hand in hand with a providentialist glorification of the Spanish branch of the Habsburg dynasty. For many of these apologists of the Catholic monarchy, this was the fifth kingdom prophesied in the Book of Daniel, the one that after four kingdoms symbolised by monstrous beasts would, according to the Bible, have "an everlasting kingship whom all dominions shall serve and obey" [Daniel, 7:27].

To authors like Juan de Salazar, the Habsburg line is that *nobilíssima y felicíssima familia [...] a quien parece que fue sublimando Dios para defensa de su Iglesia* ("most noble and happiest family [...] who seems God to have sublimated to defend his Church"), a monarchy which the Benedictine priest equated with the fifth kingship in Daniel's dream, which *durará muchos siglos i que será la última*[19] ("will last many centuries and will be the last").

However, it was particularly after 1635, when the decisive phase in the struggle for European hegemony between the Habsburgs and Bourbons got underway, when these biblical identifications became more frequent and gave rise to more propagandistic texts. Among the men of what was called the "generation of 1635", the idea gained solid ground, especially public exaltation that the Habsburgs were the dynasty God had chosen to ecumenise the world[20]. Thus, shortly after the French-Spanish rupture,

---

Causa y origen de las felicidades de España y la Casa de Austria... (Madrid: Gregorio Rodríguez, 1652). See: Ángel Ferrari, *Fernando el católico en Baltasar Gracián* (Madrid: Espasa Calpe, 1945), p. 322 and following. For an analysis of the iconographic expressions of this mythification of the Habsburgs, see: Marie Tanner, *The Last Descendant of Aeneas. The Habsburgs and the Mythic Image of the Emperor* (New Haven: Yale University Press, 1993), especially, p. 67 and following.

19 Juan de Salazar, *Política española...*, pp. 199 and 229. Regarding this biblical legitimisation of the Habsburg dynasty by authors like Juan de Salazar, Juan de la Puente and Juan de Garnica, see: Eva Botella, "'Exempt from time and from its fatal change': Spanish imperial ideology, 1450-1700", *Renaissance Studies*, 26/4 (2012), pp. 580-604, especially, pp. 595-599; Eva Botella, *Monarquía de España...*, pp. 34 and following.

20 See: José M. Jover, *1635. Historia de una polémica y semblanza de una generación* (Madrid: Consejo Superior de Investigaciones Científicas, 1949), pp. 166 and following.

Juan de Herrera saw Philip IV as the successor of David's monarchy and the champion in the struggle against heresy:

> *Este trono empezó en Christo y se ha proseguido en los Pontífices y reyes christianos, y [h]emos llegado al tiempo presente; del qual que los reyes que oy biben en la Iglesia se puede verificar, sino el gran monarcha [Felip IV] y defensor de la Fe con tanta pureza, sin consentir que aya algún herege en su reyno, siendo el martillo de todos los hereges del mundo [...] De todo lo qual y de otras razones, muchas que se pueden allegar, se collige que los Reyes de España y la Casa de Austria son figurados por el rey David*[21].

> This throne began with Christ and has continued in Pontifices and Christian kings, and we have come to the present time; in which the kings who today live in the Church can be verified, but the great monarch [Philip IV] and defender of the Faith with such purity, without allowing any heresy in his kingdom, being the scourge of heretics of all the world [...] from all these and other reasons, many that can be alleged, it follows that the Kings of Spain and the House of Austria rank with King David.

Around the same time, the Valencian priest and jurist Francisco Mateu published an *Antipronostico* which sought to refute the triumphant military prophecies made by the French polemicists when the war between the Spanish Habsburgs and French Bourbons broke out; Mateu's optimistic auguries were grounded upon the *la Monarquia Cristiana y universal del mundo, está prometida a la Corona de España*[22] ("the Christian and universal Monarchy of the world, is betrothed to the Crown of Spain").

Apparently, precisely in 1640, when the Spanish monarchy was in turmoil over the rebellions in Portugal and Catalonia, the Aragon native Baltasar Gracián stated in *El político don Fernando el Católico* that the Habsburgs had been chosen by God to put an end to the internal divisions in Christendom and to halt Turkish power. Gracián repeated the idea that while in the times of the Written Law the House of Abraham was Yahweh's favourite, the Habsburgs had been chosen by Providence to spread the

21 BNE, ms. 2366; Juan de Herrera, *Querella y pleyto criminal contra los delictos enormes que Xatillón, capitán general del rey de Francia...*, reproduced by José M. Jover, *1635. Historia de una polémica...*, pp. 530-531.

22 Francisco Mateu, *Antipronóstico a las vitorias que se pronostica el reino de Francia contra el de España en el manifiesto de las guerras publicado en 6 de Junio 1635*, Valencia, 1636 (first edition). Cited by: José Maria Jover, *1635. Historia de una polémica...*, p. 379.

Catholic faith around the world in the time of the Law of Grace, a choice which linked up with Ferdinand the Catholic's wise decision to merge the Spanish Trastámara dynasty and the German Habsburgs:

> *Casa que la estendió Dios por toda la redondez de la tierra para dilatar por toda ella su Santa Fe y Evangelio. Casa que la escogio Dios en la Ley de Gracia, assí como la de Abraham en la Escrita, para llamarse Dios de Austria Dios de Rodolfo, de Felipe y de Fernando. Esta pues escogió el Cathólico y sabio rey [Ferran el Catòlic] para sucessora de augusta de su cathólico zelo, para heredera de su gran potencia, para conservadora de su prudente govierno, para dilatadora de su felicíssima Monarquia que el Cielo haga universal. Amén*[23].
>
> [The] house that God spread around all the earth to dilate throughout it his Holy Faith and gospel. [The] house that God chose in the Law of Grace, like like Abraham in the Scriptures, to be called their God of Austria God of Rudolph Philip and Ferdinand. This therefore chose the Catholic and wise king [Ferdinand the Catholic] to succeed his august and Catholic zeal to inherit his great power, in order to serve his prudent government, to stretch out his very happy Monarchy that the Heaven let do Universal. Amen.

In the mid-17th century, the Catholic faith of the Spanish monarchy supported by authors like Francisco Enríquez, Juan de Palafox, Juan Baños de Velasco, Agustín de Castro and Andrés Mendo would cement the idea that the Spanish Habsburg dynasty was the dynasty chosen by God to defend the Catholic faith against heresies and apostates[24].

Thus, in the midst of negotiating the Treaties of Westphalia, when arguing the fifth chapter of his *Conservación de monarquías* that *Las batallas en que oy está empeñada España, son propiamente de Dios, porque son por causa de Religión* ("The battles that today Spain is committed

23 Baltasar Gracián, *El Político don Fernando el Católico* (Saragossa, 1640). Facsimile edition with a prologue by Aurora Egido: Baltasar Gracián, *El Político don Fernando el Católico*, ed. Aurora Egido. (Saragossa: Institución "Fernando el Católico", 1985), pp. 221-222.

24 Regarding this ideological-political context, see: Julián Viejo, "'Contra Políticos Atheístas'. Razón católica y Monarquía Hispánica en la segunda mitad del siglo XVII", *Prudencia civile, bene comune, guerra iusta. Percorsi Della ragion di Statu tra Seicento e settecento*, Gianfranco Borrelli, ed. (Naples: Archivio di Stato-Adarte, 1999), pp. 85-95, by the same author: Julián Viejo, "El contexto de recepción de Grocio a mediados del siglo XVII en la monarquía hispana", *Espacio, Tiempo y Forma. Historia Moderna*, 11 (1998), pp. 265-280.

to, are really God's, because they are for the cause of Religion"), Father Francisco Enríquez stated that the Spanish monarchy was the same as that of *Iesucristo* and that conserving it depended on *que el Sacro Imperio no salga de la casa fidelísima de Austria* ("the Holy Empire not leaving the very loyal house of Austria"), because over the course of more than two hundred years, the princes of this lineage had served as a *duro freno y fuerte muro* ("a hard brake and strong wall") to the spread of apostasy and heresy in Europe[25]. Following Enríquez, the Spanish branch of the Habsburgs sustained all the Catholic princes that were fighting for God's cause, including the emperor: *La corona de España es auxiliar a todos los príncipes católicos y enemiga declarada de los hereges*[26] ("The crown of Spain is to assist all Catholic princes and declared enemies of the heretics"), a role for which they had been chosen by Providence, a choice similar to the one Yahweh made of King Jehu and the priest Jonadab to put an end to the idolatry of Ahab, Jezebel, Ahaziah and all worshippers of Baal.

4. The massive spread of the idea of the divine choice of the Habsburgs. Theatre, sermons and biblical prophecies

The biblical cultural legacy is quite prominent in Spanish Baroque literature from the Baroque. Obviously we can find it in the extensive, varied, ascetic-spiritual literature from the time of the Counter-Reformation, yet it also appears in lyrical and epic poetry, theatre, novels and in all registers of both cultivated and popular prose[27]. While all of these literary genres contributed to the societal dissemination of biblical culture to a greater or lesser degree, and through this to certain political values, the best literary vehicle to massively disseminate this biblical and biblical-political

25 Francisco Enríquez, *Conservación de monarquías, religiosa y política* (Madrid: Domingo Morrás, 1648), part 1, f. 2v.

26 Francisco Enríquez, *Conservación de monarquías...*, part 1, f. 13.

27 A two-set work has recently been published on the presence of the bible in Spanish Golden Age literature: Gregorio del Olmo, dir., *La Biblia en la literatura española. Siglo de Oro*, 3 vols. (Madrid: Trotta, 2008), vol. 1; Ignacio Arellano, Ruth Fine, eds., *La Biblia en la literatura del Siglo de Oro* (Madrid: Iberoamericana-Vervuert, 2010).

culture was unquestionably theatre, especially in the successful formulas of the *comedia nueva* ("new comedy") and the *auto sacramental* ("mystery play").

Simon A. Vosters stressed that in the biblical symbolism of Lope de Vega's work there was an excess exaltation of the values of God, the king and the Spanish fatherland, which appeared strictly intertwined in Lope's idea that the Catholic Spain of the Habsburgs would be *nou poble electe de Déu*[28] ("God's new chosen people"). Vosters noted that in the biblical-political allegories of "Fénix" there was a broad mixture of referents from the Bible and the ancient world with the historical Habsburg figures: *Deliberadamente confunde los triunfos de David, de Cristo y todos los miembros de la Iglesia Militante, con las victorias de Hércules, protorrey de España, y de Atlante, su gran ayuda, siendo los dos héroes antiguos figuras de la casa de Austria, lo mismo que David i Salomon*[29] ("Deliberately confusing the triumphs of David, Christ and all the members of the Militant Church, with the victories of Hercules, pre-king of Spain, and of Atalanta, his great help, the two heroes being ancient figures of the house of Austria, the same as David and Solomon").

However, Calderón de la Barca is probably the author whose entire oeuvre shows the most elaborate, mature theological-political view of the Spanish Habsburg monarchy[30]. In *autos sacramentales* ("mystery plays") like *El Gran Teatro del mundo, Los misterios de la misa* and *Psiquis y Cupido*, Calderón reveals a historical-religious conception according to which the world had undergone three major stages or "ages": paganism, the Written Law of Judaism and finally the age of the Law of Grace, which was initiated by the coming of Christ and his doctrine, which were to be

28 Simon A. Vosters, *Lope de Vega y la tradición occidental. El simbolismo bíblico de Lope de Vega*, 2 vols. (Madrid: Castalia, 1977), vol. 1, p. 508.

29 Simon A. Vosters, *Lope de Vega y la tradición occidental...*, p. 501.

30 On this point we are following the works of: Enrique Rull, "Hacia la delimitación de una teoría político-teológica en el teatro de Calderón", *Calderón. Actas del Congreso Internacional sobre Calderón y el teatro español del Siglo de Oro*, 3 vols., Luciano García, ed. (Madrid: Consejo Superior de Investigaciones Científicas, 1983), vol. 2, pp. 759-767; Ignacio Arellano, "Notas sobre la Biblia en los autos de Calderón", *V Simposio bíblico español. La Biblia en el arte y en la literatura I. Literatura*, Vicente Balaguer, Vicente Collado, eds. (Pamplona: Universidad de Navarra, 1999), vol. 1, pp. 17-52, especially, pp. 46-49.

propagated to all of Humanity[31]. And, according to Calderón, since Rudolf of Austria (1273-1291), the first emperor of the Holy Roman Empire, this divine mission had befallen the dynasty of the golden eagles.

This idea that the Habsburgs were the lineage chosen by God to propagate the Catholic faith all over the world appears in *autos sacramentales* ("mystery plays") like *El primer blasón del Austria*, *Segundo blasón del Austria*, *El nuevo Palacio de Retiro*, *El nuevo hospicio de pobres*, *El indulto general* and *El primer refugio del hombre*, and in the panegyrics *El arca de Dios cautiva* and *El verdadero Dios Pan*. In all of these works, Calderón uses the biblical passion from the Book of Habakkuk, which in the vulgate edition says *Deus ab astro veniet*, to interpret the word *astro* in a symbolic, prophetic way, which was then transformed into *austro* and equated with the Austrian Habsburgs, who were predestined to spread the Christian faith in the third age of the world.

The panegyric entitled *El verdadero Dios Pan* is perhaps where Calderón most neatly expresses this biblical-political transposition. Through the allegorical character of "History", which is speaking to "Poetry" and "Music", the Spanish playwright says the following:

El celo	Heaven
la devoción y la Fe,	devotion and faith
de tanto historial ejemplo	of such great historical example
como tiene el mundo al Alto,	as the world has of High
al Divino Sacramento	of the Divine Sacrament
que hoy se celebra, bien como	that is celebrated today, as
Misterio de los Misterios,	Mystery of Mysteries,
principalmente en España	principally in Spain
adónde, heredado afecto,	where, inherited affection,
patrimonio es de sus reyes;	is the heritage of its kings;
no sin autoridad, puesto	not without authority, given
que como Historia lo afirmo	that as History I affirm
yo en católicos acuerdos	in catholic agreements
de la Imperial Casa de Austria.	of the Imperial House of Austria.
Y las dos debeís hacerlo:	And both of you should do so:
tú como Poesía, pues	you as Poetry, given that
compusiste el Himno tierno	you composed the tender anthem
de cántica de Habacuc;	of the song of Habakkuk;

31 Regarding these historical conceptions in medieval and modern historical-philosophical thinking, see: José Antonio Maravall, *Antiguos y modernos…*, the section on "las edades del mundo y la diferente estimación de las épocas", pp. 46-49.

y tu entonaste los versos	and you intoned the verses
como Música, en que ambas	as Music, en which both
profetizasteis diciendo	prophesised saying
que el Austro vendría el Rey	that the Austrian would become King
que ha de dominar los imperios[32].	that has to dominate the empires.

In addition to the allegorical possibilities of the word *austro*, Calderón's choice of this short biblical book is no coincidence. The verses from the Book of Habakkuk start with the prophet's complaint to Yahweh about the violence and injustice from which Israel suffers as a result of the invasion of the Chaldeans. Yahweh, who determines the history of the peoples, as made clear in the Bible, responds to the prophet's grievance by saying that he will save fair men of his people and that ultimately they will defeat and punish the enemies of Israel with his intercession.

It is not too difficult to compare the difficult, tumultuous situation of the Spanish monarchy in the central years of the 17th century with that of the people of Israel oppressed by their Chaldean enemies[33]. Yet nor is there too much distance between Calderón's theological-political world view and the ideals of a universal theocratic monarchy expressed in the aforementioned works by Tomasso Campanella, Juan de Salazar and Benito Peñalosa.

In addition to theatre, sermons were another way of massively spreading the idea that the Habsburgs were the dynasty chosen by Divine Providence to ensure and expand the Catholic faith, and one that was well integrated into the propagandistic machinery of the Spanish monarchy[34]. As proclaimed by the *Oración fúnebre* preached by the Jesuit Juan de Avellaneda at El Escorial in 1654, the sovereigns from the Habsburgs were *principes por Dios, principes con Dios*[35] ("princes

32 Cited by: Enrique Rull, "Hacia la delimitación…", p. 764.

33 The idea of a messianic redemption of the Spanish people using the prophetic texts of Habakkuk can be found in other *autos sacramentales* by Calderón such as *Mística y real Babilonia*, see: Françoise Gilbert, "Las primeras réplicas de los profetas Abacuc y Daniel en el auto *Mística Real y Babilonia*: prefiguración de dos trayectorias complementarias", *Criticón*, 83 (2001), pp. 125-132.

34 See: Gwendolin Barnes, *Sermons and the Discourse of Power: The Rhetoric of Religious Oratory in Spain (1550-1900)* (Ann Arbor: University of Michigan, 1988).

35 Cited by: Fernando Negredo, "La palabra de Dios al servicio del Rey. La legitimación de la casa de Austria en los sermones del siglo XVII", *Criticón*, 84-85 (2002), pp. 295-311. Cited on p. 297.

for God, princes with God"). The charismatic nature of the monarchy was underscored in the sermons preached, and often printed, to commemorate the births and especially funeral rites and deaths of kings and princes[36]. Likewise, through their comparisons with characters or symbols from the Holy Scriptures, many of these sermons strove to bring the members of the royalty closer to divinity, thus setting them apart from other mortals[37].

5. The "Catalans": Branches of the vine of the Lord and the cedars of the Temple of God

In the case of Catalonia, the idea was that the Catalans were God's chosen people, and we can find the political derivations of this holiness primarily in the sermons and religious-political preachings that the Catalan institutions – the Generalitat and the *Consell de Cent* ("Council of One Hundred") sponsored in the decades prior to the 1640 revolt.

As is common knowledge, Baroque sermons were a powerful means of cultural transmission, as well as social and political indoctrination[38]. In a society with a culture that was still primarily oral, the sermon became an

36 In addition to the article cited in the note above, see: Antonio Álvarez-Ossorio, "Virtud coronada: Carlos II y la piedad de la casa de Austria", *Política, religión e inquisición en la España moderna*, Pablo Fernández, José Martínez, Virgilio Pinto, eds. (Madrid: Universidad Autónoma de Madrid, 1996), pp. 29-57; by the same author: Antonio Álvarez-Ossorio, "La sacralización de la dinastía en el púlpito de la Capilla real en tiempos de Carlos II", *Criticón*, 84-85 (2002), pp. 313-332.

37 José Antonio Maravall cites three examples of sermons containing these biblical comparisons: one from the death of the Infanta Margarita of Austria (1633); another from the death of Queen Elisabeth of France (1645) and a third sermon delivered to celebrate the birth of Prince Philip (1658), José Antonio Maravall, *La cultura del barroco: análisis de una estructura histórica* (Esplugues de Llobregat: Ariel, 1976), pp. 296-298; there is also a host of other examples.

38 Specifically regarding sacred oratory in Catalonia, see: Henry Kamen, *Canvi cultural a la societat del Segle d'Or* (Lleida: Pagès Editors, 1988 [first original English edition, 1993]), pp. 468 and following; and Martí Gelabertó, *La palabra del predicador. Contrarreforma y superstición en Cataluña (siglos XVII-XVIII)* (Lleida: Milenio, 2005).

effective instrument for spreading ideas and messages, not only religious ones because of both its use of the art of eloquence and the ascendance and credibility that the preacher could attain. Likewise, the possibility that the oral discourse could be reinforced by its subsequent publication enhanced the communicative power of the sermon. And institutional sermons with a strong political and ideological content were precisely the ones that more readily reached the press.

There are a host of examples showing the important role that preaching and sermons played in propagating the ideas and political notions of Europe under the Old Regime, in both the Catholic and Protestant worlds. Specifically in Catalonia, as part of the celebrations of the Feast Day of Saint George, in the early 17th century the *Diputació del General* ("General Deputation") instated the practice of political-religious sermons devoted to the patron saint of Catalonia, as well as other sermons, usually delivered on the 24th of April or after the Feast Day of Saint George, which were devoted to the deceased deputies or auditors[39]. In turn, the Council of One Hundred also held sermons in honour of King James II, at least until the late 14th century[40]. Likewise, to commemorate certain extraordinary events or at the solemn funerals of certain prominent figures, the sermons of the Catalan institutions might have also contained a strong political message, reached the press and had major social penetration.

In these sermons and in other samples of cultural output from that period, we can find the glorification of the Catalan "nation" through various historical-mythical re-creations, with endless inventories of the wealth of the land of the Principality, and with equally inexhaustible lists of Catalan saints and martyrs. Alternatively, they might praise the language and compare Catalan to the *llengua santa* ("holy language") of the Jewish

39 The diaries of the Generalitat contain references to the offices of the Feast Day of Saint George and to the anniversaries on the 24th of April after 1600, but the sermons did not appear until 1606. These preachings seemed to have permanently disappeared in the 1660s. After the *Guerra dels Segadors* ("Catalan Revolt"), very few sermons were preached, and the diaries often state that the *General* was "exhausted" *Dietaris de la Generalitat*, dir. Josep Maria Sans (Barcelona: Generalitat de Catalunya, 1996-2002), vols. 3, 4, 5, 6 and 7.

40 We do not know exactly when the practice of these sermons started, which reached the press less often than the Generalitat's sermons from the Feast Day of Saint George. In any event, we have proof of them after the end of the 17th century.

people, as Onofre Manescal did in the late 14th century[41]. However, as in the case of the glorification of the Spanish nation, the political and military tensions of the mid-17th century were what made the most decisive contribution to the surge in biblical symbolism and nationalistic providentialist legitimisations[42].

After the years preceding the English Revolution of 1640, the Saint George feast day sermons followed a biblical-political discourse clearly aimed at strengthening the idea of the Catalan nation based on its ties with Divine Providence, an idea which was primarily used to defend the constitutions and privileges of the Catalan pactist system against the attacks from the central government of the Spanish monarchy.

Through the biblical allegory of the grapevine and its shoots – "I am the vine, you are the branches" – repeated in several sermons, the idea is conveyed of a Catalan nation linked to Divinity through Saint George, its patron. Proof of this tie is the victories of the Catalan armies in all stages of history, which had not always been sufficiently publicised. As the canon of the cathedral of Barcelona, Miquel Joan Osona, explained in the sermon he preached on the Feast Day of Saint George in 1638, the Catalans were *ínclita y esforçada nació unida com pàmpol bisarro, no ab Fe sola,*

41 Onofre Manescal, *Sermó vulgarment anomenat del serenísimo senyor don Jaume Segon, i història de la pèrdua d'Espanya, grandeses de Cathalunya, comtes de Barcelona i reis d'Aragó* (Barcelona: Sebastià Comelles, 1602), f. 77v. The precocity of this "sacralisation" of the cultural and political discourse was noted by: Pep Valsalobre, "Elements per a una Catalunya sacra: sobre alguns aspectes de l'hagiografia de l'Edat Moderna catalana", *Vides medievals de sants: difusió, tradició i llegenda*, Marinela García, Maria Àngels Llorca, eds. (Alicante: Institut Interuniversitari de Filologia Valenciana, 2012), pp. 99-122, see p. 101. In general, on Manescal's sermon, see: Lurdes Estruch, "El Sermó patriòtic d'Onofre Manescal (1597/1602)", *Butlletí de la Reial Academia de Bones Lletres de Barcelona*, 51 (2009), pp. 145-197.

42 Antoni Simon, "Un *alboroto católico*. El factor religiós en la revolució catalana de 1640", *Pedralbes*, 23/2 (2003), pp. 123-146; Andrew Joseph Mitchell, "Una nueva perspectiva sobre la Guerra dels Segadors: en búsqueda de la 'limpieza de sangre'", *Pedralbes*, 23/2 (2003), pp. 367-374; the Doctoral thesis: Andrew Joseph Mitchell, *Religion, Revolt and the Formation of Regional Identity in Catalonia 1640-1643* (Columbus: Ohio State University, PhD Dissertation, 2005) of which I was only able to see an abstract available online; and Xavier Torres, "La nació i el temple. Patriotismo i Contrarreforma a la Catalunya moderna", *Pedralbes*, 28 (2008), pp. 85-102.

sinó ab fruyt de heroycas obras a la divina Cepa[43] ("illustrious and valiant nation united like a rare vineyard leaf not with faith alone, but with the fruit of heroic works to the divine Stump"). However, this speech had a political purpose that went beyond the goal of exaltation so characteristic of the struggles for pre-eminence in the Renaissance and Baroque, since based on this historical-religious argumentation, Miquel Joan Osona was defending the freedoms and privileges of the Principality, which were then being called into question by the political directives of Olivares' Ministry:

> *Y axí nos maravella las altras nacions que tinga y gose aquest Principat insigne tants y tan singulars privilegis, que lo mateix podria tenir, si·ls aguessen guanyats ab la punta de la llança, y ab lo valor de la espasa, donant la sanch y tantas vidas en servey de són rey per argumentar-li la Corona*[44].

> and thus the other nations marvel at what we have and enjoy in this distinguished Principality insigne so many singular privileges, that they could have the same, if they had earned it with the point of the lance, and with the valour of the sword, giving blood and so mnay lives in the service of their king in order to broaden his Crown.

The 1639 sermon preached by the Capuchin Pau de Sarrià once again opened with the biblical citation of the vine and the branches from the Gospel of Saint John, and he stressed that through their feats on behalf of the faith and their kings, the Catalans had proven that they were *también ellos sarmientos luzidos y pomposos de la cepa Christo* ("also lucid and opulent vine shoots from the Christ Stump"). In his sermon, Pau de Sarrià vehemently defended the Principality's regime of constitutions and privileges. After an explanation of the passage on the flying scroll in the fifth vision of the Book of Zechariah, and basing his interpretation on the authorities Nicolau de Lira and Saint Jerome, the Capuchin friar stated that Zechariah's apocalyptic dream represented the danger of losing the statutes of the temple of Jerusalem, which were compared to the privileges and constitutions of Catalonia:

> *Entiendan los que aquí goviernan una Ciudad o Principado que la falta y descuydo en sustentar sus privilegios, en guardar sus constituciones y estatutos, es la mayor maldición y desdicha que pueden incurrir.*

43 Miquel Joan Osona, *Sermó del invicto y gloriós màrtyr Sant Jordi, patró insigne del Principat nobilíssim de Cathalunya…* (Barcelona: Gabriel Nogués, 1638), f. 21.

44 Miquel Joan Osona, *Sermó del invicto y gloriós màrtyr Sant Jordi…*, f. 21.

Those who here govern a city or Principality should understand that the lack and neglect in sustaining its privileges, en protecting its constitutions and statutes, is the greatest curse and misery that they can incur.

And to do this he called for steadfast, resistant action among the leaders of the Principality when dealing with the attacks from the court of Madrid. In this case, using the example of Moses contradicting the Yahweh's instructions in Sinai to exterminate the people of Israel for having worshipped the golden calf, Pau de Sarrià drew from Saint Gregory's explanation of this biblical episode to claim that:

y es fineza de la fidelidad de un vasallo resistir suplicando y suplicar resistiendo a su mismo rey, y siendo en favor de los privilegios de su patria dignamente concedidos, pues todo viene a resultar en abono del mismo príncipe y conservación de su reyno[45].

and it is a act of the loyalty of a vassal to resist begging plead resisting his own king, and being in favour of the privileges of his homeland worthily granted, as all became fertilizer for the same prince and for the conrservation of his kingdom.

The allegory of the vine and branches was not the only one used in these political-religious preachings linking the Catalans with the Divinity. Additionally, shortly before 1640 in the *Panegyrico Aniversario de los Heroes Catalanes difuntos inmortales en sus hazañas* the Augustinian friar Gaspar Sala compared the Catalans to the majestic cedars of Lebanon and Palestine which in biblical times had been used to build the temples devoted to Yahweh:

llamé a los defuntos Catalanes, hermosos cedros, porqué dellos en la real Sala de la fe formó Dios los artesones. Y assí, aunque este Principado en este edificio Cathólico no es lo más extenso y dilatado, pero hallareys que es lo más primoroso o, por dezir mejor, lo primero[46].

45 Pau de Sarrià, *Panegyrico de las grandezas del inclyto y gloriosissímo martir San Jorge, gran patrón del nobilíssimo Principado de Cataluña* (Barcelona: Gabriel Nogués, 1639), f. 10, 22v, 23, 24.

46 Gaspar Sala, *Panegyrico Aniversario de los heroes catalanes difuntos inmortales en sus hazañas* (Barcelona: Gaspar Nogués, 1639), f. 7v. Regarding Gaspar Sala, see primarily: Antoni Simon, Karsten Neumann, "Estudi introductori", *Proclamación Católica*, eds. Antoni Simon, Karstern Neumann (Barcelona: Editorial Base, 2003), pp. 3-49.

> I called the defunct Catalans, lovely cedars because from them God created in the Faith's Saloon, the coffered ceiling. And so, although the Principality in this Catholic building is not the most extensive and lengthy, but you will find that it is the most exquisite or, to state it better, the first.

According to the biblical text, the sacred space of the "Holy of Holies" in Solomon's temple where the Arc of the Covenant was kept was totally clad in cedar wood, and Gaspar Sala used this to note both the ancientness of the Catalans' faith and their proximity to divinity: *que siempre Cataluña en materias de Fe fue la primera y, como cedro de Líbano, sobre las eminencias de otras naciones se descuella*[47] ("that in matters of Faith Catalonia was always the first and like the cedar of Lebanon it excels over the eminences of other nations") This divine proximity also had a political repercussion: the eminence and perfection of the laws and governing system of the Principality, which not only governed the Catalan nation but was also to serve as a mirror and model for other nations: *al olor y frangancia del buen govierno y polytica deste Principado, acudían a pedirle sus leyes para gobernar sus tierras. Evidente señal de que, en esta materia, era Cataluña cedro eminente entre las demás naciones*[48] ("to the scent and fragrance of good governance and politics of this Principality, they came to ask for its laws to govern their lands. Evidente signal that, in this matter, Catalonia was a noble cedar among the other nations").

6. Peoples who defended the Faith, enemy peoples and rebel peoples: Judah Maccabee, zealots and Philistines

The heavy intertwine between religion and politics in Europe under the old regime can be seen in many aspects, including the importance of the religious factor in the uprisings and revolutions that shook up the stability of the monarchies of that period, as well as the abundant biblical references that appear in texts generated by these revolutionary movements to both justify ideology and serve as propaganda.

47 Gaspar Sala, *Panegyrico Aniversario de los héroes...*, f. 9.
48 Gaspar Sala, *Panegyrico Aniversario de los héroes...*, f. 11v.

For the specific case of the Catalan Revolt, the strength and potentiality of the religious feeling of the peasant uprising which broke out in the spring of 1640 was captured perfectly by the ruling class that spearheaded the revolutionary movement and advocated Catalonia's separation from the Spanish monarchy. After burning and destroying the towns of Santa Coloma de Farners and Riudarenes, where the Spanish *tercios* had set fire to the holy forms and churches, the General Deputation headed by Pau Claris spread a *paper* or *sumari* ("brief") where the criticism of the ill-fated policy of billeting pursued by Minister Olivares was accompanied by strong religious argumentation. According to this report, which was sent to the Court of Madrid, behind the burning of the sacred forms in Riudarenes, it seemed that *nos quisieren dar a bever la doctrina de Lutero i Calvino* ("they wanted to give us the doctrine of Luther and Calvin to drink"), meaning that the Catalans were left with no choice but to act like the Maccabees who rose up and died against the Seleucid kings' attempts to Hellenise the Jewish religion[49].

Subsequently, the reference to the Maccabees was used profusely by the Dutch rebels in their struggle against the Spaniards, by the Catalan revolutionaries in both of the major texts justifying the revolution in the second half of 1640 (*Proclamació Catòlica* by Gaspar Sala, *Notícia de Catalunya* by Martí Viladamor and *Justificació en conciència* ["conscious Justification"] by the board of theologians) and in the different political-religious sermons of the Catalan revolutionaries preached and published in 1641, as highlighted by Xavier Torres[50].

Generally speaking, the ideological justification of the Catalan revolt and the subsequent war propaganda were imbued with a strong religious tone. One feature of these texts is the multiplication and politicisation of biblical referents. Thus, for example, in the sermon that Josep Pont

49 The text of the "sumari" ends by saying: *Ha sido asote de Dios para corrección nuestra, del qual podemos decir aquello de los macabeos: 2ª Macha 6* ("It has been the scourge of God for our correction, which we can say that of the Maccabees: 2nd Maccabees 6"). *Obsecro eos qui hunc librum lecturi sunt ne abborrescont propter adversas casus, sed reputent ea que occiderunt non ad intentum, sed ad correpcionem esse generis nostri* (*Dietaris de la Generalitat*, dir. Josep Maria Sans…, vol. 5, p. 1885).

50 Xavier Torres, "Nosaltres, els macabeus: el patriotisme català a la Guerra dels Segadors", *Una relació difícil. Catalunya i l'Espanya Moderna*, Joaquim Albareda, ed. (Barcelona: Editorial Base, 2007), pp. 85-107.

preached on the anniversary of the souls of the deputies and auditors who died in 1641[51], which was politically targeted at justifying Catalonia's rupture with the Spanish monarchy and its alliance with France, he compared Pau Claris, the recently deceased leader of the Catalan revolution, to Elias, the biblical prophet who ascended into heaven[52]. In this same sermon, the figure of the deputy who had saved Barcelona from Spanish repression was also compared to Samson, the popular Israeli hero who faced down the Philistines. Catalonia was also compared to Jerusalem, the city of God which could never be annihilated. Meanwhile the Spanish, who had not only razed Catalan towns but had also sacrilegiously burned the temples of God, were equated with the 600 men in the tribe of Dan who robbed the sanctuary of the Ephraimite Micah, spurring his indignation.

This sacralisation of the Catalan revolutionary movement and the simultaneous accusations that the royal troops were behaving heretically and sacrilegiously because the Court of Madrid had strayed from the Catholic reason of state and was following the *rasón de estado iniqua y monstruosa de Nicolás Machiavello*[53] ("unrighteous and monstrous reason of state of Nicholas Machiavelli"), entailed a direct attack on one of the foundations legitimising the Spanish monarchy. Thus, it should come as no surprise that Spain responded radically to the religious accusations of the Catalan revolutionaries, or that the political treatise-writers at the Castilian Court would review to paroxysm the explanation of the alliance between the Spanish monarchy and Divine Providence, or that the Spanish political thinking and publicity in the 1640s would frame the war in Catalonia as a religious war, turning the arguments on their head, as

51 BC, F. Bon. 2839; Josep Pont, *Sermó predicat en lo aniversari que ab ejemplar devoció y ab majestosa ostentació, celebra cada any la Casa il·lustre de la Diputació...* (Barcelona: Gaspar Nogués, 1643). A modern edition in: Eva Serra, *Escrits polítics del segle XVII*, 2 vols. (Vic: Eumo, 1995), vol. 2, pp. 137-186, from which we have taken our citations. This sermon has been studied by: Rosa Maria González, "Los predicadores y la Revuelta Catalana de 1640. Estudio de dos sermones", *Actes del Primer Congrés d'Història Moderna de Catalunya*, 2 vols. (Barcelona: Universitat de Barcelona, 1984), vol. 2, pp. 435-443.

52 Eva Serra, *Escrits polítics...*, p. 156, 157, 185, 183 and following.

53 This was the accusation levelled by the anonymous author of the *Desenganyos del Principado de Cathalunya y su Rey, y avisos para los dos*, (BC, ms. 211, 1640, f. 205). In numerous passages of the *Proclamación católica*, Gaspar Sala had more or less explicitly levelled the same accusation.

they did with the biblical references which the Catalan revolutionaries had bandied about on matters of faith.

Thus, in the aforementioned *Conservación de monarquías*, Father Francisco Enríquez compared Catalonia's War of Separation with Philip IV's war against the Dutch, Germans or Swiss; he claimed that the Catholic King was trying to save the Catalans from the heresy introduced by the French, as according to Enríquez the Principality was a *región de católicos que ha vuelto centina de infieles* ("a region of Catholics that has turned into a centre for infidels"). Following this apologia for the Catholic monarchy, in these struggles the officers from the Spanish armies were *más a propósito sacerdotes que capitanes*[54] ("more apropos priests than captains"), and he compared them to the valiant warriors of the Maccabees who, led by Judah Maccabee with Yahweh's assistance, defeated Nicanor, Demetrius' impious and blasphemous general. In the biblical episode which Enríquez compared to the Spaniards' struggle against the heretics, their ultimate fate was quite dramatic, as according to the Holy Bible Judah Maccabee ordered first Nicanor's head and then his arm be cut off, and then his tongue be severed so it could be eaten into bits by birds.

In the Spanish treatises from the war years, the Catalans were not compared to the Maccabees but to the Philistines[55], that is, to the enemies, by antonomasia, of the Israelites who were defeated by King David, as well as to the zealots[56], that sect of extremist fanatical agitators whose insurrection had led to Roman repression and the fall of Jerusalem.

54 Francisco Enríquez, *Conservación de monarquías...*, Part 1, f. 3v, 3, 13.

55 As the Mercedary Father Marcos Salmerón said, the Catalans were *Vanos Gigantes como el Filisteo, que perderán la cabeça con las mismas armas que pretenden usurpar la Corona* ("Vain Giants like the the Philistine, they will lose theirt heads with the same weapons with which they seek to usurp the crown"), in: Marcos Salmerón, *Recuerdos históricos y políticos de los servicios que los generales y varones ilustres de la religión de Nuestra Señora de la Merced* (Valencia: En Casa de los Herederos de Chrysostomo Garriz, by Bernardo Nogues, 1646), p. 505.

56 As the exiled Philip supporter Alexandre Ros said, *los que drestruieron a Ierusalem se llamaron zelotes y los que pusieron a Cataluña en este estado tiranizaron el glorioso nombre de patricios* ("those who destroyed Jerusalem was called"). Alexandre Ros, *Cataluña desengañada* (Naples: Egidio Longo, 1646), pp. 273-274.

7. The two sides to Moses and Pharaoh. The shifting shapes of Jerusalem

As mentioned above, the clearly religious tone of the ideological and propagandistic struggle that accompanied the war in Catalonia led to an increasing use of political discourse tinged with biblical symbolism and allegories. Just as in 17th century England, they were used to legitimise quite contradictory political positions[57]. In fact, certain characters, cities or episodes in the Holy Bible were used by both the Catalan revolutionaries and the pro-Philip Spaniards. Even though there is a plethora of examples of this ambivalence, we shall focus on two of them: the episode of Moses and the liberation of the people of Israel from slavery in the lands of the pharaoh, and the city of Jerusalem, holy and rebellious at the same time. These referents not only have a heavy symbolic-political charge but also occupied a prime place in the Bible stories and were thus quite widely known.

As mentioned above, the figure of Moses as the liberator of the Jewish people from the tyranny of the Egyptian pharaohs was widely used in the political symbolism of the Renaissance and the Baroque. What is more, in Spain Moses had been chosen as an example of virtue to support some of the more successful and influential biblical-political guides of the treatises of the Spanish Counter-Reformation, such as the *El Governador Christiano deducido de las vidas de Moysen y Josué, príncipes del pueblo de Dios*, which the Augustinian Juan Márquez published in 1612[58].

57 Christopher Hill, *The English Bible and the Seventeenth-century Revolution* (London: Penguin Press, 1993). Hill's book demonstrates how the Bible played a key role in all aspects of social and political life in revolutionary England, but that after 1660: it lost its universal power once it had been demonstrated that you could prove anything from it (p. 426).

58 This work, printed by Francisco de Cea, was addressed to Gómez Suárez de Figueroa, the son of the deceased Lorenzo who had commissioned Márquez to write it. A defender and prior in the Order of Saint Augustine, Juan Márquez (Madrid 1565-1621) was also appointed royal preacher to Philip III of Castile and consultant to the Inquisition. Regarding his biography and works, see: Javier López de Goicoechea, *Juan Márquez. Un Intel·lectual de su tiempo* (Madrid: Editorial Revista Agustiniana, 1996). Specifically on *El Governador Christiano*, the same author has written: Javier López de Goiciechea, "Juan Márquez (1565-1621): influjo y proyección

As we have seen above, at the start of the Catalan revolt, the figure of Pau Claris was compared to numerous biblical characters in the sermons that were preached on the occasion of his death on the 27th of February 1641, that is, just one month after the liberating battle of Montjuïc (26th of January) which had saved Barcelona from the punitive Spanish expedition ordered by Philip IV and Count-Duke Olivares.

In these sermons, Pau Claris is compared to the prophet Elias who ascended into heaven, to the priest Azarias who opposed King Uzziah, or the hero Samson who defeated the Philistines. However, the analogy to Moses is clearly the most frequent. This biblical referent makes it easy to understand the idea that thanks to Pau Claris, Catalonia and the Catalans had been saved from the repressive violence of the Spaniards (the pharaoh and his armies), and that his political conduct had led to them to the alliance with France (the Promised Land). This analogy had previously been used liberally by the Dutch rebels[59] and, as Michael Walzer proved, it had been a metaphor shared by many revolutionary processes[60]. In 1641, the Augustinian friar Gaspar Sala drew this succinct parallelism:

> *!O ilustre Claris, Moysés del pueblo catalán! Encomendole Dios por medio de la suerte (que está en sus manos, in manibus tuis fortes mea) el officio de deputado eclesiástico, presidente de la Deputación, para que librasse a Cataluña de las opresiones de los castellanos; opúsosse a las órdenes de los prefectos opressores, libró al pueblo*

historiográfica de 'El Governador Christiano"', *Revista Agustiniana*, 37 (1996), pp. 93-126; and Javier López de Goicoechea, "Génesis, estructura y fuentes de *El Governador Christiano* (1612) de Juan Márquez", *Revista Agustiniana*, 39 (1998), pp. 499-556. Also: Harald E. Braun, "The Bible, reason of state and the royal conscience: Juan Márquez's El Governador Christiano", *Renaissance Studies*, 23/4 (2009), pp. 552-567. The Aragonese jurist Antoni Fuertes also used the figure of Moses to support his treatise: Antoni Fuertes, *Vida de Moysen. Parte primera. Glosada con sentencias y aforismos políticos* (Brussels: Gvilielmo Lehey-Cels, 1657).

59 See: Lea Campos, "La *Respublica Hebraeorum* nell tradizione olandese", *Il Pensiero politico*, 25/3 (2002), pp. 431-463, especially, pp. 437-441; Simon Schama, *The Embarrassment of Riches. An Interpretation of Dutch Culture in the Golden Age* (London: Fontana Press, 1987), pp. 104 and forward.

60 Michael Walzer, *Exodus and Revolution* (New York: Basic Books, 1985). Walzer notes that this metaphor was profusely used in the revolutionary movements prior to 1789 and by the theoreticians of these movements, such as Savonarola, Calvin, Knox, the French Huguenots, the Scottish Presbyterians, the English Puritans and the American revolutionaries, pp. 5 and forward.

de la opresión, púsole en campaña precediendo la justificación de la conciencia, capitaneole, acudió con provisiones con tal arte que, en materia de dineros, para los gastos se puede decir que sacaba agua de las peñas, expúsose a riesgos y peligros, guió al Principado a la tierra de promisión (que es el vasallaje del rey, nuestro señor Luys XIII) para que bajo su real sombra descansemos y respiremos de los trabajos passados[61].

Oh illustrious Claris, Moses of the Catalan people! May God entrust him through luck (which is in his hands, in manibus tuis fortes mea) with the office of ecclesiastical deputy, president of the Deputation, so he may free Catalonia of the oppressions of the Castilians; who opposed the orders of the oppressor prefects, freed the people from oppression, set him in campaign preceding the justification of the conscience, leading it, he came with provisions with such skill that, in questions of money, for the expenses it can be said that he squeezed money from the rocks, exposing himself to risks and dangers, guided the Principality to the promised land (which is vassalage to the king, our lord Louis XIII) so that under his royal shadow we rest and breathe from the past works.

However, in Spanish treatises the roles were reversed. In chapter XXVII of Father Francisco Enríquez's *Conservación de monarquías*, when he stressed that *Los monarcas a quien han acudido los rebeldes a la Corona Católica, estos mismos le sirven de açote* ("The same monarchs who have attended the rebels to the Catholic Crown were their scourge") he also noted, as many other authors did, that the French action in Catalonia was so harmful for the natives that either it would lead to the total destruction of the Principality or it would nudge the Catalans' return to the benevolent domain of the Catholic monarchy. In this case, the Egypt of the Pharaohs was Bourbon France, while Philip IV was the Supreme Pastor who was waiting the rectification of those rebel subjects who, just like the Jewish people, had strayed from the pathway marked by Yahweh and would thus suffer from the penalties:

Era antiguamente el reyno de Egipto para el pueblo de Israel el assylo de sus rebeldías contra su natural señor, que era Dios. Pecavan digo, y provocavan su enojo en confiança de que los avia de recibir el Egipcio debaxo de su protección, y los avia de

61 Gaspar Sala, *Lágrimas catalanas al entierro y obsequias del ilustre deputado eclesiástico de Cataluña, Pablo Claris* (Barcelona: Gabriel Nogués, 1641). Edited by: *Panegíric a la mort de Pau Claris de Francesc Fontanella*, eds. Montserrat Clarasó, Maria-Mercè Miró (Barcelona: Editorial Curial, 2008), pp. 135-170), appendix 3. The quote is on p. 169.

> *librar de los amorosos assaltos con que Dios intentava no tanto castigarlos, quanto reducirlos al deber [...] porque a esos mismos Franceses a quien se ha entregado esta infelice Provincia o la destruiran totalmente, o la obligaran a malos tratamientos a que se rinda a su Rey y señor natural*[62].
>
> It was formerly the kingdom of Egypt for the people of Israel the asylum for their rebellion against their natural lord, who was God. They sinned I say, and provoked his anger in the belief that the Egytion had to receive them under his protection, and had to free them of the amorous attacks with which God attempted not so much to punish them, but to reduce them to the duty [...] because these same French to whom this unhappy Province has been handed will either destroy it totally, or oblige it by ill treatment to surrender to their King and natural lord.

This analogy was completed in October 1652, when Barcelona was conquered by John Joseph of Austria, the bastard son of Philip IV, whom the sermons and treatises of Spain proclaimed to be the *Moyses de esse Principado* ("Moses of this Principality") who had rescued the Catalans from their captivity under Pharaoh's rule[63].

While in the example of Moses and pharaoh the reversal of roles was the way that the same biblical story could be used twice in opposing ways, the reference to the city of Jerusalem offered a host of possible interpretations depending on the episode chosen because in the Holy Bible, Jerusalem appears as both a city of sin and of apostasy punished by divine will and as a rebellious city or the celestial eternal city saved by Yahweh's favour.

In Francesc Fontanella's *Panegiric* devoted to Pau Claris, Barcelona threatened by the army of the Marquis of Los Vélez is compared to Jerusalem from the Book of Isaiah which was saved by Yahweh from the Assyrian army of King Senaccherib, a parallelism that Fontanella made by citing the biblical text in which Yahweh warns the King of Assur that *No entrarà lo enemich en esta ciutat – digué la pietat soberana – no llançarà dintre d'ella ses fletxas, no l'occuparà ab sos escuts ni la cenyirà ab són exèrcit; ans bé per lo camí que es vingut se'n tornarà sens invadir la ciutat*[64] ("The enemy shall not enter this city – said the sovereign piety – they

62 Francisco Enríquez, *Conservación de monarquías...*, Part 2, f. 47v.

63 Francisco de San Agustín, *Sermón en acción de gracias por la salud que alcanzó Su Majestad...* (Valencia: Estampat per Silvestre España, 1653), no number.

64 Montserrat Clarasó, Maria Mercè Mirò eds. *Panegíric a la mort de Pau Claris...*, p. 106.

shall not shoot their arrows into it, they shall not occupy it with their shields nor surround it with their army; but by the same way they came, they shall leave without invading the city").

Likewise, in the sermons from the start of the revolution and war, Catalonia is compared to the subjugated, profaned Jerusalem from the Books of Jeremiah and Lamentations which reacted to the profanations of the temples of God perpetrated by the Spanish armies. In the sermon on the anniversary of the deceased deputies and auditors in 1643, the Carmelite friar Josep de Jesús i Maria claimed that

> *està Catalunya en aquell lamentable estat en què veié lo profeta Jeremies a Jerusalem, quan plorà lo mateix que nosaltres i deia que estava lo temple de Déu aprofanat:* Portae eius destructae, Sacerdotes eius gementes, virgines eius squalidae et ipsa oppresssa amaritudine. *I tenint nosaltres presents les mateixes calamitats, i sentint Déu les mateixes ofenses, no ha de ser cada u dels catalans un Jeremies en lo sentiment, un Mataties en lo zel i un Gedeó en les armes?*[65]

> this Catalonia in that lamentable state in which the prophet Jeremiah saw Jerusalem, when he wept and said the temple of God was prophaned: Portae eius destructae, Sacerdotes eius gementes, virgines eius squalidae et ipsa oppresssa amaritudine. And us having the same calamities, and God hearing the same offences, does each of the Catalans have to be Jeremiah in his feelings, a Mattathias in his zeal and a Gideon in the arms?

However, as mentioned above, Jerusalem also had other profiles in the Bible. In his *Cataluña desengañada* (1646), the exiled pro-Philip Catalan Alexandre Ros compared the city of Barcelona, as well as the ruling class that had spearheaded the rupture with the Spanish monarchy and the alliance with France, to the rebellious Jerusalem of the fanatical sect of the zealots, whose mutinies had brought about Roman repression and the destruction of the city by Titus in AD 70. The doyen of Tortosa told a story comparing the events in Catalonia in 1640-1641 to those in Jerusalem in the years AD 66-70, saying that *los que destruieron a Jerusalem se llamavan zelotes y los que pusieron a Cataluña en este estado, tiranizaron el glorioso nombre de patricios y libertadores de la patria* ("those who destroyed Jerusalem were called zealots ands those who put Catalonia in this state, tyrannising the glorious name of patricians and liberators of the homeland"); and claiming that the patricians in their duty to free Catalonia

65 Eva Serra, *Escrits polítics...*, p. 185.

from the tyrannical rule of the King of France were just like the zealots of Jerusalem: responsible for the destruction of the Principality as a consequence of the war. *Estos son tus enemigos (Catalunya), estos los zelotes del Principado y los patricios de Barcelona; estos son los homicidas de tus privilegios, los asesinos de tu República, los verdugos de tu libertad y la causa de tu desdichada esclavitud*[66] ("these are your enemies (Catalonia), these the zealots of the Principality and the patricians of Barcelona; these are the murderers of your privileges, the assassins of your Republic, the executioners of your freedom and the cause of your wretched slavery").

In the Spanish treatises from the 1640s, Barcelona is often cited as the paradigm of a rebellious city, particularly harking back to the 15th-century war against King John II. This restless, unruly personality could be compared to the fame that Jerusalem had among the Persian kings, as attested to in the Bible in the Book of Ezra[67]. Father Francisco Enríquez made this comparison by saying:

> *que aquella ciudad de Ierusalem cabeça de aquel reyno de Iudea se avia preciado siempre de ser rebelde a aquella corona [...] devia ser como Barcelona y el Principado de Cataluña, infausto origen de tantas miserias*[68].

> that that city of Jerusalem head of that kingdom of Judea had always cherished being rebellious to that crown [...] it must have been like Barcelona and the Principality of Catalonia, infamous origin of so much misery.

8. Epilogue and conclusion

In the late decades of the 16th century and early years of the 17th century, when Castilian national identity metamorphosed into Spanish identity and Catalan national identity was likewise gaining strength, we can find the first comparisons of both national collectives with the peoples "chosen" by Divine Providence. However, unlike in Holland and England, this sacralisation of identity did not entail a direct or total comparison

66 Alexandre Ros, *Cataluña...*, pp. 273-274, 280.
67 Ez 4:11-16.
68 Francisco Enríquez, *Conservación...*, Part 2, p. 47.

of "Catalans" and "Spaniards" with the Jewish people; rather, differences were underscored or particular biblical-symbolic ties were sought. Thus, the Castilian-Spanish line of thinking noted the superiority of the Spanish people over the Jews in the realm of religious orthodoxy, while the Catalans used biblical symbols (the cedars or the branches of the grapevine) which avoided a direct comparison between both peoples.

The heavy political tensions and fighting of the Spanish monarchy in the mid-17th century, both abroad and at home, led the sacralisation of political discourses to become more heated, especially through varied biblical symbolism. Specifically, in the Catalan Revolt from 1640-1652, one can appreciate how both sides used the same biblical references for completely opposite discourses. In this phase, the biblical comparisons are more direct, and the need for ideological and propagandistic justification seemed to have overcome any qualms that might have arisen from the anti-Judaism of the Hispanic societies of the day.

Thus, the multiplicity of ways that the Holy Bible was used, which Christopher Hill examined for revolutionary England in the 17th century, interpreting it as the fundamental reason why the biblical referents remained central to the political discourse after 1660, can also be seen in the Spain and Catalonia in the mid-17th century. However, unlike in England, we can see that in the War of the Spanish Succession the ideological and propagandistic clash once again took on a heavy religious tone in Spain, and that biblical references were once again used extensively by both the pro-Bourbon and pro-Habsburg camps[69].

Likewise, in the dimension of "national" confrontation that the conflict took on in Catalonia, especially in the final stages of the war, we can see a widespread use of biblical symbolisms to justify and encourage the Catalans' resistance to the armies of Philip V, just as in the Catalan Revolt from 1640-1652. Thus, once again, the comparisons between the Catalans and the Israelites are quite direct. In texts like the *Despertador de Catalunya*, the *Respuesta de un aragonés a un amigo suyo en Barcelona sobre la defensa de Cataluña* and Emmanuel Ferrer i Sitges' *Discurs*, all of them from 1713, the Catalans' bitter struggle for their freedoms is compared

69 See primarily: David González, *Guerra de religión entre príncipes católicos* (Madrid: Ministerio de Defensa, 2002); and the text in the classical work by: María Teresa Pérez, *La publicística española en la Guerra de Sucesión*, 2 vols. (Madrid: Consejo Superior de Investigaciones Científicas, 1966).

to David's struggle against the Philistines, to the Maccabees' fight against the Seleucid kings, to Joshua's struggle against the Amalekites and the Gibeonites, to Moses' fight against the Midianites and to Ezequiel's fight against the Assyrians, all of them disputes in which the Jewish people, despite their adverse circumstances or military inferiority, triumphed in war thanks to divine favour[70].

In short, in Catalonia and Spain, the political, ideological, military and identity confrontation kept the use of biblical symbolisms alive in the ideological and propagandistic discourse. This leads us to interpret that first, there was a close relationship between the sacralisation of identity and the episodes of internal conflict of the composite monarchies that were "national" in nature; and that secondly, the distancing from religious ideals of power in favour of other ideals based on the "rational virtue" of the state, as noted by authors like Paul Kléber Monod to ideologically describe the period after the major revolutionary cycle of 1640-1660[71], had quite distinct timeframes.

70 The text of the *Despertador de Cataluña* and Ferrer i Sitges' *Discurs* were edited by: Joaquín Albareda, *Escrits polítics del segle XVIII. Tom I* (Vic: Eumo-Institut Universitari d'Història Jaume Vicens i Vives, 1996), for the bibliographic references cited, pp. 142, 146, 147. The text of the *Respuesta de un aragonés a un amigo suyo en Barcelona sobre la defensa de Cataluña* was edited by: Joaquim Albareda, *Escrits polítics del segle XVIII. Tom V* (Vic: Eumo-Institut Universitari d'Història Jaume Vicens Vives, 2011), for the bibliographic references cited pp. 119-123.

71 Paul Kléber, *El poder de los reyes. Monarquía y religión en Europa 1589-1715* (Madrid: Alianza Editorial, 2001), especially, p. 378.

Catholics and Catalans: Religion in Catalan Identity in the 16th and 17th Centuries

Ignasi Fernández Terricabras
Universitat Autònoma de Barcelona

Catalunya serà cristiana, o no serà ("Catalonia will be Christian, or it won't be"). This quote, traditionally attributed to Torras i Bages, is totally apocryphal: it is found in none of the writings by that celebrated bishop of Vic. And yet it reflects an opinion that was widely shared for centuries: Catalan-ness entails a given religious affiliation such that Catalan identity and the Catholic faith seem to be connatural.

Without underestimating the role that the struggle against the Saracens in the Middle Ages might have played in shaping this identity. I would like to draw attention to the origin of this identity in the Modern Age within the context of the Counter-Reformation.

In recent years, the historians of this period have often used the notion of "confessional identity". However, this concept has almost always been applied to lands where populations with different credos coexist with greater or lesser degrees of violence. One example is France, where the Calvinists had gained a group consciousness, a collective memory and specific cultural and behavioural patterns that the pastors and consistories took pains to preserve[1]. Following the criteria of social psychology, among the Huguenots this confessional identity has been viewed as a significant minority's desire to gain internal cohesion, political acceptance and social visibility in a hostile atmosphere, as it was primarily Catholic[2].

1 Raymond A. Mentzer, *La construction de l'identité réformée aux XVI et XVIIe siècles: le rôle des consistoires* (Paris: Honoré Champion, 2006); Olivier Christin, *Confesser sa foi. Conflits confessionnels et identités religieuses dans l'Europe moderne (XVIe-XVIIe siècles)* (Seyssel: Champ Vallon, 2009).

2 However, Mark Greengrass questions the "international" nature of Calvinist identity, which, he claims, was always tied to other identities: Mark Greengrass, "The French Pastorate: Confessional Identity and Confessionalization in the Huguenot Minority, 1559-1685", *The Protestant Clergy of Early Modern Europe*, C. Scott Dixon, Luise Schorn-Schütte, eds. (Houndmills: Palgrave Macmillan, 2003), pp. 176-195.

It is difficult to transfer this concept wholesale to 16th century Catalonia, where the expulsion of the Jews in 1492, the virtually marginal presence of Protestants and the degree of assimilation of the Morisco[3] population make it difficult to highlight unique external features of such harshly oppressed minorities. However, perhaps it could be applied to the majority group: the Catholics. Indeed, in the early Modern Age the Catalan people developed a strong awareness that their identity necessarily entailed the acceptance of post-Tridentine Catholicism and even the defence of this belief anywhere, as unequivocally expressed by numerous external signs.

1.

In 1517, when Martin Luther published his thesis against indulgences in Wittenberg (Saxony), he sparked a movement which would have profound consequences in European history. The swift expansion of the Reformation and the Catholic Church's response (the Counter-Rreformation or the Catholic Reformation) would shape a new religious map in which the different peoples had to choose – willingly or by force – one of the different denominations.

This process dovetailed with the consolidation of the absolutist states which were developing their mechanisms of power in the 16th century. The desire of the religious reformers (both Catholic and Protestant) to condition all aspects of collective life (political and religious, but also cultural, moral and economic) required the political powers to intervene in these

3 A memorial from 1610 said that *todos hablan la lengua catalana, como los demás poblados de cristianos viejos de Cataluña, sin que ninguno de ellos hable ni sepa hablar lengua arábiga [...] no visten ni usan ropas o vestiduras a la morisca, sino a la catalana* ("They all speak the Catalan language, like the other villages of old Christians in Catalonia, without any of them talking or knowing how to speak Arab language [...] they do not wear or use clothes or garments like the Moors, but rather like the Catalans"); Josep Serrano Daura, "Usos i pràctiques socials i religiosos dels moriscos d'Ascó, Benissanet i Miravet (1610)", *Miscel·lània del Centre d'Estudis Comarcals de la Ribera d'Ebre*, 9 (1993), pp. 31-42. More generally: Ignasi Fernández Terricabras, "Los moriscos en Cataluña: entre asimilación y destierro", *La expulsión de los moriscos*, Antonio Moliner, ed. (Alella: Nabla, 2009), pp. 211-233.

spheres in order to stave off a serious decline or even annulment of their decision-making capacity. In the early Modern Age, the king who wanted to secure his power had to choose a religion and work actively to consolidate it in his kingdom, because this was the only way he could guarantee his control over the process. At the same time, thanks to the clergy's resources the sovereign could increase his holdings and make use of the church networks to spread his messages. The result of this is "confessionalisation", which is a process of "social discipline" and religious intolerance in which churches and monarchies acted together to impose certain belief and behaviour patterns from above[4]. There were consequences of this which, beyond any territorial or theological variations, are structurally similar in the Protestant and Catholic worlds: religion – whichever one was accepted – and political power worked shoulder to shoulder in a cultural, social and political process that was supposed to benefit both the church and the prince.

One of the traits of confessionalisation is intolerance: only one religion is accepted in each territory; the others are banned and persecuted by repressive institutions (in Catalonia, primary the Inquisition[5]) which are

4 There is a large body of literature from the 1970s on the processes of confessionalisation and social discipline by scholars of the German Empire, which has been extensively debated among historians. Wolfgang Reinhard, "Pressures towards Confessionalization? Prolegomena to a Theory of the Confessional Age", *The German Reformation: The Essential Readings*, C. Scott Dixon, ed. (Oxford: Blackwell, 1999), pp. 17-192; Heinz Schilling, *Religion, Political Culture and the Emergence of the Early Modern Society* (Leiden-New York-Cologne: E. J. Brill, 1992); Paolo Prodi, *Disciplina dell'anima, disciplina del corpo e disciplina della società tra medioevo ed età moderna* (Bologna: Il Mulino, 1994); Federico Palomo, "Disciplina Cristiana. Apuntes historiográficos en torno a la disciplina y el disciplinamiento social como categorías de la historia religiosa de la alta edad moderna", *Cuadernos de Historia Moderna*, 18 (1997), pp. 119-136; Ronald Po-Chia Hsia, "Disciplina social y catolicismo en la Europa de los siglos XVI y XVII", *Manuscrits. Revista d'Història Moderna*, 25 (2007), pp. 29-43; José Ignacio Ruiz-Rodríguez, Ígor Sosa Mayor, "El concepto de confesionalización en el marco de la historiografía germana", *Studia Historica. Historia Moderna*, 29 (2007), pp. 279-305; José Martínez Millán, Carlos Javier de Carlos Hernández, *Religión, política y tolerancia en la Europa moderna* (Madrid: Polifemo, 2011).

5 The first inquisitorial trial over Protestantism initiated by the Inquisition of Barcelona took place in 1539. Joan Bada, *La Inquisició a Catalunya, segles XIII-XIX* (Barcelona: Barcanova, 1992), p. 62.

almost always both religious and political in nature. In the mind-set of this era, the prince's intolerance became the very source of his power[6].

Another consequence, the one I wish to highlight here, is the religious homogenisation of peoples. The political and church apparatuses contributed to making religion a constituent element of regional identity. Confession practically became an element that delimited nationality: almost by definition, the Swedes had to be Lutherans, the English had to be Anglicans and so forth[7]. Even though some historians have recently drawn attention to initiatives allowing confessional coexistence[8] in contrast to the paradigm of confessionalisation, we have to acknowledge that religious uniformity was the norm in virtually all the kingdoms during the Modern Age. Even in the particular case of France, Alain Tallon has underscored the importance of Gallicanism in the formation of a clearly unique national consciousness[9]. In the eyes of the vast majority of European men and women of the 16th and 17th centuries, apparently there could be no nation without religious unity. In fact, the link between religion and nationality is one of the strongest arguments in Adrian Hastings' famous response to Eric Hobsbawm's no less famous thesis regarding the non-existence of nations prior to the 19th century. Hastings himself stresses, for example, the relationship between English nationalism and the Anglican Reform, and between Serbian nationalism and Orthodox Christianity[10].

When the same sovereign has to reign over diverse lands that have come under his power by either genetics or force, as was the case of the

6 Ignasi Fernández Terricabras, "Les bases ideològiques: la confessionalització i la intolerància religiosa a l'Europa moderna (segles XVI-XVII)", *Per bruixa i metzinera. La cacera de bruixes a Catalunya*, Agustí Alcoberro, ed. (Barcelona: Museu d'Història de Catalunya, 2007), pp. 56-69.

7 A survey of the different situations in Europe, with an extensive bibliography, can be found in: Pierre-Jean Souriac, René Souriac, *Les affrontements religieux en Europe du début du XVIe siècle au milieu du XVIIe siècle* (Paris: Belin, 2008), pp. 320-405.

8 C. Scott Dixon, Dagmar Freist, Mark Greengrass, *Living with Religious Diversity in Early-Modern Europe* (Surrey: Ashgate, 2012).

9 Alain Tallon, *Conscience nationale et sentiment religieux en France au XVIe siècle* (Paris: Presses Universitaires de France, 2002). The author does not share the ideas of Myriam Yardeni, *La conscience nationale en France pendant les guerres de Religion (1559-1598)* (Leuven-Paris: Nauwelaerts, 1971).

10 Adrian Hastings, *The construction of nationhood: ethnicity, religion and nationalism* (Cambridge: Cambridge University Press, 2001).

Spanish monarchy, one cannot ignore this religious factor in the attempts to forge a shared political identity.

Even though Pope Alexander VI granted Ferdinand of Aragon and Isabel of Castile the title of Catholic Monarchs in 1496, primarily thanks to their actions against the Muslims and Jews, the Habsburgs filled this title with new content as part of the Counter-Reformation[11]. To the king's councillors, opposition to the Protestants (the heretics) was compared to the struggle against Islam (the infidels), and the Spanish monarchs would become the Catholic Monarchs by antonomasia, to such an extent that today many historians use both expressions synonymously. As devout Catholics, the Habsburgs saw religion as a binding, unifying force in the different lands they governed[12].

Following the medieval political ideas which made the Emperor the military leader of Christendom, Charles V warmly embraced the defence of Catholicism. He felt sorely disappointed with the Peace of Augsburg of 1555, which sought Catholic and Lutheran coexistence within the Holy Roman Empire and thus sanctioned the motto *cuius regio, eius religio*. It should be understood that this principle did not rest on individual factors but instead primarily on an institutional foundations: the religion of the

11 Pablo Fernández Albaladejo, "Rey Católico: gestación y metamorfosis de un título", *El Tratado de Tordesillas y su época. Congreso Internacional de Historia*, 3 vols., Luis Antonio Ribot, ed. (Madrid: Sociedad Estatal V Centenario del Tratado de Tordesillas, 1995), vol. 1, pp. 209-216.

12 Christian Hermann, "Multinationale Habsbourg et universalisme chrétien", *Le premier âge de l'État en Espagne*, Christian Hermann, ed. (Paris: Centre National de la Recherche Scientifique, 1990), pp. 407-414; Pablo Fernández Albaladejo, "Católicos antes que ciudadanos: gestión de una 'política española' en los comienzos de la Edad Moderna", *Imágenes de la diversidad. El mundo urbano en la Corona de Castilla (siglos XVI-XVII)*, José Ignacio Fortea, ed. (Santander: Universidad de Cantabria, 1997), pp. 103-127; Laura Manzano, "Los fundamentos de la obediencia: la religión como máximo vínculo entre los reinos de la Monarquía Católica. El ejemplo de los Países Bajos en la década de 1640", *Servir al rey en la Monarquía de los Austrias. Medios, fines y logros del servicio al soberano en los siglos XVI y XVII*, Alicia Esteban, ed. (Madrid: Sílex, 2012), pp. 147-161. The construction of the monastery of San Lorenzo de El Escorial and the collection of relics from all the lands safeguarded by Philip II have been interpreted as an instrument used to construct a "monarchic, spiritual and national identity"; Guy Lazurg, "Possessing the Sacred: Monarchy and Identity in Philip II's Relic Collection at the Escorial", *Renaissance Quarterly*, 60/1 (2007), pp. 58-93.

subjects was not at the mercy of the monarch's (more or less arbitrary) personal decision; rather the state imposed by the monarch governing the *regio* was equated with the church preached by the *religio*. In the eyes of all Europeans, the example of France, which was haemorrhaging from eight cruel religious wars from 1562 to 1598, was clear proof of the disasters that can befall a kingdom when weak monarchs do not impose a single faith and instead have to tolerate different ones within their kingdom.

In the Spanish monarchy, when Charles V abdicated in 1556, his son Philip II, the leader of the Spanish branch of the Habsburgs, was the one who clearly adopted an openly *imperial* discourse in steely defence of Catholicism. In Vienna neither Ferdinand I (the mastermind of the peace of 1555) nor his son Maximillian II were able to do it for fear of destroying the delicate balance negotiated in Augsburg[13]. The decrees issued by the Council of Trent (1545-1563) were quickly accepted by Philip II; in 1564, the king ordered them to be applied not only to the bishops and superiors of the religious orders but to lay judges and delegates of royal power as well[14]. In the entire Spanish monarchy, the Council of Trent was not only the religious norm but also civil law. Sin and crime were equated with each other, and likewise revolt and heresy seemed to go hand in hand.

Philip II's propaganda apparatus ceaselessly praised this figure of the *Paladín de la Cristiandad*, even though, as proven by María José Rodríguez Salgado and others, the monarch's political practice in international relations obeyed pragmatic concerns more often than once believed[15]. And the king's biographers are wont to recall the famous phrase that Philip II wrote

13 Sylvène Édouard, *L'Empire imaginaire de Philippe II. Pouvoir des images et discours du pouvoir sous les Habsbourg d'Espagne au XVIe siècle* (Paris: Honoré Champion, 2005); Friederich Edelmayer, "El Sacro Imperio y la Monarquía Católica", *Las vecindades de las Monarquías Ibéricas*, José Javier Ruiz Ibáñez, ed. (Madrid: Red Columnaria-Fondo de Cultura Económica, 2013), pp. 81-101.

14 Ignasi Fernández Terricabras, *Felipe II y el clero secular. La aplicación del concilio de Trento* (Madrid: Sociedad Estatal para la Conmemoración de los Centenarios de Felipe II y Carlos V, 2000). What is more, in Catalonia the provincial council of 1564-66, held under the presidency of the Archbishop of Tarragona and with heavy royal control, accepted the decrees of Trent as the ecclesiastic norm: Joan Bada, *Situació religiosa de Barcelona en el segle XVI* (Barcelona: Facultat de Teologia de Catalunya, 1970), pp. 181-211.

15 María José Rodríguez-Salgado, *Felipe II, el "paladín de la Cristiandad" y la paz con el turco* (Valladolid: Universidad de Valladolid, 2004).

to Pope Pius V when the uprising in the Netherlands broke out with strong Calvinist motivation: *antes preferiría perder mis Estados y cien vidas que tuviese, que reinar sobre herejes*[16] ("I would rather lose my States and a hundred lives than have to reign over heretics").

2.

Upon the death of Ferdinand II in 1516, the Principality of Catalonia and the countships of Roussillon and Cerdagne were yet another part – and not the most influential one – of the vast Spanish monarchy which was steadfastly committed to the defence of Catholicism. After the end of the Council of Trent, if not before, the religious and political authorities worked actively throughout the entire monarchy to implant a clearly Tridentine Catholicism. However, many testimonies prove that in the eyes of the monarch and his councillors, Catalonia found itself in dire circumstances that required an additional effort at religious indoctrination.

The first circumstance was its proximity to France, where Calvinism had penetrated deeply, especially among the elites, and religious wars were causing upheaval in the kingdom. In Madrid, the risk that the Huguenots would enter Catalonia seemed real. One example is the story that in 1566 a man far from Catalonia, the Bishop of Córdoba, Francisco de Rojas y Sandoval, when asking the King to reinforce the Inquisitorial structure in the Pyrenees, justified this move by saying:

> *Porque la mayor fuerza de estos Reinos son los Montes Pirineos, y si estos se dañasen con la herejía, la libertad que con ellos predican es tan pegajosa como hemos visto, pues en tan breve tiempo se ha dañado todo, considere Vuestra Majestad cuán dañoso sería esto para los negocios de la Iglesia y de Vuestra Majestad, pues se apoderaban los herejes de las mayores fuerzas de estos reinos y de gente muy hábil y muy útil para el servicio de Vuestra Majestad, así por la tierra como por la mar*[17].

16 Manuel Fernández Álvarez, *Felipe II y su tiempo* (Madrid: Espasa, 1998), p. 382. The best biography is by Geoffrey Parker, *Felipe II. La biografía definitiva* (Barcelona: Planeta, 2010).

17 Archivo Francisco de Zabálburu (Madrid), Folder 129, f. 153 (Warnings from the Córdoba's Bishop).

> Because the greatest strength of these Kingdoms are the Pyrenean Mountains, and if these were damaged by heresy, the freedom that they preach is as catchy as we have seen, so that in such a brief time everything has been damaged, Your Majesty should consider how harmful this would be for the business of the Church and of Your Majesty, as the heretics would take over the greatest forces of these kingdoms and very skilful and useful people for the service of Your Majesty, both on land and by sea.

The Catalan prelates also asked for royal assistance. In 1561, after having crossed all of southern France to attend the Council of Trent, the Bishop of Barcelona, Guillem Cassador, wrote to Philip II, alarmed at everything he had witnessed:

> *Sols suplicaré a Vostra Majestat [...] se recorde quant veïna sia Catalunya en aquest tan horrible incendi, del qual se ha de tenir molt gran temor en tots los regnes d'Espanya*[18].

> I will only plead that Your Majesty remember [...] what a neighbour Catalonia is in this terrible conflagration, of which all the kingdoms of Spain should feel great concern.

The presence of many Occitan immigrants in modern Catalonia, who arrived regularly between 1490 and 1630, seemed to be a serious aggravating factor. There were Catholic parishes where the number of French men in the marriage records exceeds 20%. Even though modern studies have proven that the vast majority of these immigrants came from the Catholic regions in France, the fear that Calvinists pastors and preachers would infiltrate with them was ever-present. As Òscar Jané Checa explains in this same book, throughout the Modern Age the French counter-identity worked as a stereotype that served to reinforce Catalan identity. And the French were systematically seen as Protestant heretics[19], which almost automatically set them in opposition to the Catalans, who were devout Catholics.

And if that were not enough, Catalonia's problem were compounded by the problem of banditry, which was widespread there in the 16th and

18 Archivo General de Simancas, Estado-Aragón, 328, without number (the Bishop of Barcelona to Philip II, 30-11-1561).

19 Bertrand Haan, "L'affirmation d'un sentiment national espagnol face à la France du début des guerres de religion", *Le sentiment national dans l'Europe méridionale aux XVIe et XVIIe siècles*, Alain Tallon, ed. (Madrid: Casa de Velázquez, 2007), pp. 75-90 and particularly, pp. 79-82.

17th centuries. Without entering into the debate on its causes, here we are only interested in noting that the violence and conflict spread by banditry hindered not only political but also religious control over the territory[20].

We have numerous testimonies from rectors of parishes that had to flee or were affected by the division between gangs: *será imposible poder dar un paso por este obispado que no demos en las manos de los bandoleros* ("it will be impossible to take a step in this bishopric without falling into the hands of the bandits"), the Bishop of Urgell, Andreu Capella, warned Philip II in 1589. One year earlier, his cathedral chapterhouse had written:

> *Estan les coses de la comarca i frontera de França tan mal parades que puix la gent facinerosa i gascons amb gran seguretat i sens recel de contradicció captiven los capellans, oprimint-los en gran manera per conseguir d'ells majors rescats, obligant als Rectors dels llogarets que escapen d'apartar-se, deixant ses Residències. Tenim por no sie principi d'algun error en la Fe*[21].
>
> The things in the district and the frontier with France are so bad that the wrongdoers and Gascons with great confidence and no risk of contradiction capture priests, oppressing them greatly achieve higher ransoms for them, forcing the Rectors of the villages who escape to leave, leaving their Residences. We are afraid that it could be a begining of some mistake in the faith.

In 1615, the Bishop of Vic, Andrés de San Jerónimo, bemoaned the fact that the rectors in his diocese, having received death threats from the bandits, did not dare to live in their parishes or even travel to the cathedral to meet with the bishop[22].

20 Xavier Torres, "Bandolerisme catalan et protestantisme français (XVIe-XVIIe siècles). Image et réalité", *Tolérance et solidarités dans les Pays Pyrénéens*, Michel Brunet, Serge Brunet, Claudine Pailhes, dirs. (Foix: Archives Départementales de l'Ariège, 1998), pp. 391-412; Patrice Poujade, "Conflictualité, solidarités et relations frontalières dans les Pyrénées (v. 1550-v. 1650)", *Tolérance et solidarités dans les Pays Pyrénéens*, Conseil Général Ariège, dir. (Foix: Archives Départementales de l'Ariège, 1998), pp. 431-447; Patrice Poujade, *Le voisin et le migrant: hommes et circulations dans les Pyrénées modernes, XVIe-XIXe siècle* (Rennes: Presses Universitaires de Rennes, 2011).

21 Archivo Zabálburu (Madrid), folder 177, f. 75 (The Bishop of Urgell to Philip II, 12.02.1589) and 79 (Cathedral Chapter of the la Seu d'Urgell to Philip II, 10.11.1588).

22 Cited by Henry Kamen, *The Phoenix and the Flame. Catalonia and the Counter Reformation* (Yale Universtiy Press: New Haven & London, 1993).

In short, there were fears in the Court that the French Protestants, present in considerable numbers in nearby territories, e.g. the Countship of Foix, could seize upon the Occitan immigrants, the bandit gangs, the authorities' lack of control over certain regions and the supposed "ignorance" of the rural people, mainly mountain folk, to lay down roots in Catalonia the way they had in France. Indeed, the descriptions that reached them could not have been more alarming: *Lo que más me angustia es que estamos vecinos de los luteranos y témese que so color de bandoleros no entren este verano [...] Témese que no traigan algunos predicadores luteranos para del todo pervertir la tierra, que está llena de ignorancia*[23] ("What most distresses me is that we are neighbours of the Lutherans and the fear is that under the guise of bandits they enter this summer [...] The fear is that they will bring some Lutheran preachers to pervert the land completely, it being full of ignorance"), a Dominican friar from Puigcerdà wrote to his provincial in 1565.

Catalonia appeared to be a particularly vulnerable region not only from the political and military standpoint but also in religious terms, and this led the Church and the Crown to step up their Catholicisation measures in Catalan society, measures which were also applied elsewhere but with particular zeal in the Principality.

Thus, the inquisitorial network in Catalonia was systematically reinforced, despite the resistance to the Inquisition from the Catalan ruling classes, which regarded it as a legal and political institution serving the Crown that infringed on the Catalan constitutions. All the historians of the Inquisition stress that the tribunals of Barcelona and Saragossa (whose district included the diocese of Lleida) stood out from the other tribunals in the district because of their almost obsessive concern with the French, which were the target of particular vigilance: according to figures from Joan Bada, 13.86% of the trials in the Tribunal of Barcelona were for Lutheranism, a word that the Inquisition used to refer to all Protestant denominations[24]. The history of the Reformation in Catalonia still remains

23 Archivo General de Simancas, Estado-Aragón, 332, without number (letter to provincial Juan Izquierdo, 01-06-1565).

24 Joan Bada, *La Inquisició...*, p. 134. To give a counter-example, in the tribunal of Toledo only 7.3% of the trials between 1561 and 1620 were against "Lutherans". Elisabeth Balancy, "Les immigrés français devant le tribunal de l'Inquisition de Barcelone", *Les Français en Espagne à l'époque moderne* (Toulouse: Centre National

to be written. In the vast majority of cases, the Inquisitorial trials were against foreign soldiers or merchants, leading to the surmise that the Reformation did not lay down deep roots in Catalonia. However, recent studies on the heterodox networks in Aragon or an occasional reformed Catalan also lead us to believe that this hypothesis must still be confirmed or refuted through new archival research[25].

Yet repression was not enough. In the second half of the 16th century, the Crown embarked upon a process of reorganising church resources in Catalonia in order to make them more effective in indoctrinating the people and detecting heresy. From this standpoint, the most radical action was the monastery reform of 1592, when Clement VII authorised an operation that was largely planned by Philip II and his councillors[26]. The Pope eliminated the regular canons of Saint Augustine, which had 43 churches in Catalonia, and prescribed new rules for the Benedictines from the Cloistered Congregation of Tarragona and Saragossa, which included around 60 Benedictine monasteries in Catalonia, approximately 20 of which disappeared. This not only allowed the monks to be concentrated in a smaller number of monasteries which were easier to control, but it also

de la Recherche Scientifique, 1990), pp. 45-69; Miguel J. Blázquez, *La Inquisición en Cataluña. El Tribunal del Santo Oficio de Barcelona, 1487-1820* (Toledo: Arcano, 1990); William Monter, *La otra Inquisición. La Inquisición española en la Corona de Aragón, Navarra, el País Vasco y Sicilia* (Barcelona: Crítica, 1992); Henry Kamen, *The Phoneix...*, pp. 211-274. This attention is also found in the tribunal of the Inquisition in Saragossa: Christine Langé, "L'immigration française en Aragon, XVIe siècle et première moitié du XVIIe siècle", *Les Français en Espagne à l'époque moderne* (Toulouse: Centre National de la Recherche Scientifique, 1990), pp. 25-43.

25 The most important reformed Catalan was Pere Galès, originally from Ulldecona (1537-1595), who became a professor in Geneva and died imprisoned by the Inquisition: Antonio Fernández, Doris Moreno, *Protestantes, visionarios, profetas y místicos* (Barcelona: De Bolsillo, 2005), pp. 127-133. Regarding Aragon: Michel Boeglin, "Aspectos de la Reforma en Aragón a finales del reinado del Emperador. El proceso del rector Miguel Monterde", *Manuscrits. Revista d'Història Moderna*, 30 (2012), pp. 139-159.

26 Ignasi Fernández Terricabras, "Catalunya, 'frontera d'heretges'. Reformes monàstiques i reorganització dels recursos eclesiàstics catalans per Felip II", *Pedralbes. Revista d'Història Moderna*, 18/1 (1998), pp. 547-556. See also: Antoni Pladevall, "Les transformacions i canvis en l'estructura monàstica de Catalunya l'any 1592", *Miscel·lània en honor del Dr. Casimir Martí*, Josep Maria Sans, Francesc Balada, eds. (Barcelona: Fundació Salvador Vives i Casajuana, 1994), pp. 390-397.

freed up a series of church revenues which were earmarked to reform projects. Thus, the assets from the shuttered monasteries were used to finance the creation of a new diocese in Solsona, founded in 1593 to reduce the size of the bishoprics of Urgell and Vic in a move to help to enhance vigilance over the people and the ability to react to French Calvinism. A new school in Lleida, Sant Benet, was also funded, where the Benedictine monks could reside as they were being educated in the most prestigious university in the Principality. Afterward, these monks would be charged with instructing the residents of the villages near the monasteries. Other monastic revenues were annexed to the salaries of the *mestrescola* of the cathedral of Lleida, the canon who had jurisdiction over the students in the city and numerous professors at the university. Other aims were to create a diocesan seminary in Urgell, which sought to supply the parishes with well-trained clergy, and to boost the revenues of the Augustine convent in La Seu d'Urgell and the Dominican convent in Tremp, which sent preachers to the neighbouring counties.

3.

The process of equating Catholicism with Catalan identity, upheld in such a sustained fashion, was successful. By the 17th century, the Catholic religion was fundamental, unequivocal and inevitable component of Catalan identity, along with other elements like language and its own constitutional legal culture[27]. Texts, sermons, processions and festivities of all sorts were occasions to express and consolidate this identity through religiosity[28].

27 Antoni Simon i Tarrès, *Els orígens ideològics de la Revolució Catalana de 1640* (Barcelona: Publicacions de l'Abadia de Montserrat, 1999).

28 Especially the sermon that the *Diputació del General* ("General Deputation") commissioned every 23rd of April to a distinguished preacher to celebrate the feast day of Saint George, which was often printed: Xavier Torres, Ricard Expósito, "Els sermons de Sant Jordi de la Diputació de Catalunya: literatura i religió cívica", *Literatura en la Guerra de los Treinta Años*, Sònia Boadas, ed. (Vigo: Academia del Hispanismo, 2012), pp. 129-150.

Let us examine, for example, the worship of the saints, which in all of Catholic Europe became an issue through which religious devotion was easily linked to political identity, or, as Xavier Torres and Ricard Expósito show, with a "civil religion" that reinforced social and political cohesion[29]. And Catalonia, where the saints were omnipresent even in everyday life, both in their orthodox interpretation and in other interpretations labelled superstitious[30], was no exception.

Clement VIII's 1601 canonisation of the Dominican Ramon de Penyafort, a Catalan saint, led to an unprecedented outpouring of festivities in Barcelona. From the 10th of May until the 10th of August, there were all sorts of celebrations and processions in parishes, guilds and corporations, and people flocked to the city from all over Catalonia to venerate the mortal remains of the saint conserved in Santa Caterina convent[31]. The numerous texts printed to report on the occasion stress the saint's Catalan origins and the preeminent place that his canonisation gave to Barcelona above other cities in the world[32].

After that, Xavier Torres explains, the city of Barcelona and, by extension, the entire Principality, set out on a campaign to find relics and requests for canonisation in a further bid to serve as expressions of the grandeur of the city and the religious piety of its inhabitants, whose Catholicism was practically an act of identity: never having known heresy became *de facto* one of the utmost distinctions of Barcelona natives[33].

29 We should add to article cited in precedent footnote, in order to know the situation in the whole Europe, the following book: Sofia Boesch, Raimondo Michetti, eds., *Europa sacra. Raccolte agiografiche e identità politiche in Europa fra Medioevo ed Età Moderna* (Rome: Carocci, 2002).

30 Martí Gelabertó, *La palabra del predicador. Contrarreforma y superstición en Cataluña (siglos XVII-XVIII)* (Lleida: Milenio, 2005), pp. 176-225.

31 Iayme Rebullosa, *Relación de las grandes fiestas que en esta ciudad de Barcelona se han hecho a la canonización de su hijo San Ramon de Peñafort, de la Orden de Predicadores* (Barcelona: Impremta de Jaume Cendrat, 1601).

32 Henry Ettinghausen, "De la noticia a la prensa. (San Raimundo de Peñafort, Barcelona, 1601)", *Actas del V Congreso de la Asociación Internacional Siglo de Oro*, Christoph Strosetzki, ed. (Madrid-Frankfurt: Editorial Iberoamericana-Vervuert, 2011), pp. 490-502.

33 Xavier Torres, "La nació i el temple: patriotisme i Contrareforma a la Catalunya moderna", *Pedralbes. Revista d'Història Moderna*, 28/1 (2008), pp. 85-102; Xavier Torres, "La ciutat dels sants: Barcelona i la historiografia de la Contrareforma", *Barcelona. Quadrens d'Història*, 20 (2014), pp. 77-104.

Adding to all this hagiographic fervour, in 1602 the Dominican Antoni Vicenç Domènec wrote the *Historia general de los santos del Principado de Cataluña*, after, he said, seven years of work *por todos los lugares, iglesias y archivos de Cataluña* ("around all the places, churches and archives of Catalonia"), and he published a corrected and augmented edition in 1630. In this book, he tallies 84 canonised saints and 34 who were worshipped even though they had not been officially recognised by Rome[34]. It is clear that, paraphrasing Orwell with a touch of irony, in Catalonia there are more saints than anyone else: certain devotions with clearly more public connotations (Our Lady of Montserrat, Saint George and Saint Eulàlia) were extremely popular.

Yet this feature is not exclusive to Barcelona or Catalonia. In 1596, another Dominican, Juan de Marieta, had published a list of 17,780 Spanish saints[35]. In modern Europe, many cities and monarchies tallied their holy people to demonstrate the superiority of their Catholicism: the oldest, the most genuine, the least corrupted by heresy[36].

The association between this worship of the saints to the struggle over denominations was spread by preachers and artists, by processions and informational texts or images[37]. For example, in 1614, upon the beatification of Saint Theresa of Avila, celebrations were held throughout the entire Spanish monarchy with festivities primarily promoted by the Crown and the Carmelites. In Perpignan, there were two opposing stages in Plaça del Puig: the first had a space containing images of Our Lady

34 Antonio Vicente Domènech, *Historia general de los santos y varones ilustres en santidad del Principado de Cataluña* (Girona: G. Garrich, 1630 (2nd ed). The tally of the saints is in: Martín Gelabertó, "Culto de los santos y sociedad en la Cataluña del Antiguo Régimen (s. XVI-XVIII)", *Historia Social*, 13 (1992), pp. 3-20 and José Luís Betrán, "Culto y devoción en la Cataluña barroca", *Jerónimo Zurita. Revista de Historia*, 85 (2010), pp. 95-133.

35 Cited by: Xavier Torres, "La ciutat dels sants...", p. 77-104. In general: José Ignacio Gómez, "Los santos patronos y la identidad de las comunidades locales en la España de los siglos XVI y XVII", *Jerónimo Zurita. Revista de Historia*, 85 (2010), pp. 39-74.

36 Ignasi Fernández Terricabras, "La foi et le rang: l'argumentation religieuse dans les traités pour la préséance du roi de France de François Pithou et d'Eustache de Refuge (XVIe-XVIIe siècles)", *Revue d'Histoire de l'Église de France*, 96 (2010), pp. 415-428.

37 Pep Valsalobre, "Elements per a una Catalunya sacra: sobre alguns aspectes de l'hagiografia de l'edat moderna catalana", *Vides medievals de sants: difusió, tradició i llegenda*, Marinela Garcia, M. Àngels Llorca, eds. (Alicante: Institut Interuniversitari de Filologia Valenciana, 2012).

of Mount Carmel and Saint Theresa, while the second held two figures depicting Martin Luther and John Calvin, the Protestant leaders, surrounded by their followers. When night-time fell, the masses who gathered there witnessed how:

> *por un cordelito muy sutil partieron a un mismo tiempo dos rayos de fuego de la imagen de Nuestra Señora y de nuestra Santa Madre (Santa Teresa), y con grandísima presteza se prendió en las figuras de los dos herejes, los cuales comenzaron a disparar de sus cuerpos tantos tiros y a despedir tanta cantidad extendiendo el fuego a los demás herejes y arrojando mucho por sus bocas y despidiendo infinidad de cohetes tronadores, se prendió también en la nao, haciéndose todo ceniza, con grande gusto y grita de la gente que allí estaba. Parecieron en la otra nave muchas luces de cera blanca, con que las dos imágenes quedaron como dos resplandecientes soles, tañéndose muchos juegos de chirimías*[38].

> along a subtle chord came two beams of fire at the same time from the image of Our Lady and of our Holy Mother (Santa Teresa), and with the greatest alacrity, set fire to the figures of the two heretics, who began firing from their body so many shots and give off so much, spreading the fire to the other heretics and throwing a lot from their mouths and firing countless thunderous rockets, the ship also caught fire, all turning to ash, to the great pleasure and shouts of people who were there. They looked from the other ship like many lights of white wax, with the two images like two blazing suns, playing many chalemie's songs.

Stagings of battles were common in popular festivals at the time, but the most common were the battles between the Moors and the Christians[39]. The propagandistic meaning of the pyrotechnical display in Perpignan, near the French border, seems clear: the victory of the Virgin Mary and a saint with close ties to the Spanish monarchy over the Protestants who defied the Catholic Church and, among other things, challenged the proper veneration of their victors.

38 Diego de San José, *Compendio de las solenes fiestas que en toda España se hicieron en la beatificacion de N.B.M. Teresa de Jesús* (Madrid: Viuda de Alonso Martín, 1615).

39 Maria Gargantè, *Festa, arquitectura i devoció a la Catalunya del Barroc* (Barcelona: Publicacions de l'Abadia de Montserrat, 2011).

4.

However, in the Modern Age, the efforts to make a common project coalesce in the different regions within the same monarchy also generated in reaction the need to reinforce local identity and distinguish it from that of the other subjects in the shared monarchy[40]. And while Catholicism acted as a factor unifying the heterogeneous territories under the Spanish monarchy, many Catalan thinkers defended the specificity and supremacy of the Catholicism of their land. This served to even further strengthen the identification between religious denomination and the Catalan nature, and, by extension, to distinguish it from a Castilian Catholicism which had been more damaged throughout history.

In the late 16th and early 17th centuries, chroniclers and historians like Jeroni Pujades, Esteve de Corbera and Martí Viladamor took it for granted that Saint Paul and Saint James had travelled to Catalonia before Castile and established Christianity there, meaning that the Catalans were the first Christian people on the Iberian Peninsula[41]. The claim that the Catalans were God's chosen people, which Antoni Simon i Tarrés examines in this book, can be understood within this context. Similarly, the legends of Wilfred the Hairy and Otger Cataló to explain the origin of the Catalan nation, constitutions and nobility had not only a political meaning; they were also a way to claim that Christianity had never been expelled from Catalonia. This clearly distinguishes it from Castile, which experienced ignominious void in the guise of Muslim domination[42].

40 Numerous examples can be found in: José Javier Ruiz Ibáñez, "Las percepciones de la Monarquía Hispànica como un proyecto universal", *Antonio Vieira, Roma e o universalismo das monarquias portuguesa e espanhola*, Pedro Cardim, Gaetano Sabatini, eds. (Lisbon: Biblioteca do Centro de História de Além-Mar, 2011), pp. 29-52.

41 However, Pedro Calixto Ramírez made exactly the same claims about the Kingdom of Aragon in 1616; Pablo Fernández Albaladejo, *Materia de España. Cultura política e identidad en la España Moderna* (Madrid: Marcial Pons, 2007), p. 75.

42 Jordi Cortadella, *La història antiga en la historiografía catalana* (Bellaterra: Publicacions de la Universitat Autònoma de Barcelona, 1992); Jesús Villanueva, *Política y discurso histórico en la España del siglo XVII. Las polémicas sobre los orígenes medievales de Cataluña* (Alicante: Publicacions de la Universitat d'Alacant, 2004); Antoni Simon i Tarrès, *Els orígens*....

For example, the sermon by Onofre Manescal in memory of the soul of James II which the members of the General Deputation commissioned in 1597, and printed in 1602, says:

> *Ninguna cosa ennobleix tant una terra com professar-se en ella molta virtut i recolliment. Per lo qual no pot deixar de ser alabada Catalunya, per la molta virtut que en ella sempre s'ha professat. La fe ha estat sempre en son punt, que és lo fonament de tota virtut i santedat. En lo que és recolliment, ha portat sempre ventatge a les demés nacions, la Catalana, com l'experiència pot mostrar, y hauran pogut advertir los qui són anats per altres regnes. Bé mostren esta virtut los sants naturals y indígenes de Catalunya*[43].

> Nothing so ennobles a land as to profess in it virtue and contemplation. So Catalonia must be praised, for the great virtue that has always professed in her. Faith has always been in the point, which is the foundation of all virtue and holiness. About the contemplation it has always had an advantage over other nations, the Catalan, as experience can show, and those that have gone to other realms could have been warned. So, the natural and indigenous saints Catalonia show this.

Likewise, Esteve de Corbera makes it clear that in the Principality of Catalonia, *en la antigüedad y pureza de la Fe, en el culto y observancia de la Religión, en la majestad y adorno de los Templos, en la devoción y puntualidad al servicio de las cosas divinas ninguna se le aventaja* ("in the antiquity and purity of the Faith, in the worship and observance of the Religion, in the majesty and decoration of the Temples, in the devotion and punctuality in the service of the divine things no-one led it") as shown, for example, by the name of the saints: *¿qué mayor gloria de la Nación Catalana que verse favorecida con tantos Patrones Tutelares en el Cielo?*[44] ("What greater glory for the Catalan Nation than to be seen to be favoured with so many Guiding Patrons in Heaven?").

The ideas that were somewhat tentatively debated by these historians, albeit always limited by the epistemological frameworks of the

43 Onofre Manescal, *Sermó vulgarment anomenat del Serenissim Senyor Don Iaume Segon* (Barcelona: Sebastià de Cormellas, 1602), f. 72. Regarding this text: Lurdes Estruch, "El Sermó Patriòtic d'Onofre Manescal (1597/1602)", *Butlletí de la Reial Acadèmia de Bones Lletres de Barcelona*, 51 (2007-2008), pp. 145-198.

44 Estevan de Corbera, *Cataluña ilustrada* (Naples: Antonino Gramiñani, 1678), p. 3 and 15. The manuscript was written in around 1630.

historiography of the period[45], were later popularised by preachers and writers without such caution. And we thus reach the claim that there had never been Catalan heretics. The idea is obviously false[46], but its potential to foster cohesion and identity was extraordinarily powerful.

In 1600, the Jesuit Pere Gil, one of the most influential ecclesiastics and intellectuals of the day, expressed this clearly when he described the character of the Catalans in his *Geografia de Catalunya*:

> *En lo que toca a la fe catòlica i religió cristiana són tan ferms i tan enemics de les noves invencions dels infidels i heretges que, havent tants anys com ha que tenen per espai quasi quaranta llegües veïns als heretges de França, mai l'heretgia és entrada en Catalunya, ni s'és trobat algun català que's sia fet heretge. La qual firmesa i constància en la fe i religió cristiana, que se funda en la naturalesa, però, no's deu atribuir tant a la inclinació natural e indústria humana, quant a la gràcia sobrenatural y misericòrdia divina, y per ço a Déu principalment, y no a la nació catalana, s'ha de dar esta alabança*[47].

> In what concerns the Catholic faith and Christian religion they are so firm and so against the new inventions of infidels and heretics, having had for many years as they have a space of almost forty leagues with as neighbours the heretics in France, heresy has never entered in Catalonia, nor has nay Catalan been found who is a heretic either. This firmness and perseverance in the faith and Christian religion, which is based on nature, it should not be attributed, however, both to the natural inclination and human industry, but rather to the supernatural grace and divine mercy, and so this praise must be given to God principally and not to the Catalan nation.

45 Xavier Baró, *La historiografia catalana en el segle del Barroc (1585-1709)* (Barcelona: Publicacions de l'Abadia de Montserrat, 2009), especially, pp. 73-75; Pep Valsalobre, "La historiografia literària catalana moderna: un passat difícil, un present prometedor", *Del Cinccents al Setcents. Tres-cents anys de literatura catalana*, Eulàlia Miralles, ed. (Bellcaire d'Empordà: Vitel·la, 2010), pp. 111-122.

46 Recall the impact caused by the publication of: Jordi Ventura, *Els heretges catalans* (Barcelona: Editorial Selecta, 1963), with a letter-prologue by P. Miquel Batllori.

47 Josep Iglésies, *Pere Gil (1551-1622) i la seva Geografia de Catalunya. Seguit de la transcripció del Llibre primer de la historia Cathalana* (Barcelona: Institut d'Estudis Catalans, 2002), p. 272. Encomiastic descriptions of the character of the inhabitants of a given territory are common in these texts called "corographies", which mix history and geography: Agustí Alcoberro, ed., *Identitat i territori. Textos geogràfics del Renaixement* (Barcelona-Vic: Universitat de Barcelona-Eumo Editorial, 2000); Vicenç M. Rosselló, "Al servei de la història. Els cronistes (entre les "excel·lències" valencianes i Ptolemeu)", *Afers*, 74 (2013), pp. 35-50.

Gil's text was handwritten, but other authors made the same claims in print. One example is the Dominican Jaume Rebullosa, a friend of Pere Gil; in his Spanish translation of *Relationi Universali* by the celebrated Piedmontese Jesuit Giovanni Botero, published in 1603, he adds numerous fragments of his own on Catalonia. Thus, Rebullosa praises Catalonia's religiosity:

> *como lo muestra su entereza en la fe, estando tan vezina de herejes, las enormes cruces levantadas por las encrucijadas y caminos, los muchos lugares píos y de devoción que hay por todas partes, la magnificencia de sus Templos y el particular gusto con que acuden a ellos para oir la palabra de Dios*[48].

> as shown by its confidence in the faith, being so close to heretics, the huge crosses erected at the crossroads and by roads, the many pious and devotional places found everywhere, its magnificent temples and particular pleasure with which they flock to them to hear the word of God.

In 1628, the Perpignan-based jurist Andreu Bosc claimed that *des de dita predicació de S. Pau i S. Jaume fins la present era, mai s'és perduda la Fe de Crist* ("Since that preaching by Saint Paul and Saint James until the present, the Faith in Christ has never been lost") in the Principality and particularly in the countships, because after the Muslim invasion the Christians took refuge in the Pyrenees, were never conquered and then expelled the Muslims from their mountain redoubts. Even the Spanish Inquisition, founded in Catalonia, heard hardly any trials in Catalonia compared to in the *nacions estranyes* ("foreigns nations"). That is:

> *evident prova quan Zeladors i observants són (els catalans) de la Fe, tenint l'ocasió i perill tan veí de la nació Francesa tan infecta i contaminada com tots sabem. Tot s'ha d'atribuir a la ferma, constant i antiquíssima Fe, puix poden blasonar, no sols de les primícies de la Cristiandat d'Espanya, com està provat, però també del principi que es rebé la Santa Inquisició en tota Espanya*[49].

48 Montserrat Casas, "Recepción e influencia de las Relaciones Universales de Giovanni Botero en España", *La traduzione della letteratura italiana in Spagna (1300-1939)*, María de las Nieves Muñiz, ed. (Barcelona: Universitat de Barcelona, 2007), pp. 405-428. Rebullosa's translation was reissued in 1622.

49 Andreu Bosc, *Sumari, Index o Epítome dels admirables i nobilíssims Títols d'honor de Catalunya, Rosselló i Cerdanya (Perpinyà, 1628)* (Barcelona: Curial, 1974), pp. 33, 35.

clear proof of how Zealous and observant of the Faith (the Catalans) are, having such a nearby danger as the French nation so infected and contaminated as we all know. It all has to be attributed to the firm, constant and ancient Faith, because they can brag not only of the first fruits of Christianity in Spain, as is proven, but also of the beginning of the Holy Inquisition in all Spain.

The popular spread of these ideas is proven by the fact that they were mentioned as pure fact in the Catalan propaganda surrounding the *Guerra dels Segadors* or Catalan Revolt[50]. The pamphleteers of the day repeatedly used the presence of Protestant soldiers in the Spanish armies, the attacks against the people and especially episodes like the looting and burning of churches to support religious argumentation: the fight was necessary to defend the true Catholic faith against the army of heretics which was setting fire to churches, profaning the Eucharist and insulting the images of the saints[51].

The *Proclamación católica*, written in 1640 by the Augustine priest Gaspar Sala at the request of the councillors of the city of Barcelona, unequivocally attributes the Catalans' victories over the armies of Philip IV to God's providence, as a way to thank them for their fidelity to the Catholic faith. His text is neither a theoretical nor historical treatise but a battle leaflet, propaganda, reissued several times and translated into French, Portuguese and Dutch. In it, Sala gathers all the theories about the unique, singular origin of Catalan Catholicism without a historian's moderation: not only are the Catalans the successors of the son of Noah who did not participate in building the diabolical Tower of Babel, not only had they freed themselves from Muslim bondage before asking for the French kings' assistance, but they were also the first Christians on the continent:

Apenas llegó la fama del Mesías a Cataluña, cuando partieron muchos de esta Provincia para verle, como lo testifican escrituras auténticas y tradiciones muy recibidas [...] Por esta Provincia dio principio Santiago a la cosecha apostólica, consagró el primer Obispo de España, etc. Ni hay [que] decir que lo dejó para la vuelta, pudiéndole dar principio en el primer ingreso: porque en la conversión de las almas, lo que hoy se podía hacer, no lo dejaban los Apóstoles para mañana. Desde

50 Xavier Torres, "La nació i el temple...".

51 The Catalan Revolt of 1640 was not a religious war but a clash with clearly political and social causes. However, the religious factor often arose, as analysed in: Antoni Simon i Tarrès, "Un alboroto católico. El factor religiós en la revolució catalana de 1640", *Pedralbes. Revista de Historia Moderna*, 23/2 (2003), pp. 123-145.

> *aquella antigüedad hasta estos tiempos, jamás se eclipsó la fe en Cataluña [...] Por los Catalanes goza España el santo Tribunal de la Inquisición.*
>
> Hardly had tidings of the Messiah reached Catalonia, when many left this province to see him, as witnessed by authentic documents received traditions [...] For this Province Santiago started the apostolic harvest, consecrated the first Bishop of Spain, etc. Nor is there to say left him to return beings able to start in the first stay: because in the conversion of souls, what could be done today, the Apostles did not leave for tomorrow. Since that antiquity to these times, faith was never eclipsed in Catalonia [...] Through the Catalans Spain enjoys the holy Tribunal of the Inquisition.

And, of course,

> *No se conoce ningun Catalán heresiarca: porque Vigilancio, que comenzó a derramar su ponzoña en este Principado, san Jerónimo declara que era Francés, y que los Catalanes, en descubrir su venenosa doctrina, le desterraron a Francia. Es Cataluña piedra de toque, donde los fingidos sectarios muestran presto la bajeza del metal de sus errores: es sol resplandeciente su fe, y a sus rayos, cual Águila examina los polluelos, arrojando de sí los que degeneran de la católica casta [...] porque así como hay islas que ni crían sabandijas ponzoñosas ni en ellas viven las advenedizas, así Cataluña, ni produce sectarios, ni los sufre mucho tiempo*[52].
>
> There is no known Catalan heretic: for Vigilantius, who began to shed his poison in the Principality, Saint Jerome states that he was French, and that the Catalans, when they discovered his poisonous doctrine, exiled him to France. It is Catalonia touchstone, where feigned sectarian soon showed the baseness of the metal from their mistakes: its faith is the brilliant sun, and its rays, like an eagle watching its chicks, rejecting those who degenerate from the Catholic sect [...] For there are islands that neither raised poisonous vermin nor they live upstart, Catalonia neither produce sectarian neither suffer much time.

5.

The Catalan rebels' embracing of the ideal of the defence of the Catholic faith against heresy in 1640, a stance which until then had characterised the Spanish monarchy, leads us to believe that the process of the

52 Gaspar Sala, *Proclamación Católica a la Magestad Piadosa de Filipe el Grande*, ed. Antoni Simon i Tarrés, Karsten Neumann (Barcelona: Editorial Basc, 2003), pp. 8, 11.

confessionalisation, or Catholicisation, if you will, of Catalan-ness had been successful. Catalan identity was identified with Tridentine Catholicism, among other elements.

The purpose of this paper is not to trace the course of this identification in subsequent centuries, although it has had a clear influence on many episodes and texts in the history of Catalonia. Religious argumentation was used by the Bourbon and Habsburg camps in the War of the Spanish Succession in an effort to equate their cause with that of God and the Church[53]. The relationship between religion and nationality was still crucial in the Contemporary Age, and not only in conflicts like the Peninsular War, the Carlist Wars or the Civil War. In times of peace, too, the Catalan church also stressed its national identification, now not so much to halt Protestantism as to grapple with liberalism, secularism and the workers' movement. The statements by Bishop Torras i Bages in 1892 are reminiscent of those uttered by the Jesuit Pere Gil in 1600:

> *Potser no hi ha altra nació entera i sòlidament cristiana com fou Catalunya. La infusió de la gràcia divina es féu en una raça forta, entenimentada i activa, per la qual cosa l'element humà, fecundat en aquell element diví, produí una virtut i energia que es desenrotllà en una organització resistent i harmònica*[54].

> Perhaps there is no other nation as whole and solidly Christian as Catalonia was. The infusion of divine grace was made in a strong, active and prudent race, so the human element, fertilized in that divine element, produced a virtue and power that developed in a strong and harmonious organization.

The claim for a glorious Christian past becomes clear in the reconstructions of the monasteries of Ripoll[55] and Sant Martí del Canigó. The latter, which got underway in 1902, was zealously spearheaded by the Bishop of Perpignan, Carsalade du Pont (1900-32), with the goal of stimulating

53 David González Cruz, *Guerra de religión entre príncipes católicos. El discurso del cambio dinástico en España y América* (Madrid: Ministerio de Defensa, 2002); Guillaume Hanotin, "Dimension religieuse et accents prophétiques de la guerre de Succession d'Espagne", *Revue d'Histoire Diplomatique*, 126 (2012-2013), pp. 265-282.

54 Josep Torras i Bages, *La Tradició Catalana* (Barcelona: Edicions 62-La Caixa, 1981), p. 33.

55 Jordi Figuerola, *El bisbe Morgades i la formació de l'Església catalana contemporània* (Barcelona: Publicacions de l'Abadia de Montserrat, 1984), pp. 399-463.

the Catalanist sentiment of his flock against the secular legislation of the French Third Republic[56]. The prevailing nationalism among the Catalan clergy was a motive of constant concern in both Madrid and the Vatican, especially under the Primo de Rivera and Franco dictatorships, when it also served to provide refuge to movements in political opposition to the regime[57]. The identification of the Catalan as a fervent Catholic, unequivocally shaped in the 16th and 17th centuries as part of the struggle against Protestantism, still had a long road ahead.

56 Jean-François Galinier-Pallerola, "Le Canigou: précipice affreux ou montagne sacrée? Ruine et reconstruction de l'abbaye Saint-Martin", *Montagnes sacrées d'Europe, actes du colloque «Religion et montagnes»*, Serge Brunet, Dominique Julia, Nicole Lemaitre, eds. (Paris: Université Paris I, 2005), pp. 325-337.

57 This concern becomes clear in the articles compiled by: Joan Bada, *Societat i Església a Catalunya. Cent anys entre constitucions i dictadures (1876-1978)* (Barcelona: Facultat de Teologia de Catalunya, 2011).

France and the Formation of Political and Social Identities in 17th Century Catalonia

Oscar JANÉ
Universitat Autònoma de Barcelona

The study of politics in France and southern Europe has (re-)kindled European interest in what happened on the Iberian Peninsula, especially in Catalonia. The evolutions in military habits, the social and cultural world and political culture spark a variety of analyses around a kind of incipient international diplomacy. This is the teleological evidence through which the survival of the perception and identity of territories like Catalonia necessarily find more or less solid origins in time. For this to happen, the length and intensity in certain historical times has to have led to the survival or, more accurately, the crystallisation of (more or less) heterogeneous collective identities[1].

In any event, the Modern Age is one of the key eras in the political and institutional world characterised by the monarch's desire to create powerful states free of seigniorial burdens; furthermore, it was a period in which war came to the people with devastating, counter-identity effects. France's policy in Catalonia in the 17th century and onwards signals a turning point in the consolidation of a Catalan identity which until then, also according to the historiography of the past few decades, was affected more by pressure from the Spanish monarchy. In this sense, we can explain the factors that shape a collective and socio-territorial identity, always according to a political and military entity that captured the collective imagination of peoples who had always been somewhat heterogeneous. This also shaped spaces with a degree of evolution in this identification that was obviously determined precisely in relation to pressures and threats from the outside.

1 Abbreviatons used: AMAE, Archives du Ministère des Affaires Étrangères; ANF, Archives Nationales de France.

1. France's hostilities and intentions in Catalonia

Spain's hostility toward the French, a constant feature throughout the 16th century, did not predict the transformations and political avenues developed in Catalonia in the 17th century. The cards on the table could have given a glimpse of the new alliances and political constructions in Europe. However, despite the efforts of a veritable Catalan Francophile party in the 1640s, the distance between the Catalan and French positions regarding the Principality's needs and the experiences of the Catalans who lived near the French did nothing other than magnify the traditional Francophobia, which was even more pronounced in the border areas and in Roussillon after the Treaty of the Pyrenees (1659)[2].

However, this very hostility to which we attach a great deal of importance in the creation of collective identities and their consolidation over time also differs depending on the land. In this sense, the heterogeneity of Catalonia could be seen in the diverse reactions to French aggressions at certain points in time. These responses took shape when the attacks became recurring and when they were always waged in the same regions. In this sense, we can witness the appearance of an anti-French sentiment which verged on xenophobia, along with exacerbated ties of solidarity among the peoples that were the most seriously affected, namely, as mentioned above, the northern half of Catalonia. Therefore, was it possible for the counter-identity reactions, along with the military laxness of the Spanish monarchy and its violation of the constitutions, to forge a collective sentiment of identity reaffirmation in the most affected regions? First, let us examine the relationship between the French presence, its political and military interest in the country and its use of this interest depending on its needs at different points in time.

The root of France's intentions in Catalonia lay essentially in a desire to conquer it, and above all to gain a buffer, that is, a bit of distance from the Spanish threat. The geostrategic decisions by the crown of France led it to expand its territory in Alsace, Franche Comté and Roussillon. Yet the

2 Oscar Jané, *Catalunya i França al segle XVII. Identitats, contraidentitats i ideologies a l'època moderna (1640-1700)* (Catarroja-Barcelona: Editorial Afers, 2006); Antoni Simon, *Construccions polítiques i identitats nacionals. Catalunya i els orígens de l'estat modern espanyol* (Barcelona: Publicacions de l'Abadia de Montserrat, 2005).

assimilations were only partial. The first, for example, was the assimilation of the Catalan elite, a group that was foreign in Roussillon and came from the Principality, but that despite its service to France kept enough roots in its Catalan fatherland to only be considered a collective involved in a gradual, active assimilation. Of course, their descendants were the ones who played the role of assimilated and "natural" actors of Frenchness in Roussillon. As for the rest, neither the Church nor the general populace, nor even the cultural and artistic world, underwent major transformations. However, this does not mean that the French authorities did not try to erase some of their traditions. The conditions only allowed for the gradual, necessary introduction of pro-French elements (language, teachers, Jesuits, etc.). Assimilation only came in the elite, but the elite did not regard assimilation of the popular classes as necessary, since the stability of the province allowed for this.

Roussillon was considered to be partly assimilated, but after the leaders of the country and the upper echelons were in the hands of the French – in the sense that they came from the north – and the concept of "pro-French" disappeared, it was politically integrated into France, despite the fact that it was regarded as a "reputed foreign" province until 1785. The initial doubts on whether to keep or exchange the province led to the survival of its specific religious, cultural and societal traits.

At the same time, also worth noting is the evolution in France's view of Catalonia, a third-party perspective that is often ignored. This is one aspect that takes into consideration the opinion of the other on the conditions of the Catalans, but from the standpoint of the newly-arrived power. Perhaps the most noteworthy of all, which reveals a clearer conception of Roussillon's assimilation into France 40 years after it was annexed, was the testimony by the intendant Ponte d'Albaret, the successor of the Catalan intendant Ramon Trobat, in 1698. He clearly defined the reason behind Roussillon's difficult integration into France and the remedies that should have been taken to fix this, only a few of which he actually carried out: the customs union (that is, eliminating taxes between Languedoc and Roussillon), creating trading companies, attributing the province's Church benefits *à des Français 'naturels' en dédommageant les Catalans par des bénéfices dans l'intérieur du royaume* ("for the people who are natural French, damaging the Catalans though benefices in the interior of the kingdom"), requiring the nobility and elite of the country to send their sons to study in France and serve with the French troops, and having Roussillon rejoin the Parliament of Toulouse and the province of Languedoc[3]. In fact, the intendant only managed to get the French currency circulating, to convince an increasing number of Catalans to send their sons to *França* (recall that in 1709 Jacint Rigau was decorated in Perpignan in reward for a race in France) and to raise the Church allocations to the French. He condemned the fact that in his eyes, governance over a province that in many respects escaped France or was "controlled" from the outside, such as by the Church or its ties with the Principality, was a contradiction. In fact, the intendant himself kept making a distinction between native French and Catalans and the latter's failure to adapt because they had their own identity. In reality, the French had planted the roots of an obsession with the representation of Roussillon and its Spanishness. This can be seen when there is talk of its inhabitants and the nobility of Perpignan, which the intendant believed had *le sang espagnol* ("Spanish blood"). In short, the intendant's language demonstrates the amalgam that existed between Spanishness and Catalanness, when ultimately they were synonymous with the antithesis of Frenchness: *le peuple de Roussillon se nomme et s'estime Catalan, et regarderoit comme une dégradation et une injure le nom de françois ou de Catalan francisé* ("The people of Roussillon called themselves and feel Catalan and regard beung called French or French Catalan as degradation and an insult").

Therefore, the best way to get the Roussillon natives to feel French was not to force them to do so but to eliminate the barriers that led them to perceive that they were different in both customs and justice. As Albaret said: *le droit français s'establiroit peu à peu chez cette nation qui seroit a la fin obligée de cesser de se regarder comme totalement séparée du reste des sujets du Roy*[4] ("French law was gradually established in this nation that would end up compelled to cease to regard themselves as completely separate from the rest of the subjects of the King"). Regardless, the French presence and its political and military actions during the second half of the 17th century – and much earlier in Roussillon, since it was a border area and had suffered from repeated incursions – led certain solidarities and

3 Marquis de Roux, *Louis XIV et les provinces conquises (Artois, Alsace, Flandres, Roussillon, Franche-Comté)* (Paris: Les Éditions de France, 1938), p. 89.

4 ANF, MM.972, *Extrait de la Généralité de Perpignan ou Province de Roussillon, dressée par M. de Ponte d'Albaret, intendant par l'ordre de Mgr. le Duc de Bourgogne en 1710.*

collective representations to emerge, essentially in the northern part of the country.

The possible existence of a contradiction on keeping or trading Roussillon could clearly be seen. Either option led one to believe that the French monarchy had a keen interest in it, primarily to counter Spain from close up. However, the French administration had always given off the idea that Roussillon was a territory that had been conquered by arms, and that therefore it could be kept[5], an idea that Marca expressed for Catalonia as a whole when it was occupied by France in 1647: *les terres sont à celuy qui les occupe, avec des forts et des garnisons*[6] ("the land is for those who occupy it with forts and garrisons").

Regarding France's general, constant interest in the Principality, the following factors should be borne in mind: military and cultural policies, taking advantage of prime moments, like the 1640 uprising; the use of firearms (fortifications, troop subsistence, position of strength regarding Spain, possibility of trading Roussillon); and personal actions. This set of factors was part of France's real interest. The political acts and games of people like Ramon Trobat might have accelerated certain actions[7]. The historiography discusses the concept resulting from this interest: was there an intention to assimilate, annex or fully acculturate Roussillon and its population? David Stewart mentions what he regards as two fundamental French policies in Roussillon: political assimilation and acculturation. In fact, his entire work consists of a demonstration of the policies implemented by France to attain these objectives[8]. Other authors distinguish between assimilation and integration and believe that there might have been many levels of assimilation, which was the case of Roussillon, with its "gradual assimilation". At the same time, definitive administrative acculturation and annexation projects did not actually materialise until 1789, when the Sovereign Council was abolished and the department

5 *Mémoires pour l'année 1661. Mémoires de Louis XIV*, ed. Jean Longnon (Paris: Tallandier, 2001), p. 104 (*Mémoires pour l'année 1661*).

6 AMAE, CP, Espagne, 27, *Mémoire pour les limites de la Catalogne*, on 28/09/1647, ffº 331r-344r.

7 Regarding Ramon Trobat, see: Oscar Jané, *Catalunya sense Espanya. Ramon Trobat: catalanitat i ideologia a l'empara de França* (Catarroja-Barcelona: Editorial Afers, 2009).

8 David Stewart, *Assimilation and Acculturation in Seventeenth-Century Europe. Roussillon and France, 1659-1715* (Westport-London: Greenwood Press, 1997).

of the Pyrénées-Orientales was created, eliminating all historical-toponymic symbolic references[9]. However, based solely on France's pretensions, without analysing the consequences for Roussillon, we can say that with no initial planning yet with increasing interest, it tried to attract the Catalan elite – its offspring – from Roussillon, control the Church and cut off trade with the south. What were its real objectives? To distance Roussillon from the Spanish world, both culturally and politically, under the baton of a Catalan elite (from the Principality) which the French (erroneously) believed was more influential than it actually was.

Despite this, at no time did the French monarchy give up on the possibility of conquering the Principality yet again: for some it was the main goal, with the idea of reunifying Catalonia and annexing it to France, while for others it was a tactic aimed at incapacitating Spanish military policy.

2. Violence and creation of identities

Languages and figures form the collective imagination and mythical discourse of peoples; that is, their mental representation of themselves and their prejudices about the other[10]. But what is a mental representation? How can it be captured in the everyday life of a specific society? France was a pioneer in the cultural and mental spread of ideas and policies. Regarding language, the notion of the linguistic takeover of French at the expense of other languages – started by Francis I in Villers-Cotterêts and carried out by successive royal administrations in France, including most importantly Richelieu's – worked towards the expansion of a certain French nationalism (although this term was not yet coined), that is, a strengthening of the

9 Didier Baisset, *Politique et religion dans le diocèse d'Elne (1659-1715). Contribution à l'étude du processus d'assimilation de la province du Roussillon au Royaume de France* (Toulouse: Université de Toulouse 1, PhD Dissertation, 1997), pp. 10-11; Narcís Iglésias, *La llengua del Rosselló, qüestió d'Estat [La integració lingüística del Rosselló a França (1659-1789)]* (Girona: Eumo Editorial, 1998).

10 Suzanne Gély, "Figures et langages de l'idée européenne, de Ramon Llull à Komensky: du mythe au projet", *L'Europe à la recherche de son identité* (Paris: Le Comité des Travaux Historiques et Scientifiques, 2002), pp. 361-374.

identity feeling of the linguistic nation of the elites linked to the monarchy of France: with its self-awareness, France managed to surpass limits that had been set by always looking into the mirror of the Spanish monarchy[11]. Language and concepts, territory and community, and finally the creation of identities through war are the main strands in the analysis of the incipient emergence of collective consciousness in the Modern Age.

Concepts and language

Written statements or those transcribed from oral language during the period when France occupied or was at the threshold of the Principality might be a sign of the concept that was held reciprocally, since without this presence or any reason to speak about it, conceptual opinions and reflections might have never had a literary translation. Therefore, language was important when expressing everyday opinions regarding the foreign, but also of any element foreign to the society where the communication was taking place. Thus, even though many of the trials in Roussillon involved locals, and they had an interest in avoiding retaliation, some expressions and concepts used shed light on their opinion of the French in general, and, in contrast, the representation of themselves contained in the testimonies, particularly of themselves as a people.

The mirror effect also plays an important role. Having a referent to recognise and portray situated the entire ethnic group in question in a position of self-recognition. However, the written and oral language and the legal elements, among others, made this group increasingly homogenous. France's presence – and politics – unquestionably stepped up the crystallisation of the national consciousness of the Catalans living in the countships, and eventually among all the communities in the Principality that suffered continuously from the effects of the French throughout the second half of the 17th century.

Likewise, France's language policies had a clear target in the countships of Catalonia, namely the favoured groups and ruling classes, thus ignoring the populace as a whole. It is difficult to deny the effects that

11 Jean-Frédéric Schaub, *La France espagnole. Les racines hispaniques de l'absolutisme français* (Paris: Seuil, 2003).

this might have had on these elites' change in ascriptive mind-set with the monarchy. First, they could no longer ask for any more privileges, given the disappearance of the Catalan institutions, and secondly language became a social distinction and yet another means of social promotion and appearance.

On the social, political or literary level, maintaining Catalan may seem insignificant. However, the different episodes of French interference, especially in the administrative and religious realms, made the Catalan language a part of the identity under attack. After the first French rules, the use of Catalan in writing or in the other areas covered – that is, in all spheres in general except in the communities – entailed not only a defiance of French authority but also, more importantly, a newfound awareness among large swaths of the population of their own language, a language which had been written for years and served for more than oral communication. Despite this, the evolution of the language in Roussillon seems to show two things: the common practice of writing Catalan both in wealthier homes and more prominently in Church circles (*goigs* ["religious couplets"], sermons and other writings)[12].

The space: Between land and community

The examples of the Cerdagne and Roussillon enable us to pinpoint the majority of symptoms which researchers into national identity claim shape the emergence of a group consciousness that goes beyond the restricted community, with identification referents that go beyond the *land* in the strict sense. Peter Sahlins extends the identity of Cerdagne natives to other places in Catalonia in terms of their preference for the Spanish monarchy. We believe that while this does indeed seem true, during the second half of the 17th century it is truer in the north of the Principality than in its more southern lands. In this historian's opinion, the opposing force between these groups and the obligation to elect a governor might explain Catalan identity[13].

12 Enric Prat, Pep Vila, *Mil anys de llengua i literatura catalanes al Rosselló* (Canet: Trabucaire, 2002), pp. 174-283; Narcís Iglésias, *La llengua del Rosselló...*

13 Peter Sahlins, *Frontières et identités nationales. La France et l'Espagne dans les Pyrénées depuis le XVIIe siècle* (Paris: Editions Belin, 1996), p. 126 (original

We must thus evoke collective representations of communities like those in the Cerdagne or Vallespir regarding models of social belonging, for example. That is, this is a model where the sense of belonging to an identity-based supra-group emerges from the inside out. This would be the classic pattern of concentrically-shaped ethnocentrism. However, Sahlins mentions the disadvantages of this system for being able to observe identities globally: *ce système a l'inconvénient de ne pas rendre compte de tout ce qui, dans un sentiment d'identité, relève de l'opposition à l'autre, si patente dans les zones frontalières et notamment dans la zone catalane*[14] ("this system has the disadvantage of not being accountable, in a sense of identity, for responsibility for opposition to the other, so patent in border areas, and especially in the Catalan area"). The community sees itself represented in its peers through an entire series of elements – language, religion, customs, etc. – and thus abandons the sole notion of ties to the land.

Therefore, the appearance of identity expressions in these places near the Pyrenees border, since they were near the French presence, was somehow an initial local reaction to the monarchy's desire to transform the administrative and ideological structures of the kingdom into a true State where internal discord had no place. Obviously, France displayed this trend before Spain, a fact that did not go unnoticed in the potentially affected areas, especially when mirrored by the changes in Roussillon. What came into play then was a set of national identifications that Sahlins comments on by saying *l'identité nationale consiste à substituer à l'amour du territoire local celui d'un territoire national*[15] ("national identity consists of replacing a love for the local territory for that of a national territory"). Seeking a centralised identification in the monarchy, the State thus gradually became an oppressive – military and fiscal – apparatus in a bid to demonstrate vertical control over the territories, even the faraway

version: Peter Sahlins, *Boundaries: The Making of France and Spain in the Pyrenees* [Berkeley: University of California Press, 1989]).

14 Peter Sahlins, *Frontières et identités nationales...*, pp. 128-129; Peter Sahlins, "Centrar la periferia: la Cerdaña entre Francia y España", *España, Europa y el mundo Atlántico. Homenaje a John H. Elliott*, Richard L. Kagan, Geoffrey Parker, eds. (Madrid: Marcial Pons-Historia-Junta de Castilla y León, 2001), pp. 299-317; Marshall D. Sahlins, *Las sociedades tribales* (Barcelona: Editorial Labor, 1984), p. 31; Claude Lévi-Strauss, *Raza y Cultura* (Madrid: Cátedra, 2000), p. 47 (1st edition: Claude Lévi-Strauss, *Raza y Cultura* [Madrid: Editorial Unesco, 1952]).

15 Peter Sahlins, *Frontières et identités nacionales...*, p. 24.

ones. Zones like the Cerdagne lived under the shadow of war for over 60 years, but also it spanned the border, a border which became a space that the people made their own: *s'approprient de leurs frontières et identités pour s'en servir –contre ou en collaboration avec– des centres politiques éloignés*[16] ("they take over their borders and identities to use them -against or in collaboration with- distant political centers"). This was one of the options we had analysed in the case of certain families who owned properties on either side of the border. However, throughout the second half of the 17th century, the lands of the Cerdagne, just like those of the Empordà, proved to be steadfastly against France and enraged with their oblivion in the capital of the Principality. The integration and identity of the individual in society came through levels of belonging and proximity, giving rise to a shared crystallisation of identity in developed pre-modern societies, that is, in those that had a political system, a legal system, myths and a written language[17].

Identities and counter-identities

The source of identities in the Modern Age came primarily from the offensive identities confronting them. For this reason, we shall schematically cite the most important and necessary aspects to be highlighted, such as the relationship between society and political consciousness, yet also and more importantly the inextricable ties between war and identity. It is possible to find first-hand testimonies in personal diaries and account books of individuals who experienced this and conveyed what they saw subjectively[18].

Political consciousness spread at a time when there was a desire for assembly, that is, a desire to gather with one's peers in the community in order to deal with an external aggression. The more threatening the

16 Peter Sahlins, *Frontières et identités nacionales…*, p. 15.

17 François-Pierre Gingras, Jean Laponce, "A la recherche des représentations d'appartenance", *L'individu et le citoyen dans la société moderne* (Québec: Les Presses de l'Université de Montréal, 2000), pp. 165-184.

18 Among others, we have analysed the identity-war relationship and personal writings in: Oscar Jané, "L'identité et la guerre dans les livres de raison catalans au XVII siècle", *Annales du Midi*, 270 (2010), pp. 251-278.

prospect, the more the range of what community encompassed had to expand. Thus, the (physical and temporal) dimensions of the conflicts in the late 17th century led some zones of Catalonia to search for shared identities as an unconscious, counter-identity remedy. The formation of its own identity could thus emerge from the notion of traumatic repetition. This simple idea conceals the complexity of social relations and the awakening of a consciousness of belonging. A sense of co-belonging develops between the territory and the community which is indispensable for developing a collective identity through an intuitive consciousness that the individual may have of belonging to a relatively heterogeneous community: *le sentiment de l'appartenance avait accompagné la trajectoire subjective d'un peuple ou d'une nation, encore que le 'peuple' soit un mauvais conducteur de cette subjectivité et la 'nation' le creuset idéal, voire le sillon de tout sentiment de co-appartenance vécu à l'échelle collective*[19] ("the feeling of belonging accompanied the subjective path of a people or a nation, although the 'people' is a poor conductor of this subjectivity and 'nation' the ideal crucible or the furrow of any sense of co-ownership experienced on a collective scale").

In turn, war is clearly involved in promoting hatred, fear and counter-identities. The idea of the relationship between war – in all its violence aspects – and identity is a fundamental cornerstone of the relationship between Catalonia and France between 1640 and 1697, the date when the French completed their seizure of the capital of the Principality by force[20]. The historiography of identity regards war and aggressions – and

19 Malek Chebel, *La formation de l'identité politique* (Paris: Presses Universitaires de France, 1986), pp. 78-79.

20 Antoni Simon had studied this relationship for a shorter time, around the era of the Catalan Revolt (v. 1630 - v. 1640) and more generically for the entire Modern Age: Antoni Simon, *Els orígens ideològics de la revolució catalana de 1640* (Barcelona: Publicacions de l'Abadia de Montserrat, 1999), pp. 219-230; Antoni Simon, "'Catalans' i 'francesos' a l'edat moderna. Guerres, identitats i contraidentitats. Algunes consideracions", *Pedralbes*, 18/2 (1998), pp. 391-401, and even more strikingly in: Antoni Simon, *Construccions polítiques i identitats nacionals…*; Antoni Simon, *Pau Claris, líder d'una classe revolucionària* (Barcelona: Publicacions de l'Abadia de Montserrat, 2008). In turn, Antonio Espino was the first to mention this analysis for the late 17th century: Antonio Espino, *Cataluña durante el reinado de Carlos II: política y guerra en la frontera catalana, 1679-1697* (Bellaterra: Universitat Autònoma de Barcelona, 1999).

we should add ones that continue over time – as a crucial factor in turning ethnic communities into nations.

Under these conditions, although it is true that collectives like those in Roussillon seemed to have a greater identity consciousness than any in Catalonia, the lack of a political referent and the presence and extent of the perennially strong image of the king of France might have created identity schizophrenia. In the south, the explicit reactions to the War of the Spanish Succession confirmed a prior collective ideological entrenchment, and in addition to the Castilians and the chronic policy of confrontation, the French became the referent of a warring and cultural enemy, allowing for the gestation of independent and politically innovative pathways[21].

3. Adaptation and consciousness of identity

In Catalonia, there was a political and social adaptation to the aggressor which did not exist as such throughout the entire country in 1640. The situation felt at first in Roussillon spread around the Principality, especially in northern Catalonia, including the Pyrenees, the inland regions and part of the Girona coastline. The issue of socio-territorial adaptation is fundamental: this north had an interrelationship with the presence and attacks of the French throughout the entire second half of the 17th century and became the most affected part where the strongest rejection or at least the most consideration of the French emerged. The acceptance of reality led to different kinds of battles: from Roussillon inland, and from the south of L'Albera defensively, and through compromises with Barcelona and Girona. The consolidation of a national consciousness zone by zone is one of the adaptations and consequences of France's pressure on the new border at the Pyrenees.

Another adaptation was the mental representation of the new foreigners in Spain: the people from Roussillon and part of the Cerdagne, when in reality they demonstrated that their ties with the Principality were

21 Antoni Simon, *Del 1640 al 1705. L'autogovern de Catalunya i la classe dirigent catalana en el joc de la política internacional europea* (València: Publicacions de la Universitat de València, 2011).

stronger than ever. There thus developed the case of double foreignness for many, and triple for some of the elites in the Principality – those who left and returned. So why evoke Roussillon if it was a foreign territory after 1659? First, for years this has been the attitude of Catalan historiography of the Principality. And, in fact, in the Modern Age, Perpignan, the capital of Roussillon, became the second most important city in Catalonia after Barcelona in terms of its economic and political clout. Thus, omitting or forgetting what happened in that territory and that society would be tantamount to neglecting the reality of the period.

Finally, it is worth determining the structural and/or ideological values that France promoted with its policy in Catalonia in the late 17th century, which would demonstrate an identity cohesion among the Catalan people and especially their newfound awareness. In addition to natural factors like space, constructions and climate – see the thought-provoking contributions by Henry Kamen and Fernand Braudel[22] – certain factors were fundamental in shaping this identity:

a. Language was one of the policies to which the Catalan elites in Roussillon had to adapt, as did other institutions like the Church and politics. It went from being a natural factor to a fundamental element of France's policies, both to get the elites on board and to spread the image of a king united with his peoples and land. In turn, it was a tripartite element: French was the language of power, cohesiveness (solidarity) and discrimination against foreigners or anyone speaking other languages.
b. Religion or religiosity: This is one of the main elements binding people together. It was fundamental in rural life and highlighted differences (such as when the French were popularly rejected after the late 16th century as being suspected of being Huguenots). In wars and conflicts it became a political and social element more than just a purely religious one. The resistance could be either active or passive, although the main problem of adaptation in France was that the Church

22 Henry Kamen, "Cultura i solidaritats dels catalans: època moderna", *Actes del IV Congrés Internacional d'Història Local de Catalunya: El cor urbà dels conflictes: identitat local, consciència nacional i presència estatal* (Barcelona: L'Avenç, 1999), pp. 7-20; Fernand Braudel, *L'identité de la France* (Lonrai: Flammarion, 2000), pp. 32-177.

powers in Roussillon were Spanish. In other cases, the reaction was more violent. Finally, religious cultural and artistic representations filled peoples' everyday lives, spreading a local religiosity that ran counter to the desires of the French monarchy.

c. Wars: The counter-identities promoted by wars, and especially by their extension over time (60 years of war and intermittent superimposed threats) in the same territory, are one of the prime factors in the "adaptation" to France. Solidarity overcame the limits of the "land" (proximity, markets, mountain- and coastal-dwelling peoples) and gained ground as a shared element against the French all over the most affected Catalan lands.

d. Tradition, customs and memory: The referent of both collective and individual memories was France's actions against Catalonia since the Catalan Revolt, just as earlier the referent had been the actions of the Castilian troops in the Catalan countryside, as they trampled upon the Catalans' constitutional privileges and rights. Memory creates myths and legends in which everyone, based on self-hatred or even phobia of the (known) other, belongs to a homogeneous group in terms of both political and cultural characteristics[23].

e. The prince: This is the element of balance in the midst of rejections and hatreds. Now we know, as was known then as well, that the king was still a mythical, superior figure whom everyone exculpated of all evil. However, in view of this Francophobia, the announcement of a *French* king in the kingdom of Spain was a real trial. The quest for an alternative within the Habsburgs seemed to demonstrate attachment to the princely conditions of the old regime. The origins of the "vanquished Catalonia" can be found in this identity *adaptation* to France after 1640.

23 Maurice Halbwachs, *La mémoire collective* (Paris: Albin Michel, 1997) (1st edition: Maurice Halbwachs, *La mémoire collective* [Paris: Presses Universitaires de France, 1950]). The idea of collective memory and its relationship with time, space and history are fundamental in the formation of group identity.

Conclusion

These ideas and explanations indicate, if you will, the evolution of the ethnic community, as it was known until then, and its transformation into a nation[24]. The continuity over time enables us to say that a consciousness of collective identity was forged, albeit by geographic zones. The actions of the French monarchy – and that of its most direct representatives – could not have gone unnoticed in the eyes of the Catalan peoples, even less so bearing in mind the local institutions' early involvement with France. The peak of Francophobia in Catalonia came with the seizure of Barcelona in 1697, after several years of propagandistic attacks against France and the military in the opposite direction, and Philip d'Anjou's pretensions for the Spanish crown. The shift to hatred stemmed from fear, from exhaustion after so many years of war and threats, from political intoxication, from a failure to respect the pacts and alliances, and finally from the familiar example of Roussillon, where French policies were taking root. Faced with an increasingly powerful enemy, the sociological explanations gain strength alongside the purely political ones, no doubt leading to a crystallisation of collective consciousness and unique identity, especially in the northern half of Catalonia in the late 17th century. The "weight" of the border marked the identity dynamic of northern Catalonia in all senses.

24 The personification of the collective is one of the characteristic features that verifies a common identity assimilated in the individuals that make up the ethnic community (associated with a specific territory): Edmond Marc Lipiansky, "Comment se forme l'identité des groupes", *L'identité. L'individu, Le groupe, La société*, Jean-Claude Ruano-Borbalan, ed. (Auxerre: Editions Sciences Humaines, 1999), pp. 143-147.

Catalan National Identity in the 18th Century. The War of the Spanish Succession and the Bourbon Regime

Cristian Palomo Reina
Universitat Autònoma de Barcelona

1. Approach

The purpose of this chapter is to analyse the national identity of Catalans during the 18th century, with special attention on the period of the War of the Spanish Succession. To do this, we shall focus on the main features displayed by the national/patriotic collective identities[1] and their corresponding patriotisms[2] in Europe and the Old Regime and apply them to Catalonia during this time period[3]. Calling these collective identities national forces us to take a stance in the complex debate on the

1 We shall use the expressions "national identity" and "patriotic identity" synonymously and alternate them throughout the text.

2 Even though the word "patriotism" did not appear until the 18th century, in the preceding centuries it was historiographically used by many others to refer to what Eulalia Duran has described as: *el sentiment d'amor a les coses pròpies, terra, institucions, llengua, etc.* ("the feeling of love of one's own things, land, institutions, language, etc."). Eulàlia Duran, "Patriotisme i mil·lenarisme al segle XVI", *Recerques: Història, economia i cultura*, 32 (1995), pp. 7-18. The quote is from p. 7.

3 For a clear-sighted overview of these features which reveals how contemporary national identity and today's nationalisms differ, see the presentation of the monographic dossier that the "Grup de Recerca Manuscrits" from the Universitat Autònoma de Barcelona devoted to this topic: Antoni Simon, "Presentació", *Manuscrits. Revista d'història moderna*, 19 (2001), pp. 17-20. For a similar study centred specifically on Catalonia during the Catalan Revolt, see: Xavier Torres, "Un patriotisme sense nació: què va ser l'anomenada Guerra dels Segadors (1640-1652/1659)?", *Notícia nova de Catalunya*, Josep Maria Fradera, Enric Ucelay, eds. (Barcelona: Centre de Cultura Contemporània de Barcelona, 2005), pp. 61-96.

contemporariness or ancientness of nations[4], without losing sight of the fact that ultimately this is a conceptual debate that depends both on the meaning we assign to words or expressions today and the historical meanings they had in the past[5].

We first consider national or patriotic identities in the late Middle Ages and Modern Age, at least those found in Western Europe, as collective identities of human groups whose individuals, for a variety of reasons, felt like, identified themselves as and were identified by others as members of a more or less abstract entity with more political than cultural-linguistic underpinnings, called terms like *patria* ("fatherland") or "nation" depending on the place, time and context. This generated in these individuals feelings of loyalty to this entity, its symbolic elements and other people regarded as fellow members.

Secondly, we view the formation and consolidation of patriotic identities, at least in the aforementioned territorial sphere, as long-term historical processes whose roots were in the late Middle Ages and which evolved over time, transforming, being reinvented and expanding until reaching the mass society of the contemporary centuries. Nonetheless, we do not necessarily have to regard this as a predetermined, linear, or simply accumulative process[6].

4 Approaches to this debate can be found in: Anthony D. Smith, *Nacionalismo y Modernidad: un estudio crítico de las teorías recientes sobre naciones y nacionalismo* (Madrid: Istmo, 2000); Xavier Torres, "La historiografia de les nacions abans del nacionalisme (i després de Gellner i Hobsbawm)", *Manuscrits. Revista d'història moderna*,19 (2001), pp. 21-42; Oscar Jané, *Catalunya i França al segle XVII: identitats, contraidentitats i ideologies a l'època moderna: 1640-1700* (Catarroja-Barcelona: Editorial Afers, 2006), pp. 35-70.

5 The importance of knowledge of historical vocabulary is crucial because we need this knowledge in order to better grasp the mind-set of the men and women who came before us and to thus understand their way of living and their historical realities perhaps not fully but at least less from our own time perspective.

6 About the historical evolution of the patriotic/national Catalan Identity we share the theses of Pierre Vilar and Antoni Simon i Tarrés specifically for Catalonia: Pierre Vilar, *Estat, nació, socialisme: estudis sobre el cas español* (Barcelona: Curial, 1982); Antoni Simon, *Construccions polítiques i identitats nacionals. Catalunya i els orígens de l'estat modern espanyol* (Barcelona: Publicacions de l'Abadia de Montserrat, 2005). We share also the interpretative and chronological model applied by the medievalist Vicent Baydal over the evolution of the patriotic Valencian Identity throughout the Late Medieval and Modern periods because we think that a very

Finally, we believe that these ancient national identities coexisted with, were mixed with, were grounded upon, fed and sometimes clashed with other collective identities that were based on other family, religious, professional, estate, local, seigniorial and dynastic factors held by the very same individuals, leading to multiple loyalties.

Regarding the timeframe of the analysis, the first period we shall analyse is the War of the Spanish Succession in the Spanish kingdoms of the Iberian Peninsula (1705-1714). This war was first and foremost a conflict among the great European powers, primarily France and England, which happened because of the clash between the French Bourbon and Holy Roman Empire Habsburg dynasties over who would occupy the throne of the Spanish monarchy, which was clearly in the midst of international decline but still had world-encompassing territory and trade. Yet it was also a conflict among the kingdoms of Spain, most of which showed their support of the cause of the Bourbon Philip, Duke of Anjou, as the conflict wore on or, to the contrary, the Archduke of Austria, Charles, a clash of two political conceptions that affected the organisation and form of governance of the monarchy and its kingdoms[7].

---

similar evolution was done in the Catalan Case (Vicent Baydal, "'Què som, i per què som com som'. Un nou model interpretatiu per a l'evolució històrica de la identitat col·lectiva valenciana", Vida amunt i nacions amunt. Pensar el País Valencià en temps de globalització, Manuel Lanusse, Joan A. Martínez, August Monzón, eds. [València: Publicacions de la Universitat de València, 2008], p. 179-213). We believe that these more accurately reflect the reality than the contemporary thesis on nations, because even though these often have well-founded arguments, they seem deficient to us. Exclusive axioms arose (such as the one that asserts that without contemporary nationalism there could be no nation) based on one of the conceptual interpretations of the term "nation" which ignores pre-contemporary identities, which leads to a limitation in the perspective they afford as they are insufficient to realistically encompass such complex historical processes that spanned so many years, such as the formation and evolution of modern states and nations. Nor do we support the interpretations by historians who find no differences between medieval and/or modern nations and those from the contemporary period. Our disagreement with this view stems from the fact that, even though we believe that feelings of national or patriotic identity in the late Middle Ages or Modern Age might be similar or equal to the ones today, the political, social, economic, cultural and legal context that generated and modulated them has totally changed, meaning that the identity conceptions, symbols and values have also mutated.

7 Joaquim Albareda, *El "Cas dels catalans": la conducta dels aliats arran de la Guerra de Successió: (1705-1742)* (Barcelona: Fundació Noguera, 2005), p. 12.

The second period we shall focus on, albeit more briefly, begins with the resolution of this war, one of whose consequences was an in-depth political reformulation of the Spanish monarchy to make it more uniform and absolutist, especially on the Iberian Peninsula. Indeed, the Bourbons' victory on the peninsula led to the dismantlement of the state structures of Valencia, Aragon, Catalonia and Mallorca, which had been based on their own institutions and legal systems. In their place, the institutions and systems of Castile were imposed, rendering them conquered provinces where the Bourbon King Philip V and his successors would enjoy much more absolute sovereignty than the Spanish monarchs before them had. This marked an extraordinarily important turning point in the historical evolution of identity in Catalonia and Aragon. In the case of the Principality of Catalonia, the elimination of its own institutions and laws, one of the main underpinnings of the Catalan national/patriotic identity in the Middle Ages and early Modern Age, was coupled with systematic, omnipresent oppression perpetrated by the new regime over the population after the war and throughout most of the 18th century.

This long historical process of forming national identities was closely tied to the chronologically prolonged concurrent process of constructing state political forms: public governance regimes with the power to exercise exclusive sovereignty over a territorial domain and its inhabitants, some of which, after numerous transformations, ended up becoming the contemporary states in the 19th century[8]. In consequence, in order to understand any pre-contemporary national identity, we must first properly define these political structures. In some cases, such as Catalonia, the problem arises when attempting to define this state framework.

8 About the medieval bases of European States, see: Esteban Sarasa, "Fundamentos medievales del Estado Moderno", *Ius Fugit*, 3-4 (1994-1995), p. 487-498; Max Turull, "La formació del poder polític als segles XII-XV i els orígens medievals de l'Estat. Història política i història del dret: Bibliografia recent en llengua francesa (1984-1994)", *Anuario de Estudios Medievales*, 25 (1995), pp. 761-809. It is crucially important for historians to use both the concepts and the historical terminology carefully and properly, as they are fundamental tools in the cultivation of history. For this reason, we do not share many historians' reluctance to talk about the "state" in the Modern Age. The word "state" was used in that period and was even applied to many political communities, as we shall see. Therefore, we believe that what we should do is place the emphasis on explaining that the state in the Modern Age should not be confused with the contemporary state.

2. A Catalan state within a Spanish empire

Until the Bourbon victory in 1714, the state framework of the Catalans was the Principality, despite the existence of a Spanish empire of which it had been entailed since 1479, with the exception of a hiatus lasting a little over a decade in the wake of the Catalan Revolt. This statement itself could spark controversy because it contradicts the definition sustained by the majority of Spanish historiography on the structure of the monarchy of Spain, which views it as a single institutionally, culturally and legally plural federal state made up of lower-ranking, semi-autonomous political communities: the kingdoms, principalities or provinces. We find this conceptualisation of the Spanish empire of the Early Modern period a state difficult to accept, not only because of the term "state" in the current sense of public political system of governance applied to all of Spain as a single political community, which was not found on the peninsula until well into the 18th century[9], but also because we believe it springs from the classical theory of the Modern State[10]. This, despite having been deeply questioned and, seems that it has been overcome in some aspects such as the immediate assimilation among the concepts "centralization", "absolutism" and "progress"[11] is still entrenched in the vision of the Spanish monarchy, both

9 Jesús Lalinde, "Depuración histórica del concepto de Estado", *El Estado español en su dimensión histórica*, Jesús Lalinde, Antonio Pérez, eds. (Barcelona: Promociones y publicaciones universitarias, 1984), pp. 17-58, especially, pp. 50-54.

10 This is the predominant historical interpretation in the two preceding centuries which is still upheld by many others, even though in some respects it entails explaining the past based on the contemporary nation-state, taking for granted that the same structure had existed in the centuries of the Old Regime, while also equating absolutist, unifying and centralising historical deeds with progress and modernity. Regarding the classic theory of the Modern State see: Agustí Alcoberro, "Poder i societat al Renaixement: Estat modern i identitats nacionals", *Itineraris. Nou estudis sobre cultura al Renaixement*, Eulàlia Duran, Maria Toldrà, eds. (Valencia: Tres i Quatre, 2012), pp. 69-97, especially, pp. 69-71; Francesco Benigno, *Las palabras del tiempo. Un ideario para pensar históricamente* (Madrid: Cátedra, 2013), pp. 199-222.

11 For a debunking of the classical Modern State interpretation with regard to Catalonia, see: Josep Fontana, "La Guerra de Successió i les Constitucions de Catalunya: una proposta interpretativa", *Del patriotisme al catalanisme: societat i política (segles XVI/XIX)*, Joaquim Albareda, ed. (Vic: Eumo, 2001), pp. 13-29; Antoni Simon, "El moment d'Espanya. La guerra de Successió i la imposició d'un model polític

the Catholic Monarchs and the Habsburg monarchy, as a single "modern state" based on the Crown as an institution which developed a large bureaucratic administration, centralised taxation, permanent embassies and the logistics to assemble and maintain armies with hundreds of thousands of troops. Therefore, we share the reluctance of John H. Elliott and Núria Sales to call the Spanish monarchy a "state" in the early Modern Age[12], because envisioning it as a single decentralised state with more or less autonomous territories is incongruous from the perspective of the present[13]. By this, we do not mean the term "state" has never been used when talking about composite monarchies but that, when it was used, it didn't mean the same as for referring to political entities as Catalonia. In consequence, according to specialized bibliography that about the historical origin of the term when it appears in historical documentation referring to dynastic conglomerates such as the one of the Spanish monarch is to make reference to the hereditary/patrimonial power that a monarch executes or its dynasty over one or a union of different politic communities. This is why the Spanish king was counselled to guarantee the preservation and expansion of the hereditary states in a *Consejo de Estado* ("State Council"), which suggested him a series of political guidelines (*Razón de Estado*) focused in increasing its dominions and the power that was executed over them. However, since the 16th century, we can find the word *state* applied generically, although not usually, to approximately 500 political domains in which Europe was divided. These were the states in which the public power was executed legitimately over the population there and it was considered their own, regardless of being republican or monarchies, including in the last one kingdoms, principalities, dukedoms and earldoms with sovereign prince, in which many of them could be considered one-single state monarchies or be linked to one of the many dynastic conglomerates that existed in the continent. For example this is what happened with the Kingdom of Navarra, the Principality of Catalonia, the Duchy of Milan

nacional d'estat. Una valoració historiogràfica", *Afers: fulls de recerca i pensament*, 56 (2007), pp. 131-144.

12 John H. Elliott, "Catalunya dins d'una Europa de Monarquies compostes", *Pedralbes: Revista d'història moderna*,13/1 (1993), pp. 11-24. Specifically p. 17.

13 Núria Sales, "Podem parlar de la Catalunya dels Àustries com d'un estat? I on rau l'estatalitat, en les monarquies compostes?", *Manuscrits: Revista d'història moderna*, 15 (1997), pp. 23-32.

and the Countship of Flanders within the Spanish Habsburg monarchy[14]. According to this, in the second half of 16th century, the basque chronicler Garibay wrote the following statement with utter normality: *Cathaluña es uno de los poderosos Estados que en nuestros días hallamos en los Reinos de España* ("Catalonia is one of the powerful states that in our days we find among the Kingdoms of Spain"). Also, after a few decades, the publicity that was contrary to the one from the Count-Duke of Olivares asked King Philip IV to guarantee the total preservation of the Catalan constitutions, stating that: *en todas las edades, Reynos, señorías, y estados han sido las novedades y mudanças en el gobierno odiosas y ocasión de alborotos y motines*[15] ("the changes in the government had been hateful

14 The aforementioned states, or any other from their political category, should not be confused with the seigniorial or jurisdictional states granted by the prince as privileges to the nobility, such as the Duchy of Cardona or the Countship of Santa Coloma de Queralt, both located in the Principality of Catalonia. Nor should they be confused with the old vanished states, even if the sovereign prince kept the old titles out of tradition, such as the Kingdoms of Seville or Córdoba, which were absorbed by the Kingdom of Castile in the 13th century.

15 The quotes in: Esteban de Garibay, *Los XL libros del compendio historial de las chronicas y universal historia de todos los reynos de España*, 4 vols. (Barcelona: Edición de Esteban de Cormellas, 1628), vol. 4, p. 13 (available online); Ricardo García, "El concepte d'Espanya als segles XVI i XVII", *L'Avenç: revista d'història i cultura*, 100 (1987), pp. 38-51. Besides those already mentioned, in the Modern Age, the term "state" had a variety of meanings which had gradually accumulated since the Middle Ages. For example, it could indicate how to be or situation. Both, it could indicate the individual's condition as the holder of a set of privileges which placed them within the social hierarchy in the Old Regime. It could also refer to political estates (also known in Catalonia as the *braços* or branches) into which societies were divided; the assembly of these estates to politically represent a kingdom, principality or domain was called, among other things, the Estates-General, *General* or *Juntes de Braços*. At the same time, the term "state" was used to refer to the jurisdictional and fiscal seigneuries, both secular and ecclesiastic, in their territorial dimension. Regarding the semantics of the word "state" during these centuries, see: Bernard Gunée, *Occidente durante los siglos XIV y XV, los Estados* (Barcelona: Labor, 1973); Jesús Lalinde, "Depuración histórica...", pp. 32-36; Bartolomé Clavero, *Tantas personas como estados: por una antropología política de la historia europea* (Madrid: Tecnos, 1986), pp. 80 and 81; Pablo Fernández, *Fragmentos de monarquía: trabajos de historia política* (Madrid: Alianza, 1992), pp. 86-88; Charles Tilly, *Coerción, capital y Estados europeos: 990-1990*, (Madrid, Alianza, 1992); Maurizio Viroli, *De la política a la razón de Estado. La adquisición y transformación del lenguaje político (1250-1600)* (Tres Cantos: Akal, 2009).

and caused uproar in all the ages, kingdoms, lordships and states"). Compared to this, despite the historiographic interpretations which were based solely on the absolutist discourses of the period[16], statality and sovereignty in the Modern Age did not require –anywhere or totally– only a prince and his administration, who were, incidentally, charged with the foreign relations and justice in the kingdom. Instead, it also required other institutions representing the interests of the subjects, such as parliaments, deputations and municipal governments. For this reason, despite the polysemy of the word "state", only those political communities with public regimes made up of a royal administration and local institutions can be considered states in the Modern Age within the sphere of empires or composite monarchies. That is, the states were the kingdoms, principalities and provinces making up the empires or composite monarchies, while in many states, just as in the late Middle Ages, sovereignty was exercised to the binomial monarch-estates in the Courts[17]. The fact is that, in Spain,

16 See, for example: Aquilino Iglesia, "Sobre el concepto de Estado", Centralismo y autonomismo en los siglos XVI-XVII: homenaje al profesor Jesús Lalinde Abadía, Aquilino Iglesia, Sixto Sánchez-Lauro, eds. (Barcelona: Universitat de Barcelona, 1990), pp. 213-240; Aquilino Iglesia, "La realidad estatal catalana", Manuscrits: Revista d'història moderna, 13 (1995), pp. 123-142.

17 In fact, in the late medieval centuries in Western Europe, setting aside the casuistics of the republics, there was a state-like political structure of many historical monarchic communities assembled around a royal power that served as the backbone of the public regime in each of its main domains. In this period, these public regimes were called expressions like *res publica*, "kingdom" or "principality", among other terms, and they were represented by the oligarchic elites of the three or four estates making up the feudal society in each domain. In these incipient medieval states, sovereignty was exercised according to the degree of absolute power that the prince was able to impose on his subjects, which was more or less limited by the strength of the estates to counterbalance him. This often gave rise to a constitutional system, that is, a system of institutional and legal controls over the monarch's exercise of political power, and to mixed government between the prince and the states. These two poles of power (sovereign prince and representatives of the people) were explained using the corporativist metaphor of *corpus mysticum*, comparing the monarch to the head and the estates to the parts of the body, with the entire political body being what we understand as the medieval state. Regarding the dialectic of sovereignty in the Principality of Catalonia during the late medieval centuries, see: Flocel Sabaté, "El poder soberano en la Catalunya bajomedieval: definición y ruptura", *Coups d'État à la fin du Moyen Âge? Aux fondements du pouvoir politique en Europeoccidentale*, François Foronda, Jean-Philippe Genet, José Manuel Nieto, eds. (Madrid: Casa de Velázquez,

just as in so many other powers of the day, because of the historical precedents of inheritances, marriages and conquests, the sovereign prince did not rule over a single kingdom/principality rather over several, giving rise to a pluri-state empire[18]. As the Castilian jurist Juan de Solórzano stated in

---

2005), pp. 484-498. In the Modern Age, the corporativist metaphor was still used, as clearly seen by Roussillon native Andreu Bosch in the 17th century: *Los estats o estaments de Cathalunya, Rosselló y Cerdanya dividits en tres ordens en son origen formaren un cos o Republica general per lo cap lo Princep, per Brassos los tres estats Eccleciasitich, Militar y Reyal* ("The states and estates of Catalonia, Roussillon and Cerdanya divided into three orders in their origin are made up of a body or general Republic headed by the Prince, by Arms the three estates Ecclesiastic, Military and Royal"), cited by: Núria Sales, "Abans de 1714: cap a una democratització de les institucions catalanes", *La Commemoració de l'Onze de Setembre a Barcelona* (Barcelona: Ajuntament de Barcelona, 1994), pp. 96-104 (the quote is on p. 96). It was also used to explain composite monarchies like Spain's, where the king was the head and each principality, kingdom or province was part of the body. Xavier Gil, "Un rey, una fe, muchas naciones", *La Monarquía de las naciones: patria, nación y naturaleza en la monarquía de España*, Antonio Álvarez-Ossorio, Bernardo José García, eds. (Madrid: Fundación Carlos de Amberes, 2004), pp. 39-76, especially, p. 52. The dialectic which we mentioned above in this footnote continued into the early Modern centuries, and in many states, such as the ones in the Crown of Aragon, mixed government took root since both poles of power continued to jointly legislate, the foremost attribute of sovereignty. However, in other states, such as the Kingdom of Castile, the sovereignty was executed almost exclusively by the prince since this process of imposition and attraction of the elites to the monarchic administration which got underway in the late Middle Ages and gained momentum with a number of events such as the defeat of the Communes in 1521, the clergy's and nobles' failure to attend the Courts since 1539 and the centralist, royalist programme of Olivares. And while this does not mean that there was no Castilian constitutionalism and that the Castilians did not sometimes advocate mixed government as the best form of government for Castile, it never took root. Regarding these issues related to constitutionalist thinking, mixed government in Castile and the kingdoms of the Crown of Aragon, see: Joan Pau Rubiés, "La idea del gobierno mixto y su significado en la crisis de la Monarquía Hispánica", *Historia Social*, 24 (1996), pp. 57-81. For a comparative look at other European states, by the same author: Joan Pau Rubiés, "El constitucionalisme català en una perspectiva europea: conceptes i trajectòries, segles XVI-XVIII", *Pedralbes: Revista d'història moderna*, 18 (1998), pp. 453-474.

18 The marriage between Ferdinand of Aragon and Isabel of Castile and the subsequent dynastic union consolidated in the figures of Joanna I of Castile and Aragon and the Habsburg Charles V, which gave rise to the Spanish monarchy, took place under Catalan-Aragonese political and legal principles, despite the de facto Castilian hegemony. Antoni Simon, "Patriotisme i nacionalisme a la Catalunya moderna.

the 17th century, there were two ways of unifying territories to form these empires. The first was as an "accessory", that is, by annexing all or part of a kingdom or province to another such that the former became politically and legally part of the latter. One example is Castile and León, which since the late Middle Ages was legally a single state whose legal system was spread to the kingdoms of the Indies as if they were part of it. The second was the formula of *eaque principaliter*, that is, forming a binomial or conglomerate of political communities or different states, each keeping their own legality and political system[19]. This was the formula with which Castile as a whole was united with the kingdoms of the Crown of Aragon and the difference provinces of the Netherlands. In this way, despite the ideological construct of a united Spain, as perceived outside the monarchy because of the joint, coordinated foreign policy among all the Spanish kingdoms by the royal administration[20], the *Hispaniarum Rex* was not the monarch of any Spanish kingdom or state, rather he was, separately, the monarch of the different kingdoms, principalities and provinces of the Crowns of Aragon, Castile, Burgundy, Austria and Portugal –these last two lasted between 40 and 80 years, respectively– which was extended among territories from the Iberian Peninsula, the islands of the western

Mites tradicions i consciències col·lectives", *L'Avenç*, 167 (1993), pp. 8-16, especially, p. 9. As Jon Arrieta notes, these were the principles that had been developed between the 12th and 15th centuries, a precedent of composite monarchy in the western Mediterranean that was the basis of the composite Spanish monarchy in the early Modern Age. The same author tells us that the deputies from the territories of the defunct states of the Crown of Aragon which submitted the *Memorial de Greuges* to Charles III Bourbon in 1760 clearly understood this: that the legal and political model of the monarchy as a whole during the Habsburg period originally came from the Crown of Aragon. Jon Arrieta, "Entre Monarquía Compuesta y estado de las autonomías, rasgos básicos de la experiencia histórica española en la formación de una estructura política plural," *Ivs Fvgit*, 16 (2009-2010), pp. 9-72, especially, pp. 13-18 and 25-28.

19 Regarding Solórzano and the types of unions, see: John H. Elliott, *España, Europa y el mundo de ultramar: (1500-1800)* (Madrid: Taurus, 2009), p. 34. The quotes are from: Xavier Gil, "Un rey, una fe...", pp. 56 and 57.

20 Despite the fact that there was not always a perception of strong unity from abroad, as revealed by Xavier Gil in: Xavier Gil, "Visió europea de la monarquia espanyola com a monarquia composta segles XVI i XVII", *Recerques: història, economia, cultura*, 32 (1995), pp. 19-43.

Mediterranean, the Italian peninsula and Central Europe[21]. The multi-state structure of Habsburg Spain becomes clear due to existence of the lieutenants/viceroys and governors, that is, the monarch's *alter nos* functionaries who dealt with the different territorial domains, but, specially, due to the lack of the elements that belonged to the kind of state-like political communities of the period: general courts, a currency and an own tax system, a series of higher laws and a supreme court that ruled over the whole, an official language and even its own unique succession criteria. These elements did exist within each kingdom or principality, along with the old legal nationality called *natura*, which consisted of enjoying the prerogatives and privileges of a political community. Of course, this did not exist in common for all Spaniards but only privately for the Catalans, Aragonese, Valencians, Castilians, etc[22]. For this reason, it was necessary to create substantial legal fictions in both the multiplicity of the royal figure, which had as many natures as states[23], and in the fact that the territorial supreme councils situated in Madrid were part of the territory of the kingdoms on

21 We have not mentioned the islands and viceroyalties of the Atlantic, the Americas and the Pacific due to the fact that they have not been considered states from the Catholic King, considering that they were pagan states, their juridical and political arrangements that already existed were not respected, becoming territorial incorporations and accessorizes of Castile. As a consequence, they did not dispose of institutions such as the general court, the parliaments, deputations, etc, being from the other European states of the Spanish Monarchy.

22 Regarding the Catalan *natura*, see: Núria Sales, "Naturals i alienígenes: un cop d'ull a algunes naturalitzacions dels segles XV a XVIII", *Studia in honorem prof Martín de Riquer*, 3 vols. (Barcelona: Quaderns Crema, 1986), vol. 1, pp. 675-705. To learn about the difference between this *natura* and nationality today, see p. 691. However, this is a polysemic concept which was also applied to the relationship of loyalty among the subjects of each of a prince's domains (native vassals), who were faithful to their local prince because he was the hereditary prince, or because he was fair and respectful with his prerogatives, or because he was ethnically similar to his native vassals. Xavier Torres, "Els naturals i el rei natural en la Catalunya de la Guerra dels Segadors: a propòsit d'un sermó de Gaspar Sala (1641)", *Estudi General*, 21 (2001), pp. 221-240.

23 Jon Arrieta, "Formas de vinculación a la Monarquía y de relación entre sus reinos y coronas en la España de los Austrias. Perspectivas de anàlisis", *La Monarquía de las naciones: patria, nación y naturaleza en la monarquía de España*, Antonio Álvarez-Ossorio, Bernardo José García, eds. (Madrid: Fundación Carlos de Amberes, 2004), pp. 303-326 and 308.

which they advised Catholic King[24]. Therefore, the Spanish monarchy which reigned during the War of the Spanish Succession was legally and officially an empire made up of kingdoms, principalities or legal estates that were legally independent of each other[25] and that only shared the same sovereign prince and his monarchic administration[26]. This becomes clear in the British leaflet from 1714, *The case of catalans considered*, whose first page says:

> It's sufficient to observe, That the Province, of Catalonia, ever since its Subjection to the Crown of Spain, and becoming a Part of the Dominion, has always been govern'd by particular Laws of its own, Independent of any other Kingdom[27].

Despite this, in practice the unions between equals which made up the composite monarchies never remained in balance and instead one of them gained hegemony over the whole[28], usually the one with the most resources and legal facilities that could be used by the Crown. These territories were where the different princes established their permanent courts.

24 Xavier Gil, "Un rey, una fe...", pp. 49-54.

25 Pere Molas, *Manual de historia de España, Edad Moderna (1474-1808)*, 4 vols. (Madrid: Espasa Calpe, 1988), vol. 3, p. 107.

26 There can be a certain conceptual confusion due to the fact that the historiography often talks about kingdoms, principalities or provinces from the Old Regime that became independent from composite monarchies. At the same time, those states cannot become independent since they did not legally depend on any other state. As a consequence, when those monarchic states deposed their sovereign princes and dissociated them from their dynastic conglomerates, new states were not created *ex nihilo* but rather the dissociated states became: 1) free republics such as the brief Republic of Catalonia from 1641 or the one that created the seven united provinces from the Netherlands which did not manage to consolidate a substitute for Philip II; 2) crowns of one-single state, such as the kingdom of Portugal since 1640 or 3) monarchic states linked to another monarchy that already existed such as the case of the ephemeral Catalan Republic which, in order to confront the Spanish military power, was obliged to become a principality again in order to be connected to monarchy of France in 1641.

27 *The case of the Catalans consider'd. You gain, your ends, and damn them when you've done* (London: J. Baker, 1714). Cited by: Michael B. Strubell, ed., *Consideració del cas dels Catalans seguit de La deplorable història dels catalans* (Barcelona: Curial, 1992), p. 5: *Només cal constatar que el Principat de Catalunya, des de la seva subjugació a la corona d'Espanya, quan va esdevenir una part d'aquell domini, sempre ha estat governat per lleis pròpies, independents de qualsevol altre regne.*

28 John H. Elliott, "Catalunya dins d'una Europa...", p. 14.

In the case of Spain, the state where the central government of the monarchic institution was located was Castile, meaning that the other kingdoms or principalities largely became dependent on it, or at least on the Castilian elite at court. Under the control of the ruling class of Madrid, the state-like mechanisms of the royal administration developed over the course of the 16th and 17th centuries: embassies, armies, navies, royal taxation and bureaucracy. They grew incessantly apace with the constant wars in which the Spanish monarchy was enmeshed, while the other kingdoms of Spain found that the prince, one of the crucial components of their statality, lived and governed from abroad[29]. This meant that the political and institutional life of each state was experienced both in the state and in Castile.

3. Catalan national identity during the War of the Spanish Succession

In any event, the principality of Catalonia was not only the structure and political community of reference for Catalans, rather it was also their nation in the political sense of the term: an imaginary corporative person, independent of its members or individual components, liable to becoming a political subject or the subject of collective rights[30] which was capable of feeding a strong enough patriotism to militarily mobilise people under slogans like "defending the fatherland or dying for the fatherland". Nonetheless, it is imperative that the early modern semantics of the words *nació* ("nation") and *pàtria* ("fatherland") be clarified. Both were polysemic terms that had accumulated meanings throughout the ancient and medieval centuries. As Xavier Torres explains, the word "nation" was primarily used to designate a group of people who may share the same geographic provenance (from a village or city to a large territory or country), the same sovereign or feudal lord, the same genealogy and the same estate. Additionally, it was also used to refer to foreigners, as well as those

29 The monarch's absence could be buffered though never replaced with lieutenants/viceroys and governors.

30 Xavier Torres, *Naciones sin nacionalismo: Cataluña en la monarquía hispánica (siglos XVI-XVII)* (València: Universitat de València, 2011), p. 89.

who spoke the same language, even though there was not always an exact match between language and nation given that speakers of the same language may also be considered members of different nations. In short, the author asserts that the "Catalan nation" referred to the Catalans but did not denote a collective national identity that reflected any deed or political aspiration[31]. These conclusions seem overly univocal because of the different testimonies from the 17th and early 18th centuries that used the term "nation" to refer to Catalonia as a political structure or community, especially in the periods of conflict and war between Catalonia and the Crown. This is revealed in the 1714 leaflet entitled *Lealtad Catalana purificada de invidiosas calumnias*, which reads: *Sólo las resoluciones que se toman en Cortes de un Reino o provincias, son las que se atribuyen a la nación [...]. La nación, que sólo se representa en sus Brazos unidos. Toda la nación catalana, junta en los Brazos resolvió el defenderse por el rey en cuyo dominio estaba*[32] ("Only those resolutions that are taken in

31 Xavier Torres. *Naciones sin nacionalismo: Cataluña…*, pp. 56-57 and 79-89.

32 Cited by: Joaquim Albareda, "El XVIII: un segle sense política?", *Pensament polític als Països Catalans, 1714-2014: història i prospectiva*, Jaume Renyer, Enric Pujol, eds. (Barcelona: Centre d'Estudis de Temes Contemporanis-Pòrtic, 2007), pp. 71-92 (the quote is from p. 75). Another good example would be the anonymous leaflet from 1640 entitled *Cataluña defendida de sus emulos. Ilustrada con sus hechos. Fidelidad, y servicio à sus reyes* ("Catalonia defended from its rivals. Enlightened by its facts. Royalty, and service to its kings"), where we can read: *Assi en un mismo cuerpo de Reyno* (this expression was used to refer to the composite monarchy of Spain), *ha de haber Repúblicas, y Naciones adelantadas a las otras, en fueros, y Privilegios, concedidos del mismo, por los mayores ò menores servicios, que le han hecho. Y en esta parte, (como veremos) como Cataluña excedes à las demás Naciones de la Corona, ha sido también en esta parte, aventajada, à todas ellas* ("Thus in a sole body of Kingdom, there has to be Republics, and Nations more developed than others, in charters, and Privileges, conceded by the same, for greater or lesser services, that they have given. And in this part, (as we shall see) how Catalonia exceeds the other Nations of the Crown, it has also been in this part, at an advantage, over all of them"). Borja de Riquer, dir., Història, política, *societat i cultura dels* Països Catalans, 4 vols. (Barcelona: Enciclopèdia Catalana, 1995), p. 77. Another example is the 1705 expression by Manuel Coloma, Marquis of Canales, who when analysing the causes of the loss of Barcelona by Archduke Charles said to the Council of the Bourbon State: *La revelión de Cathaluña no [es] cosa nueva en aquella nazión, pues apenas se hallará en las historias algún siglo en muchos de los passados donde no haya subscedido algún acaestecimiento desta naturaleza (y son frecuentes en todos los principios de nuevos reynados, de que están llenas las historias que escusa acordar).*

the Courts of a Kingdom or provinces, are those that are attributed to the nation [...]. The nation, that is only represented in its united Arms. All the Catalan nation, together in the Arms resolved to defend itself for the king in whose domain it was").

With regard to the word "fatherland", the same author explains that for the Catalans of those centuries, in addition to meaning paradise (celestial fatherland) or referring to one's native village, city or region, it also unequivocally alluded to the Principality of Catalonia as a political entity, synonymous with or containing the pact-based Catalan laws[33]. Therefore, the *Despertador de Catalunya*, another sample of printed propaganda from 1714, exhorts the Catalans to follow the example of the Maccabees and be *forts i constants per les lleis i constitucions de sa pàtria*[34] ("strong and constant for the laws and constitution of theor homeland"). Other words

Pués aún en tiempos de los reyes de Aragón no estuvo quieto aquel Principado, sinó quando se halló oprimido de guarniciones y presidios ("the rebellion of Catalonia [is] not something new for that nation, as hardly a century in many will be found where nothing of this nature had occurred (and they are frequent in all the beginnings of new kingdoms, accord what the books of history has a lot of examples what I excuse to remember. So still in the times of the kings of Aragon, that Principality was not calm, but when it was oppressed by garrisons and prisons"), cited in: Antoni Simon, *Del 1640 al 1705. L'*autogovern de Catalunya *i la classe dirigent catalana en el joc* de *la política internacional europea* (Valencia-Barcelona: Universitat de València-Institut d'Estudis Catalans, 2011), p. 97. Finally, we shall mention the 1709 *Anales de Cataluña*, where Narcís Feliu de la Penya speaks about how national political communities, and not just a group of people, had reacted when writing their own history: *El cuidado de todas las naciones más políticas de Europa como Españoles, Italianos, Alemanes, Franceses y otros, fue descuido en la nación Catalana, que siempre supo obrar, pero jamás escrivir* ("The care of all the most political nations of Europe like the Spanish, Italians, Germans, French and others, was neglected in the Catalan nation, that always knew how to act, but never write") Cited by the aforementioned author in: Antoni Simon, *Construccions polítiques...*, p. 376.

33 For a more thorough explanation with examples of the word "*pàtria*" (fatherland) in medieval and early modern Catalonia, see: Flocel Sabaté, *El territori de la Catalunya medieval: percepció de l'espai i divisió territorial al llarg de l'edat mitjana* (Barcelona: Rafael Dalmau, 1997), pp. 349- 351; Xavier Torres, *Naciones sin nacionalismo. Cataluña...*, pp. 104-113.

34 The quote is from: Joaquim Albareda, ed., *Escrits polítics del segle XVIII. Tom 1. Despertador de Catalunya i altres textos* (Barcelona-Vic: Institut Universitari d'Història Jaume Vicens and Vives-Eumo, 1996), p. 145.

were also applied to Catalonia as a political entity, such as *terra* ("land") and *província* ("province")[35].

The fact that Catalonia was the fatherland and political nation of the inhabitants of the Principality does not mean that there was not a Spanish collective identity, nor that the Catalans were not part of it. We only have to refer to the last document published by the Catalan authorities on the 11th of September 1714, which says that the defenders of Barcelona, among them many refugees from other parts of Spain, were fighting: *a fi de derramar gloriosament sa sang i sa vida, per son Rei, per son honor, per la Pàtria i per la llibertat de tota Espanya* ("to spill their blood and their lives gloriously, for their King, for their honour, for the Homeland and for the freedom of all Spain"). Still, the fact that this was a collective identity does not mean that it forcibly had to be national, at least not in all the Hispanic political communities. For example, on the eve of the War of the

35 Just like the previous terms, the words "land" and "province" had also accumulated meanings in the ancient and medieval centuries. In addition to the more agricultural and local geographic meanings, as a region or territory within a city or county, "land" was also synonymous with peasants or rural folk and was a way of referring to Catalonia as an entity or political structure. Finally, in this sense, it was also synonymous with the three branches of the estates that represented the Catalan state. "Province" was a word that, like "nation", could be used to refer to a community of people. Still, it was primarily used to designate homogenous geographical divisions (counties or very extensive territories) or political divisions (administrative regions, states) that fell within a higher territorial or political entity. Thus, geographically Catalonia could be a province of (Peninsular) Spain or Europe, and Spain could be a province of Europe or the world, while politically the Kingdoms of Valencia and Aragon and the Principality of Catalonia could be called "provinces" of the monarchy of Spain without losing any degree of sovereignty. What is more, just like the word "land", "province" could also refer to the *res publica*; that is, the laws and estates representing these states could also be called "provinces". These politically-tinged meanings were extraordinarily successful in Catalonia as the 17th century wore on because of the snowball of constant clashes with the administration of the Spanish branch of the Habsburgs. For a more thorough explanation with examples of the use of the terms "land" and "province" in the Catalonia of the House of Aragon and the House of Habsburg, see: Flocel Sabaté, *El territori de la Catalunya medieval: percepció de l'espai i divisió territorial al llarg de l'edat mitjana* (Barcelona: Rafael Dalmau, 1997), pp. 352 and 366; Xavier Torres, *Naciones sin nacionalismo. Cataluña...*, pp. 89-104 and 114-120.

Spanish Succession, there were vivid imperial political-ideological aspirations[36] in Castile which, taking the part for the whole, equated Castile with all of Spain, replacing Castilians with Spaniards and at the same time continuing to seek unification through the political Castilianisation of the entire peninsula[37], despite the failure of the reformist programme of the Count-Duke of Olivares[38]. In contrast, the Catalans were considered

36 As Elliott tells us, these were common in the thinking generated in the central states of composite monarchies, especially if they exploited overseas imperial colonies, which not only highlighted their power over the other states in the monarchy but also helped them to think in terms of domination and subordination, which ran totally counter to the *eaque principaliter* union. John H. Elliott, "Catalunya dins d'una Europa...", p. 18.

37 With late-medieval forerunners, through the early modern period there had been a nominal assimilation of the concepts of "Castile" and "Spain" as historical, which ended up replacing the former with the latter in the Castilian collective imagination, while since the turn of the 16th century, different factors like the multiplication of war fronts overseas, the dissociation of the Spanish Habsburgs from the imperial title, the advance of the Protestant Reformation all over Europe, the rebellion in the Netherlands, the addition of Portugal into the Crown of Spain, the crisis in the human and material bases of Castile and the enormous costs of conserving a planet-wide empire led the intelligentsia in the Court of Madrid to seek a political ideal focused on the absolutist strengthening of royal power in order to transform the centre of the empire, the Iberian kingdoms, into a single Spanish state which was territorially compact and endowed with shared cultural ties and a Castilian matrix. Eulàlia Duran, "El comienzo de la modernidad", *Cuenta y Razón*, 36 (1988), pp. 25-32; Antoni Simon, *Construccions polítiques...*, pp. 30-38 and 42-133. With regard to this idea, a new meaning of the expression "Spanish nation" emerged. During those centuries, when speaking about the Spanish nation, this usually alluded to a set of people: both all the subjects of the King of Spain and only the habitats or people of the Iberian Peninsula, or the people from the Castilian territories or those who spoke the Castilian language. In contrast, when it had a political meaning it was generally used to refer to the Crown of Castile as a political community. The new meaning was political in nature and sprang from the Castilian elite at court such as the Count-Duke Olivares, who began to speak about the "Spanish nation", equating it with the political-territorial whole of the Iberian kingdoms, as if they were a single entity. Mateo Ballester, *La identidad española en la Edad Moderna (1556-1665). Discursos, símbolos y mitos* (Madrid: Tecnos, 2010), pp. 430-443.

38 The main purpose of the desire to Castilianise Spain was the spread of the Castilian legal system to the other kingdoms in order to make it easier for the king to extract their resources, while the Castilian cultural expansion towards the peripheral elites was tantamount to fostering their collaboration with the Court in the eyes of the monarch's functionaries.

Spaniards first because of geography, since they inhabited the Iberian Peninsula; secondly because of religion, since the Catalans and the other Spaniards shared the same faith, which at that time was regarded as an essential requirement for the community to live in peace and harmony; thirdly, because the sovereign prince of Catalonia was the monarch of the other kingdoms and provinces in an empire whose centre was the territory of Spain; and fourthly, because of the monarchy's imperial policy, which joined the Catalans with the other Spaniards against external powers and their interests. This struggle against the French enemy, which was particularly harsh and incessant during the second half of the 17th century, reinforced the Spanish identity of both the Catalans and the natives of the kingdoms of the Crown of Aragon[39]. However, unlike the Castilians, until well into the 18th century the Catalans lacked a political conceptualisation of Spain that would make it their national/patriotic referent[40]. This enables us to conclude that the Spanish identity of Catalans was geographic, Catholic, monarchic and primarily imperial, which was not incompatible with their Catalan national identity, whose main patriotic referent was the Principality and whose objective was to maintain its independence within the Spanish empire. Likewise, there was no national Catalan-Aragonese identity shared by the Iberian and Balearic subjects of the Crown of Aragon, since despite Catalonia's role as the hegemonic territory in the dynastic agglomeration under the dominion of the monarchs of Aragon during the late Middle Ages, this did not translate into a well-articulated and sufficiently powerful notion of a Catalan empire to politically unify the states governed by the Catalan House of Aragon. Thus, unlike the territories of other monarchies, such as Castile, there was no process of homogenisation and centralisation of the kingdoms in the Catalan-Aragonese states and they instead remained independent of each other, without shared political structures, besides the king and the institution of the monarchy, capable of creating shared adhesion[41]. Indeed, the natives of each territory were

39 Antonio Espino, *Guerra, fisco y fueros. La defensa de la Corona de Aragón en tiempos de Carlos II, 1665-1700* (Valencia: Universitat de València, 2007), p. 307.

40 Antoni Simon, *Construccions polítiques...*, p. 371.

41 In the 14th century there was an attempt to economically and administratively centralise the Catalan-Aragonese states by Catalan initiative carried out by King Peter III of Aragon, called Peter the Ceremonious, who tried to create a *Diputació del General* ("General Deputation") and a single economic and fiscal state common to all the

considered foreigners in the eyes of the others. Nor did this uniformity take place after the dynastic union of the Crowns of Aragon and Castile. What is more, throughout the Modern Age the process of dismantlement of the states of the Crown of Aragon intensified, not only because of the different internal evolutions in each kingdom but also because of the separate way each of them interacted with Madrid. At least after Olivares' ministry, the court sought to break the solidarities and common interests of the Catalan and Aragonese kingdoms and principality, each of which, in turn, yearned for royal favour in order to improve its position compared to the others[42], especially in the periods of crisis between some of the states and the Crown. Yet this does not negate the fact that at times of great shared danger, such as the invasions of Louis XIV and the War of the Spanish Succession, they worked together intensely[43] without ultimately sacrificing their unique interests. Nor did it prevent there from being a

kingdoms. This centralising policy, along with Peter's authoritarian reign, failed because of the needs created by the war with Castile, which led the king to depend on the courts of each state, consolidating a unique economic and taxation system in each of the kingdoms. Antoni Furió, Ferran Garcia-Oliver, "Temps de dificultats (1348-1400)", *Història de la Corona d'Aragó. Vol. 1: L'època medieval (1137-1479)*, Ernest Belenguer, dir. (Barcelona: Edicions 62, 2007), pp. 254-285. Regarding the numeration we have used, see the painstakingly documented article by the archivist and erudite medievalist (Jaume Riera, "La correcta numeració dels reis d'Aragó i comtes de Barcelona", *Afers*, 69 (2011), pp. 485-521), where it is clear that this was the historical numeration conceived by King Peter for himself and his dynasty and not the king who centuries later would be called Peter IV of Aragon, which is currently the name used the most outside of Catalonia. The numeration we use which King Peter said was the one that corresponded to him because of his lineage was also used by a wide variety of institutions and scholars and other monarchs, such as John I of Aragon when speaking about his ancestors Peter II "the Great" and his son James II the "Just" and Peter IV of Aragon, the constable of Portugal who when named king of Aragon and Count of Barcelona by the Council of the Principality of Catalonia during the Catalan Civil War used this numbering to legitimise himself as the successor of the sovereigns from the Barcelona line. Jaume Riera, "La correcta numeració...", pp. 500-518.

42 On this topic, see: Àngel Casals, "Del nom i la identitat de la Corona d'Aragó a l'edat moderna", *L'Avenç: Revista de història i cultura*, 275 (2002), pp. 29-35; Antoni Simon, *Construccions polítiques...*, pp. 148-154.

43 Antonio Espino, *Guerra, fisco y fueros...*, 2007; Carme Pérez, "Catalunya i València durant la Guerra de Successió. La comuna empresa de la llibertat", *Manuscrits. Revista d'història moderna*, 30 (2012), pp. 77-97.

similar shared identity to the one held with the King of Spain's other peninsular territories because they shared the same land, religion, monarch and outside enemies, although the link is stronger among closer religions. Indeed, Catalonia, Aragon, Valencia and Mallorca shared not only a long history of peaceful coexistence within the same composite monarchy but also greater political and cultural affinities among each other than with the other communities with which they interacted inside or outside the Spanish empire. In this sense, the documentation reveals clear signs of a Catalanic linguistic-cultural identity which included all Catalan speakers, including Mallorcans, Menorcans, Ibizans, Valencians and Catalans, who shared the same monarch or dynasty and were identified by the name of "Catalan nation", at least in the non-Catalan speaking world[44]. Despite this, the political-institutional uniqueness enjoyed by the inhabitants of the kingdoms of Valencia and Mallorca gave rise to the development of different patriotic identities than that of the Catalonia natives. Therefore, even though there was sometimes a kind of political-linguistic indeterminateness[45], because since the medieval centuries the Mallorcan and Valencian nations had appeared in the documentation referring to the natives of those territories or their respective kingdoms, the expression "Catalan nation" meant less and less the entire Catalanic ethnic whole and instead the Principality of Catalonia or its inhabitants[46]. One sign of this indeterminateness can be captured in the words addressed in 1713 by the representations of the finished *reino de Valencia, representado por los valencianos que se hallan en este Exmo. Fidmo. Principado* ("kingdom of Valencia, represented by the Valencians that are in this Most Excellent and Faithful Principality") to the authorities of Catalonia. To recover their own freedom and self-governance, the Valencians demanded that they include *en todas las instancias que mandará interponer en alivio de este Fidmo. y Exmo. Principado la reintegración de lo que de honores gracias y privilegios ha gozado el reino de Valencia, asegurando a V.E.F. en nombre y de orden de la nación valenciana* ("on all the occasions that he order to impose for relief of the Most Excellent and Faithful Principality the reintegration of those honours and privileges the kingdom of Valencia has

44 Antoni Mas, *Esclaus i catalans. Esclavitud i segregació a Mallorca durant els segles XIV i XV* (Palma de Mallorca: Lleonard Muntaner, 2005), pp. 141-146.

45 Antoni Simon, *Construccions polítiques...*, p. 27.

46 Antoni Mas, *Esclaus i catalans...*, pp. 141-146.

enjoyed, ensuring the Most Excellent and Faifhful Principality in name and by order of the Valencian nation") while when defending the city of Barcelona they also demanded to be considered *como nativos de este E. y F. Principado, y ya que el reino de Valencia debió la mayor parte a las armas gloriosas de este Exmo. Fidmo. Principado en la feliz expulsión de los moros de su patria* (natives of this Most Excellent and Faithful Principality, and that the kingdom of Valencia owed the greater part of the glorious arms of this Most Excellent and Faithful Principality in the happy expulsion of the Moors from their homeland)[47].

It is imperative that we now focus on the most relevant factors that generated the old national identity of the Catalans without neglecting other elements, such as language and economics. Although the former did not have the importance it has today, it was not a politically neutral factor, since as the Modern Age wore on, governors and institutions tended to institutionalise their vernacular languages[48]. In Hispanic Catalonia in the early 18th century, Catalan remained virtually the only language of oral communication among Catalans, and it was also the official language in the sense that it was the language with which the king judged the Catalan legislation and the one used by the councils of both large institutions and local governments. Nonetheless, since the 16th century a diglossic process had gotten underway with Spanish and Catalan in the terrain of literature, either because of the international prestige of Spanish, as it was the language of the most powerful courts of the period, or for commercial reasons, since it was the language that spread the most widely as Spain's empire expanded. This did not prevent numerous authors like Cristòfor

47 The quotes are from the following documents: *Representación que en 16 de junio dieron los valencianos en Barcelona a los tres comunes de Cataluña en nombre de su nación*, and *Representación que en 12 de julio dieron los valencianos a los tres comunes de Cataluña ofreciéndose a la defensa de Barcelona*. The texts can be viewed in: Francesc de Castellví, *Narraciones Históricas*, 4 vols., eds. Josep M. Mundet, José M. Alsina (Madrid: Fundación Francisco Elías de Tejada-Erasmo Pèrcopo, 1999), vol. 3, pp. 813-815.

48 Oscar Jané, *Catalunya i França...*, pp. 52-53. Languages were seen to have huge disciplinary potential for linguistic unification, and the written language was considered a more effective tool for conserving the shared historical memory, symbols and myths, as well as for the cohesive power, thanks to the printing press, to make many people imagine themselves part of a national community by reading the same texts. Antoni Simon, "Presentació...", p. 19.

Despuig, Jeroni Taix, Pere Gil, Andreu Bosc, Pere Nicolau and Josep Elies Estrugós from displaying a protesting, patriotic attitude toward the use of Catalan, nor did it prevent the existence of pretensions and projects to make Catalan a valid instrument of literary expression according to the tastes of the period, nor the fact that almost all the propaganda targeted at internal consumption in the Principality, which we shall discuss below, was printed in the native language of Catalonia[49]. Politically, even though there had been some controversy[50], the first compulsory change in the Catalans' linguistic behaviour did not come until the repressive era after the 1652 conquest of Barcelona[51], the foreshadowing of forthcoming events[52].

Regarding the economy, we should note that parallel to many places around Europe, mercantilist thinking[53] also developed in Catalonia precisely in the early decades of the 17th century, when the general crisis of that century began to constrict, characterised by revolving around the existence of Catalonia's own economic space. In this period, the weakening of trade relations with the lands of the Crown of Castile and alienation from the monarchs of Madrid made the principality and countships its own

49 Antoni Simon, *Construccions polítiques...*, pp. 200-202; Antoni Simon, "La historiografia del segle del Barroc (de Jeroni Pujades a Narcís Feliu)", *Història de la historiografia catalana*, Albert Balcells, ed. (Barcelona: Institut d'Estudis Catalans [Secció Històrico-arqueològica], 2004), pp. 93-116.

50 Like the one within the Provincial of the region of Tarragona in 1635-36 and 1636-37, in which much of the Catalan clergy, backed by both the *Diputació* ("General Deputation") and the *Consell de Cent* ("Council of One Hundred"), defended the use of Catalan when preaching to the faithful. The Castilianising positions were upheld by Antonio Pérez, the archbishop of Tarragona, and Alexandre Ros, the canon of Tortosa, who used the pseudonym Gómez Adrín. The most prominent protests in defence of Catalan came from Justino Antolínez de Burgos, the bishop of Tortosa, Pau Duran, the bishop of Urgell and the doctor in law Dídac Cisteller. Antoni Simon, *Construccions polítiques...*, pp. 195-199.

51 Antoni Simon, "La historiografia...", p. 116

52 For an overview of the language issue in Catalonia prior to 1714, see: Mila Segarra, "El conflicte lingüístic català-castellà als segles XVI i XVII", *Història de la cultura catalana, volum 2, Renaixement i barroc, segles XVI-XVII*, Pere Gabriel, ed. (Barcelona: Edicions 62, 1994-1999), pp. 167-192; Joan Lluis Marfany, *La Llengua maltractada: el castellà i el català a Catalunya del segle XVI al segle XIX* (Barcelona: Empúries, 2001); Joan Lluis Marfany, *Llengua, nació i diglòssia* (Barcelona: L'Avenç, 2008).

53 An overview of mercantilist thinking in Europe and Catalonia can be found in: Lluís Argemí, *Història del pensament econòmic a Catalunya* (Lleida-Vic: Pagès-Eumo, 2005).

economic fatherland, thus making the economy an element of identity. This line of thinking was developed primarily by lawyers and merchants like Jaume Damians, Francesc Gilabert, Narcís Peralta, Jaume Dalmau and Francesc Magarola, who shaped protectionist theses which distinguished between outsiders and native-born Catalans. They had their own economic space and therefore their institutions had to defend them from the invasion of foreign merchants and goods which caused the decapitalisation of the country and the ruin of its manufacturing[54]. By the second half of the 17th century, at the onset of the War of the Spanish Succession, it should be noted that despite the historiography that claims that one of the core motives for the Principality's libel of the Habsburgs was the Catalan ruling class's economic designs to economically run the monarchy of Spain, Antoni Simon has shown that the space of reference of economic interests was still Catalonia, not Iberian Spain or its world-wide empire[55].

In addition to the two aforementioned elements, language and the economy, we believe that there were four major pillars upon which the old national identity was built. The first was religion. A powerful cohesive element, as well as a factor in the clash of different cultures, nations and states, religion is mentioned by the majority of researchers since it was always one of the prime instruments used to create collective identity in the hands of different power nuclei[56]. In the Catalonia of Baroque, Counter-Reformation Catholicism, the religious issue was quite weighty during the War of the Spanish Succession, not only because of the prominent displays of religious fanaticism among the defenders of the resistant

54 Antoni Simon, *Construccions polítiques...*, pp. 187-188.

55 Simon clarifies that even though it is true that the in the late 17th and early 18th centuries a sector of the Catalan commercial bourgeoisie, represented by the eminent figure of Narcís Feliu de la Penya, had the clear objective of expanding its penetration into the American market and that its interests were linked to other broader sectors that mistrusted France and wanted to draw closer to the maritime powers (England and the United Provinces of the Netherlands), this does not mean that these pro-Habsburg sectors had strength, ambitions and a programme that could influence the political and economic directions of the Court of Madrid, or that it was necessary, given that these objectives were feasible to achieve in Catalonia by calling the Courts. Antoni Simon, *Del 1640 al 1705. L'autogovern de Catalunya i la classe dirigent catalana en el joc* de *la política internacional europea* (Valencia-Barcelona: Universitat de València-Institut d'Estudis Catalans, 2011), pp. 9-18.

56 Oscar Jané, *Catalunya i França...*, pp. 53-54.

Barcelona, so harshly criticised on the one hand by a steadfast sympathy of the Catalan love for freedom, such as by Voltaire in *Le siècle de Louis XIV* (1751), but because the publicists and preachers on both sides turned what began as a dynastic conflict between two Catholic princes into a religious war with special prominence for the issue of alliances with heretics. This war of roles was a triumph on the Peninsula because of the Bourbons' religious propaganda on the notorious, numerous presence of Protestants among the allied ranks, but not in the Principality, where the heretics and sacrilegious were the French by antonomasia, an image from the Catalan collective imagination which France unquestionably earned in its constant invasions and raids throughout the 17th century. The prime role of the influence of the Catalan clergy, the vast majority of whom were in favour of the emperor's son, with the exception of much of the hierarchy, over the natives of the country deserves no further comment than noting that their dynastic position was clearly influenced by widespread Francophobia within the estate and the rejection of Bourbon royalism which modified the style of the traditional relationship between the Spanish churchmen and the Crown[57].

The second pillar can be found in the long list of higher privileges that affected the population at large in each state, extending above and beyond the local and seigniorial boundaries[58]. In Catalonia, the *Constitucions i*

57 Regarding religious fanaticism in Barcelona in 1713-1714, see: Joaquim Albareda, "Dinasticismo, política y religión en la Guerra de Sucesión de España", *Les Altres guerres de religió: Catalunya, Espanya, Europa (segles XVI-XIX)*, Xavier Torres, ed. (Girona: Documenta Universitaria, 2012), pp. 285-313. Regarding religions and the War of the Spanish Succession on Spanish territory, see: David González, *Guerra de religión entre príncipes católicos: el discurso del cambio dinástico en España y América, 1700-1714* (Madrid: Ministerio de Defensa, 2002). Regarding the behaviour of the Catalan clergy in this conflict, see: Joaquim Albareda, *Els Catalans i Felip V: de la conspiració a la revolta, 1700-1705* (Barcelona: Vicens Vives-Fundació "La Caixa", 1993), especially, pp. 248-272; Joan Bada, "L'Església catalana davant la dinastia borbònica i el decret de nova planta (1701-1726)", *Del patriotisme al Catalanisme: societat i política (segles XVI/XIX)*, Joaquim Albareda, ed. (Vic: Eumo, 2000), pp. 239-261.

58 Thus, in the corporativist societies from the Middle Ages and Modern Age, the defence and preservation of the privileges, customs, freedoms and rights was a common, constant feature around Europe, since these privileges, which consisted of dispensations to fulfil shared norms, brought benefits to those who had them and distinguished them from others. These historical provisions, which were private law

altres drets de Cathalunya or the *llibertats dels catalans* ("freedoms of the Catalans"), by definition the laws of the Principality of Catalonia and the countships of Roussillon and Cerdagne, legally and politically distinguished the Catalans and their state from the other subjects and kingdoms in the Crown of Aragon and later from the monarchy of Spain and logically from the other external political communities of these dynastic conglomerates. For this reason, in 1705, Mitford Crowe, the plenipotentiary of the Kingdom of England in the negotiations with the early Catalan pro-Habsburg faction, said that the Catalans were a separate people living under their own laws and privileges, who would readily support any king who undertook to restore and uphold their ancient rights[59].

In the Principality, these laws were generated by the monarch in conjunction with the Catalan representatives within the General Courts, and in their absence by institutions like Catalonia's *Diputació del General* ("General Deputation") and Barcelona's *Consell de Cent* ("Council of One Hundred"); after the late 17th century, the *Tres Comuns*[60] ("Three Commons") ensured their compliance. These institutions, which were considered *de la terra* ("from the land"), just like the Catalan elite that peopled them[61], had gradually distanced themselves from the royal power

by nature, were granted by a sovereign or agreed to in the Courts. There were many different kinds of privileges, and they could be granted to a person, a family, a church, a school, a brotherhood, a city or village, an estate or a group of inhabitants of a state, and they therefore affected not only those which the historiography has called the privileged classes (the secular aristocracy and the members of the Church), which were logically the groups that had the most privileges, but in general all the members of an estate-based society who were affected by some privilege. Xavier Torres, *La Guerra dels Segadors* (Vic: Eumo, 2006), pp. 22-24; Xavier Torres, *Naciones sin nacionalismo: Cataluña...*, p. 133; Oscar Jané, *Catalunya i França...*, p. 49; and Antoni Simon, "Presentació...", p. 18.

59 Alan David Francis, *The first Peninsular War 1702-1713* (London-New York: Ervest Benn, 1975), p. 177.

60 The *Tres Comuns* ("Three Communes") were the Council of One Hundred, the General Deputation and the new *Braç Militar* ("Military Branch"). Regarding this institution, see: Eduard Martí, *La Conferència dels Tres Comuns (1697-1714): una institució decisiva en la política catalana* (Vilassar de Mar-Lleida: Fundació Ernest Lluch-Pagès Editors, 2008).

61 The Catalan ruling class in the 17th and early 18th centuries was characterised by being first a mesocratic elite which fused elements from the traditional petty nobility and honorary citizens with canons, merchants, jurists and other members of the

that had generated them in the 13th and 14th centuries and became more representative of the Catalan political community than the monarch, at least as the early modern centuries wore on. On the one hand, these institutions upheld the interests of this community while also advocating respect of the constitutions by the sovereign and his officers, and they often sought more autonomy from the monarch, especially in periods when there was a distancing between the ideals and interests of the prince and of the Catalans[62]. Likewise, they coalesced large swaths of society by getting the middle classes to participate in politics and creating or reinforcing the Catalan national identity by intervening in commercial, monetary and economic-tax matters[63], as well as by creating legal, historical, linguistic, literary, ritual and symbolic cultural productions[64]. The organic and jurisdictional invigoration of the institutions was accompanied by incipient geographic thinking[65] in the 15th, 16th and 17th centuries, as well as historical and linguistic thinking opposed to Castilian cultural assimilation through a long list of authors including Francesc Calça, Rafael Cervera, Jeroni Pujades, Andreu Bosc, Esteve de Corbera, Narcís Feliu de la Penya, Josep Romaguera, Manuel Marcillo and Pere Serra i Postius. The legal and constitutionalist thinking also evolved, especially in the decades between 1590 and 1650[66], through doctors in law

middle classes, which gave it a wider, more open social base than many European urban oligarchies. Secondly, it was a cohesive group, since its members shared strong inter-family connections, a deeply rooted pactist culture and weak adhesion to the Crown caused by fairly widespread marginalisation from the benefits of royal patronage, as well as the poor payment of services rendered for the sovereign. Antoni Simon, *Pau Claris. Líder d'una classe revolucionària* (Barcelona: Publicacions de l'Abadia de Montserrat, 2008), pp. 25-33 and 48-57.

62 Antoni Simon, "Presentació…", p. 18.

63 For a much more detailed explanation, see: Miquel Pérez, *Entre el Rei i la Terra: el poder polític a Catalunya al segle XVI* (Vic: Eumo, 2004).

64 Antoni Simon, *Construccions polítiques...*, pp. 136-137; Anthony D. Smith, *Nacionalismo...*, p. 346.

65 Agustí Alcoberro, *Identitat i territori. Textos geogràfics del Renaixement* (Vic: Eumo, 2000).

66 Víctor Ferro, *Dret públic català: les institucions a Catalunya fins al Decret de Nova Planta* (Vic: Eumo, 1987); Joan Lluís Palos, *Els Juristes i la defensa de les Constitucions: Joan Pere Fontanella (1575-1649)* (Vic: Eumo, 1997); Antoni Simon, "El pensament polític català a l'alta edat moderna: una aproximació", *Pensament polític als Països Catalans, 1714-2014: història i prospectiva*, Jaume Renyer, Enric

and jurists like Joan Pere Fontanella, Josep Queralt, Pere Antoni Jofreu and Francesc Martí Viladamor, who developed patriotic legal-political theorisations which posited the Catalan political community's unique, enhanced level of sovereignty before the prince[67]. They even went as far as to uphold theories like popular sovereignty[68] and carry out actions like deposing Philip V and forever excluding the Bourbons from the *llegitima Successió dels Comtats de Barcelona, Rosselló, Serdanya, Principat de Cathalunya, y del (SIC) demès Regnes, Estáts, Dominis y Senyorias de dita Monarquia de Espanya*[69] ("legitimate Succession of the Counties of Barcelona, Roussillon, Cerdanya, Principality of Catalonia, and the (sic) other Kingdoms, States, Domains and Lordships of this said Monarchy of Spain"). Thanks to the printing press, especially after the 17th century, all of this production of historicist and legal postulates was consumed not only by the more elitist sectors, but it was also widely disseminated throughout society, particularly after the Catalan Revolt[70], which had no precedents in earlier periods. This dissemination permeated both the middle and lower echelons of society thanks to smaller printed items: gazettes, lists of deeds, notices or other kinds of printed leaflets devised in the propaganda

---

Pujol, eds. (Barcelona: Centre d'Estudis de Temes Contemporanis-Pòrtic, 2007), pp. 17-38.

67 Antoni Simon, *Construccions polítiques...*, p. 162.

68 The thesis of popular sovereignty posits that sovereignty lies with the community, not the prince, or with both the community and the prince. According to this thesis, the community granted the prince power and was always and ultimately the repository of sovereignty. Jesús Villanueva, *Los Orígenes carolingios de Cataluña en la historiografía y el pensamiento político del siglo XVII* (Bellaterra: Universitat Autònoma de Barcelona, 1994).

69 The quotation is from: Germán Segura, "Cataluña contra la Monarquía Borbónica: La primera constitución de las Cortes Catalanas de 1705-1706", *Tiempos Modernos: Revista Electrónica de Historia Moderna*, 13/1 (2006), pp. 1-21, especially, p. 20.

70 In the Hispanic era after the internal inter-war period (1652/9-1705), the avenues of dissemination were highly restricted by repression, and it was not until the start of the 18th century that short and mid-length political writings began to circulate again with vigour. For an explanation of propaganda in the Principality in the second half of the 18th century, see: Antonio Espino, "La publicística catalana y el cambio dinástico: el ocaso de la dinastía de los Austria", *Cuadernos de Investigación Histórica*, 19 (2002), pp. 287-312. For the era of the War of the Spanish Succession, see: Maria Rosa Alabrús, "Informació i opinió a la Catalunya de la Guerra de Successió", *Política, economia i guerra. Barcelona 1700*, Albert Garcia, ed. (Barcelona: Ajuntament de Barcelona, 2013), pp. 152-173.

workshops at the request of the General Deputation and the Council of One Hundred. This brought greater accessibility to scholarly works which until then had remained outside the reach of the public at large because of their price, length and intellectual level[71].

With regard to the War of the Spanish Succession, the defence of this legal and political system is crucial to understanding Catalonia's participation in favour of the Habsburg archduke, since throughout half a century the Catalan ruling class strove to recover its self-governance which had been stolen by the Spanish monarchy in 1652[72] by sacrificing the Catalan people during the constant wars against France with Louis XIV. The refusal of the Habsburgs Philip IV and Charles II, as well as the Bourbon Philip V, to return self-governance to Catalonia despite its sacrifices did nothing other than stir up a feeling of frustration among its ruling class[73]. This frustration, magnified by the absolutist, hapless dynamic of government management by the Bourbon viceroy Fernández de Velasco between 1703 and 1705, were some of the initial reasons that led Catalonia to favour the Germanic candidate, Charles, in the international war for the throne of Spain that devastated Europe starting in 1702. In 1706, as Charles III he would return the self-governance that had been almost completely lost[74]. The importance of these laws became even more pronounced as the war wore one, with a gradual radicalisation of the defence of the fatherland and the constitutions which in 1713-1714 led to the choice to fight to the bitter end, not only to be under the mild dominion of the emperor but also *per la conservació de les llibertats, privilegis i prerrogatives dels catalans que nostres antecessors a costa de sa sang gloriosament alçaren i*

71 However, we are largely unaware of the degree to which the propagandistic press circulated in and penetrated the lower classes given the obvious difficulty in ascertaining figures on this genre. Antoni Simon, "La divulgació social del discurs històric a la Catalunya del Barroc i l'ús de la història com a arma política", *Butlletí de la Real Acadèmia de Bones Lletres de Barcelona* (forthcoming).

72 After the return of Barcelona under the sovereignty of Philip IV, in order to control the actions and attitudes of the ruling class of the Principality, he cut back the self-governance which it had enjoyed prior to the Catalan Revolt through royal control over access to the lists of possible candidates to hold posts in the prime institutions in Catalonia. Antoni Simon, *Del 1640 al 1705...*, p. 63.

73 Antoni Simon, *Del 1640 al 1705...*, p. 318.

74 Antoni Simon, *Del 1640 al 1705...*, p. 81.

nosaltres devem, així mateix mantenir[75] ("for the conservation of the freedoms, privileges and prerogatives of the Catalans that our ancestors at the cost of their blood gloriously rose and we must, also maintain").

In any event, if we claim that the constitutions were one of the underpinnings of Catalan identity during this period, this means that in spite of a considerable part of the Spanish historiography, which, induced by the statalist paradigm, regards the defence of local codes of laws as something that only interested the dominant elite and the Catalan-Aragonese constitutional systems as aristocratising, corrupt and anachronistic, there is proof that these supposedly elitist rights were defended not only by the ruling class but also by the upper echelon of the popular estate, often called the *populus*[76]. This *populus* was made up of the urban and rural

75 The quote is from: *Crida dels diputats del 12 de juliol de 1713*. See: Joaquim Albareda, ed., *Escrits polítics del segle XVIII...*, pp. 193 and forward.

76 In contrast, the Spanish national historiography has traditionally stressed, and still stresses, the idea that the Bourbons' Nueva Planta was a political and administrative rationalising measure, a prior step needed for the subsequent appearance of modern Spanish democratic constitutionalism years later and for the industrial and economic development of Catalonia. Currently, this thesis is difficult to be defended due to the following reasons. The first is the political model, since it points to absolutism and centralisation as the only pathways to modernity, ignoring the historical evolution of England, the United Provinces of the Netherlands, the Helvetic Confederation, the United States of America and other political formations. This is compounded by the assumption of the inability of the pactist system of the Crown of Aragon to evolve towards modern parliamentary systems, ignoring both its potentialities in the early 18th century and the fact that the real motive preventing it from developing was, unlike the other cases cited above, military defeat. In addition to these reasons, as Antoni Simon has mentioned, it is paradoxical to consider the absolutist regime, which is characterised by the denial of the balance of powers and the defence of despotism, as the best way to evolve towards political modernity. What is more, the historian Santos Madrazo has proven that during the reign of Philip V, the corruption and inefficacy was equal to or higher than what had existed in the regimes prior to the Nueva Planta. Secondly, with regard to the economic systems of absolutist regimes, Hilton L. Root has made it clear that parliamentary systems offered better conditions for economic development since they paved the way for an economy with a lower interest rate. Regarding the economic growth of Catalonia in the 18th century, it is necessary to explain that it stemmed from a process of agricultural spread, intensification and specialisation, the integration of wine-making culture into the world market, and the regional specialisation of manufacturing, as well as the decentralisation of manufacturing from Barcelona, all of these processes that got underway in the 16th and 17th centuries and had nothing to do with the administrative measures of either

middle classes, that is, wealthy farmers, merchants, artisans and professionals who were socially situated between the elite and the poor, who had a substantial degree of material wellbeing and limited but effective participation in local politics. With access to reading materials, they were the consumers of the cultural and propagandistic productions generated by the ruling class[77]. And yet the spectre of the social penetration of the freedoms was yet even broader, since at the major points of conflict and upheaval, even the lower class protested and fought in defence of *sas constitucions, privilegis i llibertats* ("their constitutions, privileges and freedoms"). From their vantage point, violations of the laws of the Principality gave rise to tyranny because these laws, which were often ignored by the king's functionaries and collaborators, prevented – among other things – the royal forces' depredations with impunity of the timber of the forests and the harvests of the country estates, the improper use of draught animals, retaliation and the destruction of houses with no knowledge of the cause, forced levies on the peasants and artisans, and regulation of the billeting of the Spanish troops in Catalans' homes[78]. Precisely what concerned the authorities of the Castilian elite which fed the royal administration, the people who designed the Nueva Planta, was the weakness of the aristocratic presence in the institutions of the Principality and the weight of the Catalan middle classes in political participation[79]. Illustrative examples of all of this can be found in the War of the Spanish Succession. For example, in their objections to the Habsburg arguments in favour of the Catalan

the Habsburgs or the Bourbons. Santos Madrazo, *Estado débil y ladrones poderosos en la España del siglo XVIII* (Madrid: Catarata, 2000); Hilton L. Root, *The Fountain of Privilege. Political Foundations of Markets in Old Regime France and England* (Berkeley: University of California Press, 1994); Antoni Simon, "El momento d'Espanya...", pp. 142-144.

77 Xavier Torres, *Naciones sin nacionalismo: Cataluña...*, pp. 258-264.

78 Eva Serra, "Estudi introductori. Les Corts Catalanes. Una aproximació històrica", Antoni de Capmany, *Práctica* y estilo de celebrar cortes *en el reino* de *Aragón, principado* de *Cataluña* y *reino* de *Valencia* y *una noticia* de *las* de *Castilla* y *Navarra*, eds. Eva Serra, Josep Fontana (Barcelona: Base, 2007), p. 24.

79 Antoni Simon, "Mitos historiográficos sobre la relación Cataluña España en la construcción del estado moderno. Una lectura crítica de la historiografía nacionalista española", *Mitificadores del pasado, falsarios de la historia: Historia Medieval, Moderna y de América*, José Antonio Munita, ed. (Bilbao: Univeridad del País Vasco, 2012), pp. 91-107, epecially, p. 99.

freedoms, the Bourbons argued that *los privilegis de Catalunya solament serveixen per los nobles i gaudins, i que sols estos se miren exempts de tributs, no emperò los plebues* ("the privileges of Catalonia are only for the nobles and 'gaudins', and only these are seen as exempt form taxes, but not the plebs"), a thesis which was denounced as false in 1713 by the Catalan resisters in the *Despertador de Catalunya*, where they claimed that the privileges belonged to everyone; even though the upper classes had more and better privileges, which was *conforme en les demés parts del món*[80] ("like the other parts of the world"). We can also clearly observe this in the profound lamentations that the farmer Joan Esteve Llandrich from Santa Coloma de Farners wrote in his diary shortly after the 11th of September 1714: *la Ciutat de Barcelona estigué asitiada 14 mesos sens tenir ajuda de ningú, antes no se volgué donar y después se agué de entregar, y se romperen tots los privilegis de Cataluña, de aon ploram y plorarem, nosaltres y els nostres desendens*[81] ("the City of Barcelona was besieged for 14 months without the help of anyone, first not wanting to give up and then having to hand itself over, and all the privileges of Catalonia were broken, for which we weep and will weep, ourselves and our descendents"), while in the same period, the collaborationist and senior Bourbon functionary Francesc Ametller, when designing the Nueva Planta that would be instated in Catalonia in 1716, claimed that the seigniorial social hierarchy would remain untouched: *con los señores feudales no se deve innovar cosa*[82] ("with the feudal lords no innovations should be applied").

The third pillar of patriotic identity was the figure of the sovereign prince. In the Europe of the composite monarchies divided into widely diverse territorial domains, loyalty to this figure or his dynasty was of prime importance[83]. This loyalty was deliberately cultivated by the powers-that-be

80 Cited by: Xavier Torres, "Identitat i llibertats a la Catalunya dels Àustries. Assaig sobre els privilegis", *Miscel·lània Ernest Lluch i Martín*, 2 vols. (Vilassar de Mar: Fundació Ernest Lluch, 2006), vol. 1, pp. 551-560 (the quotes are on p. 551).

81 Xavier Torres, "Reis pagesos i llibertats: La fi de les Constitucions Catalanes segons els memorialistes de pagès", *Del patriotisme al Catalanisme. Societat i política (segles XVI/XIX)*, Joaquim Albareda, ed. (Vic: Eumo, 2000), p. 217.

82 Joaquim Albareda, *La guerra de successió i l'Onze de Setembre* (Barcelona: Empúries, 2000), p. 139.

83 Even in republics there were grand aristocratic figures who boasted enormous power and became referents similar to sovereign princes in monarchies. Just to cite a few

using formulas like the divine origin of the temporal sovereign's power or comparisons with the traditional figure of the *pater familias*, which turned the prince into the father of the homeland, giving rise to major difficulties envisioning or allowing for a homeland without or against a sovereign prince[84]. Thus, a high degree of loyalty was generated among the subjects, and even fanaticism in some cases, as recalled by the Bourbon marshal the Viscount of Puerto: *yo he visto miquelete que expirando de las heridas en lugar de recomendarse a Dios gritaba que moria por Carlos III*[85] ("I have seen Catalan militia men who expiring form their wounds instead of placing themselves in God's hands shouted that they were dying for Charles III"). And even though it is true that patriotic identities, like the Catalan identity we are analysing, were generally opposed to the absolutist-style offences committed by the princely administrations against the states' own laws and institutions, it is also true that channelling this resistance into veritable political revolutions organised against the royal figure, where the sovereign and the fatherland were dissociated with each other, was not a very common phenomenon and resulted from many factors which should be analysed on a case-by-case basis. Regardless, when this did happen, it led the majority of people to consider the defence of the fatherland a higher duty than loyalty to the king[86]. Still, this revolutionary divorce between the monarch and the fatherland was usually undertaken somewhat reluctantly, to such an extent that once consummated a new monarch was usually sought who was more respectful of the state's constitutional system in terms of both the conception of power of the day and the contribution to the military needs when dealing with the aspirations of the dethroned prince[87]. Nevertheless, the entire population did not renounce the prince who had been expelled by the institutions of the fatherland. In Catalonia, either for short-term personal reasons[88] or because of absolutist convictions, some

examples, we can mention the dukes of the Most Serene Republic of Venice, the Medici family which governed the Florentine republic for centuries and the Nassau "Stadhouders" from the House of Orange in the Republic of the United Provinces.

84 Xavier Torres, "Un patriotisme sense nació...", pp. 79-80.

85 Cited by: Joaquim Albareda, *Els catalans i Felip V...*, p. 254.

86 Xavier Gil, "Un rey, una fe...", pp. 65 and 66.

87 Xavier Torres, "Nacions sense nacionalisme: pàtria i patriotisme a l'Europa de l'Antic Règim", *Recerques*, 28 (1994), pp. 87-88.

88 The range of possibilities is broad: from being a mercenary who chose sides based on the profit they could earn to supporting the king because a rival supported the other

people maintained their loyalty to the king who had been rejected by the fatherland. These Catalans nurtured the forces of the defeated monarch – Aragonese in the Catalan Civil War, Habsburg in the Catalan Revolt or Bourbon in the War of the Spanish Succession – in opposition to the *bons patricis, bons catalans* ("good patricians, good catalans") or Catalan *patriotes* ("patriots")[89] who remained loyal to the Catalan fatherland represented by the local laws and institutions, revering the kings chosen by them. The adjectivisation of absolutists by the supporters of John II of Aragon, the Habsburg Philip IV and the Bourbon Philip V reflects the fact that they believed that observance of the laws of the fatherland could not precede nor be equated with nor contradict the monarch's ultimate will[90]. This does not mean that they necessarily had to be anti-constitutionalist, nor that among the patriots there were not supporters of the new princes with absolutist ideas or behaviours[91]. If we focus on the War of the Spanish Succession to shed light on the ideological underpinnings of the *botiflers* ("Bourbon supporters")[92] of Catalonia, we can see that in addition to the

side, or because a given social sector supported the opposing monarchy, or out of simple vengeance prompted by war atrocities, etc.

89 The use of the word *patriotes* ("patriots") is not a caprice. Without delving into the 15th century conflict, we should note that in both the Catalan Revolt and the War of the Spanish Succession, the Catalans who were on the side of the institutions of the Principality were called *bons catalans* ("good Catalans"), *bons patricis* ("good patricians"), *els de la terra* ("people of the land") or *els de la pàtria* ("people of the fatherland"). Thus, in the opinion of Núria Sales when referring to the War of the Spanish Succession, it is much less faithful to their time to call them patriots than to call them Austriacists, Habsburgists or archdukists. Núria Sales, *Els Botiflers: 1705-1714* (Barcelona: Rafael Dalmau, 1981), p. 8.

90 Xavier Torres, *Naciones sin nacionalismo: Cataluña...*, p. 254.

91 Just to cite a specific example, Núria Sales classified the legal consultant and Austriacist from Reus Francesc Grases i Gralla as an absolutist. Núria Sales, Els Botiflers..., p. 7.

92 A disparaging name given in the Catalan-speaking lands to the supporters of Philip of Bourbon after 1704, along with the names *gavatxos* ("frogs"), *bugres* ("rascals") or *traïdors* ("traitors"). However, after 1707, it was adopted by Philip's supporters themselves in contrast to the terms *catalans* ("Catalans"), *vigatans* ("Vic natives"), *imperials* ("Imperials"), *austríacs* ("Austrians"), *alemanys* ("Germans"), *aligots* ("buzzards") or *maulets* ("tricksters") (the last one in the kingdom of Valencia), which they used to describe the supporters of the Habsburg Charles III. Joaquim Albareda, "Aproximació a les idees del Filipisme català durant la Guerra de Successió", *Una relació difícil. Catalunya i l'Espanya moderna*, Joaquim Albareda, ed. (Barcelona:

short-term arguments, such as the validity of the designs of the Habsburg Charles II, the vindication of the Catholic faith when confronted with the English, Dutch and imperial Protestant troops and the abuses committed by the Austriacist government, the Catalan Bourbon discourse was characterised by the exaltation of a Bourbon dynasticism that recriminated the pro-Habsburg's betrayal of the Duke of Anjou to defend the maximum royal attributes, and by a clearly elitist, conservative set of ideas that made them abominate the greater attributions of the Catalan institution in the power of the Austriacists, equating them with a lack of control over the popular classes. In this sense, the Catalan *botiflers* protested Catalonia's own laws by arguing that if the patriots defended them so zealously, their rejection of King Philip V was illogical, given that he was the one who had sworn on them while also allowing the government posts of the institutions to be occupied by foreigners or by perfidious bourgeoisie from the popular estate, even if they were natives of the country. Even though this was a self-interested defence, it would seem somewhat complicated to label the Catalan *botiflers* ("Bourbon supporters")[93], who also criticised the nefarious policy of the Viceroy Velasco[94], as anti-constitutionalist or anti-foralist, were it not for the fact that after the destruction of the legal codes of Valencia and Aragon, what was difficult was not to label them thus in view of the clear-sightedness of the 1707 decree to abolish the legal codes of Valencia and Aragon, although some *botiflers* did help to salvage certain aspects of private Catalan law after the Nueva Planta[95].

The fourth pillar was the one that most strongly conferred a national Catalan identity on the popular classes: the violence from the incessant wars. Rapes, mobs and excesses pitted the natives of the Principality and the countships against the Spanish and French armies (either as billeted allies or as invading enemies) and generated feelings of opposition and enmity that led to a clear distinction between "us" and "them". This meant that as the conflicts wore on, both urban and rural, the original factors behind them, such as the defence of either dynasty in the War of the Spanish Succession, ceased to be of prime importance among broad swaths of the popular classes

Base, 2007), pp. 181-194; Jesús Mestre, dir., *Diccionari d'història de Catalunya* (Barcelona: Edicions 62, 1992), pp. 79 and 146.

93 Ernest Lluch, "De noms i de 'modernors'", *L'Avenç*, 253 (2000), pp. 60-63.

94 Joaquim Albareda, "Aproximació a les idees...", pp. 181-182.

95 Ernest Lluch, "De noms...", p. 62.

while national/patriotic counter-identities became more important[96]. Let us examine a few examples from the War of the Spanish Succession[97]:

According to the Austriacist captain and Catalan chronicler Francesc Castellví, the Bourbons' 1706 advance in Austriacist Catalonia aroused among the Catalans *más el amor al rey Carlos y hicieron más odioso el nombre de francés y castellano*, while *crecía más cada día el odio a la persona del Rey y a los castellanos, y* (the Catalans) *sacrificaban sus vidas gustosos* ("more the love of king Charles and made the names of French and Castilian more odious while every day the hatred of the person of the King and the Castilians grew more and (the Catalans) sacrificed their lives happily") according to the pro-Bourbon chronicler Vincenzo Bacallar, the Marquis of San Felipe, who claimed that the Castilians mainly supported the Bourbons in order *no ser conquistados de aragoneses y catalanes, y ultrajados de portugueses, a los quales despreciaban y aborrecían* ("not to be conquered by the Aragonese and Catalans, and defiled by the Portuguese, who they despised and hated"). However, the armies in the Habsburg cause aroused aversion among the natives of the Principality, who saw how as allies *no repararen en fer mal y desviar donas casadas y doncellas si los tenian paraules* ("they did not care about hurting and deviating married women and maidens in case these said some words to them") or to extort through *cartas incognitas de desafio y composit al qui coneixian tenia diner* ("through anonymous letters challenging and accosting those who were known to have money"), according to the testimony of the priest Ombravella from the Collell sanctuary. The Catalans had a worse image, *que.s levantaren en lo any 1705 en títol de Miquelets* ("who rose in the year 1705 under the name of Miquelets") because of the fact that, as the peasant Aleix Ribalta from Palau d'Anglesola tells us in 1708, the *miquelets pararen en lladres, y estos eran los que feian més mal en lo pahís* ("the miquelets became thieves, and it was they who did most damage to the country") In turn, the Austriacist peasant Francesc Gelat,

96 Antoni Simon, *Construccions polítiques...*, p. 437. Nevertheless, the hatred or rejection was not exclusively ethnic/cultural; rather it stemmed from the important political facet of nations in the Modern Age, giving rise to the fact that the traitors of the homeland were also enemies, even if they were culturally the same as its defenders.

97 All of the following examples and citations can be found cited and explained, along with many other testimonies, in: Antoni Simon, *Construccions polítiques...*, pp. 443-447.

who was a member of the militia that aided besieged Barcelona in 1706, had shed his Habsburg dynasticism in 1707, as gleaned from an annotation in his diary: *totom diu que la corona d'Espania toca a Carles Terser i no an al duch d'En Jou. Al fin Déu vulla donar la corona d'Espania a lo qui tòquia per a que se puga conseguir pau i quietud* ("everyone says that the crown of Spain is for Charles [the] Third and not for the duke of Anjou. In the end let it be God who gives the crown of Spain to who has the right so that he may achieve peace and calmness"). These counter-identities were even further exacerbated when the Catalans were abandoned by their allies and their king against Bourbon Spain and France, revealing that the only alternative left to them in order to conserve their independence, government and freedom was to resist and win or else be subjugated by the enemy, *deixant Catalunya per a Castella* ("leaving Catalonia for Castile"), as noted by a friar in Barcelona's Santa Caterina convent. Thus, they would lose their native-born rights and acquire those of the Castilians, and be condemned to live, *una vida que parece muerte* ("a life that seems like death"), without freedoms and subjected to harsh taxes and billeting, as expressed in the leaflet *Lealtad Catalana Purificada de invidiosas calumnias* ("Catalan Loyalty Purified of envious slander"). The furore of war became ferocious and increased the Catalans' aversion towards the Bourbons, and especially against the Castilians. Thus, in early 1714, while many songs written in Catalonia included lyrics like *Anem a dar batalla/als cruels castellans/y visca Cataluña/visca la llibertat* ("Let's go fight/the cruel Castlians/and long live Catalonia/long live freedom"), and the Catalans from many towns occupied by the French and Castilians revolted against the taxes they imposed with cries of *fora lladres, visca la pàtria* ("out with the thieves, long live the homeland") and *via fora moros* ("Moors out"), the Castilians persecuted Catalan patriots and *si cap ne podían agafar, o passàvan mal i molts que'n penjavavan. I lo pijor, que las pobras vilas o pagaven, perquè per totas las vilas que los castellans trobàvan voluntaris i posàvan foch, que era la més llàstima del mónt* ("and if they could catch any, they had a bad time and many were hung. And the worst, that the poor villages paid for it, because in any place where the Castilians found volunteers they set fire to, that was the saddest for the forest") according to the testimony of the frightened peasant Gelat.

4. A long epilogue: Catalan national identity in Bourbon Spain

In the states within the Crown of Aragon, the outcome of the War of the Spanish Succession meant the imposition of a political model which interplayed the Bourbons' absolutist aspirations with the political and ideological ideals of the court of Madrid with the goal of turning the Spanish kingdoms on the Iberian Peninsula into a single political community unified around a Castilian core. The Bourbon conquest of Valencia, Aragon, Catalonia and Mallorca between 1707 and 1715 allowed the structures of the autochthonous states to be abolished, and instead of annexing these territories as accessories to Castile they became regions ruled under Castilian forms of governance. The local laws, general courts and deputations of each country were destroyed, and the Catalan and Aragonese subjects had to attend the Castilian courts. Likewise, the Council of Aragon, which was charged with advising the king on issues that affected the territories in the Crown of Aragon, was dissolved and its functions were shifted to the Council of Castile. The viceroys were replaced by General Captains who became the top authorities in the different Catalan and Aragonese countries. The Bourbons' new Royal Audiences, each presided over by one of the four General Captains, replaced the former supreme courts of justice and took on governing roles. In Catalonia, Aragon and Valencia, the traditional divisions of the land into *vegueries* ("vicaries"), *juntes* and *governacions* ("governations"), respectively, were replaced by Castilian territorial demarcations called *corregiments* or townships. The council-based municipal governments, grounded upon the system of representation and election via balloting, were transformed into town halls with Castilian-style councillors, giving rise to an in-depth aristocratisation of the local administration. In short, this is how the peninsular heart of the vanished Habsburgs' composite monarchy in Spain became the united kingdom of Bourbon Spain[98]. In the Principality of Catalonia, this entire

98 The only autonomous regions left on the Iberian Peninsula were the Kingdom of Navarra and the Basque provinces; although they had been territories of the Crown of Castile centuries past, they retained their legal codes in reward for their loyalty to Philip V.

process was accompanied by the exile of thousands of people in the territories under imperial dominion[99], the permanent military occupation of the territory over the course of a century[100] and horrible systematic, omnipresent repression which consisted of summary executions, rapes, prison sentences, banishment, property confiscations, a fearful climate of denunciations and accusations, impositions of extraordinary taxes and the Royal Land Registry, a new tax that was outrageously high in a country devastated by war, which was added to the ones already traditionally paid[101], and the persecution of the Catalan language in an effort to destroy it[102]. All

99 Agustí Alcoberro, *L'exili austriacista, 1713-1747* (Barcelona: Fundació Noguera, 2002).

100 This is proven by deeds like the construction of the Ciutadella (citadel) in Barcelona, and a number of Spanish troops posted in Catalonia that fluctuated over the course of the entire century between 20,000 and 30,000. Lluís Roura, "Subjecció i militarització a la Catalunya del segle XVIII", *Del patriotisme al catalanisme: societat i política (segles XVI/XIX)*, Joaquim Albareda, ed. (Vic: Eumo, 2001), pp. 289-315, especially, p. 296.

101 Josep M. Torras, *Felip V contra Catalunya: testimonis d'una repressió sistemàtica: 1713-1715* (Barcelona: Rafael Dalmau, 2005).

102 Apparently, in the 18th century the Spanish ruling class firmly believed that languages were a crucial component of a national consciousness and that any languages which were not an inherent part of the statist, Castilian ideal were a disturbance. For this reason, they tried to erase them from the map in all the territories under the reign of the King of Spain. If we specifically examine Catalonia, we have to say that since they knew that this policy would come upon resistance by the inhabitants of the Principality, it was not implemented all at once but instead gradually. In this way, even though the Nueva Planta decree only stipulated that the cases before the Royal Audience be tried in Spanish, throughout the 18th century and in the early 19th century, Catalan still suffered from attacks by the Bourbon administration, such as limitations or prohibitions on using it to preach sermons or as the language of communication among the clergy, and a ban on using it to teach, print books or publish romances, put on plays or even make annotations in accounting books. On this subject, see: Francesc Ferrer, *La Persecució política de la llengua catalana: història de les mesures preses contra el seu ús des de la Nova Planta fins avui* (Barcelona: Edicions 62, 1985); Francesc Ferrer, "Resistència a la substitució lingüística al Principat", *La Llengua catalana al segle XVIII*, Pep Balsalobre, Joan Gratacós, eds. (Barcelona: Quaderns Crema, 1995), pp. 429-435; Josep Maria Ainaud, *El Llibre negre de Catalunya: de Felip V a l'ABC* (Barcelona: La Campana, 1995); Antonio Muñoz, Josep Catà, Repressió borbònica *i resistència catalana: (1714-1736)* (Madrid: Muñoz-Catà, 2005); José María García, "Revisión de algunas ideas sobre política e ideología lingüísticas en el siglo XVIII español", *Cuadernos de Ilustración y Romanticismo. Revista Digital*

of this leads us to wonder what happened to the Catalan national/patriotic identity in a context in which its own institutions and laws were eliminated and repression was exerted over the course of an entire century[103].

The religious sphere was still equally important since the Catalans held onto their Catholicism as a basic feature of their identity throughout the 18th century. Regarding the churchmen in Catalonia who had caused so many problems for the Bourbons, many of them suffered from repression, while the *botifler* clergy devoted their efforts to legitimising King Philip

---

del Grupo de Estudios del Siglo XVIII, 17 (2011). Regarding the Catalan language in the 18th century, see: Mila Segarra, "Una llengua d'us estrictament popular", *Història de la cultura catalana, volum 3: El Set-cents*, Pere Gabriel, ed. (Barcelona: Edicions 62, 1994-1999), pp. 143-162. However, according to Joan Lluis Marfany, it would be erroneous to consider external imposition as the only reason behind the spread of Spanish in Catalonia. Thus, without ever underestimating the role of Spain's prohibition of Catalan, this author tells us that we should first bear in mind the internal desire for the expansion of diglossic behaviour not only among the ruling class but also in other new and rising sectors, a phenomenon that precisely reached its feverish peak in the 19th century through the mythicized Renaixença (Renaissance) movement. Secondly, we should not automatically construe the use of Catalan as an act of resistance, since the wealthy Catalans in the 18th century never stopped using their mother tongue in family relations and when dealing with the subordinate classes. Nor did they ever abandon it in their daily religious practice, and they also took pains to study it. In this author's opinion, these actions (at least the first two) were clearly motivated by a classist ideology of blocking knowledge of the language considered the language of success and by the Church hierarchy's concern with people properly understanding the Catholic rites and dogmas. Joan Lluís Marfany, *La Llengua maltractada...*; Joan Lluís Marfany, Llengua, nació... With regard to the scholarly studies and dissertations on Catalan performed at the Reial Acadèmia de Bones Lletres of Barcelona, see: Mireia Campabadal, *La Reial Acadèmia de Bones Lletres de Barcelona en el segle XVIII: l'interès per la història, la llengua i la literatura catalanes* (Barcelona: Reial Acadèmia de Bones Lletres de Barcelona-Publicacions de l'Abadia de Montserrat, 2006), especially, pp. 211-260.

103 To answer this question, as this chapter is being written we lack a monograph that could provide a realistic global overview of the issue of Catalan identity in the 18th century, although such a volume does exist for the two preceding centuries. However, we do have the research by Ernest Lluch, who highlighted interesting issues which are worth delving into further: Ernest Lluch, *La Catalunya vençuda del segle XVIII: foscors i clarors de la Il·lustració* (Barcelona: Edicions 62, 1996); and especially a brief but particularly useful report on the state of the matter: Joaquim Albareda, "El XVIII...".

and his dynasty among extensive swaths of the population who rejected them, seeking the peace and subjugation of the country[104].

The figure of the sovereign prince remained an important part of Catalans' collective notions of their identity, personified in the imposed Bourbons. This can be seen, for example, in the story from the Royal Audience of Barcelona which recounts the 1743 mutiny of Cervera against the local Bourbon aristocratic regime, in which the inflamed lower classes cried: *Visca el rei i les calces d'estopa, morin els traïdors*[105] ("Long live the king and burlap pants, death to the traitors").

With regard to the Catalan ruling class, we should say that those who went into exile in Vienna retained not only their Austriacism or Habsburg dyanasticism but also their parliamentarist ideology, their commitment to the abolished legal system and their plural, composite conception of the Spanish monarchy[106]. This led them to take advantage of moments of international instability among the powers to try to convince their former allies in the War of the Spanish Succession to unite once again in an effort to expel the Bourbons from the peninsula[107]. The most prominent intellectual from this group was the Aragonese Juan Amor de Soria, whose work *Enfermedad chrónica, y peligrosa de los Reynos de España y*

104 Josep M. Torras, *Felip V contra Catalunya…*, pp. 325-336.

105 The expression *calces d'estopa* ("flaxen stockings") was a form of self-affirmation among the plebes. Peasants, artisans, minor merchants and cart drivers wore this rough fabric, unlike the wealthier classes. Enric Tello, *Visca el rei i les calces d'estopa: reialistes i botiflers a la Cervera set-centista* (Barcelona: Editorial Crítica, 1990), pp. 205-206.

106 Ernest Lluch, *L'Alternativa catalana: 1700-1714-1740: Ramon de Vilana Perlas i Juan Amor de Soria: teoria i acció austriacistes* (Vic: Eumo, 2000).

107 See the propagandistic texts: *Via fora els adormits* (1734), *La voz precursora de la verdad pregonando la esclavitud de Europa por las injustas invasiones de la Real Casa de Borbón clama para redimirla del cautiverio* (1734) and *Record de l'Aliança fet al Serm. Jordi Augusto, Rey de la Gran Bretanya, etc. etc., ab una carta del Principat de Cataluña y Ciutat de Barcelona* (1736). The first can be found in: Ernest Lluch, ed., *Escrits polítics del segle XVIII. Tom 3. Via fora els adormits* (Barcelona-Vic: Institut Universitari d'Història Jaume Vicens and Vives-Eumo, 2005); the second in: Ernest Lluch, Aragonesismo austracista *(1734-1742). Conde Juan Amor de Soria* (Saragossa: Institución Fernando el Católico, 2010); and the third in: Josep Maria Torras, ed., *Escrits polítics del segle XVIII. Tom 2. Documents de la Catalunya sotmesa* (Barcelona-Vic: Institut Universitari d'Història Jaume Vicens Vives-Eumo, 1996).

de Indias: sus causas naturales, y sus remedios[108] ("Chronic disease, and dangerous for the Kingdoms of Spain and the Indias: its natural causes and its cures") (1742) offered a political project for Spain that consisted not only of returning the Peninsula to the political situation prior to the Nueva Planta but also implementing new and fairer tax measures for the different Iberian kingdoms, calling the General Courts of the states periodically, and creating a General Parliament of the monarchy which would have to be held once a decade to *hermanar y concordar las dos coronas* (Aragon and Castile) *y sus naciones, deshaciendo y destruyendo una de las causas de la enfermedad de la monarquía por la discordia y la antipatía que entre ellas ha reinado*[109] ("bringing together and matching the two crowns [Aragon and Castile] and their nations, breaking and destroying one of the causes of the disease of the monarchy through the discord and antipathy that has reigned between them"). In contrast, the dominant classes who remained in the Principality, most of whom had not been loyal to Philip V until 1713 or even 1714, adapted to the new Bourbon regime in the most advantageous way possible. As they saw Catalonia stripped of its traditional local institutions and the highest magistracies and posts in the country occupied by early *botiflers* and especially Castilian military officers, the Catalan elites, especially the nobility and rising bourgeoisie, bought off the baillages and councillorships of the new Bourbon town halls, the bottom rung in the absolute monarchy's ladder of power over the land. Proof of this is that more than half the members of the new town halls were the same people who had occupied the posts in the municipal governments before the Bourbon victory[110]. This same ruling class yearned for the creation of a peninsular and American Spanish domestic market and sought to profit from the expansive effects of the economic upswing experienced

108 This text can be found in: Ernest Lluch, Aragonesismo austracista..., pp. 173-372.

109 Cited in: Joaquim Albareda, "L'austriacisme, una visió alternativa", *Barcelona. Quaderns d'Història*, 7 (2002), pp. 23-50, especially, p. 41.

110 Josep M. Torras, "La fi de l'autogovern", *Història, política, societat i cultura dels Països Catalans. Desfeta política i embranzida econòmica: segle XVIII*, Borja de Riquer, dir. (Barcelona: Enciclopèdia Catalana, 1995-2008), vol. 5, p. 218. Regarding the origin, consolidation and evolution of the Bourbon town halls, see, by the same author: Josep Maria Torras, *Els Municipis catalans de l'antic règim: 1453-1808: procediments electorals, òrgans de poder i grups dominant* (Barcelona: Curial, 1983); Josep Maria Torras, *Los Mecanismos del poder: los ayuntamientos catalanes durante el siglo XVIII* (Barcelona: Crítica, 2003).

by the Principality in the 18th century, the one that, as Joaquim Albareda and Lluis Roura have revealed, linked the polysemic words "fatherland" and "nation" with the Spanish state in the second half of the century, that is, with the political representation of Spain and the monarchic administration[111]. However, this Spanish conception of identity, just like its revolutionary and liberal version from the early 19th century which we shall discuss further on, shows few signs of having reached the lower classes[112].

Having said this, it seems to be a century in which, as Ferran Soldevila declared, Catalonia made an effort to become a province[113]. Nonetheless, the vanquished Catalonia of the 18th century was not an oasis of peace and obedience. Throughout the entire 18th century, Madrid still doubted Catalonia's loyalty. The Principality was regarded as conquered, hostile territory. This seemed to be a well-grounded opinion, because there was indeed resistance to the new state of affairs after 1714. There was armed and violent resistance, such as the guerrilla insurrection led by the Austriacist Pere Joan Barceló, nicknamed "Carrasquet", who recruited thousands of men in an attempt to free Catalonia in 1719, protected from the invasion of the Quadruple Alliance's forces against Philip V's Mediterranean policy[114]. This was followed by several uprisings by minor troops and bands in the 15 ensuing years. Likewise, the general tenor after the 1740s was characterised by claims of how beneficial the old Catalan regime destroyed by the French-Spanish conquest had been via the recollection of how things used to be done and the tendency to reconstruct the traditional structures, as noted by Ramon Grau. These claims were both bottom-up through numerous popular revolts against the system imposed by the Nueva Planta

111 Joaquim Albareda, "El XVIII...", pp. 83-86; Lluís Roura, "El 'segrest' del concepte 'nació' al tombant del segle XVIII", *Una relació difícil. Catalunya i l'Espanya moderna (segles XVII-XIX)*, Joaquim Albareda, ed. (Barcelona: Editorial Base, 2007), pp. 293-327, especially, p. 298.

112 Joaquim Albareda, "L'austriacisme, una visió...", p. 49; Josep Fontana, *Història de Catalunya. La fi de l'Antic Règim i la industrialització, 1787-1868* (Barcelona: Edicions 62, 1988), vol. 5, pp. 180-181.

113 Ferran Soldevila, *Història de Catalunya*, 2 vols. (Barcelona: Alpha, 1962), vol. 2, p. 1170.

114 Enrique Gimenez, "Conflicto armado con Francia y guerrilla austracista en Cataluña (1719-1720)", *Hispania: Revista española de historia*, 220 (2005), pp. 543-600.

around all of Catalonia, led by the guilds[115], and top-down with reformist projects envisioned by the Catalan Bourbon elite which consisted of reviving the old models of local governance and pluralising and decentralising the monarchy in view of the enlightened despotism of Madrid, which ran counter to the interests of Catalonia[116].

This situation did not go unnoticed by foreign travellers, military officers and government officials who were around the Principality of Catalonia in the 18th and early 19th century. In their reports or travelogues, they wrote about the pronounced identity contrast that existed between the Spaniards as a whole and Catalans, who were often characterised by a collective desire to be free, with separatist ideals and a deep aversion to the French and Castilian[117].

In conclusion, despite the fact that many of these topics on the century of Bourbon absolutism still require more in-depth study, it should be said that not only was there a national or patriotic Catalan identity through the centuries of the Old Regime, but despite the repression and lack of local state structures and the adaptation to the new imposed regime, at the dawn of the 19th century this identity still survived among most peoples of the Principality. And it survived thanks to the maintenance of the culture, to the reactions against oppression and especially to the historical memory of what Catalonia had been before the 11th of September 1714. The change of this state of affairs was fostered by the liberal revolution which expanded the new Spanish national identity, both the revolutionary and the reactionary[118], among the Catalans, which made their Catalan-ness a way of being a member of the contemporary Spanish nation. However, this is a phenomenon which lies beyond the scope of this analysis.

115 Josep Maria Torras, *Els Municipis catalans...*, pp. 321-325; Josep Maria Torras, *Los Mecanismos del poder...*, pp. 125-142.

116 Ramon Grau, "L'experiència del despotisme il.lustrat a Catalunya, 1759-1775", *L' Avenç: Revista de història i cultura*, 254 (2001), pp. 8-17. A summary of these projects can be found in: Joaquim Albareda, "El XVIII...", pp. 82-83.

117 Pere Anguera, "Entre dues possibilitats: espanyols o catalans?", *Del patriotisme al Catalanisme: societat i política (segles XVI/XIX)*, Joaquim Albareda, ed. (Vic: Eumo, 2000), pp. 317-337.

118 Lluis Roura, "El 'segrest' del concepte...", pp. 307-327.

Contemporary History

The Contemporary World: An Increasingly Noticeable Distinct Identity

Jordi Casassas
Universitat de Barcelona and Institut d'Estudis Catalans

The main purpose of the following pages is to outline the distinct features of the Catalan historical dynamic during the contemporary period. First off, we should consider that it was a vindicatory regional area in a historical period characterised by the gelling of national states and then gradually by the uniformising and later nationalising effort of these states over all the inhabitants under them. An analysis of the distinct features of the Catalan dynamic is precisely what will determine the initial chronology and the internal rhythms of the period.

Setting aside the historiographic controversies regarding where we should place the boundary between the modern and contemporary worlds, we should bear in mind that a number of unique features converged in Catalonia: the memory of a defeated, lost past (primarily in 1714 and with the *Nueva Planta* decree), a process of structural differentiation and territorial integration (hinted at in around 1680 and a reality by the middle of the following century) and its own cultural, academic and institutional dynamic which strained to coexist with the directives emanating from the central power. All of this together leads us to place the starting point in the 17th century and to identify a major crossroads in the international shift in course marked by Spain's decolonisation in South America and the impact of the Napoleonic Wars on the Peninsula. As a modern economic area and export zone, these two major points of upheaval totally affected Catalonia, but just like in the early 18th century in the wake of the huge defeat and repression after 1714, the desire to rally appeared once again early in the next century, now with modern industry as the main distinct feature.

In 1906 the Catalanist leader Enric Prat de la Riba published one of the seminal books of Catalanism, *La Nacionalitat Catalana*[1], in which he

1 Enric Prat de la Riba, *La Nacionalitat Catalana* (Barcelona: Edicions 62-La Caixa, 1978).

identified these 17th century changes as the origin of the revival of the distinct modern consciousness. And for the 19th century he added Catalonia's enormous influence over the European Romantic movement, the rising importance of cities and industrialisation. This series of factors should be joined by the rising tensions stemming from Catalonia's relations with the state, which were fraught because of the discrepancies between an industrial area and a fundamentally agricultural state (a constant claim of fiscal protectionism for Catalan industry), and owing to the poor or non-existent state management of Catalan public affairs. Some historians have even pointed to this lack of state action as one of the explanations behind the origin of Catalan nationalism. We do not agree with this outlook, but it does serve to illustrate how a distinct feeling took root in Catalonia to make up for everything that the state did not do or did poorly.

Even though it is becoming more and more common to talk about a continuum between the culture of the 18th and 19th centuries, the importance of the Romantic movement in Catalonia seems indisputable: the late Romantics would later talk about a *Renaixença* ("Renaissance") of unique consciousness, and some even claimed that the goal was to consolidate Catalonia's cultural independence since this was impossible via political means. The difference was based not only on language and history but also on unique ways of thinking, particular institutions and the dawning awareness of this difference. The Romantic mobilisation of the intellectuals, literati and liberal professionals was notable: with their institutions and publications, they put all the main arguments of uniqueness into circulation, which some historians have described as the great invention of the national tradition.

Another of the leaders of Catalanism who was also a noteworthy historian, Antoni Rovira i Virgili, saw the onset of Catalanism as the confluence of four main currents: the aforementioned cultural Renaissance and the protectionist claims of the bourgeoisie, plus the social mobilisations of Carlism and federal republicanism. The advent of these distinct movements, which are viewed as essential elements in the dawning of national consciousness, have sparked heated historiographic controversies. Regarding Carlism, some historians have denied its relationship with early Catalanism, although they do recognise the unique features of Catalan Carlism in relation to the swift deterioration of the traditional rural world in this region. Regarding the participation of federalism and, by extension, the popular urban mobilisations in the first half of the 18th century, the controversy finally surfaced in 1974, pitting those who viewed Catalanism as a reflection of bourgeois domination against those who, conversely, defended the current's popular roots.

Apart from this complex process of national awareness (initially more diffuse but openly political by the last quarter of the 19th century) which gained ground in contemporary Catalonia, there is another distinct feature which we cannot ignore. Since this was a region experiencing swift changes, powerful industrialisation and urbanisation, social tensions soon became one of the defining features of this contemporary Catalan dynamic, even more so after the mid-19th century when very low birth rates were recorded, only surpassed by France. Thus, the industrial regions became poles that attracted people from elsewhere. The phenomenon of immigration is one of the characteristics of Catalonia even today, and it is often a cause of instability which is difficult to assimilate because of the lack of regional and state and legislation on the matter. Mobility and social tensions turned Catalonia into a veritable crucible of modern violence (with such harsh junctures as the late years of the 19th century, the years after World War I and the early months of the Civil War in 1936-1937). It is common to speak disparagingly about the predominance of anarcho-syndicalists in the Catalan labour movement (the early rebels), but the fact is that since its origins in the 19th century this movement (along with other republican-based grassroots movements) showed very high levels of class consciousness and a notable ability to survive in an aggressive environment stemming from harsh political, social and labour repression.

Another unique characteristic is the political dynamic. Catalonia, and Barcelona as its capital, is very far from the central executive and legislative power, that is, from the centres where the country's major policies are devised. Since 1833, what have operated in Catalonia are four *diputacions* ("provincial councils"), but it soon became clear that Barcelona, the capital of Catalonia, is more than just a provincial capital. Since the conception of the city's modern enlargement in 1959, the hosting of the Universal Exposition in 1888 and the subsequent annexation of the surrounding towns in 1897, Barcelona has become a Mediterranean metropolis and has called for a kind of double Mediterranean-capital status within Spain. This process, along with the organisation of political Catalanism and the launch of modern republicanism, gave the Catalan urban world a political peculiarity that it still holds onto today. We can even talk about a unique feature through the relationship of the two 20th century dictatorships

(1923-1930 and 1939-1976). From the very start, these anti-parliamentary experiments revealed themselves to be particularly openly anti-Catalan and anti-Catalanist, and they strove to eradicate what they considered to be the dangerous separatist vein threatening Spain's national unity.

First Catalan culture, and then gradually its unique political organisation (especially Catalanism) have managed to react and confer distinct features compared to Spain as a whole which are so noticeable that they have given credibility and a rising social acceptance of the Catalanists' claims.

Catalonia: Unique Consciousness and Collective Identity in the First Half of the 19th Century Notes and Considerations

David Cao Costoya
Universitat de Barcelona

1. The Catalan identity between the old regime and nascent contemporary society: A pending challenge, in part, in our historiography

Until relatively recently, the analysis of collective identities in Catalan historiography has been little more than the exclusive terrain of contemporary historians[1]. In the past few years, however, this has begun to change notably. Many modern historians have given the political and ideological formation of collective identities a prime place in their research programmes and historiographic reflections[2]. And many of the resulting publications have focused on 17th-century Catalonia and to a greater or lesser extent have revolved around the centre of gravity of the Catalan Revolt in 1640 and the political and ideological dynamics associated with it. For all of these historians – and we shall not inquire into their different approaches in this article – the 17th century represents a crucial period in the crystallisation of these political-cultural constructs, a process that ran

1 One recent product of this concern can be found in the collective volume: Jordi Casassas, coord., *Les identitats a la Catalunya contemporània* (Barcelona: Galerada, 2009).

2 See, for example: Xavier Torres, *Naciones sin nacionalismo. Cataluña en la monarquía hispánica (siglos XVI-XVII)* (Valencia: Universitat de València, 2008); Antoni Simon, *Construccions polítiques i identitats nacionals. Catalunya i els orígens de l'estat modern espanyol* (Barcelona: Publicacions de l'Abadia de Montserrat, 2005); Òscar Jané, *Catalunya i França al segle XVII: identitats, contraidentitats i ideologies a l'època moderna: 1640-1700* (Catarroja-Barcelona: Afers, 2006).

parallel to the emergence of modern states and their rising political, fiscal and military demands.

One of the authors to whom I am referring, Xavier Torres, stresses the fact that at that time, the Catalan identity and its political expression in the guise of patriotism was not primarily grounded upon strictly cultural or identity factors (although they were not totally innocuous) but that it was basically "constitutionally-based", linked to the existence of a political community articulated by a web of laws and privileges. The key, in this author's opinion, can be found in the institutional sphere, in *las distintas formas de articulación política de un territorio* ("the different forms of political articulation of a territory"). Thus, even though Torres notes the existence of *nacions abans del nacionalisme*[3] ("nations before nationalism"), he clearly distinguishes between old patriotism and modern nationalism and rejects the existence of a simple, linear or necessary transition between the two. However, at the same time he suggests the possibility that those old precedents were not entirely immaterial in shaping contemporary political and cultural dynamics.

Yet here we come upon a serious difficulty. At this moment there are no studies similar to the ones mentioned above for the 18th century, and this prevents us from confidently explaining the possible continuities or disruptions between those old phenomena and contemporary identity dynamics. While Catalan historiography has shown considerable interest in studying certain economic and social transformations precisely in this phase of transition which we have agreed to call – with variations – the shift from the old regime to nascent contemporary society, the same cannot be said for the issue of identities. We are largely unaware of what distinct idea of community existed among the Catalans in the course of the 18th century and in the transition to the contemporary world; therefore, it is impossible to precisely outline how the old collective identities and pre-existing forms of social and territorial cohesion morphed under the new historical conditions (if, as we assume, they did).

If, as some studies claim, the Catalan identity under the old regime was grounded particularly upon the constitution, closely linked to the existence of the institutional and legal structure that governed the community, we can assume that its dismantlement after the outcome of 1714

3 Xavier Torres, *Naciones...*, p. 347.

and the Nueva Planta decrees must have drastically affected this identity. Which factors were determining after that pivotal point, in the context of Catalonia's increasing integration within the Spanish political and administrative structures as part of a Bourbon monarchy whose goal was to centralise and unify the country?[4] Perhaps these factors were the survival of private law, the still-widespread use of the Catalan language in the majority of spheres, the historical memory of the lost institutions, the awareness of being a defeated community and the sense of victimhood, the economic and social development that Catalonia experienced in that century or the existence of regional collective dynamics indisputably led by Barcelona?[5] If, as claimed by Salvador Sanpere i Miquel (1840-1915), a positivist historian and republican politician, the Bourbon Nueva Planta meant the death of the State but not the end of the Catalan people, we should be able to explain why this is so and weigh the factors that made it possible. Sanpere's claims that *un pueblo vive mientras su lengua vive* ("a people lives while its language lives") is valuable in that it is representative of the Catalanist perspective from the early 20th century, when the Catalan language had already been made a fundamental attribute in the shaping of the Catalan identity, but it does not explain the survival and evolution of that unique consciousness once self-governance was lost[6].

Pierre Vilar (1906-2003), a French Hispanicist with a lasting influence on our historiography, set out to study *els fonaments econòmics de les estructures nacionals* ("the economic bases of the national structures") and conferred a great deal of importance on Catalonia's growth in the

4 Joaquim Albareda asks this and other questions in: Joaquim Albareda, *El XVIII: un segle sense política? Pensament polític als Països Catalans, 1714-2014*, Jaume Renyer, Enric Pujol, dirs. (Barcelona: Centre d'Estudis de Temes Contemporanis-Pòrtic, 2007), pp. 71-92.

5 Regarding the formation of a system of Catalan cities and the articulation of a domestic market coordinated by Barcelona, albeit regarding a previous historical period, see: Albert Garcia, *Un siglo decisivo. Barcelona y Cataluña, 1550-1640* (Madrid: Alianza, 1998). See, too: Jaume Dantí coord., *Ciutats, viles i pobles a la xarxa urbana de la Catalunya moderna* (Barcelona: Rafael Dalmau, 2005); Jaume Dantí ed., *Les xarxes urbanes a la Catalunya dels segles XVI i XVII* (Barcelona: Rafael Dalmau, 2011).

6 Salvador Sanpere, *Fin de la nación catalana* (Barcelona: L'Avenç, 1905), p. 690. Facsimile edition with introductory study by: Salvador Sanpere, *Fin de la nación catalana*, ed. Joaquim Albareda (Barcelona: Base, 2001).

18th century (the region's rising demographic and economic influence on Spain as a whole), since that was when the foundation of unequal capitalist development around Spain was laid, a factor which he considered essential when explaining the future accentuation of Catalonia's regional personality and the emergence of a unique group consciousness in the 19th century[7]. Vilar remarked on the dynamic correlation between *l'estructura econòmica* ("the economic structure") and *sentiment de grup* ("group feeling") and advised about the need to bear this duality in mind when striving to analyse the existence of the nation. Yet at the same time, the French historian noted that for much of the 18th century, the *intensa vida regional* ("intense regional life") fit comfortably within Spain as a whole, a far cry from the conflictive relations in the ensuing century[8]. He even claimed that the 18th century had been *estèril per a l'esperit de grup dels catalans*[9] ("sterlie for the group spirit of the Catalans"), a stage in which collective consciousness had gone through a process of *afebliment* ("weakening") and had been at *risc de desaparició* ("extinction risk"), at least among the *classes emprenedores i acomodades*[10] ("entrepreneurial at wealthy classes").

Ferran Soldevila (1894-1971) believed that the 18th century was largely a period in which *desnacionalització* ("denationalisation") efforts intensified, and in which the Catalans *anaven a assajar d'esdevenir província, essent la seva voluntat fondre's dins Espanya, d'assimilar-s'hi, d'esborrar, doncs, la diferenciació existent, profunda encara*[11] ("were going to try to become a province, their desire being to melt into Spain, to assimilate themselves, so to erase the existing, still deep, differentiation"). This perspective was deeply indebted to the kind of discourse that had been crystallising since the 19th century with the *Renaixença* movement, which dramatically contrasted an 18th century marked by the culmination of secular decline and collective alienation with a more or less glorious period in

7 Pierre Vilar, *Catalunya dins l'Espanya moderna. Recerques sobre els fonaments econòmics de les estructures nacionals*, 3 vols. (Barcelona: Edicions 62, 1964), vol. 1, pp. 15-87.

8 Pierre Vilar, *Catalunya dins l'Espanya moderna...*, vol. 1, p. 79 and following.

9 Pierre Vilar, *Catalunya dins l'Espanya* moderna..., vol. 2, p. 419.

10 Pierre Vilar, *Estat, nació, socialisme. Estudis sobre el cas espanyol* (Barcelona: Curial, 1982) p. 75.

11 Ferran Soldevila, *Història de Catalunya*, vols. 3 (Barcelona: Alpha, 1962-63), vol. 3, p. 1168.

the revival of Catalan culture and *esperit* ("spirit") launched in the middle decades of the 19th century. Ernest Lluch (1937-2000) explicitly criticised this kind of approach and sought to reveal that during the 18th century there had been an entire series of political, cultural and economic expressions and projects which evidenced that it was not a *segle nacionalment perdut per a Catalunya* ("not a century nationally lost for Catalonia"). Indeed, he borrowed the words of Jordi Rubió i Balaguer (1887-1982) when he defended the inheritance of the 18th century as a way to better understand the cultural phenomenon of the *Renaixença*[12]. Thus, Lluch particularly underscored the survival of a local political tradition alternative to centralist absolutism (which would somehow be associated with some Catalan leaders' "claims for the old codes of law" in the constitutive period of the Courts of Cádiz) and the existence of an "enlightened project for Catalonia" forged in around 1780, which was grounded upon its own history and literature and on a vision of the present and future of the Catalan economy aimed at conferring a "global consciousness of being a country". The roles of the Junta de Comerç ("Board of Trade") and individuals like Jaume Caresmar (1717-1791) and Antoni de Capmany (1742-1813) were fundamental in the materialisation of these projects. In short, the image of a quiet 18th century and a Catalan society that had permanently lost its memory of the old laws and institutions and had happily and fully assimilated within the structures of the Bourbon centralist absolutism has been seriously called into question in numerous studies[13].

According to Pere Anguera (1953-2010), in 1800 the *pòsit diferencial era viu i poderós* ("differential sediment was alive and powerful"), and a Catalan identity grounded upon a variety of elements like language, civil law and the *consciència col·lectiva de formar part d'una comunitat derrotada* ("collective awareness of forming part of a degerated community"), he claimed, *persistia* ("persisted"). According to this historian's interpretation, the implosion of the Peninsular War (1808-1814) signalled a major

12 Ernest Lluch, *La Catalunya vençuda del segle XVIII. Foscors i clarors de la Il·lustració* (Barcelona: Edicions 62, 1996); Jordi Rubió, *Història de la literatura catalana*, 3 vols. (Barcelona: Departament de Cultura de la Generalitat de Catalunya-Publicacions de l'Abadia de Montserrat, 1986), vol. 3, p. 19.

13 See, for example: Lluís Roura, *Subjecció i revolta en el segle de la Nova Planta* (Vic: Eumo, 2005); Josep Maria Torras, *Els municipis catalans de l'Antic Règim (1453-1808)* (Barcelona: Curial, 1983).

turning point in that *per primera vegada s'evidencià en un conjunt significatiu de catalans un sentiment espanyol* ("for the first time a Spanish feeling was shown by significant proportion of Catalans"). However, this same author noted that the conflict acted in a *manera doble i contradictòria* ("double and contradictory way") because it fed a particularist historical consciousness that was susceptible to more political considerations which somehow gained momentum alongside the rising pressure from the modern liberal state to homogenise[14].

The fact is that the Peninsular War was soon mythologised as a moment of sentimental communion and brotherhood among the different regions and peoples of Spain, all galvanised against a common enemy. The collective resistance against the French became the founding myth of a shared national Spanish project[15]. Today we know that a wide range of movements and political projects were concealed under the much-heralded unanimity. If there was a vigorous unique Catalan identity back then, Anguera asked, what exactly were its fundamental defining attributes, how did it fit within the new political context and how did it coexist with other loyalties and frames of integration?[16] Did Catalan patriotism play a major role in the uprising and in determining the political dynamic of the period, or did it play a totally marginal role compared to other principles of cohesion and mobilisation? Soldevila noted that Catalan and Spanish patriotic feelings mixed in a way that was difficult to extricate from each other, and he identified expressions of a *tímid regionalisme*[17] ("timid regionalism"). Joan Mercader (1917-1989) described the ideology of the

14 Pere Anguera, "Entre dues possibilitats: espanyols o catalans?", *Del patriotisme al catalanisme. Societat i política (segles XVI-XIX)*, Joaquim Albareda, dir. (Vic: Eumo, 2001), pp. 317-337. See, too: Pere Anguera, *Els precedents del catalanisme. Catalanitat i anticentralisme: 1808-1868* (Barcelona: Empúries, 2000), pp. 27-88.

15 Regarding this myth, see: Álvarez Junco, "La invención de la Guerra de la Independencia", *Studia Historica. Historia Contemporánea*, 12 (1994), pp. 75-99; Lluís Ferran Toledano, "La Guerra de la Independencia como exponente de la unanimidad espanyola", *A Guerra da Independencia e o primeiro liberalismo en España e America*, José M. Portillo, Xosé Ramon Veiga and Maria Jesús Baz, dirs. (Santiago de Compostela: Universidade de Santiago de Compostela, 2009) pp. 69-101.

16 See several reflections on this issue in: Albert Ghanime, "Reflexions al voltant de la Guerra del Francès i la identitat catalana", *Les identitats a la Catalunya contemporània*, Jordi Casassas, dir. (Barcelona: Galerada, 2009), pp. 183-200.

17 Ferran Soldevila, *Història de Catalunya...*, vol. 3, p. 1266 and following.

leaders of the Principality as *particularisme provincial* ("provicial particularism") and the position of the Junta Superior de Catalunya as *federalista*[18] ("federalist"), while Jaume Vicens i Vives (1910-1960) detected a *caliu provincialista* ("provincialist warmth") in Catalonia during this period and pointed out that the memory of the former governing institutions remained alive, although this in no way prevented the Catalans from feeling totally Spanish[19]. Vilar, in turn, believed that it was the historical period with the greatest affirmation of Spanish national unity and that the events revealed that there was not necessarily an opposition between anti-centralism and unity[20].

More recent studies have stressed the fact that the Catalan patriotism of this period and the existence of awareness of a unique identity were not obstacles to participating in the resistance and constructing a Spain-wide political project in a more or less coordinated fashion[21]. Thus, according to Maties Ramisa, the *identificació política de Catalunya amb Espanya* was *compatible amb el manteniment de la pròpia identitat en el substrat bàsic de la consciència col·lectiva* ("political identification of Catalonia with Spain" was "compatible with the maintenance of its own identity in the basic substrate of the collcetive awareness"). This historian states that the Napoleonic agents and officers kept underscoring the strong particularisms in the Peninsula and noting the *diferent idiosincràsia dels catalans i la resta d'espanyols: els bonapartistes tenen molt clara l'entitat geohistòrica i lingüística de Catalunya, que sempre consideren un objectiu militar específic dins d'Espanya*[22] ("different idiosyncracy of the Catalans and the rest of the Spaniards: the Bonapartists see the geo-historical and linguistic entity of Catalonia very clearly, that they always consider a specific

18 Joan Mercader, "La ideologia dels catalans del 1808", *Miscellanea Aqualatensia*, 5 (1987), pp. 83-98.

19 Jaume Vicens, "La Guerra del Francès", *Moments crucials de la història de Catalunya*, Ramon d'Abadal, Jaume Vivens, dirs. (Barcelona: Vicens-Vives, 1962), pp. 283-285.

20 Pierre Vilar, "Ocupació i resistència durant la Guerra Gran i en temps de Napoleó", *Assaigs sobre la Catalunya del segle XVIII* (Barcelona: Curial, 1973), pp. 126-128.

21 Antoni Moliner, *La Catalunya resistent a la dominació francesa. La Junta Superior de Catalunya (1808-1812)* (Barcelona: Edicions 62, 1989).

22 Maties Ramisa, *Els catalans i el domini napoleònic (Catalunya vista pels oficials de l'exèrcit de Napoleó)* (Barcelona: Publicacions de l'Abadia de Montserrat, 1995), pp. 359-372.

military target within Spain"). This would probably partly explain the *Catalanist essay* with which Marshal Augereau tried to attract Catalonia to the empire during the first half of 1810. With it, he strategically appealed to the particularist feeling of the Catalan people with proclamations that glorified the Catalans' hardworking character and historical gestures and promoted the public, official use of the Catalan language. This translated, for example, into the bilingual Catalan-French publication of the *Diario de Barcelona* (*Diari de Barcelona y del Gobern de Catalunya*) and the drafting of the minutes of the Barcelona Town Council in the local language[23]. One of the main collaborators and inspirations behind that policy was the Frenchified liberal Tomàs Puig (1771-1835), whose biographer, Lluís M. de Puig (1945-2012), stressed his clearly Catalanist orientation[24]. The same author identified clear signs of Spanishness among Catalans in this period, yet he also underscored the *presència d'un fet diferencial indiscutible i d'una consciència de grup molt profunda* ("undeniable presence of a differential and a very deep group awareness"), grounded upon attributes like language, a *comunitat de cultura* ("community of culture") and the *fet economic* ("economic fact")[25]. However, other historians believe that the broader spheres of political and territorial identification did not play as relevant a role as they have been assigned and that community dynamics and more strictly local loyalties are what mobilised and articulated the resistance following a self-defensive logic[26].

Still within this same time period, which was characterised by accelerated fraying of the structures of the old regime and the constituent process underway, it has been shown that historicist arguments were frequent

23 Joan Mercader, *Catalunya i l'imperi napoleònic* (Barcelona: Publicacions de l'Abadia de Montserrat, 1978) pp. 79-133. Mercader reported on the meagre consequences of the campaign. Josep Fontana believes that this stage has been mythologised by Catalan historiography; see: Josep Fontana, "La fi de l'Antic Règim i la industrialització (1787-1868)", *Història de Catalunya*, 10 vols., Pierre Vilar, dir. (Barcelona: Edicions 62, 1998), vol. 5, p. 169.

24 Lluís Maria de Puig, *Tomàs Puig. Catalanisme i afrancesament* (Barcelona: Institut d'Estudis Catalans, 1985).

25 Lluís Maria de Puig, "Invasió napoleònica i qüestió nacional a Catalunya", *La invasió napoleònica. Economia, cultura i societat*, Josep Fontana dir. (Bellaterra: Universitat Autònoma de Barcelona, 1981), pp. 55-79.

26 John Lawrence Tone, *La guerrilla española y la derrota de Napoleón* (Madrid: Alianza, 1999). The study primarily centres on Navarra.

among Catalan politicians and played a core role in the discourse on reinstating the old laws and institutions of the Principality of Catalonia and the Crown of Aragon[27]. The most famous case is Capmany, who in that context of negotiation and recomposition of the Spanish political space tried to bargain for a reformist, moderate solution grounded upon the historical tradition and legal and institutional background of the former kingdoms of the Crown of Aragon[28]. As history has shown, this was not the road taken. What is more, it seems clear that Catalonia's historical, legal and institutional referents did not achieve an appreciable place within Spain's national discourse. Still, the constitutional tradition and the Catalan historical memory forged their own pathway. This is proven by the fact that during the Liberal Triennium (1820-1823), appeals to the old laws and institutions of the Principality recurred frequently in the discourse of Barcelona liberalism, especially among the moderates, who praised the old constitutional system and drew parallels and affiliations with the new system of freedoms to seek the legitimisation and consolidation of Spain's liberal regime and the reinforcement of a provincial space which would guarantee them some degree of political capacity. However, this objective was somewhat at odds with the centralising, unitarist momentum which had been revealed in Cádiz[29].

27 Lluís Ferran Toledano, "Historicisme i política de la classe dirigent catalana en el debat constitucional gaditià", *Entre la construcció nacional i la repressió identitària. Actes de la primera trobada Galeusca d'historiadores i d'historiadors. Barcelona, 10 i 11 de desembre de 2010*, Agustí Alcoberro, Giovanni C. Cattini, dirs. (Barcelona: Museu d'Història de Catalunya, 2012), pp. 203-218.

28 Ramon Grau, Marina López, "Antoni de Capmany: el primer model del pensament polític català modern", *Història del pensament polític català del segle XVIII a mitjan segle XX*, Albert Balcells, dir. (Barcelona: Edicions 62, 1988), pp. 13-40; Ramon Grau, *Antoni de Capmany i la renovació de l'historicisme polític català* (Barcelona: Ajuntament de Barcelona-Quaderns del Seminari d'Història de Barcelona, 2006); Francisco José Fernández de la Cigoña, Estanislao Cantero, *Antonio de Capmany (1742-1813). Pensamiento, obra histórica, política y jurídica* (Madrid: Fundación Francisco Elias de Tejada, 1993).

29 Jordi Roca, *Política, Liberalisme i Revolució. Barcelona, 1820-1823* (Barcelona: Universitat Autònoma de Barcelona, PhD Dissertation, 2007), pp. 430-463; Jordi Roca, *Tradició constitucional i història nacional (1808-1823). Llegat i projecció d'una nissaga catalana, els Papiol* (Vilassar de Mar-Lleida: Fundació Ernest Lluch-Pagès Editors, 2011); Ramon Arnabat, *La revolució del 1820 i el Trienni Liberal a Catalunya* (Vic: Eumo, 2001), pp. 82-87; Ramon Arnabat, "Territoris i sensibilitats

2. Industrialisation, a distinguishing feature

As mentioned above, during the 18th century Catalonia underwent a series of economic and social transformations that gradually turned it into a relatively developed region in material terms, one that experienced early modernisation in line with the prevailing paradigms in its most immediate environs. That century witnessed strong demographic growth, agricultural development characterised by specialisation and market orientation, the arrival of a remarkable industrial manufacturing base and the expansion of trade. A fairly well-articulated Catalan market was strengthened by a notable urban network led by Barcelona, which was gaining ground as the indisputable backbone of its economic area. This series of transformations – rooted in the previous century – fostered the appearance of a unique society with its own partly specific features and needs.

In the course of the 18th and early 19th centuries, the Catalan elites launched a series of economic, cultural, technical and scientific institutions aimed at fostering this modern development and setting up valid local instruments to manage and distinguish a unique reality. The Junta de Comerç ("Board of Trade") and its chairs and the Reial Acadèmia de les Bones Lletres ("Royal Academy of Belles-Lettres") were the key players, but not the only ones. The actions of this institutional complex combined fostering economic prosperity, exerting pressure in defence of local interests and implementing educational actions aimed at meeting the educational needs that were not properly covered by the State, with a focus on the historical and economic specificities of Catalan society[30].

---

nacionals Catalunya-Espanya durant el Trienni Liberal", *Projectes nacionals, identitats i relacions Catalunya-Espanya. Homenatge al doctor Pere Angera (II)*, Ramon Arnabat, Antoni Gavaldà, dirs. (Catarroja-Barcelona: Afers-Ideologies i societat a la Catalunya contemporània-Universitat Rovira i Virgili, 2012), vol. 2, pp. 33-48. Regarding the concept of nation, see: Xavier Arbós, *La idea de nació en el primer constitucionalisme espanyol* (Barcelona: Curial, 1986).

30 Jordi Monés, *L'obra educativa de la Junta de Comerç 1769-1851* (Barcelona: Cambra Oficial de Comerç, Indústria i Navegació de Barcelona, 1987); Mireia Campabadal, *La Reial Acadèmia de Bones Lletres de Barcelona en el segle XVIII. L'interès per la història, la llengua i la literatura catalanes* (Barcelona: Reial Acadèmia de Bones Lletres-Publicacions de l'Abadia de Montserrat, 2006).

Based on the aforementioned transformations, Catalonia developed a modern industrial economy starting in the 1830s, although more clearly in the ensuing decades[31]. The country was the site of a major industrial revolution based on the production of consumer goods, primarily grounded upon the textile sector. Its engine was private initiative, and it was nudged along by the new legal-political framework and rising involvement in the Spanish economy. These intense transformations situated Catalonia among the pioneering industrial regions in Europe and accentuated its uniqueness within Spain at that time, where the Industrial Revolution was a failure, to use an uncompromising, expressive and historiographically controversial term[32]. The accentuated geographic concentration of industrial activity in Catalonia within Spain explains the coining of the slogan *Catalunya, fàbrica d'Espanya* ("Catalonia, workshop of Spain"), which is even more meaningful when applied to the second half of the century[33].

The economic transformations to which we are alluding also meant that the liberal revolution in Catalonia had a pace and intensity different to the rest of Spain, which resulted in uneven political processes. This led what is called the modern social question to emerge earlier and relatively more strongly in Catalonia. Jaume Balmes (1810-1848), a Catholic priest and thinker and one of the most lucid analysts of this time, is an exceptionally brilliant witness to these issues[34]. Balmes, who held openly industrialist positions, pledged himself to the Spanish national project and rejected blind provincialist attitudes which could distort it. He believed that the Principality's political independence was not only undesirable but also *impossible de realitzar* ("impossible to carry out"), and that the desire to revive the *antics furs* ("ancient law") ran counter to *l'esperit del segle* ("the spirtit of the century"). Yet he also remarked on Catalonia's *estat excepcional* ("exceptional state") compared to the other Spanish

31 Jordi Maluquer de Motes, Jaume Torras, "La formació d'una societat industrial", *Història econòmica de la Catalunya contemporània*, 6 vols., Jordi Nadal, dir. (Barcelona: Enciclopèdia Catalana, 1994), vol. 1.

32 Jordi Nadal, *El fracaso de la Revolución industrial en España, 1814-1913* (Barcelona: Ariel, 1987).

33 Jordi Nadal, Jordi Maluquer de Motes, *Catalunya, la fàbrica d'Espanya. Un segle d'industrialització catalana, 1833-1936* (Barcelona: Ajuntament de Barcelona, 1985).

34 Josep Maria Fradera, *Jaume Balmes. Els fonaments racionals d'una política catòlica* (Vic: Eumo, 1996).

provinces[35], *así en lo tocante a la riqueza pública, como en lo relativo a las ideas, costumbres, hábitos e índole de los habitants*[36] ("as well as in that concerning public wealth, and things related to the ideas, customs, habits and nature of the inhabitants"). In a series of articles that the thinker from Vic published under the title of *Cataluña* ("Catalonia") in the magazine *La Sociedad* in 1843, a context marked by urban upheaval and intense social and political conflict, Balmes contributed an entire series of extraordinarily interesting observations and reflections. He stressed that the modern economic development of Catalonia was unique in southern Europe and exceptional within Spain. One result of this unique development was the relative *oposició d'interessos* ("difference of interests") with the other *províncies* ("provinces")[37]. Balmes' description of this situation, though perhaps too simplistic, is nonetheless highly expressive.

> *Conviene no perder de vista que Cataluña es la única provincia que participa, propiamente hablando, del movimiento industrial europeo, y así sólo en ella se presentarán los nuevos problemas sociales; no en las demás, que, a excepción de cierto movimiento febril y somero que se observa en la estrecha esfera de la política, continúan en todo lo demás como allá en el reinado de Carlos II. Cuando se pasa de Cataluña al extranjero nada se observa que no sea una especie de continuación de lo que aquí se ha visto. Diríase que el viaje se hace dentro una misma nación, de una a otra provincia; pero al salir del Principado para lo interior de España, entonces parece que en realidad se ha dejado la patria y se entra en países extraños*[38].

> It is worth keeping in mind that Catalonia is the only province that participates, properly speaking, in the European industrial movement, and thus only in it will the new social problems arise, not in the others, that except for a certain feverish and superficial movement that is seen in the narrow sphere of politics, all the others continue as they were under the reign of Charles II. When one moves abroad from Catalonia nothing is seen that is not a kind of continuation of what one has seen here. One could say that the journey is done within the same nation, from one province to another; but on leaving the Principality for the interior of Spain, then it seems that in reality one has left the homeland and entered into foreign countries.

35 Jaume Balmes, *Escrits sobre Catalunya* (Vic: Eumo-Institut Universitari d'Història Jaume Vicens Vives, 1998), p. 71.

36 Jaume Balmes, *Escrits sobre Catalunya...*, p. 44.

37 Jaume Balmes, *Escrits sobre Catalunya...*, pp. 47 and 57.

38 Jaume Balmes, *Escrits sobre Catalunya...*, pp. 82-83.

Drawing from an organicist approach, he claimed that *la vida de España está en las extremidades; el centro está exánime, flaco, frío, poco menos que muerto* ("the life in Spain is in the extremities; the center is lifeless, thin, cold, little more than dead"). Madrid, a *centre sense vida* ("centre without life"), was *incapaz de dar impulso y dirección al movimiento de un gran pueblo* ("unable to provide impetus and direction to the movement of a great people"). The Catalan elites could not afford to wait for the stimuli and solutions from the centre of the State. Balmes claimed that *hace ya mucho tiempo que está acostumbrada Cataluña a hacer grandes cosas por sí misma, marchando por el camino de la prosperidad, sin que le sirva de mucho la dirección del gobierno* ("for a long time Catalonia is used to doing great things for itself, marching down the path of prosperity, without the management of the government being of much use"). In short, in another series of articles entitled "Barcelona", which came a bit later (1844), he stressed the uniqueness of the capital of Catalonia, which more closely resembled some northern European cities its Spanish counterparts. Therefore, he believed that it was logical that the revolution (or counter-revolution) that had been affecting the country since 1833 had *particularitats característiques* ("characteristic particularities") in Catalonia in the *part política* ("political part"), because Catalonia's *organització social* ("social organisation") was also unique[39].

This disparity in the forms of economic and social development to which Balmes alluded has been pointed out by some contemporary Catalan historiographers as a fundamental fact when explaining the limitations of the Spanish State's success in its nationalisation efforts and the survival of a Catalan identity that was later susceptible to being politicised. There have been discussions of the profound opposition of structures, unequal development, the bourgeoisie or divided business class and, in short, the inability to articulate a collective project capable of bringing together the interests of a ruling class with overly divergent objectives[40].

39 Jaume Balmes, *Escrits sobre Catalunya...*, p. 53-54, 65 and 146.

40 See, for example: Pierre Vilar, *Catalunya dins l'Espanya...*, vol. 1, pp. 53-93; Josep Fontana, *La fi de l'Antic Règim...*, p. 453 and following. By the same author, see, more recently: Josep Fontana, "Les dificultats polítiques de la industrialització", *Una relació difícil. Catalunya i l'Espanya moderna (segles XVII-XIX)*, Joaquim Albareda, dir. (Barcelona: Base, 2007), pp. 399-413.

The debate between those in favour of free trade versus the protectionists is, therefore, nothing more than a partial reflection of this structural disparity. In Catalonia, there were insistent claims for an economic and tariff policy that suited the needs of its industrial development. Without delving any further, Balmes wrote some of the articles mentioned above in a context in which there was a great deal of concern in Catalonia over the potential signing of a free-trade agreement between the Spanish and British governments which threatened to seriously jeopardise Catalan industry. In direct reference to that issue, Balmes showed his support of nationalising Catalonia's interests (in favour of Spain) and of convincing the other provinces of Spain that what was being proposed was not a monopoly in favour of the Principality but a *sistema de compensacions recíproques* ("system of reciprocal compensations"), that is, a joint development programme based on a protected domestic market. In short, this is the argument that was articulated and disseminated in the early decades of the 19th century by people like Antoni Bonaventura Gassó (1752-1824?), Guillem Oliver (1775-1839) and Eudald Jaumeandreu (1774-1840), and which mid-century was propounded particularly by Joan Güell i Ferrer (1800-1872) and Joan Illas i Vidal (1819-1876), who used platforms such as the Institut Industrial de Catalunya, *El Locomotor* and *El Bien Público*. The main features of this line of political thinking could be identified earlier in Campmany, Caresmar and Francesc Romà i Rossell (1725-1784), whose industrialist mercantilism projects and concerns contrasted with the prevailing agrarianism in other regions of Spain[41].

Further examples of the expressions and implications stemming from the existence of this unique economic and social physiognomy in Catalonia within the context of Spain could be cited, but it is not always easy to properly weigh them or even less to determine their specific influence on and interaction with more strictly identity-related factors. For example, there was an idea fostered by locals and outsiders alike, which can be detected quite long before the onset of the Industrial Revolution, of the proverbial hardworking, active personality of the Catalans, making this one of their

41 Ernest Lluch, *El pensament econòmic a Catalunya (1760-1840). Els orígens ideològics del proteccionisme i la presa de consciència de la burgesia catalana* (Barcelona: Edicions 62, 1973); Lluís Argemí, *Història del pensament econòmic a Catalunya* (Vic-Lleida: Eumo-Pagès, 2005); Joan Fuster, *Barcelona i l'Estat centralista. Indústria i política a la dècada moderada (1843-1854)* (Vic: Eumo, 2005).

fundamental attributes as a people. To what extent did the existence of certain social institutions and distinct economic development contribute to generating a culture of work that could feed a unique collective consciousness like this?

There was also a more or less well-founded and precise idea of a Catalonia that was used to standing on its own and that was rarely able to find a sufficiently solid ally within the State for its moral and material progress. We have seen this partly reflected in Balmes' words. For example, the State was unable to take a proactive enough role in the realm of communication infrastructures, which were fundamental in consolidating the modern process of economic development in Catalonia, among other reasons because of the chronic weakness of the public treasury. The construction of railway infrastructures in Spain depended heavily on foreign investment, but not so much in Catalonia where, for a variety of reasons, the initiative and participation of Catalan capital was important enough to spur the construction of the regional railway network[42]. In terms of roads, it is interesting to examine the creation of the Junta de Carreteres de Catalunya (Motorway Board of Catalonia), a supra-provincial entity made up of representatives of the four Catalan provincial councils[43]. It was set up in 1848 along with the design of a plan for motorways around the Principality with the mission of spearheading improvements in the Catalan roadway network via extraordinary regional excise taxes. In view of the State's inhibition or inability to act decisively in this sphere, the Catalan institutions took the reins. Despite the episodes of inter-provincial tensions and the limitations in both competences and effective action, this experience was quite important because it enabled Catalonia to have an administrative body between 1848 and 1868 which was superimposed over the provincial division and was charged with planning and operating in the entire Principality.

In short, there is yet one final note that is not totally foreign to the issues we are examining. The Catalans' political, administrative and

42 Pere Pascual, *Los caminos de la era industrial. La construcción y financiación de la Red Ferroviaria Catalana (1843-1898)* (Barcelona: Edicions Universitat de Barcelona, 1999).

43 Pere Pascual, "La Diputació i la modernització de la xarxa viària catalana: 1840-1868", *Història de la Diputació de Barcelona*, 3 vols., Borja de Riquer, dir. (Barcelona: Diputació de Barcelona, 1987), vol.1, pp. 141-195.

professional participation within the State during the 19th century has been noted as being much lower than what it should have been proportionally given its population and economic clout within Spain as a whole[44]. From this we can infer that Catalonia had little political influence in the construction of the liberal State, at least in the more institutional behaviours that are organically dependent upon the administrative apparatus. Probably the most striking figure is the number of Catalan ministers, which did not even reach 3% of the total between 1814 and 1900, most of them during the Sexenni Democràtic (Six Years of Democracy, 1868-1874). Regarding Catalans' scarce presence in the civil and military administration, it has been pointed out that this may be explained by the fact that Catalonia's society and economy offered more varied prospects and possibilities for work and professional promotion other than public service. It is difficult to weigh to what extent this contributed to the perception of the State as a relatively foreign entity to the reality in Catalonia and how this somehow compromised its success at nationalising Catalonia.

3. Historical awareness and the use of the past

In the sections above we have discussed the apparent importance of history as a fundamental factor reinforcing Catalans' collective consciousness. In the 1830s and especially during the decades immediately thereafter, there was a rising interest in the history of Catalonia, and this only intensified the literary and political use of the Catalan past, especially from the Middle Ages. This same period is when we can find the first expressions of a Romantic Catalan historiography (written in Spanish) which emerged from the heat of the emerging Romanticism. History became a basic component of a higher cultural agenda that sought to restore the Catalan personality. It is interesting to note that this historicism, which is essential to the process of identity differentiation, emerged the most strongly in the

44 Borja de Riquer, Manel Risques, "Participació administrativa, professional i política en l'Estat", *Els catalans a Espanya, 1760-1914*, Mª Teresa Pérez, Antoni Segura, Llorenç Ferrer, dirs. (Barcelona: Universitat de Barcelona-Generalitat de Catalunya, 1996), pp. 83-93.

key years when the Spanish liberal state was being consolidated and developed as the political and legal framework of reference[45].

The years of the liberal revolution shaped a period when political uses of the past proliferated. Setting aside for now the contributions which we could more or less accurately describe as historiography per se, we can find numerous examples in the publications and printed matter that fuelled the liberal discourse, which stressed establishing affiliations among the new and old institutions and freedoms. The taste for and use of the historical past could also be seen in the sphere of literary creation (just as it could in other artistic disciplines). One prominent development in this vein is the emergence of the historical novel set in the Middle Ages. A pioneer in this genre was Ramon López Soler (1799-1836), who introduced the works of Sir Walter Scott to Catalonia. Following his example, Joan Cortada (1805-1868) wrote numerous historical novels set in the Middle Ages, some of which, such as *La heredera de Sangumí* (1835), contributed to the thematic Catalanisation of the literary output and fostered an interest in Catalans' own history[46]. In the sphere of Romantic drama, the same holds true for Jaume Tió (1816-1844), who stands out as the person who introduced French Romantic literature and edited and completed the *Historia de los movimientos, separación y guerra de Cataluña en tiempo de Felipe*, a work by Francisco Manuel de Melo (1608-1666)[47]. As the

45 Regarding the historiography of this period, see: Ramon Grau, "La historiografia del romanticisme (de Pròsper de Bofarull a Víctor Balaguer)", *Història de la historiografia catalana*, Albert Balcells, dir. (Barcelona: Institut d'Estudis Catalans, 2004), pp. 141-160; Ramon Grau, "L'aportació dels historiadors romàntics", *Història de la Cultura Catalana*, 10 vols., Pere Gabriel, dir. (Barcelona: Edicions 62, 1995), vol. 4, pp. 221-248; Josep Fontana, "El romanticisme i la formació d'una història nacional catalana", *El segle romàntic. Actes del col·loqui sobre el Romanticisme. Vilanova i la Geltrú 2, 3 i 4 de febrer de 1995* (Vilanova i la Geltrú: Biblioteca-Museu Víctor Balaguer, 1997), pp. 539-549; Pere Anguera, "Españolismo y catalanidad en la historiografía catalana decimonónica", *Hispania*, 209 (2001), pp. 907-932; Josep Maria Fradera, "El passat com a present (la historiografia catalana de la revolució liberal a la Renaixença)", *Recerques*, 23 (1990), pp. 53-71. For the general context: *Els intel·lectuals i el poder a la Catalunya contemporània (1808-1975)*, Jordi Casassas, coord. (Barcelona: Pòrtic, 1999), p. 49 and following.

46 Albert Ghanime, *Joan Cortada: Catalunya i els Catalans al segle XIX* (Barcelona: Publicacions de l'Abadia de Montserrat, 1994).

47 Regarding Jaume Tió, see: Francesc Mestre, *Temps, vida i obres del polígraf D. Jaume Tió i Noé, 1816-1844* (Barcelona: Balmes, 1927).

author of *Pedro el Católico* (1842), *Roger de Flor* (1844) and *El Consejo de Ciento* (1846), Antoni de Bofarull (1821-1892) played an important role in the effort to thematically Catalanise drama in Catalonia and to spread cognizance of the episodes, characters and institutions from the Principality's medieval past[48].

The work by Pròsper de Bofarull (1777-1859) entitled *Los condes de Barcelona vindicados* (1836) was essential to the birth of Catalan Romantic historiography from the liberal revolution[49]. Its author stressed that the Principality of Catalonia had a past as an independent political entity. He emphasised the need to make this history known and spotlighted the role that the House of Barcelona and the Crown of Aragon had played in the construction of Spain. A perusal of the justification of the work makes it crystal clear that this stance was not agenda-free from the political or ideological perspective. Thus, Bofarull stated that Wilfred the Hairy (9th century) and his successors had founded

> *Una Patria, Soberanía y Constitucion civil que nos han transmitido, y cuyo origen y vicisitudes conviene tener muy presentes, mayormente cuando se trata de uniformidad civil Española, de reformas y de regeneracion de fueros, libertades ó* privilegios *que el antiguo Condado y Marquesado de Barcelona no desconocia muchos siglos atrás á pesar de los embates del feudalismo.*

> A Homeland, Sovereignty and civil Constitution that have been transmitted to us, and whose origin and vicissitudes should be kept well in mind, mainly when it is a question of the Spanish civil uniformity, of reform and regeneration of charters, liberties or privileges that the ancient County and Marquisate of Barcelona was not unaware of centuries ago despite the ravages of feudalism.

In this vein, he recalled that at that time, in around 1833, Catalonia was *una de tantas provincias de la Monarquía continental Española* ("one of so many provinces of the Spanish continental Monarchy"), but that in the past it had been a *pequeño Estado independiente* ("small independent

48 Jordi Ginebra, *Antoni de Bofarull i la Renaixença* (Reus-Lleida: Associació d'Estudis Reusencs-Pagès Editors, 1988).

49 Próspero de Bofarull, *Los condes de Barcelona vindicados, y cronología y genealogía de los reyes de España considerados como soberanos independientes de su marca*, 2 vols. (Barcelona: Imp. de J. Oliveres y Monmany, 1836), vol. 2. Regarding the Bofarulls, see: Ramon Grau, "El pensament històric de la dinastia Bofarull", *Barcelona Quaderns d'Història*, 6 (2002), pp. 121-138.

state"). Bofarull, who dedicated the work to Ferdinand IV of Barcelona and Aragon and VII of Castile (this order is quite meaningful), ended by expressing his desire for the work to be a contribution to the *Historia general de España y particularmente de la de Cataluña nuestra Patria*[50].

At that time, Bofarull, the first in a prominent family of archivists and historians, was one of the members of the restored Acadèmia de les Bones Lletres of Barcelona, which was futilely attempting to revive the old project of spearheading and coordinating the development of a history of Catalonia. Along with Fèlix Torres i Amat and Albert Pujol, he was in charge of the complete edition of the *Crónica universal del Principado de Cataluña* written by the jurist Jeroni Pujades (1568-1635)[51]. Years earlier, this had meant opposing the transfer of the extraordinarily important Archive of the Crown of Aragon to Madrid, stating that there were still important ties between people and institutions located in the Principality and that documentation centre because until that constitutional period *jamas ha podido considerarse la península como una sola nacion ó reyno sino como un conjunto de estados independientes gobernados por un mismo principio*[52] ("the peninsula could never have been considered as a singlke nation or kingdom but rather as a set of independent states governed by a single principle"). Keeping the Archive in Barcelona was essential to making it possible to perform historical studies and issue documentary publications such as the one Bofarull himself undertook in 1847, entitled *Colección de documentos inéditos del Archivo General de la Corona de Aragón.*

Some of the contributions that went the furthest towards consolidating this Romantic, historicist cultural climate include the 1839 publication of the volumes devoted to Catalonia within the work *Recuerdos y bellezas de España*, spearheaded by illustrator Francesc X. Parcerisa (1803-1876).

50 Próspero de Bofarull, *Los condes de Barcelona vindicados...*, vol. 1, pp. 5-6 and 12.

51 Gerónimo Pujades, *Crónica Universal del Principado de Cataluña*, 8 vols. (Barcelona: Impr. de José Torner, 1829-1832); Eulàlia Miralles, *La Crónica Universal del Principado de Cataluña de Jeroni Pujades a l'Acadèmia de Barcelona (1700-1832)* (Barcelona: Ajuntament de Barcelona-Arxiu Històric de la Ciutat, 2003).

52 Felix Fluralbo [Pròsper de Bofarull], *Reflecsiones sobre los perjuicios que ocasionaría á algunas provincias de España y en particular á la de Cataluña la traslación de sus archivos á Madrid que propuso la Comisión de Cortes en su dictamen y minuta de decreto presentado a las mismasen 19 de marzo de 1814* (Barcelona: Imprenta de José Torner, 1821), p. 4.

Likewise, Pau Piferrer (1818-1848), a writer and prominent theatre and music critic with the *Diario de Barcelona*, was charged with the first volume and part of the second, which was completed by an extremely young Francesc Pi i Margall (1824-1901)[53]. Influenced by Hugo and other European Romantics, Piferrer's work, a hybrid of literature and history, emanates the Romantic aesthetic sensibility and reveals a desire for patriotic affirmation and a clearly conservative ideological bent. The text prioritises the aim to emotionally stir its readers through evocative re-creation and narrative efficacy rather than critical analysis and dry erudition. The reassessment of the past, especially the Middle Ages, and the synthesis between landscape, history, tradition, nature and monumental heritage is one of the most noteworthy features of the work, a formula that was copied and endured for a long time.

During those same years, Pròsper's nephew, Antoni de Bofarull, who we mentioned above, made a decisive contribution to establishing a historical-cultural Catalan identity[54]. His contribution to shaping the contemporary Catalan mythical-symbolic identity was extremely important[55]. Fully drawing from the Romantic and historicist atmosphere and the rising fondness of knowledge and dissemination of the Catalan past, a phenomenon on which its main proponents conferred a clearly patriotic meaning aimed at restoring a damaged collective personality, in 1846 he published *Hazañas y recuerdos de los catalanes*, a collection of stories which blend legend and real historical events from the Middle Ages[56]. The author himself acknowledged the influence of the German Romantics like Klopstock, Goethe and Schiller in his literary re-creation of Catalan medieval history.

This historian and writer from Reus was also the editor and translator of the chronicles of James I, Ramon Muntaner and Peter III the Ceremonious, crucial players in Catalan medieval historiography from

53 Regarding Piferrer, see: Ramon Carnicer, *Vida y obra de Pablo Piferrer* (Madrid: Consejo Superior de Investigaciones Científicas, 1963).

54 Jordi Ginebra, *Antoni de Bofarull...*

55 Magí Sunyer, *Els mites nacionals catalans* (Vic: Eumo-Societat Verdaguer, 2006).

56 Antonio de Bofarull, *Hazañas y recuerdos de los catalanes, ó coleccion de leyendas relativas a los hechos más famosos, a las tradiciones más fundadas, y a las empresas más conocidas que se encuentran en la historia de Cataluña, desde la época de la dominación árabe en Barcelona, hasta el enlace de Fernando el católico de Aragón con Isabel de Castilla* (Barcelona: Juan Oliveres, 1846).

the 13th and 14th centuries. While in the last two chronicles, bilingual Catalan-Spanish editions enabled readers to access the documents' original language, the same did not hold true with the first one, which was only published in Spanish translation. This is clear proof of the deep-seated diglossia which prevailed in Catalan society and culture during that period and of the circumstances in which the restoration movement developed. In the introduction to the chronicle of Peter III the Ceremonious, Bofarull started with the following excerpt, in which he revealed himself to be somewhere between peevish and resigned about the former Principality's progressive deterioration and political and cultural subordination:

> *Cuando un pais, por desgracia, deja de ser nacion independiente y pasa tan solo á figurar confundido entre los estados de una gran monarquía, su preponderancia antigua queda olvidada por la que ejerce el estado dominante, su idioma de corte, si lo ha tenido particular, pasa á ser vulgar en sus pueblos, sus usos y costumbres van desapareciendo, al alternar con los de sus nuevos hermanos, y hasta sus glorias y hazañas se oscurecen, por no ser ya mas que parte en la historia general del reino á que se ha unido. En este caso, para el que conoce el valor del suelo que le vió nacer, solo queda, en consuelo, el estudio de las crónicas que se escribieron en pasados siglos y, sobre todo, el entusiasmo que estas graban en el corazon del que lee*[57].

> When a country, unfortunately, ceases to be an independent nation and becomes only mixed among the states of a great monarchy, its ancient preponderance is forgotten by that which the dominant state exercises, its court language, if it has had its own, becomes the vernacular of its peoples, its uses and customs gradually disappear, through alternating with those of its new brothers, and even its glories and exploits fade, to become no more than part of the general history of the kingdom it has joined. In this case, for those who know the value of the soil that saw its birth, all that remains, as consolation, is the study of the chronicles that were written in past centuries and, especially, the enthusiasm that these engrave in the hearts of those who read them.

In the prologue to Muntaner's work, Bofarull underscored the existence of a *verdadera* [Catalan] *nacionalidad* ("true [Catalan] nationality") in the Middle Ages and roundly criticised the vision of a uniform past on the

57 Antonio de Bofarull, *Crónica del rey de Aragón D. Pedro IV el Ceremonioso, ó del Punyalet, escrita en lemosin por el mismo monarca, traducida al castellano y anotada por Antonio de Bofarull* (Barcelona: Impr. de Alberto Frexas, 1850), p. 5.

Peninsula. He thus stressed that the 15th century Spanish monarchy was made up of different states that obeyed a common power but were in no way homogeneous in their *costumbres, leyes, idiomas, caractéres y hasta tendencias políticas*[58] ("customs, laws, languages, characters and even political tendencies"). In his justification of the work, he argued quite clearly its purpose and somehow also the cultural agenda which he was propounding along with other contemporary intellectuals:

> *España, como he defendido en otras ocasiones, no es una nacion, y sí un conjunto de nacionalidades, cada una de las cuales tiene su historia y su gloria particular, que las demás no conocen, originandose de esta ignorancia que solo prepondere y se tenga por única buena y capaz la que ha tenido medios para absorver toda la importancia. Esfuérzense, pues, en cada una de esas antiguas nacionalidades, para resucitar todo lo bueno que guardan dormido y olvidado, y así se logrará que la nacion española brille con todas las bellezas de su heterogeneidad, y así se le devolverá su verdadero tipo nacional, mas propio que el exclusivo que de mucho tiempo la domina [...]*[59].

> Spain, as I have defended on other occasions, is not a nation, but it is a set of nationalities, each of which has its own history and its particular glory, that the others do not know. It is for ignorance that some people accept the predominance of just one nation, the one who had more facilities for absorbing all the importance. Strive then, in each of these ancient nationalities to resurrect the good they keep dormant and forgotten, and so it will be ensured that the Spanish nation shines with all the beauties of its heterogeneity, and thus will return it its true national type, more appropriate than the exclusive than has long dominated it.

In line with this discourse (and we have already seen that the boundaries between literary practice and historiography were quite porous), it has been noted that many Catalan historians of that period tended to show some resistance to accepting the perspective of a uniform past for Spain without nuances, and that they were striving to devise a particular vision of Spain which stressed the diversity of its internal composition and its plurinational origin[60]. It is in this framework that the existence of a political, legal and institutional tradition and personality unique to Catalonia

58 Antonio de Bofarull, *Crónica catalana de Ramon Muntaner: Texto original y traduccion castellana. Acompañada de numerosas notas, por Antonio de Bofarull* (Barcelona: Imprenta de Jaime Jepús, 1860), p. 7.

59 Antonio de Bofarull, *Crónica catalana de Ramon Muntaner...*, pp. 23-24.

60 Ramon Grau, "L'aportació dels historiadors...", p. 240 and following.

and the Crown of Aragon was underscored until relatively recently, with 1714 as the cut-off point. The distress over the marginal place occupied by non-Castilian referents in the Spanish nation culture under construction and the desire to lambast the simultaneous attempt to craft an official vision of the past that served to legitimise the centralist, uniformist policy driven by Madrid partly explains the existence of Catalan formulations like this one. The origins of this kind of utterance and historical argument had a solid forbearer in the figure of Capmany. Certainly the "revival" of a unique history did not question the Spanish legal-political nation as a framework of reference or Catalans' belonging and adhesion to this project[61]. Nonetheless, the rediscovery of the Catalan historical referents, particularly those from the Middle Ages, was fundamental in the formation of a particular political culture which enabled the ruling class of the country to develop their own discourse which matched their needs and the unique position that Catalonia occupied within liberal Spain[62].

From a more historiographic sphere, the contributions of Joan Cortada, whom we mentioned above, Ferran Patxot (1812-1859) and Víctor Gebhardt (1830-1894), who are quite dissimilar from each other (just as their points of departure were also ideologically distinct), illustrate this desire to interpret the history of Spain from the Catalan periphery, to underscore the constituent plurality of the Spanish political nation and to undo, albeit to disparate degrees, the exclusive and abusive equation of this Spanish political nation with Castile. For example, Tomàs Bertran i Soler (1791-?) criticised the work by Modesto Lafuente (1806-1866) on the history of Spain by based on secular, liberal-democratic and federalising postulates. Bertran i Soler disapproved of Lafuente for many reasons, including his providentialism and Castilian-centralism: *pretender que todas las glorias de España se refunden en*

61 Josep Maria Fradera, "La política liberal y el descubrimiento de una identidad distintiva de Cataluña (1835-1865)", *Hispania*, 5 (2000), pp. 673-702.

62 Albert Ghanime, "Apunts i reflexions al voltant dels referents medievals en la política catalana de la primera meitat del segle XIX", *L'edat Mitjana. Món real i espai imaginat*, Flocel Sabaté, dir. (Catarroja-Barcelona: Afers, 2012), pp. 205-215; Giovanni C. Cattini, David Cao, "La cultura del constitucionalisme i els intel·lectuals catalans del Vuit-cents", *Afers*, 77 (2014), pp. 173-193.

Castilla, es una impertinencia y la mayor necedad[63] ("to pretend that all the glories of Spain are forged in Castile, is an impertinence and most foolish"). The multifaceted and influential Víctor Balaguer (1824-1901), the author of an extraordinarily important history of Catalonia, claimed in 1860 that:

> *salva* [sic.] *alguna honrosa escepcion, Castilla es España para los historiadores generales. Hablan siempre del pendon castellano, de los leones y las torres, de las glorias y libertades castellanas, y escriben muy satisfechos la historia de Castilla creyendo escribir la de España. Es un grave error. La España es un compuesto de diversas nacionalidades. Hoy son provincias los que, hace pocos siglos aun, eran reinos y naciones*[64].
>
> except [sic.] some honourable exceptions, Castile is Spain for general historians. They always speak about the Castilian banners, the lions and the towers, the Castilian glories and liberties, and write self-satisfiedly the history of Castile, believing that they are writing the [history] of Spain. This is a serious mistake. Spain is made up of various nationalities. What are nowadays provinces, were, a few centuries ago, kingdoms and nations.

Balaguer is a brilliant example of the political use of history to serve a progressive, decentralising liberal programme which sought to be an alternative to the centralist, uniform and exclusionary model of state instated

63 Tomás Bertran, *Cuchilladas á la capilla de Fray Gerundio* (Valencia: Imprenta de la Regeneración Tipográfica, 1858), p. 159. Even though Modesto Lafuente's influential *Historia general de España* (1850-1867) is usually taken as an example of this fundamental assumption that Castile equals Spain, the historian Mariano Esteban de Vega sustains that this claim does not fit reality and that an exclusionary historiographic Castilianism did not exist during the Elizabethan era. See: Mariano Esteban de Vega, "Castilla y España en la Historia general de Modesto Lafuente", *¿Alma de España? Castilla en las interpretaciones del pasado español*, Antonio Morales, Mariano Esteban de Vega, dirs. (Madrid: Marcial Pons, 2005), pp. 87-140; Mariano Esteban de Vega "Castilla en la configuración de la Historia Nacional Española", *Castilla y León en la historia contemporánea*, Manuel Redero, María Dolores de la Calle, dirs. (Salamanca: Universidad de Salamanca, 2008), pp. 41-70. Regarding Lafuente and his work, see: Juan-Sisinio Pérez Garzón, "Modesto Lafuente, artífice de la historia de España", *Historia general de España desde los tiempos más remotos hasta nuestros días. Discurso preliminar*, Modesto Lafuente, dir. (Pamplona: Urgoiti, 2003), pp. 7-97.

64 Víctor Balaguer, *Historia de Cataluña y de la Corona de Aragón*, 5 vols. (Barcelona: Librería de Salvador Manero, 1860), vol. 1, pp. 11-12.

by the Elizabethan moderates[65]. The plural vision of the Peninsula's past, the positive view of the confederal model of the Crown of Aragon, the claims for the history of Catalonia and the exaltation of the old Catalan constitutional system are crucial features of his discourse, a stance with clear political implications which bound together the concepts of freedom, progress and political decentralisation[66]. Some of his historical works, such as *Bellezas de la historia de Cataluña* (1853), *La libertad constitucional* (1858) and the aforementioned *Historia de Cataluña y de la Corona de Aragón* (1860-1864), disseminated and amplified a series of ideas and conceptions on Catalonia's past which would prove themselves to be quite enduring in the historical and political discourse. Balaguer insistently claimed that counter to what the absolutist, Caesarist *enemics de la llibertat* ("enemies of freedom") propounded, the country's true traditional governing system was constitutionalism. Along these lines, he noted that the Catalan people were characterised by the precocity, intensity and lastingness of their worship of freedom. Thus, according to Balaguer, the Catalan spirit was synonymous with constitutionalism and liberalism[67]. Therefore, once again the love of freedom was posited as a fundamental component of the Catalans' collective identity. The stance was not new, but Balaguer expressed it and disseminated it better than anyone else.

65 Joan Palomas, *Víctor Balaguer. Renaixença, Revolució i Progrés* (Vilanova i la Geltrú: El Cep i la Nansa, 2004). For an analysis of Balaguer's historiographic output, see: Ramon Grau, "Les coordenades historiogràfiques de Víctor Balaguer", *Víctor Balaguer i el seu temps* (Barcelona: Publicacions de l'Abadia de Montserrat, 2004), pp. 41-68.

66 Regarding "provincialist" approaches and the historicist discourse of progressive liberalism in the years of the revolution, see: Josep-Ramon Segarra, "Liberales y fueristas. El discurso 'neofuerista' y el proyecto liberal de la nación española (1808-1868)", *Provincia y nación. Los territorios del liberalismo*, Carlos Forcadell, María Cruz Romero, dirs. (Saragossa: Institución Fernando el Católico-Consejo Superior de Investigaciones Científicas-Diputación de Zaragoza, 2006), pp. 73-99.

67 Víctor Balaguer, *La libertad constitucional. Estudios sobre el gobierno politico de varios paises y en particular sobre el sistema por el que se regia antiguamente Cataluña* (Barcelona: Imprenta Nueva de Jaime Jepús y Ramon Villegas, 1858), p. 226.

4. Language, another factor. The Romantic spirit and the *Renaixença*

From today's vantage point, regarding the Catalan language as a basic attribute of a unique collective identity may seem obvious. However, viewing it as such is the outcome of an ongoing historical process in which language has been reframed as a sign and fundamental component of a human collective with a personality of its own. The arrival of Romantic thinking in Catalonia had an influence on this kind of conception, and its influx could be noted in the conception of the nation and the approach to the phenomena of language, literature and art. In no way does this mean that language was an irrelevant factor in identification and cohesion until then, or, for example, that no interest had been shown in the country's literary tradition. However, Romanticism had a particular bearing on the importance of language, and it conferred transcendence and a sense of unity on the claims, concerns and initiatives related to language. Thus, the acceptance of the concept of *Volksgeist*, which posited that peoples were endowed with a unique spirit or soul expressed in the different facets of human activity, provided intellectual justification for a process of rediscovering and properly valuing the local historical-cultural legacy which was linked to a decisive process of defining the Catalan identity[68].

Within this framework, the archaeological and artistic remains could be seen as material vestiges of a shared past, the testimony of a given collective idiosyncrasy which could be more or less idealised. The popular tradition was apparently reassessed and became a subject of study by academicians and scholars. Proof of this is the studies by the Universitat de Barcelona professor Manuel Milà i Fontanals (1818-1864) and the writer and bibliographer Marià Aguiló (1825-1897), who undertook a major effort to research and compile popular songs and poems[69]. Catalan law, too, was the focus of special attention. Somewhat in line with the

68 See the intersection of these elements in: Manuel Jorba, "Literatura, llengua i Renaixença: la renovació romàntica", *Història de la Cultura Catalana...*, pp. 77-132.

69 Llorenç Prats, *El mite de la tradició popular. Els orígens de l'interès per la cultura tradicional a la Catalunya del segle XIX* (Barcelona: Edicions 62, 1988).

postulates of the Historical School of Law represented by Savigny, a group of prominent Catalan jurists, including Francesc Permanyer (1817-1864), Estanislau Reynals i Rabassa (1822-1876) and Manuel Duran i Bas (1823-1907), worked particularly actively to uphold and defend the Catalan legal tradition, which they viewed as a prime manifestation of the spirit of the nationality. Consequently, they claimed the validity of Catalan civil law, which they strove to shield from the uniformising codification initiatives being driven by the State during this period and stressed the need for legal unity to be respectful of regional law[70]. As an involved party, from the perspective of 1883 Duran spoke of the existence of a "Catalan legal school". Tellingly, he pinpointed its emergence in the start of the second third of the century, dovetailing with the literary rebirth, and he cited the debate on the Draft Civil Code of 1851 as the decisive impetus.

Language played a crucial role in this process of defining and distinguishing the Catalan identity, which did not reject belonging to a common Spanish fatherland but was instead viewed as a reencounter with or restoration of the collective Catalan personality. We mentioned this at the start. In this sense, the *Renaixença* is usually regarded as a gradual process of rehabilitating Catalan language and literature which got underway in the second third of the 19th century in response and opposition to a state of a profound secular linguistic and cultural decline, which would be substantiated in a vigorous collective recovery. One of the scholars who is the most familiar with the *Renaixença*, Manuel Jorba, has described it as a *moviment complex i plural, no reduïble a una única opció cultural, la literària, ni a una única direcció ideològica* ("plural and complex movement, not reducible to a single cultural option, the literary one, or a single ideological direction") and has stressed its determination to *seleccionar i recuperar els signes considerats caracteritzadors d'una identitat nacional catalana diferenciada i de definir-la*[71] ("to select and retrieve signs considered characteristic of a distinct Catalan national identity and to define this"). From quite a different perspective, another researcher,

70 Lídia Arnau, "L'Escola Històrica del Dret a Catalunya", *Barcelona Quaderns d'Història*, 15 (2009), pp. 153-170; Lídia Arnau, "El moviment codificador de mitjan segle XIX: la defensa del dret propi des de Barcelona", *Barcelona Quaderns d'Història*, 10 (2004), pp. 203-217.

71 Manuel Jorba, "La Renaixença", *Història de la literatura catalana. Part moderna*, 10 vols., Joaquim Molas, dir. (Barcelona: Ariel, 1986), vol. 7, p. 10.

the anthropologist Llorenç Prats, also agrees on this globalising dimension, as he defines the *Renaixença* as a *moviment ideològic, d'expressió fonamentalment literària, que propugna una determinada definició i representació simbòlica de la idea de Catalunya i de la catalanitat*[72] ("ideological movement, basically of literary expression, which advocates a specific definition and symbolic representation of the idea of Catalonia and Catalanism"). Generally speaking, there is widespread consensus in viewing the *Renaixença* as a far-reaching phenomenon which cannot be reduced solely to a literary movement.

This relative agreement, however, cannot be extended to other fundamental factors, all of which are intertwined, such as the scope and specific meaning of the concept, its timeline and period, the kind of literary and cultural expressions that fit within it, its usefulness as a literary descriptor (the expression is borrowed from the Josep M. Domingo)[73], its real role in the rehabilitation of the language and the consolidation of modern Catalan literature and its implications and political projection. The debate is in no way new[74], but in recent years an entire series of diverse studies have subjected the movement to profound criticism and revision[75]. In this sense, without delving too deeply, it is clear that the contributions that have required us to rethink many assumptions include those by Albert

72 Llorenç Prats, *El mite de la tradició popular...*, p. 33.

73 Josep M. Domingo, "Renaixença: el mot i la idea", *Anuari Verdaguer*, 17 (2009), pp. 215-234.

74 Jordi Casassas, *La fàbrica de les idees. Política i cultura a la Catalunya del segle XX* (Catarroja-Barcelona: Afers, 2009), p. 113 and following.

75 Without striving to be exhaustive, we could cite: Josep Fontana, *La fi de l'Antic Règim...*, p. 429 and following; Josep Maria Fradera, *Cultura nacional en una societat dividida. Patriotisme i cultura a Catalunya (1838-1868)* (Barcelona: Curial, 1992), pp. 127-233; Albert Rossich, "La literatura catalana entre el barroc i el romanticisme", *Caplletra*, 9 (1990), pp. 35-57; Albert Rossich, "Les arrels literàries de Verdaguer", *Ausa*, 17/136 (1996), pp. 39-60; Joan-Lluís Marfany, "En pro d'una revisió radical de la Renaixença", *Professor Joaquim Molas. Memòria, escriptura, història*, 2 vols. (Barcelona: Publicacions de la Universitat de Barcelona, 2003), vol. 2, pp. 635-656. Some of these issues are echoed in: Jordi Ginebra, "La ideologia de la Renaixença: col·lisions entre llengua, nació i modernitat", *Llengua, nació i modernitat. Projectes i conflictes en la Catalunya dels segles XIX i XX* (Valls: Cossetània, 2010), pp. 31-51. See, too, the assessment by: Margarida Casacuberta, "Els valors de la Renaixença: sobre Barcelona, l'orgull burgès i el treball dels catalans", *Barcelona Quaderns d'Història*, 12 (2005), pp. 53-79.

Rossich, which fundamentally refute the concept of decline, the necessary correlate to the *Renaixença* or rebirth, coupled with the rising evidence that the decades from 1830 to 1850 were characterised more by continuity of the previous literary tradition and the rising abandonment of Catalan as a cultivated language.

As is common knowledge, the status of the Catalan language was seriously damaged in the early 19th century by an advanced state of diglossia, and Catalan played a clearly subordinate role to Spanish as a cultivated language[76]. Capmany is credited with a famous declaration that in the late 18th century Catalan was *un idioma antiguo provincial, muerto hoy para la República de las letras*[77], *meramente provincial y plebeyo*[78] ("a former provincial language, dead nowadays for the Republic of Letters, merely provincial and plebian"). In the early 19th century, Catalan was indisputably the language of the people, the only one that was massively known and used. Despite the constrictions of the Bourbon monarchy, there is proof that Catalan still had a more or less estimable presence, depending on the case, in certain spheres of local administration, Church governance and education, and commercial and notary activity. We also have evidence of its use – albeit waning – in account books and private correspondence, and in a variety of publications and printed matter, most of it targeted at popular consumption. It has been stressed that particularly after the second third of the 19th century, dovetailing with the consolidation of a new liberal political atmosphere in Spain, there was greater language shift and diglossia, which were already well-entrenched but accelerated and intensified at that time. This phenomenon is not only because linguistic and

76 Regarding the state of the Catalan language in the 19th century, see: Pere Anguera, *El català al segle XIX. De llengua del poble a llengua nacional* (Barcelona: Empúries, 1997); Joan-Lluís Marfany, *La llengua maltractada. El castellà i el català a Catalunya del segle XVI al segle XIX* (Barcelona: Empúries, 2001); Joan-Lluís Marfany, *Llengua, nació i diglòssia* (Barcelona: L'Avenç, 2008); Jordi Ginebra, "Una època de crisi: la llengua catalana en el primer terç del segle XIX", *Llengua, nació i modernitat..*, pp. 11-29; Josep Moran, "Consideracions sobre els liberals espanyols i la llengua catalana", *Treballs de lingüística històrica catalana* (Barcelona: Publicacions de l'Abadia de Montserrat, 1994), pp. 169-185.

77 Antonio de Capmany, "Apendice de algunas notas", *Memorias historicas sobre la marina comercio y artes de la antigua ciudad de Barcelona*, 2 vols. (Madrid: Imprenta de D. Antonio de Sancha, 1779), vol. 2, p. 54.

78 Antonio de Capmany, "Prologo", *Memorias historicas...*, vol. 4, p. 14.

cultural homogenisation became a programmatic goal and because the State had increasingly effective instruments for grounding and imposing it, but also because certain sectors of the Catalan population had been embracing this process as a logical and irreversible part of political and cultural modernity.

Historians of Catalan language and literature have noted the apparent paradox which arose precisely in the middle decades of the century, with the consolidation of a fully diglossic sociolinguistic scene and the clear recession of the Catalan language in a number of spheres, which was actually what sparked the first symptoms of a desire to rehabilitate Catalan as a cultivated literary language and to improve its status in society[79]. To wit, the prologue-manifesto that Joaquim Rubió i Ors (1818-1899) wrote for his volume of poetry in 1841 seems to reveal the start of a major shift in attitude. Rubió claimed that he was trying to *recordar á sos compatricis llur passada grandesa, y desterrar la vergonyosa y criminal indiferencia ab que alguns miran lo que pertany á sa patria*[80] ("remind his compatriots about their great past and to expel the shameful and criminal indifference with which some regard what belongs to their homeland"), he criticised those who *se avergonyeixen de que se los sorprengue parlant en català* ("feel ashamed before those who are surprise them speaking Catalan") and he proposed working to produce a *lliteratura propria, a part de la castellana* ("its own literatura, apart from the Castilian"). The shift in stance compared to Capmany, for example, is significant. Obviously, the process was slow and not bereft of qualms and contradictions. For example, in the *Diario de Barcelona* in 1854 one of the leaders of the movement, Milà, succinctly expressed his lack of confidence in the potential of the Catalan language as a vehicle of modern literature and culture[81].

79 In the words of Josep Murgades, it was a *revaluació literària* ("literary revaluation") and *devaluació funcional* ("functional devaluation") in *relació directament proporcional* ("directly proportional relation"). Josep Murgades "La Renaixença o l'inici d'una singular paradoxa", *Llengua i discriminació* (Barcelona: Curial, 1996), p. 139.

80 Joaquim Rubió, *Lo Gayté del Llobregat. Poesias de Don Joaquim Rubió y Ors* (Barcelona: Estampa de Joseph Rubió, 1841), p. 4, 7 and 10-11.

81 Manuel Milà, "Cultivo de la literatura provincial", *Obras completas del Doctor D. Manuel Milá y Fontanals catedrático que fué de literatura en la Universidad de Barcelona. Coleccionadas por el Dr. D. Marcelino Menendez y Pelayo* (Barcelona: Librería de Álvaro Verdaguer, 1892), vol. 4, p. 174. Cited in: Manuel Jorba, *Manuel*

One noteworthy milestone in the consolidation of the movement was the definitive instatement of the Jocs Florals annual poetry competitions in Barcelona in 1859, which became a central platform in the country's literary life. Despite all its limitations, the institution proved to be a major stimulus to the Catalan-language poetry output and played a crucial role in the enshrinement and social projection of writers in this language[82]. In the *Revista de Cataluña* in 1862, the young Terenci Thos i Codina (1841-1903) mentioned the trajectory of the Jocs Florals after its first three editions and noted that, to him, that "restoration" evidenced *un revifament del esperit nacional* ("a revival of the national spirit") in Catalonia. However, this did not call into question its belonging to Spain: *Catalunya es y vol esser are y sempre espanyola, mès sens deixar de esser per aixó catalana*[83] ("Catalonia is and wants to be now and forever Spanish, but without for this reason ceasing to be Catalan").

The Jocs Florals were immediately criticised and satirised from certain ideologically advanced cultural and literary spheres, which labelled it anachronistic, elitist and ideologically conservative and repudiated its model of archaic, artificial language, a far cry from the Catalan spoken on the streets. Still, the tension and conflict between these two distinct realms should not conceal a kind of osmosis. Regardless, it is clear that if the revived use of Catalan in the world of literature ended up being a fact (with all the instability inherent in it), it is because there was simultaneously vigorous popular cultural and literary activity, represented by Anselm Clavé (1824-1874) and his working-class choral societies, Frederic Soler *Pitarra* (1839-1895) in the theatre, and Conrad Roure (1841-1928) and others who established a prolific and effective partnership with the publisher Innocenci López (1829-1895) and earned a significant audience and market. Especially after the second half of the 1860s, the appearance of periodical publications like the *Calendari del Pagès*, *Lo Noy de la Mare*

Milà i Fontanals en la seva època. Trajectòria ideològica i professional (Barcelona: Curial, 1984), p. 173.

82 Regarding the Jocs Florals, see: Josep Miracle, *La Restauració dels Jocs Florals* (Barcelona: Aymà, 1960). A more recent publication is: Josep M. Domingo, ed. *Barcelona i els Jocs Florals, 1859. Modernització i romanticisme* (Barcelona: Ajuntament de Barcelona-Institut de Cultura-Museu d'Història de Barcelona, 2011).

83 Terenci Thos, "Restauració dels Jochs Florals de Barcelona", *Revista de Cataluña*, 1 (1862), pp. 254-262.

and *Lo Gay Saber* was a clear symptom of a kind of rehabilitation of the Catalan language. And all of this fostered the shaping of a local culture in Catalan.

5. Around 1860

Lately it has been stressed how in a context of deep-seated cultural, political and urban transformations, the Jocs Florals was a *suggestiu instrument intel·lectual de representació i de monumentalització* ("stimulating intellectual instrument of representation and monumentality") and an *exponent i escena de l'ambició de les elits locals* ("exponent and stage for the ambition of the local elites")[84]. It is worth recalling that in 1859, the same year that the Jocs Florals got underway, the Cerdà Plan to urbanise Barcelona's Eixample, a symbol of the expansion and modernisation of the most industrial Spanish city of the era, was approved. Balaguer, who at that time was the official chronicler of the city and one of the masterminds of the "restoration" of that literary competition, received the commission from the Town Hall to propose the names for the new streets in the city. The project that Balaguer submitted to Barcelona's Town Hall, approved with just a few changes, shaped a veritable *toponímia identitària*[85] ("identity toponymy"). According to *Las calles de Barcelona* (1865-66), with his choices he was trying to clearly lay out the *fisonomía histórico-política de Cataluña* ("historical-political physiognomy of Catalonia"). Balaguer's decision to include references to the historical past of the Countship of Barcelona and the Crown of Aragon commemorated *las glorias populares y cívicas de la nacionalidad catalana y sus libres Instituciones* ("popular

84 Josep M. Domingo, "Barcelona i els Jocs Florals, 1859. Literatura, modernització urbana i representació col·lectiva", *Barcelona i els Jocs Florals, 1859. Modernització i romanticisme* (Barcelona: Ajuntament de Barcelona-Institut de Cultura-Museu d'Història de Barcelona, 2011), pp. 46-67.

85 Joan Palomas, "Víctor Balaguer i la toponímia identitària: formació del primer nomenclàtor de l'Eixample de Barcelona", *Les identitats...*, pp. 293-316. See, too: Stéphane Michonneau, *Barcelona: Memòria i identitat: Monuments, commemoracions i mites* (Vic: Eumo-Universitat de Vic, 2002), pp. 35-55.

and civic glories of the Catalan nationality and its free institutions") and offered a sweeping gallery of personalities that invoked the military, scientific and literary glories of the Principality[86]. Nor did he omit references to economic activities in the street names, such as Comerç (Trade), Marina (Seafaring) and Indústria (Industry). In short, he shaped a public discourse which sought to express a certain historical personality of Catalonia and connect the image of a magnificent past with the country's contemporary *ressorgiment* ("resurgence"). It was unquestionably a way of exhibiting its merits, of fostering the self-esteem of the collective, of representing Catalonia and of symbolically capitalising on this representation.

86 Víctor Balaguer, *Las calles de Barcelona. Origen de sus nombres, sus recuerdos, sus tradiciones y leyendas…* (Barcelona: Salvador Manero, 1865), vol. 1, pp. 434-435.

The Advent and Politicisation of Distinct Catalan Identities (1860-1898)

Giovanni C. Cattini
Universitat de Barcelona

The last third of the 19th century in Spain was characterised by two pivotal events: first, the frustrated attempt to modernise the entire state during the years of the *Sexenni Revolucionari* ("Revolutionary Six Years", also called the *Sexenni Democràtic*, or Six Years of Democracy, 1868-1874), and secondly the Bourbon Restoration and the consolidation of the political system initiated by Cánovas del Castillo. This period witnessed a plurality of approaches which contributed to the crystallisation and politicisation of a Catalan identity that was distinct from its Spanish counterpart. Intellectuals and liberal professionals played a prominent role in this effort, and their reflections should be framed within the context of French culture from the last three decades of the 19th century, which was characterised by both the collapse of Sedan in 1870 and the struggles between the hegemonic positivist culture and irrationalist sparks in the late 19th century. Catalan intellectuals reflected based on the coeval European currents and synthesised heterogeneous responses to the problems of their day and their society. Some of these contributions harnessed Catalonia's uniqueness as an argument which could serve both the republican-federalist nuclei and the Catholics, both the progressives and the conservative Catalans. Thus, we can claim that one of the defining features of the period spanning from 1860 to 1898 was unquestionably the consolidation of a Catalan identity which for the first time translated into an increasingly popular cultural and political movement characterised by the defence of Catalonia's unique features. Just like all phenomena of modernity, this Catalanist movement cannot be considered either unique or exclusive to the interests of an industrial society which was grappling with heightened social conflict during those years.

On the other hand, the period also witnessed repeated economic crises which came hand in hand with breakneck growth interrupted by two financial crises (1866 and 1882): the free-trade policies of the Spanish government ended up giving way to a protectionist bent (1891), and the arrival of phylloxera, which was a true calamity for wine production in the Principality. These late years in the century also witnessed the population's first exodus from rural areas to urban centres, especially Barcelona, as well as rather large-scale transatlantic emigration. However, the period analysed was also characterised by an entrenchment of the centralist, uniformist policies of the Spanish state, which attempted a reform of the civil code especially after the 1880s which threatened the survival of Catalan laws and sparked the first grassroots mobilisations in defence of Catalan law. Likewise, the mobilisations to secure protectionist tariffs also played a key role in the claims of the nascent Catalanist movement. The politicisation of this movement underwent a series of milestones throughout the 1880s: two Catalanists Congresses were held (1880 and 1883); the first political associations were founded and soon joined forces, including the Centre Català (1882) and the Lliga de Catalunya (1887); the seminal doctrinaire texts appeared, such as *Memorial de Greuges* (1885) and *Lo Catalanisme* (1886) by Valentí Almirall; and different messages were formulated with the support of hundreds of Catalanists (to Ireland and Charles Parnell in 1886 and to the Queen Regent in 1888). Finally, the 1890s were characterised by the formation of the Unió Catalanista and the calling of this movement's first almost unitary meeting, which drafted the project to support Catalan autonomy (*Bases de Manresa*, 1892).

In addition to this political organisation, Catalanism was also fed by a rich and heterogeneous associationist movement which spanned everything from *excursionisme* (hiking and nature appreciation) to choral singing, from adopting the *sardana* as the Catalan national dance to the dissemination of nationalising symbols and elements, like the anthem, flag and patriotic festivals. Likewise, the last 25 years of the 19th century witnessed the consolidation of local literary and artistic tastes, an expression of the influx and spread of the leading European currents of the day. The wave of terrorist violence and the colonial defeat in 1898 contributed to the definitive politicisation of this movement and its gradual conquest of political hegemony after the first decade of the 20th century.

The years that we are taking into consideration are a key period which has been the subject of interpretations by contemporary Catalan historiographers to explain the birth of the Catalanist movement. The interpretation of one of the top scholars of this phenomenon, the historian and politician Antoni Rovira Virgili (1882-1949), pinpoints the emergence of this movement in the confluence of different factors: the literary Renaixença, federalism as reformulated by Valentí Almiral, the conservative Catholic tradition which had turned its back on fundamentalism and a bourgeoisie that had become disillusioned by the politics of Spain's ruling class[1]. Some years later, the reviser of Catalan historiography Jaume Vicens Vives stated that Catalanism had been defined by four specific reactions: first he claimed that Catalonia was formed by a specific social structure different to the rest of the state and characterised by a deeply rooted feeling of the validity of its laws and customs, the fondness of its history and institutions and the awareness of its economic awakening; the second element was awareness of the inefficiency of the contemporary Spanish state, which was always enmeshed in periodic dangerous crises; third, the liberal Jacobin state had sacrificed the most intimate and respect-worthy interests of the Catalan people; and finally, the Catalan people found the systematic corruption in the operation of the Spanish administrative machinery repugnant. According to Vicens Vives, these elements shaped the generation of 1901, which had taken the leap to political nationalism[2]. During the same period, the French Marxist historian Pierre Vilar read his widely cited doctoral thesis which was published in Catalan in four volumes as *Catalunya dins l'Espanya moderna* ("Catalonia into modern Spain"), subtitled *Recerques sobre els fonaments econòmics de les estructures nacionals.* ("Research into the economic basis of national structures") In the first introductory volume, he spent the second chapter reflecting on the different historical phases and social structures that had characterised the relations between Catalonia and Spain, emphasising the role of the middle classes in the historical development of Catalan nationalism[3].

However, the monograph that would become the canonical reading on Catalanism was not published until the late 1960s: Jordi Solé Tura's *Catalanisme i revolució burgesa. La síntesi de Prat de la Riba*[4]

1 Antoni Rovira, *Resum d'història del nacionalisme català* (Barcelona: Editorial Barcino, 1936).

2 Jaume Vicens, *Industrials i polítics (segle XIX). Biografies catalanes* (Barcelona: Teide, 1958).

3 Pierre Vilar, *Catalunya dins l'Espanya moderna. Introducció al medi natural*, 4 vols. (Barcelona: Edicions 62, 1964), vol 1.

4 Jordi Solé, *Catalanisme i revolució burgesa* (Barcelona: Edicions 62, 1967). Regarding the impact of this book on Catalan historiography, see: Giovanni C. Cattini,

("Catalanism and the bourgeois revolution. The synthesis of Prat de la Riba") which was published in June 1967. This book became the paradigm of a certain culture of anti-Francoism whose point of reference was somewhat simplified readings and Marxist leaflets against Catalan nationalism as used by the so-called bourgeois sectors, which he contrasted with socialism as another national liberation movement. In the book's conclusions, Jordi Solé Tura claimed that Catalan nationalism can be explained by two main strands of argumentation: the structural differences between Catalonia and Spain, and the weakness of the hegemonic Catalan class when undertaking the bourgeois revolution by trying to impose itself upon the entire state. Solé Tura stressed that throughout the 19th century, the construction of the liberal Spanish state was the job of rural landowners, both the kind that resulted from disentailment and the kind that stemmed from earlier rural land ownership. The Catalan industrial bourgeoisie never managed to play a decisive role within this framework, and instead it promoted a kind of nationalism whose purpose was to achieve solidarity between the privileged and exploited classes so that the workers would not join forces against the owners of the factories where they worked.

The most often argued response to these interpretations comes from the reflections of Josep Termes (1936-2011), who used a more heterodox Marxist perspective to underscore the grassroots nature of the origins of Catalanism, a thesis based upon his studies of the Catalan workers' movement and anarcho-syndicalism in the Principality. Termes formulated this theory for the first time in 1971, and it was widely disseminated after his participation in a Historians' Colloquium promoted by the Fundació Bofill in 1974. These studies reflected the civic concern with overcoming the *Marxism-Lerrouxism* instigated by Solé Tura's work, which equated nationalism with the bourgeoisie. Over the years, Josep Termes reiterated his theses in different articles, and their essence was that Catalanism had emerged as a movement with an antagonistic attitude towards Madrid's centralism that demanded a democratic reform of the Spanish state, and that Catalanism had first emerged federalist (both the kind that had emerged in traditionalist [formalism] movements and those that were rooted in populist republicanism), advocating a Spain built upon free peoples. According

Prat de la Riba i la historiografia catalana. Intel·lectuals i crisi política a la fi del segle XIX (Catarroja: Afers, 2007).

to Termes, the success of this movement was due to the deeply rooted Catalan-ness of Catalonia's working classes. In this sense, this historian harshly criticised the Marxist historiographic currents as being formalist and failing to understand anything other than theory. Termes claimed that Catalanism was a social phenomenon that had been embodied in different political currents which spanned the entire range of political forces in the Principality, from conservatism to the extreme Marxist, anarchist left. All of these currents were upheld on a deeper reality: the survival of Catalan particularism (linguistic, cultural, psychological and symbolic) among the working classes. Within this framework, he synthesised a scheme of Catalan nationalism and its perception among the Catalan working classes that was divided into four historical junctures: from the 18th century to the *Sexenni Democràtic* ("Six Years of Democracy", 1868-1874), from the beginning of the Restoration to 1898, from 1901 to 1931 and finally the Republic and the Civil War. Even though it does not ignore the above-cited traditional arguments, this interpretation managed to launch an entire prominent school of historians who divulged and further examined the thesis of the grassroots origins of the Catalanism that still survives today, providing a more comprehensive overview of the explanation of the roots of Catalanism in contemporary history[5].

1. The *Sexenni Revolucionari* (Revolutionary Six Years, 1868-1874) and the Catalan political forces between decentralisation, federalism and *foralism*

The 1860s were characterised by heavy tensions, both internal and external. These tensions helps us to understand this crucial stage in the modernisation processes of the Western world which, of course, also affected Catalan and Spanish society in general. The Catalan economy was suffering from

5 Josep Termes' different contributions are compiled: Josep Termes, ed., *Història de combat* (Catarroja: Editorial Afers, 2006). The debate on the popular roots of Catalanism can be found in: Agustí Colomines, "La historiografia del catalanisme posterior al 1936", *Diccionari d'historiografia catalana*, Antoni Simon, dir. (Barcelona: Enciclopèdia Catalana, 2003).

the economic impact of the American Civil War as well as the bankruptcy of the railway companies, which also brought down the Spanish financial system backing them[6]. This resulted in different attempted uprisings, declarations and Carlist Wars, and the Carlist generals' very rupture with Isabella II's regime was a crucial backdrop to General Prim's conspiracy, the Cádiz proclamation in September 1868 and the queen's exile[7].

The new political scene in Catalonia was characterised by broad support of a possible decentralisation of the state. Since the *Bienni Progressista* ("Progressive Biennium", 1854-1856), a large swath of Catalan liberals had referred to Víctor Balaguer, who under the new order adopted General Prim's line in his newspaper *La Montaña Catalana*. Balaguer supported a progressive monarchic tendency and the decentralisation of the state. Generally speaking, the Catalan monarchists viewed federalism with mistrust, as they regarded it as a threat to the unity of the fatherland and to maintaining the public order[8].

On the other hand, the Catalan republicans and federalists equated the old centralist monarchic order with the reign of Isabella II, which is why they supported its replacement even though this did not necessarily mean that they also supported Catalanism. Indeed, some of them mistrusted the obstinacy of a group of Barcelona youths who were clamouring on behalf of Catalan. The powerful federalist current became hegemonic in Catalonia in the first elections in January 1869, when the federalist republicans became the leading force in the Principality with a voter turnout of 70%: they won 28 of 37 seats. This figure contrasted with the tenor in the rest of Spain, where the republicans earned 57 out of 304. Within this framework, the Catalan federalist republicans accounted for 40% of the republicans in the Congress in Madrid. In the majority in Catalonia, at that time they were in the minority in the rest of Spain, so the plans for Spain they were promoting, and Catalonia's concomitant fit within a federal system, would have entailed a reconstruction of the state grounded upon the

6 See: Albert Carreras, Xavier Tafunell, *Historia económica de la España contemporánea* (Barcelona: Crítica, 2006), pp. 134-163.

7 Marició Janué, *Els polítics en temps de revolució. La vida política durant el Sexenni revolucionari* (Vic: Eumo, 2002); Maurició Janué, *La Junta Revolucionària de Barcelona de l'any 1868* (Vic: Eumo, 1992). See, too: Maurició Janué, *La Diputació revolucionària 1868-1874* (Barcelona: Diputació de Barcelona, 2003).

8 Maurició Janué, *La Junta Revolucionària...*, pp. 73-78.

ancient peninsular or regional kingdoms, with municipality autonomy at the core. In this sense, the leaders of Catalan federal republicanism, Valentí Almirall and Josep Anselm Clavé, spearheaded the Federal Tortosa Pact on the 18th of May 1869 with the goal of forging bonds among the federalist forces in Catalonia, Aragon, Valencia and the Balearic Islands. The pact was a bid on behalf of and a celebration of the old freedoms in the regions that were part of the former Crown of Catalonia and Aragon[9]. The historical Catalan identity was at the root of the approach taken by the majority of Catalan federalists, but the problem was that identity was not as deeply rooted in the rest of Spain as it was in Catalonia. Within the federalist spectrum, there was a division between its milder and more intransigent supporters: the former were gradualists and supporters of top-down federalisation from the centre, while the latter believed that the federal republic was the only expression of democracy and that it had to be imposed bottom-up, from the periphery, with a revolution if need be. Given this, it is fascinating that the supporters of the milder approach labelled their more intransigent counterparts as Catalanists. The reign of the Savoy King Amadeus I was characterised by rising clashes, and in 1870 the republicans led a mutiny against the draft. Meantime, the electoral results of the Catalan republicans left them in a more hegemonic position, so in the 1871 general elections, with 30% voter turnout, 16 seats out of 39 were won; while in 1872 this figure was 22 out of 41. The proclamation of the Republic was also characterised by extraordinarily low voter turnout and by rigged election results.

It should be noted that the Catalan federalists from the *Sexenni Democràtic* also had an explicitly Catholic, conservative branch, with Romaní Pugidengolas as the author of a seminal text, *El Federalismo en España*. This author soon abandoned the federalists and led the Catholic unity list in the January 1869 elections. Finally, many of the exponents that would wave the legitimist flag in the last Carlist War came from this

9 The text of the Federal Pact of Tortosa can be found in: José Antonio González, *Federalisme i autonomia a Catalunya (1868-1938)* (Barcelona: Curial, 1974), pp. 436-441. Regarding Catalan republicanism, see: Àngel Duarte, *Història del republicanisme a Catalunya* (Lleida-Vic: Pagès Editors-Eumo, 2004); Josep Pich, *Valentí Almirall i el federalisme intransigent* (Catarroja: Afers, 2006).

platform, which had encompassed everything from the old moderate guard to the neo-Catholics and Carlists[10].

Within this framework, the Carlist sector[11] also experienced a major revival during the years of the *Sexenni Democràtic*: during the period from 1869 to 1872, it played the electoral card and earned almost spectacular results in the Basque Country and Navarra, tempered by disappointing results in much of Catalonia. On the 15th of April, Charles VII published a declaration of war in Geneva, while in May 1872, he also swore that he would give Catalonia, Valencia and Aragon back their old *furs* ("codes of law"). Yet he was nonetheless quite reluctant: in 1874 he allowed a Diputació General ("General Deputation") of Catalonia to be formed, which was set up in Sant Joan de les Abadesses on the 1st of November and dissolved in August of 1875 when La Seu d'Urgell was occupied by the army of Alfonso XII. It was presided over by Rafael Tristany (1874-75), the head of the Carlist army in Catalonia and, in the later months, by Francesc Savalls. It published a *Boletín Oficial del Principado de Cataluña* ("Official Gazette of the Principality of Catalonia") The Carlist pretender to the throne tried to frame it as the first step towards restoring the Catalan *furs*. Thus, historiographers have constantly debated the contribution to Catalanism by these sectors in a thread of interpretations that argue in favour of or shade or deny the proto-Catalanist traits of these movements, as mentioned in the introduction. In any event, today there is unanimity in recognising that both federalism and Carlism had their own

10 The author of this chapter has written two articles on Romaní Puigdengolas and the Unitat Catòlica (Catholic Unity) platform: Giovanni C. Cattini, "La construcció de l'Estat nacional espanyol i els intel·lectuals perifèrics. La crítica regionalista d'en Francesc Romaní Puigdengolas", *L'Estat nació i el conflicte regional: Joan Mañé i Flaquer, un cas paradigmàtic 1823-1901* (Barcelona: Publicacions de l'Abadia del Montserrat, 2004), pp. 33-62; Giovanni C. Cattini, "Les eleccions del gener de 1869: la plataforma per a la Unitat Catòlica i la politització del regionalisme catòlic", *Església, societat i poder a les terres de parla catalana*, Lourdes Plans, ed. (Valls: Cossetània Edicions, 2005), pp. 279-290.

11 Regarding Carlism in the *Sexenni Democràtic*, see: Lluís Ferran Toledano, *Entre el sermó i el trabuc. El carlisme català contra la revolució setembrina (1868-1872)* (Lleida: Pagès Editors, 2001); Lluís Ferran Toledano, *Carlins i catalanisme. La defensa dels furs catalans i de la religió a la darrera carlinada 1868-1875* (Manresa: Farell, 2002); Lluís Ferran Toledano, *La muntanya insurgent. La tercera guerra carlina a Catalunya 1872-1875* (Girona: Quadern del Cercle, 2004).

unique expressions in Catalonia. Their failures allowed a Catalanist pathway to be paved within the political framework of the Principality[12].

2. *La Jove Catalunya*, the birth of pre-political associationism and the end of the *Sexenni Democràtic*

The years of the *Sexenni Democràtic* paved the way for an early coalescence of pre-political associationism, which would figure prominently among the unique features of a specific Catalan identity. In around February 1870, with a few harbingers in the spring of 1868, *Jove Catalunya*[13] was formed in Barcelona. It was the expression of a heterogeneous group of youth linked to the world of Catalan culture and the Jocs Florals. The ideological backdrop spurring the publication was a radical Catalanism verging on pro-independence stances which was expressed in articles by personalities like Francesc Ubach Vinyeta, one of the first authors to suggest the need for secession given the economic and cultural offenses suffered by the Catalans at the hands of the Spanish state, and Narcís Roca Farreras, who suggested secession to free the Principality from a "unitary Castilian despotism" in favour of a federal republic. The youth who spearheaded *La Jove Catalunya* soon created the newspaper *La Gramalla* (1870), which was replaced by *La Renaixensa* (1871) after a few months, which in turn advocated for a national recovery project, with the cultural and literary revival of Catalan as the means to achieve it. Further forging ahead along the pathway laid by the founding fathers of the rebirth of the Jocs Florals, who had revived the value of Catalan language and literature, a political movement was now being pursued which sought to re-establish the political entity of Catalonia in a new decentralised Spain. This group was planting the seeds of a restoration of Catalonia's lost sovereignty, the purpose to which all of the new association's cultural and

12 See: Albert Balcells, dir. *Història de Catalunya* (Barcelona: L'Esfera dels Llibres, 2004).

13 Margalida Tomàs, *La Jove Catalunya. Antologia* (Barcelona: La Magrana-Diputació de Barcelona, 1992); Carlota Duran, *"La Renaixensa", primera empresa editorial catalana* (Barcelona: Publicacions de l'Abadia del Montserrat, 2002).

political expressions were devoted. The members of this group included personalities who stood out prominently in the history of Catalan culture and politics, including Pere Aldavert, Àngel Guimerà, Francesc Matheu and Francesc Ubach i Vinyeta, among others. Assembled around them was a large number of authors who shared their romantic Catalanism, often more nostalgic than activist, and who sought to champion the ties among the Latin races. In this sense, they wanted to follow the patterns set down by the Félibriges led by Frederic Mistral, but they also wanted to become a movement that sought to recover Catalan identity and respond to the crisis in the Latin world spurred by France's decline after 1870. The young proponents of Catalan culture modernised the strategies in a regenerationist vein, and despite their divergences in both political and literary choices, they shared the project of channelling the political, social and cultural aspirations of Catalonia within Spain and of achieving a state organisation that recognised Catalonia's unique status. This associationism was not yet a true political party, but it did represent the seed from which the Catalanist organisations founded soon thereafter would germinate.

The different contributors to *La Renaixensa*, the mouthpiece of La Jove Catalunya, included the aforementioned Josep Narcís Roca i Farreras (1894-1891), a doctor and republican who suggested the need to promote a "progressive Catalanism" which represented the future, instead of a fossilised, clichéd past upheld by what he called the *jocsfloralescos* sectors. Roca i Farreras was upholding the ideals of democracy and Catalan-ness from the perspective of a reform of Spain to a more federal model[14].

The rising tensions in the years of the *Sexenni Democràtic* led to the abdication of King Amadeus I and prompted the assembled Spanish Courts to vote in favour of the proclamation of the Republic on the 11th of February 1873. This was the point when Catalonia had the clearest presence at the helm of Spanish politics, resulting in a wave of profoundly virulent anti-Catalan phobia which spread through the rest of Spain. In this sense, *El Eco de España* claimed that the Republic had become Catalonia's realm, and it accused the other Spaniards of allowing this to happen. The revival of the Carlist War on the one hand and the cantonalist federal uprisings on

14 See: Jordi Llorens, "Estudi Preliminar", *El catalanisme progressiu*, Josep Narcís Roca, dir. (Barcelona: La Magrana, 1983); Toni Strubbel, *Josep Roca i Ferreras i l'origen del nacionalisme d'esquerres. Assaig basat en l'obra de recopilació duta a terme per Fèlix Cucurull* (Arenys de Mar: Els Llibres del Set Ciències, 2000).

the other undermined the political stability of the First Spanish Republic, which came to a definitive end with General Arsenio Martínez Campos's pronouncement of the restoration of the Bourbon monarchy in the person of Alfonso XII in December 1874.

3. The beginning of the Bourbon Restoration in Catalonia and the first steps in the Catalanist political movement (1875-1882)

The regime change happened with the support of the major Catalan bankers, including Manuel Girona and Evarist Arnús, who created the Banco Hispano Colonial along with the Santander native Antoni López. The Bourbon Restoration was actively supported by the most important economic agents in the Principality. There was economic euphoria between 1876 and 1882 for a variety of reasons: the rise in wine exports, the resumption of the building of railways and so-called *vias ferratas* (Portbou 1878, Sant Joan de les Abadeses 1880, Vilanova i la Geltrú 1882, Berga 1887, Flix 1892); the manufacture of the first locomotives in Barcelona; the development of the electricity industry after 1875; and the construction of the first telephone line in the kingdom between Barcelona and Girona in 1877. Despite these advances in the late 19th century, metallurgy and chemicals accounted for 11% of the industrial production, while textiles accounted for 54%.

However, Catalonia's support of Cánovas del Castillo's political and institutional project was another matter. This politician from Málaga spearheaded a conservative, centralised liberal regime with open goals of homogeneity. One of its challenges was putting an end to the military's pronouncements and interventions in political affairs. The peaceful alternation of the two main parties in the government, the reconciliation between the Crown and the more liberal sectors and the participation of the Catholics in political life, which came with a gradual distancing from Carlism, were just some of the main achievements. Despite this, the elections were characterised by irregular mechanisms which created distance between the political system and the electorate and existed within a network of political cronyism which extended around all of Spain[15]. For all practical purposes, democratic representation was virtually non-existent in Europe at that time, and clientelism, fraud and election manipulation were quite widespread.

Within this context, the main Catalan political parties in favour of the Restoration suffered from a major defeat in the constituent elections of January 1876, a symptom of the disorganisation and state of prostration of the conservative classes in Barcelona[16]. What is more, the new Spanish Constitution enacted the following July abolished the Basque codes of law as the last measure against the most recent Carlist War uprising. The survival of a legal corpus from the old Basque freedoms had motivated an agitation campaign in the Principality, with the prestigious director of the Diario de Barcelona, Joan Mañé i Flaquer, as the main player along with prominent intellectuals and professionals from the Catalanist world and politics in general[17]. There was also a group of intellectuals and historians who attempted to influence into the Spanish constitutional works throughout publications devoted to reclaim the Catalan legal body and its modernity. This is the important case, among other authors, of Josep Coroleu Pella and Josep Forgas, authors of works such as *Las Cortes Catalanas* (1876) or *Los Fueros de Cataluña* (1878), looking for the promotion of the State's decentralization[18].

These factors helped lead the most prominent conservative intellectuals to cool towards the new political system launched with the Restoration; they maintained a position that was hostile to the regime, either by themselves or actively within the ranks of moderate Catalanism. This cooling-off was soon shared by the economic and political sectors that viewed

15 Manuel Suárez, *La España liberal: 1868-1917: política y sociedad* (Madrid: Síntesis, 2006); José Varela, coord., *El poder de la influencia. Geografía del caciquismo en España (1875-1923)* (Madrid: Centro de Estudios Constitucionales-Marcial Pons Historia, 2001).

16 See: Jordi Casassas, *Entre Escil·la i Caribdis. El catalanisme i la Catalunya conservadora de la segona meitat del segle XIX* (Barcelona: La Magrana, 1990), pp. 108-134; Jordi Casassas, *Els intel·lectuals i el poder a Catalunya* (Barcelona: Pòrtic, 1999), pp. 125-180.

17 For the history of the solidarity campaigns of the ancient codes of law from Catalonia to the provinces, see the article by: Jordi Bous, "Joan Mañé i Flaquer i el conflicte foral al territori basc", *L'estat nació i el conflicte regional. Joan Mañé i Flaquer, un cas paradigmàtic (1823-1901)* (Barcelona: Abadia del Montserrat, 2004), pp. 91-131.

18 Giovanni C. Cattini, *Historiografia i catalanisme. Josep Coroleu i Inglada (1839-1975)* (Catarroja: Afers, 2007).

the ambiguity of Cánovas' tariff policy with hostility, which was only further aggravated by Sagasta's rise to power in 1881. The new Minister of the Treasury, Juan Francisco Camacho, was a convinced supporter of free trade, and this was viewed in Catalonia as a terrible sign that engendered a climate of intense mobilisations by the major Catalan corporations[19]. These initiatives shaped the formation of an intellectual sector which, just like with the protectionist campaigns of 1848-1849, contributed to spurring much of Catalan society's protest against the customs tariffs, leading to the 1882 reform[20]. These reforms triggered massive demonstrations which degenerated into riots, leading to the proclamation of a state of war. The indignation of Catalan public opinion could be summarised by the words of Joan Mañé i Flaquer, as he reminded the Madrid-based leaders that trade treaties were an open vexation of Catalonia's interests: *el puñal que han clavado en el pecho de Cataluña clavado queda y la herida sigue manando sangre, y esta sangre enrojecerá el Ebro trazando una línea divisoria entre Cataluña y el resto de España*[21] ("The dagger they have stuck in the chest of Catalonia remains stuck there and the wound is still dripping blood, and this blood will redden the Ebro drawing a line between Catalonia and the rest of Spain").

4. The Catalanist movement between the first doctrinaire formulations and the quest for a public space (1882-1892)

These events had received the active support of the earliest articulations of what was already known as the Catalanist movement, which after the 1820s entered into a spiral of politicisation, leaving behind the simple goal

19 See: Joaquim Coll, *Narcís Verdaguer i Callis (1862-1918) i el catalanisme possibilista* (Barcelona: Publicacions de l'Abadia de Montserrat, 1998), pp. 41-42.

20 For the economic policies of the Spanish governments from 1875-1886, see: Joan Palomas, *Els rerafons econòmics de l'activitat dels parlamentaris catalans (1876-1885)* (Bellaterra: Universitat Autònoma de Barcelona, PhD Dissertation, 2002), pp. 97-153; José María Serrano, *El viraje proteccionista de la Restauración* (Madrid: Siglo XXI, 1989).

21 Juan Mañé, "Cataluña independiente", *Diario de Barcelona* (14 May 1882).

of cultural promotion which it had had until then. This was possible because of the crisis in the large Spain-wide political parties in Catalonia due to their inability to influence the policies of the Spanish rulers who were promoting both campaigns aimed at legal uniformisation, which was threatening the continuity of Catalan civil law, and free-trade measures, which were prompting a crisis in the Catalan textile industry. In this framework, it should be borne in mind that there were three large political families that could be defined as Catalanist in the early years of the Restoration. The first were the federalists led by Valentí Almirall, who in 1879 spearheaded the *Diari Català*, the first Catalan-language newspaper. The second was the intellectual circle linked to the *Renaixensa*, whose main proponents were the playwright Àngel Guimera and the writer Pere Aldavert. The third was known as the Vic-based sector, led by Father Jaume Collell, which articulated a Catholic Catalanist regionalism around the weekly *La Veu de Catalunya*, supported by a broad swath from the Catalan Catholic Church who had supported the legitimist candidate in the last Carlist War.

The coexistence of such different veins was not simple; however, the first unitary milestones organised by the Catalanist movement were two Catalanist congresses in 1880 and 1883 and the creation of the Centre Català in 1882[22]. The first major event that gave this sector visibility was the meeting that the Centre Català called at Barcelona's Llotja del Mar on the 1st of January 1885, which ended up producing the famous *Memorial de Greuges*[23]. This text was written to garner the king's explicit support for the Catalans' requests and signalled the convergence of different sensibilities

22 Jordi Galofré, *El Primer Congrés Catalanista (1880)* (Barcelona: Rafael Dalmau, 1979); Josep Maria Figueres, *El Primer Congrés Catalanista i Valentí Almirall. Materials per a l'estudi dels orígens del catalanisme* (Barcelona: Generalitat de Catalunya, 1985); Josep Maria Figueres, *El primer diari en llengua catalana. Diari Català (1879-1881)* (Barcelona: Institut d'Estudis Catalans, 1999), pp. 341-347; Juan Trias, *Almirall y los orígenes del catalanismo* (Madrid: Siglo XXI, 1975), p. 278 and forward; Carlota Duran, *"La Renaixensa", primera empresa...*, p. 75 and forward; Josep Pich, *El Centre Català. La primera associació política catalanista (1882-1894)* (Catarroja: Afers, 2002); Maria Carme Illa, *El Segon Congrés Catalanista. Un congrés inacabat. 1883-1983* (Barcelona: Generalitat de Catalunya, 1983).

23 Josep Termes, *Història del Catalanisme fins a 1923* (Barcelona: Pòrtic, 2000), pp. 171-179; for the story of the *Memorial de Greuges*, see too: Joaquim Nadal, *El memorial de Greuges i el catalanisme polític* (Barcelona: Magrana, 1986); Joaquim Camps, *El Memorial de Greuges* (Barcelona: Editorial Dalmau, 1968).

which had banded together with the goal of defending the decentralisation of the state, a protectionist economic policy for the Catalan economy and recognition of the cultural, linguistic and legal uniqueness of the Principality[24].

During the early 1880s, the key figure and impetus to the discourse and practice of the Catalanist movement was clearly Valentí Almirall (1841-1904), a former federalist republican who had been quite active in the *Sexenni Democràtic*. His most famous works include *Lo Catalanisme* (1886)[25], the first benchmark doctrinaire text of the Catalanist movement. In this book, Almirall posits the scholarly foundations of the Principality's claims and the practical solutions that could resolve Catalonia's fit within Spain. In line with his federalist past, Almirall believed that asymmetrical federalism was precisely the tool that could resolve the frictions between the Principality and the capital of the state. He saw this solution as possible in both a republican system and a monarchy. What is more, Almirall suggested the need to restore the Courts in order to ensure the country its legislative power. These Courts would not be formed through either direct suffrage or the military and Church but through varied elements that would emerge from one-third of the representatives voted in through direct suffrage, another third of the representatives from the districts and a final third from the corporations. Almirall constantly repeated that it was important to avoid *les anomenades pràctiques parlamentàries* ("The so-called parliamentary practices")[26]. *Lo Catalanisme* closed by recalling that the reform of the state would only be possible by creating a far-reaching movement that could summon a general groundswell of public opinion. This statement seemed to seal the experience of the *Memorial de Greuges*, which had been successfully submitted the previous year, of which Almirall had been one of the main driving forces.

24 *Memoria en defensa de los intereses morales y materiales de Cataluña, presentada directamente a S.M. el Rey, en virtud de acuerdo tomado en la reunión celebrada en la Lonja de Barcelona, el día 11 de enero del año 1885* (Barcelona: Imprenta Barcelonesa, 1885), p. 70 and forward.

25 Valentí Almirall, *Lo Catalanisme. Motius que'l legitiman. Fonaments cientifichs i solucions practicas*, (Barcelona: Llibreria de Verdaguer and Llibreria de Lopez, 1886).

26 These statements must be understood within the broader framework of the late 19th-century crisis in European liberalism. See: Giovanni C. Cattini, *Prat de la Riba...*, pp. 157-311.

Besides *Lo Catalanisme*, Almirall also wrote a series of articles originally published in the French *La Revue du Monde Latine* between 1885 and 1886, which he later compiled under the title of *L'Espagne telle qu'elle est* ("Spain such as it is")[27]. In these articles, Almirall denounced the boss system in Restoration Spain 15 years before Joaquín Costa wrote his famous *Oligarquia i caciquisme*. The success of the articles published in *La Revue du Monde Latin* and their repercussions in Spain motivated Almirall to assemble this book, which was issued in 1887 thanks to the French publisher Albert Savine. The French publisher's perspicacity enabled the French and international audience to become familiar with the existence of this criticism of Cánovas' Spain. Three years later, Savine published another book with a similar title on the reality in Italy; however, its author, the libertarian lawyer Francesco Saverio Merlino, made an economics-based, anti-capitalist criticism of the history of the new Kingdom of Italy, even though it was possible to note echoes of Almirall's criticisms of the centralist, bureaucratic state[28].

In any event, Almirall's trial by fire was his attempt to get the Centre Català to participate in the elections in order to create a possible Catalan political front in Madrid's Congress. His failure in the 1886 political elections was the beginning of his decline, as proven by the ensuing fracture within the Centre Català stemming from the fact that two candidates were simultaneously proposed for the directorship of the Centre. Finally, the sector opposed to Valentí Almirall, almost 40% of the members, decided to split off and form the Lliga de Catalunya, with clear echoes of the Irish cause. The Lliga had the support of the more radical elements linked to the group at the magazine *Renaixensa*, as well as the affiliation of different exponents from the magazine *La España Regional* linked to the business circle of Güell Bacigaluppi and the Marquis of Comillas[29]. Even more importantly, it was backed by the university students at the Centre Escolar

27 Valentí Almirall, *L'Espagne telle qu'elle est* (Paris: Albert Savine Editeur, 1887).

28 In this sense, see: Giovanni C. Cattini, "La recepció de l'Europa mediterrània en la França de final del segle XIX. L'Espanya de Valentí Almirall i la Itàlia de Francesco Saverio Merlino en els llibres de l'editorial parisenca d'Albert Savine", *Miscel·lània en homenatge al professor Santiago Riera Tuèbols. Revista d'Història Cultural*, 9 (2006), pp. 44-65.

29 Giovanni C. Cattini, "Los regionalistas catalanes en la España de la Restauración: la plataforma de La España Regional (1886-1893)", *Bulletin d'Histoire Contemporaine de l'Espagne*, 45 (2011), pp. 19-42.

Catalanista, who had the support of Enric Prat de la Riba, Francesc Cambó, Josep Puig i Cadafalch and Lluís Duran Ventosa, among others[30].

The 1888 Barcelona Universal Exposition was held within this historical juncture[31]. The impetus from Barcelona's leading groups to organise this event stemmed from a broad series of reasons that ranged from the desire to impose the economic importance of Barcelona and Catalonia over the rest of the backward state to making the birth of a rising metropolitan pole visible to the international community, without losing sight of the fact that this event might also serve to conclude the period encompassing much of the 1880s in which Barcelona had been a provincial capital of Spain, perhaps different because it was an industrial centre, yet nonetheless far from the centre of political power. Within this context, the Queen Regent's arrival in Barcelona to officially open the Universal Exposition was used by the members of the Lliga de Catalunya to organise a protest on behalf of the defence of the moral and material interests of the Principality. To this end, the Lliga gave Maria Cristina of Habsburg-Lorraine the *Missatge a la Reina Regent*[32]. The Catalan collective imagination identified Alfonso XII's widow as the descendant of the Archduchess Elisabeth Christine, the wife of Charles of Habsburg who had opposed Philip V during the War of the Spanish Succession, who had promised never to abandon the Catalans. It goes without saying that the princess was unable to keep her word. Yet with a text reminiscent of the *Memorial de Greuges*, the Lliga requested the introduction of a dual system in the style of Austria-Hungary, which provided room for and recognition of the Principality. It openly claimed that Hungary was the mirror of Catalonia.

30 Jordi Llorens, *La Unió Catalanista i els orígens del Catalanisme polític* (Barcelona: Publicacions de l'Abadia de Montserrat), pp. 50-55; Jordi Llorens, *La Lliga de Catalunya i el Centre Escolar Catalanista. Dues associacions del primer catalanisme polític* (Barcelona: Rafael Dalmau, 1996).

31 Jordi Casassas, "La Exposición Universal de Barcelona de 1888. Notas para un estudio de historia cultural", *Haciendo historia (Homenaje al profesor C. Seco)*, Teresa Martínez, ed. (Barcelona: Universitat de Barcelona, 1989), pp. 401-408; Jordi Casassas, *Entre Escil·la...*, pp. 231-273. Regarding the Exposition, see, too: Ramon Grau, *Exposició Universal de Barcelona. Llibre del centenari 1888-1988* (Barcelona: L'Avenç, 1988).

32 *Missatje a S. M. donya Maria Cristina de Habsburg-Lorena, reyna regent d'Espanya, comtesa de Barcelona* (Barcelona: Impr. Renaixensa, 1888).

In any event, in the late 1880s, the main upheaval in the Catalanist movement was the discussions on the interpretations of the Civil Code kindled by the Basic Law dated the 11th of May 1888, which threatened the survival of the different *furs* or regional codes of law present in Spain[33]. Spain's attempt to standardise the country's laws stirred up Catalan society, which submitted reports to the government through a variety of organisations and mobilised with a wave of demonstrations in defence of Catalan law, which spread through the towns and county capitals all around Catalonia (and in Aragon, the Balearic Islands, Galicia, Navarra and the Basque Country as well)[34]. The mobilisations and protests led José Canalejas, the new Attorney General, to revise the controversial articles. According to the young politician Narcís Verdaguer i Callís, it was *la primera victòria del catalanisme* ("the first victory of Catalanism").

This movement of patriotic stirrings reached its peak in the creation of the Unió Catalanista (1890) and in its first public assembly held on the 25th to 27th of March 1892, which sought to set out the organisation's agenda. The document that resulted from this assembly was not a Constitution but an instrument for spreading the Catalanist credo in the Principality[35]. In any event, the first statement explained the competences of the central power, while the remaining sixteen referred to the regional power.

The different points called for the following: the defence of Catalan laws (point two); the normalisation of the Catalan language as the only official language in Catalonia and the means of communication with the state (three); the Catalan-ness of the administrative staff and thus the official and military posts in the Principality (four); a new territorial division based on the *comarques* ("counties") and municipalities (five); sovereignty in Catalonia's internal governance, with far-reaching legislative, fiscal and economic self-governance (six); the establishment of the legislative

33 Àngel Comalada, *Catalunya davant al centralisme* (Barcelona: Sirocco, 1984), pp. 127-229; Joaquim Coll, *Narcís Verdaguer i Callis (1862-1918)* (Barcelona: Publicacions de l'Abadia de Montserrat), pp. 186-212.

34 Maites Ramisa, *Els orígens del catalanisme conservador i "la Veu del Montserrat"* (Vic: Eumo, 1985), pp. 101-105.

35 Josep Termes, Agustí Colomines, *Les Bases de Manresa de 1892 i els orígens del catalanisme polític* (Barcelona: Generalitat de Catalunya, 1992); Josep Termes, Agustí Colomines, *Patriotes i resistents* (Barcelona: Editorial Base, 2003), p. 159 and forward; Joan Lluís Pérez, *Les Bases de Manresa i el programa polític de la Unió Catalanista (1891-1899)* (Manresa: Fundació Caixa de Manresa, 1992).

power of Catalan Courts as expressions of organic and guild-based suffrage (seven); legislative power which would restore the Audiència de Catalunya as its highest court (eight); the creation of five or six functionaries elected by the Courts as the representatives of executive power (nine); the retention of a broader range of competences by the natural *comarques* and municipalities (ten and eleven); contribution to the army of the land and sea with volunteers (twelve) and monetary compensation like prior to 1845; public order through the militia and Mossos d'Esquadra (local police) (thirteen); its own monetary system in harmony with the system in the other regions within the state and with international treaties (fourteen); public education to be organised by the municipality or, in its absence, by the *comarca*; and finally the last two points guaranteed that the Catalan Constitution and the rights of Catalans were safeguarded by the Catalan executive power, and that there were plans to reform the civil laws of the Principality in accordance with its historical roots and the requirements of the new society.

As historiographers have recalled[36], the *Bases de Manresa* were not the origin of political Catalanism; rather they reflect the end of an era marked by Romanticism, which then translated into programmatic principles which were, however, lacking doctrine, the potential for execution and policy. However, we should stress that this assembly highlighted the importance of defining the role of Catalonia in Spain's political life, while it also sparked and demonstrated the vitality of a nationalist protest movement which in subsequent years would become one of the leading actors in the Principality's political life.

5. In the quest for transversality: Catalan church, republicans, modernist intellectuals and the labour movement

Likewise, as mentioned above, there were other sectors in the social, political and cultural life of the Principality who had a fairly receptive attitude towards Catalonia's uniqueness. Worth noting among them is the role played by the Catalan Catholic Church, which in the last two decades of

36 See: Josep Termes, Agustí Colomines, *Patriotes...*, pp. 169-173.

the 19th century did not hesitate to use Catalan identity elements to carry out re-catholisation campaigns in the Principality, which it believed was enmeshed in a dire process of secularisation.

In turn, upon the suggestion of Pope Leo XIII, the Catholic Church was characterised by the heterogeneity of stances towards Catalan society and Catalanism. There was one sector that sought to moderate its aspirations which mainly emanated from the bishop of the city of Barcelona and had the support of the *Diari de Barcelona*. Meanwhile the group from Vic, with *La Veu del Montserrat* as its mouthpiece, was outrightly Catalanist and proclaimed the traditional, Catholic roots of the movement. Prominent members of this latter group were Josep Torres i Bages (1846-1916), Jaume Collell (1846-1932) and the bishop Josep Morgades (1826-1901).

This sector was actively involved in the activities that the Catalan Church undertook to revive Catholicism in the country, in the sense that they wanted to stop and invert the trend towards secularisation in Catalan society. Patriotic-religious festivals were held with this goal in mind; the first was the Millennial of Montserrat in 1880 and then came the restoration of the monastery of Ripoll (1892).

In Montserrat, the abbot Miquel Muntadas spearheaded a committee to celebrate the millennial of the creation of the monastery with the intention of making it a benchmark religious centre in Catalonia. The *La Veu del Montserrat* sector managed to fully Catalanise the event by imposing the Catalan religious song, *El Virolai*, instead of the Castilian *Firme la Voz*, and the coat-of-arms of the Principality next to that of the Virgin of Montserrat, the embodiment of the religious and patriotic spirit of Catalonia. The Catalan Church's other prime moment came when the bishop of Vic, Josep Morgades, aided by Jaume Collell, secured the complicity of the local and Catalan elites to physically reconstruct the monastery of Ripoll, whose destruction was a symbol of the violence unleashed by the liberal revolution. The monastery of Ripoll had been founded by Count Wilfred and Abbot Oliva, and its restoration secured its status as the cradle of Catalan nationality[37].

37 Josep Junyent, "Jaume Collell i Bancells: les campanyes patriòtico-religioses (1887-1888)", *Ausa*, 13/122 (1989), pp. 14-20; Jordi Figuerola, *El bisbe Morgades i la formació de l'Església catalana contemporània* (Barcelona: Publicacions de l'Abadia del Montserrat, 1994).

We should note that this sector also fed off the prestige of Father Jacint Verdaguer (1845-1902), the author of works like *L'Atlàntida* (1877) and *Canigó* (1886), which transformed him in life into the utmost representative of the Catalan poetic Renaixença or rebirth. Josep Murgades himself crowned Verdaguer as the *Poeta de Catalunya* at the monastery of Ripoll (1886).

On the other hand, from the political standpoint this Catholic sector very carefully tracked the steps of the Catalanist movement; for example, in the early 1880s the presbyter Jaume Collell tried to approach to Almirall's discourse[38], but the secular state hegemonically promoted in the Catalanist movement by the latter led the former and his sector to support Catholic Catalanism. It is telling that to respond to Valentí Almirall's *Lo Catalanisme*, the presbyter published articles in *La Veu de Montserrat* that were eventually included in his seminal work: *La Tradició Catalana*[39]. This book, which appeared in 1892, was a condemnation of liberal states for their uniformising policies which led the inhabitants to be uprooted from their respective homes and thus from the cultural and legal legacy that had characterised a Catholic life for centuries. These policies thus opened up a new historical period in which there was nothing that could guarantee human harmony. For this reason, the erasure of regional life meant the breakdown of the traditional family and their religious beliefs. Defending regionalism was synonymous with defending the traditional, agrarian Catalonia and its Catholic values.

On the side diametrically opposed to the Church we find the complex web of Catalan republicanism, in which the federalists had been the first political force during the *Sexenni Democràtic*. After a few years of retreat from political life, the federalists returned to action by holding a regional congress of the federalist party in Catalonia, which ended by approving a *Projecte per a la constitució de l'Estat català*, or draft constitution for

38 Josep Junyent, "De la gran dignitat de l'acostament entre Jaume Collell i Valentí Almirall en 1882-1885", *Revista de Teologia de Catalunya,* 27 (1992), pp. 215-256; Benjamí Montserrat, *Jaume Collell i Bancells (1846-1932). Perfil biogràfic d'un activista catòlic del catalanisme* (Barcelona: Institut Universitari d'Història Jaume Vicens Vives-Universitat Pompeu Fabra, PhD Dissertation, 2003), p. 177.

39 José Torras, *La Tradició Catalana* (Barcelona: Biblioteca Balmes, 1935).

Catalonia (1883)[40]. This charter was signed by a series of proponents of republicanism from the *Sexenni Democràtic*, led by the young lawyer Josep Maria Vallés i Ribot (1849-1911). Despite this, the draft constitution faithfully reflects the federal party's uncertain phase in its quest to lay down more solid roots in Catalonia. On the other hand, the draft constitution is the most vigorous bid for federalism and autonomy in Catalonia within a Spanish federal state. This congress primarily helped to consolidate the Partit Republicà Democràtic Federal as the majority party at the republican end of the political spectrum. Its hegemony was possible thanks to the alliance it forged between a group of young professionals with uncertain jobs (journalists and writers) and a series of local notables who had participated in the *Sexenni Democràtic*[41]. Republicanism was still an important referent among the artisan and working classes in Catalonia, as proven by the second elections with universal suffrage, which witnessed the triumph of the candidacy of the Unió Republicana in the Barcelona district (1893), and it continued to be referent in the early decades of the 20th century.

A generation of young Catalanist, avant-garde republicans who spearheaded the modernist movement also crystallised in the 1890s[42]. The ideological features of modernism were defined around *L'Avenç* (1889-1893), led by Joaquim Casas-Carbó along with authors like Jaume Massó i Torrents, Pompeu Fabra, Jaume Brossa and Alexandre Cortada. They were a combination of cultural Catalanism and ethical universalism, which served as the foundation of what we could call an early cultural nationalism which lay at the root of left in favour of autonomous regional goverment. The *Foc Nou* group, led by Pere Coromines, Ignasi

40 José Antonio González, "Estudi Introductori", *Memorial de Greuges de 1760. Projecte de Constitució de l'Estat català de 1883. Memorial de Greuges de 1885. Missatge a la Reina Regent de 1888. Bases de Manresa de 1892*, 6 vols., Josep Maria Font, dir. (Barcelona: Generalitat de Catalunya, 1990), vol 1, pp. 11-40, follows the patterns of the famous text: José Antonio González, *Federalisme i autonomia a Catalunya (1868-1938)* (Barcelona: Curial, 1974). See, too: Pere Gabriel, *El catalanisme i la cultura federal. Història i política del republicanisme popular a Catalunya el segle XIX* (Reus: Fundació Josep Recasens, 2007).

41 See: Àngel Duarte, *Història del republicanisme...*, pp. 129-130.

42 Eduard Valentí, *El primer modernismo literario catalán y sus fundamentos ideológicos* (Barcelona: Ariel, 1973); *El temps del Modernisme* (Barcelona: Publicacions de l'Abadia de Montserrat, 1985); Joan Lluís Marfany, *Aspectes del Modernisme* (Barcelona: Curial, 1990).

Iglesias and especially Jaume Brossa, was the most radical sector in modernism and sometimes showed affinities with the labour movement. This can be seen in their contributions to *Revista Blanca*, which showed a radical reivindication of autonomy that stemmed from a Europeanism that contrasted with the Decadent Movement in Southern Europe, although with a focus on its Latin roots. What is more, these modernists played a crucial role in Catalan culture by promoting translations of authors like Ibsen and Maeterlinck, among others. The Festes Modernistes de Sitges promoted by Santiago Rusiñol also helped to disseminate these currents among Catalan artists.

On the other hand, the Catalan labour movement had its own dynamics as it organised itself independently in those years, gradually detaching from historical republicanism, although always maintaining an open dialogue with it. The gestation of an intellectual labour discourse emerged in parallel with the theoretical configuration of anarchism as part of an eclectic culture permeated with different cultural suggestions and traditions, in which anti-centralist approaches played a core role, a stance shared by both the federalists and the Catalanists. The world of labour had a positive view of Catalanism and worked to give shape to a popular form of Catalanism despite the many discrepancies it had with the movement as a whole[43].

In the 1880s, anarchism split off into two currents. Bakunin's collective anarchism was spurred by the direct intervention of the upper crust of Catalan anarchists, with leaders and publicists like R. Farga Pellicer, A. Pellicer, A. Lorenzo, E. Canivell and especially J. Llunas i Pujals. Contrasting with that was anarchism as defined by Kropotkin, anarchist communism, which despite its slow spread became more popular in the 1890s due to the tactical failure of the large union centrals, especially after the dissolution of the general strikes of 1890 and 1893, events which lay at the root of the individualist terrorism of the 1890s. In the 1890s, there was a new convergence between ideological neophytes to anarchism and young Catalanist

43 Josep Termes, *Federalismo, anarcosindicalismo y catalanismo* (Barcelona: Anagrama, 1976); Teresa Abelló, *Les relacions internacionals de l'anarquisme català (1881-1914)* (Barcelona: Edicions 62, 1987); Teresa Abelló "El moviment anarquista (1874-1914): entre el catalanisme i l'internacionalisme", *Afers*, 7 (1992), pp. 131-141; Ferran Aisa, *La cultura anarquista a Catalunya* (Barcelona: Edicions de 1984, 2006); Josep Termes, *Història del moviment anarquista a Espanya (1870-1980)* (Barcelona: L'Avenç, 2011).

intellectuals, which survived until World War I, except for the dramatic hiatus of the Montjuïc Trial (1896). In its late phase, the unifying force was not those old federalists seduced by Bakuninism but young intellectuals from "good families" influenced by Nietzsche, who synthesised an amalgam of modernism and feelings and ideas closer to anarchism. They sought to destroy society intellectually while also aiming to bring culture to the masses and Catalanise the labour movement, which they claimed had been blinded by the internationalist culture. Despite this, with the organisational and intellectual repression that came in the wake of the Montjuïc Trial, the more ideological stage of anarchism came to a close, followed in the early years of the 20th century by a praxis of this ideology and its re-adaptation to the organisational models imposed by the triumph of capitalist society.

6. Catalan symbolic and cultural nationalisation at the turn of the 19th century

In the last few decades of the 19th century, the aforementioned modernisation of Catalan politics came hand in hand with the nationalisation of the most important cultural elements from the country's history and the creation of symbols, festivities and identity features that still survive in the 21st century[44]. Their dissemination and consolidation was possible because of the spread of a heterogeneous web of associations that propounded a transversal Catalanness and were centred everywhere from *centres excursionistes* ("hiking and nature centres") to popular choral societies. Among the most effective symbols and myths, we should highlight the consolidation of the features most needed to organise a political mobilisation and coalesce mass politics: a flag, a national day and an anthem. Regarding the flag[45], we should stress that the four red stripes on a yellow background had historically existed in the

44 On the relations between myths and symbols of Catalan political culture see: Giovanni C. Cattini, "Myths and symbols in the political culture of Catalan nationalism (1880-1914)", *Nations and nationalism*, 21/3 (2015), forthcoming.

45 Pere Anguera, *Les quatre barres. De bandera històrica a senyera nacional* (Barcelona: Rafel Dalmau Editor, 2010); Jordi Albertí, *La bandera catalana: mil anys d'història* (Barcelona: Pòrtic, 2010).

Principality and Barcelona with the flags of Santa Eulàlia and Saint George, whose symbolism (the red cross over a white background) had traditionally represented the governing institution, the Generalitat de Catalunya. However, the flag began to take on a more prominent place in the Catalan identity after the reinstatement of the Jocs Florals poetry competition in 1859. Writers like Víctor Balaguer and Josep Coroleu, poets like Jacint Verdaguer and playwrights like Àngel Guimerà, among others, made a crucial contribution to ensuring that the story behind the four stripes became the symbolic referent of the Catalanist movement. However, this movement was not limited to the world of literature, as it also expanded to the sphere of choral singing and the nascent *excursionisme*, which became the propaganda tool of Catalan symbolism by antonomasia. The very politicisation of the Catalanist movement during the *Sexenni revolucionari*, and especially at the beginning of the 1880s, confirmed the consolidation of the four stripes as an identity feature: they also appeared in the headline of the *Diari català* (1879-1881), in the commemorative images of the two Catalanist Congresses (1880 and 1883) and in the coat-of-arms of the Centre Català (1882). Four-striped flags began to appear in all Catalanist events or events defending the Principality's economic and/or legal interests, such as the protests against the free trade agreements and the reform of the civil code. Likewise, in a more historical-cultural vein, in 1893 the transfer of the remains of Ramon de Berenguer II from Barcelona to the restored monastery of Ripoll was accompanied by numerous flags from the most important towns in Catalonia. In 1896, the *Cant de la Senyera* ("Song of the *Senyera* ["Catalan flag"]") was performed for the first time at the benediction of the standard of the Orfeó Català. This song, which was written by Joan Maragall and set to music by Lluís Millet, immortalised the *senyera* forever.

During those years, the groundwork was also laid for the siege and fall of Barcelona on the 11th of September 1714 to become the founding myth of contemporary political Catalanism[46]. The War of the Spanish Succession had been one of the major themes in the works by the writers, historians and intellectuals behind the Renaixença. Given this backdrop, the politicisation of the Catalanist movement in the 1880s led the date to gain even more significance. The patriotic events began in 1886,

46 Pere Anguera, *L'Onze de Setembre. Història de la Diada (1886-1938)* (Barcelona: Publicacions de l'Abadia de Montserrat, 2008); Albert Balcells, *Llocs de memòria dels catalans* (Barcelona: Proa, 2007).

when different Catalanist groups and organisations tried to hold a mass for the martyrs of 1714. The authorities forbid Father Jaume Collell, who was known for his Catalanist militancy, from officiating over a mass in memory of those who perished in this event. The monument to Rafael Casanova, the last chief councillor of the Generalitat from the War of the Spanish Succession, was erected in 1888 and became a referent, even though the traditional floral offerings did not begin until six years later.

Around this same time, *Els segadors* officially became the national anthem, almost historically dovetailing with the recognition of the 11th of September as the national day[47]. In 1892, Francesc Alió set to music the song *La guerra de los segadores*, which Manuel Milà Fontanals had published in 1882. Milà himself claimed that he had learned about this song thanks to Jacint Verdaguer, who had heard it on the plain of Vic or in Les Guilleries between 1860 and 1870. It should be noted that historian Ernest Moliné i Brases tinkered with the lyrics of the song to make it more combative and appropriate for Catalanist claims by adding the refrain: *bon cop de falç, defensors de la terra, bon cop de falç* ("Strike with your sickle, defenders of the land! Strike with your sickle!"). The anthem began to become popular the following summer when the Orfeó Català added it to its repertoire. Despite this, it took a few more years to officially become Catalonia's national anthem. The different Catalanist organisations began to use *Els segadors* systematically after 1897, and the Orfeó Català itself definitively chose it as the final piece performed in its concerts. Emili Guanyavents' condensation of the song (1899) was particularly effective as it made it easier for people to learn the lyrics. In the late 19th century, every 11th of September the Catalanist associations started to use the song in their traditional floral offering to the monument to Rafael Casanova. Despite this, the song did not have an easy time, as the Spanish authorities believed that the bellicose lyrics were a provocation to Spain because of its rejection of Castilians and its negative references to Philip IV and the 18th century war. Because of this, the authorities repeatedly intervened to ban it from being performed. During the years of the Second Republic,

47 Josep Massot, Salvador Pueyo, Oriol Martorell, *Els Segadors: Himne nacional de Catalunya* (Barcelona: Generalitat de Catalunya, 1983); Pere Anguera, *Els Segadors com es crea un himne* (Barcelona: Dalmau, 2010); Jaume Ayats, *Els Segadors. De cançó eròtica a himne nacional* (Barcelona: l'Avenç, 2011).

the top authorities of the Generalitat tried to spread a new anthem with more joyous lyrics, but they were not successful since *Els segadors* had already become an unrenounceable part of the popular Catalan collective imagination.

Along with these referents, which were crucial to bringing the political message to the masses, we should also mention the nationalisation of folkloric elements such as certain dances (the *sardana*) and the wearing of the traditional Catalan cap (the *barretina*). The *sardana* is emblematic: there were references to this dance, known as a traditional dance in the region of La Selva and the Empordà, as far back as around the mid-19th century[48]. Its spread was possible thanks to Josep Maria (Pep) Ventura's energetic efforts to promote the modern longer version of the *sardana*, which unleashed a revolution in the musical scores and bands which quickly took root and became crucial to the spread of the dance in the regions of Empordà, La Selva, Gironès, La Garrotxa, Ripollès and Alt Maresme after the 1850s. However, the Catalanist movement only began to proclaim the Catalan-ness of the *sardana* after the 1880s. Noteworthy factors in this were the success of a *sardana* contained in Tomás Bretón's work *Garin* (1892) and the celebrated poetry also finished, in its definitive version, in 1892 by Joan Maragall, which celebrated the *sardana* as *la dansa més bella / de totes les que danses que es fan i desfan* ("the most beautiful dance / of all the dances that you do and undo"). In 1894, the *sardana* was declared the national dance. With the new century, the dissemination of this dance went hand in hand with the growth of Catalanism in all the regions of the Principality, the clearest sign of this being the advent of Solidaritat Catalana, which reached most towns in Catalonia and encouraged the local townspeople to learn the dance. After that time, the *sardana* became a symbol of Catalan-ness, and this is precisely how it was perceived during the Primo de Rivera and Franco dictatorships.

On the other hand, the traditional Catalan cap, the *barretina*, was also important and used for symbolic purposes in the politicisation of

48 See: Jaume Ayats, *Córrer la sardana: balls, joves i conflictos* (Barcelona: Rafel Dalmau Editor, 2006); Pere Anguera, *La nacionalització de la sardana* (Barcelona: Rafel Dalmau Editor, 2010).

the Catalanist movement[49]. It was in open decline as a headpiece when a young poet, Father Jacint Verdaguer, appeared at the Jocs Florals in 1865 to collect a prize dressed like a peasant and wearing a red *barretina*. In the eyes of the intellectuals of the Renaixença, that image of youth amounted to proof of a popular Catalan culture, one that was alive and noble, far from the customs of the city with its essence uncorrupted. The *barretina* soon became more than a cap and began to be used in different Catalanist manifestations. The multitudes wore the *barretina* as a symbol of protest in the demonstrations against free-trade policies and the attempts to homogenise the laws counter to the interests of Catalonia. As Ramon Albero recalled in the obituary of the regionalist politician and industrialist Lluís Ferrer Vidal i Soler, during those years of mobilisation against the new draft civil code promoted by Manuel Alonso Martínez, Lluís Ferrer,

> *com els altres estudiants patriotes, portava la barretina vermella a les manifestacions, i quan s'acostava a casa la canviava pel capell. Un dia el pare lo descobrí el fet i digué al seu fill en to de consell: 'Bé noi, la barretina no està malament, però pensa que segons com es posa sembla un barret frigi.' I un barret frigi, per a un home de la Restauració, que havia vist la situació de 1873, venia a ésser quelcom terrible*[50].

> like the other student patriots he wore a red beret to the demonstrations, and when he approached the house he changed it for a hat. One day the father discovered the fact and said to his son as advice 'Well boy, the beret is not bad, but think that depending on how you put it on it looks like a Phrygian cap.' And a Phrygian cap, for a man of the Restoration, who had seen the situation in 1873, was something terrible.

Barretina also became the title of a Catalanist weekly and the characters who symbolised important magazines in the Catalan nationalist movement like *Cu-Cut!* and *Patufet* also wore a *barretina*. According to Tísner, Noucentisme and its elitist pretensions dealt the *barretina* its death blow and reduced it to a folkloric element, yet despite its disuse today, it still survives as an indisputable symbol of Catalan identity.

49 Pere Anguera, *La Barretina: la imatge tòpica del pagès català* (Barcelona: Rafel Dalmau Editor, 2009).

50 Ramon Albero, "Ha mort Lluís Ferrer Vidal i Soler", *La Veu de Catalunya* (16 April 1936), p. 11.

7. Associationism, the struggle for the Catalanisation of the country's institutions and the impact of 1898

These identity elements were able to survive because they earned the acceptance of a broad swath of the population, and if this was possible it was clearly thanks to the richness of association life in Catalonia, which after the Bourbon Restoration contributed to cementing the sense of a unique Catalan identity. One eloquent example of this was the nascent *excursionisme* (a hiking and nature appreciation movement), which under the guidance of mountaineering clubs all over Europe encouraged a love of nature among young people and worked together to promote and disseminate all kinds of knowledge related to the local land. The Associació Catalanista d'Excursions Científiques was founded in 1876 following these premises, although it soon had a competitor in the Associació d'Excursions Catalana in 1878, until they merged in 1890 to create the Centre Excursionista de Catalunya[51]. Its rank-and-file members included prominent representatives of Catalan culture who got directly involved to achieve the purposes of these hiking and nature associations, which included safeguarding and restoring Catalonia's artistic heritage, as well as supporting all expressions of the Catalanist movement then and in the ensuing years. Another example of this associationism, this one with more grassroots participation, was the choral societies promoted in the second half of the 1850s by Anselm Clavé, which were a significant model of socialisation for the Catalan working-classes during this period[52]. After Clavé's death, the choral societies continued, but they were really revived in 1891, when the Orfeó Català was created upon the initiative of the young musicians Lluís Millet and Amadeu Vives. It soon earned the favour of Catalan audiences, especially thanks to its own anthem, *El Cant de la Senyera*, which was created for the Orfeó by the poet Joan Maragall and set to music by Millet himself. This song premiered at the monastery of Montserrat in

51 Agustí Jolis, *Centre Excursionista de Cataluya. 120 anys d'història. 1876-1996* (Barcelona: Centre Excursionista de Catalunya, 1996).

52 Josep Maria Roig, *Història de l'Orfeó Català: moments cabdals del seu passat* (Barcelona: Publicacions de l'Abadia del Monserrat, 1993); Manuela Narváez, *L'Orfeó Català, Cant Coral i Catalanisme (1891-1951)* (Barcelona: Universitat de Barcelona, 2005) <http://diposit.ub.edu/dspace/handle/2445/35524>.

1896. The Orfeó Català also made a notable contribution to disseminating the song *Els Segadors*, which became Catalonia's national anthem within a few years. The Catalunya Nova choral society promoted by Enric Morera in 1895 was much more politicised, as it was directly affiliated with the Unió Catalanista. What is more, a variety of hiking and nature groups also had their own choral societies which spread the songs that were to become Catalonia's national songs.

The pathway to the Catalanisation of the different spheres of public life in Catalonia also included its ruling classes' rising recognition of the socioeconomic and political-historical uniqueness of the Principality, as well as what was known as the *assalt catalanista* ("Catalanist assault") on the most prestigious institutions of the country via the presidency of prominent Catalanists at the helm of Barcelona's most emblematic corporations, from the Ateneu Barcelonès to the Acadèmia de Jurisprudència de Barcelona.

In the first case of self-recognition, we should stress the role played by the revival and consolidation of the project *Galeria de Catalans Il·lustres*, which the Barcelona Town Hall restored in 1877. It was designed to represent not only the great figures in the nation's historical past but also the new contemporary bourgeois heroes who would become the prototypes of the new nascent political society[53]. Meanwhile, the *assalt catalanista* on the emblematic corporations began with the Ateneu Barcelonès, a meeting point of Barcelona's elite since 1872 whose board was presided over by the poet and playwright Àngel Guimerà (1895). Guimerà raised quite a racket when for the first time he spoke Catalan in his presidential speech to kick off the year. It was the first time that the country's own language had been used at the Ateneu, and this sparked indignation among many members of the organisation, who believed that the official language of the Ateneu, just like all the organisations representing the state, was Spanish and that consequently all the events had to be conducted in that language. From then on, Catalan started to be used more often in private and public corporations, giving an unmistakable signal of the transversality of Catalan-ness, which was slated to be one of the backbones of 20th century Catalan society[54]. Despite this, the pathway to normalisation in the use of

53 Jordi Casassas, *Entre Escil·la i Caribdis...*, p. 200 and forward.

54 See: Jordi Casassas, *L'Ateneu i Barcelona. Un segle i mig de vida cultural* (Barcelona: RBA-La Magrana, 2006).

the Catalan language was not so simple, as shown by the speech of Joan Josep Permanyer, the new president of the Acadèmia de Jurisprudència de Barcelona (1896), when he spoke out in favour of the Catalanisation of all legal life in the Principality. This request was obviously met with an insurmountable refusal from the authorities of the Spanish state.

The end of the 19th century marked the patterns in the later socio-political development of Catalan: the loss of the Spanish state's last colonies triggered a profound crisis in the public treasury on the one hand, while the recovery of Catalan capital invested in the Antilles until 1898 meant an important injection of capital in Catalan industry. The events of 1898 led to a radicalisation of the Catalanist world (exemplified by *Missatge a la Reina Regent* and the *Als Catalans* and *Al Poble de Catalunya* manifestos), which in September 1899 led to the creation of the Centre Nacional Català (CNC) by Prat de la Riba's group. At this time of crisis, two crucial events defined Catalonia's politics: the *Concert Econòmic* ("Economic Agreement"), which Polavieja's eventual rise to power in Madrid seemed to make possible, and the closure of the savings banks when not only were these agreements not implemented but, quite to the contrary, Villaverde's budgets increased the fiscal pressure (1899). Precisely the closure of the savings banks heightened the tensions significantly and led the Catalans to demand active intervention on behalf of Catalan interests in state policies. Prat de la Riba understood that times were evolving and that he had to distance himself from the more dogmatic positions of the non-politicians in the Unió Catalanista who were against participation in the elections. The merger of the CNC and the Unió Regionalista, which sprang from the remains of the movement supporting General Polavieja in Catalonia, paved the way for the formation of the Lliga Regionalista in 1901, which went on to play a key role in all Catalan public life until 1931. This party, which had modern political ranks, defeated the system of dynastic parties in Catalonia and embarked upon the unprecedented modernisation of the country[55].

55 Santiago Izquierdo, *La primera victòria del catalanisme polític* (Barcelona: Pòrtic, 2001).

What Made Catalonia Unique (1901-1939)

Jordi Casassas
Universitat de Barcelona and Institut d'Estudis Catalans

1. Catalanism's difficulty attaining a political profile of its own

In 1901, a new stage got underway in the history of contemporary Catalonia, and especially in Catalanism[1]. This current, which until then had primarily encompassed culture and cultural policy agitation, was finally able to connect with a small part of Barcelona's electorate (and prominent representatives of industrial leaders) and won four deputy seats in the Spanish Courts under the slogan of *L'enemic és el cacic*[2] ("The enemy is the cacique"). Shortly afterward came an attack on the hegemony of electoral cronyism, and the Catalanists were able to secure several councillorships in the Barcelona Town Hall. However, in the early years of the century, the Catalanist presence was quite meagre and always trailed

1 Many years ago there was a historiographic controversy between those who pinpointed the origin of Catalanism in 1901 as the outcome of the colonial crisis, and those who said that the process had gotten underway during the *Sexenni Democràtic* ("Six Years of Democracy", 1868-1874) with the actions of Valentí Almirall and especially the efforts of the Unió Catalanista (1891) and the *Bases de Manresa* (1892). Among the former, adhering strictly to the thesis put forth by: Jordi Solé Tura, *Catalanisme i revolució burgesa. La síntesi de Prat de la Riba* (Barcelona: Edicions 62, 1967), we can highlight: Borja de Riquer, *La Lliga Regionalista. La burgesia catalana i el nacionalisme (1898-1904)* (Barcelona: Edicions 62, 1977); and among the latter, we can cite: Jordi Llorens, *La Unió Catalanista i els orígens del catalanisme polític* (Barcelona: Publicacions de l'Abadia de Montserrat, 1992); Joaquim Coll, *Narcís Verdaguer i Callís (1862-1918) i el catalanisme posibilista* (Barcelona: Publicacions de l'Abadia de Montserrat, 1998).

2 The candidates elected were: Bartomeu Robert (Societat Econòmica d'Amics del País), Albert Rusiñol (Foment del Treball Nacional), Lluís Domènech i Montaner (Ateneu Barcelonès) and Sebastià Torres (Lliga de Defensa Industrial i Mercantil). See: Santiago Izquierdo, *El doctor Robert (1842-1902). Medicina i compromís polític* (Barcelona: Proa, 2002).

behind the Spanishist republicans from the *Unión Republicana,* which Alejandro Lerroux had begun to lead, and which had solid roots in the city's working-class neighbourhoods. In the rest of Catalonia, monarchic cronyism was still largely in the majority; it was very hard for the Lliga Regionalista (the name that this Catalan group adopted) to be taken into consideration and it often had to secure this consideration in alliance with the local caciques[3].

The situation that prompted this definitive advent of political Catalanism was not so much the colonial crisis itself as the economic and fiscal policy which the central government implemented in a bid to deal with the disasters of the war with the colonies and against the USA (closure of the savings banks in 1899 and creation of the Unión Regionalista management organisation). This created initial confusion between the defence of the city's economic bourgeoisie's interests and the defence of the nationalist ideals (which were called regionalist at that time)[4]. Regarding the latter, years earlier Catalonia had been defined as a nation (natural fact) and Spain as a state (arbitrary construct that always came after the nation)[5]. Regarding the objectives of the Catalanist organisations, there was a rising controversy between those in favour of limiting themselves to cultural agitation and national awareness-raising and those called the Possibilists, who were politically in favour of running in the elections to – generically – work towards and defend the moral and material interests of Catalonia *per tots els mitjans legals possibles*[6] ("by all possible legal means"). Both sectors justified their claims by harking back to the history of the country's medieval glories and the origin of the loss of the freedoms in 1714. On the other hand, Catalanism also began to have hindsight and awareness of having

3 See the classic: Isidre Molas, *Lliga Catalana: un estudi d'Estasiologia*, 2 vols. (Barcelona: Edicions 62, 1972), vol. 2.

4 See: Enric Jardí, *El doctor Robert i el seu temps* (Barcelona: Editorial Aedos, 1969).

5 See: Narcís Roca, *El catalanisme progressiu*, ed. Jordi Llorens, 2 vols. (Barcelona: La Magrana, 1983), vol. 2.

6 See: Jordi Llorens, *La Unió Catalanista i els orígens…*; see too: Lluís Domènech, *Escrits polítics i culturals (1875-1922)*, ed. Maria Lluïsa Borràs (Barcelona: La Magrana, 1991).

a history of its own, and the first histories of the movement began to appear (Enric Moliné i Brases)[7].

Among the national symbols, the Eleventh of September began to gain ground as a unitary festival that was increasingly used to express Catalonia's claims, against which the authorities tended to react with differing degrees of harshness, depending on the intensity of the political juncture on which the *Diada*, Catalonia's national day, fell. In the *Diada* of 1901, in this tense situation of post-colonial crisis, around 30 radical youths putting laurel wreaths at the foot of the statue of Rafael Casanova were arrested, while on the 15th of the same month a demonstration of around 10,000 people confirmed the appeal of the Rafael Casanova statue, which came above specific organisations and parties[8].

The shift in the political climate of Barcelona was perfectly reflected in the generational change: in 1901 three main players from the 19th century died: the federalist Francesc Pi i Margall, the liberal Víctor Balaguer and the conservative regionalist Joan Mañé i Flaquer. The next year, the great national poet Father Cinto Verdaguer died, along with the doctor and noted Catalanist Bartomeu Robert (and Valentí Almirall died in 1904). In parallel to political action, we cannot fail to mention the leading role played by the intellectual-professional sector in the entire national movement in Western Europe during this decisive period falling between 1870 and 1914[9]. In 1902, the economist Guillem Graell reformulated Catalonia's economic claims against the central power in *La cuestión catalana*[10]. In 1903, intellectuals of many stripes founded the Ateneu Enciclopèdic Popular, an organisation with a particularly pro-worker sensitivity and

7 For the dynamics of Catalanism until the Primo de Rivera dictatorship, the following is essential: Josep Termes, *Història del catalanisme fins el 1923* (Barcelona: Pòrtic, 2000).

8 See: Pere Anguera, *L'Onze de Setembre. Història de la Diada (1886-1938)* (Barcelona: Centre d'Història Contemporània de Catalunya-Publicacions de l'Abadia de Montserrat, 2008); see too: Albert Balcells, *Llocs de memòria dels catalans* (Barcelona: Proa, 2008).

9 For the overall evolution of this sector, see: Jordi Casassas, coord., *Els intel·lectuals i el poder a Catalunya (1808-1975)* (Barcelona: Pòrtic, 1999).

10 See: Òscar Costa, *L'imaginari imperial: el noucentisme català i la política internacional* (Barcelona: Alpha, 2002).

the desire to democratise culture and sympathies towards Catalanism[11]. In 1903, too, the first Catalanist workers' union was founded, the Centre Autonomista de Dependents del Comerç i la Indústria[12], and the Primer Congrés Universitari Català was held. The intellectuals and many of the leaders of Catalanism were young men who had just graduated from university and were fully aware of the importance of having a leading educational institution. However, since they were unable to affect this in 1903 they created the para-university structure of the Estudis Universitaris Catalans (which remained an important actor in cultural resistance and university activities during the Franco regime), which taught different disciplines applied to the reality of Catalonia (economics, history, language, literature, etc.)[13]. In 1904, two important publications were created: *El Poble Català*, the republican, Catalanist alternative to the conservative *La Veu de Catalunya*, the mouthpiece of the Lliga Regionalista[14]; and the children's magazine *Patufet*, an initiative by the radical Catalanist Josep Maria Folch i Torres with a clear mission of social integration and the nationalisation of youth[15]. Finally, in 1906 this interventionist, modernising and normalising zeal manifested by Catalan intellectuals materialised in the Primer Congrés Internacional de la Llengua Catalana, which marked the beginning of the modern efforts to normalise Catalan[16].

In the political sphere, in 1904 an apparently anecdotal affair precipitated the inevitable when Francesc Cambó violated the agreement to boycott the visit by the young Alfonso XIII and the head of government

11 See: Ferran Aisa, *Una història de Barcelona: L'Ateneu Enciclopèdic Popular (1902-1992)* (Barcelona: Ateneu Enciclopèdic Popular-Virus, 1992); Pere Solà, *Els ateneus obrers i la cultura popular a Catalunya (1900-1939). L'Ateneu Enciclopèdic Popular* (Barcelona: La Magrana, 1978).

12 See: Manuel Lladonosa, *Catalanisme i moviment obrer: el CADCI entre 1903 i 1923* (Barcelona: Publicacions de l'Abadia de Montserrat, 1988).

13 See: Albert Balcells, *Els Estudis Universitaris Catalans (1903-1985). Per una Universitat Catalana* (Barcelona: Institut d'Estudis Catalans, 2011).

14 See: Joan Baptista Culla, Àngel Duarte, *La premsa republicana* (Barcelona: Diputació de Barcelona-Col·legi de Periodistes de Catalunya, 1990).

15 See: Enric Jardí, *Els Folch i Torres i la Catalunya del seu temps* (Barcelona: Publicacions de l'Abadia de Montserrat, 1995).

16 See: Pompeu Fabra, *La llengua catalana i la seva normalització*, ed. Francesc Vallverdú (Barcelona: Edicions 62, 1980); see too: Maria Pilar Perea, *Llums i ombres en el primer Congrés de la Llengua Catalana (1906). La resposta dels intel·lectuals* (Palma de Mallorca: Institut d'Estudis Baleàrics, 2007).

Antonio Maura by making a brief welcoming speech (in a clearly protesting vein, which perennially bothered the monarch) at the Barcelona Town Hall: the Lliga split off from the majority republican and democratic sector, leaving regionalism barely represented. The second event happened in November 1905, when around 300 officers from the Barcelona garrison attacked the studios and editorial office of the satirical magazine *Cu-Cut!* and *La Veu de Catalunya* and beat anyone near them. The officers claimed that they were responding to the affront caused by a graphic joke: a military officer and a civilian were in front of a restaurant where a huge celebration was taking place; the officer asked what was happening and the civilian told him that it was a victory banquet (an electoral victory of the Catalanists over the republicans), to which the officer responded: *Ah! Doncs no deuen ser militars* ("Ah! So they must not be in the military") (in clear allusion to the Spanish army, which was only suffering from defeats). The events sparked a huge wave of indignation and a protest among the Catalanist deputies in the Spanish Courts, which responded by condemning the Catalanists and approving a Law on Jurisdictions which placed crimes against the fatherland and its symbols under military jurisdiction. The Catalan deputies and several others (including the old Spanish republican Nicolás Salmerón) left the deputies' chamber as a sign of protest[17].

This circumstance was seized upon by those remaining in the Lliga Regionalista, who were preparing a huge party to welcome the deputies in May 1906 under the leadership of the young activist Francesc Cambó: their goal was to resume contact with the public and gain political ground while subordinating the other sectors of Catalanism[18]. To fully capitalise on the initiative, some intellectuals (primarily Eugeni d'Ors and Josep Pijoan) convinced the young lawyer and leader of the Lliga Regionalista, Enric Prat de la Riba, to publish a short book in which he definitively set forth the doctrine of Catalanism[19]. This book was *La Nacionalitat Catalana* (1906), which d'Ors called the *llibre de capçalera* ("header book") of the Catalan people. The book was divided into three main parts: an analysis

17 See: Jordi Casassas, ed., *Els fets del Cu-Cut!, cent anys després: taula rodona organitzada pel Centre d'Història Contemporània de Catalunya el 24 de novembre de 2005* (Barcelona: Centre d'Història Contemporània de Catalunya, 2006).

18 See: Francesc Cambó, *Memòries (1876-1936)* (Barcelona: Alpha, 1981).

19 An overview can be found in: Enric Ucelay, *El imperialismo catalán. Prat de la Riba, Cambó, D'Ors y la conquista moral de España* (Barcelona: Edhasa, 2003).

of the identifying features upon which Catalanism was grounded (social, legal, geographic, character, historical and linguistic); a study of the historical process of restoring the national sentiment based on Catalonia's resistance against Bourbon absolutism, the people's Romantic rediscovery and the move throughout the 19th century towards full political authority represented by his generation; and finally a strategic conclusion entitled *Imperialisme.* In this final part, also the last to be written, Prat changed register and made a very modern synthesis between regenerationalist theories and the new imperialist formulations. Supporting himself on theoreticians from the United States, the author explained the need to link the national claims to the process of modernisation, a prior, necessary step for Catalonia to exert influence abroad and make claims for a state of its own. To Prat, the Catalan people were equated with the cultural and commercial dynamism of the small ancient Mediterranean peoples (Phoenicians and Greeks), as well as with a high degree of Romanisation. They reached their peak with the medieval expansion and were reduced to a situation of decline and subordination to Spain with the onset of the Modern Age due to general political causes and geographic marginalisation. However, at all times the Catalan people had shown their loyalty to their own unique language, institutions and legal customs, as well as a recurring desire to defend them from Spanish assimilation[20].

The welcome celebration for the deputies, which is known as the Festa de l'Homenatge (20 May 1906) was a resounding success, and it marked the first time that Catalanism entered into contact with the urban masses, especially the middle classes, liberal professionals, petty bourgeoisie and artisans. The culmination of that day was a huge demonstration which the propaganda boldly claimed 200,000 people had attended (in a city that had 533,000 inhabitants in 1900, with the majority of the working class suspicious of Catalanist ideas)[21]. This success enabled a platform called Solidaritat Catalana to be created in which all the Catalan groups banded

20 See: Jordi Casassas, "Estudi introductori a Enric Prat de la Riba", Enric Prat de la Riba, *La Nacionalitat Catalana*, ed. Jordi Casassas (Barcelona: La Magrana, 1993).

21 Reflections on the contacts between Catalanism and the working class can be found in: Josep Termes, *Les arrels populars del catalanisme* (Barcelona: Empúries, 1999); Josep Termes, *Històries de la Catalunya treballadora* (Barcelona: Empúries, 2000); Josep Termes, *La catalanitat obrera: la República catalana, l'Estatut de 1932 i el moviment obrer* (Barcelona: Afers, 2007).

together except the Lerroux republicans. Solidaritat Catalana earned its first win at the urns in the provincial elections of March 1907[22]. At that time, they agreed upon a common platform (Tivoli Programme) on which to run in the general elections scheduled for April. Written by Prat de la Riba, the Tivoli Programme focused on the demand for the Law on Jurisdictions to be derogated, the struggle against election cronyism, the reform and modernisation of the state, the recognition of Catalonia and provincial and municipal autonomy in education, social work and public works. The success of Solidaritat Catalana was resounding: it won 41 of the 44 available seats in Catalonia with 70% voter turnout (an unheard-of figure which was not repeated until the Second Republic)[23].

In 1907, Prat de la Riba was elected president of the Diputació de Barcelona (Provincial Council of Barcelona), so thanks to Solidaritat Catalana, Catalanism had finally managed to touch the masses, earn election wins and gain control over an institution with provincial competences within the peripheral state administration. There is no doubt that Prat de la Riba had a vision of the Catalan state (a regional vision, given that he never promoted political secession) with an ambitious agenda and a clear idea of the priority spheres of action[24]. To achieve this, a disciplined party was needed (in 1907 he launched the Lliga's supervisory body, political committee and youth section as a means of giving prepared middle-class youth a place within the organisation), and the mobilisation of intellectualism embodied in the current of what was called Noucentisme had to be subordinated[25]. This movement, which was initially poetic, can be considered part of the huge wave of symbolist subversion against the previous hegemony of positivism and reality, as well as a uniquely Catalan manifestation of the trend of intellectuals responding to the crisis of classic liberalism with steadfast intervention in public affairs and even in politics. The main Catalan disseminator of this new intellectual morality was Eugeni d'Ors, and it is telling that he spread his ideas via a daily column in *La Veu*

22 See: Albert Balcells, Joan Baptista Culla, Conxita Mir, *Les eleccions generals a Catalunya de 1901 a 1923* (Barcelona: Fundació Jaume Bofill, 1982).

23 See: Isidre Molas, *Lliga Catalana…*, vol. 1, pp. 63-81.

24 See as a whole: Albert Balcells, Josep Maria Ainaud eds., *Enric Prat de la Riba. Obra Completa*, (Barcelona: Institut d'Estudis Catalans-Proa, 1998).

25 See: Jordi Casassas, "Els quadres del regionalisme. L'evolució de la Joventut Nacionalista de la Lliga fins el 1914", *Recerques*, 14 (1983), pp. 7-32.

de Catalunya entitled *Glosari*[26]. The uniqueness of Catalonia lay in the fact that these intellectuals always acted primarily with the goal of modernising and cleaning up the liberal system and did not allow themselves to be tempted by the anti-parliamentarianism advocated by many of their fellow southern Europeans[27].

The new buzzwords were *civilitat (ciutat versus ruralia), ètica de la responsabilitat, cultura, voluntat, arbitrarietat, mediterraneitat, imperi, tradició, continuïtat, nació, joventut, esperit del temps (del nou-cents), etc.* ("civility [city versus ruralism], ethics of responsibility, culture, will, arbitrariness, Mediterranean-ness, empire, tradition, continuity, nation, youth and spirit of the times [20th century], etc."). And in Catalonia, this current merged with Catalanism, and after the Festa de l'Homenatge and the appearance of Prat's *La nacionalitat catalana*, it was almost unanimously subordinated to the directives of the nationalist leader and the governing role he soon undertook in the Barcelona Provincial Council[28]. This practical action in perspective was soon joined by the mobilisation of young professionals from all fields (doctors, educators, sociologists, economists, urban planners, architects, etc.). Together they combined the new ideas with the old postulates of regenerationism and Latinism from the last quarter of the 19th century, and spurred by the political possibilities, they believed that they could modernise Spain from Catalonia. For this reason, between 1907 and 1914 they gradually outlined their programme to regenerate Spain in the magazine *La Cataluña* (written in Spanish to accomplish their goal of intervention in Spain)[29].

All of this euphoria ground to a halt between 1908 and 1909 with the crisis in Solidaritat Catalana and especially the outbreak of the Setmana Tràgica (Tragic Week) and its after-effects[30]. The crisis in the Solidaritat

26 See: Enric Jardí, *Eugeni d'Ors: obra i vida* (Barcelona: Quaderns Crema, 1990).

27 Maximiliano Fuentes, "La particular dimensión europea de Eugeni d'Ors durante la Primera Guerra Mundial", *Ayer*, 76 (2009), pp. 209-243.

28 See: José Luís Martín, "Dinàstics i regionalistes (1898-1913)", *Història de la Diputació de Barcelona*, 3 vols., Borja de Riquer, dir. (Barcelona: Diputació de Barcelona, 1987), vol. 2.

29 See: Antoni Guirao, "*La Cataluña.* Ideologia i poder a la Catalunya Noucentista", *Cercles*, 1 (1998), pp. 64-66; Antoni Guirao, "El procés nacionalitzador a *la Cataluña*", *Cercles*, 5 (2002), pp. 104-115.

30 Solidaritat Catalana had also spurred the creation of a Solidaritat Municipal in the Barcelona Town Hall, which led to the election of the first people's mayor, the

Catalana movement once again revealed the tensions and difficulties stirring inside Catalanism, which led to a gulf between the more conservative and progressive sectors (including most prominently the doctrinal efforts of the Mallorcan Gabriel Alomar)[31], spurred by the different stances on Antonio Maura's Law to Reform the Local Administration with Cambó's clear support[32]. The second event, which was much more serious, affected Catalan life in general and especially the bourgeois world and middle classes where Catalanism had taken root. In July 1909 a clash between the rising social mobilisation (unionism and Lerroux republicanism) and an exceptional situation linked to a new colonial crisis in North Africa broke out in four or five days of extreme violence, with hundreds of barricades and the burning of around 80 religious buildings, along with numerous deaths and injuries, all of which totally paralysed the city. Troops were called in from Valencia to restore peace and return Barcelona to some semblance of normality[33]. Afterwards, the repression was extremely harsh and even impacted European public opinion (especially because of the shooting of the educator, Mason and closer to anarchism Francesc Ferrer i Guardia, who was unfairly accused of instigating the events). A handful of newspapers and politicians from Madrid spread the notion that the events in Barcelona were an expression of Catalan separatism[34].

In inland Catalonia, the effects of the Tragic Week were truly profound. For a few months, the clash of social identities and their respective political cultures resurged[35]. The working class waged its fraught struggle

republican and nationalist Albert Bastardas. See: Alfred Pérez-Bastardas, *Els republicans nacionalistes i el catalanisme polític: Albert Bastardas i Sampere (1871-1944)* (Barcelona: Edicions 62, 1987).

31 Gabriel Alomar, *Negacions i afirmacions del catalanisme: catalanisme socialista* (Barcelona: Fundació Rafael Campalans, 1989).

32 Francesc Cambó, *Discursos parlamentaris: 1907-1935*, ed. Jordi Casassas (Barcelona: Alpha, 1991).

33 See the classic accounts: Josep Benet, *Maragall i la Setmana Tràgica* (Barcelona: Edicions 62, 2009); Joan Connelly, *La Setmana Tràgica* (Barcelona: Ediciones B, 2009); Ignasi Moreta, *La Setmana Tràgica i tres articles de Joan Maragall* (Barcelona: Fragmenta, 2009).

34 See: Patricia Gabancho, *Despert entre adormits. Joan Maragall i la fi de segle a Barcelona* (Barcelona: Proa, 1998).

35 Of the extensive literature, see: Soledad Bengoechea, *Barcelona i la Setmana Tràgica de 1909: arrels i conseqüències* (Barcelona: Museu d'Història de Barcelona-Institut de Cultura-Ajuntament de Barcelona-La Central, 2012).

to create a union structure following the mandates of France's Amiens Congress (1906), and after 1910 this would become the CNT[36]. In turn, the majority republicanism continued to be politically organised by the radicals who followed Alejandro Lerroux[37], while the leftist Catalanists created a platform called the Unió Federal Nacionalista Republicana, which was somewhat successful in the 1910-1911 elections[38]. Nonetheless, the republican culture was still expressed through a growing network of casinos, centres and athenaeums of all sorts, which were a mix of politics (albeit not electoral), free-time activities, education and consumer cooperatives[39]. The Lliga Regionalista suffered from significant electoral setbacks resulting from its connivance with the repression that came in the wake of Tragic Week: Cambó lost his seat as a deputy and Prat de la Riba was showered with criticism and discredit from all sides, to such an extent that a tribute was held for him in December 1910 to make amends. In turn, the young professionals associated with *La Cataluña* and Spanish collaboration were dealt a heavy blow with the fall of Maura as the head of government and Cambó's defeat in the elections.

They were clashing political cultures, yet they also had many commonalities. Catalan territory fostered internal circulation, especially in the northern regions (Catalunya Vella) and the littoral and pre-littoral area. Since the second half of the 18th century, with the entire process of modernisation that culminated in industrialisation in the ensuing century, mobility flows of the population from the countryside to the urban zones had been increasing in Catalonia. On the other hand, economic modernisation had distanced the dynamic in Catalonia from the rest of Spain, and there were often joint demonstrations by management and labour demanding protection for Catalan industry. A clear anti-state feeling had also been inherited from the

36 See: Pere Gabriel, *Classe obrera i sindicats a Catalunya (1903-1920)* (Barcelona: Universitat de Barcelona, PhD Dissertation, 1981); see too, the classic: Josep Maria Huertas, *Obrers a Catalunya. Manual d'Història del moviment obrer (1840-1975)* (Barcelona: L'Avenç, 1982).

37 Joan Baptista Culla, *El republicanisme lerrouxista a Catalunya (1901-1923)* (Barcelona: Curial, 1986).

38 See: Santiago Izquierdo, *El republicanisme nacional a Catalunya. La gestació de la Unió Federal Nacionalista republicana* (Barcelona: Societat Catalana d'Estudis Històrics, 2010).

39 See: Pere Gabriel, *El catalanisme i la cultura federal: història i política del republicanisme popular a Catalunya el segle XX* (Reus: Fundació Josep Recasens, 2007).

19th century, as well as a cultural substrate which embodied a diffuse feeling of separation that each aggression by the state magnified. The historicist feeling was omnipresent in all social sectors, and collective referents did take root even though they often appealed to contradictory historical traditions. From 1907 to 1913 the celebration of the *diada nacional* ("national holiday") on the day of Barcelona's fall to the Bourbon troops on the 11th of September 1714 became more widespread, and more political institutions called to participate in the ceremonies (Lliga Regionalista, UFNR), as did unions (CADCI) and cultural-political organisations (Unió Catalanista) among others.

2. The *palaeo-statalisation* of Catalonia and the political hegemony of Catalanism

In July 1911, the presidents of the four provincial councils of Catalonia met in Barcelona and charged Prat to draw up the internal regulations of the Mancomunitat de Catalunya, as called for in Maura's Law to Reform the Local Administration. It was soon ready, and in early December a committee delivered it to the head of the central government, José Canalejas. Canalejas' murder in November 1912 delayed its way through Parliament (which often became quite tense), and the decree creating the Mancomunitat de Catalunya was not approved until December 1913[40].

It is important to note that the struggle to create this regional body was capitalised upon by the Lliga Regionalista, which after 1912-1913 became the hegemonic electoral force in Catalonia. Catalanist euphoria was unleashed in the 1913 celebration of the Eleventh of September, and the Barcelona Town Hall officially participated in the celebration for the first time[41]. The spectacular surge in regionalism alarmed the Catalanist republicans of the UFNR, and on the initiative of its president, Pere Coromines, they strove to counterbalance it by reaching an electoral pact

40 Albert Balcells, Enric Pujol, Jordi Sabater, *La Mancomunitat de Catalunya i l'autonomia* (Barcelona: Proa, 1996).

41 See: Jaume Sobrequés, "El segle XX. I. De les annexions a la fi de la Guerra Civil", *Història de Barcelona*, 8 vols. (Barcelona: Enciclopèdia Catalana-Ajuntament de Barcelona, 1995), vol. 7.

with Lerrouxism (the Sant Gervasi Pact of 1914), which had always been profoundly anti-Catalanist. When it ended in utter failure, republican Catalanism entered a phase of organisational fragmentation from which it never truly recovered until March 1931 with the creation of Esquerra Republicana de Catalunya[42]. What is true, however, is that in just eleven years, and with little effort, political Catalanism had become the leading force in the Principality and had set forth its political agenda. This disproportion can be explained by noting how the political organisation of the elections was only part of this movement's potential; the other part of the formula can be found in civil society and its rising institutionalisation which had begun with the Restoration and was an extremely powerful avenue of social penetration. The discrediting of official cronyist politics in Catalonia contrasted with this other system which was clearly distinguished from the rest of the state and was an atomised atmosphere with great cultural (popular or not) wealth and political dynamism.

There was yet another component of the Catalan political culture inherited from the 19th century which we could generically call anti-statism. This feeling, at first somewhat diffuse but gradually cutting across society, gradually came into focus throughout the 19th century. In the last quarter of the century the content of regenerationism was expanded so much that it could be called Catalanism, whose institutions had to develop a modernising (and Europeanising) activity which made up for the shortcomings of the central state's actions in Catalonia[43].

Between the increasing activity of political Catalanism, the support from the rich web of institutions in Catalonia which spurred it on and the prominence of an intellectual-professional sector which was increasingly aligned with Noucentisme, the outcome was the ideal situation to begin to give content to the Mancomunitat de Catalunya, which was officially established on the 6th of April 1914. It had an action plan contained in the *Memòries presidencials* which Prat de la Riba had written at the beginning of each political race in his role as president of the Provincial

42 See: Pere Coromines, *Apologia de Barcelona i altres escrits*, ed. Àngel Duarte (Barcelona: La Magrana, 1990).

43 See: Agustí Colomines, *El catalanisme i l'estat. La lluita parlamentària per l'autonomia (1898-1917)* (Barcelona: Publicacions de l'Abadia de Montserrat, 1993).

Council of Barcelona.[44] These reports discussed issues like spiritual culture and material culture, high culture and popular culture, the need to have modern infrastructures that would encourage modernisation and the real integration of the entire territory. Specific actions had also been advanced, including the *Servei d'Higiene* ("Hygiene Service") and the *Museu Social* ("Social Museum"), the latter to encourage improvements in the living and working conditions of the working class, along with the *Junta de Museus* ("Board of Museums")[45]. The most spectacular actions came in the realm of high culture with the creation of the Institut d'Estudis Catalans (1907), the only academy of sciences recognised by the International Union of Academies that does not correspond to a state; and in 1914 the Biblioteca de Catalunya (Library of Catalonia) began operating. One of the most important initiatives spearheaded by this Institute was positioning modern Catalan as a political tool to unify Catalan society and a necessary vehicle for consolidating and projecting its culture. In January 1913, the first orthographic rules were approved, and a few days later Prat de la Riba officially incorporated them into his policies, which helped to ensure that they were adopted by the two leading Catalanist newspapers: *La Veu de Catalunya* and *El Poble Català*. In 1918, the *Gramàtica catalana* was published, and in 1932 the *Diccionari de la llengua catalana* came out. The mastermind behind this linguistic normalisation was Pompeu Fabra[46].

The Mancomunitat de Catalunya was also the only such body created in the Spanish state, and it was proof of the density that the Catalan and Catalanist political culture had achieved[47]. Even though it was founded when the Great War was causing heavy tensions and changes, and even though it had meagre authority and budgets, the efforts of this internal governing body were extraordinarily notable. It

44 Jaume Bofill, *Prat de la Riba i la cultura catalana*, ed. Jordi Casassas (Barcelona: Edicions 62, 1979).

45 This was inherited from earlier times; see: Maria Ojuel, *La Barcelona prodigiosa de Carles Pirozzini (1852-1938)* (Lleida: Pagès Editors, 2012).

46 See: Albert Balcells, Enric Pujol, *Història de l'Institut d'Estudis Catalans* (Barcelona: Institut d'Estudis Catalans-Editorial Afers, 2002).

47 Aside from the monographic work cited above in note 40, see, too: Enric Ucelay, "La Diputació i la Mancomunitat (1914-1923)", *Història de la Diputació de Barcelona*, 3 vols., Borja de Riquer dir. (Barcelona: Diputació de Barcelona, 1987), vol. 2, pp. 37-177.

stood out in the fields of education and culture, yet we cannot forget the actions of pedagogy and training of teachers and the institutions it founded, such as the *Escola de Funcionaris* ("Civil Servants' School"), the *Servei de Conservació i Catalogació de Monuments* ("Monument Conservation and Cataloguing Service"), the *Servei del Mapa Geològic* ("Geological Map Service") and the *Servei d'Estudis Sanitaris* ("Health Studies Service"), among many others. We should also spotlight its effort to encourage agricultural cooperatives, the *Escola d'Agricultura* ("Agriculture School"), the creation of a secondary network of roads and railways to help connect the country, the arrival of the telephone to all villages in Catalonia, the creation of a network of popular libraries and the design and slow launch of a *Comissió d'Educació General (o Nacional)* ("General [or National] Education Committee"), which was supposed to serve as the seed of a modern *Ministeri* ("Regional Ministry") of Culture and Propaganda.

In addition to this governmental action, the Great War also spotlighted another element of Catalan uniqueness. It extraordinarily promoted industrial activity and boosted immigration to the Barcelona region like never before, leading the city to definitively consolidate its status as the head of all of Catalonia: Barcelona went from having 533,000 inhabitants in 1900 to one million in 1936, with the steepest rise after the Great War (628,000 inhabitants in 1917)[48]. The extraordinary surge in economic activity, especially after 1916, always associated with the war (the high growth rates of electrical production are a clear reflection of this), that is, with exports, led to vast accumulations of wealth, yet also shortages and price inflation (of basic foodstuffs, housing and energy, primarily coal). This furthered the distance between the social classes: the *nouveau riche* abounded with their ostentation and dissipated morality, while the working class and middle class increasingly suffered from poverty and hardship. During the years of the Great War, unprecedented numbers of the working class were joining the unions: the CNT went from 15,000 members in 1915 to 74,000 in 1918 and would grow even more spectacularly the following year. However, this was not true of the middle classes,

48 Regarding the tensions sparked by the Great War in the demographic, cultural and political dynamic of Catalonia, see: Josep Termes, *La immigració a Catalunya i altres estudis d'història del nacionalisme català* (Barcelona: Empúries, 1984).

which had no union tradition and instead responded to the tensions in those years with rising radicalisation[49].

This kind of tension, which we could call structural, could also be seen in politics and ideology: even the central politicians responded to the new tensions by closing the Courts, revealing that the crisis in the Restoration regime was irreversible. In Catalonia, the hegemony of the Lliga Regionalista seemed a fait accompli. In 1915, it warned the government of the need to modernise the state's economic policy and adapt it to the extraordinary circumstances of the war (*El pensament català davant el conflicte europeu)*[50] ("Catalan thought regarding the European conflict"). When it got neither results nor a positive response from the Conservative Party, a frontal clash with cronyist politics got underway in late 1915, especially after the Liberal Party came to power in December[51]. This party, the traditional enemy of Catalanism, reached an alliance to oust the Lliga in April 1916. In turn, Prat de la Riba responded by writing the manifesto *Per Catalunya i l'Espanya gran*, where he reiterated Catalonia's aim to intervene within the scheme of a federation of Iberian peoples. The Lliga was victorious in the 1916 elections after vying against small republican groups in inland Catalonia, too (the Bloc Republicà Autonomista organised by Layret or M. Domingo called Bloc Republicà Català since 1917[52] and the revamped Unió Catalanista led by Domènech Martí i Julià), and Cambó declared 1916 the Lliga's *any heroic* ("heroic year"). At the Festa de la Unitat Catalana held in Barcelona's Parc Güell, Cambó made a rhetorical cry to Europe asking for its intercession so that all Spaniards could feel welcome in Spain and to secure guarantees that in the future reconstruction of Europe the Catalans did not have to express their disagreement

49 See: Soledad Bengoechea, *Organització patronal i conflictivitat social a Catalunya: tradició i corporativisme entre finals de segle i la dictadura de Primo de Rivera* (Barcelona: Publicacions de l'Abadia de Montserrat, 1994).

50 See: Francesc Cambó, *Política Econòmica*, ed. Alfons Almendrós (Barcelona: Alpha, 1999); see too: Jordi Casassas, "Introducció als grans temes cambonians", *El món de Cambó. Permanència i canvi en el seu 125è aniversari*, Jordi Cassasas, dir. (Barcelona: Institut Cambó-Alpha, 2001), pp. 13-36.

51 See: Francesc Cambó, *Discursos i conferències*, ed. Jordi Casassas (Barcelona: Alpha, 2007).

52 For further information on the career of this influential republican, see: Xavier Pujadas, *Marcel·lí Domingo i el marcel·linisme* (Barcelona: Ajuntament del Vendrell-Ajuntament de Barcelona-Publicacions de l'Abadia de Montserrat, 1996).

with being represented by Spanish delegates. That year, too, the regionalist councillors in the Barcelona Town Hall submitted a proposal to the town council asking that the sessions be held in Catalan[53]. The year 1916 also marked the founding of *Nostra Parla*, an organisation whose mission was to disseminate the national sentiment in Valencia, the Balearic Islands and Roussillon based on the linguistic unity of these lands[54].

The war had provided yet another front of ideological and political confrontation between supporters of either side[55]: the supporters of the allies and the Germans clashed with enormous zeal, and only a handful had declared themselves to be neutral (the members of the Comitè d'Amics de la Unitat Moral d'Europa were roundly labelled pro-German)[56]. The press, especially the general and enlightened press, reported in detail about the events in the war, and chroniclers like Agustí Calvet (Gaziel) at *La Vanguardia* became quite famous. The progressives and republicans (with mouthpieces such as the magazine *Ibèria*, promoted by Claudi Ametlla) unanimously supported the allies, and the desire to collaborate with France led to the formation of a Corps of Volunteers who fought as part of the French Foreign Legion. Doctor Solè i Pla organised a Comitè de Germanor (Brotherhood Committee) to help the Catalan Volunteers; in it, there was open talk of how Catalonia could ask for support for the Catalan cause after an allied victory. Within this context, the prestige of the historian of worldwide national movements, Antoni Rovira i Virgili, was consolidated.

Cambó translated the consolidation of the Lliga and the political radicalisation of these years into a twofold initiative aimed at first seeking regionalist complicities in the outlying areas of Spain (initially in Valencia and the Basque Country) and secondly forging the alliances needed to assemble the critics of the Restoration and those who were at odds with its economic policy in order to force a constitutional reform. This initiative

53 See: Jordi Casassas, *Jaume Bofill i Matas (1878-1933). L'adscripció social i l'evolució política* (Barcelona: Curial, 1980).

54 Lluís Duran, *Breu història del catalanisme. I. Del segle XIX a la Dictadura de Primo de Rivera* (Barcelona: Publicacions de l'Abadia de Montserrat, 2009), pp. 179-182.

55 Jordi Albertí, "Els amics d'Europa (1915-1919) una veu a contravent 1", *Revista de Catalunya*, 180 (2003), pp. 90-106; Jordi Albertí, "Els amic d'Europa (1915-1919) una veu a contravent 2", *Revista de Catalunya*, 181 (2003), pp. 85-103.

56 See: David Martínez, ed., *El catalanisme i la Gran Guerra (1914-1918)* (Barcelona: La Magrana, 1988).

was declared unlawful by the government, but it took shape in an Assembly of Parliamentarians gathered temporarily in Barcelona due to the political hiatus of the 19th of July 1917. Given the urgency of the moment, Cambó's intention of discussing the political aspects of the territorial division of Spain (to attain a system with broad autonomy) was once again postponed. Nonetheless, the government's dissolution of the Assembly triggered a climate of immense Catalanist unrest in Barcelona[57].

The Assembly of Parliamentarians became even more prominent when it dovetailed in Barcelona with the mobilisation of local officers (from colonels upward) who were complaining about the rising cost of living and their marginalisation by the Ministry of War. Organised into Juntes de Defensa (Defence Boards), they made a great ruckus calling for political reforms and the regeneration of Spain; however, ultimately they were nothing other than a corporate mobilisation which spread around all of Spain, leading to a ministerial crisis.

The political reformism, and the apparent military reformism, were ultimately conditioned by the rising social mobilisation, with such important milestones as the 1916 Saragossa Pact between the UGT and the CNT unions, the huge railway strike in Valencia in 1917 and constant strikes in Barcelona, Sabadell, Girona and other cities. The Lliga Regionalista was alarmed by this rising revolutionary wave (Europe's situation in 1917 contributed a great deal to it) and began direct governmental collaboration with the monarchy (the ministries of Ventosa i Calvell and Felip Rodés), generating a dangerous schism within Catalanism.

In August 1917, Catalanism was forced to cope with Prat de la Riba's premature death. The Mancomunitat was left stranded without the person who had first defined it and its main referent at a very delicate juncture. Prat was replaced in the presidency of the Mancomunitat by an early colleague in political Catalanism, the prestigious architect Josep Puig i Cadafalch[58]. We could say that his presidency was a continuation of Prat's, a praiseworthy feat given the difficulty of the moment and the constant boycott by the central government, as well as the fact that his mandate

57 For Cambó's thinking on the impact of the Great War, see: Francesc Cambó, *El catalanisme regeneracionista*, ed. Jordi Casassas (Barcelona: La Magrana, 1990).

58 See: Josep Puig i Cadafalch, *Memòries*, eds. Núria Mañé, Josep Massot (Barcelona: Publicacions de l'Abadia de Montserrat, 2003); see too: Albert Balcells ed., *Puig i Cadafalch i la Catalunya contemporània* (Barcelona: Institut d'Estudis Catalans, 2003).

dovetailed with the most complex and fraught moments in the entire first third of the 20th century in Catalonia[59], namely the period that started upon the end of the Great War, when the extraordinary stimulus that this had brought to Catalonia was brought to an abrupt end, leading to a ferocious wave of class struggle and revealing the political system's inability to manage an area like Catalonia, which had changed radically over those years. The rising aggressiveness of the Federació Patronal, or management organisation, was confronted with the powerful machinery of the anarcho-syndicalist Sindicats Únics (1918)[60], and the civil government's exclusively repressive actions on the side of management, coupled with the unheard-of mobilisation of the Sometent (a civilian militia in reserve for emergency situations in the countryside), only served to even further radicalise the situation. Between 1919 and 1921, these tensions erupted in a wave of extreme violence which is known as the *guerra social*[61] ("social war").

The transformations and ambient radicalism affected the Mancomunitat, which was even further thwarted by the constant hurdles being put up by the central government. To respond, the Escola de Funcionaris was mobilised to help draft the bases of the autonomous regime, which was approved by the Catalan municipalities and submitted to Madrid in November 1918. In the Courts, Cambó defended Catalonia's project for autonomy by presenting Catalonia's claims as the reflection of a natural national reality which should be dealt with by granting it political sovereignty. The official policy and press in the capital reacted violently, prompting the withdrawal of the Catalan Parliamentarians from the deputies' chamber and a strong grassroots reaction in Catalonia. The Mancomunitat's response was not to wait but instead to write a draft charter and declare its readiness to implement it (the repression of the grassroots demonstrations in support of it resulted in two deaths). This text was approved by 1,046 of the 1,072 town halls in Catalonia (representing 99%

59 See: Enric Jardí, *Puig i Cadafalch: arquitecte, polític i historiador de l'art* (Mataró: Caixa d'Estalvis Laietana, 1975).

60 See: Magda Sellés, *El Foment del Treball Nacional (1914-1923)* (Barcelona: Publicacions de l'Abadia de Montserrat, 2000).

61 See: Albert Balcells, *El pistolerisme: Barcelona (1917-1923)* (Barcelona: Pòrtic, 2009); and the more general: Albert Balcells, *Violència social i poder polític: sis estudis històrics sobre la Catalunya contemporània* (Barcelona: Pòrtic 2001).

of the total population) and ratified by the Assembly of the Mancomunitat in January 1919. The Spanish Courts once again closed ranks on the discussion of the Catalan text and categorically denied the possibility of a popular referendum in Catalonia[62].

Therefore, in these three long years after the war, social violence, institutional instability, the political and moral crisis, social transformations and the central government's constant refusal to listen to the claims of Catalanism had profound effects on this current, leading to changes destined to become extremely important within Catalanism. Among the most important changes was the forceful outbreak of broad swaths of the lower middle class, which had gradually become more radical and spurred the first separatist political formulation led by Francesc Macià (a former colonel separated from the army after the events of *Cu-Cut!* in 1905): the goal was to establish the Federació Democràtica Nacionalista (1919) as well as to revitalise the clubs and centres that were increasingly widespread in Catalonia (such as the group *La Falç*), all of which were openly at odds with the moderation and governmental collaboration that Cambó was imposing on the Lliga[63]. We should also mention the schism within the Lliga itself and the calling of a Conferència Nacional Catalana (June 1922) by the people who were at odds with Cambó's leadership and instead proposed following the nationalistic line imposed by Prat. They created a new party, Acció Catalana, which seemed to win broad acceptance in the last elections before the dictatorship. Taking advantage of this mobilisation, in 1922 Macià also transformed his federation into a party called Estat Català. The following year, Rafael Campalans, Gabriel Alomar and Manuel Serra i Moret created the first nationalist socialist party, the Unió Socialista de Catalunya. The ensuing year, Campalans published *El socialisme i el problema de Catalunya*[64].

Before the dictatorship, the political map of Catalanism had been revamped to adapt to the transformations prompted by the war; its approaches

62 Albert Balcells, Enric Pujol, Jordi Sabater, *La Mancomunitat de Catalunya i l'autonomia...*, pp. 108-178.
63 Francesc Macià, *Francesc Macià: polític, teòric, agitador. Documents (1907-1931)*, ed. Josep Maria Roig (Barcelona: Generalitat de Catalunya-Departament de la Vicepresidència, 2010).
64 See: Antoni Fabra Ribas, Rafael Campalans, *Catalanisme i socialisme. El debat de 1923* (Barcelona: La Magrana, 1985).

and strategies had also radicalised considerably. One of them, which dovetailed with the tense commemoration of the Eleventh of September in 1923, consisted of signing a tripartite pact between Galicia, the Basque Country and Catalonia known as the Galeusca Pact which sought to pressure Spain to recognise its plurinationality.

3. *Resistentialist* Catalanism and political autonomy

As the Captain General of Catalonia, Miguel Primo de Rivera promised the bourgeoisie and local personalities that his coup d'état would be transitory, that it sought to preserve the public order and clean up politics from the corruption of cronyism, and that would be respectful of the country's administrative decentralisation, while mercilessly condemning separatism, that is, in practice any form of nationalism after the war. The coup, waged on the morning of the 12th and 13th of September 1923, was particularly the response to the tense patriotic celebration on the 11th. This bourgeois world, which included the president of the Mancomunitat, agreed with everything in exchange for having the public order secured. The CNT had emerged severely weakened from the years prior to the social war (in March 1923 the main CNT leader, Salvador Seguí, nicknamed the "Noi del Sucre", had been murdered), so the Primo de Rivera coup met with no opposition. A handful of Catalanist leaders (such as the separatist Francesc Macià) went into exile, and members of Acció Catalana founded a secret radical group, the Societat d'Estudis Militars, which actually accomplished little.

Once he was in power in Madrid, Primo de Rivera dispelled all doubts. On the 19th he passed the *decret contra el separatisme* ("decree against separatism") targeted exclusively against Catalan nationalism, which marked the start of systematic persecution against the presence of the Catalan language (*delitos por la palabra, oral o escrita*) ("crimes by the word, oral or written"), Catalanism in any of its manifestations and the use of its symbols in education (ban on teaching in Catalan at schools, December 1923), public space and official institutions and bodies. In January 1924, Alfons Sala from the Unión Nacional Monárquica was appointed president of the Mancomunitat, the step prior to permanently shuttering other private and official entities. In Barcelona in January 1924, Alfonso XII praised the accomplishments of his ancestor Philip V, and the dictator proclaimed his desire and determination to put an end to Catalanism and to reduce it to yet another regional folktale. In December 1923, Primo de Rivera had published yet another of his numerous public letters in the press, in which he bemoaned the weakness of the successive governments before his coup, which had made it possible for *se recudreció la extravagancia de predicar que los catalanes tienen distinta espiritualidad que el resto de los españoles [...] infausta labor de divorciar los sentimientos de unas y otras regiones* ("the extravagance of preaching that the Catalans have a different spirituality that the rest of the Spaniards was intensified [...], work infamous feelings about divorce and other regions"), without understanding that *en cada variedad regional está uno de los grandes atractivos de la nación Española* ("in each regional variation [lies] one of great attractions of the Spanish nation"). Thus, all Spaniards, the state and Catalans of good faith could see how Catalonia *se asemeja cada dia a las otras regiones*[65] ("resembles the other regions every day").

Institutions like CADCI were overseen; others like the Orfeó Català were closed, and even the F.C. Barcelona football pitch was closed (June 1925) on the pretext of whistling during the Spanish national anthem. All told, around 150 entities in all of Catalonia and around 20 suspect local newspapers were closed. In turn, the CNT was outlawed in May 1924 and the group for which it served as the mouthpiece, Solidaridad Obrera, was banned[66]. The attacks against Catalan language and culture were so draconian that a group of Castilian intellectuals mobilised by Giménez Caballero and his magazine *La Gaceta Literaria* signed a manifesto in support of Catalan language and culture (March 1924). What is more, a major exhibition on Catalan books was promoted at the Biblioteca Nacional in Madrid (1927). On the other hand, radical nationalism was reactivated during this period with manifestos, acts of force (such as the failed Garraf Conspiracy against the king in May 1925) and most notably the aborted attempt to invade Catalonia from Prats de Molló organised by Macià in November 1926 (it was initially planned for the 11th of September) to materialise

65 See: Jordi Casassas, *La dictadura de Primo de Rivera (1923-1930)* (Barcelona: Anthropos, 1983), pp. 114-115.

66 See: Josep Maria Roig, *La dictadura de Primo de Rivera a Catalunya, un assaig de repressió cultural* (Barcelona: Publicacions de l'Abadia de Montserrat, 1992).

the Catalan people's right to national sovereignty and to proclaim the Independent Catalan Republic[67]. Despite the failure of this action, the subsequent trial of the conspirators in Paris gave visibility to Catalonia's claims and brought a great deal of fame to Macià, who from then on conducted a far-reaching campaign to raise funds and secure aid for the proclamation of a Catalan Republic. The peak came in 1928 in Cuba, with the preparation of the Constituent Assembly of Separatism and the approval of the Provisional Constitution of the Catalan Republic (with a previous draft by Josep Conangla), which declared *la voluntat i la decisió fermes de valer-se dels mitjans revolucionaris per a independitzar-se de l'Estat espanyol*[68] ("the firm will and determination to use revolutionary means to gain independence from Spain").

The dictatorship fell in January 1930 and was replaced by a slightly more permissive military regime which was soon known as the *dictablanda* ("soft dictatorship"). In this new framework, the Catalan political forces started to reassemble after years of being totally underground. There also developed a clear trend to seek platforms of citizen mobilisation that allowed the social support available to be gauged, a key factor given that the years prior to the dictatorship, years of electoral corruption, social war and heavy repression, had been characterised by rising absenteeism in the elections. The emergence from the dictatorship facilitated contacts between the more radical sectors from this opposition and the world of anarcho-syndicalism. In the later years of the dictatorship, Partit Comunista Català had been founded in Lleida by Jordi Arquer, a defender of the dictatorship of the proletariat. This was the first communist organisation in Catalonia (just as socialism had arrived in 1923), and in 1930 it merged with Joaquim Maurin's Federació Comunista Catalano-Balear to found the Bloc Obrer i Camperol[69].

Of the previous forces, the Lliga Regionalista is the one that emerged the most weakened by the dictatorship, largely because its leader, Francesc Cambó, had to recover from a delicate operation on his vocal chords in London. Acció Catalana managed to reorganise its alliance with the

67 Giovanni Conrad Cattini, *El gran complot: qui va trair Macià?: la trama italiana* (Barcelona: Ara Llibres, 2009).

68 See: Josep Conangla, *La Constitució de l'Havana i altres escrits*, ed. Joaquín Roy (Barcelona: La Magrana, 1986).

69 Albert Balcells, *Marxismo y catalanismo (1930-1936)* (Barcelona: Anagrama, 1977).

republicans of Rovira i Virgili, and they started the process of creating the Partit Catalanista Republicà, which commentators predicted would gain political hegemony[70]. On the left, Estat Català (a faction of which had set up the Partit Comunista Català), represented inland by Jaume Aiguader, along with the social-democratic group *L'Opinió*[71] and republican nuclei created the "Intel·ligència d'Esquerres" platform, the soul behind the mobilisations that called for amnesty for social and political prisoners and democratic elections, and that eventually asked that an autonomous regime be granted. In March 1930 another significant event happened: the journey by Spanish intellectuals to Catalonia invited by the Catalans in appreciation of the support they had provided during the difficult years of the dictatorship[72]. All of this served to weave contacts between Spanish personalities that were taking up positions in favour of the Republic and the anti-monarchic and the Catalanist political organisation in Catalonia, the most dynamic in Spain. This goodwill facilitated Catalonia's participation in what was called the Sant Sebastián Pact in August 1930. The Catalan delegates went there to actively support a coup d'état being prepared for the month of December, and they received a pledge that the constituent period to ensue would include automatic acceptance of the charter of self-governance that Catalonia had submitted to the Spanish legislature.

Catalonia's unique status was strongly felt during the call for municipal elections for the 12th of April 1931[73]. The Lliga chose to reach an understanding with Spanish liberals and run as the Centro Constitucional with the goal of propping up the monarchy, although it ended in a resounding failure. The Partit Catalanista Republicà ran by itself with a Catalanist agenda, but one that was not very politically and socially radical. The other republican and socialist groups called a Conferència d'Esquerres in March to agree on minimum points for the forthcoming elections. They took advantage of Macià's noteworthy ability to bring people together, just

70 See: Montserrat Baras, *Acció Catalana (1922-1936)* (Barcelona: Curial, 1984).

71 See: Joan Baptista Culla, *El catalanisme d'esquerra: del grup de l'Opinió al Partit Nacionalista Català d'Esquerra (1928-1936)* (Barcelona: Curial, 1977).

72 Albert Balcells, *Cataluña ante España: los diálogos entre intelectuales castellanos y catalanes (1888-1984)* (Lleida: Milenio, 2011).

73 The following is essential reading on this entire period: Amadeu Hurtado, *Quaranta anys d'advocat, Història del meu temps (1931-1936)* (Mexico: Xaloc, 1967). New edition: Amadeu Hurtado, *Quaranta anys d'advocat. Història del meu temps (1894-1936)* (Barcelona: Edicions 62, 2011).

after his return from exile, and outlined a platform (Esquerra Republicana de Catalunya) that was radical in the political and national sense and, as was said at that time, was social-leaning following in the footsteps of the most advanced countries in Europe[74]. The ERC was the major winner in the elections, which had high voter turnout in the Barcelona area: it captured the aspirations of change which spanned from the middle class to working-class sectors who were excited about change given the CNT's traditional apoliticism. However, most importantly, the new Esquerra managed to connect with the age bracket that had joined the election census since 1923 and had never voted before yet was quite active in the rich web of institutions (casinos, athenaeums, centres, etc.) and had a clear republican, nationalist bent[75].

Without a doubt, Catalonia's uniqueness on the 14th of April stemmed from the precocity of a double republican proclamation: the first without attributes, that is, the Spanish proclamation by Lluís Companys; and then Macià proclaiming the Catalan Republic as an *estat integrant de la Federació Ibèrica* (and therefore, confederal). This latter act prompted alarm in the provisional government of the Republic, and precisely on the 17th it sent a three-minister committee (the decisive one was the Minister of Justice, Fernando de los Ríos) to convince Macià to hold back, to give him the presidency of a provisional Generalitat and to accept the primacy of the constituent period above all other considerations[76]. Macià's refusal unleashed heavy tensions within Estat Català and opened up a controversy which is the focal point of Jaume Miravitlles' book *Ha traït Macià?* (1932). Despite this, the constituent elections in June were yet another triumph for the ERC.

In parallel, the Generalitat set out to draw up the text of its charter according to the agreements reached in San Sebastián; it did so quickly because it drew from the statutory text from 1919. On the 2nd of August,

74 Maria Dolors Ivern, *Esquerra Republicana de Catalunya (1931-1936)*, 2 vols. (Barcelona: Biblioteca Abat Oliva, 1988-1989).

75 Jordi Casassas, "El triomf d'Esquerra Republicana de Catalunya a les eleccions de 12 d'abril de 1931", *Esquerra Republicana de Catalunya. 70 anys d'història (1931-2001)*, Ramon Alquézar, dir. (Barcelona: Columna, 2001), pp. 93-98.

76 Josep Maria Roig, "La Generalitat republicana, del 14 d'abril de 1931 al 6 d'octubre de 1934", *Història de la Generalitat de Catalunya. Dels orígens medievals a l'actualitat, 650 anys*, Maria Teresa Ferrer, Josep Maria Roig, dirs. (Barcelona: Institut d'Estudis Catalans-Generalitat de Catalunya, 2011), pp. 299-328.

what was called the "Estatut de Núria" (Núria Charter) was approved in a plebiscite with 75% voter turnout and 99.45% of the votes in favour. Even though women did not yet have the right to vote, they mobilised and gathered around 100,000 signatures in support of the text. However, the Spanish Courts dawdled on the issue, to which people like Azaña attached no more importance than to agricultural reform. In January 1932, a parliamentary committee was established to study the proposal, although its work did not reach until the end of May. According to the new Constitution that defined Spain as an *estado integral compatible con la autonomia de los municipios y las regiones* ("an integral state compatible with the autonomy of the municipalities and regions"), Catalonia was treated as an autonomous region, while the state reserved a large capacity for intervention, offered no guarantees of stability and restricted the use of Catalan. The atmosphere in Madrid bore a great deal of hostility towards Catalonia, the press poisoned the atmosphere, boycott campaigns of Catalan products were waged, demonstrations against education in Catalan were held and the number of manifestations of intellectuals (euphoric in 1930, including Unamuno, Ortega y Gasset and Royo Villanova) against political autonomy multiplied[77].

The Charter was ultimately approved on the 9th of September 1932 thanks to the alarm triggered by General Sanjurjo's coup d'état the previous August. The climate of national mobilisation which enveloped the processing of the Charter was accurately described by Rovira i Virgili in *Catalunya i la República* (1931)[78]. Yet this constituent process also prompted a dire political crisis in Catalonia: the Lliga was reorganised and adapted to the new republican, autonomous situation in late 1932 and was renamed Lliga Catalana; moderate, Catholic-leaning republican Catalanism created the Unió Democràtica de Catalunya[79]; tensions within the ERC between the "L'Opinió" group and Estat Català (which was itself

77 See: Manuel Gerpe, *L'Estatut d'Autonomia de Catalunya i l'Estat integral* (Barcelona: Edicions 62, 1977).

78 See: Albert Manent, *Obra cultural de la Generalitat* (Barcelona: La Gaia Ciència, 1977).

79 See: Hilari Raguer, *La Unió Democràtica de Catalunya i el seu temps (1931-1939)* (Barcelona: Publicacions de l'Abadia de Montserrat, 1976); Joan Baptista Culla, *Unió Democràtica de Catalunya (1931-2001)* (Barcelona: Unió Democràtica de Catalunya, 2002).

in the midst of an internal crisis) were magnified, creating a crisis in governance and within the party itself. In December, those from *L'Opinió* were expelled and created the Partit Nacionalista Republicà d'Esquerra[80]. On the other hand, Macià's death on Christmas day in 1933 left the ERC without the leader who managed to unite most of its factions, and his successor, Lluís Companys, was a clear exponent of the *Spanishist* line of Catalan republicanism.

Companys' presidency began fraught with difficulties: on the international scene, Hitler's ascent to power challenged the continental balance and was calling democracies into question; in Spain, the triumph of the right-wing coalition (CEDA) foreshadowed a clear reformist shift; and in Catalonia, the Lliga Catalana earned the most votes, even though the ERC still governed thanks to its alliance with Acció Catalana and the USC[81]. On the other hand, the effects of the worldwide crisis were being felt, social tensions remained intact and the Catalan countryside was being mobilised by the *rabassaires* ("tenant farmers on vineyards") against the landowners owing to their desire to put an end to the traditional *rabassa morta* contract (which remained in effect until the vine died)[82]. The Catalan parliament approved a Law on Cultivation Contracts to resolve this issue, but it was appealed by a coalition led by the Lliga Catalana with the support of the Institut Agrícola Català de Sant Isidre and the Partido Agrario Español before the Constitutional Guarantees Court, which ruled in their favour[83]. This precipitated the seditious confederal proclamation on the 6th of October 1934[84].

After the military neutralisation of the sedition in Catalonia and the imprisonment and condemnation of President Companys, much of his government and other authorities, the government's reaction meant that

80 See: Isidre Molas, *El sistema de partidos políticos en Cataluña (1931-1936)* (Barcelona: Ediciones Península, 1974); Enric Ucelay, *La Catalunya populista. Imatge, cultura i política en l'etapa republicana (1931-1939)* (Barcelona: La Magrana, 1982).

81 Heribert Barrera, *Lluís Companys. Trajectòria d'un president* (Barcelona: l'Avenç, 1990).

82 See: Albert Balcells, *El problema agrari a Catalunya: la qüestió rabassaire (1890-1936)* (Barcelona: Nova Terra, 1983).

83 See: Ismael Elies Pitarch, *L'estructura del parlament de Catalunya i les seves funcions polítiques (1932-1939)* (Barcelona: Curial, 1977).

84 See: Joan Costa, *La veritat del sis d'octubre* (Valls: Cossetània Edicions, 2006).

autonomy was overturned for all practical purposes, the government was replaced by a Governor General of Catalonia, Spanish was imposed as the official language of the Generalitat and the Catalan flag was banned, among other measures. Fortunately, the Lliga Catalana somehow acted as a moderating factor in this anti-autonomy campaign. Another front affected was the job of nationalising Catalonia, an action initiated by the Mancomunitat which was still underway during the republican period despite the rising difficulties and tensions. Within this effort, the Associació Protectora de l'Ensenyança Catalana continued with its courses, campaigns to disseminate Catalan culture, its 8,000 members and its educational publications spearheaded by Pompeu Fabra. Another organisation, Palestra, was founded in 1930 by J. M. Batista i Roca to train young people and future citizens regardless of their parties and religious beliefs, with the aim of disseminating the national history, geography and economy of Catalonia. Generally speaking, the Generalitat promoted the dissemination of Catalan culture among the masses who until then had been excluded from access to culture.

During the two and a half years of the Civil War[85], any analysis of the uniqueness of Catalonia was subordinated to the exceptionalism of the period, despite the republican authorities' and cultural and educational elites' desire to maintain some semblance of institutional normality[86]. First the revolutionary outburst, then the shock of May 1937, beyond the central government's intervention to limit autonomy, and finally the arrival of the war front on Catalan lands in the spring of 1938 are all situations that explain this exceptionalism.

85 We can refer to: Josep Termes, Arnau Cònsul, *La Guerra Civil a Catalunya (1936-1939)* (Barcelona: Edicions 62, 2008).

86 A reading on the government of the Generalitat is fascinating: Govern de la Genrealitat-Josep Tarradellas, *Crònica de la Guerra Civil a Catalunya*, ed. Jordi Casassas (Barcelona: Edicions Dau, 2008).

Catalan Identity in the Years of a Spanishist Dictatorship

Carles Santacana
Universitat de Barcelona

The end of the Spanish Civil War, which lasted from 1936 to 1939, and the definitive instatement of the Franco dictatorship radicalised the identity conflicts in Catalonia. On multiple occasions during the war, the Franco side had stated that one of the motivations that had pushed them to wage the coup d'état was precisely the rise in national affirmation projects like the one in Catalonia, which in regions like the Basque Country and Galicia were at different stages on the road to achieving political autonomy within the Spanish republic. In this sense, the underlying factors in the Civil War included not only social conflict and the stormy clash between democracy and authoritarianism but also, hovering above it, the clash between different ways of envisioning Spanish identity and the role that complementary and/or alternative identities could play in it. It should be noted that during the Second Republic, Catalan political affirmation was not necessarily the corollary of a pro-independence political stance. However, the cultural affirmation, the fundamental underpinning of Catalanism, was complete, paving the way for engagement with formulations all over the world based on a proposal of modern culture. Yet this mainstay of Catalanism was perfectly compatible with a focus on achieving political autonomy within the modernisation aims of the Spanish Republic. What is more, during the early months of the Civil War, the collapse of the republican state and the revolutionary wave pushed Catalonia to expand beyond the boundaries of the statute of autonomy and operate virtually independently, precisely at a time when the war itself meant that Catalonia's future would depend on the outcome of a Spanish civil war.

These paradoxes stemmed from a twofold dynamic, which on the one side heightened Catalonia's affirmation while it also exercised co-responsibility with the Spanish dynamic. This process came to a sudden halt with the victory of Franco's army and the instatement of his dictatorship. The state that emerged from this military victory took shape as a ruthless dictatorship primarily based on a military victory and harsh repression of all the sectors that had opposed the military coup. From the ideological standpoint, the state became a single-party dictatorship, similar to the fascisms of the day, albeit with one feature that heavily conditioned any comparison: the central role of the Catholic Church in the discourse that legitimised the Franco dictatorship, which curtailed the omnipresence of the Falange, the regime's only party. In this sense, the Spanish identity[1] formulated by the new regime was indebted to numerous components. The first and foremost was the military mentality, which had always equated the army with the Spanish nation and had been particularly belligerent towards any affirmations that might be critical of a traditional view that associated the Spanish nation with the grandeur of its conquests. The second was the Falangist discourse against any social division, denying social classes and disallowing any group it viewed as against a discourse of Spanish national unity. The third was a strongly Catholic identity which sought referents in which the state and religion had maintained common positions, always seen from the standpoint of Spanish unity. And we can also add the self-attribution of leadership of the Hispano-American community, in which the claims for Spanish as a universal language played a key role. All of these lines of argumentation existed prior to the Civil War but now converged in a common strategy to manage the Francoist discourse and power, and they did so after the radicalisation brought about by the war itself, which opened up a profound chasm between the winners and losers. The confluence of all of these factors gave enormous force to Spain's unitary discourse, which divided Spain into good and evil Spaniards. Naturally, the good Spaniards were the ones who upheld a unitary, Catholic vision of the state, whereas the others were everyone who endowed Spanishness with other contents or who rejected it with alternative identities, which naturally were subjected

1 Regarding the different interpretations of Spanish nationalism during this period and the role played by identities like the Catalan identity, see the fascinating book: Ismael Saz, *España contra España. Los nacionalismos franquistas* (Madrid: Marcial Pons, 2003). The corresponding chapters in the following book offer a great deal of insight on the interpretations made by Spanish intellectuals: Santos Juliá, *Historias de las dos Españas* (Madrid: Taurus, 2004).

to iron-fisted repression, which was systematic in the case of the Catalan culture[2] and Catalanism[3].

1. Between denial, evasion and resistance in the 1940s

We must understand and analyse the evolution in Catalan identity during the Franco regime within this context, bearing in mind the doctrinal statements, political formulations and cultural referents, or the forms of representation designed especially for the masses. In any of these spheres we can find three possible options. First, there was pure and simple denial of the existence of a unique Catalan identity. For those who upheld this thesis, the inhabitants of the four provinces of Catalonia were Spaniards just like the residents anywhere else, with the only unique feature being a local identity which connected directly to the superior Spanish identity in a subordinate way. In order to forward this thesis, it was useful to have local identities[4] that would blur and/or contradict the Catalan identity, because the dismemberment of the Catalan reality was a goal in itself. There were several attempts to do this, that is, to glorify local particularisms. It is no coincidence that the most notorious attempts occurred at the extreme ends of the Principality, where it was always easy to exploit the physical distance from Barcelona to activate a feeling of alienation from the dynamic in that city. The two most obvious cases were *tortosinismo*, which claimed that the city of Tortosa and the lands of the Ebro River were not Catalan, and even claimed that they did not speak Catalan but

2 A compilation of articles from the era, which lists Catalan intellectuals and politicians who were regarded as responsible for the "red-separatist" vein in Catalonia, can be found in: Eulàlia Pérez, *Fantasmones rojos. La venjança falangista contra Catalunya (1939-1940)* (Barcelona: A Contra Vent, 2009).

3 The seminal book on this cultural and political repression is: Josep Benet, *L'intent franquista de genocidi cultural contra Catalunya* (Barcelona: Publicacions de l'Abadia de Montserrat, 1995).

4 An examination of this thesis can be found in: Carles Santacana, "L'espai local en el franquisme. Aportació historiogràfica i utilització política", *Identitat local i gestió de la memòria. Actes del VII Congrés d'Història Local de Catalunya*, Carles Santacana, dir. (Barcelona: L'Avenç, 2004), pp. 61-80.

a purported Tortosan language. The other was *leridanismo*[5], which also questioned Lleida's fit within Catalonia and at some point gave rise to the creation of a province called *Valle del Ebro*, which would separate the lands of Lleida from Catalonia. In the same vein, the authorities also tried to strengthen the role of the provincial institutions, which could trigger the acceptance of a provincialism alternative to the global Catalan conception. Questioning the unity of Catalonia and its language while fostering localisms and territorial dismemberment was a strategy that at times became prominent but ultimately failed, most likely because the idea of Catalonia as a unit, regardless of its identity character, was quite well entrenched. The phenomenon of *barcelonismo* was another more ambivalent issue: while sometimes the name Barcelona was used intentionally to make a veiled reference to Catalonia, other times it became a substitute which some authors used when they did not want to refer to Catalan issues, turning them into Barcelona issues.

While the first course consisted of denying the existence of Catalonia, the second entailed recognising the existence of a Catalan territory and community with unique features, but with a purely regional identity which fit in perfectly, albeit subordinately, with the Spanish national identity of which it was part. The goal was to harness certain elements of Catalan culture which were easily integrated into this discourse and exclude all the other elements that had historically tilted that culture towards the formulations of Catalanism, which was wholly proscribed. Therefore, the most important goal was to eliminate works and people that had become the referents of this Catalanism, especially in its republican vein[6]. In this stage, especially in the 1940s and 1950s, this Catalan regional identity[7] was gradually defined

5 The following book is quite interesting on this topic: Miquel Pueyo, *Ni blancs ni negres, però espanyols* (Barcelona: Edicions 62, 1984).

6 An interesting survey, through its reinterpretation of the republican past, can be found in: Francesc Vilanova, *Una burgesia sense ànima. El franquisme i la traïció catalana* (Barcelona: Empúries, 2010). A summary can be found in: Francesc Vilanova, "Recordar y no olvidar. La construcción de una memoria antirrepublicana en el franquismo catalán", *Ayer*, 77 (2010), pp. 227-260.

7 This idea is extensively examined with numerous examples of authors, commemorations and places of memory in: Carles Santacana, "Una lectura franquista de la cultura catalana als anys quaranta", *Entre el malson i l'oblit. L'impacte del franquisme en la cultura a Catalunya i les Balears (1936-1960)*, Carles Santacana, dir. (Catarroja: Afers, 2013), pp. 45-70.

by the authorities and intellectuals with ties to local power. If we trace the intellectuals' discourse, we can distinguish the *Falangistes*, whose discourse made few appeals to Catalonia, very similar to what their Castilian counterparts might have done beyond their rhetoric on the hard-working nature of Catalans; the newspaper *Solidaridad Nacional* was the top exponent of this vein. On the other hand were an entire list of writers and journalists who had forged their careers in conservative Catalanism prior to the Civil War and now used a discourse that abjured their identification with Catalanism. Their top exponent, Ferran Valls i Taberner, proclaimed that Catalan society had embarked upon a "false route" by being deceived by Catalanism. This movement had falsified the true history of Catalonia, which made no sense as anything other than a region of Spain. It is impossible to truly discern some of these authors' degree of conviction or adaptation to the new reality, such as the journalist Carles Sentís, but ultimately this regional affirmation was grounded upon Catalan referents which could, in any event, be reinterpreted. Throughout this entire operation, the role of intellectuals and publicists had been essential. More or less explicitly, the underlying thesis was that they had deceived a public that was very sensitive to its traditions, so much so that they actually came to believe in a "separatist delirium".

At the end of World War II, the dictatorship's need to improve its international image translated into not only an emphasis on the Catholic component of the regime but also a desire to ease up on the repression of non-Castilian cultures. In Barcelona, the arrival of governor Bartolomé Barba in 1945 embodied this change in tack. Barba[8] believed it was clear that the regime had to foster folkloric Catalan expressions as well as any other cultural expressions that could be integrated into a healthy regional spirit. What is more, Barba believed that the regime could not afford to leave these assets in the hands of the resistance. For this reason, he had no qualms about commemorating the anniversary of poets like Jacint Verdaguer (1945) and writers like Jaume Balmes (1948)[9], which allowed him to define the Catalonia being disseminated, one that was always

8 See his own testimony in: Bartolomé Barba, *Dos años al frente del Gobierno Civil de Barcelona y varios ensayos* (Madrid: Javier Morata, 1948), p. 27.

9 With regard to Balmes, we have followed the seminal article by professor: Conrad Vilanou, "Jaume Balmes i el franquisme: a propòsit de les dues visites de Franco a Vic (1947 i 1949)", *Ausa*, 25/167 (2011), pp. 8-49.

Catholic and traditional, with *seny* (loosely translated as "wisdom") as the perennial basic trait of Catalans. And through this same policy, the Orfeó Català[10] was authorised, after having been banned in 1939.

Finally, the third option could only be exercised underground or in exile. Through nuclei that gathered in Catalan *casals* or in the limited political activities carried out in exile, significant groups of exiles kept up a Catalan identity grounded upon the everyday use and worship of the Catalan language, open discussions on the causes of the Civil War and its effects on Catalonia, and discussions on the role that political Catalanism should play in the event of a possible fall of the Franco regime and its relations with republican institutions abroad. Certainly, especially in the 1940s, activism in exile was essential to keeping the culture alive through the cultivation of literature and the annual Jocs Florals literary competitions, along with regular publications of magazines and the creation of publishing houses, not to mention reflections on identity with publications such as the work by the young philosopher Josep Ferrater Mora, *Les formes de vida catalanes*, published in Chile in 1944.

2. The 1950s: Beginning to rethink

In 1947, the construction of a throne for the Virgin of Montserrat became the excuse for a sizable grassroots mobilisation. Obviously, it was a festival to offer this new throne to the most popular Virgin in Catalonia, and for this reason it lent itself to a stress on the discourse of Catholic Catalonia. However, the authorities' vision and the organisers' agenda were quite different. Officialdom highlighted the Virgin that the Catalans venerated the most and the monastery that Franco had given back to the monks in 1939. However, since it was a religious affair, the monastery allowed for a citizen committee, the Abat Oliba Committee, which was able to include people from both the winning and defeated sides in the Civil War. This reconciliation in the social base and the profuse use of Catalan lent

10 The significance of this authorisation and an overview of this entity can be found in: Josep Maria Roig, *Història de l'Orfeó Català. Moments cabdals del seu passat* (Barcelona: Publicacions de l'Abadia de Montserrat, 1993).

major symbolic value to both the Committee and the enthronement ceremony, with interpretations that differed significant between officialdom and these dynamic grassroots nuclei[11]. In the mid-1950s, small sectors of the Catholic Church began to distance themselves from the regime, albeit quite slowly, especially from the doctrine of national-Catholicism[12].

On the other hand, in the cultural sphere, the 1950s was a time of increased publications in Catalan, which contrasted with their rarity in the early 1940s. Given the symbolic value of the Catalan language, these publications took on a significance beyond their literary value, which in practical terms was restricted to poetry and novels, with very few essays. One of the exceptions was the book by the historian Jaume Vicens[13], who in 1954 published *Notícia de Catalunya*, an essay in which he offered an interpretation of Catalonia's past which framed it as a community with specific features and a history of its own, which led to its conflicts today. Vicens analysed the elements of continuity and change in Catalan society, but the most important part of the book was clearly its very existence. A few years later, Vicens supervised the first history of post-war Catalonia, even though he had to call the volumes in that publishing project "Catalan biographies". All together, the resurgence of Catalanism during those years necessarily took on a cultural guise, a culture that had to avoid any political identification, even though the connections in the midst of the dictatorship were obvious to everyone. With regard to Catalanism in the late 1950s and early 1960s, everyone was reaching the same conclusion. Despite the attempts to annihilate Catalanism and later discredit the remnants of Catalan culture that were publicly authorised, a consistent enough minority had maintained a minimum of underground activity and was beginning to reappear with specifically cultural expressions[14] through several lawful structures, especially using Catholic platforms (magazines,

11 See: *Les Festes de l'Entronització de la Mare de Deu de Montserrat (1946-1947)* (Barcelona: Publicacions de l'Abadia de Montserrat, 1997).

12 See the chronicle by: Josep Maria Piñol, *El nacionalcatolicisme a Catalunya i la resistència (1926-1966)* (Barcelona: Edicions 62, 1993).

13 Regarding this prominent historian and cultural and political activist, see the recent biography by: Cristina Gatell, Glòria Soler, *Amb el corrent de proa. Les vides polítiques de Jaume Vicens Vives* (Barcelona: Quaderns Crema, 2012).

14 A complete description of Catalanist cultural activities, both legal and underground, can be found in: Joan Samsó, *La cultura catalana entre la clandestinitat i la represa (1939-1951)* (Barcelona: Publicacions de l'Abadia de Montserrat, 1994-1995).

congregations, etc.), the only lawful ones that were exempt from the most direct control by the authorities. We could say that everyone was reaching this conclusion because those who were spearheading the resurgence spoke about a New Renaixença, but it is also quite telling that officialdom witnessed this new situation with alarm, stressing that it would be worthwhile for the regime to lead and head this resurgence of Catalan culture to prevent it from becoming a channel of political claims[15].

The redefinition of Catalanism in these years also influenced the new referent that was Europe. Certainly prior to the Civil War, Catalanism had keenly tracked the development of the nationalist claims in Europe, such as the Irish and Czech peoples', as well as political solutions like the dual monarchy. In the inter-war period, it had closely monitored the Society of Nations within the context out the rally around self-determination. Europe was also synonymous with modernity. Now, in the context of the Cold War, Europe had been divided into two blocs and Western Europe felt the need to reassert itself between the two great international poles of the United States and the Soviet Union. The notion of Europe then took on a new meaning whose doctrine was captured at the 1st Congress of Europe held in The Hague in 1948. After that, Western Europe was perceived as a whole and identified with democratic values. Despite the extremely slow evolution of the states, European construction was given a body called the European Movement, which accepted the participation of national councils made up of exiles from the dictatorial countries. Through this means, Europe was identified with democracy and took an explicit stand against the Franco dictatorship. What is more, Spain participated through a federal council with a structure that allowed for the existence of a Catalan council within the European Movement. All of this together added positive reasons for more strongly integrating Europeanism into the image of a Catalanism that sought to be identified with the *nord enllà* ("northern beyond"), as described by the poet Salvador Espriu in his famous 1954 *Assaig de càntic en el temple*[16]. Therefore, beyond each state's economic and technical interpretations of the 1957 Treaty of Rome, which the

15 See the studies by the Consejo Nacional del Movimiento in: Carles Santacana, *El franquisme i els catalans. Els informes del Consejo Nacional del Movimiento, 1962-1971* (Catarroja: Afers, 2000).

16 An interpretation of Espriu's literary and social role can be found in the recent biography by: Agustí Pons, *Espriu, transparent* (Barcelona: Proa, 2013).

Franco regime wanted to join, Europeanism clearly became an inherent new part of the reformulation of Catalanism. However, for some years Europeanism was not a common thread throughout all of Catalanism because the Cold War distanced the PSUC from these postulates, as they believed that European construction was purely a capitalist market. In this vein, the Catalanist republican, liberal and social-democratic nuclei, both in the country and in exile, were the ones who most avidly followed the new European concept, and they tried to influence it through the Catalan Council of the European Movement, a non-governmental organisation led by the socialist Enric Adroher "Gironella". What is more, the Catalanists believed that Europe would also allow the central role of states to be superseded, and they preached a certain vision of a federal Europe in which the stateless nations could play some role. This hope, coupled with Catalonia's traditional Europeanism, conferred a great deal of appeal on the new concept of Europe, so much so that it became a hallmark of anti-Franco Catalanism[17].

3. The 1960s: Mass culture and anti-Franco Catalanism

In the 1960s, the novel presence of television, with just a single officially-run station, afforded vast possibilities of disseminating a given vision of Spanish identity, which in popular culture was primarily associated with certain forms of traditional Andalusian music, which became the archetype of Spanishness. Some authors[18] have pointed out that the official

17 See: Pilar de Pedro, Queralt Solé, *30 anys d'història d'europeisme català 1948-1978* (Barcelona: Mediterrània, 1999). A more far-reaching idea than is reported here can be found in: Carles Santacana, "Europeísmo y catolicismo en el discurso cultural y político catalán de la posguerra", *Cercles. Revista d'Història Cultural*, 14 (2011), pp. 25-37. See, too: Carles Santacana, "La dimensió europea de la política catalana al llarg del segle XX", *Els Països Catalans i Europa durant els darrers cent anys*, Albert Balcells, dir. (Barcelona: Institut d'Estudis Catalans, 2009), pp. 255-265.

18 Years ago this was explained by: Juan Pablo Fusi, *Un siglo de España. La cultura* (Madrid: Marcial Pons, 1999). A reflection on the interactions of different cultural strata can be found in: Vicente Sánchez, "Las culturas del tardofranquismo", *Ayer*, 68 (2007), pp. 89-110.

cultural policy of the Franco regime was grounded primarily upon a mass culture of evasion more than on the generation of discourses developed by intellectuals with ties to the dictatorship. The power of television, along with the radio stations, which were naturally also officially controlled, had a clear capacity to influence the creation of cultural and identity universes. These powerful mouthpieces constantly disseminated a unitary concept of Spain in which Catalan culture and its referents appeared sporadically as the sign of the integration of a region within the Spanish nation. The references mainly included appeals to the *timbaler del Bruc* ("drummer boy from Bruc"), who had defended the Spanish fatherland from the French, religiosity as exemplified in Montserrat[19] and folkloric elements like the *sardana* dance.

However, the reality was that the same Franco officials knew that despite their discourses, Catalan integration was relatively limited[20]. In fact, one of their concerns was the scarce presence of Catalan leaders in the Franco regime's power structures. This is easy to see just by examining the lists of the council of ministers, the Spanish Courts or the leading organisations within the Falange. This was viewed by the Franco elites as a failure, which was magnified by their consternation at the slow but unstoppable revival of Catalan culture, which was trying to assert itself in any lawful venue it could find, sometimes taking advantage of the schisms within Church institutions, which were under a special regime thanks to an agreement with the Holy See. The turning point in this situation came in 1959 and 1960. First, the regime organised a long visit by Franco to Catalonia, which was meant to launch what was called *Operación Cataluña*, aimed at attaching a great deal of importance to three concessions that the government was to make to the Catalans as a sign of its goodwill. It was called

19 With regard to the complex meaning of Montserrat, one interesting read is the book by: Antoni Batista, *Montserrat. Els misteris de la Muntanya Sagrada* (Barcelona: L'Arquer, 2008). Regarding its conversion into a symbol, see: Jordi Figuerola, "Montserrat, símbol religiós i nacional", *L'Avenç*, 150 (1991), pp. 70-150. And for a perspective on Montserrat specifically as a place of memory, see: Albert Balcells, *Llocs de memòria dels catalans* (Barcelona: Proa, 2008), p. 209-233.

20 What is particularly interesting is the statement made secretly in different deliberations of the Consejo Nacional del Movimiento, in both 1962 and 1971, which clearly expressed the Catalan elites' lack of political integration, as well as the political momentum that Catalan culture might gain. An analysis of these documents can be found in: Carles Santacana, *El franquisme i els catalans....*

the campaign of the three "C's": two had to do with the city of Barcelona, namely the cession of the Montjuïc castle to the city, from which it had been bombarded, and the approval of the Municipal Charter. The third was the approval of the compilation of Catalan civil law. The Franco government wanted to imbue these three operations with great symbolic value, even though their scope was, in fact, quite limited. Indeed, the cession of the castle did not stop it from being used by the army; the Municipal Charter primarily meant giving the mayor, the mover and shaker Josep Maria de Porcioles[21], more leeway; and the compilation of Catalan civil law had little bearing on citizens' day-to-day lives. However, all three were framed as a symbol of how well Franco treated Catalan society. Despite the propaganda campaign, new generations of Catholic Catalanist activists[22] joining in anti-Franco actions had been gaining momentum for some time. In 1959, a campaign against the editor-in-chief of *La Vanguardia Española*, Luis de Galinsonga, captured the news reports after he reacted to a church sermon in Catalan with the cry of *Todos los catalanes son una mierda* ("All Catalans are shit"). After many months of protests, Galinsonga was dismissed shortly before Franco's visit. Dovetailing with this visit was another incident at the Palau de la Música, where part of the audience sang *El cant de la senyera*, the banned Catalanist anthem, leading to the arrest of several activists, including a young leader named Jordi Pujol[23]. Thus, the gestures by the Franco government and the incorporation of Catalanist Catholic sectors into anti-Francoism were happening at the same time. Virtually at the same time, in 1961 a small core of businessmen created the Òmnium Cultural. This organisation's mission was to disseminate Catalan language and culture; it had been suspended by the authorities in 1963 and was not authorised again until 1967, proof of the limitations

21 The figure of Porcioles summarises the local Franco authorities' strategies in the 1950s, a mixture of private interests and adaptation of the official structures. See: Martí Marín, *Josep Maria Porcioles. Catalanisme, clientelisme i franquisme* (Barcelona: Base, 2005).

22 A vision from the standpoint of the main players in this process can be found in: Enric Cirici, *La generació dels fets del Palau* (El Prat de Llobregat: Rúbrica Editorial, 2001).

23 The documentation from the war council to Jordi Pujol has recently been published and is highly illustrative of the objectives that guided those young activists as well as the police's perspective on the onset of this movement. See: Enric Canals, *Pujol Catalunya. El consell de guerra a Jordi Pujol* (Barcelona: Pòrtic, 2013).

that the dictatorship placed on Catalanist cultural initiatives, even if they were promoted by people coming from the bourgeois world who had been pro-Franco in the post-war years[24]. That was also when the magazine *Serra d'Or*[25] was launched, which starting in 1959 became a decisive tool in the confluence of authors and readers who wanted to remake and update Catalan culture in a modern, national vein, using a publication under the aegis of the monastery of Montserrat to avoid official censorship.

4. Catalonia, Catalan-speaking lands

In the early 1960s, Catalan society once again experienced an economic surge, began to welcome a large number of immigrants from the poorer regions of Spain and sought to solidify its orientation towards Europe, where a highly developed society would emerge. In this new context, there was a relative easing up on censorship, especially in initiatives that were not very widely known and were specifically intellectual. The social changes and the need for reflection among the new generations of intellectuals were behind the resurgence of two issues which sought to resolve the collective definition of Catalans at that time. While language and history played an essential role in the formation of Catalan identity – just as in so many other places – the unique circumstance was that the Catalan language during the period of Catalonia's highest political projection of did not strictly match the territory of the Principality of Catalonia today. Since the Middle Ages, the Catalan language had been spoken in a broader geographic region than Catalonia per se, spanning from the towns of Salses to and Guardamar from Fraga to Mahon. Likewise, the utmost expression of a political power emanating from Catalonia also dated back to the Middle Ages, with the Crown of Aragon and the Catalan-Aragonese

24 A chronicle of this organisation can be found in: Josep Faulí, *Els primers quaranta anys d'Òmnium Cultural* (Barcelona: Proa, 2005).

25 This magazine played a key role in bringing together people of all cultural and political stripes, from Catholics to communists. An analysis of its operation and contents can be found in: Carme Ferré, *Intel·lectualitat i cultura resistents. Serra d'Or (1959-1977)* (Cabrera de Mar: Galerada, 2000).

Confederation, which vanished in 1714. In this case as well, the territorial domain encompassed the areas where the Catalan language was spoken, as well as Aragon, where Spanish was spoken. Since the Renaixença, Catalanism had often used references to the brotherhood of the different Catalan lands, which included Catalonia proper, Valencia, the Balearic Islands and the counties under French administration. The territory of Catalan language and culture had been given different names, including *Països de Llengua Catalana* ("Lands of Catalan Language"), but the stress was always on cultural and linguistic unity, with few political-institutional references. In the 1960s, some Catalanist nuclei believed that a New Renaixença was beginning to emerge, grounded upon the cultural revival, but it implicitly entailed overcoming the social and ideological divisions that the Civil War had wrought in Catalan society. They looked into the past to explain contemporary Catalonia, a project which can be seen quite clearly in Jaume Vicens Vives' *Notícia de Catalunya* (1954), and his later *Industrials i polítics* (1958), which not only is a book on 19th century history but also projects the same concerns on contemporary Catalan society and its conflicts. Vicens was a key *guide* in this New Renaixença, but he died prematurely in 1960, just when a project and spheres of action were being defined (such as *Serra d'Or*, Cercle d'Economia and contacts with exiled leader Josep Tarradellas). The issue of the Catalan reality, swinging between history and the current reality, also inspired authors elsewhere, like Joan Fuster, who published *Nosaltres els valencians* in 1962, and later Josep Melià, who wrote *La nació dels mallorquins*, which had initially been titled *Els mallorquins* (1967). It is clear that this was a time when the country was being redefined[26], which entailed not only a specific look at each territory but also the formulation of the concept of the Països Catalans (Catalan Countries). We owe this concept primarily to Joan Fuster[27], who used it naturally in his aforementioned book and

26 Despite the years that have gone by, the following book is still a highly useful basic guide to the political reformulations of Catalanism: Josep Maria Colomer, *Espanyolisme i catalanisme. La idea de nació en el pensament polític català (1939-1979)* (Barcelona: L'Avenç, 1984).

27 The figure of Joan Fuster is extremely important not only in Valencia but in Catalonia as well. Recently, on the occasion of Fuster Year, many works have been published on his thinking and cultural activities, including debates on their relevancy today, such as the monographs by the Valencian magazines *Afers* (71-71) and *L'Espill* (40). In addition to these collective works, one of the most important books is: Ferran

in *Qüestió de noms* (1962), where he tackled the issue directly with an adamant defence of the name using arguments that combined the affirmation of the cultural unity of the entire linguistic sphere and the diversity of each territory within it. Naturally, before the Civil War there had been numerous culture-based unity initiatives, but they had never managed to coin a single name, nor had that been considered essential. Fuster's words in 1962 fell within a different kind of discourse. He said:

> *I millor encara, la de 'Països Catalans', que tant s'ha estès en els últims deu anys, i que amb això mateix ha fet la prova de la seva viabilitat. Països Catalans té, en primer lloc, l'avantatge de la concisió i de la 'normalitat'. En té, de més a més, un altre, que provisionalment salva i acull les persistències dels particularismes tradicionals: és un plural. He dit abans que hi ha particularismes perquè hi ha particularitats. Negar que, dins la nostra radical 'unitat de poble', no existeixen uns matisos regionals de perfil decidit, seria estúpid i suïcida. La història i les estructures socioeconòmiques ens han marcat, fins avui, amb un 'caràcter' local lleugerament distint. La 'unitat' que som abraça i tolera una pluralitat perceptible. És lògic que el nom que pretenem imposar-nos reflecteixi aquesta pluralitat alhora que afirmi i afermi la nostra unitat. Per això Paisos Catalans és el terme més oportú que hi podríem trobar. Estic persuadit que no sols és el més oportú: crec, que és l'únic que, en les nostres circumstàncies actuals, pot servir-nos*[28].

> And better yet, that of the 'Catalan Countries', which has spread so much in the last ten years and with that, has passed the test of its viability. Catalan Countries has, firstly, the advantage of brevity and 'normality'. It has, moreover, another that temporarily saves and holds the persistence of traditional particularisms: it is plural. I said earlier that there are particularisms because there are particularities. Denying that, within our radical 'unity of the people', there are no marked regional nuances, would be stupid and suicidal. History and the socio-economic structures have, until today, marked us with a slightly different local 'character'. The 'unit' that we are tolerates and embraces a perceptible plurality. It is logical that the name we want to impose on ourselves reflects this diversity while affirming and strengthening our unity. So Catalan Countries is the most appropriate term that we could find. I am convinced that not only is it the most appropriate: I think that it is the only one that can work for us in our current circumstances.

Archilés, *Una singularitat amarga. Joan Fuster i el relat de la identitat valenciana* (Catarroja: Afers, 2012). Focused on identifying the discourses that Fuster used to define Valencian identity, the interrelations with Catalonia figure quite prominently.

28 Joan Fuster, *Qüestió de noms* (Barcelona: Aportació catalana, 1962).

Certainly, the bounds of the Catalan Countries clearly delineated the entire new Catalanist cultural universe which was emerging in the 1960s; the most important point is not that Fuster and friends spearheaded it, but that there were stable initiatives that followed this proposal, including the magazine *Serra d'Or*. This magazine, promoted from the monastery of Montserrat, where all the anti-Franco cultural sectors found a home, was putting this definition into practice by welcoming writers and cultural proposals from the entire linguistic area, which launched a parallel recovery process with many intersections. We should stress that the most important point was not defining the concept but really using it in the new cultural world that was emerging, as proven by the fact that Fuster's book was the first to be published by Edicions 62, and that the Catalan Countries was also the territory chosen by Badia i Margarit to start the divulgation of *Llengua i Cultura dels Països Catalans*. Even more importantly, however, exchanges and complicities rose steadily, and, in fact, an alternative cultural circuit stretching across the entire Catalan-speaking territory was created. In this sense, the *Gran Enciclopèdia Catalana* project of the Països Catalans was further proof of a real, practical commitment also gestated in the mid-1960s, and with palpable results starting with the first instalment in 1969. The last great project of this era, the 1975-1977 Congrés de Cultura Catalana, was also hatched along these lines. In short, therefore, the launch of the notion of the Països Catalans become one of the main strands in the cultural resurgence of the 1960s, which curiously lost momentum with the shift to the period of the Spain of the autonomous communities.

5. Who is Catalan? The challenge of immigration

Apart from this need to redefine itself, Catalonia's action against Spanish regionalisation sparked another reflection on the human transformation of Catalan society, which was experiencing an immigration process that was changing the physical and human landscape of Catalonia. This is a crucial issue for many reasons, partly because the immigrants during this stage had no chance to get to know Catalan culture; rather, they reached Catalonia with the official Franco discourse as their only referent. During the republican era, the debate had chiefly been oriented towards a discussion on the relationship between immigration and anarchism. However, now the terms were quite different, primarily because anarchism had almost entirely vanished from the landscape[29]. In contrast, the demographic impact of this wave of migration was extraordinarily powerful; it entailed the arrival of more than one million people over a pre-existing population that did not quite total four million people. What is more, the new arrivals were concentrated in clearly defined areas, where their own numbers were an objective hindrance to interactions with the local people, especially when, in terms of urban planning, new neighbourhoods tended to be built where the vast majority of residents were immigrants. These factors forced the issue to be reframed. The proposal that was the most functional in social-political terms was the one set forth by writer Francesc Candel in *Els altres catalans* (1964), which placed the immigration that had begun during the years of the Republic, albeit of a different sort, at the heart of the debate. We should note that Candel's book was more intuitive than theoretical; it was actually a long report, a sketch of the harsh reality in the new ghettos which he had, in fact, presented in 1957 in the guise of a novel entitled *Donde la ciudad cambia su nombre*. One year later, he published an article entitled *Los otros catalanes*, which was a harbinger of the book that would make him more famous and had a huge impact among its audience (it was the bestselling book in Catalan on Sant Jordi – the day of the book – in 1964). Moreover, the slogan-like nature of its title made it quite famous. The most pressing underlying issue which required the Catalonia that was emerging at the time to be rethought was the risk of a social fracture, and the majority of Catalanists wanted to counter this with image of a single people. *Els altres catalans* sought to state that the new arrivals should also be allowed to be considered Catalan, that is, that they should be helped in their integration. All of this was clearly an act of will, since there was no instruments to achieve it, but it was understood to be an issue of extreme importance. Jordi Pujol had also referred to it: with the sensitivity of the social Catholicism that permeated the neighbourhoods of immigrants, he had proclaimed that anyone who lives and works in Catalonia is Catalan, if they want to be. In this sense, Pujol and Candel became fully complementary to each other, although they did not necessarily wholly agree. In

29 The causes of this process can be found in the last chapter of the book by: Josep Termes, *Història del moviment anarquista a Espanya (1870-1980)* (Barcelona: L'Avenç, 2011).

fact, Pujol was behind Candel's work from the very start, and many sectors of Catalanism believed that it was vital to respond to this huge challenge, which came hand-in-hand with an analysis of the living conditions of the new arrivals and the factors that had expelled them from their homelands. Within this backdrop of social criticism, it is important that the Franco regime's censorship[30] was more interventionist precisely in the parts of Candel's book that referred to the social situation in Andalusia, the origin of many of the immigrants. Even though Candel's book had become a common reference (often times only its title) in the Catalan collective imagination on this issue, this did not mean that there was unanimity. From a radical nationalist stance, Manuel Cruells published *Els no catalans i nosaltres* (1965), a clear retort that expressed a radically opposite position which somehow dovetailed with some sectors' approach to the issue prior to the war. In any event, the issue[31] was expressed strongly, and there were even official publications that evaluated the phenomenon, albeit without any reference to identity problems, along with numerous examinations of the issue from the social sciences[32].

6. The reformulation of Catalan identity at the end of Francoism

Along with these evolutions in the more intellectual, reflective formulations[33], which reached very small nuclei of the population, there is no doubt that if these Catalanist positions wanted to project a given vision

30 The recent edition by Jordi Amat highlights the circumstances under which the book was published and the intervention of censorship. See: Francesc Candel, *Els altres catalans* (Barcelona: Edicions 62, 2008).

31 A sweeping survey of the interrelations between immigration and Catalanism throughout the 20th century can be found in: Josep Termes, *La immigració a Catalunya i altres estudis d'història del nacionalisme català* (Barcelona: Empúries, 1984).

32 See: Clara Parramon, "La contribució de la immigració en la construcció identitària: interpretacions i fets", *Les identitats a la Catalunya contemporània*, Jordi Casassas, dir. (Cabrera de Mar: Galerada, 2009), pp. 635-667.

33 A recent overview can be found in: Andrew Dowling, *La reconstrucció nacional de Catalunya, 1939-2012* (Barcelona: Pasado & Presente, 2013).

of Catalonia they needed platforms of dissemination. In this sense, we have already noted that the Franco regime was gradually abandoning the pretence of hegemony in cultural circles, although it was not willing to do away with all the instruments at its disposal to reach the population as a whole. Thus, the dictatorship controlled the only television channel that existed, from which it disseminated a certain archetype of Spanishness and a Catalan-ness that could be subsidiary to it. A similar mission was expected of the radio stations, which spread a mass culture. Despite the stringent limitations caused by direct or indirect state control over the ways in which mass culture was disseminated, Catalanists nonetheless strove to affect these expressions, particularly by trying to modernise the initiatives that sought to disseminate Catalan culture, disassociating them solely with tradition and instead seeking to connect with the new generations. The phenomenon of the *Nova Cançó* ("New Song") was extremely important in this aim. It sprang from a group of young singers who expressed themselves in Catalan and linked their cultural product to modern forms, with references to French chanson and American folk music, meaning that the most socially popular cultural expression in Catalan was linked to newness and openly progressive values. This phenomenon was extraordinarily important because it broke with the association of ideas between Catalanness and folklore and brought a modern, innovative element of mass culture closely tied to the international phenomena of singer-songwriters and protest songs. From this standpoint, singers like Raimon, Lluís Llach and Joan Manuel Serrat become cultural icons who brought a language and culture that had primarily been for private use into the public sphere. It also launched a bare-bones Catalan record industry, which was needed in order to reach a larger public. Likewise, other actions were gradually set into motion designed for children and young people who were being educated in Spanish with contents that reflected Spain's world view, with the goal of counterbalancing them with initiatives like the magazine *Cavall Fort*, created based on Catalan contents and language. Cultural organisations and excursionist centres were the focal points of a cultural and identity circuit alternative to the official one, and they sponsored lectures, music and theatre performances, along with a series of activities that served as the mouthpiece of a young generation, especially university students. In the sphere of mass culture, too, we should note the role played by a sports club, Futbol Club Barcelona, during those years. This club had taken on significant symbolic value prior to the Civil War, which had only been heightened by the politicisation stemming from the direct control that the official structures of the Franco regime exerted over sports. In the 1960s, Barça accentuated a discourse which linked the club to a Catalan-ness that stretched beyond the bounds of the dictatorship. On the one hand, it dared to publicly protest its discriminatory treatment by the sports authorities (who were also political), a challenge that surprised the dictatorship precisely because it came from a sports club. At the same time, this club[34] which dared to criticised the sports authorities also strengthened its civic and cultural role, and thus in the early 1960s it used the Catalan language on a regular basis in its publications and even in the loudspeaker system in the stadium, which led to government retaliation. Thus, in league with a sector of Catalanist, leftist intellectuals, a sports club also became a symbol of a Catalan identity in protest of the dictatorship, meaning that the *més que un club* ("more than a club") slogan uttered by Narcís de Carreras in 1968 was loaded with real meaning.

Somehow, either through more or less widespread publications, publishing houses, creators of theatre or phenomena like the *Nova Cançó*, Catalan culture was forging ahead despite the hurdles, fines and prohibitions. As a whole, it shaped a militant culture which was affirmed not only by its own initiatives but also by the hostile response from the authorities. This generated complicities that often managed to overcome the logical differences in the ideological interpretations of many deeds and situations. From this vantage point we can interpret the 1967 controversy around the publication of the book by the intellectual and communist militant Jordi Solé Tura, *Catalanisme i revolució burgesa*, which posited that the emergence of Catalanism in the late 19th century had primarily stemmed from the frustration of a Catalan bourgeoisie which did not get the Spanish state to act according to its class interests. This interpretation clashed with that of other authors who were also members of nuclei of resistance, such as Josep Benet, who was radically opposed to this interpretation, and historian Josep Termes, who countered with a theory on the prime role of the Catalan working classes in the survival of Catalan-ness and the impetus behind the Catalanist movement. Regardless, this controversy over the interpretation of Catalanism did not end up having direct, immediate, negative effects

34 See: Carles Santacana, *El Barça i el franquisme. Crònica d'una dècada decisiva per a Catalunya (1968-1978)* (Barcelona: Mina, 2005).

on the coalescence of a least common denominator of Catalan identity forged in anti-Francoism. Obviously this socially cross-cutting nature was limited by ideological differences, but the limitations placed by the Cold War, which slowed the process down, were even more important. However, in 1966 the underground parties from the entire political spectrum created the first single platform that included the communists, called the *Taula Rodona* ("Round Table"). Yet the most important step came in 1971 with the clandestine founding of the Assemblea de Catalunya[35], a single body which brought together parties, unions and a wide variety of groups, from professional organisations to neighbourhood associations. The Assemblea gathered together a series of sectors mobilised against Francoism, and its actions were grounded upon a programme of claims that could be summarised as a call for freedom, amnesty for political prisoners, the reinstatement of the autonomy embodied by the republican Generalitat and the coordination of the struggle with the other anti-Franco groups in Spain. From this perspective, the claims for autonomy gave militant Catalanism all its political, anti-Franco meaning, while it also linked it, albeit just tactically, with all the other anti-Francoist demands. The Catalan language remained a defining feature of the Catalan identity it sought to project. In around 1975, a few months before the dictator's death, a heated controversy broke out when the Barcelona Town Hall refused to provide financial assistance for extracurricular Catalan courses. Even though Francoism was ebbing, the local authorities were incapable of forging a minimally attractive Catalan regional identity. In fact, the dictatorship was still referring to the Catalans with the same clichés as always, with the usual reference to their hardworking nature and the appeal to *seny* and tradition. All of these clichés continued to characterise the official discourse in which the Catalans were simply the hardest workers in Spain. To the contrary, the more active cultural world and the underground parties had gradually woven a new story of Catalan identity in which intellectuals played a highly active role. In fact, many of these intellectuals had already earned considerable recognition and played a prominent role in the press and cultural circles, and they were the spearhead of shifting into the sphere of politics the entire web of publications, publishing houses and cultural, professional

35 See the importance of this group in: Antoni Batista, Josep Playà, *La gran conspiració. Crònica de l'Assemblea de Catalunya* (Barcelona: Empúries, 1991).

and citizen organisations whose voices were increasingly being heard. It is quite telling of the political value of all these actions that the extreme right-wing groups associated with the authorities targeted their punitive actions at bookshops associated with this cultural movement or at publishers that were supporting the local culture, not to mention the attack on the sites where the *Enciclopèdia Catalana* was produced.

Precisely in 1975, an initiative was launched that perfectly captured the efforts to rethink the country from the vantage point of anti-Franco Catalanism. It was the Congrés de Cultura Catalana[36], an initiative first launched by the Col·legi d'Advocats de Barcelona but which soon became a broad-based platform. Despite its name, the congress had special features. It was held until 1977, two years filled with debates and presentations all around the Catalan-speaking lands which set out to determine the state of the issue in all spheres of action, from the economy to the theatre to the environment, science and literature. Each of these spheres was to analyse and assess the situation in their field at that time and to propose future pathways. The death of Franco in November 1975 gave the Congress even more prominence, and it especially allowed it to be held in a climate of widespread citizen participation. All the sectors that had taken an active part in the cultural and political dynamism since the early 1960s participated actively in the Congress, which defined an integrative, progressive Catalan identity with language at the core, and with a considered reflection on immigration, a heavy focus on education, an interest in recovering the republican past, support of Europe and a spirit of conserving the land. What is more, the Congress also sought to restore knowledge of the republican past among citizens who had been denied this knowledge for decades.

The death of General Franco and the proclamation of King Juan Carlos de Bourbon happened in these conditions. Despite the fact that the official discourses during the Franco regime denied the existence of Catalonia's claims, we know that the authorities were aware of them and for that very reason combatted them. However, if the new monarch's choice was to open up a process of democratisation, he needed to offer some kind of solution that would allow a Catalan identity at odds with the one he represented

36 Regarding this initiative, see: Jaume Fuster, *El Congrés de Cultura Catalana. Què és i què ha estat?* (Barcelona: Laia, 1978). The documents can be seen more extensively in: *Congrés de Cultura Catalana* (Barcelona: Curial, 1978).

as the sovereign of Spain to be integrated or neutralised. Given this, it is quite significant that the king's first official trip outside of Madrid was precisely to Barcelona. It was February 1976, a time when the police were repressing the demonstrations in favour of amnesty for political prisoners called by the Assemblea de Catalunya. On that trip, the king explicitly acknowledged Catalan language and culture, as well as Catalans' desire for autonomy, and he launched a study commission for a special regime for Catalonia, perhaps somewhat similar to the Mancomunitat for the four provinces of Catalonia. From then until the elections in June 1977, the governments of the monarchy and the parties created by Francoism – the Alianza Popular and the Unión de Centro Democrático – always advocated that recognition of the uniqueness of Catalonia should come via a Consejo General de Cataluña, the outcome of that study commission. In contrast, all the opposition groups that had operated underground against Franco were calling for the restoration of the 1932 charter of self-government and the return of Josep Tarradellas, the president of the Generalitat in exile. The line between the two proposals was clearly drawn. The Spanish government's was coherent with the notion of a regional Catalonia which had held throughout the years of the Franco regime, while the common thread in the notions put forth by the groups that had resisted the dictatorship was the idea that Catalonia was a nation and that political autonomy within Spain was the best way to guarantee its identity. The results of the elections held on the 15th of June 1977 signalled a notable victory for this second option, and thus a few months later the Generalitat was reinstated. The almost 40 years of the Franco dictatorship had not managed to erase Catalan culture and Catalanist feeling, but the sociological changes that the society had experienced indicated that in no way could it simply pick up where it had left off in 1936.

Cross-cutting topics

The Language: Vehicle for Transmission of Catalan Identity throughout History

Josep MORAN and Joan Anton RABELLA
Universitat de Barcelona and Institut d'Estudis Catalans

1. The formation of the language and the earliest texts in Catalan

Just like all Romance languages, Catalan was formed between the late 7th and early 8th centuries. That was the period when we can consider that the language that the people living in the northeast part of what is Catalonia today were speaking had become something so different to Latin that it could no longer be called by that name.

This was the moment when Catalan was formed; however, there are no written documents in the Romance language. Instead we would have to wait a few more centuries before Romance began to be used in writing and gradually displaced Latin from a sphere in which it was the exclusive language, since at that time Latin was the only one taught and written in all of Western Europe, even in the Germanic lands. Therefore, we are starting with a language system that we could describe as diglossic, because while the spoken language was Romance, for centuries the only written language was still Latin.

However, during that same period, knowledge of Latin must have gradually shrunk to the Church and legal spheres, as confirmed by the rise in preaching in the vernacular, which must have been necessary because the people were not competent enough in Latin. However, the scribes must have served as interpreters of the legal and juridical texts written in Latin so that people were able to understand their content, because they contained very important information for the people involved (wills, donations, oaths of loyalty, record books, etc.). This situation must have also been one of the reasons why after the 10th and especially 11th centuries, words and fragments in the vernacular began to appear in the Latin texts, since they were terms that might reflect the fact that the scribes had translated them to make them more understandable.

The birth of written Catalan is a crucial issue because, strictly speaking, the history of the language begins with the earliest texts where it appears, since the study of early Catalan relies entirely on the material samples conserved.

This is an important issue not only from the linguistic and historical standpoints but also from the symbolic standpoint. Precisely these implications, which extend beyond the scientific realm, have also influenced academia, such that in the past the study of the earliest documents has often concentrated on the search for the first text written in Catalan.

Yet when analysing the first texts written in Catalan, confusion between the history of the language and the history of the literature has also been a negative factor, since historically prime value has been placed on literary documents, meaning that legal or economic texts, such as feudal oaths, grievances, record books or wills, were undervalued because they had no aesthetic or literary value. This situation helps us to understand why we have so often read – and even today we can find some works that contain this outdated information – that the *Homilies d'Organyà*, certainly the oldest document known to most people, was the first text written in Catalan, while in reality it is the first literary text. And even so, this descriptor is quite relative, since those sermons can hardly be described as literature.

Today the nature of the texts (whether they are literary, legal or economic) and the determination of which is the oldest document (in the sense that the oldest is considered more important than the others) are no longer priority issues. To the contrary, the prime endeavour is to further study the documentation from the archaic period, which in the case of Catalan is extraordinarily rich.

Another factor that should be borne in mind is that the documents which have survived until today should not be confused with the ones that existed in ancient times. Even though it is not very likely, a new ancient document might still be found, as happened in 1992 with Cebrià Baraut's discovery of a new fragment from *Liber iudiciorum* or *Llibre dels judicis*[1].

One of the most controversial issues has been establishing a criterion to determine the first texts written in Catalan, a problematic issue because

1 Cebrià Baraut, Josep Moran, "Fragment d'una altra versió catalana antiga del 'Liber iudiciorum' visigòtic. 1 Edició, contingut i datació. 2. Estudi lingüístic", *Urgellia*, 13 (1996-1997 [2000]), pp. 7-35.

the oldest documents are written in a hybrid language. It has traditionally been considered that the entire text, or almost all of it, should be written in the Romance language in order to be able to consider it written in Catalan. However, today we believe that the first or first few texts in Catalan are those that have a significant part written in the Romance language, even if the rest of the document is in Latin[2].

Catalan did not appear suddenly in one or several written texts with a precise language that mastered all the expressive resources; rather, it gradually blossomed after the 9th century, but especially throughout the 11th century, within documents written in Latin.

Thus, during the 9th century we can find documents like *Acta de consagració de la catedral de la Seu d'Urgell*, which includes toponyms that reveal names that have completed the evolution to Romance (such as *Ferrera* [<FERRARIA] or *Palomera* [<PALUMBARIA]). In the 10th century, in addition to toponyms, we can also see common words in Catalan (such as *escudella* ("bowl") in a will from 986), and we do not find texts with entire phrases or fragments in Catalan until the 11th century.

Even though, as mentioned above, today we can still read in manuals and reference books that the earliest texts in Catalan are the *Liber iudiciorum* (the misnamed *Forum iudicum*) from the 12th century[3], and the *Homilies d'Organyà* from the early 13th century[4], for many years now linguistic studies specialising in this period have stated that these are not the first texts in Catalan but that there are many earlier texts, most of them feudal, which were written primarily or largely in Catalan. A precise date cannot be pinpointed in these texts – they often have no date, so it has to be determined by the characters that appear in it – and it is difficult to determine a chronological order because some dates overlap. Therefore, today we generally do not speak about a specific document but about a body of feudal texts from the 11th century.

2 Joan Bastardas, "Quan el llatí esdevingué català?", *La llengua catalana mil anys enrere* (Barcelona: Curial, 1995), pp. 73-105; Josep Moran, "La llengua catalana en els seus orígens i en relació amb les altres llengües de l'Europa carolíngia", *Catalunya a l'època carolíngia, art i cultura abans del romànic (segles IX i X)* (Barcelona: Museu Nacional d'Art de Catalunya, 2000), pp. 129-130

3 *Fragment d'una versió catalana del Liber Iuciorum visigòtic (Forum Iudicium)* (Alacant: Biblioteca Virtual Joan Lluís Vives, 2006).

4 *Homilies d'Organyà*, eds. Amadeu Soberanas, Andreu Rossinyol, Armand Puig (Barcelona: Editorial Barcino, 2001).

During that century, we can find oaths, such as the *Jurament feudal de Radulf Oriol* (1028-1047) and the *Jurament de compareixença* (1031-1035), along with agreements and wills in which significant parts are written in Catalan[5].

And shortly thereafter, but during the same century, we have extensive texts written primarily in Catalan, with the exception of the more formulaic parts – like the beginning and end of the document – such as the *Greuges de Guitard Isarn, senyor de Caboet* (1080-1095) and the *Jurament de pau i treva del comte Pere Ramon de Pallars Jussà al bisbe d'Urgell* (1098-1112)[6].

However, the information on these feudal texts is not a new development in late 20th century studies; rather many of these documents had already been known since the late 19th and early 20th centuries, when scholars like Julià Bernat Alart (1881)[7], Pere Pujol (1913)[8] and especially Joaquim Miret i Sans (1904 i 1908)[9] recovered and published them.

The process of developing written Catalan took place primarily during the 11th century, probably through a confluence of factors.

The most decisive factor was probably the consolidation of feudalism in Catalunya Vella ("Old Catalonia"), a new society that led to the creation of new values and new concepts which often had no set name in Latin. In this case, therefore, social events must have had linguistic consequences, such that the new elements gradually appeared in documents written in Latin in their Romance names. For this reason, the earliest words in Catalan

5 Josep Moran, Joan Rabella, *Primers textos de la llengua catalana* (Barcelona: Proa, 2001).

6 Joan Rabella, "'Greuges de Guitard Isarn, senyor de Caboet' (1080-1095)", *Estudis de Llengua i Literatura catalanes. XXXV. Homenatge a Arthur Terry*, 4 vols. (Barcelona: Publicacions de la Abadia de Montserrat, 1997), vol. 1, pp. 9-49.

7 Julià Bernat Alart, *Documents sur la langue des anciens comtés de Roussillon et de Cerdagne* (Paris: Maissonneuve, 1881).

8 Pere Pujol, *Documents en vulgar dels segles XI, XII-XIII procedents del bisbat de la Seu d'Urgell* (Barcelona: Biblioteca Filològica de l'Institut de la Llengua Catalana, 1913).

9 Joaquim Miret, "El més antic text literari escrit en català precedit per una col·lecció de documents del segles XIè, XIIè i XIIIè", *Revista de bibliografia catalana*, 5/47 (1904), pp. 215-222; Joaquim Miret, "Documents en langue catalane (Haute Vallée du Sègre, XIe-XIIe siècles)", *Revue Hispanique*, 19 (1908), pp. 6-19.

– if we ignore toponyms – are feudal, such as *comanar*, "place under the stewardship of a feudal lord", and *atendre*, "fulfil a feudal obligation".

Another factor that must have pushed this process was the low literacy level existing at the onset of feudalism, since it was a time when there was little knowledge of Latin except in the most enlightened church centres. Thus, while a more polished Latin remained in use in the centres with the best education (such as in the countships of Barcelona and Empúries), in others with lower levels, such as some in the western Pyrenees, Romance began to filter into the written language earlier.

Thus, the production of a high number of documents during this period combined with the poor training of some scribes and the difficulty translating the new terms used in the laypeople's declarations led the Catalan language to gradually encroach into the documentation.

And there is yet another factor worth bearing in mind that has rarely been given its due: the degree of Romanisation. In this sense, it is quite telling that the vast majority of the earliest texts in Catalan appear primarily in the bishopric of Urgell, which encompassed lands such as El Pallars which combined lower Romanisation – and, therefore, lower Latinisation as well – with higher survival of the pre-Roman linguistic substrate. These factors must have led the Catalan language be applied in writing earlier because Latin must have been less prevalent.

As we can see in the documentation that still survives, the process of becoming a written language must have been lengthy because for Catalan it implied an adaptation process so that it could be used for purposes for which it had not been used until then. Therefore, written Catalan did not appear suddenly with a perfectly established writing system and expression; rather it did so gradually and at first had limited linguistic resources at its disposal.

Therefore, it is a language that shows not only vacillations in spelling but also fairly undeveloped syntax. In this sense, the most characteristic aspect of the earliest texts has been considered parataxis, that is, the lack of sentence connectors and the repetitive use of just a handful of elements, like the copulative conjunction *i* ("and"). This lack of connectors gives the earliest texts a very primitive expressiveness and a rather discontinuous discourse.

Throughout the 11th century, the use of Catalan in writing spread so much that in some documents the Latin part is actually quite minor. We have no text without any Latin, but we can note that this language is limited to the beginning and end of the documents, the parts we can consider the most formulaic.

2. The expansion of written Catalan (13th and 14th centuries)

The earliest texts span the period from the 11th century (the documentation from the 9th and 10th centuries primarily contains only isolated words) to the first half of the 13th century. After that time, between the second half of the 13th century and the early 15th century, Catalan managed to establish a model of written language that gradually came to occupy many fields of culture and knowledge, in addition to administrative and legal affairs.

Thus, in a relatively brief period of time, a model of educated or formal language was established which quite clearly contrasts with the language found in the documentation from the archaic or pre-literary period. This formal model did not appear suddenly but gradually evolved in feudal texts and chancery prose, which gained momentum after the second half of the 14th century.

Raymond Lully (Ramon Llull in Catalan) has traditionally been considered the founder of literary Catalan and, by extension, what we can regard as the model of cultivated language appropriate for the different fields of knowledge. However, today we know better: the specific studies on Lully's oeuvre, as well as studies on medieval written output in Catalan, demonstrate that despite the important implications of his work in the use and evolution of written Catalan, there are many other factors which contributed to the development of written Catalan during that period. Back in the 13th century, texts were being produced that were gradually gaining distance from the parataxis of the feudal documents, such as the *Costums de Tortosa* (1272)[10], which already shows greater expressive and syntactic ductility.

This situation is not specific to Catalan, since the vernacular versions of scientific and technical texts developed considerably all over Europe after the late 13th century. However, what is indeed remarkable is that

10 Jesús Massip, *Costums de Tortosa* (Barcelona: Fundació Noguera, 1916).

Catalan was one of the earliest, most active vernacular languages in the production of both translations and original scientific and technical texts.

Thus, to a large degree, Raymond Lully dovetailed and coexisted with this juncture and cannot be regarded as the sole or even most important factor in the development of written Catalan. At a time when a new secular public was asking for works related to trade, legal affairs, politics and technical matters in urban society, essentially functional and practical works, Raymond Lully was also suggesting that a writing model appropriate for its target be adopted, which was neither literary nor linguistic but instead philosophical-religious and proselytising in nature. Lully's uniqueness lies not in the purported innovation that has often been attributed to him – which also occurred at the same time in other fields like science, technology, jurisprudence, history, homilies, etc. – but in the scope of his endeavours and his vast written output.

However, when examining the early Catalan language, we should bear in mind that Occitanian also experienced a similar circumstances in the writing of practical texts in Romance at that time, and that during Lully's lifetime Montpellier belonged to the Kingdom of Mallorca.

In addition to the factors we have just mentioned, there are two others which made a decisive contribution to the formation of a model of cultivated language appropriate for different fields, from science to administration, from literature to trade: first, the prestige of the monarchy, and secondly, the extensive, continued use of written Catalan by the Royal Chancellery.

At that time, not only was the vernacular the language spoken by the Catalan count-kings but it was also used in their speeches, documentation and chronicles. Martí de Riquer called it the "king's Catalan" in his *Història de la literatura catalana*, and we could also call it the "royal Catalan"[11]. This public use made a crucial contribution to legitimising and conferring prestige on written Catalan.

However, this is not an isolated factor; rather it compounds the role of the Royal Chancellery in the formation and spread of this model of cultivated language. The Royal Chancellery was an institution created by James I in the mid-13th century which was in charge of the royal

11 Martí de Riquer, *Història de la literatura catalana*, 3 vols. (Esplugues de Llobregat: Ariel, 1964), vol. 2, p. 336.

documentation and correspondence and established the roles of the notaries, secretaries and scribes. These scribes and secretaries were the ones who gradually forged the Chancellery's specific style by writing a vast amount of documentation which would contribute to the spread of a model of written language that was increasingly well established.

The operations of the Chancellery – which in addition to administrative tasks also became a veritable cultural hub, especially after the mid-14th century – were determined by Peter III the Ceremonious in his 1344 *Ordinacions*, which were an adaptation of the *Leges palatinae* of James III of Mallorca, excellent proof of the detailed organisation of the royal bureaucracy[12]. During that century, a model of what we would call today administrative or State language gradually took shape and was used in everything from official correspondence to justice. It would come to extend beyond the strictly royal sphere and become a model for other administrations, such as municipal documentation.

From the linguistic standpoint, this language model was enriched after the second half and especially the end of the 14th century through sound knowledge of Latin rhetoric among the scribes and secretaries of the chancelleries, and a high level of purity and homogeneity would be achieved. In this sense, the Royal Chancellery became more than an administrative institution and was joined by great writers, translators and intellectuals such as Bernat Metge, Guillem Nicolau and Jaume Conesa.

The job of the Chancellery was essential to explaining why historically the medieval Catalan language been considered very united, since the homogeneity still shown by the spoken language – because most of the most important dialect differences did not appear, or did not spread, until the end of the Middle Ages, especially throughout the 15th century – required the use of a *scripta* that had highly stable features along with a large output and considerable prestige.

Therefore, this was a time in which a formal model appropriate for the majority of spheres of writing, including the administration, literature, science and trade, was generated and consolidated. Thus, during this period Catalan came to occupy almost all the fields corresponding to the formal, cultivated registers.

12 Próspero de Bofarull, *Procesos de las Antiguas Cortes y Parlamentos de Catalunya, Aragón y Valencia,* 8 vols. (Barcelona: Establecimiento litográfico y tipográfico de José Eusebio Monfort, 1850), vol. 5.

Judging from the importance of the feudal texts, the formation of this cultivated model most likely started through the development of legislative documentation, which began with the early (mid-12th century) translation of the *Usatges de Barcelona*[13] (a compilation of laws, customs and constitutions) from Latin into Catalan. It continued with the translation of texts like the *Furs de València*[14] (1261) and the writing of other texts directly in Romance, like the aforementioned *Costums de Tortosa* (1272). It reached its fullness with texts like the *Llibre de Consolat de Mar* during the 14th century[15].

Thus, Catalan became the general language used in administration – or officially, according to the modern terminology – so not only was the first compilation of the *Constitucions de Catalunya*, completed in 1418, written in Catalan but the second ones, dating from 1588, and even the third and last ones from 1704, at the beginning of the reign of Philip V, continued to be written in this language[16].

In addition to the legislative documentation is the juridical and administration output, which includes texts issued not only by the Royal Chancellery but also by other institutions, such as the Generalitat de Catalunya, the Generalitat del Regne de València and the Gran i General Consell del Regne de Mallorca. Catalan was also used in other jurisdictions, such as the seigniorial, in areas such as criminal trials; books of the Court (that is, "justice", both royal and seigniorial), the royal bailiff, the *mostassaf* ("market officer") and the division; municipal orders, etc. Many of these kinds of texts have been preserved, and some have even been published, such as the *Procés de la Guardialada (1396)*[17], the *Llibre de*

13 *Usatges de Barcelona. El codi a mitjan segle XII*, ed. Joan Bastardas (Barcelona: Fundació Noguera, 1991).

14 Germà Colón, Arcadi Garcia, *Furs de València* (Barcelona: Barcino, 1970), vol. 1; Pedro López Elum, *Los orígenes de los 'Forum de Valéncia' y de las Cortes en el siglo XIII* (Valencia: Generalitat Valenciana, 1998), pp. 105-298.

15 Germà Colón, Arcadi García, *Llibre del Consolat de Mar* (Barcelona: Fundació Salvador Vives Casajuana, 1981-1987), 4 vols.

16 *Constitucions i altres drets de Catalunya* (Barcelona: Generalitat de Catalunya-Departament de Justícia, 1995).

17 Francesc Carreras Candi, "1396.- Procés en la Guardia Alada, d'un misteriós crim, descobert meravellosament", *Boletín de la Real Academia de Buenas Letras de Barcelona*, 10/77 (1922), pp. 404-424.

batlle reial de Barcelona Berenguer Morey (1375-1378)[18], the *Processos de crims del segle XV a Lleida*[19], the *Un llibre de cort reial mallorquí del segle XIV*[20], the *Procés contra els consellers, domèstics i curials de Joan I, entre ells Bernat Metge*[21], the *Llibre de Cort de Justícia de Cocentaina (1269-1295)*[22], the *Procés criminal barceloní del segle XIV*[23], the *Llibre de cort de justícia de València (1279-1321)*[24] and the *Llibre de mostassaf d'Eivissa*[25], among others.

One the earlier administrative and historiographic texts is the royal oratory, from which a large sample of speeches remains; they were written not only by the secretaries and scribes but in some cases the king himself, as in the case of Peter III (a good example is the Montsó proposition of 1383)[26]. This kind of text is the best example of what was called the language of state; they are brilliant documents written to be read on special occasions such as the opening of the Courts, and they had a clearly

18 Josep Maria Casas, *Llibre del batlle reial de Barcelona Berenguer Morey (1375-1378)* (Barcelona: Fundació Salvador Vives Casajuana, 1976).

19 Maria Dolors Farreny, *Processos de crims del segle XV a Lleida: transcripció i estudi lingüístic* (Lleida: Institut d'Estudis Ilerdencs, 1986).

20 Joan Miralles, *Un llibre de cort reial mallorquí del segle XIV (1357-1360)* (Palma de Mallorca: Institut d'Estudis Baleàrics, 1984).

21 Marina Mitjà, "Procés contra de consellers domèstics i curials de Joan I, entre ells Bernat Metge", *Boletín de la Real Academia de Buenas Letras de Barcelona*, 27 (1958), pp. 375-417.

22 Joan J. Ponsoda, *El català i l'aragonès en els inicis del Regne de València segons el Llibre de Cort de Justícia de Cocentaina (1269-1295)* (Alcoi: Marfil, 1996); Josep Torró, *Llibre de la Cort de justícia de Cocentaina (1269-1290)* (Valencia: Universitat de València, 2011).

23 Joan Anton Rabella, *Un matrimoni desvingut i un gat metzinat. Procés criminal barceloní del segle XIV* (Barcelona: Publicacions de l'Abadía de Montserrat, 1998).

24 M. Àngels Diéguez Seguí, *El llibre de cort de justícia de València (1279-1321). Estudi lingüístic* (Alacant-Barcelona: Institut Interuniversitari de Filologia Valenciana-Publicacions de l'Abadia de Montserrat, 2001); M. Àngels Diéguez Seguí, *Clams i crims en la València medieval segons el* Llibre de cort de justícia *(1279-1321)* (Alacant: Universitat d'Alacant, 2002); Enric Guinot, M. Àngels Diéguez, *Llibre de la Cort de la Justícia de Valencia (1280-1282)* (Valencia: Publicacions de la Universitat de València, 2008).

25 Antoni Ferrer, *El llibre del mostassaf d'Eivissa. La vila d'Eivissa a la baixa edat mitjana* (Eivissa: Editorial Mediterrània, 2002).

26 Josep Maria Sans, coord., *Cort General de Montsó. 1382-1384* (Barcelona: Generalitat de Catalunya- Departament de Justícia, 1992), pp. 78-81.

institutional tone, often verging on propagandistic, which often surveys the common history. Probably the most famous piece of Catalan parliamentary oratory which follows this pattern is Martin I's proposition to the Courts of Perpignan on the 26th of January 1406, which is known by the "title" of *Gloriosa dicta sunt de te*[27].

And finally we have the historiographic output, which is basically made up of the four major chronicles: the *Llibre dels Fets* of James I (from the late 13th century, but conserved in a manuscript from 1343), the chronicle of Bernat Desclot (between 1283 and 1288), the chronicle of Ramon Muntaner (between 1325 and 1328) and the chronicle of Peter the Ceremonious (the most complete version of which was revised in around 1385)[28], in addition to annals and account books.

The Catalan chronicles are a magnificent example of what we could describe as official historiography because they describe the royal history: they were either written by the king – such as James I or, to some extent, Peter III – or used as a mechanism of propaganda around them.

This prestige as a language of culture, with a well-entrenched model legitimised by the authority of the king, is a factor that fostered the spread of written Catalan not only in literature but also to the majority of fields of knowledge (in addition to becoming a language we could call official or administrative in Sicily, Sardinia, Naples and even Greece, where, for example, the *Capítols d'Atenes* were written in 1380), at a time when, as noted above, other European languages were also undergoing the same process.

In this sense, in addition to being used quite early in spheres that had been reserved for Latin until then, such as philosophy, as in Raymond Lully's *Art*, it was also used in technical and practical works in fields such as astrology (like *Astronomia* by Jacob ben David Bonjorn [1361][29] and the *Taules de Barcelona* by Jacob Corsuno [14th century][30]), mathematics

27 Ricard Albert, Joan Gassiot *Parlaments a les corts catalanes* (Barcelona: Els Nostres Clàssics, 1928), pp. 56-72.

28 *Les quatre grans cròniques*, ed. Ferran Soldevila (Barcelona: Editorial Selecta, 1983).

29 Josep Chabàs, *L'astronomia de Jacob ben David Bonjorn* (Barcelona: Institut d'Estudis Catalans, 1992).

30 Josep Maria Millàs, *Las tablas astronómicas del Rey Don Pedro el Ceremonioso* (Barcelona: Consejo Superior de Investigaciones Científicas, 1962), pp. 121-138.

(like the *Summa de l'art d'Aritmètica* by Francesc Santcliment [1484][31] and the *Aritmètica* by Siena [15th century][32]), cooking (like the *Llibre de sent Soví* [from the 14th century], the *Llibre del coc* by Robert de Nola [*ca.* 1458-1491][33] and the cookery books by Pere Castell [14th century], Mestre Miquel [*ca.* 1407], Ponç Deslledó [1438] and Joan Martina [before 1439]), medicine (such as the *Regiment de preservació de pestilència* by Jacme d'Agramont [14th century][34], the *Speculum al foder* [14th century][35] and the *Regles per a metges novells* by Felip de Soldevila [*ca.* 1465-1490]), sailing (like the nautical chart by Guillem Soler [1380], the one by Gabriel de Vallseca [1439-1449] and the one by Jaume Bertran [1456-1491]) and geography (such as the atlas by Cresques Abraham [*ca.* 1375)[36] and the mapamundis by Macià de Viladesters [1423] and Joan de Viladesters [1428]), as well as texts related to trade (such as the *Tarifa dels corredors de Barcelona* from 1271 or the municipal ordinances of the different guilds, such as the one of the butchers of Perpignan from 1303). Historically, this facet has not been properly valued, from the perspective of the language, but today we now have detailed studies that reflect the vast wealth of documents in such a wide variety of fields.

And the range of written uses of the Catalan language during that period should be filled out with private letters, which, though less formal and closer to the private sphere and individuals, continued to retain the fundamental features of the formal written language. We have numerous publications of medieval correspondence in Catalan, most of it private, such as the *Documents històrichs catalans del sigle XIV. Colecció de cartas*

31 Joana Escobedo, *La 'Summa de la art de arismètica' de Francesc Santcliment* (Madrid-Barcelona: Biblioteca de Catalunya, 2004).

32 *Llibre de Sent Soví (receptari de cuina)*, ed. Rudolf Grewe (Barcelona: Editorial Barcino, 1979); *Llibre de Sent Soví*, ed. Joan Santanach (Barcelona: Editorial Barcino-Restaurant de les Set Portes, 2014).

33 Robert de Nola, *Llibre de Coch*, ed. Veronika Leimgrober (Barcelona: Curial, 1996).

34 Jacme d'Agramunt, *Regiment de Preservació de la Pestilència*, ed. Joan Veny (Tarragona: Publicaciones de la Excelentisima Diputación de Tarragona, 1971; 2nd edition: Barcelona: Enciclopèdia Catalana, 1998).

35 Anna Alberni, *Speculum al foder* (Bellcaire d'Empordà: Edicions Vitel·la, 2007).

36 Abraham Cresques, *El Atlas catalán de Abraham Cresques* (Barcelona: Diàfora, 1975).

familiars corresponents als regnats de Pere del Punyalet i Johan I[37], the *Epistolari del s. XV. Recull de cartes privades*, the *Cartes privades*[38] *del segle XV a l'Arxiu de Santa Maria del Mar*[39], the *Cartes d'una catalana del segle XIV al seu marit*[40] and the *Epistolari de la València medieval*[41].

3. The spoken language in the Middle Ages

Just as research in the field of literature has traditionally focused primarily on specific periods and authors, the history of the Catalan language has also chiefly analysed the language of the most significant texts and authors (Raymond Lully, the *Homilies d'Organyà*, the chronicle of James I, etc.), while less literary texts have been less thoroughly examined. It was not until the 1980s that this began to change and that studies of these texts became more widespread. Specifically, scholars began to examine texts closer to the oral language in the quest for the features of medieval speech.

Even though we cannot have direct knowledge of the language spoken in the past, we have been able to determine some of its aspects and characteristics through the written documentation, via both texts that copy some fragments of it quite literally (such as direct declarations in criminal trials) and texts that deliberately reproduce the spoken language for a given purpose (such as the sermons of Saint Vincent Ferrer). Likewise, there are also texts more closely related to the private sphere (such as private letters).

37 Josep Coroleu, *Documents historichs catalans del segle XIV. Colecció de cartas familiars correspondent als regnats de Pere del Punyalet i Johan I* (Barcelona: La Renaixensa, 1889).

38 Francesc Martorell, *Epistolari del segle XV. Recull de cartes privades* (Barcelona: Barcino, 1926).

39 Manuel Riu, "Cartes privades del segle XV a l'Arxiu de Santa Maria del Mar", *Estudis Universitaris Catalans*, 23 (1979), pp. 501-506.

40 Teresa Vinyoles, "Cartes d'una catalana del segle XIV al seu marit", *Estudis Universitaris Catalans*, 26 (1984), pp. 387-420.

41 Agustín Rubio, *Epistolari de la València Medieval* (València: Institut de Filologia Valenciana, 1985).

Within this kind of text, fragments in a direct style from criminal trials – such as those that copy the declarations of witnesses in the first person – are the documents that shed the most light on the former spoken language.

The analysis of these texts has enabled us to learn some specific characteristics: in the vocabulary, we see words and expressions that do not commonly appear in cultivated texts, such as insults and blasphemies, which were punishable by law; in morphology, we see aspects like the oral use of the ending *-eu* for the second person plural, whereas *-ats/-ets/-its* was exclusively used in the written language during the 14th century and well into the 15th century; and in syntax, we see several such important features as the living use of the article derived from IPSU in the spoken language in Barcelona at the end of the 14th century, a feature of the oral language that is virtually never reflected in writing because it was frowned upon as being overly familiar or popular. Syntactic information is particularly interesting and meaningful because it is more difficult to modify than the vocabulary or morphology. This also confirms the reliability of the oral information that can be found in some of these texts (such as the use of the passive voice, which does not appear in direct excerpts because, just like today, it was not used in the spoken language in an informal register).

Many of these characteristics match some of the traits of today's colloquial language, which confirms the existence of constant features in the colloquial, spoken language over the course of the centuries.

4. Spread of the use of the Catalan language

In addition to reflecting several specific features of colloquial or popular speech, this documentation shows us that the Catalan language was used widely, and almost exclusively, among the country's inhabitants, precisely at a time of extraordinary population mobility. And it was used not only by aristocrats (Christian and Jewish, the latter of whom were quite numerous) but also by people from other countries (primarily Occitanians and Genovese) and even slaves.

The Genovese often appear in the documentation, usually associated with trade, despite the long and returning war with Genoa in the 14th century, just as sometimes there are Pisans, English or Normans. However, the

Occitanians were the largest group of immigrants to the Catalan-speaking lands.

To contextualise, we should mention the continuity of Catalonia's relationship with Occitania since the pre-Roman era, especially in the Principality. This relationship continued with similar Romanisation on either side of the Corbières; it remained in place later during the Visigothic and Frankish periods and then became even more pronounced during the early Middle Ages, when the counts – and later the count-kings – focused their territorial expansion northward, not by means of armed struggle but through marriages and pacts. This northward expansion towards Occitania achieved its peak geographic reach during the government of Ramon Berenguer III, with his marriage to Douce de Gévaudaun of Provence in 1112, such that virtually more territory was held in Occitania than in Catalonia.

After Muret's defeat in 1213, and despite the shift in the direction of the expansion, this time southward towards the Mediterranean, relations with the territories to the north continued to be important, also through the migratory flow of Occitanians southward, which had been significant since the Frankish period and continued until the Modern Age.

This human contribution with European roots is a fascinating fact during the Middle Ages, especially during the time of the conquest of the Catalan-speaking domain, most notably the Principality. One of the most significant examples was the seizure of Tortosa (1148) during the reign of Ramon Berenguer IV, in which English, Normans, Pisans, Lorrainers, Genovese (who played a key role and were given one-third of the city), Templars and a few Aragonese participated, along with the repopulation of the city and region of Tarragona organised by the Norman Robert Bordet (or Robert de Culley), whom Bishop Oleguer gave the title of Prince of Tarragona in 1129. Many of these foreigners must have had quite sporadic relations with the locals (even the Genovese of Tortosa ended up selling their estates because they were not as profitable as they had calculated they would be), but in other cases they were lasting, as proven, for example, by onomastics. The surname *Anglès* must have come from some of the English who participated in these conquests and later stayed in the country, as in the case of a document of the diplomat of the monastery of Santes Creus (specifically the will of Gilabert Anglès, from 1172)[42].

42 Joan Papell, *Diplomatari del monestir de Santa Maria de Santes Creus (985-1225)* (Barcelona: Fundació Noguera, 2005), pp. 244-246.

With onomastics, we can see the significant influx of people from Occitania through the existence of surnames that now we regard as fully Catalan but which originally came from Occitania, such as *Xirinacs, Pàmies, Llaudet* or *Jassans*.

Regarding the slaves, who were quite numerous during the Middle Ages and from widely divergent backgrounds, including Armenians, Tartars, Wallachs, Albanians, Greeks and Bulgarians, just as with the Europeans from different places we can see that they, too, spoke Catalan, even though they came from such faraway lands, like the Tartars. Even the Muslim slaves spoke Catalan, which contrasts with the reports on the Moriscos from the south of the region, which we know continued to speak Arabic, and most of them only Arabic, until almost the time of their expulsion in 1609. Here there must be a major contrast between the Muslims who lived as slaves in the cities and the Moriscos who lived in rural areas in an almost feudal regime grouped into – and isolated in – fairly large communities.

5. The evolution of the Catalan language: The 15th century and the shift to the 16th century

The political and territorial spread of the Crown of Catalonia-Aragon during the 13th and 14th centuries led to the expansion of the domain of the Catalan language, and through transposition, consecutive dialects (the region of Valencia and the Balearic Islands during the 13th century, and Alghero during the 14th) emerged there. However, from that time on, geographic, historical, social and internal factors differentiated the dialects of Catalan, yet without ever rupturing the structural unity of the spoken language. This situation became evident after the end of the Middle Ages, with a language that had several more innovative features in the central area compared to the lateral areas and those that were colonised at a later date, which would retain forms that were lost in the most dynamic region. One example is the conservation of a term like *arena* in the northwest and Balearic Islands and *eixir* in Valencia and Roussillon, words that were common throughout the entire domain until then.

Thus, after the end of the 14th century and especially in the 15th century, varied examples of diatopic differences began to appear in the medieval language, and even a few examples of the existence of geographic varieties.

At the end of this period, the distance between the spoken language – at a time when it was regionally differentiated – and the written language became accentuated because a new model of formal language that would capture the linguistic innovations gaining ground never formed. This situation fostered the appearance of the terms *valencià* and *mallorquí* to designate those dialectal varieties, as compared to the codification of other European languages (especially after the Renaissance: Juan de Valdés[43], Pietro Bembo[44], etc.) which during the Middle Ages did not have such fixed, stable writing systems as Catalan.

However, during this period, the fact that a corrective work was written is remarkable; it stemmed from a convergence of the need to formulate a modernising language model and the need to declare the existence of dialectal variation – which was clear to its speakers. This text was the *Regles d'esquivar vocables o mots grossers o pagesívols* (from the late 15th century)[45]. It did not formulate a modernising language model in an organised fashion, but through the forms it condemns it does shed light on which forms were used orally, which at times dovetail with the colloquial solutions that are still used today (such as *gavinet* instead of *ganivet* or *Toni* for *Antoni*). The aim of the *Regles* was to maintain a *sermo urbanus*, that is, a single formal language based on the languages of the two main cities, Barcelona and Valencia, which would avoid the most colloquial and dialectal characteristics, from phonetics to lexis.

After the 16th century, precisely a very brilliant century in literature, there was a decline in the written language. This situation is one of the main reasons leading the period from the 16th to 17th centuries to traditionally be

43 Juan de Valdés, *Diálogo de la lengua* (Madrid: Clásicos Castellanos, 1928).

44 Pietro Bembo, *La Prosa* (Venice: Iacomo Vidali, 1575).

45 Antoni Maria Badia i Margarit, "Regles de esquivar vocables o mots grossers o agresívols. Unas normes del siglo XV sobre la pureza de la lengua catalana", *Boletín de la Real Académia de Buenas Letras de Barcelona*, 23 (1950), pp. 137-152; 24 (1951-1952), pp. 83-116; 25 (1953), pp. 145-163; Antoni M. Badia i Margarit, *Les Regles de esquivar vocables i 'la qüestió de la llengua'* (Barcelona: Institut d'Estudis Catalans, 1999).

known as the Decadència ("Decline"), particularly based on the contrast between the output until the 15th century and in the ensuing centuries.

During the 15th and 16th centuries, Catalan remained the only language known orally, even though after the enthronement of a Castilian dynasty, the Trastámaras, and different political and sociocultural factors, contact with the Castilian language began at a time when it was quite prestigious, especially in the region of Valencia and certain spheres. Thus, we cannot state that contact with Castilian was either widespread or in all spheres.

The failure to create a new model of written language that reflected the most important changes in the spoken language until the late Middle Ages ended up generating the perception that the written language system inherited from the Middle Ages was obsolete. Thus, between the late 15th century and especially during the 16th century, there was clearly a chasm between the written and spoken languages. And this sensation that the written model still used was inadequate for that point in time can be seen by works that showed the desire and need to modernise the written language, such as the *"Traducció" valenciana del Blanquerna* by J. Bonllavi in 1521[46], which is actually not a translation but an adaptation to the language of the early 16th century in a specific geographic area.

Thus, we can note that on the one hand there was a change in the oral language which was quite important in terms of dialects. As the outcome of these diatopic changes during the 16th century, the first classifications of the Catalan dialects began to emerge, such as the one by Francesc Calça, who distinguished the dialects of Roussillon, Urgell (what we call today north-western Catalan), Tortosa, Empordà and Barcelona (today's central Catalan). Meantime the use of the old model of written language continued, and would continue even longer, despite the fact that it was gradually gaining distance from the spoken language[47].

46 Ramon Llull, *Blanquerna* (Barcelona: Biblioteca Hispànica Puvill, 1973); Beatrice Schimd, *Les 'traduccions valencianes' del Blanquerna (València 1521) i de la Scala Dei (Barcelona 1523)* (Barcelona: Curial Edicions Catalanes-Publicacions de l'Abadia de Montserrat, 1988).

47 Francesc Calça, *De Catalonia, liber primus* (Barcelona: Typographia Iacobi Cendrat, 1588).

6. The Modern Age (16th century)

The union of the Crown of Aragon and Castile with the Catholic Monarchs, which became permanent under the Habsburgs, accentuated the castilianising trend which had gotten underway in the previous century with the Trastámara dynasty. What is more, this union led the monarchy's decision-making centres to move outside Catalonia.

With this union, the autonomous institutions remained intact, at least formally, but the Court, which was in Castile, fully adopted Castilian as its own language at a time when absolutism and the regal nature of the superior culture was being accentuated. What is more, the Catalan-speaking nobility gradually became castilianised, especially in the region of Valencia under the influence of the royal or viceroyal court during the mandate of Germana de Foix. With regard to the bourgeoisie, the prince was notably weakened after the war against John II and the plagues and social conflicts of the 15th century. In the 16th century, the region of Valencia suffered from the upheaval of the Revolt of the Brotherhoods, so no local cultural movement was able to take root anywhere. This action alleging Catalan's inferiority compared to Castilian can be seen quite clearly in the *Col·loquis de Tortosa* by Cristòfol Despuig, without a doubt the most interesting work written in Catalan during the 16th century[48].

Regarding the Church, this institution's position on language was not uniform. We should first mention the Inquisition as a centralising, Castilianising factor which was exempt from diocesan jurisdiction and exerted heavy ideological repression during the reign of Philip II. The archbishopric of Valencia was also a hub of castilianisation, especially after Saint John de Ribera, even though Catalan remained the language of parish administration and popular preaching there, as shown by the fact that the Valencian rituals from the 16th and 17th centuries exclusively used Catalan in catechism and admonitions.

In the Tarraconense Ecclesiastical Province, which encompassed the land of the Principality from Ibiza (which at that time belonged to the archbishopric of Tarragona) to the Catalan lands of Aragon (which were part of the bishopric of Lleida) and the northern part of the region of

48 Cristòfol Despuig, *Los Col·loquis de la insigne ciutat de Tortosa* (Barcelona: Publicacions de l'Abadia de Montserrat, 2011).

Valencia (diocese of Tortosa), the attitude towards the Catalan language was more favourable. Thus, in 1591 this province's Council approved preaching solely in the native tongue, in accordance with the provisions of the Council of Trent. What is more, Catalan was the vernacular language used along with Latin in the Church's pastoral administration (parish books, education, catechism). These provisions were extraordinarily important in maintaining Catalan as a language of social interaction, both oral and written, during the period of the Decline.

With regard to the internal history of the language during this period, we can state that despite the cultural difficulties, modern Catalan took shape grammatically and lexically during this century.

7. The Baroque (17th century)

After a slow economic recovery throughout the 16th century, in the following century there emerged a new ruling class in the Principality made up primarily of the bourgeoisie and mid-level clergy, who reacted adamantly against the assimilationist aims of the monarchy and tried to recover political and social initiative through autonomous institutions.

Politically, this attempt was not entirely successful, yet nor was it an utter failure that put a halt to new attempts, as shown by the outcome of the Reapers' War (1640-52), with the absolutely negative exception regarding the unity of Catalonia of the cession of Roussillon and part of the Cerdagne to the kingdom of France (1659).

Apparently, during that century there was an attempt to recreate an educated local literature that would go beyond the continuity that had characterised the previous century. This, too, was not wholly successful, but at least a modest literary model was created that lasted a long time.

From the linguistic standpoint, we should note the effort to recreate a modern literary language in Catalan, despite the fact that the Castilian influence would lead to considerable interference, especially in the lexis but also in the syntax. This phenomenon, noted by historians of literature, was so widespread that it became a cliché which for many years discredited the works of the best representatives of this literary current, including Francesc Fontanella, Josep Romeguera and Francesc Vicent Garcia, the rector of

Vallfogona de Riucorb. The latest studies on the Catalan Baroque in general, and particularly on the rector of Vallfogona, and about the castilianisms of the authors on the Balearic Islands provide more reliable information on the language from this literary period. For example, we can see that many of the castilianisms found are occasional and never became entrenched.

Regarding the language in other popular literary genres, whose cultivation had never stopped and which had no direct influence from the Castilian models, it is clear that they show greater linguistic purity than the cultivated literary language.

But if we examine other non-literary language uses (administrative, juridical, notarial, educational, etc.), which were also outside the direct Castilian literary influence, they also continued a local tradition unabated and show considerable linguistic purity and accuracy. Even orthographically, we can see that a normative model of language use was taking shape. This written Catalan was still quite uniform, or standard, throughout the entire linguistic domain from Roussillon to the region of Valencia, and therefore the dialectal variations that appear in them are quite limited.

Through the Treaty of the Pyrenees (1659), the countship of Roussillon (including Conflent, Capcir and Vallespir) and part of the Cerdagne went to the kingdom of France, which soon exerted an assimilationist policy. It began with the introduction of French in teaching and preaching, followed by the first legal provisions expressly against Catalan: in 1682 knowledge of French was obligatory to hold a public post or honorary degree, and in 1700 the oral or written use of Catalan was banned in public acts or documents.

Thus began the legal restrictions on the use of Catalan and the goal of language replacement depending on the affiliation with different absolutist, uniformising states, which would continue throughout the rest of the language domain in the ensuing century with the Bourbon provisions after the War of the Spanish Succession.

8. The 18th century

While Castilian cultural pressure had occurred without any legal measures against Catalan except in French Roussillon during the preceding centuries, with the rise of the Bourbons the first measures appeared as a consequence of the shift in political regime. However, Catalan did not suddenly entirely vanish from the administration or public use during the 18th century. With the Nueva Planta decree, Spanish was introduced into the administration of the new territorial bodies which depended directly on the Crown: the Audience, the administrative division, the Army and higher education, all in Cervera. They mostly used Latin, while the local administration was organised by townships.

However, Catalan remained the written language in the institutions which were not so directly related to the royal administration and instead still operated under a seigniorial regime. Thus, it remained the language of the local administration, even in towns under royal jurisdiction which were not the heads of townships under the new districts called *corregiment.*

Since the Nueva Planta in the Principality of Catalonia preserved Catalan civil law, notaries, who were closely associated with this law, continued to use Catalan.

This situation spread to Ibiza under the civilian and church jurisdiction of the archbishopric of Tarragona. As far as we can tell, a similar situation could also be found on Mallorca. In the region of Valencia, Philip V's Bourbon uniformism was backed by the aristocracy, which, in turn, abandoned the cultivation of the vernacular language and instead adopted Spanish to better distinguish themselves from a people who had rebelled against them. Nor was the local civil law maintained, and this led to the castilianisation of the notaries.

In Northern Catalonia, the pressure to adopt French continued. French was imported as the language of civil administration, but Catalan lasted a while longer in the local administration and seigniorial jurisdiction.

In Sardinia and therefore in Alghero as well, Catalan, which had remained the main administrative and notarial language, was replaced in these roles first by Spanish and then by Italian after this island's integration into the political domain of the House of Savoy in 1720 as the result of the Peace of Utrecht.

To the contrary, on Menorca, which was under English domination, Catalan was respected as a local language without impediments, and it thus produced the best Catalan literature during this period.

The language use during the Enlightenment, the characteristic cultural current of this century, was conditioned by political limitations. In the past, the field of science had suffered the most intensely from castilianising pressure, but there was no dearth of books in Catalan on agriculture or medicine, for example, that were more or less popular in style.

On Mallorca, the proponents of the Enlightenment had a greater interest in language, particularly during the second half of the century, dovetailing with the revival of the castilianising repressing during the reign of Charles III. The most representative figure of this movement was Josep de Togores, the Count of Aiamans, a Catalan writer and grammarian.

The Enlightenment found Menorca to be the most favourable atmosphere to develop the local language, and despite the modest physical and demographic dimensions of the island it also yielded the most brilliant results, at least during the periods of British rule. One example was the Societat de Cultura de Maó, which used Catalan and whose members included Enlightened Menorcans, literati and grammarians such as Febrer i Cardona and the Ramis i Ramis brothers.

In Catalonia, the institutions generally had to operate within the contradiction of having to respect the uniformist, castilianising policy of the Bourbon monarchy while seeking to defend and promote the local culture. For this reason, they adopted a possibilistic, noncommittal attitude. One exponent of this was Barcelona's Reial Acadèmia de Bones Lletres.

In Northern Catalonia, which was subjected to strong pressure to adopt French, for some time the possibilities of creating cultivated literature in Catalan seemed to be non-existent, but surprisingly there was an active neoclassical theatre, which virtually ground to a halt after the French Revolution. In addition to their literary value, these plays, at least the better-known ones, show notable linguistic quality without too many dialectalisms or foreign borrowings, and they do deserve specific linguistic study of their own.

The Nueva Planta did not directly affect the Church, which continued to retain Catalan as its language in the Tarraconense Province, following provisions approved in 1591. Spanish had been introduced in the more important preaching, but not in a widespread fashion because it was actually looked down up by the nobles from the Bourbon tradition such as Rafel d'Amat, Baron of Maldà. Primary education, which was provided by the parishes or controlled by the Church, continued to take place in Catalan; for this reason, educational and grammatical works appeared in Catalan in the 18th century, such as the ones by Josep Ullastre and Baldiri Reixach, written according to the new pedagogical currents.

Middle school was also taught by the regular and secular clergy. The basic language at this educational level was Latin, but the use of the vernacular, primarily Catalan, was on the upswing.

In theory, this situation extended to Mallorca as well. Regarding the diocese of Valencia, we have already said that the Castilian influence had been strong during the Habsburgs, but Catalan was still the language of parish administration until Archbishop Mayoral imposed Spanish in 1744. But the most popular preaching must have been done in the local language. Despite the castilianising pressure, written Catalan was still used by the town clergy.

The legal measures against Catalan were stepped up during the reign of Charles II. The 1766 *Real Cédula de Aranjuez* required Spanish teaching to be introduced into Church centres after the expulsion of the Jesuits. This provision even had to be respected by the anti-royal bishops like Josep Climent in Barcelona. It led to the castilianisation of seminaries, where secondary education was taught, along with the publication of grammars and bilingual dictionaries with the purpose of facilitating an understanding of Spanish. However, Catalan was not fully excluded from primary education, which was still poorly regulated and provided by local clergy and teachers, until the end of the next century, at least in the Principality.

Taking advantage of the provision handed down by Charles III, some royalist bishops imposed Spanish in the parish administration, such as Juan Díez de la Guerra on Mallorca, despite the opposition of the canons. In the region of Valencia, too, all the parish books had to be converted into Spanish and therefore personal names did as well. Regarding the Tarraconense Ecclesiastical Province, the Castilianisation of these books depended on the royalist zeal of the bishops; thus, in the diocese of Tortosa they were Castilianised early on, as they were in Vic by bishop Francisco de Veyán. However, in Barcelona and Girona, the parish registries were written in Catalan until the following century.

Charles III's provisions did not affect the local and seigniorial administration, as we know because there still remain local acts and ordinations written in Catalan which date from after this provision. Notaries in Catalonia were not affected either.

These provisions handed down by Charles III seriously affected the language precisely at a time of economic and cultural expansion. However, at the same time, in reaction to this negative dynamic, the movement to defend and apologise for the language was also revitalised. It had ancient forerunners in figures like Carles Ros, Lluís Galiana and Manuel J. Sanelo, who revealed an interest in the language of the region of Valencia parallel to the activity of the enlightened circles in the Principality and the Balearic Islands.

In Barcelona, in addition to the activities of the Acadèmia de Bones Lletres, a Council Seminary was formed, reorganised by Bishop Climent; this was a circle of enlightened clergy such as Josep Ballot and Fèlix Amat who were interested in Catalan language and culture, and whose work would be the precursor to the 19th century Renaixença.

There was notable lexicographic and grammatical activity, primarily orthographic, focused on normalising the language use, but all of these efforts were individual and were bereft of any authority that could gradually flesh out the modern language. The political and cultural limitations within which the Catalan academies had to operate made it impossible to do this, despite several attempts by the Reial Acadèmia de Bones Lletres.

9. The Napoleonic period

Even though it was not extraordinarily important, it is quite interesting to note the way the Catalan language was treated during this period, which illustrates that a swift normalisation process was possible if the political regime allowed and encouraged it.

During the Napoleonic regime, the Girona native Tomàs Puig induced Marshal Augereau to make a Catalan language revival policy for public use, and official notices and the *Diari de Barcelona* were thus published in both Catalan and French. Likewise, the minutes of the Barcelona Town Hall were published in Catalan at the behest of the councillor Antoni de Ferrater. Despite Tomàs Puig's political speculations, the French occupiers' adoption of Catalan was pure strategy, because their intention was to bring Catalonia fully into the French Empire[49].

49 Lluís Maria de Puig, *Tomàs Puig: catalanisme i afrancesament* (Barcelona: Institut d'Estudis Catalans, 1985).

Nonetheless, this assimilation had to be somewhat gradual, and in the meantime the French codes had to be translated because the majority of inhabitants of the Principality did not understand French. The French administration inquired a commission of collaborationist jurists as to whether the codes should be translated into Catalan or Spanish. These jurists, who came from the Bourbon regime and had been used to writing in Spanish, even though they were Catalans, recommended that they be translated into Spanish. The reasons they mentioned were evidently not their ineptitude in Catalan but instead pretexts such as their claim that:

> *la llengua castellana és la llengua de les Acadèmies i dels espectacles. Té una gramàtica, una ortografia i un diccionari, i no hi ha en canvi cap gramàtica ni ortografia catalana, i els diccionaris catalans són molt incomplets*[50].
>
> Castilian is the language of the Academies and the spectacles. It has a grammar, an orthography and a dictionary, and in contrast, there is no Catalan grammar or orthography, and the Catalan dictionaries are very incomplete.

However, counter to the opinion of these jurists, the Baron of Gérando, a French administrator from the Upper Cerdagne who was a prominent member of the French Enlightenment at the time, wrote to the French minister Regnier,

> *que l'ús de la llengua castellana o espanyola no havia estat introduït a Catalunya fins a l'època de la submissió d'aquesta província a les lleis generals d'Espanya [...] l'època en què les places de la magistratura arrabassades als catalans foren reservades als castellans sols; una època de la qual els catalans conserven un dolorós record [...], que els juristes del país prefereixen el castellà perquè estan més acostumats a escriure'l [...] Però la llengua catalana té les seves gramàtiques, els seus diccionaris, la seva literatura. Les Constitucions de Catalunya, que contenen els codis d'aquesta província, estan escrites en català. Els notaris redacten quasi totes les escriptures en català*[51].
>
> that the use of the Castilian or Spanish language had not been introduced in Catalonia until the epoch of the submission of this provinve to the general laws of Spain [...] the epoch when the posts in the magistracy seized from the Catalans were reserved

50 Joan Mercader, "L'oficialitat del català sota la dominació napoleònica", *Butlletí de la Societat Catalana d'Estudis Històrics*, 2 (1953), p. 19.

51 Carles Rahola, "El baró de Gérando i la llengua catalana", *Proses històriques* (Barcelona: La Revista, 1933), pp. 49-51.

> only for Castilians; an epoch of which the Catalans retain a painful memory [...] that the country's jurists prefer Castilian because they are more accustomed to writing it [...] But the Catalan language has its own grammar, its own dictionaries, its own literature. The Constitutions of Catalonia, that contain the codes for that province, are written in Catalan. The notaries drew up almost all the scriptures in Catalan.

In this sense, we should say that the fact that Josep-Pau Ballot, a professor of rhetoric, Castilian grammar and Latin at the Seminary of Barcelona, undertook the writing of his *Gramàtica i apologia de la llengua catalana* during the Napoleonic period was no coincidence; rather it was a response to the discussion on the literary viability of the Catalan language, which was scorned by many learned people of his day[52].

10. The constitutional regime

The redress of the previous status of the Catalan language might have been assimilated by the Spanish liberal stream, which strove to overcome the absolutism of the Old Regime after the Courts of Cádiz. However, the victorious trend of Spanish (and French) liberalism was centralist and uniformist, a continuation of the regime that they were supposedly replacing. In fact, as Alexis de Tocqueville stressed regarding France, the uniformising centralism that characterised the Jacobin movement which emerged during the French Revolution had not been invented by this political current; instead it dated back precisely to the Old Regime.

Yet if the policy of the Old Regime had been based on imposition and was therefore viewed as oppression, with the liberal regime the people theoretically held the sovereignty, and thus any Constitutional provision had to be gratefully accepted. The centralism of the Spanish liberals viewed even the provincial boards that had been created to counter Napoleonic domination with mistrust; therefore, in his manifesto published on the 28th of October 1809, the poet and liberal politician from Madrid Manuel José Quintana claimed that *la hidra de federalismo, acallada felizmente en el*

52 Josep Pau Ballot, *Gramàtica i apologia de la llengua catalana* (Barcelona: Alta fulla, 1987).

año anterior, osa otra vez levantar sus cabezas ponzoñosas ("the hydra of federalism, happily silenced the previous year, dares again to raise its poisonous heads"), even though at that time federalist ideas inspired by the political regime of the United States had not yet developed in Spain[53].

Therefore, the new liberal regime, especially after Isabel II (1833-1868), promoted the formation of a political-economic oligarchy while also imposing Spanish in the new bodies that the constitutional regimes established to replace the ones from the Old Regime, including all levels of the local administration and education, especially after the Moyano law of 1857. Spanish was also imposed in the Church administration in the dioceses where Catalan was still used, generally surreptitiously, such as Barcelona, taking advantage of the implementation of the Concordat of 1851.

The new trade laws (Trade Code of 1829) also required trade documentation to be written in Spanish, even though it had been drafted in Catalan until then. This measure had a significant effect on the process of industrialisation and the spread of trade derived therefrom; despite the fact that it was a clearly Catalan phenomenon, judging from the written documentation it took place entirely in Spanish. This notably conditioned the use of written Catalan and, in general, any subsequent normalisation process of the Catalan language.

What is more, in 1870, precisely during the mandate of General Prim, the Civil Registry was created, which exclusively used Spanish, leading to the castilianisation of Catalan personal names. The official toponyms were also abusively made Spanish or disfigured in the cartography and official nomenclatures of the time, with aberrant forms like *San Baudilio*, *San Cucufate* and *Villanueva* instead of Sant Boi, Sant Cugat and Vilanova.

11. The *Renaixença*

Parallel to this wholesale imposition of Spanish in official activities and education (which would result in the spread of written Spanish in

53 Richard Hocquellet, *Resistencia y revolución durante la segunda guerra de independencia. Del levantamiento patriótico a la soberanía nacional* (Saragossa: Prensas Universitarias de Zaragoza, 2008), p. 231.

all spheres, even private correspondence), the earliest representatives of this movement adopted a contradictory stance on the use of language: they loved Catalonia, its language and its particular features in general, especially its laws, but they did not formulate any coherent programme to normalise Catalan. Instead they somehow participated in the activities of the new regime, which totally banished Catalan from public life. This is the case, for example, of Antoni Puigblanch, Aribau and even Milà i Fontanals, who went no further than a purely diglossic system: Catalan had to be reserved for personal communication or for more affective literary works.

The Renaixença emerged under these conditions, and in the prologue to his 1841 poems, Joaquim Rubió i Ors was the one to express it the most lucidly. After making a claim against *la vergonyosa y criminal indiferencia ab que alguns miran lo que pertany á sa patria* ("the shameful and criminal indifference with which some regard what belongs to their homeland"), he described past splendours, expressed the ethical attitude of writing in Catalan and formed a possibilistic action programme adapted to the political circumstances: *Catalunya pot aspirar encara á la independència no á la política [...], però si a la lliterària, fins a la qual no s'estén ni se pot estendre la política del equilibri*[54] ("Catalonia can still aspire for independence not political [...] but rather to the literary, to which the policy of balance does not reach nor can reach").

A few years later, in 1859, the Jocs Florals were launched following this agenda. They were the maximum public expression that the liberal regime allowed Catalan culture and language. However, it is clear that this initial approach was not enough to ensure the survival of the language in the modern world, as can clearly be seen in the contemporary history of Occitanian. The process of normalisation had to go further and could not be limited to the literary use.

Concomitant to literary development, the Renaixença promoted the study of the language, a continuation of the activity from the Enlightenment. This was fostered by the birth of modern linguistics, particularly Romance linguistics, which Milà i Fontanals introduced in Catalonia.

What is more, the development of Catalan literature after the Renaixença had not only aesthetic and intrinsically linguistic value but

54 Josep Moran, *Treballs de lingüística històrica catalana* (Barcelona: Publicacions de l'Abadia de Montserrat, 1994), p. 183.

also considerable sociolinguistic value as it contributed to maintaining the prestige and social use of the language in the numerous social, scientific and artistic associations which were created under the impetus of Catalanism. It also fostered its maintenance as an informative and cultural written language, despite the lack of schooling in Catalan. In this sense, the activity of scientific excursion organisations which were emerging under the impetus of the Renaixença were important, as they adopted Catalan as their own scientific language, overcoming the inertia of the old academies.

12. Political Catalanism and language claims: Federalism

Fortunately, the Renaixença was not limited to becoming an exclusively literary and cultural movement with no political ambitions, at least in the Principality. Instead, due to federalism and primarily the efforts of Valentí Almirall, it expanded its scope to develop a political action plan aimed at dealing with the regime's centralism and advancing towards political catalanism. But when and from where did federalism reach Catalonia?

It does not seem to have come or at least transcended federalist ideas before the "Glorious" September Revolution of 1868, which ousted Queen Isabel II. At that time, there were two modern federalist models, republican and democratic: the former was created in the United States of America in 1783, that is, before the French Revolution, while the latter was the Swiss model established through the 1843 Constitution, which stipulated three official languages.

Though it was the first to appear, the American model apparently did not have as much initial influence in Catalonia, or at least it was not taken into account when writing the Constitution of Cádiz. Nor did political analysts like Jaume Balmes or the main players in the Catalonia of the Constitutional or Liberal Triennium of 1820 to 1823 mention it, nor did the republican Abdó Terrades (1812-1856). In fact, the first federalist Catalan political association was the Club dels Federalistes (1868-1869), which predated the 1868 creation of the Partit Republicà Democràtic Federal, of whom Valentí Almirall was a founder and prominent member, the mentor of political Catalanism. We shall not enter into the details of this process, which experts like Josep Pich i Mitjana[55] are more familiar with, but given the information available we can deduce that the model on which it was inspired was the Swiss. In this sense, it may be no coincidence that Almirall and his coreligionist radical politicians met in a venue called Cafè Suís.

The first person to introduce federalist republicanism in Catalonia was probably the democratic politician José Maria de Orense, the Marquis of Albaida, upon his return from exile. He was the one who motivated Almirall to study *la constitución de la Confederación suiza y la de la Federación norteamericana* ("Constitution of the Swiss Confederation and the American Federation"). Other democratic republican politicians of the day, such as Josep-Narcís Roca i Farreras and Conrad Roure, also praised the Swiss system. It should be noted that the federalist seed planted by Orense blossomed in fertile soil in Catalonia, perhaps more than anywhere else, not only in Barcelona but also in other Catalan counties or towns where a progressive political attitude predominated, such as in the Empordà, with figures like Joan Tutau from Figueres and Pere Caimó from Sant Feliu de Guíxols.

We shall not go into detail about the shift of one sector of federalism led by Valentí Almirall which, disillusioned by the division of the federalists and the failure of the First Republic, posited Catalanism as a distinct political force not linked to any Spanish party. However, according to Conrad Roure, in 1882, that is, right in the midst of the Bourbon Restoration, Valentí Almirall gave a lecture on Switzerland, which he had visited several times. And in the 20th century Josep M. Corredor, who had stayed in Geneva for prolonged periods of time after 1954, published a 1971 study on *La Unió Americana i la Confederació Suïssa vistes per Valentí Almirall*[56].

In any event, political Catalanism strove to frame Catalonia as fully equal within Spain or the Iberian Peninsula. Therefore, it should come as no surprise that these federalist ideas were taken into account by politicians such as Enric Prat de la Riba, such as in the articles on federalism and nationalism published in 1897 in the *Revista Jurídica de Catalunya*.

55 Josep Pich, *Valentí Almirall i el federalisme intransigent* (Catarroja-Barcelona: Editorial Afers, 2006).

56 Josep Maria Corredor, *De Casa i d'Europa* (Barcelona: Selecta, 1971).

13. The Restoration

The 1874 Bourbon Restoration was a movement that emerged in reaction to the First Republic, which was federal, and it was the heir to the traditional centralist, unitary system of liberalism (or Spanish pseudo-liberalism), while also consolidating the political and economic oligarchy centred in Madrid, where territorial clientelism assured its predominance.

This regime consummated the banishment of Catalan in the administration and education. Thus, in 1881 the new law on civil prosecution required all documentation to be written in Spanish, such that any text written in another language had to be translated for it to have legal value.

Thus, these circumstances witnessed the contradictory fact that as the literary Renaixença was gaining momentum and developing, the Catalan language was totally excluded from the official realm and largely from the private written realm as well because of exclusively Spanish-language education. Yet despite these unfavourable conditions, the Renaixença unquestionably contributed to maintaining the social prestige of Catalan so that this language was not abandoned by its speakers but instead remained their native language, even among the bourgeoisie and intellectuals in the Principality and Balearic Islands. In the region of Valencia, the native language did not achieve the same prestige among the bourgeoisie, who had close ties to the Spanish political and social system and started quite a widespread process of castilianisation, especially in the cities of Alicante and Valencia.

At the beginning of the Restoration, the literary Renaixença seemed to be viewed with curiosity and high hopes in an attempt to equate it with a broad concept of Spanish nationality which was more theoretical and opportunistic than real. This can be seen in Víctor Balaguer's initiation speeches into the Royal Academies of History and Language in 1875 and 1883, respectively. In his 1875 speech, Balaguer examined the topic of *De la literatura catalana*, where he reported on the birth of a literature that was not in the "national" language. In response to this speech, after wondering whether this was a "natural revolution" or "archaeological reconstruction", José Amador de los Ríos, a professor of Spanish literature at the Universidad de Madrid, stated that he saw nothing incompatible between this literary renaissance and *las leyes fundamentales del genio y de la cultura españolas*[57] ("the fundamental laws of genius and Spanish culture").

In 1883, Balaguer spoke on *El significado e importancia de las literaturas regionales*. According to this speech, regional literatures have their place within the *gran nacionalidad Española* ("great Spanish nationality"), since Spain's unity must be a plural unity. The response this time came from Emilio Castelar (another politician who started out progressive but had adapted to the regime of the Restoration), who in a grandiloquent way made a laudatory but not overly committal description of the history of Catalan literature and justified its modern existence within the "unity and variety" of Spain[58].

Other Spanish literati and intellectuals from this period, like Juan Valera and especially Marcelino Menéndez y Pelayo, initially viewed the Catalan Renaixença sympathetically. However, as this literary movement gained ground and broadened its social base, mistrust and even hostility began to appear as it became associated with the development of political Catalanism.

This became clear not only in Valera's private correspondence but also in the controversies between Gaspar Núñez de Arce, Valentí Almirall and Joan Mañé i Flaquer in 1886 and 1997, and between Leopoldo Alas and Pompeu Gener in 1894, as well as in Francisco Tubino's 1880 study of the Renaixença. Even the most sympathetic Spanish intellectuals, like Menéndez Pelayo, a disciple of Milà i Fontanals, and P. Francisco Blanco García, never went further than accepting a cultural – but not political – compromise. They accepted the existence of Catalan literature but not political Catalanism, which they always viewed as a threat to Spanish unity.

It is clear that no movement favourable to the normalisation of the Catalan language beyond the Jocs Florals or the greater or lesser tolerance of literary production in general would emerge from either the Restoration regime or Spanish liberalism in general, alarmed by the war in Cuba, because they were based on a rigid centralism and a desire to achieve

57 Víctor Balaguer, *Discursos leídos ante la Real Academia de la Historia* (Madrid: T.Fortanet, 1875), pp. 12-86.

58 *Discursos de D. Víctor Balaguer y D. Emilio Castelar leídos en la recepción pública del primero el Domingo 25 de febrero de 1883* (Madrid: Real Academia de la Lengua, 1883).

a state that was unified linguistically, primarily via schools. They were thus consummating the legislative and administrative process initiated by the *Real cédula* ("royal warrant") issued by Charles III, as shown by the fact that the Basque codes of *fueros* ("law") had been abolished and the attempts to suppress private civil legislation, in Catalonia as well.

For this reason, in 1881 Valentí Almirall rebuked Víctor Balaguer, who was trying to harmonise Spanish liberalism with Catalanism:

> *Lo Catalanisme no és l'Espanyolisme, per la senzilla raó que les dues paraules expressen idees distintes [...] Desenganyi's lo senyor Balaguer [...] Los espanyolistes aspiren a una pàtria gran, unificada y centralitzada [...]*[59].
>
> Catalanism is not Spanishness, for the simple reason that the two words express different ideas [...] Let's disillusion you, Mr. Balaguer [...] The Pro-Spanish aspire to [have] one great united and centralised homeland [...].

At this point we will not go into a detailed description of political Catalanism, but we should note that Catalan was this movement's preferred language of expression and that its claims explicitly included the demand for the Catalan language to be given official status. Thus, Catalan was the language of the Catalanist press after *La Renaixença* (1871) and *Diari català* (1879), and of doctrinal expositions such as Valentí Almirall's *Lo catalanisme* (1886)[60] and Torras i Bages' *La tradició catalana* (1892)[61]. Regarding programmatic documents or claims, in 1888 the *Missatge a la Reina Regent* demanded *que la llengua catalana sia la llengua oficial a Catalunya per a totes les manifestacions de la vida d'aquest poble. Que l'ensenyament a Catalunya sia donat en llengua catalana* ("that the Catalan language be the official language of Catalonia for all aspects of the life of this people"), and in the 1892 Bases de Manresa, base 4rt was devoted to this issue: *La llengua catalana serà l'única que ab caràcter oficial podrà usarse a Catalunya y en les relacions d'aquesta regió amb lo Poder central*[62] ("The Catalan language shall be the only one that can

59 Josep Moran, *Treballs de lingüística històrica catalana* (Barcelona: Publicacions de l'Abadia de Montserrat, 1994), p. 283.

60 Valentí Almirall, *Lo catalanisme* (Barcelona: Edicions 62-La Caixa, 1979).

61 Josep Torres, *La tradició catalana* (Barcelona: Selecta, 1966).

62 Francisco Flos, *Lo regionalisme esplicat* (Terrassa: L'Ateneu Tarrassench, 1895), p. 28.

be used officially in Catalonia and in the relations between this region and the central Power"). This base, which was defended by Ramon Picó i Campamar, was approved unanimously with no emendations.

What is more, the first Catalanist Congress held in 1880 proposed creating an Acadèmia de la Llengua Catalana, which would be entrusted with the mission of establishing the language norms in an effort to overcome the hindrance to the full normalisation of the use of the language caused by the lack of spelling and grammar rules.

The reaction of the Spanish political and intellectual class after the First Republic, that is, during the Bourbon Restoration, was mostly a lack of understanding and hostility towards the Catalanist claims, including those referring the Catalan language, which were regarded as separatist[63]. This reaction created an anti-Catalanist current which has strongly influenced the history of Catalonia and Spain and has conditioned – and still conditions today – the process of linguistic and political normalisation in general.

63 Josep Grau, *La lliga regionalista i la llengua catalana (1901-1924)* (Barcelona: Publicacions de l'Abadia de Montserrat, 2006), pp. 89-98.

A Survey of the Legal History of Catalonia and its Historical Rights

Tomàs de Montagut
Universitat Pompeu Fabra and Institut d'Estudis Catalans

From the material standpoint, historical rights are naturally traced back to their origins, to the evolution and history of Catalan law, that is, to the history of the law and institutions of Catalonia viewed as a political entity with its own personality that stood apart from other communities after a given historical period.

As is known, we have to seek the historical antecedents of the birth of Catalonia, as a political community with full public power endowed with its own legal system, in the process of independence from the Carolingian empire which the Catalan counts, led by the Count of Barcelona and carried out over the course of a long period of time[1].

Thus, over time the Count of Barcelona became the prince of Catalonia under the authority of the *Usatges de Barcelona*, the first code that contained the general laws of Catalonia which began to be put into writing in the 12th century[2]. However, the prince's power ran more deeply, specifically in feudal processes of private power represented by the legal figures of oaths of loyalty and homage, as well as in the earlier tradition of private law, represented by the survival of Visigothic law contained in the epitomes of the *Liber Iudiciorum* of its former monarchs[3].

The 12th century also witnessed how the notion of jurisdiction was used in Europe in the construction of valid processes of public power (Empire and Church). Soon this concept was able to be transferred effectively to different emerging Christian monarchies and became a useful

1 Ramon d'Abadal, *Els primers comtes catalans* (Barcelona: Editorial Teide, 1958).

2 Joan Bastardas, *Usatges de Barcelona. El Codi a mitjan segle XII* (Barcelona: Fundació Noguera, 1984), pp. 7-38.

3 *El Liber Iudicum Popularis*, eds. Jesús Alturo, Joan Bellès, Josep M. Font, Yolanda García, Anscari Mundó (Barcelona: Generalitat de Catalunya, Departament de Justícia i Interior, 2003).

legal-political instrument for the monarchs who led these national communities, which were *de jure* but not *de facto* part of the Christian empire[4]. Over the course of the Middle Ages, the lower political entities that were more personal or territorial in scope, such as municipalities, baronies, guilds and other kinds of universities or corporations, also gained the title of jurisdiction, albeit with a special nature at a lower rank than the monarch and only in certain matters, since the monarchy reserved some of them for itself as royalty.

In the 13th century, the *Commemoracions de Pere Albert*, which complemented and updated the Usatges, granted the Count of Barcelona – now also the King of Aragon – the overall jurisdiction over the entire Principality of Catalonia[5].

However, this jurisdiction was doubly conditioned, first by the configuration of the Crown of Aragon as a territorial union made up of the kingdoms and lands of the monarch, one of whose founding members was the Principality of Catalonia

This union meant that the monarch had a certain universal jurisdiction which extended over all the territories in the Crown in certain matters like war, justice and foreign relations, while it respected and protected the general jurisdiction of each of them and the independence of their respective legal systems[6].

Likewise, the general jurisdiction of the Count of Barcelona – the prince of Catalonia – was soon conditioned by some of Catalonia's constitutions and by pactism, the contractual doctrine according to which some jurists established a range of constitutional principles that affected the nature of the supreme political power of Catalonia and the production,

4 Pietro Costa, *Iurisdictio: Semantica del potere politico en la pubblicistica medievale (1100-1433)* (Milan: A Giuffrè, 2002), pp. 63-91.

5 Elisabet Ferran, *El jurista Pere Albert i les Commemoracions* (Barcelona: Institut d'Estudis Catalans, 2006), pp. 233-256.

6 Tomàs de Montagut, "La Justicia en la Corona de Aragón", *La administración de justicia en la historia de España: actas de las III Jornadas de Castilla-La Mancha sobre investigación en archivos (novembre 1997)* (Guadalajara: Junta de Comunidades de Castilla-La Mancha, 1999); Tomás de Montagut, "La Constitució política de la Corona d'Aragó", *El Compromiso de Caspe (1412), cambios dinásticos y Constitucionalismo en la Corona de Aragón*, Isabel Falcón, coord. (Saragossa: XIX Congreso de Historia de la Corona de Aragón, 2013), pp. 104-116.

application and interpretation of Catalan law[7]. Thus, the necessary intervention of the leading social estates in Catalonia was established in the operation of its supreme governance at the hands of the prince, and the monarch was required to swear his observance of Catalan law if he wanted to earn authority over the general jurisdiction in Catalonia. In this sense, Catalan law, which is called historical Catalan law today, was made up of the Usatges of Barcelona, by the constitutions and chapters approved by the Catalan Courts, and by the other laws of Catalonia, meaning the privileges, freedoms and customs of the universities (municipalities and different corporations) and its people (as individuals or in aggregation as a plurality). Historical Catalan law also included common law (Roman – canonical) and equality and sound reason, which were determined by the jurists in the practical exercise of their professions (judges, lawyers, consultants, etc.) and when resolving the specific cases that they were familiar with and weighed or decided[8].

Therefore, historical Catalan law was characterised by being a pluralistic legal system due to the number of sources making it up: laws and customs from Catalonia, judicial and doctrinal jurisprudence from Catalonia and Europe, and civil and canonical norms common to Christian Europe. Another unique feature of historical Catalan law was the fact that it was an open legal system because its application to each specific case depended on the cultural context of the moment, and the job of the jurists and notaries involved was to interpret it. Catalan law was not closed or fully predetermined in a single code or book of laws!

During the historic process that validated pactism (13th-18th centuries), different political and administrative institutions were founded, grew and were formalised, including the Cort General de Catalunya ("General Court of Catalonia") and the Deputació del General de Catalunya ("General Deputation of Catalonia"). The General Court of Catalonia, whose origins are not yet clear[9], was the institutional framework from which, through

7 Victor Ferro, *El Dret Públic Català. Les Institucions a Catalunya fins al Decret de Nova Planta* (Vic: Eumo, 1987), pp. 295-310.

8 Tomàs de Montagut, "Els juristes de Catalunya i la seva organització col·legial a l'època medieval", *Ius Fugit*, 12 (2003), pp. 269-302.

9 Jesús Fernández "Notas en torno a las asambleas condales en la Cataluña de la Alta Edad Media", *Estudis Històrics i documents dels arxius de protocols*, 10 (1982), pp. 7-88; Gener Gonzalvo, "Les assemblees de Pau i Treva i l'origen de la

a parliamentary procedure[10], the pact between the estates of the people and the king, the branches and head, respectively, of the Principality of Catalonia was established in the guise of a corporation of corporations.

In effect, the estates that were represented in the Courts (barons and knights; prelates and men of the cloth; citizens and honorary citizens), took turns to temporarily represent the *Universitas Cathaloniae*, that is the *Populus* of Catalonia, in that a fictitious political person required that a permanent body be created which would continuously express its will. This is the origin of the General Deputation of Catalonia, the body that permanently represents the Parliament (General), which was soon also known by the name of the Generalitat. Royal Decree Law 41/1977 dated the 29th of September 1977, which created the provisional Generalitat of Catalonia, was referring to this historical and political institution when it stated that *la Generalidad de Catalunya es una institución secular en la que el pueblo catalán ha visto el símbolo y el reconocimiento de su personalidad histórica, dentro de la unidad de España*[11] ("the Generalitat de Catalunya is a secular institution in which the Catalan people have seen the symbol and recognition of its historical personality, within the unity of Spain").

In consequence, Catalonia as a Principality, that is, as a general community, was politically and institutionally represented by both the prince and the General Deputation or their Deputation (Generalitat). The prince also represented all of the Crown of Aragon and each of the other kingdoms and territories comprising it. In contrast, the Generalitat exclusively represented the Principality of Catalonia and its political community, the historical, direct forerunner of today's Catalan people.

In the 15th century, the personal union of the Catholic Monarchs led to the personal union of the Crown of Aragon with Castile, as well as the chronic absenteeism of the monarchs, who from then on lived almost permanently outside of Catalonia.

Cort General de Catalunya", *Les Corts a Catalunya. Actes del Congrés d'Història Institucional* (Barcelona: Generalitat de Catalunya, Departament de Cultura, 1991), pp. 71-78.

10 Tomàs de Montagut, "Estudi introductori", Lluis de Peguera, *Practica, forma, y estil de celebrar Corts Generals en Cathalunya, y materias incidents en aquelles*, ed. Tomàs de Montagut (Madrid: Centro de Estudios Constitucionales, 1998).

11 Joseph Benet, "Precedentes Históricos del Estatuto", *Comentarios sobre el Estatuto de Autonomía de Cataluña*, 3 vols. (Barcelona: Institut d'Estudis Autonòmics, 1990), vol. 1, p. 62. See footnote 22 below.

In this context, the Generalitat became the only higher institution with supreme representation of Catalonia that actually resided in the Principality itself.

Today we know more about the process of the formation of the Generalitat[12], the era when it was at its institutional peak[13], its reform or rearrangement by Ferdinand the Catholic, its adaptation to the universal empire of the Habsburgs[14] and its rupture with Philip IV and the return to obedience[15]. We are also familiar with the defeat in the War of the Spanish Succession[16] and the abolition of Catalan institutions and public law with the Bourbons' Nueva Planta decrees[17], which mutilated what we call today historical Catalan law, leaving only private, criminal and trial law barely subsistent and in force, mere fragments of its former legal system.

However, the vindicatory memory of the institutions of self-governance which were eliminated by the Bourbons and the process of rebirth and partial recovery of the autonomy lost in the 18th to 20th centuries took shape in critical moments of political rupture or reformist transition during this historical period, especially upon the introduction of the first Constitutional State of Spain with the approval of the Constitutions of Cádiz of 1812; and 100 years later with the fall of the monarchy and the proclamation of the Catalan Republic in Barcelona on the 14th of April 1931, just a few hours before the Spanish Republic was also proclaimed in Madrid.

12 Albert Estrada-Rius, *Els orígens de la Generalitat de Catalunya (La Deputació del General de Catalunya: dels precedents a la reforma de 1413)* (Barcelona: Universitat Pompeu Fabra, PhD Dissertation, 2001).

13 Isabel Sánchez, *La Diputació del General de Catalunya (1413-1479)* (Barcelona: Generalitat de Catalunya-Institut d'Estudis Catalans, 2004).

14 Miquel Pérez, *Entre el rei i la terra. El poder polític a Catalunya al segle XVI* (Vic: Eumo, 2004).

15 Joseph Capdeferro, "La Deputació del General al segle XVII", *L'autogovern de Catalunya* (Barcelona: Fundació Lluís Carulla, 2004), pp. 51-56.

16 Joaquim Albareda, *La guerra de Successió i l'Onze de Setembre* (Barcelona: Editorial Empúries, 2000).

17 Josep Maria Gay, "La génesi del Decret de Nova Planta de Catalunya. Edició de la consulta original del 'Consejo de Castilla' de 13 de juny de 1715", *Revista Jurídica de Catalunya*, 81/1 (1982), pp. 7-42; Josep Maria Gay, "La gènesi del Decret de Nova Planta de Catalunya. Edició de la consulta original del 'Consejo de Castilla' de 13 de juny de 1715" (segona part), *Revista Jurídica de Catalunya*, 81/2 (1982), pp. 263-348; Josep Maria Gay, *El corregidor a Catalunya* (Madrid: Marcial Pons, 1997), pp. 90-127.

In Cádiz, the defenders of the voluntaristic and philosophical postulates that came to the fore with the French Revolution which legitimised the foundational nature of national sovereignty did away with historical rights because they believed that with the approval of the Constitution, history and its power of political legitimisation were nullified.

Still, other patriots in Cádiz believed that the mission of the Constitution was to update the fundamental laws of the monarchy which resided in the traditional laws, customs and institutions of the Spanish kingdoms – especially Castile – and that monarchic absolutism had been unfairly eliminated. From this perspective, the Constitution did not nullify the political history of Spain and its peoples but instead legitimised them by restoring the fundamental laws of the monarchy and updating them within the frame of a constitutional, liberal state.

The civil wars afterward and the triumph of the moderate constitutions of 1845 and 1876 – the latter after the failure of the Spanish federal republic – meant first recognition of the historical laws of the Kingdom of Navarra and the Basque lands within the constitutional framework, and secondly the triumph of the constitutional visions of Spain with more emphasis on the abstract, unitarist Castilian matrix than on the other peoples of Spain. Consequently, there was soon a divorce between the official world of a constitutional, unitarist Spain centred in Castile and the reality of a Catalan people and historical Catalan law that strove to recover their own public personality through the models of political Catalanism that professor Isidre Molas[18] has situated in time and has studied and described in detail under the following rubrics:

1. "The birth of Catalanism as an autonomous political current: The Hungarian model. From Valentí Almirall and Jaume Collell to the Unió Catalanista".
2. "The nationalism of Enric Prat de la Riba and the Bohemian model".
3. "Cambó and the German model of shared sovereignty".
4. "Self-determination: The Irish model and the Soviet model".

18 Isidro Molas, "El concepte de sobirania en el catalanisme polític", *Les transformacions de la sobirania i el futur polític de Catalunya*, Enric Fossas, dir. (Barcelona: Proa, 2000), pp. 195-213.

The proclamation of the Catalan Republic by Francesc Macià on the 14th of April 1931 and its reduction to the Generalitat de Catalunya three days later was perfected with the express recognition by the Provisional Government of the Spanish Republic of the *hecho histórico de la restauración de la Generalitat*[19] ("historical fact of the restoration of the Generalitat"). Catalonia had to determine its attributions by proposing a Statute of Autonomy which would be submitted to the Constituent Courts and later to the sovereign decision of universal suffrage of the Catalan people.

Prestigious jurists of that time, like Francesc Maspons i Anglasell[20], made legal arguments that the initial relations between both republics – the Catalan and the Spanish – reflected *a la idea d'un pacte entre entitats sobiranes*[21] ("the idea of a pact between sovereign entities"). Even though this doctrine was not imposed, with the approval of the Constitution of the Spanish Republic in 1931 and the subsequent approval of the Statute of Autonomy of Catalonia in 1932, a period got underway in which the restored Generalitat de Catalunya symbolised the recovery of a composite model of Spanish unity that had been lost with the Bourbon dynasty and was based on respect for the diversity of its peoples. The unitary composition of the state actually included historical rights and institutions and allowed them to be expressed constitutionally and updated in an orderly fashion through statutes of autonomy.

However, the Franco dictatorship stopped this process of restoring and modernising the historical laws unilaterally and by force of weapons. The law abolishing the Statute of Autonomy of Catalonia in April 1938[22], signed

19 Josep Benet, "Precedentes Históricos del Estatuto", *Comentarios sobre el Estatuto de Autonomía de Cataluña*, 3 vols. (Barcelona: Institut d'Estudis Autonòmics, 1990), vol. 1, p. 49.

20 See the text in: Francesc Maspons, "Dictamen de Maspons i Anglasell", *República Catalana, Generalitat de Catalunya i República Espanyola. A l'entorn de la "Generalitat de Catalunya i la República Espanyola" de Francesc Maspons i Anglasell*, eds. Hèctor Bofill, Lluís Duran, Ferran Armengol (Barcelona: Generalitat de Catalunya, Secretaria de Coordinació Interdepartamental, 2006), pp. 61-101.

21 Hèctor López, "Vigència del dictamen", *República Catalana, Generalitat de Catalunya I República Espanyola. A l'entorn de la "Generalitat de Catalunya i la República Espanyola" de Francesc Maspons i Anglasell*, eds. Hèctor Bofill, Lluís Duran, Ferran Armengol (Barcelona: Generalitat de Catalunya, Secretaria de Coordinació Interdepartamental, 2006), pp. 103-127.

22 *Boletín Oficial del Estado*, year III, no. 534 (Friday, 8 April 1938), p. 6673 "Ley disponiendo la abolición del Estatuto Catalán".

by the dictator Francisco Franco and his brother-in-law and Minister of the Interior, Ramon Serrano Suñer, withdrew the abrogation of the aforementioned Statute on the 17th of July 1936, the day before the military coup d'état against the democratic legal system in force in the Second Spanish Republic. This day, *el Estatuto de Cataluña, en mala hora concedido por la República, dejó de tener validez, en el orden jurídico español*[23] ("the Statute of Catalonia, granted by the Republic at the wrong time, ceased to be valid, in the Spanish legal order"). In consequence, the military occupation of Catalonia as a result of the Civil War and during the period of the second dictatorship (1939-1975) witnessed a return to the situation prior to the divorce between official unitarist Spain centred in Castile and a real, plural and diverse Spain. The traitorous provinces of Guipuzkoa and Biscay also witnessed the abolition of their historical laws, which were only respected in the provinces that had been faithful to Franco, namely Navarra and Álava. During this period, the contents of historical Catalan civil law was reduced following the possibilistic criteria allowed by the hostile political climate of the Franco dictatorship, albeit using the more precise techniques of dogmatic legal science. The outcome of this reduction was the compilation of a body of special civil law in Catalonia which was approved as law within the national Franco state in 1960. Thus, the last remnants of historical Catalan law still in force were fossilised and could not be autonomously renewed[24].

With the death of the dictator Francisco Franco (1975), as mentioned above, the transition to democracy embarked upon by the government of Adolfo Suárez remedied the previous situation with the enactment of Royal Decree Law on the Prefecture of the State 41/1977 dated the 29th of September 1977, which restored the provisional Generalitat of Catalonia[25], and with the recognition that

> *la Generalidad de Catalunya es una institución secular, en la que el pueblo catalán ha visto el símbolo y el reconocimiento de su personalidad histórica, dentro de la unidad de España*[26].

23 *Boletín Oficial del Estado*, year III, no. 534..., p. 6674.

24 Lluís Puig, "Derecho Civil Catalán", *Comentarios sobre el Estatuto de Autonomía de Cataluña*, 3 vols. (Barcelona: Institut d'Estudis Autonòmics, 1990), vol. 1, pp. 419-420.

25 *Diari Oficial de la Generalitat de Catalunya*, no. 1, Monday, 5 December 1977, pp. 1-2.

26 Josep Benet, "Precedentes Históricos del Estatuto", *Comentarios sobre el Estatuto de Autonomía de Cataluña*, 3 vols. (Barcelona: Institut d'Estudis Autonòmics, 1990), vol. 1, p. 62.

> The Generalitat de Catalunya is a secular institution, in which the Catalan people have seen the symbol and recognition of its historical personality, within the unity of Spain.

However, in its first article, the restoration of the Generalitat was clearly limited in time (until the autonomous community system that might be approved by the Courts entered into force) and in material and organic content and competences (the Generalitat was only restored in the bodies, attributions and legal system that were regulated within the scope of the law restoring it). As a result, we cannot state that the Statute of Autonomy of 1932 went back into force, although the aforementioned Franco-era law that abrogated it with retroactive effects to April 1938 was indeed abolished[27]. Despite all of this, with all its limitations, the Generalitat de Catalunya was the only institution from the Second Spanish Republic that was actually restored, but excepting that, the transition to democracy in Spain legitimised the violent rupture of the republican democratic legal system wrought by the military coup d'état[28]. The transition was carried out in a transactional way by setting up a new democratic framework for the future that accepted but did not revise the past acts. With the 1978 Constitution, the 1979 Statute of Autonomy of Catalonia, its update in 2005 and Ruling 31/2010 by the Spanish Constitutional Court, we reach the present of the people and citizens of Catalonia as well as their historical laws which are, nonetheless, still an important part of their individual and collective identity.

27 See note 22 above and *Diari Oficial de la Generalitat de Catalunya*, no. 1, Royal Decree-Law 41/1977, dated 29 September on the provisional restoration of the Generalitat de Catalunya, second final provision: *Queda derogada la Ley de la Jefatura del Estado de ocho de abril de mil novecientos treinta y ocho* ("The Law of the Head of State of April 8 of 1938 is repealed").

28 See: *Boletín Oficial del Estado*, year III, no. 534…, p. 6674 where the law signed by Franco declares: *El Alzamiento Nacional significó en el orden político, la ruptura con todas las instituciones que implicasen negación de los valores que se intentaba restaurar* ("In the political order, the National Uprising meant a break with all the institutions that implied denial of the values that it was aimed to restore").

Architecture, Power and Identity in Medieval Catalonia: Challenges of Recovering and Re-creating Identity

Xavier BARRAL I ALTET
Universities of Rennes II, Ca'Foscari of Venice and Institut d'Estudis Catalans

The signs of national identity in art and architecture have always been the subject of controversy, debate and opposing concepts. Are the works of Joan Miró or Josep Lluís Sert made abroad Catalan art? Is the architecture of Norman Foster, Arata Isozaki or Richard Meier made in Barcelona Catalan art? Are these categories legitimate and fair at a time when many people believe that internationalism prevails over art? How can we define identity in art?

During the 19th century, choosing the architectural style that was the most national, in the sense of the most representative of the country, was a keen concern. From this standpoint, research into the sources pointed clearly towards the Middle Ages. Josep Puig i Cadafalch (1867-1956), who preferred the neo-Gothic over the neo-Romanesque as the national style, confessed that when he was a mere 36 years old he wished "to figure in this progressive work of young architects who dreamt of creating a new art for the nation". In 1904, he defined it as follows (Figure 1):

> *Allò que potser hem creat de més positiu entre tots és un art modern que ha pres per base el nostre art tradicional, adornat amb les belleses de materials nous, resolent amb l'esperit nacional del nostre art antic les necessitats actuals, impulsant-lo cap a algunes de les exuberants decoracions meridionals, i, fins i tot, infiltrant-li determinades ornamentacions morisques o algunes vagues visions d'Extrem Orient, i un segell purament local, molt diferent de tots els altres*[1].

1 Josep Puig, *Escrits d'arquitectura, art i política*, ed. Xavier Barral (Barcelona: Institut d'Estudis Catalans, 2003), p. 252.

> What we all together have created perhaps the most relevant is a modern art based in our traditional art, adorned with the beauty of new materials, solving current needs through the national spirit of our ancient art, orienting the modern art towards some exuberant Southern decorations, and even infiltrating it with certain Moorish ornamentation or some vague visions of the Far East and a purely local label, very different from any other artistic expressions.

Figure 1: *Sant Jordi* ("Saint George") by Eusebi Arnau, Casa Amatller (Josep Puig i Cadafalch, 1898-1900), Barcelona.

These issues, whether formulated more or less explicitly, can be found at the core of the reflection on identities in art. The creation of a national art history is and has been overseen by many governments through their cultural organisations, and they exercised a positive or negative role depending on how they chose to use art. It is not always clearly accepted that there is an objective art history, or that art history, like all the humanities, is a subjective discipline in which the training and stances of art historians translates into the content and orientation of their writings.

In the more specific case of Catalonia, the originality of Romanesque art has been brought to the forefront because before the first Romantics, before the start of what were called the regional schools, and before the first nationalisms which sought to base part of the historical justification of the past on art, Romanesque art was neither of interest, nor was it considered artistically important (Figure 2). On the other hand, it is quite likely that at least in architecture, the Catalan Gothic was infinitely superior in originality and quality than the much-vaunted Romanesque. The Catalan Gothic spread far and wide during the Middle Ages, especially around the Mediterranean, while the Romanesque was confined to the lands of Catalonia per se, virtually without exception (Figure 3).

Figure 2: *Brodat de la Creació* ("Creation Embroidery") (XI-XII centuries) (Cathedral Treasury, Girona).

Two other periods in the history of Catalan art might compete with this Gothic, which I uphold as the symbol of a nation that felt overly confined within its borders: Modernisme (Art Nouveau, Figure 4) and post-1992 Catalonia (Figure 5).

Figure 3: *Mare de Déu dels Consellers* ("Our Lady of the Conselors") by Lluís Dalmau, 1445 (Museu Nacional d'Art de Catalunya, Barcelona).

Figure 4: *La cançó popular catalana* ("The catalan popular song") by Miquel Blay, Palau de la Música Catalana (Lluís Domènech i Muntaner, 1905-1908), Barcelona.

Figure 5: *Mercat de Santa Caterina* ("Santa Caterina's Market") (Enric Miralles, Benedetta Tagliabue, 2005), Barcelona.

1. Medieval art and cultural identity

Art is always identity, and medieval art is particularly so because it defines the land, the will to power, the desire to be one, the fascination with the other, war and submission, yet also the aspiration towards a unique beauty shared within the framework of the general Europe-wide style of the day. Architecture was the main art in the Middle Ages, as it was in all the other periods in the history of art, first, because it is the artistic formula that requires the most economic resources, and secondly because it is the one that lasts the longest. It might also be the art that best reflects the artistic will of the person who commissions it, as they are usually cognizant that the work will last over time and aware of the repercussions of the architectural model chosen. Indeed, whether the visual expression of power confers an image of newness or tradition, of regional roots or international positioning, hinges on this choice.

Contemporary statesmen did not err when they choosing the architectural style with which they would like to go down in history, how they want to be remembered. In both the Middle Ages and today, there have been politicians and statesmen, kings and princes who have apparently taken more interest in war or the immediate economy than in the architectural image that will outlast them. Others, however, have understood that after they are no longer around, the dignitary's memory will remain in everyone's everyday life through architecture. This was shown, for example, by the French President François Mitterrand with the Louvre pyramid and by Alfonso the Magnanimous in Naples with the Triumphal Arch which precedes the entrance to his urban residence in Castelnuovo (Figure 6).

Figure 6: Alfonso the Magnanimous Triumphal Arch (1452-1471), Castelnuovo, Naples.

Defining identity with architecture entails somehow deciding what makes one different from others, or more simply defining the unique features of a social group, a region or sometimes merely a person in the case of egotistically exhibitionist patronage. Therefore, there are two ways to publicly exhibit identity via architecture: one is by following the fashions, that is, acting like others, and we would have to include drawing from past or the persistence of an obsolete taste within this category. The other clearly entails the desire to be original and to create something new.

It is very difficult to define what might be original, not to mention innovative, in the art of medieval Catalonia because it all depends on how we see ourselves, that is, on the subjectivity of the historian. Today, if we examine the Catalan studies on the medieval art of Catalonia, we can find many arguments praising the creative originality, innovations and particular features of an art which must obligatorily be defined within a Mediterranean context. When, however, we examine general textbooks on art history throughout Europe, we realise that Catalonia is usually absent, also because 20th century historiography preferred to spotlight the medieval art of France or Italy. Does this reflect the reality of medieval art? Or is it instead the outcome of nationalist operations that Catalonia has also attempted, albeit with fewer economic means and with less capacity for intellectual dissemination?

Ultimately, agreeing on whether there is some sort of medieval art model that emerged in Catalonia and spread around the world should not matter to us. We should be more interested in defining the characteristics of an artistic output which, original or not, is the art of a given land and corresponds to given political and social realities.

Today, due to circumstances that still exist and reasons that can be documented, the art of Catalonia is seen by the public at large and mass tourism through two precise monuments that in no way represent the totality of more than 20 centuries of artistic history: the Romanesque and Modernisme. The first is highly pleasing, perhaps because of its austerity, because it represents the origins of the nation or perhaps because, though deformed in order to lead people to believe that all Romanesque was solely religious, it might reflect a mysterious vision of the past full of unknown aspects (Figure 7). However, the Catalan Romanesque in the Middle Ages was not at the forefront of European architecture, nor did it export anything new or original. The other period that is associated with the tourism image of Catalonia today is Modernisme, the Catalan name for Art Nouveau, a local style spanning the 19th century and first quarter of the 20th century which sprang from the need to externally display a very small group of well-off citizens' new wealth. However, Modernisme, too, is local, geographically introverted and never served as a model anywhere else (Figure 8). In Catalonia in the Middle Ages, the Gothic, not the Romanesque, was probably the most innovative style that represented the power and expansion of the nation. Without a doubt, throughout the 20th century and the early 21st century, innovation and artistic creativity have not come through Modernisme but instead can be clearly situated within contemporary architecture and Catalan designs, which have earned a great deal more international projection than this country's Modernisme.

Figure 7: Nave of the church (11th century) Sant Vicenç de Cardona.

Figure 8: Milà House, "La Pedrera" (Antoni Gaudí, 1906-1910), Barcelona.

All of this is meant to show that we cannot define identity in art according to tourist fads or momentary times or taste that evolve and change. We should recall that the Modernisme that is so broadly admired today was largely destroyed for many decades in the 20th century because it was neither liked nor considered useful. And this is true not only in Catalonia but also in other more powerful cultures, such as France, where the iron architecture of Paris' central market, Les Halles, designed by architect Victor Baltard (1805-1874), was destroyed even recently, albeit not without fierce controversy, as were many wrought-iron underground openings designed by Hector Guimard (1867-1942), which today are protected as highly prized historical monuments.

2. Middle ages, visual expression of power and identity awareness

We can often detect a great deal of continuity in the art of every country, especially during the Middle Ages, when nations were being formed. This continuity stems from the desire to revive the past in order to create a history of its own grounded equally upon the prestige of the past and the cultural novelties of the day. This meant that the constant features in medieval Catalonia were the Mediterranean and a Roman orientation.

Probably what best defines the evolution of art in medieval Catalonia was the historical continuity of Roman art and especially the survival of the urban structure and the organisation of the land dating from Roman times. This meant walled cities, which evolved while retaining the fortified image of power encapsulated in the walls, tower and gateways. In the realm of religious architecture, the survival of the models from late antiquity through the centuries of the early Middle Ages and until fully into the medieval period offered a technical and stylistic continuity that led to Romanesque religious architecture. In many cases, the paleo-Christian basilicas remained in use, at least until the major reconstructions from the Romanesque period. For example, we can see both continuity and evolution in all the churches in Terrassa. The architecture from the early Middle Ages is usually local architecture quite far from the creations generated in the major courts of the Carolingian leaders (Figure 9).

Figure 9: Church of Sant Pere, Terrassa, Early Middle Ages apse.

Sant Miquel church in Cuixà, with its three short naves separated by rectangular pilasters and arcades, its broad transept and its wood-covered structure, is the best remaining example of a monument that reflects the sweeping architectural ambitions of the prelates in the second half of the 10th century (Figure 10). The point of departure in terms of both technique and structure was local late antiquity. The aim was the monumental ambition of the great European abbey churches; the point of reference was Rome and its great basilicas from the past.

In Cuixà better than elsewhere, we can see a highly irregular pre-Romanesque architecture in terms of its mural techniques in the architecture of the first third of the 11th century, which led to the reappearance of the vault, built with highly regular walls made of small, skilfully placed ashlars. The preceding building in Cuixà was not destroyed but surrounded by new constructions. This early Romanesque architecture in Catalonia corresponds to a widespread style in southern Europe, and it was used in the early 10th century to define a general geography of the style, placing Catalonia in a European context at a time when the southern part of the country and virtually the entire Iberian Peninsula were still under Muslim rule.

Figure 10: Nave the church of Sant Miquel de Cuixà (10th century).

Some of the most important buildings from that time in the realm of religious architecture are clearly the great cathedrals of Barcelona, Girona, La Seu d'Urgell and Vic (Figure 11). However, the site where the formulation of the concept of early Romanesque architecture from the 11th century has been best conserved is in the collegiate church of Cardona (Figure 12). At the end of the first third of the 11th century, the prestigious Abbot Oliba decided to bring his monasteries in Ripoll and Cuixà, along with the cathedral in Vic, where he served as bishop, in line with the tastes of the time. The basilica of Ripoll was consecrated in 1032, the one in Cuixà in 1040 and the cathedral of Vic in 1038. Both monastery churches had been reconstructed in the late 10th century and consecrated in 977 and 974, respectively. Therefore, they probably did not need to be reconstructed just 50 years later. However, aware of the need to impose an architectural image that would represent the country in a modern way, Abbot Oliba decided that with these architectural reconstructions he wanted to guide the religious identity of the country towards the symbols of early Christianity and the papacy, that is, towards Rome.

Figure 11: Cathedral Bell Tower of Sant Pere, Vic (11th century).

Figure 12: Church of Sant Vicenç de Cardona (11th century).

Oliba had personally gone to Rome at least twice, in 1011 and 1016, have gone back at least once. He imported architectural symbols from Rome, which he decided to introduce as publicly as possible, that is, in the visible aspects of his main churches. In Ripoll, which has the seven apses aligned over the transept of the new basilica, Oliba somehow guided the eyes and aspirations of Catalan religiosity towards the most prestigious basilica in the heart of Christianity, Saint Peter's (Figure 13). In Vic, six years after his feat in Ripoll, Oliba decided to construct a circular church devoted to the Virgin Mary across from the main building of the Sant Pere cathedral. In around 1038, it was directly reminiscent of the prestigious, monumental Roman Pantheon, which had been dedicated to Mary and all the saints since 609 with the name of Saint Mary of the Martyrs.

When building his prestigious basilicas, Oliba probably did not have the means he needed for an architectural undertaking on a European scale, such as the ones that were underway in Cluny and Saint-Bénigne in Dijon, for example. However, within his limited means he wanted to signal a pathway that was neither more nor less than what the other European prelates in the first third of the 11th century were imposing in their respective abbacies, such as Bernward in Hildesheim or Poppo in Aquileia.

Figure 13: Church of Santa Maria de Ripoll (11th century; restaured during the 19th century).

Oliba's example shows us that great architectural ventures always spring from the initiatives of unusual people. But it also reveals that these decisions always need to be complemented with the economic means to carry them out.

Later or late Romanesque architecture took off in Catalonia after the second third of the 12th century, when a novel style brimming with new technical possibilities for making larger buildings was already being developed in northern Europe, in that nucleus of power that was Paris and the Île-de-France. What is more, the new iconographies led the façade statues to be replaced with columns in the form of personages, while the murals inside the building disappeared. Thus, the walls were vacated, opening up large windows to showcase stained glass windows and ushering in a new iconography of light.

At that time, Catalonia, just like much of Europe from at least Italy to Cologne, remained loyal to the most traditional Romanesque and yet produced works of notable quality similar to what was being developed in the large complexes in Provence, such as Saint-Gilles and Saint-Trophime d'Arles, which were faithful to the taste, manners and even symbolism of the ancient monuments. As a paradigmatic example, I would, of course, like to mention the triumphal significance of the monumental doorway in Ripoll, whose architectural form and composition revealed its builders' profound knowledge of classical triumphal arches, and the way the iconography was organised into superimposed levels with small angled columns (Figure 14). This triumphal symbolism drew from religious iconography to serve the idea of power that was as secular as religious, or even more secular than religious.

Figure 14: Façade of Santa Maria de Ripoll (12th century) photograph of 1913.

When we study the art of the Middle Ages, we do not always have the written documents needed to interpret the desires of the developers or the public purposes of the major architectural works. One highly emblematic case of this gap in our knowledge is the monumental façade of the basilica of Ripoll. There, right in the middle of a huge expanse of religious images, we see on the right side of the entry doorway a depiction of Christ speaking to a man facing him, while three other anonymous adults are facing forward. One is dressed as a bishop and the other two are in such a precarious state of conservation that we cannot determine whether they are monks or princes. Numerous identities have been put forth for these figures, which are identified by no inscriptions; however, their presence and the position they occupy may explain the reason behind the doorway, the person who commissioned it and under what circumstances it was opened.

During the 13th century, a new form of religiosity began to reach Catalonia, the Cistercian order, which in France had led to architectures stripped of all decoration while adopting the basic elevation of Gothic constructions. The count-kings did not hesitate to appropriate this new religious expression for themselves and to place it at the service of the public image of power. With this purpose in mind, they transferred the family pantheons from Ripoll to Poblet (Figure 15).

Figure 15: Gothic Cloister of the Cistercian Monastery of Poblet.

However, the city was still the main site of residence and power. Destined to be a large economic and political centre in the medieval Mediterranean, in addition to a hub that integrated cultures, the city of Barcelona expressed its prestige and wealth in the sphere of art with the representation of power and the court. This reality was then translated into monuments thanks to the new architectural ambitions, from which the Palau Reial and the cathedral benefitted. While the structure of the walled city embodied the strength of power more than the fear of invaders in the collective imagination, the size of the Drassanes shipyards expressed the essential importance of the relationship between the city and the sea (Figure 16).

Figure 16: Gothic city walls of Barcelona.

Valencia and Mallorca embodied not only the spirit of conquest but also the Mediterranean side of Catalonia's will to power, and these cities should be joined by Perpignan, with its Palau dels Reis de Mallorca. We can call to mind the Consulate of the Sea, which was represented monumentally in each city by the Llotja building and more materially and mundanely by trade and goods. The first Consulates of the Sea known in the Catalan-speaking lands are the ones in Barcelona, mentioned back in 1282, even though the institution dated from before then. It was soon followed by the consulates of Valencia (1283) and Mallorca (1326). The symbol of these Consulates of the Sea is the *Llibre del consolat de mar*, which dates from the mid-14th century.

Yet some princes did not seem to view architecture as necessary to their identity, prestige or posterity. The most emblematic case is probably James I the Conqueror; we know this through the information from a story, the *Llibre dels feits*, which recounts his life and feats.

During the reign of James I, many princes expressed a clear desire to impose their own architecture in the lands they had conquered as a symbol of identity. Frederick II is a good example of this in southern Italy, a land with its own great architectural traditions where the emperor imposed artistic forms grounded upon refined military architecture with the goal of reviving the prestige of the ancient world as an essential feature of the imposition of his power. Beyond the stylistic connotations, what characterised the 30 years of governance of Frederick II (1220-1250) is the extraordinary explosion in building: castles, fortresses and palaces which have mostly been destroyed, but which we are aware of through both their monumental vestiges and text sources. Beyond a constant return to the classical naturalistic values, which is primarily manifested in the portraits of the sovereign still conserved today and are one of the features of the sculpture rendered in southern Italy during this period, one of the main original features of sculpture during the reign of Frederick II is the mixture between this glance back at the ancient world and its close ties with the transalpine Gothic. Frederick II had a veritable artistic conquest and land occupation policy which contributed to creating and disseminating his own style for posterity. Shortly before then, the Norman princes of Sicily had acted more subtly with the view that their identity on the island should adopt artistic aspects of the Muslim past while also seeking to import the refined Byzantine models.

Regardless of the decision that led to any given architectural course, it was linked to the concept of posterity and had identity consequences. All of this seems totally absent from the concerns of a colonising king like James I. The *Llibre dels feits* never mentions either observations of the monumental landscapes in the conquered lands or any deliberate state policy that would lead to a desire to export or impose an identity.

If we take the slightly later case of the arrival of Charles I of Anjou to the throne of Naples in 1266, and we consider the decade leading up to the death of James I in 1276, we find two policies that are even more distant from each other. After reaching the lands of the German Hohenstaufens, the Anjous of France quickly geared their architectural commissions toward the French style, as clearly revealed by the documents conserved from the Angevin chancellery. Charles I brought architects, engineers, carpenters and many other tradesmen from France whose names we know from their appearance on contracts and payments, such as Pierre d'Agincourt, Jean de Toul, Pierre de Chaules, Jean de Lauden, Henri d'Asson, Raoul de Corbie, Thiebaut de Saumur, Pommier d'Arras and Baucelin de Linne. The arrival of the Angevin conquerors in Naples totally transformed the city's monumental appearance. During those early years of occupation, French artists and local teams joined forces to transform the city, a city that must have still substantially and particularly visibly conserved its own Byzantine and then, briefly, Norman history.

James I does not seem to have been concerned with anything of the kind, and this is surprising. No artistic grandeur seems to have enticed the conquering king, or at least nothing of this kind can be perceived in the story that sought to give him an official image for posterity, the *Llibre dels feits*. It is as if from this point of view he was unable to prepare for the future, for posterity, by exporting his monumental realities, those of his land. Not even in September 1269, when James assembled the fleet to liberate Jerusalem, does he seem to have thought about or planned any kind of cultural colonisation, although it is difficult to speculate on the outcome of a campaign that barely started before being thwarted by the shipwreck caused by the huge storm that pummelled the Catalan coasts.

The *Llibre dels feits*, the veritable chronicle of the aspirations of James I, contains nothing that leads us to imagine any desire or strategy similar to those of the Norman princes of Sicily, the Hohenstaufens or the Angevins, or anything that even minimally resembles them. The silence of the *Llibre dels feits* is even more surprising if we consider that during

James I's period of expansion throughout the Mediterranean, the capital, Barcelona, was in the throes of urban Gothic cultural development as the city that had been transformed into the great capital of the Catalan-Aragonese Crown where the court usually resided. Barcelona would prosper throughout the entire 13th century and would definitively take off during the 14th century when, under Peter the Ceremonious, the great Saló del Tinell (Figure 17) was built in the Palau Reial in around 1359-1370 and the Gothic Drassanes shipyards were completed in around 1381.

Figure 17: Royal Palace, *Saló del Tinell* (1359-1370), Barcelona.

Under James I, Barcelona was not a modern city; instead, it looked more Romanesque and had just begun its slow march towards the Gothic. In order for this artistic progress to fully unfold, it had to await the construction of the new cathedral which got underway in 1298, along with the introduction of the new convent orders and the construction of the grand Gothic churches (Figure 18) of Santa Maria del Mar (1329), Santa Maria del Pi (1329) and Sant Just (1342). It was not yet the city that one century later offered a prestigious, authoritative, official monumental landscape with the new Palau de la Generalitat, the Hospital de la Santa Creu and the new façade of the Casa de la Ciutat. However, it is true that three years prior to the death of James I in 1273, the celebrated Saló del Consell de Cent was opened in this building (Figure 19).

Figure 18: Church of Santa Maria del Mar (14th century), Barcelona.

Figure 19: Palace Council of Barcelona, *Saló de Cent* (1369-1372)

Historians have no qualms about attributing this subsequent artistic impetus to the artistic desires and political and religious project spearheaded by Peter the Ceremonious. Destined to be a huge economic and political centre of the medieval Mediterranean, in addition to a hub of different cultures, at that point the city of Barcelona began to manifest its prestige and wealth in the realm of art with the representation of power and the court and with the monumental translation of this reality through the new architectural ambitions from which the Palau Reial and the cathedral would benefit. The onset of Gothic art also represented the aspiration to a new life of beauty within the framework of an artistic feeling that was closely tied to the courtly spirit which definitively overcame the austerity of the Romanesque.

Another quite different example of the relationship between architecture, identity and power in the Middle Ages can be found a little over a century later, when Alfonso the Magnanimous, Alfonso IV of Catalonia and Aragon (1396-1458), occupied Naples in 1442. At that time, despite its development, Barcelona could not compare with the main cities in the new Renaissance, humanistic Italy as a capital and centre of culture. Alfonso moved to the castle of the Angevins and kept its chapel and the main living and reception quarters. At times the decision to conserve a monument is also a political decision. For example, by resuming construction of Castelnuovo, Alfonso sought to maintain the Gothic chapel of his Angevin ancestors, and he did so deliberately. However, the way a prince wishes to guide his image for posterity can also be perceived through the style of a work and the choice of artists; thus, the promoter of a monumental work of art understands that it can also express a political stance. Alfonso expressed this by commissioning a triumphal arch to officially signal the entrance to the castle, an intense reflection of the Renaissance taste of the period (Figure 20). With the exaltation of his own power, the monarch was imposing his legitimacy in both the present and future history in marble. Alfonso the Magnanimous wanted to be a renowned patron of the arts and culture, a true sponsor, a man of his times in Italian humanism. He wanted to hire the best artists of the day, and he even wanted the great Donatello (1386-1466) to work on his arch at the entry to the castle.

Figure 20: Triumph of Alfonso the Magnanimous (1452-1471), Castelnuovo of Naples.

And herein lies another personality feature which leads us to reflect on the identity awareness associated with the expression of power. As we have seen, the Gothic culture in Barcelona was not the most innovative at the time, especially compared to the new tastes of the Italian Renaissance. Yet Alfonso the Magnanimous called to Naples artists like the Mallorcan architect and sculptor Guillem Sagrera and the sculptor Guillem Sagrera, the son of Jordi de Déu, who would have never been regarded as avant-garde artists in Italy. The most surprising part is that he commissioned a deliberately out of date Catalan-style Gothic arch to surmount the throne room where he was to welcome the greatest men of his day, which today seems impossible to understand either culturally or artistically (Figure 21). However, it can only be explained by the desire to express origins and identity.

Figure 21: Alfonso the Magnanimous' Saloon, called "The Barons Saloon", Castelnuovo of Naples.

3. Recovering the Middle Ages as a symbol of identity

During the 1840s, a renewed taste for the Middle Ages developed in both France and other countries in Romantic Europe. This trend tended to ignore looking back at the ancient world as neoclassicism did to instead seek the origins of the nation on both a local and regional scale at a time when the medieval nationalities were being shaped, which back then were associated with the birth and development of the Romanesque art of each specific place. This awareness, spurred by literary and artistic Romanticism, quickly led to the study of medieval art, which at that time was practically unknown, and to the creation of institutions charged with protecting and restoring this long-neglected heritage. Great names of the day, such as Prosper Mérimée (1803-1870) and Eugène Viollet-le-Duc (1814-1879), got involved in this task, which art historians like Émile Mâle (1862-1954) in France, Manuel Gómez Moreno (1870-1970) in Castile and Josep Puig i Cadafalch (1867-1956) in Catalonia transformed into a national debate based on the overarching question of Romanesque geography and claims that the art from one region predated its counterpart from another.

In Catalonia, the popular movement to revive the medieval past, primarily Romanesque at that time, came later, and the nationalist fervour at the height of the Renaixença was reinforced with the restoration of the monastery of Ripoll in 1885, even though the first project dated from twenty years earlier (Figure 22). The architect Elies Rogent (1821-1897) was the master of a generation whose energies would be spent reviving the country's artistic roots. In the early 20th century, Josep Puig i Cadafalch, an architect and politician, as the president of the Mancomunitat de Catalunya, was the erudite driving force behind this revival. He had understood and wished to demonstrate that a theory about Catalan national Romanesque art should come hand in hand with a systematic study of its monuments, an undertaking which he himself performed aided by Antoni de Falguera and Josep Goday. As a result of this undertaking, they published the four volumes of the *L'arquitectura romànica a Catalunya* between 1909 and 1918 (Figure 23).

Figure 22: Ruins of the Church of Santa Maria de Ripoll (1835).

Figure 23: Cover of the book *L'arquitectura romànica a Catalunya (1909-1918)* by Josep Puig i Cadafalch, Antoni de Falguera and Josep Goday.

In these volumes, Puig classified Romanesque art into two periods: the first was characterised by the shift from the wooden truss to the vault and was thereafter called the early Romanesque art, while in the second, starting in the 12th century, the Romanesque church was architecturally well-finished and decorated with sculptures from the façade to the cloister. When stressing the importance of Catalonia, Puig was forced to decide whether these artistic movements were generated in Catalonia itself or whether they had arisen abroad and reached Catalonia later. Out of caution, he chose the latter hypothesis. These movements had not arisen first on the Iberian Peninsula but in northern Italy or even further inside Italy. And Puig i Cadafalch did not hesitate to search for these more distant roots, travelling through today's Croatia, Armenia and even Moldova. Having emerged from these countries, the forms had travelled and had thus been transformed and fine-tuned until they reached Catalonia.

At that time, Catalonia had the institutions it needed to safeguard its cultural heritage. The revival of the Romanesque past was one of the spearheads of political projects in favour of autonomy which in the early 20th century pushed the nationalist leaders of Catalonia to create a number of cultural institutions devoted to studying and assessing its medieval past. The most notable examples are the Institut d'Estudis Catalans, following the model of the Institut de France, and the Junta de Museus ("Board of Museums"), which led to the creation of the future Museu d'Art de Catalunya ("Art Museum of Catalonia") in Barcelona. At the same time, they organised the study of the country's most distant past with the excavations in Empúries and the Museu Arqueològic ("Archaeologic Museum").

Between 1908 and 1912, the Institut d'Estudis Catalans and the Junta de Museus published a series of fascicles on Romanesque murals under the direction of Josep Pijoan. They can be regarded as the baseline, the underpinning, of a new culture that looked back at the medieval past, inspired – it should be said – by similar French undertakings that had preceded them. This formidable collective enterprise, which entailed considerable enthusiasm as well as energies, along with the desire to avoid exporting abroad a heritage which was finally beginning to be considered a founding aspect of the nation, also prompted debates among the leading scholars of the day.

Some, like Puig i Cadafalch, indeed supported the conservation of the paintings in situ for heritage reasons, but the risk of watching them disappear in the hands of antiquarians, collectors or foreign museums led to the unanimous decision to remove the paintings from Pedret, Boí, La Seu d'Urgell, Taüll and Burgal, along with many other locations, to the museum in Barcelona (Figure 24). Between 1919 and 1923, Italian technicians, accompanied by numerous Catalan experts, proceeded to undertake one of the most extraordinary operations to extract, transfer and restore huge stretches of Romanesque murals. And thus the Museu d'Art de Catalunya came to house one of the most important collections of medieval murals ever assembled in a museum to date.

Figure 24: Removing the Romanesque mural paintings in the Pyrenees (1922).

Saving the murals from the Pyrenees was tantamount to saving the nation, and it was somehow regarded as an operation aimed at recovering Catalan identity. While in France the neo-medieval movement had emerged in the 19th century under the aegis of Romanticism, in Catalonia – fully into the 20th century and within the era of the nationalisms of the first third of that century – the operation to recover the past took on a clearly political meaning.

Another aspect of the revival of the Middle Ages as a symbol of identity was restorations. Our idea of Catalan Romanesque art today, primarily architecture, stemmed from many of Josep Puig i Cadafalch's studies, which had agendas that intertwined politics and restoration. Architects' restorations have always influenced the subsequent image of a past time, and the architect's knowledge, interest or convictions have almost always affected later studies of the monument.

At that time, Catalan architects dreamed about restoring the lost monumentality of the Romanesque buildings by eliminating the superfluous, poorer-quality elements which had been added at later dates. All of the restorations by Josep Puig i Cadafalch aimed to be faithful to what he regarded as the original monument and to a Middle Age which he considered the outcome of an evolution that he himself had helped to construct.

For this reason, the architecture of the Romanesque basilica of Ripoll is not the medieval building but the outcome of how Elies Rogent saw Romanesque architecture from his vantage point in the 19th century. Likewise, the chancel in the basilica of Sant Joan de les Abadesses and the architecture of the small Santa Cecília church on Montserrat directly reflect Josep Puig i Cadafalch's vision of medieval art well into the 20th century (Figure 25). And this is neither good nor bad; rather, it is simply a fact that should be noted in history. The consequences of these interventions often lead art historians, especially with the 19th century interventions, to study a medieval monument as if it were truly medieval, when in fact it is modern or contemporary. Each monument has its own history and most recent interventions, just as those by the architect Antoni González Moreno-Navarro in Sant Quirze de Pedret or in Sant Llorenç near Bagà are already part of the monument's history (Figure 26).

Reviving the Middle Ages as a symbol of Catalan identity, recovering a medieval monument and through its restoration creating a unit representing a regional style, or at least creating it more or less consciously, fully belongs to the history of a nation, to the ideology through which we aim to regard the past, and to the everyday and cultural life of those intervening. For this reason, in Catalonia, for example, some of the interventions performed on monuments during the Franco dictatorship reflect an ideology that somehow sought to make Catalonia Spain. Yet at other points in history, the claims for the medieval artistic heritage can become a cry for independence.

Figure 25: Apse of the Church of Sant Joan de les Abadesses (12th century, restaured by Josep Puig i Cadafalch).

Figure 26: Pre-romanesque Church of Sant Quirze de Pedret (restaured by Antoni González Moreno-Navarro).

Museums are not above these problems, as museographic presentations of the medieval past guide the history of art and therefore imbue history with one meaning or another. And this is normal because both museographic agendas and the restoration of monuments entail personal or institutional decisions that reflect the political time in which they are taken and the personal positions of their authors.

The historiography of Romanesque art in Catalonia, just like everywhere, is ultimately the story of a long quest for identity. Understanding the Middle Ages, protecting its vestiges, making an inventory of them and studying, restoring and presenting them pedagogically as places that should be seen or showing them in museums are just so many other stages in decisions that entail taking a position on the past and the vestiges of history.

4. Artistic emblems of Catalan identity with medieval roots

Sometimes art histories limit themselves to regarding art as only architecture, sculpture and painting, with only cursory glances at other minor art forms, such as objects, manuscripts and ephemeral staged productions. But art is much more than this because there are many other forms of art beyond the ones that serve the power and money of the wealthiest, both religious and in secular society.

It is difficult to define the boundaries of art, meaning the limits of our cultural heritage. What is art, what should be conserved, when, how and why? We should insist on proclaiming that the notion of art is very far-ranging and covers everything that is created by the hand of man, which is sometimes called "crafts". If we expand the notion of art to our artistic heritage, then we realise that our heritage is always mementos, memories, history, inheritances and experiences, both past and present. Over the years, the notion of cultural heritage has been expanded and has even become fashionable; we have veered away from the old idea that it only covered historical monuments and architectures of the past so it now invades the fields of ethnology, society and collective identity.

Without a doubt, heritage is one of those elements that makes us a nation and serves as a vital bond in historical cohesion. Let us take the case of the monastery of Montserrat, for example. It would be very limiting to define it artistically only as architecture or the works of art that are part of it, because the monastery of Montserrat is identity and defines the nation, yet not only through its architecture, when it was built or at the different times it was improved. It is identity because the Catalan people have made it a place of memory and because all the art found there has been and still is used by people who identify with it. And this concept generates artistic creation through the new architectures needed to house pilgrimages. These forms of collective religious practice take the shape of votive offerings, souvenirs and prints and the different interpretations of the Moreneta, the medieval Virgin Mary of Montserrat. But most importantly we should mention the ephemeral stagings of collective experiences, liturgical experiences and experiences of patriotic fervour (Figure 27).

Figure 27: *La Moreneta* ("The Black Madonna"), wood sculpture 12th century, restaured (Church of Santa Maria de Montserrat).

In the early 1980s, the publication of an erudite yet also somewhat diffuse collection was launched in France under the supervision of the historian Pierre Nora. It was entitled *Les Lieux de Mémoire* ("The Places of Memory"). In this book, art was integrated into monuments, commemoration sites, landscapes, cultural heritage, the glories of the nation, traditions and places or acts which reveal a country's identity.

In the same vein, when defining artistic emblems of identity, we should consider a much broader notion of art and art history in order to embrace the entire complexity of creation, including how it is used, that is, ephemeral phenomena that turn it into identity.

The artistic emblems of identity may be linked to the land, customs or way of living. The Costa Brava, the Delta d'Ebre, the large cities and towns, the sea, rivers and mountains are all constituent elements in that they are the home to a landscape that is modified which man has influenced with architecture and ways of living. Just like the cathedral and the monastery, the country estate (*masia*), the house, the factory or the market are artistic emblems of a culture that is usually defined through periods and styles: Romanesque, Gothic, Renaissance, Baroque, Modernisme, Noucentisme, etc.

In this context of architecture, landscape and life, there are places of collective memory which serve as artistic emblems: the monasteries of Ripoll and Poblet, pantheons of the counts and monarchs of Catalonia, respectively; the Saló del Tinell in Barcelona's Palau Reial and the Saló de Cent in the Town Hall; the Palau de la Generalitat; the Gran Teatre del Liceu opera house; and the Palau de la Música Catalana: they are all obvious places which can be joined with many other more popular ones, such as the monument to Columbus and the Sagrada Família in Barcelona; several very contemporary ones such as the Miró Foundation in Barcelona and Palau Sant Jordi stadium; and places which themselves generate art, such as the town of Cadaqués.

And taking this reflection even further, we can find symbols like the four stripes of the Catalan flag, the *barretina* ("traditional Catalan cap"), the *caganer* ("a scatological figure in Catalan nativity scenes") and the Cobi mascot from the 1992 Olympics, all of which belong to an everyday reality in which creativity has been totally embraced as an even minuscule part of the collective imagination of a people. We could further add the language itself and some of its set expressions like *goigs* (religious couplets devoted to the Virgin Mary, God or Jesus Christ) and even Pompeu Fabra's dictionary of the Catalan language.

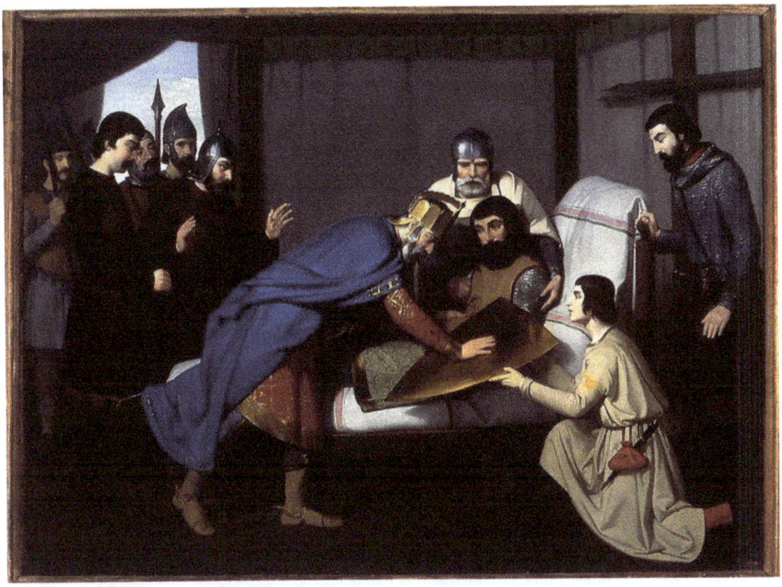

Figure 28: Painting known as *Mort de Guifré el Pilós* ("Death of Wilfred the Hairy") by Claudi Lorenzale (around 1843), Reial Acadèmia de Belles Arts de Sant Jordi, Barcelona.

Historical figures can equally be considered artistic emblems of identity through a collective imagination that has transformed the history or legend of each of them in art. Wilfred the Hairy and the legend of the four stripes were enthusiastically embraced by 19th century artists (Figure 28), while Abbot Oliba has been immortalised with monuments and public monumental sculptures, as have James I the Conqueror and Count Ramon Berenguer. The sculptor Josep Clarà made a celebrated bust of President Francesc Macià, while a statue of the great footballer Kubala is a fixture at the entrance to Camp Nou. All of this is also memory more or less directly related to the historical reality, which prompts a look back into the past.

Another aspect of these emblems which are actually places of collective memory is related to works of art that have been promoted so avidly that they have become prime collective symbols, sometimes even erroneously. This is the case of the Romanesque Christ painted in the Middle Ages to decorate the apse of Sant Climent church in Taüll, which today is an attraction at the Museu Nacional d'Art de Catalunya (Figure 29). More than any other work of medieval art, the Christ of Taüll is reproduced daily in tourist brochures on Catalonia to supposedly represent the peak of medieval creativity at the founding of the nation. That monumental Christ shown frontally, a *Maiestas Domini* who blesses and is carrying a book between the alpha and the omega inside a "mandorla", prompts a powerful visual effect because of the sobriety of the lines, the intensity of the eyes and the fact that it has been associated with the austerity of the Romanesque style. However, in this case the medieval reality was probably different, and what we regard today as a major work of Catalan medieval art may then have been a mural in a small mountain church which was probably not even comparable with the great productions that emerged from the centres of power, in this case Church power, that is, the great cathedrals or the most important monasteries.

Figure 29: Mural Painting of the apse of Sant Climent de Taüll (12th century) (Museu Nacional d'Art de Catalunya, Barcelona).

Figure 30: *Ball de diables* ("Devils dance") (Catalonia, 2013).

One of the factors that perhaps best joins the Middle Ages with today's world in the field of collective celebrations is festivals with religious or pagan origins, its image conveyed through costumes, music, games or dance (Figure 30). Each town and each social group has its own emblems of identity in the world of festivals based on celebrations of patron saints or other moments of collective exaltation and identity-based fervour. The *sardana* dance, *havanera* music, *castellers* (human towers), bonfires and *gegants* (figures of giants) are traditions that involve artistic creation in both the crafting of the objects and the rites that surround the celebration. In this sphere, we could apply the symbols of identity to a patron saint of the entire country, like Saint George for Catalonia, which generates an entire body of iconographic symbolism on the saint's day (Figure 31). There are many other examples which more or less directly hark back to the Middle Ages or the collective history. Every year, as the national day commemorating a precise event, the Eleventh of September leads to more or less ephemeral art and creativity related to the reality at that time. We could even add different sporting events, like Barça in football, which yield art in the guise of clothing, merchandising, trophies and even stadium architecture. All of these cases, involve factors which are the components of creativity, the creativity of a specific place, its geography and climate, the season of the year or the customs.

Figure 31: Small Gothic Sculpture of Saint George (Generalitat Palace, currently in the Museu Nacional d'Art de Catalunya).

5. Modifying medieval identity through contemporary religious architecture

During the 19th century, when Catalonia was emerging from neoclassicism and joining Romanticism and the new nationalisms in Europe, identity questions were in the air. Later, in his opening speech for academic year 1889-1890 at the Centre Escolar Catalanista of Barcelona, over which he presided, Josep Puig i Cadafalch strove to define what making a national art history would be to him:

> *Comença el catalanisme escorcollant arxius, fotografiant monuments, calcant làpides, classificant monedes, buscant rondalles i cançons, fent inventari dels costums i trajos, ressuscitant el llenguatge; i què és tot això sinó observar la pàtria, escorcollant la seva realitat?*[2]

> Catalanism began scrutinizing archives, photographing monuments, tracing tombstones, sorting coins, searching for stories and songs, making inventory of customs and dress, reviving the language; and what is this without observing the country, scrutinizing its reality?

Many of these issues would lead us to another debate on the past, how the ties with the present are expressed and how this should be done. Developing a national art history is and has been overseen by many governments via their cultural estates, which exercise a positive or negative role depending on what course they take. In Catalonia, the nationalist cultivation of art history is recent and dates no further back than the early 20th century. The core of its revival was medieval art. The first to follow the model of France, where this issue had been under consideration since the mid-19th century, was Father Josep Gudiol i Cunill (1872-1931). Taking advantage of the momentum caused by the work of Bishop Josep Morgades (1826-1901), the restoration of Ripoll and the creation of the Museu Episcopal de Vic, in 1902 Gudiol published *Nocions d'arqueologia sagrada catalana*[3], which was reissued in 1931-1933 (Figure 32). By sketching a timeline specifically for Catalonia superimposed upon

2 Josep Puig, *Escrits d'arquitectura, art i política...*, p. 203.

3 Josep Gudiol, *Nocions d'arqueologia sagrada catalana* (Vic: Imprenta de la Viuda de P. Anglada, 1902).

the European timeline, and by covering what at that time was understood as archaeology, especially monumental archaeology from the ancient world until the 19th century, though primarily stressing the Middle Ages, Gudiol offered the first synthesis, an educational text that was targeted at Catalans so that they could discover, learn about and love their past and the artistic originality of Catalonia. A little later, as mentioned above, between 1909 and 1918, Josep Puig i Cadafalch, who had experienced the late Renaixença, observed the actions of the architect Rogent, tracked the restorations of different monuments and aimed his life at the politics, architecture and art of Catalonia. In doing so, he became aware that the country needed catalogues of monuments and published *L'arquitectura romànica a Catalunya*. From Puig to Joaquim Folch i Torres (1886-1963), others kept reflecting on the relationship between art and nation, writing seminal works until the late 1930s. However, after the Civil War and during the Franco dictatorship, it was more difficult for Catalan art history not to be included within Spanish art history for a period, although this vision was gradually modified within the last third of the 20th century.

Between the mid-19th century and the early decades of the 21st century, we have witnessed different ways in which the Middle Ages has been more or less consciously restored. I would like to summarise some of them.

After Romanticism, the first style that looked back towards the Middle Ages is Modernisme (the Catalan version of Art Nouveau), which in Catalonia has been, was and will be a controversial artistic movement. To some people, it is a national symbol of Catalonia and nothing more. But to others it signals a break with academicism, a return to the traditional trades and the unleashing of the most exuberant fantasy. To many, Modernisme is a retrograde movement which emerged from the poor taste of a bourgeois which suddenly found itself wealthy but lacked a secular, artistic, cultural tradition. However, everyone recognises the prominent role played by the medieval heritage in Modernisme. When swept away by Noucentisme, Modernisme ceased to be practised as a style and fell out of fashion; in fact, it was reviled until its revival during the second half of the 20th century.

Figure 32: Cover of the book *Nocions d'arqueologia sagrada catalana (1902)* by Josep Gudiol.

One aspect of the contemporary view of the medieval past is religious architecture, and the most celebrated example among tourists, Barcelona's Sagrada Família, stands head and shoulders above all other constructions. It was begun in 1882 by Francisco de Paula del Villar (1828-1901) and later continued by Antoni Gaudí (1852-1926) from 1884 until his death. It is still unfinished today and has been the subject of controversy on how it is being completed, as an exact replica of Gaudí's legacy (Figure 33).

Figure 33: Church of the *Sagrada Família* ("Holy Family"), Antoni Gaudí, Barcelona.

At a time when the modern city was undergoing expansion and the development of industry, the Sagrada Família was regarded as anti-urban and anti-modern because on the one hand it ignores, destroys or downplays the modernity and rigour of Cerdà's Eixample district, while on the other it signals a return to the Middle Ages without any desire to update it, especially in terms of its iconography. Religiosity and the kind of provocative Catholicism it conveys are obsolete (Figure 34); the Sagrada Família seeks to redeem metropolitan secularism through architecture, to redeem the sins of an entire civilisation that was moving towards modernity at breakneck speed. The Holy Family, the Trinity, the Apostles and the Church are glorified in what was supposed to be the start of an expiatory temple, the clearest example of anti-modernity, especially in terms of the ideology behind it, and in the sculpture that strove to immortalise these ideas. However, while in the part that was completed, Francisco de Paula del Villar had envisioned a clearly neo-medieval basilica, Gaudí reinterpreted this architecture with this creative brilliance. With the Sagrada

Família, Gaudí changed his own life, orienting himself spiritually towards beatitude and contemplation, towards a past that would never come back. Gaudí's major innovation in the Sagrada Familia is the shift from neo-Gothic to a new architecture, without having to raze the part of the preceding project that had already been built. As the temple was erected, Gaudí shifted from the early neo-Gothic to the new forms that he was creating. Gaudí spent many years of effort and research in order to design a new column in a new order that would go beyond the classical orders (Doric, Ionic, Corinthian, composite, etc.) and their different variations developed throughout the centuries of the Middle Ages. He wanted a column that would be similar to what he observed in nature, one that had the same appearance and expressiveness and that would externalise all the strength of the support to withstand weight, as well as a growing spiral movement, similar to trees, which he viewed as a symbol of life. Thus, Gaudí updated the medieval concept of associating the symbolism of the building and architectural technique (Figure 35).

Figure 34: Façade of the Nativity, *Sagrada Família* ("Holy Family"), Barcelona.

Figure 35: Vaults of *Sagrada Família* ("Holy Family"), Barcelona.

One very different example of the return to the Middle Ages, more run-of-the-mill but no less creative, is the basilica on Tibidabo, which in the early 20th century, when construction got underway, situated the city of Barcelona on par with other European cities in terms of the cultural heritage that most directly imitated the Middle Ages (Figure 36). In neighbouring France, too, there was no dearth of models of this sort. During the entire 19th century but especially towards the end of it, numerous cities wanted to build monuments to triumphant Catholicism, expiatory basilicas and buildings whose size and location served two ideological purposes: first, to symbolically dominate the other constructions in the city, religious or not, because of their location, and secondly to ensure that as a result of this elevated location no other urban building could ever rise to their height. Somehow, the goal was to physically manifest the dream of the medieval cathedral which dominated the urban setting from the centre of the city using the higher lands that had been appropriated in the city centres as their boundaries were pushed outward.

Figure 36: Basilica of Tibidabo (Josep Maria Sagnier, started in 1902), Barcelona.

Today, in the age of travel and tourism, we are paradoxically witnessing the contradiction that the dominant basilicas are frequently visited monuments in their cities, yet this fervour is experienced with as much tourist curiosity as with the goal of pilgrimage. In addition to these general traits, I wish to recall a few of the many central monuments in collective religiosity as the Sacré-Coeur in Montmartre, Paris; the one built on the peak of Fourvière hill which dominates the city of Lyon; and Notre-Dame de la Garde in Marseille. Another symbol of the dominance of the Middle Ages over the modern city is the gigantic, pharaonic, monumental statues placed atop a mountain and illuminated by night to keep a watchful eye on the sound social morality of the city below.

The neo-Gothic basilica on Barcelona's Tibidabo was begun in 1902 by architect Enric Sagnier (1858-1931) and continued by his son; construction lasted almost 60 years. The sculptures on the doorway by Eusebi Arnau and other decorative elements in the church also hark back to the recollection of the Middle Ages. The basilica is topped by an enormous bronze statue of the sacred heart by Frederic Marès (1893-1991), which today seems like a symbol of the past that aims to engage with a nearby symbol of the present, the Collserola telecommunications tower (1988-1992) designed by British architect Norman Foster. It is more than 200 metres tall and has a curvilinear triangular metal platform with 13 storeys measuring 63 metres tall. This secular challenge clashes with the religious goal represented by the construction of the Sagrat Cor basilica. Both structures dominate the city and soar skywards. They are both emblematic and from the 20th century. Does one represent artistic progress and the other artistic anti-progress?

Just like in the Middle Ages, construction work on the basilica of Tibidabo lasted many years. Even before it was finished, the artistic taste that these constructions express had fallen out of fashion, even though major artists of the day had been called upon to both build and to decorate it with sculpture, mosaic or painting. We should say that this was also what probably would have happened in the Middle Ages. Halfway between the glorification of past styles (neo-Gothic and neo-Romanesque) and the application of new metal technologies in religious architecture, these visionary architectures have not yet found a place of their own in art history, but they do contribute to keeping alive a dream of the Middle Ages brought to fruition.

The basilica on Tibidabo is dominated by a gigantic statue, just like the aforementioned Notre-Dame de la Garde in Marseille. In Rio de Janeiro, the Christ Redeemer also dominates the city from above. In Le Puy-en-Velay, the medieval town in the department of Haute-Loire celebrated for its Romanesque monuments, the cathedral itself stands slightly beneath the salmon-coloured metal statue of Notre-Dame de France. Visitors queue up to enter it and climb the inner staircase which, just like the Eiffel Tower, leads to more than three storey height, which allowed until quite recently, after reaching the landings of the Our Lady and the Christ Child, them to emerge from the head in the middle of the crown of the Queen of Heaven. Through these grandiose examples, the Middle Ages became an everyday part of the tourism of our times.

Even today, religious architecture from the 19th and 20th centuries is generally misunderstood. During the 19th century, the construction of churches essentially looked back to the past in the belief that the Middle Ages was when the highest understanding of holy buildings and their decoration had been achieved. In Catalonia, 20th century religious architecture probably began with the commission that Antoni Gaudí received to build the church in the industrial colony that the Güell family owned in Santa Coloma de Cervelló (1908-1915); today the only part still standing is the crypt. Antoni Gaudí's two main accomplishments were examples of religious architecture in the Modernista style (the Sagrada Familia and the Güell crypt); they are joined by the restorations and reforms carried out by Josep Puig i Cadafalch (Sant Joan de les Abadesses, Sant Martí Sarroca and Montserrat). Other important stops in this journey are occasional works, such as the Sagrat Cor church on Tibidabo by Enric Sagnier, mentioned above, and the chapel at the Universitat Industrial de Barcelona (1927) by Joan Rubió i Bellver (1871-1952).

The stance on the architecture of the Middle Ages was one of the most hotly debated issues during those decades. Josep Maria Jujol (1879-1949), for instance, took different models: he got some influence from the decorativism of Baroque architectu re when he built, between 1915 and 1929, an elliptical-strapped chapel for Masia Negre in Sant Joan Despí (Baix Llobregat); and, the same time, around 1918-1919 he accepted the built a structure within an existing construction in the cubicle devoted to Our Lady of Mount Carmen in the chapel of Carmelite convent in Tarragona which was clearly neo-Gothic in design. These concerns regarding the medieval past can be clearly seen in the two great works built in the third decade of the century in the region of Tarragona (Figure 37): the monumental Sagrat Cor church in Vistabella (1918-1923) and Mare de Déu de Montserrat sanctuary in Montferri (1926-1929). The neo-medieval model had a long life in 20th century Catalan religious architecture, but among the architects working in the second half of the century it often signalled a vision of the past instead of a quest for modernity.

Figure 37: Church Basilica of Our Lady of Montserrat (Josep Maria Jujol, 1926-1935), Montferri.

Beyond Franco-style neoclassicism, the Church emerged from a long slumber on liturgical matters with Vatican II, yet doubts also arose and after 1964 the architecture of space became difficult to understand, with new structural and functional models, new aesthetic expressions, new monumental configurations and the gradual appearance of a religious architecture which fell fully within the general architectural currents of the day. The main architects of this new period wondered whether the new architectural forms or the new materials were good enough to build Christian churches; that is, they were examining the relationship between architecture, contemporary art, faith and the revival of the past.

During the 1970s, the architects who built churches continued to ponder the ideal style for a Christian church. However, the discussion did not stem from the goal of finding an ideal structure for the organisation and rites of the modern Church but from the question of whether the traditional forms should be maintained. A tendency gradually emerged to view religious buildings as adaptable multipurpose structures, in clear opposition to the typological quests of the 1940s and 1950s. Some defended an open kind of construction not designed specifically for worship, following the ideas of Mies van der Rohe (1886-1969), who first built a practical form and later adapted it to the purpose it served. In some cases, the passage of time has shown that the construction of multipurpose buildings was quite a valid solution for late-20th century religious architecture. The most obvious proof of this is churches which have been repurposed, such as Sant Sebastià parish church on Barcelona's Via Favència (designed by the Martorell/Bohigas/Mackay studio in 1958). It was built somewhat tentatively using prefabricated materials and parts, with the only symbolic element identifying it as a church being a large, freestanding concrete cross on the outside. Today this construction is used as a school.

6. Containers and exhibitors of the medieval past for the use of many

The last two centuries of Catalan art have witnessed three collective events that have generated artistic activities with far-reaching implications: the 1888 Universal Exposition, the 1929 Universal Exposition and the 1992

Olympics. The Olympics prompted a wide variety of art forms, but the most representative and coherent were industrial and graphic design and architecture and urban planning. The size of the event contributed to spreading awareness of the art of Catalonia far and wide.

At that time, within just a few years in the 1980s Barcelona took an enormous qualitative leap in the field of architecture, urban planning and the relationship between conserving the past, urban planning and contemporary art. After 1979, the Barcelona Town Hall, under mayors Narcís Serra and Pasqual Maragall, who during the planning years were advised primarily by architect Oriol Bohigas (Barcelona, 1925), began to transform the city while taking advantage of the urban framework of the General Metropolitan Plan. After 1983, Europe's attention was drawn around the monumental changes occurring in the city of Barcelona, which was trying to respond to issues that were puzzling urban planners, architects and artists everywhere: new neighbourhoods and how they interweave with the older ones, historical or not; the relationship between urban planning and monuments; and the financing of public art commissions with a mixture of private patronage and institutional orders. The goal was to ascertain whether the city itself could be a site of contemporary art installed right in the heart of the medieval quarter, whether it could become a monument of the future and whether works of art should decorate humble, peripheral districts, more privileged areas or protected historical contexts. Studies were conducted on how to prevent potential aggressions against these works. The postulate was that, just like in our most distant past, the quality of art should contribute to improving everyday aesthetics, citizen behaviour and the harmony of life.

I would like to focus on several works that refer directly to diverse aspects of the medieval past and offer different solutions. The Palau del Lloctinent, located between Barcelona's Plaça del Rei and the Museu Marès, is a site housing archives. Commissioned by the Courts of Montsó in 1547, this lieutenant's resident, which was built on a plot of land next to the Palau Reial Major between 1549 and 1557, was never actually inhabited, and some areas of it remained unfinished. In 1838, the decision was taken to house the Archive of the Crown of Aragon there, and it thus underwent several reforms between 1850 and 1853. In 1931, it was declared a historical-artistic monument along with the Palau Reial Major and was once again restored by architect Jeroni Martorell (1877-1951). In 1994, the Archive was moved to a new building located in the

Sant Martí district, designed by architects Lluís Domènech i Girbau and Roser Amadó, which had opened in 1993. This major cultural facility – it is the most important medieval archive in Barcelona – is an example of renovation by moving. The Biblioteca Nacional de Catalunya, on the other hand, is an example of the adaptation of a medieval structure in situ. Started with the Library of the Institut d'Estudis Catalans (1907), the Biblioteca de Catalunya opened in 1940 in the former medieval hospital of Santa Creu in Barcelona's Raval neighbourhood, where readers were able to work in its magnificent 15th century medieval quarters (Figure 38).

Figure 38: Nacional Library of Catalonia (Former medieval hospital 15th century), Barcelona.

Another example of a container of the past in a modernised medieval context which has been an intense witness of the passage of the centuries is Barcelona's Casa de l'Ardiaca, located at number 1 Carrer de Santa Llúcia in the Gothic Quarter across from the cathedral. Along with the adjacent Casa del Degà, originally from the 12th century, this former residence of the leading dignitaries of the cathedral was remodelled during the 15th and 16th centuries. Archdeacon Lluís Desplà i d'Oms renovated the residence

(1469-1510) and turned it into an essentially Gothic house, but with elements that had a Renaissance feel. The expansion of the Pla de la Seu in 1420 required the Casa del Degà to be transformed. The bridge that used to join the Casa de l'Ardiaca and the Roman tower was demolished in 1823, and in 1870 both buildings were purchased by Josep Altimira, who decided to join them to make a single family residence. In 1895, the house became the headquarters of the Col·legi d'Advocats of Barcelona, which charged Lluís Domènech i Montaner (1850-1923) with decorating it. Purchased by the city in 1919, the Arxiu Històric de la Ciutat was installed there and remains there today. Between 1920 and 1922, a repurposing project was performed on this building by Josep Goday i Casals (1882-1936). This project consisted of raising the façade of the Casa del Degà to the height of the rest of the building, incorporating the gallery of segmented arches from the Casa de l'Ardiaca into the whole. Declared a historical-artistic monument in 1924, Adolf Florensa i Ferrer (1889-1968) supervised the façade reform projects (1955 and 1962), both of which were planned following historicist criteria.

In this case, it was more complicated to integrate contemporary rehabilitation architecture because the medieval building was joined by the presence of the city's Roman wall. The reform, which was completed in 1996, modified the first façade by totally redesigning both the interiors and the external appearance with prominent glass and steel tribunals that prolong the plain of the mural between three of its towers (Figure 39).

Figura 39: *Casa de l'Ardiaca* (Roman wall, new container, 1996), Barcelona.

The most up-to-date showcases and containers of medieval art are museums, the true cathedrals of art 20th and 21st century art. In Catalonia, the goal has been to preserve Catalan with a new museum, the Museu d'Història de Catalunya, which is housed in the Palau de Mar located in Plaça de Pau Vila in the Barceloneta neighbourhood. Designed in 1881, the former Magatzems Generals de Comerç, which were used to store the goods that arrived by sea, was renamed the Palau de Mar when it was remodelled in 1992. The architects Josep Benedito and Agustí Mateos rehabilitated the warehouses, restoring the technical and architectural beauty of a monument that was also meant to be part of the cultural heritage. Opened in 1996, the museum analyses the history of the country from prehistory until today in chronological order.

A better example of the relationship between the medieval past and today's museums is the Museu Marítim of Barcelona, housed in the city's medieval Drassanes Reials (royal shipyards) (Figure 40). The facilities were created by Peter II the Great in the late 13th century in order to have a space where galleys that were exclusively at the service of the crown could be built and maintained. In the mid-14th century, Peter III the Ceremonious ordered the first building to be constructed on the premises, which had a series of smaller pillars and arches than the current building. Towards the end of the century, the same monarch decided to replace that first structure with two series of arches and pillars, which formed the bays on the mountain side and the bays on the sea side – two of which remain, forming the main façade – separated by a central courtyard.

This complex became one of the premises protected by the city thanks to a change in the layout of the wall during the reign of Peter III. In the mid-15th century, it was joined by a new construction: the Botiga Nova of the Diputació del General, which is wholly conserved today. This building was financed by the Generalitat to store the materials, tools and wares of the galleys owned by this institution. The main body of the building was constructed in the second half of the 16th century, as shown in recent archaeological and document studies. The eight bays are placed on top of the medieval structure. Apart from the medieval wall, the Drassanes Reials as a whole had numerous fortified elements throughout its history. Today it is an excellent example of a heritage museum.

Figure 40: Maritime Museum (Gothic shipyards), Barcelona.

Things are simpler when a medieval building is used to house a museum on medieval art and the history of the country or an institution that represents it. Next to the cathedral of Barcelona, an old building called the Canonja (because of the community of canons from the cathedral who lived there in the 14th century) is the site of the Museu Diocesà of Barcelona. The Canonja was torn down in 1400, and in around 1423 the right part of the building standing today was built in alignment with the slope of the Canonja, and Pia Almoina was installed there. Founded in 1009 to provide assistance to the poor and ill, this charitable institution had previously occupied a building which had to be torn down to build the cloister of the cathedral. The second body of the building, whose façade was on Avinguda de la Catedral, was built in 1546 by integrating the remains of older buildings, including a tower from the Roman wall. The Pia Almoina started to decline in the 18th century and ceased operating in the 19th century. In the early 1970s, upon the decision of the archbishopric of Barcelona, the building was totally remodelled and refurbished by Josep Maria Botey in order to house the Museu Diocesà.

It has two sections, the museum per se, which is based on the Canonja, and the temporary exhibition area. The architect's overarching idea was to conserve the different architectural stages in a visible way and to achieve a new architecture that was representative of today yet had medieval resonances.

The main showcase of medieval Catalan art is located atop Montjuïc mountain looking out over and dominating Plaça d'Espanya, the site of the Palau Nacional, the headquarters of the Museu Nacional d'Art de Catalunya (MNAC), created in 1990. It is made up of the pre-existing centres of the Museu d'Art de Catalunya, the Museu d'Art Modern, the Gabinet de Dibuixos i Gravats, the Gabinet Numismàtic de Catalunya and the Biblioteca General d'Història de l'Art, and it has expanded with new research, exhibition and restoration centres. The collection of the Museu d'Art de Catalunya is exceptionally important and the outcome of a long, complex history of how it was assembled. A visit to the MNAC's current collections, most of them featuring Catalan art, enable us to construct a history of the country's art from the Romanesque to the 21st century, giving it its due importance within Western art (Figure 41).

Figure 41: Romanesque Descent from the Cross of Taüll (Museu Nacional d'Art de Catalunya, Barcelona).

The Palau Nacional building is one of the city's most emblematic architectural symbols, yet also one of the most controversial. It was built very quickly for the 1929 Barcelona International Exposition. After 1934, it permanently consolidated its position as a museum when the Museu d'Art de Catalunya was installed there. The palace's Gran Saló, which was used for concerts and massive gatherings during the Exposition, was later the venue of a variety of political, literary and sporting events. In the mid-1980s, the decision was taken to restore the building, which was in quite poor shape, in order to install the new Museu Nacional d'Art de Catalunya there as part of the overall rehabilitation of the Palau Nacional spearheaded by the Italian architect Gae Aulenti (1927-2012).

Another issue we should not lose sight of is the implementation of a kind of radically contemporary architecture, in this case museum architecture, in the middle of a medieval neighbourhood and how it integrates into the historical context by transforming it. The American architect Richard Meier built the Museu d'Art Contemporani de Barcelona (MACBA) between 1990 and 1995 in the old quarter of Barcelona, the Raval, next to the Centre de Cultura Contemporània in the Casa de la Caritat, which presents not that exact problem but a similar one. With its modest profile and symbiosis with its environs, the museum was meant to imprint a new dynamic on the old neighbourhood. The architecture of this museum, which is characterised by the discretion and harmony of its shapes and by the burst of luminosity it brings, has become a paradigm within the major urban renovation that the neighbourhood has undergone in recent years. It is an international construction adapted to its site, a rectangle articulated into three volumes, elegant and pristinely white, which perfectly defines the architect Richard Meier's entire body of work.

We can find similar approaches in the field of Modernisme as well. The Fundació Antoni Tàpies, created by the Barcelona painter in 1984 to promote the study and knowledge of contemporary art, is located in the Modernista building of the former Editorial Montaner i Simon built by architect Lluís Domènech i Montaner and located right in the heart of Barcelona's Eixample, at number 255 Carrer d'Aragó. This building was constructed between 1879 and 1881 and is one of Domènech i Montaner's (1850-1923) most significant ones. It is characterised by a grid-like iron structure inside and exposed brick on the façade and thus falls fully within the development of the Modernista language. The architects Lluís Domènech and Roser Amadó rehabilitated this monument between 1986 and 1990. Their goals were to restore the essence of the technology as well as the spatial volumes and aesthetic features characteristic of Modernista structures, which had been lost after many subsequent modifications with interior rearrangements, transforming its original purpose to turn it into a museum. Domènech i Montaner's Modernista façade was preserved and crowned with the monumental wire sculpture by Antoni Tàpies called *Núvol i cadira*.

Returning to the Middle Ages, Carrer de Montcada located in in Barcelona's old quarter next to Santa Maria del Mar church. It is a street lined with palaces from the 13th and 14th centuries, most of them built for wealthy Barcelona residents in the late Middle Ages. The Museu Picasso occupies several of these palaces. Number 15, the Palau Berenguer (13th to 18th centuries), the museum's central site, owes its current appearance to the reform undertaken by nobleman Joan Berenguer d'Aguilar in the 15th century on the previous construction dating from the 13th century. It was restored between 1960 and 1963 to house the museum; it was later expanded in 1970 with the addition of the Palau Baró de Castellet at number 17 of the same street. The museum later expanded further with a third palace, the Palau Meca, located at number 19, which was donated to the city by the Caixa de Pensions in 1981. At that point, a wholesale restoration of the museum was planned, which was commissioned to architects Jordi Garcés and Enric Sòria. This restored museum was opened in 1986. In these palaces, pride of place was given to the central, open-air courtyards which are accessible from the street. The architects suggested joining the courtyards of all three buildings with a central corridor running parallel to the street, which would serve as the backbone and would unify the entire complex. Installing Picasso's important donation to Barcelona inside medieval palaces in the heart of the city means associating the identity of the artist with the most genuine image of medieval Catalonia and therefore promoting it in the eyes of the world as the most genuine bond between past and present (Figure 42).

Finally, the last example I have chosen is a prestigious medieval monument which was rehabilitated so it could better explain itself (Figure 43). The monastery of Pedralbes was founded by Queen Elisenda de Montcada, the last wife of King James II, at the foot of Tibidabo mountain. When the queen purchased the Pedralbes estate in 1326, she had a convent and church built there, the latter consecrated in 1327. That same year, the monastery was given to the Clarissan nuns, even though it was not yet finished:

the dormitory was yet to be finished in 1393, one wing of the cloister was not built until 1412 and the chapterhouse was built between 1416 and 1419. After the death of James II (1327), Queen Elisenda moved to the part of the monastery which was organised as a palace, which was later dismantled in 1363 based on a provision from her will. Thanks to the royal protection, in just a few years the monastery acquired important rights and incomes from the church of Sarrià and other parishes. With the disentailment of 1835, the monastery lost its former income, but the community subsisted and was able to keep the property. In 1897, the religious woman Eulàlia Anzizu i Vila promoted the restoration of the church, which got underway in 1894 under the supervision of Joan Martorell i Montells (1833-1906). During the 20th century, numerous restorations have been undertaken there: the first one overseen by Jeroni Martorell i Terrats in 1920, a latter one by Camil Pallàs in 1968, and finally the latest restoration by Joan Bassegoda (1930-2012) from 1979 to 1983, which enabled the Museum-Monastery of Pedralbes to be opened to the public after part of the convent was granted for the city's use.

Figure 42: Picasso Museum (Gothic Palaces Montcada Street), Barcelona.

Figure 43: Gothic Cloister of the Monastery of Pedralbes, Barcelona.

The monastery complex was surrounded by a wall and included several different buildings. The priests and the staff serving the community used to live around the current Plaça del Monestir, which can be reached through two fortified doors. The most important constructions in the complex are the church and the cloister, around which the community's other quarters are arranged. Today, the monastery of Pedralbes is a museum which explains itself, while it is also a guidebook to 14th century Catalan Gothic art which a shows strong unity of style because it was built so quickly.

Conclusions

With just a few selected examples and a brief history sketched through the medieval art of Catalonia and some of its subsequent re-creations, I have attempted to explain how the establishment of an identity in the origins of the nation is indebted to the Middle Ages, pre-Romanesque, Romanesque or Gothic art and to subsequent interpretations, both modern and contemporary, along with restorations of monuments, conservative rehabilitations and museographic presentations. Within any human community, identity is an individual issue which stems from a context, yet also – and perhaps more importantly – from the desire to belong. In the field of medieval art, this desire is expressed by both medieval creativity and the actions that we continue producing or acting on with our own perspective, sensibility and explanations, actions or interventions.

Annexe

Select bibliography (from 2000)

General series

Art de Catalunya = Ars Cataloniae, 16 vols. (Barcelona: L'Isard, 1997-2003).

Before the Romanesque

Jordi Camps, Eduard Carbonell, Montserrat Pagès, eds., *Catalunya a l'època carolíngia: Art i cultura abans del romànic (segles IX i X)* (Barcelona: Museu Nacional d'Art de Catalunya, 1999-2000, exhibition catalogue).
Gemma Garcia, Antonio Moro, Francesc Tuset, *La seu episcopal d'Ègara: Arqueologia d'un conjunt cristià del segle IV al IX* (Tarragona: Institut Català d'Arqueologia Clàssica, 2009).
Carlos Mancho, *La peinture murale du haut Moyen Âge en Catalogne (IXᵉ-Xᵉ siècle)* (Turnhout: Brepols, 2012).
Jorgina Sales, *Las construcciones cristianas de la 'Tarraconensis' durante la Antigüedad Tardía: Topografía, arqueología e historia* (Barcelona: Universitat de Barcelona, 2012).

Romanesque art

Xavier Barral, *L'art romànic català a debat* (Barcelona: Edicions 62, 2009).

Jordi Camps, Xavier Dectot, eds., *Obres mestres del romànic: Escultures de la Vall de Boí* (Barcelona-Paris: Museu Nacional d'Art de Catalunya-Musée National du Moyen Âge, 2004, exhibition catalogue).

Manuel Castiñeiras, Jordi Camps, eds., *El romànic i la Mediterrània: Catalunya, Toulouse i Pisa (1120-1180)* (Barcelona: Museu Nacional d'Art de Catalunya, 2008, exhibition catalogue).

Catalunya romànica, 27 vols. (Barcelona: Enciclopèdia Catalana, 1984-1998).

Francesca Español, Joaquín Yarza, *El romànic català* (Manresa: Fundació Caixa Manresa, 2007).

Milagros Guardia, Carlos Mancho, eds., *Les fonts de la pintura romànica* (Barcelona: Publicacions i Edicions de la Universitat de Barcelona, 2008).

Montserrat Pagès, *Pintura mural sagrada i profana, del romànic al primer gòtic* (Barcelona: Publicacions de l'Abadia de Montserrat, 2012).

Gothic art

Rosa Alcoy, ed., *El Trecento en obres: Art de Catalunya i art d'Europa al segle XIV* (Barcelona: Universitat de Barcelona, 2009).

Rosa Alcoy, ed., *Contextos 1200 i 1400: Art de Catalunya i art de l'Europa meridional en dos canvis de segle* (Barcelona: Universitat de Barcelona, 2012).

L'art gòtic a Catalunya, 10 vols. (Barcelona: Enciclopèdia Catalana, 2002-2008).

Xavier Barral, *Vitralls medievals de Catalunya* (Barcelona: Lunwerg-Institut d'Estudis Catalans, 2000).

Pere Beseran, *Jordi de Déu i l'italianisme en l'escultura catalana del segle XIV* (Tarragona: Diputació de Tarragona, 2003).

Rafael Cornudella, ed., *Catalunya 1400: El Gòtic Internacional* (Barcelona: Museu Nacional d'Art de Catalunya, 2012, exhibition catalogue).

Francesca Español, *El gòtic català* (Barcelona: Caixa Manresa-Angle Editorial, 2002).

Francesca Español, *L'art dels reis catalans: Esplendor i riquesa de la Corona d'Aragó* (Manresa: Angle Editorial, 2010).

Maria Rosa Terés, *Capitula facta et firmata: Inquietuds artístiques en el quatre-cents* (Valls: Cossetània, 2009).

Modernism

Francesc Fontbona, ed. *El Modernisme*, 5 vols. (Barcelona: L'Isard, 2003-2004).

Raquel Lacuesta, Xavier González, *El modernisme perdut: La Barcelona antiga* (Barcelona: Base, 2013).

Recovering Medieval Art in Contemporary Catalonia

Santiago Alcolea, ed., *La missió arqueològica del 1907 als Pirineus* (Barcelona: Fundació Caixa de Pensions, 2008).

Rosa Alcoy, Pere Beseran, eds., *El romànic i el gòtic desplaçats: Estudis sobre l'exportació i migracions de l'art català medieval* (Barcelona: Publicacions i Edicions de la Universitat de Barcelona, 2007).

Albert Balcells, ed., *Puig i Cadafalch i la Catalunya contemporània* (Barcelona: Institut d'Estudis Catalans, 2003).

Andreu Garcia, *Els museus d'art de Barcelona: antecedents, gènesi i desenvolupament fins l'any 1915* (Barcelona: Publicacions de l'Abadia de Montserrat, 1997).

Enric Granell, Antoni Ramon, eds., *Lluís Domènech i Montaner: Viatges per l'arquitectura romànica* (Barcelona: Col·legi d'Arquitectes de Catalunya, 2006).

Milagros Guardia, Immaculada Lorés, *El Pirineu romànic vist per Josep Gudiol i Emili Gandia* (Tremp: Garsineu, 2013).

Maria Teresa Matas, ed. *Boí, Burgal, Pedret, Taüll: Imitació o interpretació contemporània de la pintura mural romànica catalana* (Barcelona: Amics de l'Art Romànic, 2000).

Josep Maria Xarrié, *Restauració d'obres d'art a Catalunya* (Barcelona: Publicacions de l'Abadia de Montserrat, 2002).

Identity Issues

Xavier Barral, *L'art i la política de l'art* (Cabrera de Mar: Galerada, 2001).
Xavier Barral, *Història de l'art a Catalunya: Creació artística, paisatge i societat* (Barcelona: Base, 2013).
Jordi Casassas, coord., *Les identitats a la Catalunya contemporània* (Cabrera de Mar: Galerada, 2009).
Pere Lluís Font, ed. *Catalunya: origen, ciutadania i identitat: Actes de la jornada científica celebrada el 13 de desembre de 2006* (Barcelona: Institut d'Estudis Catalans, 2009).
Josep Puig, *Escrits d'arquitectura, art i política,* ed. Xavier Barral (Barcelona: Institut d'Estudis Catalans, 2003).
Jaume Sobrequés, *Espanya contra Catalunya: Crònica negra d'un simposi d'història* (Barcelona: Base, 2014).

Identities. An interdisciplinary approach to the roots of the present
Identités. Une approche interdisciplinaire aux racines du présent
Identidades. Una aproximación interdisciplinar a las raíces del presente

Individual or collective, assumed or imposed, accepted or disputed, identities mark out the basic framework that root the human being in society. Language, literature, the creation of a shared memory, social formulas and the range of all cultural expressions have contributed to articulating human life as a mixture of identities. Given these concerns, this series publishes books from the different branches of the Humanities and Social Sciences, which have taken identity as a prism through which the problems of current society and its historical roots are studied. The preferential use of English, French and Spanish ensure greater dissemination of research collected here. The series includes monographs, collected papers, conference proceedings.

Individuelles ou collectives, assumées ou imposées, acceptées ou combattues, les identités configurent le premier cadre d'enracinement de l'être humain en société. La langue, la littérature, la création d'une mémoire commune déterminée, les formules sociales et toutes les expressions culturelles ont contribué à articuler la vie humaine comme un treillis d'identités. Compte tenu de ces préoccupations, cette collection publie ouvrages depuis les diverses branches des sciences humaines et sociales qui prennent l'identité comme prisme par lequel étudier les problèmes de la société d'aujourd'hui et ses racines historiques. L'utilisation préférentielle de l'anglais, le français et l'espagnol assure une plus grande diffusion des recherches ici présentés. La collection accueille des monographies, ouvrages collectifs et actes de congrès.

Individuales o colectivas, asumidas o impuestas, aceptadas o combatidas, las identidades configuran el primer marco de enraizamiento del ser humano en sociedad. La lengua, la literatura, la creación de una determinada memoria común, las fórmulas sociales y todas las expresiones culturales han contribuido a articular la vida humana como un entramado de identidades. Asumiendo estas preocupaciones, esta colección publica obras provenientes de las distintas ramas de las Humanidades y las Ciencias Sociales que adopten la identidad a modo de prisma con que estudiar los problemas de la sociedad actual y sus raíces históricas. El uso preferente del inglés, el francés y el castellano garantizan una mayor difusión de las investigaciones aquí recogidas. La colección acoge monografías, obras colectivas y actas de congreso.

Editorial address: **Institut for Research into Identities and Society (IRIS)**
University of Lleida Plaça Víctor Siurana 1
25003 Lleida
Catalonia / Spain

Vol. 1 Flocel Sabaté (ed.)
Identities on the move
ISBN 978-3-0343-1296-7, 2014

Vol. 2 Flocel Sabaté (ed.)
Hybrid Identities
ISBN 978-3-0343-1471-8, 2014

Vol. 3 Flocel Sabaté (ed.)
Perverse Identities
ISBN 978-3-0343-1556-2, 2015

Vol. 4 Flocel Sabaté (ed.)
Conditioned Identities
ISBN 978-3-0343-1618-7, 2015

Vol. 5 Flocel Sabaté & Luís Adão da Fonseca (eds.)
Catalonia and Portugal
ISBN 978-3-0343-1650-7, 2015

Vol. 6 Flocel Sabaté (ed.)
Historical Analysis of the Catalan Identity
ISBN 978-3-0343-2010-8, 2015

www.ingramcontent.com/pod-product-compliance
Ingram Content Group UK Ltd.
Pitfield, Milton Keynes, MK11 3LW, UK
UKHW021844100926
8556IPUK00019B/1030

9 783034 320108